American
Jewish
Year Book

American

Jewish

Year Book 1979

VOLUME 79

Prepared by THE AMERICAN JEWISH COMMITTEE

Editors
MORRIS FINE
MILTON HIMMELFARB

Associate Editor
DAVID SINGER

THE AMERICAN JEWISH COMMITTEE
NEW YORK
THE JEWISH PUBLICATION SOCIETY OF AMERICA
PHILADELPHIA

Preface

The present volume features Professor Charles Liebman's "Leadership and Decison-making in a Jewish Federation." This in-depth study of the New York Federation of Jewish Philanthropies provides important insights into the changing outlook of American Jews, and the impact this is having on Jewish communal priorities. Another feature is Professor Leon Shapiro's "Soviet Jewry Since the Death of Stalin," an authoritative overview of Jewish life in the Soviet Union during the past 25 years. Particularly noteworthy is Professor Shapiro's emphasis on religious life and cultural endeavors.

The review of developments in the United States includes Milton Ellerin's "Intergroup Relations"; George Gruen's "The United States, Israel, and the Middle East"; and Geraldine Rosenfield's "The Jewish Community Responds to Issues of the Day." Alvin Chenkin and Maynard Miran provide revised U.S. Jewish population estimates.

Jewish life around the world is reported on in a series of articles dealing with Israel, Canada, Argentina, Great Britain, France, Germany, Poland, Yugoslavia, and South Africa. There is an analysis of the human rights implications of the Belgrade Conference. New estimates for the world Jewish population are given.

Carefully compiled directories of national Jewish organizations, periodicals, and federations and welfare funds, as well as religious calendars and obituary notices, round out the 1979 AMERICAN JEWISH YEAR BOOK.

We are very grateful to our colleague Joan Margules for technical and editorial assistance. Thanks are also due to Amy Carr for preparation of the index, and to the entire Information and Research staff.

THE EDITORS

Contributors

BERNARD BASKIN; rabbi, Temple Anshe Sholom, Hamilton, Ont., Canada.

ALVIN CHENKIN; research consultant, Council of Jewish Federations and Welfare Funds.

DENIS DIAMOND; executive director, South African Jewish Board of Deputies, Johannesburg.

MILTON ELLERIN; director, trends analysis division, American Jewish Committee.

GEORGE E. GRUEN; director, Israel and Middle East affairs, foreign affairs department, American Jewish Committee; adjunct associate professor of Judaic studies, Brooklyn College, CUNY.

LIONEL E. KOCHAN; Bearsted Reader in Jewish history, University of Warwick; honorary fellow, Oxford Centre for Post-graduate Hebrew Studies, England.

MIRIAM KOCHAN; journalist; translator, Oxford, England.

CHARLES S. LIEBMAN; Mendelsohn Visiting Professor of Jewish Sociology, Jewish Theological Seminary of America; on leave from Bar Ilan University.

SIDNEY LISKOFSKY; director, division of international organizations, foreign affairs department, American Jewish Committee.

MISHA LOUVISH; writer; translator; journalist, Jerusalem.

ARNOLD MANDEL; essayist; novelist; reporter and literary critic, *Information Juive* and *L'Arche;* contributor, literary supplement, *Le Monde,* Paris.

NAOMI F. MEYER; co-director, Camp Ramah, Argentina.

MAYNARD MIRAN; research associate, Council of Jewish Federations and Welfare Funds.

GERALDINE ROSENFIELD; researcher, American Jewish Committee.

FRIEDO SACHSER; political and news editor, *Allgemeine Jüdische Wochezeitung;* German correspondent, London *Jewish Chronicle,* Düsseldorf.

LEON SHAPIRO; professor of Russian and Soviet Jewish history, member of faculty on the Soviet Union and Eastern Europe, Rutgers University.

Table of Contents

Special
Articles

Leadership and Decision-making in a Jewish Federation: The New York Federation of Jewish Philanthropies

by CHARLES S. LIEBMAN

INTRODUCTION • STRUCTURE AND FUNCTIONS • POLICY AND INFLUENCE • LEADERSHIP • THE FUTURE

INTRODUCTION

THE NEW YORK FEDERATION OF JEWISH PHILANTHROPIES (hereafter referred to as Federation) was organized in 1917, following almost two years of discussion and negotiation.[1] New York thus became the 23rd Jewish community in the United States to establish a central fund-collecting society for local agencies serving Jewish health and welfare needs. Today, there are approximately 220 Jewish federations throughout the

---

Note: A large number of people helped make this study possible. My greatest debt of gratitude is to the New York Federation of Jewish Philanthropies; Federation's files, minutes, and meetings were all opened to me; every person to whom I turned for assistance was most cooperative. Three individuals who read and commented in detail on a first draft of this study merit particular mention: Sanford Solender, Federation executive vice-president; Dr. Donald Feldstein, Federation executive director for community services; and Mrs. Laurence (Billie) Tisch, immediate past chairman of Federation's Distribution Committee. None of them is in agreement with all of my conclusions, but this makes me all the more grateful to them for their help.

[1]There is no scholarly history of Federation. The most comprehensive survey is *The Golden Heritage: A History of the Federation of Jewish Philanthropies of New York from 1917 to 1967* (New York, 1969). This is surprisingly informative, considering it was published by Federation in honor of its own 50th anniversary. But it was not intended as a systematic, much less scholarly, history. On the early history of Federation see Deborah Dash Moore, "From Kehillah to Federation: The Communal Functions of Federated Philanthropy in New York City" (paper read at the annual conference of the Association of Jewish Studies, Boston, December 1976), and the bibliography cited therein, including Arthur A. Goren, *New York Jews and the Quest for Community: The Kehillah Experiment, 1908–1922* (New York, 1970), and I. Edwin Goldwasser, "Federation for the Support of Jewish Philanthropies in New York City," AJYB, Vol. 20, 1918–1919, pp. 113–146. See also Deborah Dash Moore, "The Emergence of Ethnicity: New York's Jews 1920–1940" (Columbia University, unpublished doctoral dissertation, 1975).

United States and Canada. About 200, including all but the smallest, are affiliated with the Council of Jewish Federations and Welfare Funds (CJFWF).[2]

Over the course of time, the influence of the federations has grown. Their functions have come to include increasing control over the expenditures of their beneficiary agencies. Federations today see themselves as organizations responsible for the entire Jewish population in a given geographic area.

Contributing to the growth in influence of the federations were the mergers in various communities between local federations and Jewish welfare funds, which raised money for overseas needs. The merged organization, often called the Jewish Federation and Welfare Fund, or Combined Jewish Appeal, brought new people into the federation orbit. Some of these people, activists and large contributors to the welfare funds, had previously been indifferent to the purely local agencies which the federations served. In many instances they were first- or second-generation American Jews of predominantly East European background, and were particularly oriented to support for Israel. Federation leaders, usually of German Jewish descent, were, on the other hand, often indifferent, if not hostile, to Zionism. The federation-welfare fund mergers, an outcome of the diminishing social and ideological differences between these groups, hastened the process of integration. They also increased in large measure the amount of money that the federations had at their disposal—an amount already increased by greater contributions by American Jews.

The federations' expanding involvement in local Jewish community councils contributed further to their growth in influence. Such councils, which exist in most Jewish communities, are composed of local groups as well as local chapters of national organizations, and are primarily concerned with relations between Jews and non-Jews, though some community councils also concern themselves with internal Jewish matters. In providing funds and services to these councils, and sometimes even the impetus for their creation, the federations increased their visibility, while becoming more sensitive to community needs.

In many communities the federations allocated funds to national Jewish organizations, in return for which the organizations restricted their own local fund-raising activities. Such arrangements limited the visibility of the

---

[2]For a summary treatment of the various Jewish federations and the federation movement in the context of American Jewish organizational life, see Daniel J. Elazar, *Community and Polity: The Organizational Dynamics of American Jewry* (Philadelphia, 1961). A different focus is provided in Harry L. Lurie, *A Heritage Affirmed* (Philadelphia, 1961). For financial and program information, see S.P. Goldberg, "Jewish Communal Services: Programs and Finances," AJYB, Vol. 78, 1978, pp. 172–221. A recent article of particular interest is Marc Lee Raphael, "Jewish Philanthropy and Communal Democracy: In Pursuit of a Phantom," *Response*, Fall 1977, pp. 55–56.

national organizations while enhancing Federation's importance on the local scene.

The development of New York's federation was somewhat different from that of most others. Its focus and concerns have changed in the last ten years, but, until recently, were far more narrow, at least from a Jewish perspective. In many respects it was the last to join the mainstream of federation life. This fact, the size of the New York federation, the number of people it serves, and the amount of money it allocates, all make it a significant subject for study.

In 1978–79, Federation will distribute over $27 million to some 130 agencies and institutions serving the health, welfare, recreational, and educational needs of an estimated 1,500,000 people. Most of that money will come from Jews of Greater New York and represents Federation's share of the United Jewish Appeal-Federation annual Joint Campaign. To a great extent, therefore, Federation will be exercising its own discretion in the allocation of Jewish public funds not earmarked for any particular purpose.

The sum which Federation receives is arrived at through a negotiated agreement with UJA, as the donors have not specified these funds as being for Federation. Hence the importance of a study which asks:

- To what purposes does Federation allocate its funds?
- Who are the people deciding how Federation's funds are allocated?
- How do these people arrive at their decisions?
- Given the obvious assumption that influence accrues to any institution which distributes money, how much influence does Federation really have? Over whom, how, and in what direction does it exercise this influence?
- What changes, if any, have taken place in Federation in the last few years?

This study addresses these questions, but touches only peripherally on two aspects of Federation which its leaders regard as central, and which merit independent treatment—Federation's sources of revenue, and the activities of its agencies.

Fund-raising has always been a central aspect of Jewish communal life in the United States,[3] and the Joint Campaign partnership between Federation and UJA does, indeed, exist to raise funds for local and overseas needs. However, as UJA-Federation is an independent organization, our focus will be limited to the effects of the Joint Campaign on Federation policy.

---

[3] A popular survey is Milton Goldin's *Why They Give: American Jews and Their Philanthropies* (New York, 1977). The January 1977 issue of *Moment* magazine was devoted to American Jewish philanthropy. Unfortunately there is no systematic scholarly study of the topic. Two articles which merit attention are Marshall Sklare's "The Future of Jewish Giving," *Commentary,* November 1962, pp. 416–426, and Marc Lee Raphael, *loc. cit.* Sklare's material is dated, but the article remains a landmark study.

The activities of Federation's agencies engage the greatest effort and attention of many of its leaders, with Federation allocating funds directly to roughly 80 agencies and organizations. Fifty-four of these are member agencies otherwise known as beneficiary societies. Under the terms of their membership, these societies are permitted to raise additional funds only from government, foundations, and members of their own boards—not from the community at large. The societies provide a broad range of medical, social, and recreational services. There are ten hospitals, geriatric centers serving 6,000 elderly, 30 Y's and Jewish community centers, and 24 camps. Some of the beneficiary societies are: Mt. Sinai Hospital; the Jewish Board of Family and Children's Services, which provides mental-health treatment to children, as well as adult counseling and rehabilitation services; the Altro Health and Rehabilitation Services, caring for the physically and mentally handicapped; the Federation Employment and Guidance Service; the Jewish Association for Services for the Aged (JASA), serving the aged in 18 centers and three housing developments; the Jewish Home and Hospital for the Aged; Associated YM and YWHAs of Greater New York, with 11 community centers under its aegis; and the Board of Jewish Education, which provides pedagogic guidance and supportive services of varying intensity to 640 Jewish day and supplementary schools.

In addition to its beneficiary societies, Federation allocates funds to subvented (non-member) agencies. In some cases, these are agencies which Federation itself created. Unlike the beneficiary societies, subvented agencies have no representation on the Federation board. They may, however, raise funds from the community at large. Among the subvented agencies are the Jewish Community Relations Council (JCRC), the Metropolitan New York Coordinating Council on Jewish Poverty, and the Jewish Association for College Youth (JACY). Federation also subsidizes three neighborhood service centers for inner-city Jews—centers which it established—and provides funding for such varied groups as the New York Board of Rabbis, Greater New York Conference on Soviet Jewry, and Jewish Museum.

Although this study will not deal with the various agencies per se, it will explore the relationships between Federation and its agencies, the manner in which the agencies are funded, and the direction in which Federation allocations have moved.

Federation spends over $2 million a year on administration and services to its agencies, employing 150 people (20 in its thrift shop), 55 of whom are professional staff, and involving hundreds of laymen in its activities. Even so, this study will not be an administrative one. It will focus instead on Federation's key committees, which bring it in touch with the larger community. No attempt will be made to assess the efficiency of Federation, or even describe its internal operations, except as these relate to fundamental questions.

This study is based on a variety of sources. Formal interviews were conducted with 58 individuals. Most were professional and lay leaders who had contact with Federation, and might be expected to be informed about its activities. Federation publications, minutes of committees, and other documents of the last ten years were perused selectively. The September 1975–September 1977 minutes of two committees, the Distribution Committee (Federation's allocation committee) and the Communal Planning Committee, were read carefully. Beginning in September 1977, I regularly participated in meetings of Federation's key committees and a number of subcommittees. These meetings afforded ample opportunity for discussion with Federation activists. Finally, a questionnaire was distributed to people who served on the Distribution Committee (DC) in either 1968 or 1978.

The first section of this study describes the structure of Federation and its functions, including its general relationship to its beneficiary societies, the functions of its key committees, and the formal role of the professionals. The second section explores Federation's present policy and how it emerged. The third section focuses on Federation's present leaders—who they are, how they were recruited, what motivates them, and how they compare to the leaders of a decade ago. It also deals with the role of the large contributor in Federation's decision-making, and examines the question of how much control the professionals exercise. The concluding section assesses Federation, and considers its prospects for the future.

FEDERATION: STRUCTURE AND FUNCTIONS

The Formality of Agency Control

One difference between the New York federation and that of other cities is the degree of formal control exercised by Federation's beneficiary societies. Its by-laws provide for a Board of Trustees with authority over Federation's basic decisions. The Board of Trustees is presently composed of 303 members, two-thirds of whom are designated by the beneficiary societies and called institutional trustees. The remaining trustees are either life trustees or trustees-at-large chosen by the Nominating Committee, whose members are selected, in turn, by the Board of Trustees.[4]

---

[4]Not all trustees exercise an equal vote. Beneficiary societies are accorded from one to ten votes, depending on their size. The institutional trustees present at any given Board meeting divide the votes to which the agency is entitled among themselves, so that an institutional trustee may sometimes be entitled to cast more than one vote. However, this occurs only in the case of a roll call, or what is known in Federation terminology as a weighted vote, and weighted votes are rare.

The Board also elects the officers of Federation and the members of the Executive Committee (EC). In addition, the Board approves the appointment, by the president, of members of Federation's operating committees. All basic decisions are subject to its confirmation.

The Board, when taken as a whole, is too large a body to control the operations of Federation. Hence, it relegates much of the task to its 54-member EC. The provision of a two-thirds majority of institutional trustees on Federation's Board extends to the EC as well.

The Reality of Agency Control

The theoretical control which the beneficiary societies exercise over Federation is not as crucial in determining policy as one might assume. A number of factors account for this.

First of all, while agency control is exercised through representation on the Board of Trustees, the agency representatives cannot be paid employees. Only laymen represent the agencies, and the extent to which the primary commitment of these laymen is to their agencies, as opposed to Federation interests, or to their own conceptions of the needs of the Jewish community, differs. Many of the institutional trustees are independent-minded, and do not see themselves as accountable to the agencies which appointed them.

Secondly, many institutional trustees adopt a Federation, as distinct from an agency, point of view. Meetings and materials received by Board members reflect the point of view of Federation's president and executive vice-president. There is a strong Federation tradition, enhanced by the fact that service on the Board of Trustees is considered a mark of distinction for most members of agency boards. Hence, although it is the agency and not Federation which designates the representative, even institutional trustees want to play the Federation game. This is particularly true for Board members seeking appointment to Federation's own committees. Service on these committees may confer status and distinction, bringing the appointee into contact with some of the social and financial elite of New York Jewry. The president and executive vice-president exercise a crucial voice in committee appointments.

Thirdly, some agencies are dependent on Federation for help in recruiting their own board members. In the past, Federation was instrumental in helping to raise large sums for the capital needs of many agencies. These agencies, particularly the smaller ones, are unlikely to adopt an independent point of view. On the other hand, some of the largest of the beneficiary societies, such as the hospitals, receive so small a percentage of their funding from Federation (total Federation allocations represented .7 per cent of hospital budgets in 1978) that they are relatively indifferent to Federation Board decisions.

Fourthly, neither the Board nor the EC really makes organization policy. They approve or, on rare occasions, disapprove the policy formulated by a smaller group of people. Neither Board nor EC members have the time, energy, or expertise to continually challenge the judgment of the professionals, or the small number of lay leaders engaging in Federation activity on a full-time or almost full-time basis. The agenda, framework, and decision-making premises are determined by this select group of leaders. One executive head of a large beneficiary society stated that he never bothered to read the Board minutes because, as far as he was concerned, the Board never did anything anyway.

Finally, there are not that many issues involving conflicts of interest. Generally, each agency wants more money for itself, which means less money for others. (There are rare cases of agencies requesting cuts because they have found other sources of income.) But that is something different from an interest shared by all agencies in opposition to Federation interest. Indeed, Federation leaders are very careful not to formulate issues in these terms.

Many trustees-at-large and life trustees have had some agency orientation or served at some time on agency boards. Their involvement in Federation stems from their involvement in the programs of its beneficiary societies. It would be contrary to their own convictions to act against agency interests, of which, for some of them, Federation's interest is simply the sum total. Despite the foregoing, one can point to a Federation as distinct from an agency point of view.

INSTITUTIONAL CONFLICT BETWEEN FEDERATION AND ITS AGENCIES

While Federation and its agencies may be in complete agreement on goals, they may differ on how to achieve these goals. Federation leaders stress the principle of agency autonomy. They emphasize that each agency is independent, and while Federation may seek to persuade, it can never coerce. Agency leaders, on the other hand, stress the importance of Federation planning and coordination. They acknowledge that Federation reduces competition and duplication among the agencies, and that Federation's assistance has helped them to pioneer in the fields of health and social-welfare services. They benefit from Federation's joint purchasing plan. Still, even under the most idyllic circumstances, and even within a framework of mutually acknowledged guidelines, it is only natural that agencies will seek greater autonomy, and Federation a greater coordinating role.

There is also the issue of the extent to which Federation should indent its reserves in order to maintain a certain level of grants to its agencies. The present ratio of expendable reserves to annual grants is about 100 per cent.

This is considerably lower than that of other federations in major metropolitan centers, where the ratios vary from 171 to 483 per cent. In December 1976, the Level of Grants Committee, a permanent subcommittee of the EC, recommended a one per cent decrease in the level of grants for the forthcoming year, to be followed by two and three per cent reductions in each of the next two years, subject to increase in the event of a rise in compaign contributions. The level of grants, which requires the approval of the Board of Trustees, does not determine how much each individual agency will receive. This is decided by the DC, subject to ratification by the Board of Trustees. But the level of grants does determine the total sum which the DC will have at its disposal and provides agencies with a rough estimate of what they are likely to receive.

Many agencies were extremely unhappy over this proposal, which came in the midst of New York's fiscal crisis. They complained that Federation was trying to save money when it was already badly needed. Nevertheless, the proposal was accepted by the EC and the Board of Trustees—a fact that suggests the influence of Federation's leadership. The approval was attributed primarily to a strong presentation by Federation's executive vice-president about the need for maintaining reserves. The following year, the Level of Grants Committee reversed itself, and recommended a three per cent increase, as reserves had grown from a windfall of bequests. The EC lowered this to two per cent, but the Board raised it back to three. Still, the three per cent increase fell short of the inflated cost of living, and the leadership resisted pressure for larger increases in the level of grants.

The issue of the level of grants is one of the few in which agency and Federation interests were opposed. The conflict's resolution suggests how difficult it is to determine which side is the more influential. In general, Federation interests probably prevail, within the constraints set by agency interests.

IDEOLOGICAL CONFLICT BETWEEN FEDERATION AND ITS AGENCIES

In addition to the institutional self-interests dividing the agencies and Federation, there is an ideological division. Federation agencies, almost without exception, were created to serve the needs of individuals or families. Federation was Jewish because its beneficiary societies served a Jewish clientele, who were, however, served as human beings, not Jews. A notable exception was Federation's allocation to Jewish education—an allocation which many within Federation viewed as anomalous.

By the end of the 1960's, a growing number of Federation leaders spoke in terms of the organization's communal role, having come to understand Federation's role as one including responsibility to the Jewish community as a community. Frederick P. Rose, president of Federation from 1974 to 1977, began his farewell message in 1977 with the statement: "Viewed as a tapestry, the New York Jewish community is a richly colored one, in which Federation is a dominant thread weaving itself through every aspect of Jewish communal life."[5] Such a conception is strikingly different from that which prevailed a decade earlier, although uttered by a man in the mold of the older leadership. This, then, indicates the rapidity with which the communal ideology of Federation became institutionalized. The change was to have important implications for Federation's traditional agencies.

Federation concern for the Jewish community meant support for a community relations council, for enterprises such as the Greater New York Conference on Soviet Jewry, for Jewish college youth programs, and for neighborhood stabilization projects in such middle-class areas as Flatbush in Brooklyn and Forest Hills in Queens. It added a substantial measure of legitimacy to increased Federation support for Jewish education. Many of the most significant agencies engaging in communal activity are subvented agencies, rather than beneficiary societies. Given increasingly limited resources, there is an understandable agency interest in opposing the communal thrust of Federation, and its subventions to non-members.

The resistance to Federation's communal direction has not come from institutional trustees alone. In the debates that surrounded the early subventions to the Greater New York Conference on Soviet Jewry, observers remarked that they could not distinguish institutional from at-large trustees. If all the institutional trustees had opposed the subvention, it would not have been accepted. Institutional trustees tend to be independent-minded, and agency interests are not necessarily foremost among their concerns, particularly when such interests are narrowly and parochially defined. Even among the agency executives there were those who, by virtue of their own background and perceptions, favored greater communal involvement on the part of Federation. In most instances the grants to subvented agencies were small.

The one resounding defeat for those who supported Federation's communal role came early in the period, in 1970, when the Board of Trustees rejected a proposal for a substantial increase in the support for Jewish education, a proposal which was subsequently accepted in modified form.

The role that agencies play through their institutional trustees can be of much consequence. The initial 1976 proposal to fund the Jewish Community Relations Council at $125,000 was reduced to $75,000, as a result of opposition from institutional trustees. In discussing the possibility of a large

---

[5]Frederick P. Rose, *The President's Message,* Federation of Jewish Philanthropies, May 9, 1977.

increase in the allocation to the Greater New York Conference on Soviet Jewry, objection was raised to granting a subvented agency a greater percentage increase than that which most beneficiary societies received. "Our agencies won't stand for that," one Federation member declared. Although the demands of Federation leaders are usually satisfied, structural constraints limit the recommendations and proposals they can bring before the EC and Board of Trustees. This probably accounts for the fact that while Federation is moving in the same direction as other federations throughout North America, the movement is at a slower pace.

The Committee Structure

Federation has two standing committees, the Executive Committee, with its important subcommittee on Level of Grants, and the Nominating Committee. But its operational activities are carried on primarily through six community services committees and 15 operating committees. The by-laws provide for community services committees (formerly called functional committees) in each of Federation's traditional agency areas: the aged, camping, community centers, family and children's vocational and rehabilitation services, hospital and medical services, and Jewish education. Every beneficiary society is represented on the community services committee concerned with its area of service. The committee provides a forum for the exchange of ideas and makes recommendations to the Board of Trustees and operating committees.

Some of the community services committees are very active. Their meetings are well attended, and the participating agency executives feel they benefit from the exchanges. Other committees exist only on paper, or function haltingly without the participants feeling that they are of much utility.

The 15 operating committees include some, such as the Law Committee, the Labor Relations Committee, and the Investment Committee, exclusively concerned with Federation's internal operations. The activity of these and similar committees have important consequences for Federation's internal management, but only four actually determine Federation's public posture and policies. Three of them, the Distribution Committee (DC), Communal Planning Committee (CPC), and Public Programs and Policy Committee (PPPC), represent, in Federation's own terminology, its major committees.

THE DISTRIBUTION COMMITTEE

By general consensus, Federation's most important committee is the 30-member Distribution Committee. Appointment to the DC is perceived as a mark of distinction. It is less a reward for past service than a sign that the appointee is highly intelligent, energetic, and willing and able to devote many hours a week to communal service. The DC's members, more than those of any other committee, comprise a Federation elite.

The by-laws restrict DC membership to current or former trustees-at-large. None can be institutional trustees. DC members must also resign from the boards of any beneficiary societies on which they may be serving at the time of their appointment.

The function of the DC is to prepare that portion of Federation's budget (about 90%) which deals with allocations. The budget proposal, along with the DC chairman's report, is submitted to the Board of Trustees in June of each year. Ratification is virtually automatic, although there have been exceptions. The DC takes care in the phrasing of its justifications for allocations and may even make minor allocation adjustments in anticipation of Board reaction. Nevertheless, it is the DC that determines, within the framework of the overall sum set by the level of grants, how much each agency or project funded by Federation will receive. In addition, it is the DC that allocates special funds (about $400,000 in 1978), being required only to report its decision to the Board of Trustees. The only funding activity over which the DC exercises no authority is Federation's operating budget.

For the fiscal year 1978–79, the DC will allocate roughly $27.1 million. Approximately 18 million of this will come from the Joint Campaign, about three million from the Greater New York Fund, about one million from investment income, and the remainder from unrestricted legacies, with the deficit covered by indenting reserves.

The work of the DC is carried on through subcommittees in the following fields: camping; the aged; community centers; family, children, vocational and rehabilitation services; Jewish education; medical care; and special projects, subventions and memberships. Each subcommittee is aided by a professional consultant. In general, each DC member serves on two subcommittees, with no two members serving on the same ones.

In the fall, the subcommittee members visit the agencies for which they are responsible. Discussions are conducted with each agency executive, and often with some of the agency's lay leaders. During these visits, subcommittee members learn about the agency's problems and make known to the agency leaders their own interests and concerns. These are often concerns which the subcommittee has previously presented to the full DC through a staff memorandum and subcommittee chairman's report. During the next few months, the subcommittee chairman and some members may meet with one or more agency executives to discuss a particular problem. In late winter and early spring, budget hearings are held with the agencies, whose requests are accompanied by budget information summarized for DC

members in a detailed memorandum prepared by Federation's budget director, his assistant, and four budget examiners. Thus, DC members are provided with ample budget information prior to the hearings. In addition, the
professional consultant may have prepared a brief memorandum on the
agency. At the budget hearings, subcommittee members can evaluate the
extent to which their concerns and recommendations, and the general
policy of the DC and Federation, have been reflected in agency programs.
Although the DC prides itself on not adopting an antagonistic attitude, the
hearings are often touchy.

Following the budget hearings, the DC subcommittee chairmen make a
tentative decision on the distribution of allocations to each functional field.
Each subcommittee then submits its recommendation and report to the full
DC. At the May meeting of the DC, all subcommittee recommendations are
reviewed and changes may be made not only in allocations to specific
agencies, but also in the overall distribution of allocations by functional
field.

Allocation recommendations may take a variety of forms other than
outright grants. One important variant is a reserve allocation, which provides that a sum of money be made available to a particular agency only
after it has met certain conditions or introduced a particular program.

DC procedures are not entirely satisfactory to many agency executives,
some of whom doubt whether subcommittee members are well-informed.
One agency executive characterized the visitations and budget hearings as
a "charade." No one pretends that in one visit per year to an agency, or
one budget hearing, a subcommittee member can gain detailed knowledge
of that agency's operation. However, a term of office on the DC is three
years, which means a member visits the same agency a number of times.
A DC member may serve for four consecutive terms (12 years) before he
is required to step down for one year. As of June 1978, DC members had
served an average of six years. While subcommittee assignments may be
rotated, the experience one gains in dealing with one type of agency is
helpful in understanding another. The longer one serves on the DC, the
greater expertise one acquires. DC members average a minimum of a few
hours per week on Committee matters; most subcommittee chairmen spend
an average of eight to ten hours a week on DC affairs. A few members are
less conscientious than others about attending meetings or doing their
homework. DC chairmen, alert to this, encourage such members to resign
as soon as their term of office expires, or do not reappoint them for an
additional three year term.

Some DC observers feel there is room for more in-depth studies of the
agencies, perhaps by having subcommittees focus on a limited number of
agencies each year. Agency executives sometimes complain that they have

no opportunity beyond the budget hearings to interact with DC members. They especially seek access to committee and subcommittee chairmen, in order to present their case for more money. The larger agencies with the more prestigious board members are in the best position to do so. Agency executives will, on occasion, request that their board members contact DC members on a social level, at the golf course or a luncheon meeting, to explain the agency position; but DC members view these efforts as singularly unsuccessful.

THE COMMUNAL PLANNING COMMITTEE

The Communal Planning Committee (CPC) is generally regarded as Federation's second most important committee. As in the case of the DC, all its members must be present or former members of the Board of Trustees. CPC members, however, are evenly divided between at-large and institutional trustees. There are, at present, 32 members on the CPC, whose function is to advise the Board of Trustees and DC about important communal trends and needs to be considered in the formulation of Federation and DC policy. The CPC considers the desirability of proposed beneficiary society projects, recommends modifications and additions to programs and structures, and recommends the admission of new agencies and the disaffiliation of others.

Such projects as assistance to Jews in the inner city and neighborhood stabilization must acquire CPC approval prior to funding. Projects are considered in subcommittee, and then in full committee, before detailed recommendations are made to the Board of Trustees.

A CPC meeting might consider the requests of a camp or community center to purchase new property. Members will have before them the report of a subcommittee or professional consultant on the impact of the project in terms of agency costs and community needs. CPC and DC chairmen are ex-officio members of each other's committees, and close relationships are further insured by the shared services of the same consultants.

The CPC is Federation's major instrument for communal planning. While its concerns and procedures, the intelligence of its lay members, and the quality of its professional staff are impressive, Federation's success in communal planning has not been striking. This is partly due to the fact that it is only within the last few years that Federation has defined its Jewish communal responsibilities in broad terms.

Also, Federation does not have reliable demographic data on the Greater New York Jewish population and its movements. Without such data, intelligent communal planning is virtually impossible. Community centers, for example, have been authorized in areas where many feel they are not needed, or relocated so that they hasten Jewish movement out of others. The data that the CPC requires are not only of a demographic nature, but must include information on local community sentiments and attitudes. It is only of late that Federation has become sensitive to this fact.

Federation has, also, to take account of the needs of its beneficiary societies. There is agency opposition to Federation's undertaking new projects which mean competition for funding or programming. Thus, for example, there is agency opposition to neighborhood service centers which seek to centralize in one location the social, health, and welfare services provided by different agencies in a particular neighborhood. Federation created the Metropolitan New York Coordinating Council on Jewish Poverty in 1972. The Council, in turn, was instrumental in the creation of a number of local community councils. But Federation then exercised its influence to prevent these local councils from engaging in social work or receiving government grants which might compete with its beneficiary societies. It also doubted the councils' abilities to deliver quality services. This opposition came despite Federation's own feeling that the development of strong local Jewish community institutions was necessary for neighborhood stabilization.

Finally, New York City's problems are of such a magnitude that no agency could solve them, and New York's problems are Federation's problems. Fiscal crises, changing neighborhoods, and crime all have an impact on New York City's Jews. Federation, aware of its dependence on the broader social environment, encouraged its executive vice-president to assume the chairmanship of the Task Force on the New York City Crisis. In general, however, communal planning at Federation takes place in the context of living with severe municipal crises, not of meeting them.

THE PUBLIC PROGRAMS AND POLICY COMMITTEE

The Public Programs and Policy Committee (PPPC) is the newest of Federation's three major committees. Created in 1976, it replaced two older committees, one on government programs, and another on social legislation. The by-laws require that there be a minimum of 15 members, ten of whom must be members of the Board of Trustees. There is no provision for the ratio of institutional to at-large trustees. Of its present 33 members, 13 are trustees: 8 at-large and 5 institutional.

The PPPC studies government programs and policies as they affect Federation, its beneficiary societies, and the Jewish community, and recommends action on given issues. Where policy positions already exist, the PPPC acts without consulting other Federation bodies.

Most of the issues discussed by the PPPC deal with government legislation affecting Federation's health and welfare agencies. For example, the

Committee devoted much attention in late 1977 to the Carter Administration's welfare reform proposals. After reaching a consensus on some of the issues, the PPPC expressed its opinion to local congressmen, as well as to the Washington office maintained by the Council of Jewish Federations and Welfare Funds, an office financed by special grants from some of the larger Jewish federations. During the New York State legislative session, most committee time is devoted to state matters, and PPPC leaders (its chairman and three staff members) are in frequent contact with Federation's part-time lobbyist in Albany, as well as with executive and legislative officials. At the municipal level, Federation's contacts are more direct, and matters are handled without the intervention of a lobbyist.

The importance of the PPPC reflects the increasing importance to Federation of governmental activity. Government, at all levels, is a major source of funding to most of the beneficiary societies. Regulatory and other non-fiscal legislation has an impact on the agencies, and local tax policies vitally affect Federation's camps. The assignment of children to child-care agencies and foster homes in accordance with the religion of the parents is of concern to Federation's agencies, as are the rates of government reimbursement for child care.

THE DEPARTMENT OF RELIGIOUS AFFAIRS

In 1953, Federation hired Rabbi Isaac N. Trainin as the head of a newly-instituted Department of Religious Affairs. It was Federation's hope to improve its relationship with rabbis and synagogue leaders, some of whom, incensed at what they saw as Federation's indifference to vital Jewish concerns, not only refused to support the Federation campaign, but urged Jews not to contribute.

The Department acts through two committees, the Religious Affairs Committee and the Commission on Synagogue Relations. The first, an operational committee of Federation, supervises the Department's conduct and advises Federation and its agencies with regard to religious matters. The by-laws require that there be a minimum of ten members on the committee, a majority of whom must be trustees. At present, there are 43 members, 16 of whom are rabbis. The committee deals with religious issues within Federation and its agencies, and concerns itself with such matters as the availability of kosher food in Federation agencies, the operation of agencies on Jewish holidays, and the manner in which Federation relates to other Jewish religious practices. It has a task force on medical ethics, and has prepared a handbook on the subject for hospitals and doctors.

The Commission on Synagogue Relations has a broader communal scope. Membership is open to all synagogues, rabbis, and Jewish social-work agencies in Greater New York; laymen may be invited to join. The

Commission functions through task forces, which hold conferences, publish material, and seek to involve the community. In 1977–78, the Commission had 15 task forces focusing on such matters as alcoholism, gambling, the Jewish family, mixed marriages, and singles. Some task forces have their own subcommittees; the one on mental health and Judaism has four. The Commission is governed by an executive council and a small board of governors, which is, in effect, the ruling body of the Commission.

The Department of Religious Affairs (DRA) promotes Federation's image in the synagogue world, and alerts the latter to the existence of Federation's agencies and their services. It also pressures Federation and its agencies to increase their specifically Jewish content and programming, and their services to Jews. Some of those who oppose Federation because they feel its orientation is too nonsectarian, and its control is in the hands of non-committed Jews, regard the DRA as an "apologist." In 1975, for example, the chairman of the Religious Affairs Committee wrote to a task force member asking him to withdraw publication of an article critical of Federation's financial support of Jewish hospitals. Criticisms of Federation, he wrote, should be made only from "within." On the other hand, some of those oriented to the older Federation tradition of nonsectarian service see the Department as troublesome. Federation's present leadership views it as its "eyes and ears" in the synagogue world, serving as a bridge, and alerting Federation to potential problems.

The Religious Affairs Committee and Commission on Synagogue Relations are extremely sensitive about their status within Federation. Many members feel they are "outsiders," not part of the elite whom they perceive as dominating the organization. One leader of the Religious Affairs Committee stated, "We're not Wall Street and we're not German and that's why we're on the outside. Not only are we not consulted; we aren't even informed of the reasons for crucial decisions which we could help interpret to the community." The Committee and Commission are not, however, without influence. As one observer noted, their influence rests in part on the very fact that they have not been fully incorporated into the Federation system. Among the recommendations first proposed by the DRA and subsequently adopted by Federation were assistance to inner-city Jews and local community councils, subventions to COLPA (Commission on Law and Political Action) and the Beth Din of the Rabbinical Council of America, aid to Black Jews, and special help to three fire-ravaged day schools. Federation also turns to the DRA for recommendations regarding representative leaders of the synagogue world to be appointed to its committees. Trainin exercises a virtual veto over the appointments of rabbis to Federation committees, and his recommendations with regard to laymen are given careful consideration. Paradoxically, as Federation expands its interest in Jewish matters, the Department's influence may diminish. In other words, "Yiddishkeit" in Federation may become so important that one man or department can no longer be looked to as a source of information, contacts, and support.

Apart from more manifest functions, the DRA provides the opportunity for Orthodox, Conservative, and Reform rabbis to meet together. It tends to avoid issues likely to divide rabbis along denominational lines, and the rabbis themselves are careful to keep such issues subdued, should they arise. At one point, the Orthodox chairman of the task force on medical ethics refused to address a Conservative colleague by his rabbinical title. But this incident was an exception, according to respondents, to the customary good feeling.

In most cases, the Orthodox have been pleased by the willingness of even their Reform colleagues to support them on such issues as insistence on kosher kitchens in Federation agencies, closing agencies on Jewish holidays, and protecting the rights of agency employees who do not work on the second day of Jewish holidays. The Orthodox interpretation of Jewish law is generally regarded as normative in the deliberations and decisions of the DRA and its committees. On the other hand, Reform and Conservative rabbis are pleased by the respect shown them by the Orthodox rabbis, and the consideration accorded their concerns and opinions on Jewish issues. In early 1978, this general good feeling became strained. Whether the DRA can continue to insulate itself from the denominational tensions within the broader community remains to be seen.

THE PROFESSIONALS

Federation's professional staff numbers 55, 19 of whom are executive. Since 1970, the staff has been headed by Sanford Solender, executive vice-president. The PPPC is served by three staff members who have other professional obligations within Federation. The DRA also has a professional staff of three, all rabbis, one of whom is responsible for fund-raising at the synagogue level. Relations with Federation's agencies and other beneficiaries, and services to Federation's DC and CPC are under the direction of the executive director for Community Services. Since 1976 this position has been held by Dr. Donald Feldstein. He is responsible for a professional staff of seven, and a Budget Department with its own director and additional staff of five.

The Community Services consultants owe their first loyalty to Federation. They also see themselves, however, as advocates for the points of view and needs of the agencies they serve. Community Services staff functions include advising the agencies, coordinating and facilitating exchanges between them and, in some cases, representing the agency point of view in governmental or professional organizations.

Federation is a member agency of a variety of organizations. Approximately 70 per cent of its annual membership fees (over $250,000) goes to the Council of Jewish Federation and Welfare Funds and the National Jewish Welfare Board, and the remainder to such organizations as the Community Council of Greater New York, Council of Voluntary Child Care Associations, Greater New York Hospital Association, and Council of Social Work Education. Federation consultants may be called upon to serve on these councils, or other ad-hoc committees with professional orientations. In addition, they may be called upon to act as intermediaries between government bodies and the agencies.

The Community Services staff members supply the primary link between Federation and its agencies, and, as such, are sometimes placed in a conflict-of-interest situation. Both sides assume, however, that in such instances they act on Federation's behalf. Indeed, most of their time is spent working directly with Federation's committees and subcommittees, primarily the DC and CPC.

FEDERATION POLICY AND INFLUENCES

Federation's Traditional Policy

More scholarly attention has been paid to Federation's early years than to its recent past. The following material is based primarily on memories and perceptions, rather than a rigorous study of written sources. Apparently, Federation was involved in some measure of communal planning, integration of facilities, and agency control, almost from its inception. Certainly, by the end of the 1940's, a consensus among its leadership on the function of Federation began to emerge. Federation was created to centralize the collection of Jewish philanthropic funds, maximize the amount collected, and distribute the money to beneficiary societies. These agencies were established, in turn, to provide health, welfare, and social services to Jews who required them—primarily the sick, the emotionally and physically handicapped, and the poor. Federation also assisted Jewish Y's and community centers providing recreational, educational and counseling services to middle-class Jews, as well as to the needy. Finally, some money was allocated to Jewish education.[6]

---

[6]The initial decision in 1917 to allocate money to Jewish education was a compromise between those who opposed any allocation and those who sought broad support. The final

But not all Federation leaders perceived their primary function as supporting the agencies. Indeed, more and more of them came to see their roles as maximizing the services to their agencies' clients. Where Federation leaders felt that services could be improved by the creation of new agencies or the merger of old ones, they encouraged this. The challenge was to help those in need. Then, as now, the Board of Trustees was dominated by agency representatives. But large contributors became increasingly oriented to Federation, rather than the agencies. They had a welfare and service philosophy, rather than a loyalty to specific agencies.

The agency point of view lost ground because Federation captured the imagination of the large contributors. It was Federation itself that provided the major portion of most agencies' operating expenditures, and encouraged those contributors to assist them. The 1950's and early 1960's were periods of great construction and expansion. Federation undertook two major building-fund campaigns of 50 and 100 million dollars. One result was the creation and heading of new institutions by Federation people. Federation increasingly directed the pace of its agencies' growth, and recruited wealthy contributors to serve on agency boards. The quality of Federation's professional leadership further contributed to its dominant role.

At the helm of Federation during this period stood two great leaders, each with the title Executive Vice-President. Joseph Willen was responsible for fund-raising, and Maurice Hexter for administration. Serving under Hexter were three professional consultants: Maurice Hinnenberg in the health and aging field; Graenum Berger in the community centers and camp field; and Martha Selig in the family, social-service, and child-care field. Hexter and his three lieutenants have been described by a number of respondents as "giants." They combined intelligence, detailed knowledge of their fields of service, dedication to Federation, and political savvy. Agency executives gave them genuine professional deference, and had difficulty resisting Federation staff recommendations, which were practicable and well-informed.

All of this stimulated an élan among Federation's lay leaders, especially among those on the DC. They felt that they were participating in an exciting, challenging, and supremely important enterprise. One was engaged, through contributing, fund-raising, and committee service, in providing outstanding services to people in genuine need. There was a sense

---

decision limited support to the six principal Talmud Torahs of New York. Mordecai Kaplan, founder of Reconstructionism, celebrated the decision in his diary with the notation: "It has broken the back of the assimilationist tendency." In 1939, the Jewish Education Committee was created out of a merger of the Bureau of Jewish Education and the Jewish Education Association. Federation funds for Jewish education went to this new body, rather than directly to the Jewish schools it served. The new organization, a beneficiary society from its inception, changed its name to the Board of Jewish Education of Greater New York in 1970.

that Federation's professionals, agencies, and lay leadership were the very best.

This elitism was reinforced by the backgrounds of much of Federation's lay leadership. Many came from wealthy families with a tradition of communal service. They were disproportionately of German Jewish origin, second- or third-generation Americans. Neighbors on Manhattan's Upper East Side, with second homes in Westchester, many knew one another socially, belonging to the same country clubs; if they had any synagogue affiliation, they were more likely than not members of a Reform temple—most often Temple Emanu-El of New York City. If their memberships overlapped in any Jewish organization, it was likely to be the American Jewish Committee.

Nineteen sixty-eight marked the end of this period. In December 1977, a questionnaire was distributed to the 22 living members of the 1968 DC. Fourteen responded, but some information was available for all 22. For example, four contributed $25,000 or more to the 1970–71 campaign. Three contributed between $10,000 and $24,999; six contributed from $5,000 to $9,999; and six from $2,500 to $4,999. Thus, 19 contributed $2,500 or more. In 1970–71, Federation raised $17.4 million. Given the fact that UJA and Federation today distribute their joint campaign proceeds on a roughly four-to-one basis, and given rates of inflation since 1970, it seems fair to say that 19 of the 22 DC members made contributions comparable to the $10,000 or more joint-campaign contributions of today. These contributions and, most likely, the gifts ($1,700 and $1,600) of two other DC members, fall into the category of large contributor.

Place of residence is another indication of means. Twelve of the 14 respondents had New York City residences. Eleven lived within a ten-block radius of one another, centering on Manhattan's Upper East Side in the 60's between Fifth and Park Avenues; one member lived on Central Park West. The remaining two respondents had homes in Scarsdale and Rye, wealthy suburbs in Westchester county.

Respondents were also asked to list the social clubs to which they belonged in 1968. Six of the 14 belonged to the Sunningdale Country Club in Westchester, considered one of the elite Jewish country clubs in the Greater New York area. Four respondents belonged to the Harmonie Club, the most prestigious Jewish club in the City. All belonged to at least one social club. By contrast, six of the 14 were not affiliated with any synagogue. Of the remainder, three were members of New York's Temple Emanu-El.

Respondents reported that wealth was not a criterion for DC membership, as it apparently had been in the earlier years. But if great wealth was not a necessary requirement, Federation leaders, for the most part, were certainly people of substance.

The children of East European Jews had entered the ranks of Federation's elite by 1968. Four respondents reported that their fathers were born in Russia. All, however, were themselves born in the United States, 13 of the 14 in New York. Most respondents were between 55 and 65 years of age in 1968. They would have entered college between 1925 and 1935, a period of quotas and discrimination against Jews in the prestigious American colleges and universities. Yet, of the 11 male respondents,[7] nine attended Ivy League colleges (Harvard, Columbia, Yale, University of Pennsylvania, and Cornell). By contrast, their formal Jewish education was slight. Six reported having had no formal Jewish education; five had either attended Sunday school or had some other form of weekly instruction for a few years. Only two had attended afternoon schools which met more frequently than once a week. One respondent reported he was educated in an Orthodox school.

The impression that DC members had a relatively weak Jewish identity is reinforced by other data. Respondents were asked how they would have reacted in 1968 if their child had considered marrying a non-Jew. Only one respondent would have been "strongly opposed"; four would have discouraged it; three would have been neutral; and six would have accepted it.

Many people regard the Federation leaders of this period as assimilationist, but the leaders did not perceive themselves in this light. Respondents were asked how they would have felt in 1968 and how they feel today about the statement, "Being Jewish makes a difference in everything I do."[8] No respondent reported any change in his feelings over the ten-year period. Of the 14 respondents, eight asserted (three strongly and five "somewhat") that "being Jewish makes a difference in everything I do," while six denied the statement (one "somewhat" and five "strongly"). Yet, the respondents' answers are more "Jewish" than those of comparable age and generational groups in Boston.

Maurice Hexter, in discussing his perception of the 1950's and 1960's leadership, introduced the term "assimilationist," but noted that there were few such people around, and these not particularly troublesome. He related having asked the non-Jewish wife of a Federation leader to remove a cross pendant which she had worn to a Federation dinner. She had obliged. The implication was that if one dealt firmly and politely with assimilationists, one could handle them. The troublesome element, in Hexter's view, was the "hyper-Jews," who had provoked difficulty over their insistence on more

---

[7]The 11 males out of a total of 14 respondents is proportionate to the 21 males out of a total of 26 DC members.

[8]The question was derived from the Boston Jewish community survey and used to facilitate comparisons with a larger sample.

money for Jewish education, and their request in 1948 that Federation lend one million dollars to Israel. The request was rejected.

Members of the large middle group of which Hexter was a leader were neither "assimilationists" nor "hyper-Jews." Their participation in Federation was, very probably, a surrogate to participation in the synagogue or other expressions of Jewish life. One traditional leader wrote: "For many Jews, Federation is . . . a vehicle by which the individual expresses a major part of his own Jewish fulfillment."[9] The particular attraction of Federation was that its activity best fulfilled Jewish obligations as the predominantly secularist Federation leaders perceived them, i.e. the obligation to help one's fellow man. Their philanthropic activity was an expression of their view that Judaism is not so much a common set of rituals and beliefs, as a set of ethical imperatives of universal concern. But unlike the East European secularists or Zionists, who also rejected the religious tradition, this group did not perceive itself as being in revolt. The data suggest that this was, instead, a group relatively uninformed about things Jewish. There were exceptions, of which Hexter was the most notable. Perhaps such people reconciled their knowledge of Judaism with the prevailing currents in Federation by finding support for their position in the ideology of classical Reform which prevailed in New York's Temple Emanu-El at the time. This may account for the incorrect perception of outsiders that the majority of Federation leaders were members there.

Federation's Jewishness was further expressed by the fact that its agencies, with the exception of the hospitals, served a predominantly Jewish clientele. Until the 1960's, it was assumed that only Jewish consumers of health, welfare and other social services would seek assistance from Jewish-run agencies, camps, and homes for the aged. But then this assumption became inadequate; the perception of change gave Federation leaders cause for reflection and served to divide the leadership itself. For those to whom Federation was Jewish by virtue of its humanitarian service, the change was, if anything, a source of satisfaction. For those, however, who found service to Jews of particular importance, the change in agency clientele was a cause for concern.

Another "Jewish" rationale for Federation activity was the notion that by serving all needy, regardless of race or religion, Jews enhanced their status in American society. It was felt that non-Jews would appreciate how much Jews were doing, and that this would reduce antisemitism and cement alliances between Jews and non-Jews. This argument suggests a particular sensitivity to antisemitism on the part of a group whose achievements and

---

[9]Leonard Block, "Comments Re 'Preliminary Draft' Report of the Commission on the Role of Federation," Federation of Jewish Philanthropies, January 28, 1972.

status might be thought to have insulated them. In fact, some members of this group experienced antisemitism in a more traumatic way than did the middle-class descendants of East European immigrants.

The Jewish upper classes of New York, the wealthy descendants of German Jewish immigrants who were born in the first two decades of this century, were well aware of what their families had achieved. At the same time, they were conscious of sharp barriers to the penetration of Jews into the upper circles of New York society. The best clubs were closed to them. While German Jews built their own distinguished city and country clubs, this was as much out of necessity as choice. Those who sought admittance to fine private schools and prestigious colleges were often accepted. Precisely because of their high status and sense of personal or familial achievement, however, they were sensitive to the fact that not every club, group, or type of association was open to them in these schools. The pain of discrimination, even when it assumed a petty social form, was compounded by the fact that they lacked a compensatory Jewish pride. Raised in a tradition of noblesse oblige, concern for the needy, and identification with Federation or one or more of its agencies, they knew, however, little about Judaism. It was not, in their opinion, better to be a Jew than a non-Jew; although, having been born a Jew, it was a matter of self-respect not to deny one's identity. This was thin armor with which to shield oneself from antisemitism.

Two respondents actually reported having believed that Jews weren't fully accepted by non-Jews because they were in some sense inferior. Both had identical reactions to the Six Day War, an event which, along with subsequent visits to Israel, deepened their Jewish identity. The Israeli achievement proved, they felt, that Jews weren't really inferior, and that their earlier conceptions of Judaism had been wrong.

In the final analysis, while many of the respondents' relatives—unable to accept their outsider status, find meaning in remaining Jewish, or resist the blandishments of Gentile society—converted, intermarried, or disassociated themselves from anything Jewish, Federation's leaders remained very much within the Jewish fold.

Those who would disparage the motivation of these leaders point to the fact that Federation constituted a kind of club; that entree into its leading circles may have provided the aspirant with business and social relationships. Those who took an active role in Federation might, therefore, have been concerned with their own self-interest rather than service in a Jewish context. Federation did, indeed, provide some social and business contacts for its leaders, but there were other boards, far more prestigious and socially helpful than Federation's Board of Trustees, open to wealthy Jews. According to respondents, these boards, once closed to even the wealthiest German

Jews, were certainly open by the 1960's. Federation leaders, therefore, chose a specifically Jewish forum for their activity when, in many instances, alternative forums were available. Indeed, this is what distinguished them from those who sought to assimilate.

There were some lay leaders, most likely of East European origin, who had deeper Jewish concerns, specifically that of Jewish survival. One of the professional consultants, Graenum Berger, had become, within a Federation context, radically Judaized, and he influenced others. Federation files from the late 1960's include many memoranda from Berger sharply objecting to the direction in which Federation was moving. On the other hand, the Jewish universalist outlook of the majority of Federation leaders was shared by most agency executives.

There is evidence, from a variety of studies, that many Jewish social workers, even those in such ostensibly Jewish institutions as Jewish community centers, and certainly those in psychiatric and case-work agencies, have tended to perceive their personal and professional responsibility in humanistic, universalist, perhaps even Marxist terms, rather than in terms of Jewish survival.[10] Agency executives clearly varied in their Jewish proclivities, but Federation's own lay and professional leaders found their Jewish conceptions reinforced, rather than challenged, by the executives of the beneficiary societies with whom they came in contact. The agencies were generally in sympathy with the notion of service to non-Jews as well as Jews.

How was it possible that in New York, the city with the largest Jewish population in the world, more Jewish institutions than any other American city, and the headquarters of virtually all national Jewish organizations, Federation leadership could remain so relatively insulated?

By the end of the 1950's, in virtually all communities in North America, federations had merged with the major welfare-fund agency, the United Jewish Appeal, whose leadership, at least at the local level, was frequently of Eastern European descent, had Zionist sympathies, and was committed to the survival, as a distinctive group, of American Jewry. In New York, however, Federation and UJA remained separate entities, joining together only for campaign purposes in 1973. The absence of a merger in New York

---

[10]See, for example, Oscar I. Janowsky, *The JWB Survey* (New York, 1948); Herman Stein, "Jewish Social Work in the United States, 1654–1954," AJYB, Vol. 57, 1956, pp. 3–98; and Carl Urbont, "The Purposes of the Jewish Community Center Movement: An Appraisal of its Operation," *Ibid.*, Vol. 68, 1967, AJYB, pp. 29–59. Urbont notes in his discussion of the Jewish community centers: "With the professionalization of agency staffs . . . it entrusted its value system to workers whose training and philosophy are not necessarily rooted in the Jewish community. . . . These workers have recognized social group work with its emphasis on the individual, the group, and the process of personality development, as their discipline. . . . They generally have a stronger loyalty to broader social-work aims as espoused by their national professional organization than they do to center purposes" (pp. 47–48).

was both a manifestation and further cause of major differences between UJA and Federation.

The very size of the New York Jewish community, the multiplicity of its societies, clubs, and organizations, meant that even wealthy Jews did not necessarily mix with one another as they did in other cities. In New York, German Jews maintained separate clubs and societies long after they had disappeared in other areas.[11] Only in New York City, with its large and diffuse Jewish population, could Federation ignore the wishes of the major Jewish philanthropy, UJA, and the developments taking place within significant Jewish sub-groups. Thus, for example, the increased importance of Orthodox Jews in New York went unnoticed until the late 1960's.

New York's large Jewish population, and the fact that it is the headquarters for almost every national Jewish organization, encouraged the development of a variety of independent Jewish organizational systems. In most Jewish communities, federations contribute to such national Jewish organizations as B'nai B'rith, the American Jewish Congress, and the American Jewish Committee. In return, the national organizations restrict their fundraising to special events of a limited nature. But such an arrangement never evolved in New York, where the organizations anticipate raising a significant portion of their budget. Fund-raising, in turn, requires an active organization. Consequently, organizations whose local chapters outside New York have been "smothered" by federations maintain their distance in New York. In addition, the national organizations have a special interest in recruiting a New York lay leadership for their national boards, as well as their local chapters. Thus there is competition for money and lay leaders among Federation, UJA, and a host of other groups, each of which seeks to create its own network of organizational activity. From Federation's point of view, this reduced its potential income (even the combined UJA-Federation campaign has not broken through these distinctive institutional loyalties) and insulated its leadership from trends elsewhere.

Factors Leading to Change

In 1921, Federation's combined allocations to its agencies represented 43 per cent of their expenditures.[12] That figure remained fairly constant until 1947. In that year, Federation's grant represented 40 per cent of its agencies'

---

[11]In Philadelphia, for example, the acceptance of wealthy East European Jews into the "upper class" social clubs of German Jews had occurred by 1940. In Atlanta, however, distinctive social clubs still existed in the late 1940's. Two articles on this topic are found in Marshall Sklare (ed.), *The Jews* (New York, 1958), pp. 262–287.

[12]The percentages reported in this section are derived from Federation of Jewish Philanthropies, *Financial Experience of Affiliated Societies: 1939 to 1973–1974.*

expenditures. From that point on, the proportion of Federation's contribution declined with each succeeding year. By 1951, the percentage was 30 per cent; by 1961, 17 per cent; and by 1971, 5 per cent. This transformation is attributable primarily to the enormous increase in government funding. Federation's own grants increased almost yearly, sometimes by as much as ten per cent, but generally by approximately four or five per cent. (On five occasions between 1946 and 1966, grants were reduced.) The decline in Federation's contribution was most pronounced in the case of hospitals, but other agencies were affected as well.

Table I provides information for a selected group of Federation agencies.

Table I

Federation Grant as a Percentage of the Agencies Total Expenditure

Agency	Year			
	1940	1950	1960	1970
Jewish Board of Guardians* (child care)	82	57	31	16
Jewish Child Care Association	41	47	20	8
Jewish Home and Hospital for the Aged	43	36	17	4
ALTRO Health and Rehabilitation Services	91	90	82	45
Jewish Family Service*	82**	87	75	71
Educational Alliance (community center)	77	77	66	49

*JBG and JFS merged in 1978
**In 1945

In some cases the decline in the 1950's exceeds that in the 1960's. Federation veterans, however, recall the latter decade as a time of crisis, indicating a possible turning point in the 1960's. In the opinion of agency executives, the tremendous increase in government resources in this period served to reorient agency leaders. They became growth conscious, and increasingly directed their programs to areas where funding was available. Federation encouraged this growth, not realizing perhaps that this weakened agency ties to Federation and provided a rationale for increasingly nonsectarian service.[13] Some of the Government's eligibility requirements excluded agencies which confined their services to Jews; this was also true of some non-governmental sources of funding. The Greater New York Fund (the New York counterpart of United Way), for example, allocates, through Federation, funds to some of the latter's beneficiary societies, representing about ten per cent of Federation's grants to its agencies. In the 1960's, the Fund required recipient agencies to sign an affidavit affirming that they did

---

[13]The impact of government funding is discussed in Graenum Berger, "American Jewish Communal Service 1776–1976: From Traditional Self-help to Increasing Dependence on Government Support," *Jewish Social Studies,* 1976, pp. 225–246.

not discriminate in their selection of clients, staff, or board members.[14] Federation was able to overcome the restriction, but a precedent had been set.

The changes occasioned by growing sources of outside support were accompanied by dramatic demographic changes in New York's population. Jews, along with other middle-class whites, tended to move out of the city, while Blacks and Hispanics moved in. Jewish birth rates declined. Finally, the Jewish needy, those who traditionally made use of Federation's services, were increasingly Orthodox, with a high proportion of hasidic Jews, many of whom were reluctant to turn to agencies of any kind with their problems. They did not view problems such as mental retardation or family strife as matters to be discussed outside the family circle. Nor did they expect help in vocational guidance and rehabilitation. Federation's camps and community center services, too, were so nonsectarian in character as to be effectively closed to traditional Jews.

The result was that the number of non-Jews served by Federation agencies increased. Excluding the Orthodox, of whom Federation seemed unaware, demographic changes alone pointed toward a more nonsectarian policy. This policy was further strengthened by the rise of Black consciousness and the notion of community representation, phenomena initially welcomed by many Jews.

Federation's traditional policy came under attack from two sides. The "survivalists" wondered why Federation should continue to support beneficiary societies that had become, in effect, nonsectarian agencies largely funded by the Government. Federation, they felt, should support only those agencies having Jewish programs or providing services to Jews. The survivalists were a minority among Federation leaders, but they included some people of wealth, along with many middle-class Jews who declined to contribute to Federation because of its overly nonsectarian philosophy. The second group, the "nonsectarians," felt that the very conception of a Federation of Jewish agencies had become an anachronism. They viewed the by-laws' provision that beneficiary societies be "organized primarily for the benefit of Jews . . ." as contrary to the needs of the 60's. They may have been responding, at least in part, to the assimilation and intermarriage of their own children; but the fact remains that their ranks were thinning.[15]

---

[14]*Ibid.,* p. 241.

[15]It is interesting to examine campaign income in this light. Income from the 1954 campaign was 13 per cent above that of 1949. Comparable increases for successive five-year periods were 20 per cent in 1959, 5 per cent in 1964, and 14 per cent in 1969. This means that, aside from the 1954–1959 period, campaign increases were not keeping pace with inflation. However, in addition to the annual campaign, Federation launched two successful building-fund campaigns. In the particularly lean campaign years of 1959 to 1964, when campaign income rose from 14 to 15 million dollars, close to $100 million was raised in building funds. Hence, there

The charge that increased government funding made Federation irrelevant was countered by describing the organization's role as providing the added income that permitted the agencies to experiment, carry on pilot projects, and raise the quality of their professional staffs—in short, to uphold standards of excellence. In fact, the idea of "excellence," and the Federation leadership's conception of it as something especially Jewish, was not entirely new.[15a] But nonsectarians insisted that if Federation's contribution was to upgrade service, it should not limit this contribution to any one set of agencies, or to an exclusively Jewish clientele, but should focus on the community of the needy, which cuts across ethnic-religious boundaries.

The survivalists, for their part, argued that they, too, would look beyond Federation's agencies, to the needs of middle-class people, the young, the poor, the sick, the aged, and the handicapped, on the local, national and international levels. This broad clientele, however, would be a Jewish one.

The first challenge to Federation's policy came from the nonsectarians. Early in the 1960's, Joseph Willen proposed that Federation accept, and even encourage, the shift of its agencies to a purely nonsectarian policy. With the acquiescence of Hexter, Willen proposed that Federation cease the construction of Jewish community centers in Jewish neighborhoods, and rebuild in predominantly Black areas such as Harlem and Bedford-Stuyvesant. This nonsectarian outlook was expressed in the volume *The Golden Heritage,* which Federation published in honor of its 50th anniversary. Its pictorial essay begins: "In this village, this city, in this New York, Man is our concern," and concludes: "Whatever concerns the heart and hope of Man—concerns us." The only specifically Jewish photographs, one of Temple Emanu-El and one of a hasidic prayer room, are grouped together with photographs of four churches.

The nonsectarians sought to formalize acceptance of their position in a document, "Goals and Purposes of Federation." A subcommittee of the

---

was no sense of immediate crisis. There was, however, in the opinion of those interviewed, intense concern for the future. Federation leaders had developed an impressive organization, but feared there would be no one to manage it after they retired. Although campaign income had not decreased, there was some decline in the number of very large contributors, and a sharp decline in the number of contributors in general. In the 1966 campaign, there were 84,672 gifts of more than ten dollars. The number of gifts decreased by 1,949 in 1967, 1,652 in 1968, and 3,171 in 1969. (Federation of Jewish Philanthropies, *Report of the Commission on the Role of Federation,* "Preliminary Draft," December 1971, p. 27.)

[15a]It would be interesting to trace the view of "excellence" held by a segment of German American Jews. I suspect that it carried distinctive Jewish overtones; but I hesitate to guess whether it arose out of Jewish defensiveness, a secularization of the "chosen people" concept, or some other source. In a recent unpublished paper, Gerson Cohen argues that Jews in different places and periods have had a particular need to develop a sense of self-esteem in order to protect themselves against currents of assimilation. His analysis suggests that "excellence" filled just this function for some German American Jews.

Communal Planning Committee was appointed to prepare a report to Federation's Board of Trustees. The first draft (June 1967) reflected the nonsectarian point of view, but by the time the final report was adopted in April 1969, its thrust had been neutralized, and the survivalists had taken the offensive. The early drafts recommended that some money be allocated to special programs for non-Jewish agencies, and noted that changes in the clientele of Federation's agencies warranted "reexamination of the composition of the boards of these agencies." By late 1968, the report, now in its fifth draft, paid greater lip service to Federation's Jewish goals, but retained the emphasis of earlier drafts. The nonsectarians insisted that they were merely making explicit the accepted policy of Federation. CPC Chairman David Sher, in presenting a preliminary report to the Board of Trustees, made this quite clear: "The most significant feature of the statement has to do with Federation's role in rendering services beyond those to the Jewish population. . . . What we are seeking here is a recognition of what Federation is already doing in that respect. If Federation, which is already engaged in a variety of general communal services, is to continue to engage in those services, it should do so not unwittingly, not begrudgingly, but should proclaim it proudly as a discharge of a duty which it has to the City of New York, of which it is a citizens' institution."

Sher's point of view was not shared by Federation's president, Samuel Silberman. In a seven-page memorandum dated December 1968, Silberman argued that the statement of goals and purposes had to emphasize that Federation's primary objective was to serve the Jewish community, rather than to support agency programs. He saw no possibility of drawing the nonsectarians into Federation's orbit. To the contrary, he wanted Federation to appeal to the more committed Jews. He cautioned the framers of the report against "alienating groups of worthwhile, responsible Jews because of . . . a rejection of their concerns." To Silberman, community and communal organization were foci of Jewish identity. He, therefore, viewed the entire Jewish community as the constituency of Federation.

The final draft of the Goals and Purposes report was a compromise. It retained a statement that agencies with nonsectarian clients and programs could remain affiliated with Federation, but deleted references to non-Jews serving on agency boards. In general, it eliminated the nonsectarian emphasis, and alluded to some of Silberman's points, without, however, making them the central focus.

At a Board of Trustees meeting on May 12, 1969, a number of amendments which would have strengthened the Jewish emphases of the report were defeated. These emphases, referred to by one past president as a "return to the ghetto," came in a memorandum from the Religious Affairs

Committee which called attention to Federation's role in support of Jewish education and service to Jews. But despite this defeat for the survivalists, the final report differed greatly from the original draft.

The report never played a major role in Federation's life. The language of its final draft was so vague that it could serve many purposes. It was resuscitated in 1977, for example, to legitimate the Jewish emphases of the Communal Planning Committee. The deliberations over the Goals and Purposes did, however, span a crucial period in the development of Federation's outlook. In shifting its focus of concern, Federation veered first toward a nonsectarian position, and then reversed direction. The particularly Jewish emphases of Federation still lay in the future; but the Silberman memorandum, with its communal emphasis, contained in it the core of Federation's new policy.

Silberman and his successor, George H. Heyman, Jr., were especially influential, as a result of a turnover in professional leadership. In 1967, Hexter and Willen retired under terms that assured them a role in Federation's deliberations for another ten years. The three years that followed were difficult ones in terms of professional leadership. One professional recalls that two days after Hexter's retirement, Silberman announced he was returning Federation to lay control. Two Federation executives from outside New York refused job offers because they feared that with Hexter and Willen in the background, they would be unable to act freely. The post was finally offered to an executive with no experience in the field of Jewish communal service, and his tenure was rather unsuccessful. When George Heyman assumed the presidency of Federation in 1969, he chose to leave vacant the position of executive vice-president. Only a year later did Sanford Solender, with a background in Jewish community-center work, take office as the professional head. This meant that Heyman's policies were of unusual importance in this crucial period.

Heyman has been referred to as the architect of Federation's new policies. But, as he himself notes, he would not have succeeded ten years earlier. Conditions in 1969 made Federation policy ripe for change, partly due to the changes in government funding and demography already mentioned. The reorientation of Federation policy was further facilitated by a shift in the outlook of some of its leaders.

Perhaps the most important factors in affecting such a change of outlook were the Black Power movement and manifestations of Black antisemitism. This was the era of the Teachers Strike, of Oceanhill-Brownsville, of antisemitic remarks by Black spokesmen. The assertion by Blacks of their rights led Jews to wonder why they should not think in terms of Jewish rights. Increased government responsiveness, particularly at the municipal level, to demands by ethnic groups, meant that the "rules of the game" had now changed. More and more Federation leaders believed that the growing emphasis on the distribution of resources along ethnic lines required that Jews insist upon receiving their fair share. Finally, Black antisemitism was a traumatic experience for many liberal Jews who had been deeply committed to the civil rights movement, who saw themselves and other Jews as champions of the Negro cause, and who believed that antisemitism, except from the extreme right, had disappeared in the United States.

A second factor that led at least some Federation leaders to change their Jewish outlook was the Six Day War and its aftermath. Both Israel's victory and the renewed threat to its existence contributed to their Jewish pride and concern. It is possible that perceptions of Black antisemitism heightened such feelings by serving as a further reminder that Jews were threatened in the 1960's as in the past. This time, however, Jews had shown that they could fight back and emerge victorious.

A third factor in the transformation of the outlook of some Federation leaders was the growing disenchantment with conceptions of the "common good." This disenchantment could have been a product of the war in Vietnam, a letdown from the Kennedy era, or a gradual erosion of earlier liberal political beliefs. Whatever the case, it reinforced a feeling that Jews had best be more attentive to their own interests. While Federation has not abandoned its concern for the general welfare, it now views its contribution to that welfare through the medium of group interest. Thus, for example, Solender, in urging upon Federation greater explicit concern for the needs of middle-class Jews, argues that in so doing they serve all New Yorkers, because the welfare of the city requires preserving its middle-class population.

The increased visibility of Jewish survivalists also served to alter the views of some Federation leaders. The upward mobility of East European Jews brought increasing numbers of them into professional and social contact with traditional Federation leaders. Some of the East Europeans had deep Jewish commitments and beliefs; a number were Orthodox. These were not exotic Hasidim, but people to whom Federation leaders related as peers.

A number of respondents ascribed special importance to the Commission on the Role of Federation in the conversion of some of Federation's traditional leaders to a more Jewish point of view. The Commission was appointed in 1970 by George Heyman, and was chaired by the man who succeeded him as president, Lawrence B. Buttenweiser. The Commission included both Federation leaders and a number of Jewish communal figures, including rabbis outside the Federation orbit. The Commission's deliberations extended to a weekend at a kosher hotel. Respondents felt that the resultant confrontation of Federation leaders and a number of articulate, sensitive, and deeply committed Jews made an impact on some of the less Jewishly identified leaders. The Commission saw itself as charting a new direction for Federation. Its report, a distinctly "survivalist" document, recommended strengthening Jewish communal activity and putting greater emphasis on Jewish educational and cultural programs. It was presented to the Board of Trustees in 1972. No action was taken, but its impact remained on those who participated in its formulation.

Since 1970, Federation policy has increasingly come to reflect responsibility to the Jewish community. Some of the old leaders have been converted to the new policy; some have dropped out of Federation activity; some have remained as proponents of a minority point of view; some have simply shifted with the new tide. Finally, new leaders have been found.

COMMUNAL INVOLVEMENT

The change in Federation's policy has been expressed through its support of agencies and activities of a community-building nature, rather than those serving the needs of individuals. It has, for example, increased its subventions (allocations to non-member agencies). In the five-year period of 1964–69, subventions increased by 8 per cent, from $271,974 to $295,237. The overall increase in Federation allocations during this period was 15 per cent. In the next five years, subventions increased by 27 per cent, to $396,506; overall allocations increased by only 7 per cent.

Federation created the Jewish Association for College Youth and sponsored a Metropolitan New York Coordinating Council on Jewish Poverty in 1970. The former organization's genesis was tied to a demonstration by college students in the Federation office in 1970 protesting a lack of attention to the needs of Jewish students. The latter organization stemmed from Federation's growing concern for the Jewish poor of the inner city. The council was the beneficiary of a special allocation of $1,200,000.[16]

Far more controversial was Federation's support for the Greater New York Conference on Soviet Jewry, whose task is to alert the public to the plight of Soviet Jewry through educational, cultural, and political activities. Assistance to the Conference meant not only supporting an agency engaged in helping Jews outside New York, indeed outside the United States, but also helping them in a way foreign to Federation's traditional mode of operation. The initial Federation allocation occasioned great debate. It was possible to justify it on the grounds that anything of concern to New York Jews as Jews was part of Federation's responsibility. Federation was not quite ready to accept that kind of rationale. Even today the allocation to the Conference is a matter of contention. While no one opposes the principle of assistance to Soviet Jewry, there are those who feel this should be the

---

[16]On the genesis of Federation's interest in the Jewish poor, with special attention to the role of the Religious Affairs Committee, see Trainin, *op. cit.,* pp. 85–91. See also Metropolitan New York Coordinating Council on Jewish Poverty, *Jewish Poverty Issues* (n.d.).

responsibility of UJA, not Federation. Hence, support is justified on the grounds that the organization "works closely with a number of Federation agencies and provides materials to camps, community centers, and Jewish schools in the New York area."[17]

Another expression of Federation's communal involvement, and a reversal of a previous policy, was its creation of, and support for, the Jewish Community Relations Advisory Council. Incidents of Black antisemitism, a mayor insensitive to Jewish needs, and racial tensions within the City University system in the late 1960's had led to a feeling that organizations engaged in Jewish communal relations should confer regularly with one another. Federation was willing to participate in such meetings, but declined to fund a permanent organization, following a 1968 CPC recommendation.

By 1973, attitudes within Federation had changed. A new, younger leadership, led by Daniel S. Shapiro, agitated for a formal Jewish Community Relations Council (JCRC). It felt that Federation should take the initiative in creating such a body, as it was, according to Shapiro, "the central body for Jewish communal life." This view differed radically from the earlier one. With noteworthy rapidity the new outlook had become an assumption, at least on the part of the younger element. Thus, despite some internal opposition, and the objection of some Jewish communal organizations which feared the competition, Federation was instrumental in establishing and funding the JCRC in 1976.

Close ties to the JCRC represented a whole new way of viewing society and the Jew's role in it. Jews were now viewed as a distinctive group with distinctive group interests. Such a conception carried political overtones and affected the individual's understanding of what it means to be a Jew. It stood in dramatic contrast to the traditional view of Federation leaders.

Some people have noted that Federation undertook many of its communal projects reluctantly, over internal opposition. One respondent commented that "Federation really backed into these projects." But while it is true that Federation responded to communal pressures, and in the case of its poverty program, to the availability of government money, it also responded to pressures from within, pressures wrought by changing leadership and altered attitudes.

By the late 1960's, Federation had already accepted two new reference groups. One was the national Jewish community as represented by the Council of Jewish Federations and Welfare Funds. Federation responded positively to the Council's requests for allocations and special grants, and the deliberations and decisions of the Council and its General Assembly

---

[17]Federation of Jewish Philanthropies, *Distribution Committee Report*, 1978–1979, p. 62.

provided ammunition for those who sought to change Federation's direction. Proponents of more funds for Jewish education, for example, legitimated their demands by pointing to Council statements and decisions.

Secondly, Federation became increasingly responsive to what its leaders called the "traditional" segment of the community, by which they meant primarily the Orthodox. Members of this segment were influential in that they were perceived as constituting both the bulk of the Jewish poor to whom Federation had to respond, and the anchor for Jewish neighborhood stabilization.[18] They were also represented among the wealthiest Jews in New York. In fact, the two New York gifts of $5 million to the Israel Emergency Appeal in 1973 came from Orthodox Jews. Hence, campaign needs, too, dictated greater sensitivity to their wishes and needs.

Federation's communal involvement increased along with its recognition that agencies must demonstrate community roots in order to obtain government funding. This meant establishing relationships with local Jewish community councils and seeking neighborhood support for Federation agencies. Federation was rather late in eradicating its image as a rich Jewish club removed from the reality of urban life. Other Jewish groups, particularly Orthodox ones, had meanwhile established their claims, and benefited from government assistance, before local Jewish community councils with ties to Federation could make their voices heard.[19]

The single most important Orthodox group competing with Federation for funds for employment guidance and senior-citizen services is Agudath Israel. But there are scores of smaller agencies and institutions that benefit from government assistance. Some of these, hardly legitimate, receive government money because they command, or give the impression of commanding, a constituency of potential voters. Obviously, not all the funds which have gone to them might otherwise have gone to Federation; but without these groups Federation agencies would have been greater beneficiaries of government funding.

Federation has not sought to expose the fraud in which some of these groups engage. Indeed, its policy is not to do so, although information which has led to the exposure of a few of the groups has come from people

---

[18]In supporting a proposal to help a middle-income Orthodox community, a member of the CPC commented that neighborhoods were more stable where there was "a stable Orthodox Jewish community." He pointed out the necessity, therefore, of "involving the Orthodox community in joint programs if viable Jewish neighborhoods are to remain": *Minutes of the Communal Planning Committee*, September 15, 1976.

[19]There are approximately 40 local councils of Jewish organizations located in the Greater New York area. A majority of these are connected in some way to Jewish community centers. Federation spends close to $175,000 in direct and indirect support for 27 of the councils. There are closer ties between eight Jewish community councils in poverty areas and the Metropolitan Coordinating Council on Jewish Poverty established by Federation.

in Federation or its agencies.[20] Instead, Federation sought to establish ties with that segment of the Orthodox community adept at politics and the art of securing grants, without compromising its own standards of honesty and quality service.

Federation also encouraged its own agencies to strengthen ties to local political leaders. The Public Program and Policy Committee (PPPC) became the vehicle for coordinating this activity, a fact which accounts in part for the growing importance of that committee.

JEWISH EDUCATION

The history of Federation's involvement in Jewish education is a complex one that has engendered much controversy. There is a perception within Federation that the resounding victory won by the proponents of Jewish education a few years ago left a residue of bad feeling among some who were defeated. It, therefore, comes as a surprise to learn that in 1930 Federation allocated 4.9 per cent of its total grants to Jewish education; in 1960, 4.8 per cent; in 1970, 5.5 per cent; in 1977, 6.3 per cent; and in 1978, 7.2 per cent.[21]

These figures however, are misleading. In the first place, the 7.2 per cent total allocation for Jewish education in 1978 consisted of a grant of $1,701,000 to the Board of Jewish Education, and a grant of $215,000 for tuition assistance to Jewish schools, primarily day schools, made through the Program Development Fund. The Board of Jewish Education spends most of its money on programs of consultation and guidance to most of the 210 Jewish day schools and 440 afternoon and Sunday schools in the Greater New York area. It also offers some direct support to schools through incentive grants and interest-free loans. (This was estimated at $169,000 in the 1977–78 fiscal year.) In addition to these sums, and other aid offered by the Board, such as engineering consultation or assistance in securing government aid, Jewish schools also benefited in 1977–78 from approximately $1 million in interest-free loans from the Hebrew Free Loan Society, another agency of Federation. Federation repaid the interest lost through depletion of its reserves. Finally in 1972, Federation established the Program Development Fund (PDF), presently geared to attracting large gifts. Its largest donor is Joseph Gruss. As of January 1978, Gruss had contributed $2 million of the $4.3 million raised by the Fund. There were

---

[20]The topic of Jewish corruption is discussed in Perry Davis, "Corruption in Jewish Life," *Present Tense*, Winter, 1978, pp. 19–24.

[21]A sharp attack on Federation's policy with regard to Jewish education appears in Moshe Sherer's "What is Federation doing with the Jewish Charity Dollar?" *Jewish Observer*, February-March 1977, pp. 4–6.

29 other donors, 20 of whom contributed $100,000 or more. In 1977–78, the PDF distributed $1,075,000, 90 per cent of which went directly to day schools.

Only in 1978 did Federation itself allocate a sum of money to the PDF for direct tuition aid to schools. The Fund is, however, sponsored and encouraged by Federation. In the fall of 1978, it appeared likely that Federation's assistance to the PDF would be further increased. With the exception of Gruss, few, if any, of the donors would have contributed to Jewish education were it not for Federation recruitment. The number of Orthodox contributors, in particular, has been negligible, as they generally prefer to support their favorite day schools directly.

If one combines PDF grants, allocations to the Board of Jewish Education, and allocations to Jewish schools through the PDF, expenditures for Jewish education represent 10.6 per cent of Federation's total 1978 allocations. This does not take into account indirect aid, loans, and informal programs of Jewish education. Some Jewish community center expenditures, for example, are for educational programs. The Jewish Association of College Youth also spends money on Jewish education. Many of Federation's camps have Jewish educational programs, as do many of the agencies serving children and senior citizens; the recreational facilities of various Jewish community centers are utilized by 50 day schools for their physical education programs; and Federation's family and vocational agencies provide social work and guidance in a number of day schools.

Jewish education has received a growing percentage of the Federation dollar since 1968. While the increments do not match those for community centers (which increased from 23.8 to 28.8 per cent from 1970 to 1978), they are larger than those in any other functional field. The fact that budgetary decisions are made within the confines of minor incremental changes in periods of relatively constant income makes Federation's efforts on behalf of Jewish education all the more notable.[22] Federation allocations to Jewish education, exclusive of the PDF, increased by 15.1 per cent from 1977 to 1978. Allocations to community centers increased by 5.6 per cent, and to all other functional fields by less than two per cent.

Nevertheless, Federation allocations for Jewish education fall considerably below those of federations throughout the United States. In 1976, the last year for which comparable data is available, the 15 largest federations outside New York allocated 26 per cent of their funds to Jewish education.[23] Whether one uses a 7.2 or 10.7 per cent figure for New York, the differences

---

[22]Between 1975 and 1976 the 16 largest federations increased their allocations to Jewish education by ten per cent. New York's increase (inclusive of the PDF) ranked fourth highest.

[23]"Federation Allocations to Jewish Education 1966–1976," Council of Jewish Federations and Welfare Funds, *Reports,* November 1977.

are marked, particularly as the bulk of New York's money goes to consultive services performed by the Board of Jewish Education, rather than to direct financial aid to Jewish schools.[24] Federation has, however, encouraged the Board to increase its direct assistance to these schools.

The Jewish education issue was never one of support versus non-support, but rather involved such questions as the extent to which such support should become a Federation priority, whether support for day schools should be a particular priority, and the extent to which schools should be funded directly rather than through the Board of Jewish Education.

Support of Jewish education in general, and of day schools in particular, has indeed become a Federation priority. At the same time, Federation has eschewed the radical change in policy required to increase such support dramatically. Such a change would involve either new campaign mechanisms to permit the earmarking of contributions for Jewish education (a proposal made in 1977 at an informal gathering of a few Federation leaders) or the elimination of some agencies and programs which Federation currently supports.

In 1968, Federation president Samuel Silberman appointed a Functional Committee on Jewish Education, under the chairmanship of Solomon Litt, to prepare recommendations on Jewish education for the Board of Trustees. The committee was composed of trustees and non-trustees favoring greater Federation assistance to Jewish education. The Committee's report was prepared by a consultant (Hyman Chanover of the American Association for Jewish Education) and submitted to the Board of Trustees in 1970. It reviewed the background of Federation involvement with Jewish education, cited the effort of other cities with large Jewish populations to fund Jewish education, and noted the demonstrated association between intensive Jewish education and positive Jewish identity. The recommendations called upon Federation to double its allocation to the Board of Jewish Education, and to establish a 25-million-dollar Jewish Education Endowment Fund. The Fund was to be comparable to a Federation Building Fund; that is, money was to be solicited from contributors beyond their annual campaign contributions. The report recommended that Federation provide an incentive grant by drawing upon its reserves to contribute to the Endowment Fund on a matching basis.

The Board rejected the report. The proposal that Federation indent reserves to match grants to an endowment fund was thought to be unrealistic.

---

[24]Ten federations, including New York's, spent over $500,000 on Jewish education in 1976. Baltimore and New York were the only two communities in which more funds were allocated for consultive services than for financial aid to local schools. In five communities (Cleveland, Detroit, Montreal, Philadelphia, and Toronto) the ratio of allocations for consultive services to those for direct school aid was below 50 per cent: *ibid.*

Nor could the Board accept the notion that Jewish education was an essential ingredient for Jewish survival when most Federation leadership had none.

What Federation leaders were prepared to accept was the traditional Federation philosophy of helping Jews in need. This was the argument developed by George Heyman and other proponents of increased support for Jewish education. It began with the assumption that the public schools were terrible. No Federation leader living in New York, it was argued, would send his children to a public school. Poor Jewish parents, however, could not afford private schools. Were they to be deprived of a decent education for their children? Support for Jewish education was, therefore, justified in terms of helping needy Jews. For Heyman himself, support for Jewish day schools was related, at least in part, to an assertion of Jewish pride. He reported that a turning point in his own position came when a Catholic prelate asked him, "Why are Jews embarrassed to spend Jewish money for Jewish purposes?"

A second legitimation for support to Jewish education was the fact that many of the day-school facilities were so deteriorated as to be in violation of building codes. Hence, they required support to protect the image of the Jewish community and to provide minimum sanitary and safety conditions for Jewish children.

It is ironical that the most indirect rationale for Jewish education—relegating it to an aspect of philanthropy—provided greater legitimacy to aiding Jewish day schools than to helping supplementary schools, and played down the importance of the work of the Board of Jewish Education, which sought to improve the quality of education, rather than to provide schools with direct financial aid. This may help to explain why the Program Development Fund elicited major contributions from people having neither a personal commitment to the value of Jewish education, nor any particular sympathy for the Board of Jewish Education.

The philanthropic point of view pervades a second report on Jewish education, commissioned by Federation, prepared by Eli Ginzberg,[25] and submitted in April 1972. This report reflected the view that something should be done for Jewish schools specifically, rather than Jewish education in general. It called for the phasing out of the Board of Jewish Education's consultative services and the substitution of direct support of schools, "particularly of day schools serving low-income students," and a scholarship program for needy students "primarily in day schools."

The Ginzberg report was even less acceptable to Federation than Chanover's. First of all, the Board of Jewish Education had just undergone some

---

[25]Eli Ginzberg, "Federation's Responsibility for Central Services for Jewish Education in Greater New York" (April 30, 1972).

reorganization, had hired a new executive, Dr. Alvin Schiff, and was benefitting from an improved relationship with Federation. The Board, therefore, was able to call upon friends within both Federation and the Jewish community for support. Secondly, many, even some who supported its general recommendations, felt the report was based on inadequate data. Finally, Federation was unwilling to assume the responsibility for allocating money directly to Jewish schools and fixing the criteria by which these allocations should be made. An intermediary agency was therefore necessary, and the Board of Jewish Education was the obvious candidate. Since it was to continue in existence, it made sense for it to undertake such functions as educational consultation and guidance.

Federation's present policy reflects elements of both reports. Creation of the Program Development Fund, for example, was a step in the direction recommended by the Chanover report. The spirit of the Ginzberg report is found in modified form in the Distribution Committee's attitude toward the Board of Jewish Education. While the Board's services in raising the quality of Jewish education are appreciated, there is a pressure on the Board to provide greater direct support to Jewish schools. The more indirect the services are, the more probing the DC becomes. Federation's 1978 allocation of tuition assistance to schools established distribution criteria. The Functional Committee on Jewish Education will seek to coordinate the variety of services offered Jewish schools through the Board of Jewish Education, PDF, Hebrew Free Loan Society, and other agencies. This new trend could result in greater selectivity in allocations to schools, as the Chanover report recommended, and in increased Federation leverage to encourage the coordination, even merger, of schools in many areas. These developments might presage a far more centralized authority in Jewish education in New York than hitherto. Many forces in the community view these developments with unease, and are seeking to assure themselves the greatest possible voice in any decisions that will be made.

Finally, the philosophy underlying Federation's support for Jewish education today is that Jewish education strengthens Jewish identity. In June 1977, at the introductory and concluding plenary sessions of Federation's 60th anniversary celebration, the audience heard speakers emphasize that Federation's highest priority was Jewish education as an instrument for Jewish survival.

JEWISH PROGRAMMING

Federation today insists that Jewish values and needs be reflected in agency programs. This aspect of Federation policy received emphasis in the DC report to the Board of Trustees in 1977. DC Chairman Billie Tisch noted several considerations affecting the DC's shift in funding. The first was "the Jewish purposes of Federation." Federation, she stated, could not be all things to all people. The shortage of funds had forced the DC to "focus on the places and programs where we are best able to serve, and where no one else can or will pay attention to specialized situations."

Another important concern is the proportion of Jewish clientele served by each agency. Budget reports, prepared by DC staff in anticipation of budget hearings, include information on the agency's Jewish census. Agencies serving a predominantly non-Jewish clientele, and unable or unwilling to institute changes in policy to attract more Jews, have faced cuts in allocations and, in a few cases, the threat of disaffiliation. This policy has strained Federation-agency relationships in some instances, but has been accepted by most Federation leaders.

A more subtle policy change is reflected in Federation's desire to enlarge the Jewish content of its agencies' programs. This is a touchy point for Federation leaders, since the lives of many of them are not noticeably rich in Jewish content. Should Federation encourage its agencies to maintain kosher kitchens, or close on the Jewish holidays, when the vast majority of Federation leaders do not themselves believe that Jews are obligated to eat kosher food or refrain from work on Jewish holidays? Should Federation leaders insist that the informal educational programs in its camps or child-care centers contain Jewish content when some Federation leaders are themselves ignorant of, and indifferent to, Jewish culture?

Despite the apparent incongruity, this is the direction in which Federation is moving. Federation leaders rationalize such measures with a philosophy of service to clientele. They argue that serving the needs of Jews means creating a Jewish environment and observing Jewish ritual. Thus, for example, kosher facilities must be available so as not to discriminate against Jews whose religious convictions require them to eat kosher food.[26] This argument finds reinforcement in the Jewish-census issue. Agencies are told that if they want to increase the proportion of Jews they serve they must tailor their practices to the needs of a Jewish clientele. Given the relatively high proportion of Orthodox Jews among the pool of potential agency users, this policy means accommodating the Orthodox. There is evidence that those agencies serving the Jewish poor which have taken steps to meet the needs of traditional Jews have experienced increased enrollments. And, as the evidence accumulates, Federation's staff and the DC feel justified in exerting more pressure in this direction.

---

[26]All food served in the Federation building itself is kosher, and Federation is closed on Jewish holidays.

The emphasis on Jewish content and programming is justified in part by the need to raise or maintain a high Jewish census. But the attention which DC members and staff devote to the introduction of kosher facilities or more Jewish programming in their agencies, and the pleasure they show when progress is made in this regard, indicate that their interest goes beyond the desire to increase an agency's Jewish census. It appears that many Federation leaders are increasingly committed to Jewish programming as an end in itself. Some see this commitment as a stage in the recovery of their own Jewish identity.

Indeed, another argument for greater Jewish content stresses the benefit of just such a strengthened self-identity. One child-care agency not noted in the past for its emphasis on things Jewish has argued that its professional responsibility toward the emotionally-retarded child requires providing a Jewish ambience which strengthens his sense of identity and security. This kind of programming has been indirectly challenged in the courts in the case of Wilder vs. Sugarman.[27] Federation has an important stake in the outcome.

HOSPITALS

Ten hospitals are beneficiary societies of Federation. In the 1977–78 fiscal year, they received about $4.5 million, or 17 per cent of Federation's total allocations. The money represented .7 per cent of their total budget. The hospitals are the pride of the Federation system in the general community, but they have been a source of controversy in the Jewish community.

Federation has reason to be proud of its hospitals, particularly for their pioneering work in medical research. Federation leaders like to point out that many Jews who are critical of Federation hospitals turn to them when they require medical care. On the other hand, the hospitals are the focus of criticism for many Jews who are unhappy with Federation. There is

---

[27]The suit challenges the constitutionality of the New York State child welfare system, which provides that neglected or abandoned children are, "when practicable," to be assigned to agencies of the same religious affiliation as the child. (The bulk of child care in New York is provided by religious-sponsored agencies.) Although both Jewish and Catholic agencies serve Black children, the suit charges that the religious preference clause has the effect of concentrating Black children in Protestant agencies which are overcrowded, or placing them under direct supervision of the city in conditions that are inferior to those of the voluntary agencies. If successful, the suit would force the government to assign neglected or abandoned children to agencies without regard to religion. The impact on Federation agencies could destroy whatever special Jewish nature they might have. The suit on behalf of the plaintiffs was brought by the New York Civil Liberties Union. See Richard Severo, "Church Groups See Danger in Child Care Bias Lawsuit," *New York Times,* March 16, 1975, and John R. Hale, "The Wilder Case: Threat to Child Care," *America,* April 20, 1974, pp. 304–306.

resentment that hospitals whose clientele is predominantly non-Jewish, and whose environment is in many cases indistinguishable from that of a non-Jewish hospital, are supported by Jewish public funds. To many, the hospitals epitomize an older Federation image—institutions under Jewish auspices, benefiting from Jewish money, but doing nothing in particular for the Jewish community.

There is further opposition to Federation support for hospitals as a matter of priority. It is argued that even if the hospitals were more Jewish-oriented, they would not merit Federation support, given other unmet Jewish needs. Medical care is almost by definition nonsectarian. While it would be nice to have a kosher kitchen in a hospital (five of the ten have), frozen kosher food is available in non-Jewish hospitals. While it might be reassuring to have a mezuzah on the hospital door (five of the ten have), patients are not required, under Jewish law, to utilize rooms with mezuzahs. Federation's obligation, the argument goes, is to support those Jewish activities which are specifically Jewish in nature, and which depend on the Jewish community for funding. Given the needs of Jewish schools, and the shortage of Federation money, there is resentment that large sums are allocated to hospitals.[28]

There are, however, some very practical reasons for continued assistance to hospitals. First of all, there are large contributors to the Joint Campaign who serve on hospital boards, and who might reduce their contributions if Federation were to discontinue its support for the hospitals. In one year alone, 66 members of the Mt. Sinai Board contributed over $2 million; 44 members of Montefiore's Board, about $1.3 million; and 83 members of Beth Israel's Board, over $2 million. The average contributions of members of major hospital boards were: Mt. Sinai, $31,500; Montefiore $30,000; and Beth Israel, $24,700. In contrast, the average contribution of board members of some of the largest and most prestigious non-hospital agencies were: 92nd Street Y, $14,700; Associated Y's, $11,300; Jewish Family Service, $7,200; Jewish Home and Hospital for the Aged, $6,400; Jewish Board of Guardians, $4,400; and Altro, $2,800.

Hospital participation in the Federation network benefits Federation and all of its agencies in other ways, as well. Hospitals account for some $24 million of the $27 million spent annually by Federation's joint purchasing plan. Joint purchasing provides significant discounts to Federation agencies in the purchase of various supplies, and the greater the bulk purchases, the larger the discount. (On the other hand, Federation hospitals are beneficiaries of Federation's joint insurance program, which provides hospitals with

---

[28]Cases for and against Federation support for Jewish hospitals are presented by Sanford Solender and J. David Bleich, respectively, in Sh'ma, May 2, 1975. See the rejoinder by Bleich in Sh'ma, May 16, 1975.

malpractice insurance at considerably less cost than that available to non-Federation hospitals.) Federation leaders also believe that their association with hospitals gives them increased status, which translates into political influence in representations to government agencies. Finally, hospital boards have been an important source of recruitment of Federation leaders.

Whatever the reasons, there is firm support within Federation for continued allocations to hospitals. However, three points should be noted. First, allocations to hospitals as a percentage of total allocations have declined steadily since 1960, and will probably continue to decline. In 1960, 38 per cent of Federation's funds went to hospitals. This fell to 32 per cent in 1965, 25 per cent in 1970, 20 per cent in 1975, and currently stands at 17 per cent. The decline began before basic changes in Federation's policy were introduced, and reflects a general consensus that other functional fields have greater priority.

Secondly, it is Federation policy to encourage hospitals to strengthen their Jewish ambience, and to provide special services for Jews. Brooklyn Jewish Hospital has established an outreach health center in Crown Heights for the Lubavitcher community, and Maimonides Hospital has a special program for the Orthodox Jews of Boro Park. Beth Israel Hospital, in the past two years, has undertaken an intensive program of specialized services to the Jewish community. The Distribution Committee made it known to hospitals that its level of support for each would depend in part on the availability of necessities and conveniences to Jewish patients. In 1977, the chairman of the DC subcommittee on medical care wrote to all Federation hospitals asking them about the presence of kosher kitchens, chapels, mezuzahs, sabbath lights, etc. Increments in Federation's support of hospitals is related to their Jewish programs. In 1977, for example, Federation cut its allocations to hospitals by $300,000, a reduction of six per cent. However, two hospitals, Beth Israel and Maimonides, received increases "in acknowledgement of their more intensive services to the Jewish community in the number of patients served, and in attention to traditional Jewish values."[29]

Federation's policy has had an impact on the hospitals. Some hospitals claim that their association with Federation provides them with an identity they value. Others appreciate the historical association. Perhaps some members of hospital boards have wanted to move in a more Jewish direction anyway, and their attempts have been strengthened by Federation's concerns. Finally, whereas Federation's contribution is a small portion of the hospitals' budgets, it is a substantial help in meeting deficits. Hospitals have argued that Federation's contribution makes possible the quality aspects of

---

[29]Morton Fisher, *Report to the Distribution Committee on Federation Medical Care Agencies,* September 1977.

their programs, and enables them to carry on their special functions for the Jewish community. Some Federation leaders are troubled by the possibility that if Federation support continues to decline, the hospitals themselves may lose interest in remaining part of the Federation network. Hardly anyone within Federation would welcome this development.

Still, those hospitals serving an almost exclusively non-Jewish clientele, and unable or unwilling to develop programs meaningful to the Jewish community, are being phased out. In the case of Bronx Lebanon Hospital the phasing out is almost complete.

THE JOINT CAMPAIGN

The joint campaign which Federation conducts with the United Jewish Appeal is an outgrowth of policy as well as an expression of institutional self-interest.

When the Yom Kippur War broke out on October 5, 1973, five days after Federation's opening campaign dinner, it was speedily agreed that the Federation campaign be coordinated with a special United Jewish Appeal drive. But that decision followed a year and a half of discussions on the possibility of a merger. In the 1960's, Federation had rejected a UJA proposal to merge the campaigns. The two organizations, however, had continued to provide some services to one another. In the mid-1960's, UJA had threatened to withdraw from any cooperative venture should Federation elect as its president a certain member of the anti-Zionist American Council for Judaism. Federation had acquiesced.

During Heyman's administration, Federation leaders began to reconsider a joint campaign. The Yom Kippur War, then, was the final push to a process already begun. In 1974, Federation and UJA concluded a two-year arrangement for a joint campaign. While the sums allotted are subject to renegotiation, the joint campaign seems to have become a permanent arrangement. The joint campaign cannot be understood solely as an arrangement resulting from financial need. Nonmonetary considerations played a vital role in its establishment, and in the continuing desire of both sides to maintain it.

The Joint Campaign has saved the overhead costs of two separate campaigns. UJA executive vice-president Ernest W. Michel, who serves along with Solender as executive vice-president of the UJA-Federation Joint Campaign (a new organization established for campaign purposes and directed by a 30-member board composed of 15 representatives from each side), estimates a saving of two to three million dollars in campaign costs. But there are losses as well. A few past contributors to either UJA or Federation, for example, are so unhappy about the fact that their money will go to the other side that they refuse to contribute to the Joint Campaign. The number of gifts over $10,000 has remained constant, however, as the dropouts have been replaced by new givers. Similarly, there are a few large contributors who, because of ideological dissatisfaction, have not increased the size of their gifts, although they are in a position to do so. Others, while pleased with the merger, fail to give a new contribution equal to the sum of their two previous ones. A man who had previously given one million dollars to UJA and $80,000 to Federation found it easy to round off his gift to the former figure. Campaign contributions have dropped each year since 1974, and while no one attributes this entirely to the merger, it is difficult to argue that the merger has helped.

Some UJA people attribute Federation's desire for a joint campaign to its own financial difficulties. (Indeed, the UJA national office did not favor the merger.) Federation income, they say, reached a plateau by 1973. The terms of the merger provide Federation with a minimum sum regardless of how little is raised. In 1978–79, for example, Federation is guaranteed a minimum of $17 million from the campaign; ten per cent of net cash receipts from $55 to $60 million; 20 per cent of receipts from $60 to $62 million; and 30 per cent of receipts from $62 to $65 million. Federation receives ten per cent of all net cash receipts beyond $65 million, but no one expects that level to be reached. Current estimates of net cash income for 1978–79 are 62.3 million, putting Federation's share at $18 million. Thus, not only is Federation guaranteed a certain sum, but it also can depend on a regular monthly cash flow from the campaign.

These benefits ought not to be overstated, however. Unlike UJA, Federation has never had a serious cash-flow problem, or the problem of uncollected pledges. Secondly, if one looks at Federation's cash income from 1959 to 1972, there is no evidence of a plateau. The pattern, in fact, is one of big jumps in income one year followed by small increases or declines the following year. (See Table II, p.48.)

With campaign and associated costs deducted, Federation's net cash receipts in 1972–73 were $15.4 million. There is no question that Federation derived immediate financial benefits from the Joint Campaign. It received as much as $18.4 million on three occasions since 1974, and anticipates $18 million for 1978–79. On the other hand, if one assumes that Federation's income since 1972–73 would have grown at a rate of three per cent a year, then by 1978–79 it would have reached $18.4 million, more than Federation estimates it will receive from the Joint Campaign.

In addition to the financial reasons discussed, the UJA-Federation merger was a product of ideological decisions. By 1974, Federation's conception of its Jewish communal role had taken firm root. The desire for a joint campaign with UJA reflected an awareness that Israel was the primary

Table II
Cash Receipts From Campaign Contributions to Federation, 1950–1973

Year	Campaign Income (to nearest thousand)	Annual Percentage Change
1949–1950	$10,362	
1950–1951	11,672	11.2
1951–1952	11,724	No change
1952–1953	11,341	−3.3
1953–1954	11,732	3.3
1954–1955	11,756	0.1
1955–1956	13,125	10.4
1956–1957	13,061	−0.5
1957–1958	12,885	−0.1
1958–1959	14,132	8.8
1959–1960	14,325	1.3
1960–1961	14,702	2.5
1961–1962	15,242	3.5
1962–1963	15,160	−0.5
1963–1964	15,082	−0.5
1964–1965	15,762	4.3
1965–1966	15,485	−1.7
1966–1967	15,897	2.5
1967–1968	16,862	5.7
1968–1969	17,986	6.2
1969–1970	17,496	−2.8
1970–1971	17,410	−0.5
1971–1972	16,594	6.4
1972–1973	18,765	0.9

Jewish concern of the bulk of New York's Jews. If Federation was to build a meaningful Jewish community, and play a central role in that community, it had to participate with UJA in efforts on behalf of Israel. UJA leaders agreed that there must be a united Jewish community able to express within the framework of one organization its concern for both local and overseas Jewish needs.

An additional factor leading to the Joint Campaign was each side's desire for some non-material resources of the other. Federation leaders were perceived as younger, brighter, more sophisticated, and of higher social status than those of UJA, who had, in turn, an emotional dedication in contrast to Federation's style. This passion was important in energizing campaign workers at all levels and in moving wealthy Jews to make substantial contributions.

It is difficult to measure the impact of the Joint Campaign on Federation's outlook. Many attribute the increased Jewish concerns of Federation to the merger. In an effort to strengthen ties with UJA, Federation has, indeed, appointed a number of UJA activists to its Board of Trustees and key committees. But Federation was seeking to expand its leadership base with people of deeper Jewish commitment before the Joint Campaign, and the merger is itself an outcome of Federation's growing Jewish concerns. The shift in Federation's orientation began three years before the final agreement.

Nor has the merger dissipated all the old antagonisms. Differences in the two organizations' styles are still discernible. Some UJA leaders label Federation people assimilationists and social snobs. Conversely, a few Federation leaders characterize UJA activists as "Seventh Avenue," a reference to New York's garment district, where some UJA leaders made their money.

The differences in approach which still exist between the leaders of the two organizations were reflected in a joint budget-hearing conducted in 1977. Each organization allocates its own funds independently. However, as there are two agencies which receive allocations from both UJA and Federation, it was decided to conduct a joint hearing at which representatives from these agencies could present their budget requests. One of the invited agencies was the Greater New York Conference on Soviet Jewry. UJA people focused on the needs of Soviet Jewry, on the tragedy of the "refuseniks," and on the importance of doing everything possible to aid Soviet Jews. Federation representatives, on the other hand, expressed their concerns about how the Conference was spending its money, how it justified certain expenditures, and how a small increase or decrease in income might affect its operation.

Nevertheless, all respondents report that, in general, differences and antagonisms are receding, as Federation and UJA people increasingly work together.

Resistance to the New Policy

Not everyone has accepted Federation's new policy of greater Jewish responsibility and commitment. There was resistance, as was noted, within the Board of Trustees. Some resistance continues to this day, as it does within Federation's key committees. In 1975, for example, the CPC rejected a project designed to draw unaffiliated Jews into organized Jewish life. There was objection to the merit of specific proposals, but some also felt the project's purpose was not within the scope of Federation. As late as 1976, objection was raised to Federation involvement in neighborhood-stabilization efforts. According to one CPC member, this was "an inappropriate departure from Federation's more traditional concerns with health and welfare issues." The majority, however, were recorded as feeling that "neighborhood stabilization as well as other efforts connected to the well-being of the Jewish community were indeed appropriate for Federation."[30]

Those of the older leadership who would resist Federation's increasingly Jewish commitment deserve recognition for their service in the past. They are serious about their ideological objections to Federation's new direction, even as they feel increasingly uncomfortable in articulating them. They espouse Jewish universalism, and are concerned for the needy, Jewish and non-Jewish alike. They are ready to admit that Jews are entitled to priority in benefitting from Jewish public money, but they regret Federation's reluctance to serve non-Jews. On what scale of moral values, they wonder, would such services as improving the quality of Jewish schools assume priority over the needs of homeless children, the handicapped, the retarded, or the aged poor? They see Federation's new policies—its insistence on kosher facilities in its agencies, its encouragement of Jewish programming, but, most of all, its priority support for Jewish day schools—as "a return to the ghetto." This Jewish particularism strikes them as anachronistic and as a challenge to everything on which they, as American Jews, have staked their Jewish identity.

Some former Federation leaders have withdrawn, to a greater or lesser extent, from active involvement. Others have remained active because of tradition, a commitment to the good things they see Federation doing, or the special pleasure they derive from Federation work. Finally, there are those who are less critical of the new policy per se than of the manner in which it has been implemented. This point of view is widely shared among agency executives.

The charge most frequently leveled at Federation is that it has become politicized. The charge is unfair in that people were always appointed to the Board, and even to key Federation committees, for reasons besides merit. But behind the charge of politicization is the feeling that a new set of priorities is leading to the appointment of people who would never have played a role in the past. There is more to this assertion than social snobbery or prejudice against East European or Orthodox Jews. As Federation has become more communally involved, and more concerned with Jewish matters, it has sought to recruit a leadership more representative of the Jewish community. Some people have been appointed to committees and then failed to attend meetings. A few new members of key committees have indicated that they are not concerned with the gamut of Federation activities or committee concerns, but only with specific issues. Many appointees are less knowledgeable of Federation and its activities than was the case in the past. It is asserted that the new appointees, with their parochial Jewish concerns, lack the dedication to the needy that characterized the older members. As Federation has come to appreciate the necessity for political

---

[30] *Minutes of the Communal Planning Committee,* July 13, 1976.

support, it has recruited people with political connections whose integrity is questioned by some. Finally, it is charged, the new policy has affected the allocation procedure itself, requiring Federation to direct allocations in response to communal pressure, rather than need.

The latter assertion reflects dissatisfaction with specific policies as much as with procedure. The charge is made that allocations are made to agencies, groups, or neighborhoods in order to satisfy new constituencies or potential contributors. Federation leaders, however, believe that their allocation decisions, with but a few exceptions, are justifiable in terms of objective need.

Another criticism of Federation's new policy is that the emphasis on serving Jews is counter productive. Thus, for example, one community center executive argues that if his center is to survive in a predominantly non-Jewish neighborhood it has to earn the support of non-Jews as well as Jews. This requires some provision of services to non-Jews, involving them in program planning as well. Exclusive focus on Jews would destroy the center's community roots, alienate the non-Jews, and harm the center's chances of obtaining government funding. If, the executive argues, the center is to help stabilize the Jewish population in a predominantly non-Jewish neighborhood, it can do so only through the creation of good will and a sense of common interest between Jews and non-Jews. The executive of another agency stressed that the law obligates him to serve a neighborhood constituency. His way of increasing service to Jews is to locate in Jewish neighborhoods. Federation, he feels, is pressing him into a confrontation situation with the government and the local community by seeking to impose a quota system for Jews.

Some charge that Federation's concentration on matters of Jewish concern has reduced its influence and prestige with many of its own agencies. One agency director, deeply committed to his agency's program of special services in the field of mental health, was eager to describe these services to the Distribution Committee. But, he complained, what the Committee wanted to know was how many Jews his agency served, why a particular facility didn't provide kosher food, and what was the Jewish ambience of another facility. He claimed to have no objection to such questions in principle, but maintained that they missed the point of his agency's primary purpose.

Such agency executives, by and large highly-skilled professionals, feel that Federation is less sensitive today than in the past to the quality of service. Some complain that their requests for money for pace-setting programs are rejected because of Federation's new priorities. On the other hand, they see Federation as imposing programs on them which they feel should be of lower priority.

There is also dissatisfaction on the part of some with regard to Federation's own executive staff. After Hexter's resignation in 1967, and until Solender's appointment in 1970, there was no strong professional leadership at Federation. Solender's appointment was followed by a period of tension within the professional staff. The director of Community Services during one period was perceived as especially abrasive, and many agency executives are still sensitive about his relationship with them. Furthermore, the fact that Federation's community service staff has, by and large, stronger Jewish orientations than most agency executives, coupled with the agency executives' sense that their own professional competence is greater than that of Federation's staff, makes them especially sensitive to the manner in which they are approached.

Professionals within Federation deny that their emphasis on Jewish concerns has reduced their interest in the quality of the agencies' services. They argue that many agency executives have been as resistant to discussions of service matters as to those of Jewish issues. There is a resistance, they argue, to strong guidance by Federation.

Finally, some agency executives who enjoy increased influence within their own organizations have expressed dissatisfaction with their personal, as distinct from their agencies', role in Federation's decision-making structure. The voice of the agency executives is heard through the Federation Agency Executive Meeting, convened monthly. In 1977, its participants formed a Governance Task Force which met with the DC and CPC chairmen to express their desire for greater participation in Federation decision-making. They complained that Federation was not adequately responsive to agency agenda and priorities. There is evidence that their desire for an increased role in Federation will find at least partial satisfaction. Agency executives have already been invited to appear before the CPC to discuss issues of general concern, in addition to specific agency items. Moreover, the executives have played an important role in planning the annual Sunday seminar of the CPC and DC, an event of central importance in shaping the perspectives of committee members.

Reflection of Federation Policy in Allocations

Regardless of the changes and new priorities within Federation, its daily activities continue to reflect its traditional concern for its agencies and their work. The Distribution Committee does spend time on such matters as encouraging agency use of standardized equipment and the purchases of services by one agency from another. One DC member remarked, "The agencies *are* Federation." While this statement is not quite accurate, it does reflect both an ideological conviction of some other leaders and Federation's intense involvement with the welfare of its beneficiary societies.

In addition, changes in Federation priorities have not been reflected in radical changes in allocations. This is demonstrated by the following table, which summarizes the percentage of Federation allocations to the different agencies in each functional field since 1960.

Table III
Percentage of Federation Dollar Allocated to Agencies Grouped by their Major Functional Field

Year	Care of Aged	Medical Care	Child Care; Family & Vocational Guidance	Jewish Education	Community Centers	Camps	Special Projects
1960	5.1	37.6	31.0	4.8	17.0	3.1	1.4
1965	5.4	31.7	32.8	4.6	20.3	3.6	1.6
1970	7.7	24.9	31.2	5.5	23.8	4.9	2.0
1975	7.8	20.0	32.1	5.9*	26.4	5.2	2.6
1978	7.7	17.1	30.3	7.2*	28.8	5.0	3.9

*Excludes the PDF

Noticeable changes are the decline in allocations to hospitals and the increase in allocations to community centers. The hospital decline, however, preceded the change in Federation's Jewish policy, and resulted from a sense of the hospitals' relative lack of need. The increased support for community centers, which also predates Federation's new policy, is explained by the relative absence of government funding for community centers. Since users' fees are inadequate to support the centers, and since it was Federation itself which encouraged the massive building campaign of community centers after World War II, there is a feeling that Federation has a special obligation to maintain these facilities. More recently, there has been a conviction among many Federation leaders that centers play an important role in Jewish socialization.

Federation's new priorities have found expression in other allocations. Jewish education rose from 4.8 per cent in 1960 to 7.2 per cent in 1978. (If one includes the Program Development Fund, the jump was to 10.6 per cent.) Special projects went from 1.4 to 3.9 per cent. Overall, however, the magnitude of change is not overwhelming. This stems in part from the nature of the budgetary process, in part from the DC's desire not to antagonize beneficiary societies who have strong allies within Federation, and, most of all, from the DC's faith in the value of the existing agencies and their ongoing programs. Of course, changes in allocations are only one way of reflecting new priorities. The introduction of new elements into agency programs is no less important.

How Much Influence Does Federation Exercise?

FEDERATION AND ITS AGENCIES

Observers believe that Federation no longer exercises the influence it once did over the structure and services of its agencies. The decline in Federation's contribution to agency expenditures, which began in the 1950's, was reflected even then, according to a former DC chairman, in a lessening of influence. Federation influence has also declined because the agencies find themselves increasingly involved in professional networks and associations to which they are accountable. In addition, they are increasingly accountable to government bodies, which fund their programs and seek to exercise a measure of control.

To the extent that Federation facilitates exchanges of information between agency executives, assists in the coordination of programs, eliminates duplication, and provides data useful for long-range communal planning, it is making important contributions to agency programming. A number of agency executives noted that they visited Federation headquarters far more frequently than any other office beside their own. It is to Federation that they turned for help and some of their most satisfying collegial relationships.

Many multi-purpose agencies find that Federation's consultants are useful to them in areas where the executive and his staff lack expertise. No one on the staff of the Jewish Association for Services to the Aged, for example, knows as much about medical care as Federation's consultant for medical services, according to JASA's principal executive. His advice, therefore, is actively sought.

Some agency executives report, too, that Federation's professional influence exceeds the influence of other funding agencies and departments, which may provide far more money. Precisely because Federation concerns itself with an agency's total program rather than with the detailed provisions of one type of service, or the administration of one type of grant, Federation gives the agencies a sense of participation in a larger community, and a sense of direction beyond the specific question of level of services. Many agency executives, for personal reasons or because they feel their own board members prefer it, maintain close ties to Federation, and this makes them aware of Federation's outlook on matters.

Federation is more influential today in shaping the Jewish nature of its agencies. Increasing the proportion of Jews whom the agencies serve and developing specific programs, facilities and personnel who can deliver agency services to the Orthodox Jewish community are examples. Where the agency board and the executive are at all sympathetic, either because of personal Jewish concerns or a desire to please Federation, Federation has been most influential.

Executives report that in the absence of Federation allocations, they would be forced to look elsewhere for funds, and this would compel them to increase the number of their non-Jewish clients and programs. Others report that only Federation's pressure prevents their own boards from pushing them in a more nonsectarian direction. There is no doubt that in the absence of Federation influence, the composition of the boards themselves would be affected.

Under Federation prodding, the Infants Home of Brooklyn now serves an almost exclusively Jewish clientele; the Jewish Board of Family and Children's Services is seeking a kosher facility in suburban New York and has established an office in an Orthodox neighborhood; the Jewish Child Care Association wishes to establish a kosher facility for retarded children; JASA operates a relocation service to move elderly Jews out of slums and into more Jewish neighborhoods; the Federation Employment and Guidance Service operates a program of vocational guidance aimed specifically at the Jewish community; and 13 of Federation's 17 camps have kosher kitchens. Joel Ehrenkranz, chairman of the DC's subcommittee on medical care, noted that in his group's visits to beneficiary hospitals in 1977, the executives emphasized what they were doing for the Jewish community.

Federation has even succeeded in persuading its agencies to increase the Jewish context and environment of services to Jews who simply do not care about a particular agency's Jewishness. The Lexington School for the Deaf, for example, asked Federation how it could increase the Jewish content of its school program. Many Jewish community centers, once devoid of Jewish content, now not only provide special services to Orthodox Jews, but also have a variety of Jewish educational programs for all their members. Richest in Jewish content, as a general rule, are the pre-school programs. But there are also teen, adult, and senior-citizen programs which explore different aspects of the Jewish heritage. The majority of children in Federation agency residential centers are non-Jews, 40 per cent of the Altro Health and Rehabilitation Service's clients are non-Jews, and the Federation Employment and Guidance Service serves more non-Jews than Jews; nevertheless, even some agencies serving more non-Jews than Jews may be providing important services to the Jewish community at an efficient rate of return on the Jewish dollar. For example, the nonsectarian aspects of an agency's program may make it eligible for government or foundation funds that enable it to enrich its specialized programs for Jews.

Federation cannot, however, impose policies where an agency's executives resist them. It is difficult to force a Jewish community center to undertake an outreach program for Jewish marginal youth, where the professional staff lacks the Jewish skills or the desire to undertake the program. Lack of influence is most noticeable when Federation's contribution is a small proportion of the agency's budget. It cannot force the Jewish Home and Hospital for the Aged, the one non-kosher home among Federation's four homes, to install a kosher kitchen against the wishes of an agency board that is proud of its tradition of non-kosher facilities. Yet the Jewish Home and Hospital is a showcase agency of Federation in terms of the quality of services it offers. Its clientele is 95 per cent Jewish, and no one contemplates its disaffiliation. An interesting case is Louise Wise Services, an adoption agency which offers little service to the Jewish community and is adamantly nonsectarian in its point of view. Federation cut its allocation to Louise Wise in 1977, and seems to be moving toward disaffiliation. Yet it has hesitated to take the final step. Support for Louise Wise has come from agency executives who are concerned about the precedent which such a move might establish.

In the final analysis, the ability of Federation to impose a Jewish policy, and the willingness of its agencies to accept such a policy, depends on more than allocations, sanctions, good will, or even a philosophy of Jewish life. It also depends on the demographic facts of life in New York.

FEDERATION AND GOVERNMENT

Federation's declining role in contributing to its agencies' expenditures might be offset by its ability to influence government. Agencies would like Federation support in securing government funding, and they look to Federation to assist them in supporting or opposing legislation which concerns them.

While there are many instances of Federation success in this regard, a recent instance of failure may have greater long-term significance. New York City has a certain number of federally-funded positions under the Comprehensive Employment and Training Act, which it distributes to a variety of local agencies. These positions, known as CETA slots, are a source of competition between local non-profit groups. In 1977, Federation requested 400 CETA slots for its agencies. After a long wait and subsequent negotiation, in which Federation agencies were pressured to offer political support for the incumbent mayor in the City primary, Federation was given only 80 slots. In many respects, the CETA experience may have been the straw that broke the camel's back, and led to a determination on Federation's part to organize itself to prevent a similar occurrence.

Federation leaders are treated with deference and regard by government officials. Federation people feel this stems from acknowledgement of their expertise, along with the fact that some of the most important business and professional leaders of the City are closely associated with Federation. Respect and personal deference, however, are not always translatable into political success.

At the state and national level success is more difficult to measure. Federation leaders believe that their good relationships with congressmen and state legislators assure them a voice in policy areas which directly affect Federation agencies. They are pleased with the results they have obtained since engaging a part-time lobbyist in Albany in 1976. If activity is any measure of future success, Federation influence should increase. It is inventorying its government contacts and extending its relationships with legislators. Finally, there is an awareness that since developments affecting Federation's agencies are as likely to stem from administrative decisions as legislative action, relationships have to be forged at the bureaucratic level as well.

Federation does not maintain a Washington lobbyist, but does contribute to the support of the CJFWF Washington office. That office, in turn, looks to local federations for guidance. The New York Federation sees itself as better geared to provide legislative recommendations than other federations, and, therefore, as having an especially important role in shaping the policies of the Washington office. Whether Federation can influence government on matters of general concern to the Jewish community depends not only on its contacts but also on its ability to formulate policy in this regard.

FEDERATION AND THE JEWISH COMMUNITY

The changes in the past ten years in Federation policy and in the recruitment of new leaders have certainly contributed to the integration of Federation policy-makers with other leaders of the Jewish community. Although relationships with the religio-political leadership of the Orthodox right wing, as represented by Agudath Israel and the *rashe yeshivot* (heads of advanced academies for Talmudic study), are still marginal or hostile, the Lubavitcher *Rebbe* maintains a cordial relationship with Federation. In general, Federation touches the lives of many Orthodox Jews in the inner city, and many communal leaders of modern Orthodox synagogues and organizations hold leadership positions in the organization. Finally, Federation, through the Joint Campaign, publicity in the mass media and synagogues, its association with a local newspaper *(Jewish Week),* and its activities in subcommunities of New York, serves to remind New York Jews of the existence of at least the semblance of a New York Jewish community.

Although the largest media effort in the 1977 campaign, a five-hour telethon, struck many as tasteless, the campaign itself served to arouse increased Jewish communal consciousness.

Except through the Joint Campaign, Federation is limited in its ability to reach the community directly. Its influence on communal identity and policy comes primarily through its agencies and institutions. Federation has encouraged its beneficiary societies in the direction of greater involvement with the Jewish community and has given increasing emphasis to the local neighborhood as the basis for communal organization. Whether it is possible to develop a sense of loyalty to the Jewish communities of Crown Heights, Boro Park, the West Side, or Suffolk County remains to be seen. It can be argued that Jews are no less likely to develop loyalties to such entities than to the Greater New York Jewish community. Furthermore, as long as the government distributes funds along neighborhood lines, and other ethnic groups perceive neighborhood divisions as relevant to them, Federation's policy makes a great deal of sense.

It is possible that the recently reactivated Functional Committee on Jewish Education will attempt to increase involvement in the local Jewish community. This is the first Jewish area in which Federation may attempt to play an active role in the formation of specific communal policy, because this is an area in which it can call upon people with significant knowledge, understanding, and ideological conviction. Federation has only recently evolved a policy oriented toward the creation and strengthening of a Jewish community. It does not, however, frame its positions exclusively from the perspective that asks: what are the policy implications that flow from a primary concern for a strong Jewish community, for a community committed to Judaism and the Jewish people? It has no research arm and, therefore, does not gather the kind of information that would provide a basis for such policy formation.

The second way in which Federation might exert influence on the Jewish community is through the community-wide organizations it supports. These are the Jewish Association for College Youth (JACY), the Greater New York Conference on Soviet Jewry, the Greater New York Metropolitan Coordinating Council on Poverty, and the Jewish Community Relations Council. All these are subvented agencies, not beneficiary societies. Federation has no clear-cut policy with regard to shaping these agencies' communal policies. In budget hearings with representatives of the Conference on Soviet Jewry, for example, questions focused on printing and staff costs, whether educational materials of the Conference were distributed in Federation camps, and why the Conference didn't list UJA and Federation as its major contributors. At no point did any representative of Federation or UJA ask about Conference policy.

The Metropolitan Coordinating Council on Jewish Poverty was created by Federation, and Federation representatives sit on its board. In the early years, Federation expressed concern that the Council might engage in activity which duplicated or competed with that of its beneficiary societies. But Federation evidences no interest in the Council's general communal policy. This is less true of JACY and the JCRC, both of which look to Federation as their primary source of funding. JACY has been asked to explain why it has a policy of distributing small amounts of money to many different groups, rather than larger amounts of money to fewer groups, and there is frequent discussion of such policies as serving committed youth rather than marginal Jewish students. JCRC, in its two years of existence, has had a far greater impact on Federation than vice versa. Some JCRC leaders are also Federation leaders, but Federation's official representatives do not necessarily bring a Federation outlook to JCRC.

Part of the reason for Federation's reluctance to be more active in the formulation of communal policy is its lack of experience. Some Federation leaders are also still leery of communal involvement. Others are aware of their own Jewish limitations and are reluctant to engage in a confrontation with other Jewish groups, or to assert their leadership. For example, it is left to the more committed Jews on the DC to raise questions about the funding of religious organizations.

Policy decisions frequently involve ideological choices, and Federation eschews ideological issues. It does so, in part, to avoid alienating and antagonizing various elements, particularly the element still committed to previous policies. But Federation also eschews ideological discussion because its leadership is uncomfortable with such questions. While there is no shortage of intelligence in Federation, there is an absence of intellectuality. This handicaps the organization by denying it a blueprint for planning. Avoidance of conflict may cost eventual loss of leadership and authority in the Jewish community.

In any case, there are inherent limitations to the policy innovations which any federation can or should offer. The Council of Jewish Federations and Welfare Funds emphasizes in its publications that since federations are "voluntary organizations representing broad-based support," they must operate through consensus rather than majority rule. Careful attention is paid to such matters as whether an issue divides the Jewish community, and whether the issue bears a relationship to the community's power structure.[31] Daniel Elazar suggests that, as a result of this, federations have

---

[31] CJFWF National Committee on Leadership Development, *Discussion Guide*, November 1976, p. 9.

unconsciously become the instruments of government for the Jewish community, a community which, as he observes, is "thoroughly unideological."[32] The danger rests in two directions—in failing to recognize that the absence of ideology bears distinct limitations, and in sacrificing too much for the sake of consensus, when it is not clear that all the elements in Federation are committed to Jewish survival as an operative goal.

FEDERATION LEADERSHIP

Composition

Although there are some influential Federation leaders who are not members of the Distribution Committee, the DC will once again be taken to be representative of Federation's lay leaders. Its decisions on allocation of funds are the most important ones that Federation makes on a regular basis, and its members, by virtue of their standing within Federation, are disproportionately represented among Federation officers, on the Executive Committee, and on the Level of Grants Committee.

The president of Federation and the chairman of the Communal Planning Committee are both ex-officio members of the DC, and they, along with 29 available members, were sent questionnaires. Twenty-seven responded.

Twenty-eight per cent of the members, including the immediate past chairman, are women (as compared to 19 per cent ten years earlier). Four members maintain two residences. One member commutes from Palm Beach, Florida. Another 13 live in the suburbs. Of these, one lives in Connecticut, ten in Westchester County, and two, including the present chairman, in Nassau County on Long Island. In contrast to the DC of 1968, a far higher proportion of members now live outside the City. (In 1968 all the suburban residents lived in Westchester.) Of those still in New York City, the majority live in the 60's between Fifth and Park Avenues. But one lives in Riverdale, in the Bronx; and one in Forest Hills, Queens.

In the 1976–77 campaign, four members of the DC contributed over $100,000, eleven from $10,000 to $100,000, eight from $5,000 to $10,000, and seven between $1,500 and $5,000.

The DC, then, remains a committee with a membership drawn from predominantly wealthy people. As was true ten years ago, great wealth is

[32]Daniel J. Elazar, "What Indeed is American Jewry?" *Forum* No. 28–29 (Winter 1978), p. 159.

not a necessary condition for membership, but certainly no one falls below what is generally classified as upper middle-class.

Social club membership provides an interesting contrast between 1968 and 1978. In 1968, all respondents belonged to a social club. In 1978, four of the 27 did not, and three noted on their questionnaires that their club memberships were not very important to them. Members clustered in four clubs; 26 per cent belonged to the Harmonie Club (identical to the 1968 figure), 26 per cent to the Sunningdale Club (down from 43 per cent in 1968), 18 per cent to Beech Point Club, and 15 per cent to the Century Country Club.

DC members still tend to have been educated in elite colleges. Of the 18 men who responded to a question about their undergraduate college, 12 attended Ivy League colleges or schools of a similar status. However, two attended the City College of New York, two New York University, and one Lehigh. Four of the five respondents from non-elite schools were sons of foreign-born fathers. Indeed, 44 per cent reported their fathers were foreign-born, 37 per cent from Eastern Europe. In contrast, 28 per cent of the 1968 members were children of East European fathers. A number of observations by DC members and others suggest that the 1978 members may be as wealthy as those of 1968, but a much higher proportion were born into modest, even humble, circumstances.

It is in Jewish background and identity that the sharpest contrasts are evident. Let us look first at Jewish education.

Table IV
Jewish Education of Distribution Committee Members: 1968 and 1978
(By Percentage)

Jewish Education	1968	1978
None	43	22
Sunday school or equivalent to age 13	36	22
Supplementary school or equivalent to age 13	14	26
Day school and/or formal schooling beyond age 13	7	30
Total number of respondents	14	27

A supplementary-school education to age 13 may not impart much more knowledge than a Sunday school education, and both may leave the child hardly better informed than one with no formal Jewish education. The differences, however, do indicate the kinds of homes in which the respondents were raised.

Differences were also marked in synagogue membership. Some respondents were members of more than one synagogue. In the table that follows, such respondents are listed according to the synagogue they indicated as most important to them.

Table V
Synagogue Membership of DC Members: 1968 and 1978
(By Percentage)

Synagogue	1968	1978
None	43	18
Orthodox	0	18
Conservative	21	11
Reform	36	48
Reconstructionist	0	4
Total number of respondents	14	27

Respondents were asked to indicate their reaction to the statement: "Being Jewish makes a difference in everything I do." The question replicated one asked in a 1975 study of the Jewish population of Greater Boston.[33] The Boston data are reported by age and generation in the United States. Since almost all New York respondents were between 40 and 64, and either second- or third-generation Americans, the comparison is presented. Unfortunately, in the report of the Boston study, data for some of the categories were collapsed so that the detail available for DC members is not available for the Boston respondents.

Table VI
Response to "Being Jewish Makes a Difference in Everything I do."
(By Percentage)

Response	1968 DC	1978 DC	Boston Sample Second Generation US (Aged 40–64)	Boston Sample Third Generation US (Aged 40–64)
Agree strongly	21	44	30	15
Agree somewhat	36	30		
Disagree somewhat	7	11	67	81
Disagree strongly	36	15		
No answer	—	—	3	4
Number of respondents	14	27	261	111

[33]Floyd J. Fowler, *1975 Community Study: A Study of the Jewish Population of Greater Boston* (Boston, 1977).

The importance of being Jewish has increased for 1978 DC members. However, as indicated earlier, 1968 DC members gave a more Jewish response than did the comparable age and generational group in Boston.

Respondents were also asked to check the statement which most appropriately conveyed what they would be likely to do if their child were to consider marrying a non-Jew. There are only 24 responses from 1978 DC members. Two members, instead of checking a response, wrote out answers that did not lend themselves to any simple categorization. Once again, two of the options were collapsed in the presentation of the Boston material.

Table VII
Most Likely Response to Child's Considering Marrying a Non-Jew
(By Percentage)

Response	1968 DC	1978 DC	Second Generation US (Aged 40–64)	Third Generation US (Aged 40–64)
Strongly oppose it	7	28	19	9
Discourage it	28	36	23	36
Be neutral	21	12	} 52	} 39
Wouldn't mind, accept it	43	24		
No answer	—	—	6	16
Total number of respondents	14	25	261	111

There are noticeable differences between the 1968 and 1978 DC members. Furthermore, the 1968 members, unlike the 1978 members, report they are more likely to accept the intermarriage of a child than a random sample of the Boston Jewish population in similar age and generational categories. Among the general Jewish population, opposition to intermarriage declined sharply from 1968 to 1978—not so for DC members. This reinforces conclusions that the level of Jewish identity among Federation leaders has risen in the past ten years.

The average age of the 1978 DC members was 57. They were likely, therefore, to have had college-age children during the late 1960's and early 1970's, a time of youthful rebellion. A few respondents noted that the behavior of their children had an impact on their own Jewish consciousness. In some cases, they were troubled by their children's intermarriages, and this led them to wonder if there were some ingredient missing in their own Jewish lives. In one case, the parents' acceptance of their children's right to a radically different life style led them to affirm their own right to a Jewish life style.

Other respondents, however, reported that their Jewish identities were shaken more by the Yom Kippur War than by any family situations. "I realized," wrote one, "that the whole meaning of my life would be zero if anything happened to the State of Israel."

To many DC members, Federation activity not only expresses their Jewish identity (a fact no less true of the 1968 members), but also contributes to it. Some suggested that the effect was generally intellectual, and not entirely one-directional. As one respondent put it: "On the one hand, I am more inclined to be active in Jewish matters because of the need, and on the other, I resent the religious people pushing their position over the less religious." A more typical response was the assertion that Federation activity contributed to the respondent's sense of Jewish communal consciousness: "While . . . I was interested in matters of Jewish concern, . . . most of my concern was for my congregation and my particular areas of interest. Now, for better or worse, I hardly look at the paper without seeking a Jewish impact." Some noted specific changes in the direction of that consciousness: "I am now an enthusiastic supporter of Jewish education." Most common, however, was the response that Federation activity intensified one's Jewish feeling and identity: "It has made me much more aware and knowledgeable about Jewish culture and concerns. I have been exposed to the entire spectrum of Jewish conviction and identification, and found it appropriate and necessary to reaffirm my own Jewishness."

No one reports specific changes of life style or habits as a result of Federation activity, although some of the responses hint at this possibility. No one reported that he or she had joined a synagogue, established a kosher home, begun observing the Sabbath, or even undertaken a program of Jewish study as a result of involvement in Federation. Perhaps the concrete expression of the intensified Jewishness reported by so many respondents is their own activity on the DC. The profound impact of Federation activity on the Jewish identity of the respondents is affirmed so often and so emphatically that one would be surprised if it found no expression in the life styles of at least some of the respondents.

No less interesting is the effect of Federation activity on some of the more recent DC appointees, who have backgrounds of intense involvement with Jewish matters. One noted that an important aspect of his service was trying to understand other people's concerns in areas to which he had not been exposed. Another observed, "Prior to my active participation in Federation activities, I was not aware of the commitment and dedication of so many key community leaders to Jewish causes through their active involvement in Federation's activities."

In summary, Federation's present leaders are different from those of ten years ago. They are still a wealthy, well-educated group, but they are somewhat more likely to be of Eastern European descent, far more likely to be synagogue members and to have had at least a minimal Jewish education, and far more concerned with questions of Jewish identity and survival. Six DC appointees are members of Orthodox synagogues, and are identified in one way or another with national Orthodox organizations. Federation President Harry Mancher epitomizes the new type of Federation leader. A self-made man, a graduate of the City College of New York, a member of a Reconstructionist synagogue, Mancher also serves as treasurer of the Joint Campaign, and has a history of UJA activity which parallels his active involvement in two Federation agencies.

How Representative Are Federation Leaders?

Federation has sought greater representation of the Orthodox, and of various geographical areas. It has been far more successful with regard to the former than the latter. The DC remains heavily over-representative of Westchester and Manhattan's Upper East Side. It has only one member from Queens, none from Brooklyn, and two from Long Island, although these areas contain the bulk of New York's Jewish population. The necessity that DC members be able to contribute large amounts of time works against representativeness. It means that there is a larger pool of available women than men. Billie Tisch, the DC's immediate past chairman, estimates that the proportion of women available to fill a DC vacancy, as opposed to men, is five to one. For a period of two years, until mid-1978, all three of Federation's key committees were chaired by women. The greater leisure time available to women means that, by and large, they are able to attend meetings more faithfully.

The time requirement restricts activity to those individuals who not only are economically successful, but who also hold the kind of position which does not require continued presence on the job. Federation's schedule is such that activists must be available during the working day—a result, in part, of the fact that Federation leaders live in the suburbs, making evening meetings unfeasible. This may help account, for example, for the absence of physicians or young businessmen from the ranks of Federation's leaders. There are some young lawyers, but they come mostly from law firms located on Lexington, Park, and Madison Avenues in the 50's, a few minutes' walk from Federation's offices. Less understandable is the absence of Jewish academics. Only one college professor serves on a key Federation committee.

Federation leaders are certainly not representative of New York's Jews, or of Federation's own contributors. By and large, they are more Jewishly concerned and committed. It is ironical that many Federation leaders think of most New York Jews as being more committed than they, and believe that their own heightened Jewish consciousness somehow makes them more representative of New York's Jews.

On occasion, Federation leaders pay lip service to their representative function, in order to justify what they intend to do in any case; never, it seems, as a constraint on what they would like to do. Thus, for example, an agency serving a high proportion of non-Jews will be told that Federation cannot continue to support its program, as Federation contributors expect their money to be spent for Jewish purposes. No one has ever pursued this point too far, nor has anyone ever suggested polling contributors to discover how they really want their money spent.

There is a growing feeling among Federation leaders that their function is not so much to do what the Jewish community wants as to define what it needs and to encourage its component members and organizations to meet those needs. As we noted, Federation is handicapped in this regard by the lack of an ideology. The professional staff, therefore, plays an unusually crucial role in this regard.

The Reward System

Federation has one practical incentive to offer its non-professional leaders —special entree and access to its own agencies, and to the other agencies and institutions with which it has indirect contact. According to one former professional, this service once included assistance to the children of Federation leaders in getting into the college of their choice, or even into medical school. Today it more commonly means providing help in placing someone in a home for the aged, or securing a private room in a hospital, when these are scarce. One rabbi mentioned this as an important incentive for his own activity. He noted that he called upon Federation agencies for help in securing hospital care and a variety of other services for the members of his congregation. Special access to agency services is a pleasant reward for activity, but does not seem to constitute a significant incentive to Federation leaders.

In fact, Federation has a problem generating an adequate reward system, which by its nature must be primarily symbolic. Its leaders are fairly sophisticated and more immune to the kinds of rewards that characterize the UJA and other national Jewish organizations. For example, shaking hands with the prime minister of Israel, or having one's picture taken with a general in the Israeli army, does not provide the thrill to Federation leaders that it does to others. Secondly, rewards such as honorary chairmanships and dinners tend to be distributed to campaign workers and large contributors, rather than to committee members.

Although outsiders assume the incentive of business contacts to be of importance to Federation activists, no one interviewed expressed the belief that Federation activity is very useful for business associations. At most, it was suggested, it is useful in enhancing an individual's reputation among existing clients and customers. There are those who have pointed to an occasional job or client acquired through Federation activity. Most, however, suggest that their Federation contacts are more likely to involve them in offering free advice and services. Of course, they, in turn, may have received such advice and services.

Federation itself buys and sells securities, engages in real-estate transactions, and purchases supplies. There is a potential here to benefit from Federation involvement. There have been hints of favoritism in the past. Federation leaders are confident, however, that they have protected the organization from this form of exploitation by their insistence that all transactions be open.

Another incentive is the social reward to be derived from Federation involvement. Federation's leadership has traditionally been part of a Jewish social elite. It seems, however, that neither Federation itself nor its key committees constitute social groups. This is in contrast to agency boards, which have a stronger social component. Respondents report that, at most, they have made one or two social contacts as a result of Federation activity. There are instances of large contributors finding that Federation contacts opened the doors to membership in prestigious social clubs. Respondents also report, however, that entrance into social clubs through this route rules out more intimate social contacts. Furthermore, such reported instances go back 20 and 30 years. A number of highly regarded Federation leaders report that their activity has not opened any new social horizons for them, although they would have welcomed it.

This is a weakness, as well as a strength, of Federation. It means that Federation's leaders have not exploited the social status they are able to confer on potential leaders. In this respect, Federation is unlike the UJA, whose leaders have found that the campaign merger has not appreciably increased their social contacts with Federation leaders. Some are prone to attribute this to snobbism. In fact, it is part of a Federation tradition which dissociates social life from Federation activity. Perhaps this was necessary in the past, when there were strong ties of family and friendship between Federation leaders and Jewish assimilationists who sought nonsectarian outlets for their philanthropic activity. Interestingly, this tradition not only differs from that which prevails in most voluntary Jewish organizations, but is also at variance with the style of elite cultural organizations. Symphony, opera, and museum boards in New York have a strong tradition of active socializing among board members.

There is, therefore, a measure of truth in the statement of a former Federation president that the reward for being a DC member is "a lot of hard work." In the final analysis, probably of greatest importance to members is the fact that they find their work stimulating and challenging and believe they are making a significant contribution to fulfilling Federation's purpose.

Recruitment

Many Federation leaders emerge from the ranks of the large contributors; but individuals known to Federation leaders through business or social contacts are also recruited directly to key committees. This was true of the DC even before 1968. Having agreed to join the DC, these individuals were then appointed to the Board of Trustees, to fulfill the by-law requirement that DC members be selected from at-large trustees. It was hoped that such people would then increase their contributions to the campaign, although there is no requirement to this effect.

A more common method of recruitment, relying essentially on the same social and business contacts, is the appointment of individuals to agency boards, rather than to Federation itself. Agency boards frequently serve as testing grounds for future Federation leaders, with Federation raiding the boards to secure key workers. Sometimes board members themselves express an interest in Federation activity, and transfer the focus of their activity. It is not necessary to leave an agency board to work for Federation. Indeed, two-thirds of the trustees are agency representatives, and may serve on any Federation committee other than the DC. In fact, however, most people find service on key Federation committees so time-consuming that they are able to devote little attention to the workings of the agency boards.

The manpower pool from which Federation recruited its leaders in the past was, by and large, limited to Wall Street lawyers and investors who were members of the same four or five social clubs.

Federation had a New Leadership division (now called Young Leadership and attached to the Joint Campaign), whose purpose was to introduce men and women between the ages of 18 and 35 to the aims and functions of Federation, and to place them on agency boards. The number of people successfully channeled into leadership roles, however, was limited.

The feeling that its leadership pool was drying up led Federation to seek a new direction in the 1960's, a direction initially geared to nonsectarianism. But Federation's professional leaders, even then, sought to keep their options open. The same Joseph Willen who led the move toward nonsectarianism encouraged the Religious Affairs Department to undertake a leadership-training program for young synagogue leaders. One participant recalls a remark of Willen's to the effect that as the children of Federation's founders had assimilated, the burden of leadership was now on their shoulders.

Federation was meanwhile competing with other organizations for the same potential leaders. The major competitor was, and still is, the American

Jewish Committee. There is a significant overlap between Federation and AJC activists. While this means a certain cordiality and mutuality of interest, it also means rivalry for the time and energy of the leaders. One individual who holds leadership positions in both organizations believes the AJC attracts a more reflective and issue-oriented person, who seeks an intellectual challenge. The Federation activist, he feels, still tends to be more concerned with service, although Federation has become more involved in ideological issues in the last few years. He noted that whereas Federation people tend to ask what impact a certain issue will have on their agencies, AJC people tend to ask what impact the same issue will have on the Jewish community. Another observer noted that it is cheaper to become an AJC leader. An annual contribution of $10,000 to AJC confers more status than does a similar contribution to the Joint Campaign.

Federation has considerably expanded its sources of recruitment in the 1970's. Leaders have been drawn from the Orthodox community, often through the initial recruitment of Isaac Trainin to the activities of the Department of Religious Affairs. A second significant source of leadership recruitment has been the UJA. A number of its campaign leaders have moved directly to key Federation committees.

While there are those who criticize Federation's slowness in recruiting from new segments of the Jewish community, others fear that the large influx of new people in the last few years has introduced an element which does not adhere to the Federation tradition of hard work, service, and concern for the agencies.

The Large Contributor

Federation leaders, past and present, claim that large contributors exert no special influence. They report that they cannot recall a single occasion on which any significant decision was reached as a result of pressure from contributors. There are, however, groups of contributors, as opposed to individual contributors, who are very influential. Federation's undertaking services to Suffolk County and its expansion of services to Westchester County were justifiable independently of contributor demands, but the impetus for the provision of services came from the needs of the campaign. Some allocations to Orthodox institutions, the general thrust of intensifying services to the Orthodox, and the appointment of a relatively large number of Orthodox Jews to key Federation committees are all accounted for, in part, by a desire to please a number of large Orthodox contributors and to attract more of them. It has already been noted that arguments against cuts to hospitals were based on reluctance to antagonize large contributors.

Secondly, Federation's own leaders are, for the most part, large contributors. Although a committee member who is a small contributor has the same vote as a large one, and being a large contributor does not insure one a seat on a key committee, it is obviously easier for a big giver to find a seat on Federation's highest councils than it is for a small giver.

Finally, it is difficult to assess the influence of the major contributors in that they ask for very little. Minor favors are given as a matter of course. Some professionals feel that while Federation does not respond immediately and directly to the pressures of large contributors, the latter represent a constraint on Federation's decisions.

Professional vs. Lay Control

Federation has had strong presidents, but an occasional weak one. Most of its laymen are strong personalities, but some are not. The stronger the lay leader, and the more control he exercises, the more the professional defers to him.

It is often impossible to distinguish lay from professional influence because of the continuing interaction between the two. As far back as respondents recall, a tradition of respect and even admiration has characterized lay-professional relations in Federation, with one exceptional period. Most important is the relationship between the president and executive vice-president. The two together really represent Federation leadership, and when they work together it is impossible to distinguish leader from follower, superior from subordinate.

Observers are of the opinion that the professionals in New York's Federation exercise greater control than the professionals of other federations. At the same time, it is widely believed that the executives of Federation's agencies exercise greater control over their lay boards than do Federation's professionals over Federation laymen. These observations accord with the notion that the more philosophical or ideological the matter, the more likely the layman is to assert himself; the more technically complex the matter, the more likely the layman is to defer to the professional.

New York City's federation is a far more complex one than any other, as a result of its size, the number and variety of agencies with which it deals, and its interrelationship with government and other voluntary associations. Hence, it is not surprising that New York tends to have a more dominant professional leadership. Federation's agencies, in the business of providing specialized services, are even more professionalized. After all, an agency board hires a professional on the assumption that he knows more about how its services are to be provided than anybody else. He is their major source of information and advice. Even agency boards, however, when confronted by an ideological issue, such as intake policy (e.g. Jewish or nonsectarian clients), will assert themselves.

It follows that Federation will be less professionally dominated than its agencies. Federation laymen have better contacts with their client-constituents (i.e. the agencies) and are better informed about them than are agency board members about the agencies' clients and constituents. As Federation has become somewhat more issue- and ideology-oriented in recent years, laymen have played an increasing role in decision-making.

Federation's present professional leaders contend that laymen control the organization. Some of them point to their own experience with other voluntary agencies, where they exercised far greater control. One staff member commented that while Federation leaders with whom she worked respected her and gave careful consideration to her opinion, they made the actual decisions.

Federation's 1968 communal thrust was initiated by laymen. Solender, who came to Federation from the National Jewish Welfare Board, had a communal orientation, and that was one of the reasons he was hired. However, a number of observers view Solender's emphases as more Jewish today than when he first came to Federation. Lay influence may have played a role in this regard. But Solender and his staff gave the lay-initiated policy sharper form and content, and there are those within Federation who attribute its Jewish thrust primarily to his leadership.

The executive vice-president plays a critical role in the selection and reappointment of non-institutional trustees, in the appointment of committee chairmen and members of major committees, and even in the nomination of Federation's president. He is responsible for the appointment of the professional staff, which in the last few years has become notably more Jewish in background and orientation. Two of Federation's top six community-service staff members are Orthodox Jews. A third has a background of involvement in the Conservative movement. Jewish commitment has become an important consideration in the hiring of new staff. It seems fair to say that the professional leaders of Federation have, since 1970, moved as far and as fast in a Jewish direction as they could, given the composition of Federation's Board of Trustees. But the lay leadership exercises important constraints.

The continuous interaction between laymen and professionals means a process of mutual education. It seems, however, that it is predominantly the professionals who teach the laymen. Indeed, a number of respondents mentioned the impact of the professionals, past and present, on their Jewish outlook.

It is the professionals who establish Federation's agenda of specific concerns. On the other hand, the professionals are constrained by the frequent presence of a number of lay leaders, who are consulted on a regular basis.

If nothing else, such laymen serve as sounding boards for new ideas, which will be abandoned if not well-received.

There seems to be some illusion on the part of Federation's laymen regarding their own role. Although it is a vital role, it is hardly one of control, except in the sense that they have the ultimate right to dismiss the professionals. On the other hand, laymen who cannot get along with professionals often find that their way to leadership positions is blocked. Professionals exercise their own initiative in recruiting potential activists; the professional staff is appointed with only courtesy deference to laymen. Committee meetings are governed by policy papers prepared by the professionals.

Greater lay control would probably hamper Federation's effectiveness; the degree that exists constitutes a necessary constraint on the professionals, and provides a basic incentive to lay service.

The present situation is quite satisfactory to most laymen. They do not really want the responsibility or work that greater lay control would impose on them. They are prepared to operate within the general framework that the professionals have set for them, comfortable in the knowledge that the detailed execution of that policy is in the hands of the professionals, while they have contributed in some way to the establishment of broad policy outlines. They are aware that Federation cannot recruit outstanding professionals, if the latter do not feel they have a real role in decision-making.

FEDERATION AND THE FUTURE

The Joint Campaign assures Federation a regular income, at least for the present. Should contributors lose interest in Israel, however, it is likely that the campaign will suffer dramatic reductions, and the burden of the campaign theme will shift to local needs. This may mean a focus on Jewish communal needs and problems of assimilation and spiritual survival, or an emphasis on serving needy Jews through Federation's traditional agencies.

Federation and Its Agencies

There are people who feel that the age of voluntary sectarian philanthropy is over. No agency executive or Federation leader agrees, but the question concerns them. The beneficiary societies providing social services and health care depend more and more on government funds. Executives in many agencies find themselves increasingly guided by those professional associations and government bodies that deal with their areas of specialization. Moreover, the Joint Campaign has loosened the ties of some agencies to Federation, in that some agency board members who contribute to the Joint Campaign no longer feel as close to Federation as they did when they contributed directly to it. Each side, therefore, is freer to go its own way. Finally, despite the preference of many agency executives and board members, a number of them face an increased intake of non-Jews.

Government policy is one important factor. It may change in one direction or another, by administrative fiat, as much as by legislative direction. The political climate of opinion is crucial, and no one can predict in what direction it will move. But basic demographic realities are no less important. A government-supported residential facility cannot reject applicants with demonstrated need if it is underpopulated. It would require an executive and an agency board with an extraordinary degree of Jewish particularism to do so, even if the law permitted it. Federation has, in one instance, guaranteed empty beds in a facility for potential Jewish applicants. But to do this on a broad basis, moral issues aside, is beyond Federation's means. Hence, a declining Jewish population means, in the long run, a declining need by Jews for the services of Federation's traditional agencies. Child-care agencies have been the first to experience this, but even homes for the aged are likely to feel the pressure. The Jewish Home and Hospital for the Aged has a magnificent facility in a predominantly non-Jewish neighborhood. At the present time, 95 per cent of its occupants are Jewish. But, contrary to the situation of a few years ago, there is no longer a waiting list of Jews. The Home doesn't have a kosher kitchen, but it does have a Jewish environment. There are services on the holidays, a Passover seder, and Jewish classes for residents. This has not deterred some non-Jews from applying for admission. Cultural factors, having to do with the use of such homes, have deterred others, but such factors are declining in importance. How long can the Jewish Home and Hospital for the Aged remain 95 per cent Jewish? At what point will the proportion of non-Jews become so high that one can no longer think of it as a Jewish home? Not all agencies face the same problem; but a significant number do.

The agencies are grateful for the money they receive from Federation. It gives them what some executives call "a standard of living in excess of the norm." They derive benefits from Federation's joint purchasing plan and look to Federation for other forms of help, such as advances in allocations when, as frequently happens, government agencies do not pay their bills on time. But the thrust of their funding and demographic realities direct many of them away from Federation. They, for their part, no longer supply the income to Federation which they once did.

Federation is not yet prepared, ideologically or structurally, for a basic reevaluation of its relationship to its agencies. Ideologically, Federation would have to ask itself where its basic obligations lie. Even if one such obligation is serving Jews in need, it might still want to consider a variety of alternatives to its present pattern of funding. It could consider reimbursing needy Jews for social services in nonsectarian agencies. Where an institutional Jewish ambience is considered necessary, perhaps the solution would be to encourage a grouping of Jews in a nonsectarian facility, and the provision of Jewish group-work services. This would represent a radical departure from Federation's traditional policy, and the organization would have to overcome the barrier of its agency-dominated Board of Trustees. This domination has not seriously impeded Federation in the changes it has made in the last ten years; but a change of this nature would fall beyond the present Board's limit of acceptance.

Alternatively, Federation might come to view its role as service to Judaism and Jewish values. Of course, there is only a fine line between individual and communal needs, and Jewish values certainly include helping those in need. But there is a clear distinction between providing health and welfare services, which are needs that Jews share with all people, and creating Jewish solidarity and a strengthened Jewish identity.

Providing for the human needs of Jews may be the best way to strengthen Jewish communal bonds. It can be argued, therefore, that Federation's responsibility to build a strong Jewish community requires that it provide health care and social services. But that is a different viewpoint from the one which presently guides Federation leaders, and would require a much greater emphasis on the Jewish aspect in the provision of services. In this respect, the senior-citizen program, rich in Jewish content and clear in the provision of human needs, may be the model. There are other options, but none likely to gain serious consideration until Federation begins to think along the lines of a basic reordering of its relationship to many of its agencies.

Federation and the Middle Class

Federation is paying increasing attention to the middle class. The Jewish middle class, when defined by a family income level of $12,000 to $25,000, cannot afford many of the services available free of charge to the poor. Federation senses its obligation to this middle-income group, as well as to the poor. Federation is also confronted with the problem of turning to middle-class Jews for campaign contributions, when many of them feel they derive little in the way of services from Federation.

Given scarce resources, there are distinct limits to the extension of broad human services to the middle class. But even if Federation narrows its concerns to the Jewish needs of the middle classes, it must still confront difficult choices. If Federation gives priority to community centers as institutions which strengthen Jewish identity, how much Jewish programming should they have? No doubt a center's board, executive, and users will play important roles in shaping its policy. But should Federation confine its role to a general policy concerning the Jewishness of clientele and program content, or should it also adopt a position on what it means to be Jewish? Should Federation determine what constitutes a minimal Jewish education? Having scarcely achieved consensus about the importance of "Jewish," Federation is not yet able to deal with such questions. But Federation must have at least a general sense of the direction in which it wishes to move. Without priorities and some specific sense of what being Jewish means, it will be the target and tool of whatever group happens to organize itself first, approach Federation, or raise a sum of money.

The provision of services to the middle class also raises the question of Federation's relations to synagogues.[34] Federation contributes no money to synagogues. The Commission on Synagogue Relations has proposed that Federation allocate funds to inner-city synagogues which require relatively small sums in order to survive. But the impetus here is offering services to the Jewish poor, with a secondary consideration being that Federation might eventually inherit the synagogue's assets. Federation has never considered synagogues in terms of their importance in shaping a Jewish community. The argument for funding community centers and not synagogues, namely that the former are available to all Jews without regard to religious conviction, is not as convincing as some within Federation think. In fact, Federation has approved, in principle, the establishment of a community center in Flatbush led by laymen from an Orthodox synagogue. Synagogues do provide services to Jews, and they are a factor in neighborhood stabilization, a matter with which Federation increasingly concerns itself. The Department of Religious Affairs has dealt with one aspect of this problem; but the problem as a whole, with its multiple ramifications, has yet to be confronted.

Federation and Jewish Education

Proponents of greater Federation support for Jewish education describe the condition of New York's Jewish schools as desperate, and speak about the need for tens of millions of dollars in assistance. They are convinced that Jewish education is the key to Jewish identity and survival, and that this is the area in which Federation has a primary obligation. The proponents of Jewish education are a group with a cause, a program, and an ideology. This makes them a powerful group. The sums of money which they feel are

---

[34]A fine discussion of the problem is Samuel H. Dresner's "Federation or Synagogue: Alternatives in the American Jewish Community," *Forum*, No. 2, 1977, pp. 73–95.

required to meet Jewish educational needs go far beyond the annual increments provided by Federation's present allocation procedure. If new sources of funding cannot be found, allocations to Jewish education can be increased only at the expense of other agencies. This would precipitate the kind of ideological conflict that Federation is loath to confront. There are some signs pointing toward such a conflict. On the other hand, as the proponents of Jewish education have moved into leadership positions, they have come to appreciate the needs of other agencies, and the sincerity and Jewish commitment of their advocates. Whether the socialization experience will moderate the drive for dramatic increases to Jewish education remains to be seen.

Neither Federation nor the Board of Jewish Education has sought to exercise significant influence over the direction of Jewish education. Yet, should large sums of money become available for Jewish education, Federation will demand greater accountability. This will raise some difficult ideological questions which will have to be resolved.

Conclusion

Only in the past few years has Federation begun to view itself as an institution with responsibilities to the total Jewish community. Certainly, Federation has done much to create a sense of community, and some people increasingly look to it for leadership. Although Federation eschews this role, it has established and funded agencies which may assume such leadership. However, national organizations, sensitive about their own prerogatives, especially in New York, have resisted communal centralization. Some Federation agencies have their own roof organizations which mediate between Federation and them, and dilute Federation's influence. Synagogues, major foci of Jewish identification and commitment, remain marginal to Federation. Jewish schools, perhaps the most important instruments of Jewish survival, are not really part of Federation's structure. Finally, the Jews of Greater New York do not think of themselves as an organized community. Their loyalties are either parochial (to a particular organization, school, or synagogue) and/or general (to Israel, Judaism, or the Jewish people). If Federation is to create and lead a Jewish community, it will not do so by shifting Jewish loyalties to itself, but rather by serving as an instrument for shaping loyalties. In the last analysis, Federation is an instrument, and not an end, in the creation of a Jewish community.

Soviet Jewry Since the Death of Stalin: A Twenty-five Year Perspective

by LEON SHAPIRO

FOR A PROPER PERSPECTIVE on the situation of the Jews in the Soviet Union, it is important to understand the special role that Jews play in Soviet nationality doctrine. The Bolsheviks accepted as legitimate the separate national concerns of the various nations and peoples of the former Russian Empire, and the Soviet state structure is based on the territorial principle—Ukraine, Belorussia, Georgia, Lithuania, etc. Since the Jews were without territory, the Bolshevik answer to their needs was total equality. This was to be achieved through gradual assimilation, which was to come about as a result of an "objective process." In Lenin's view, opponents of Jewish assimilation—including the socialist Bund, with its program of Jewish cultural autonomy—were clerical reactionaries and petty-bourgeois. Lenin was not anti-Jewish; he sincerely (and naively) believed that Russian Jews would be glad to merge with other national groups into a classless socialist society. In 1919, the Bolsheviks abolished the *Kehillah* (Jewish communal structure) and nationalized all Jewish communal agencies. At the same time, they created a number of specialized government organs (a Jewish commissariat, Jewish soviets, Jewish courts, etc.) which were intended to serve the needs of Jews during the period of transition from a capitalist to a socialist society. Lenin died in 1924 and, after several years of internecine strife, was succeeded by Stalin.

In his early years Stalin was not antisemitic. His views on the nationality issue, presented in *Marxism and the National Question,* were shared by many Bolsheviks and even some Mensheviks, including Jews. Later in life, however, Stalin began to exhibit a personal anti-Jewish bias, to which his daughter Svetlana Allilueva has testified. Toward the end of World War II the old Russian nationalist concept of *russkost* (the glorification of all things Russian), so dear to the hearts of 19th-century Slavophiles, began to mix with the Marxist ideology of the makers of the Bolshevik Revolution. Soviet ideology shifted from an emphasis on "socialism in one country" to a militant national communism. Stalin, a Georgian by birth, made a significant contribution to the chauvinistic mood of the Russian people. The glorification of Russia and her national past became an important aspect of

---

[1]Most of these government organs were liquidated under Stalin in the decade 1930–40.

life in the USSR. At the same time, expressions of nationalist sentiment on the part of other groups in the Soviet Union were branded as "deviationist."[2]

At the end of the 1940's Soviet officials initiated a campaign against "cosmopolitans." A large number of writers, artists, and composers were accused of being insufficiently patriotic and of following alien ideas borrowed from Western capitalist countries. It soon became evident that the campaign against "cosmopolitans" was focused on Jewish intellectuals, most of whom were, in fact, loyal to the Soviet state. In the course of the campaign the very idea of a separate Jewish group life became suspect. Jewish books and memorabilia disappeared from Soviet libraries and museums. The specter of "Sionskii Kahal," a hostile world Jewry, resurrected from the "Protocols of the Elders of Zion," became an acceptable propaganda tool in the Soviet fight against Zionism and the newly-established State of Israel. As a result, antisemitism assumed a new respectability in the Soviet Union, and spread to leftist movements in various parts of the world.

The campaign against "cosmopolitans" was followed by the infamous "doctors' plot." Six outstanding doctors, all Jews, were accused of conspiring with the American Jewish Joint Distribution Committee and American intelligence services to poison high Soviet officials. Stalin's death on March 5, 1953, the day the "show trial" was to begin, brought a halt to the matter. The trial never took place, and those physicians who had survived their detention were released and rehabilitated.

With Khrushchev's accession to power, changes came about in the social and political climate; there was a liberalization of the regime. The great fear pervading Soviet society under Stalin gradually disappeared. The situation of Soviet Jewry, however, continued to be defined within the rigid framework of xenophobia and anti-Jewish bias inherited from the Stalin era. Khrushchev was plainly not interested in revitalizing Jewish life. Indeed, he himself, as a high Party and state official, had been among the framers of many of the anti-Jewish measures taken under Stalin. To Khrushchev, who was born in a peasant village in the Kursk district on the Ukrainian

---

[2]On Stalin's nationalism see Robert C. Tucker, *Stalin as Revolutionary* (New York, 1973), and the same author's "The Emergence of Stalin's Foreign Policy," *Slavic Review,* December 1972, pp. 563–589. See also Svetlana Allilueva, *Only One Year* (New York, 1969). At the end of World War II many Russian exiles in France and elsewhere underwent a "change of direction" and accepted the Soviet regime. Some who returned to the USSR paid dearly for their patriotic gesture.

According to many observers of the Soviet scene, Stalin is enjoying renewed popularity among the masses as a symbol of patriotism. The horrors of the Stalin era are almost forgotten; survivors of the old generation do not want to remember, and the young simply do not know. A. Zinoviev, a scholar and writer who recently left the Soviet Union, has stated that if free elections were held today, the Communist Party would receive a majority.

border, Jews and Judaism were totally alien; he exhibited all the prejudices of his class, including a hostility toward Jews that he was never able to overcome. Khrushchev was overthrown by a coalition of Stalin's collaborators, and in 1964 a collective leadership, with Brezhnev as secretary-general of the Party and Kosygin as premier, took over the reins of government. Again there were changes in the direction of greater liberalization of Russian society. With respect to matters affecting the Jewish population, however, nothing changed. The old policy of "integration" remained basic to the new regime. While open, violent antisemitism disappeared, deepseated anti-Jewish bias remained. Only recently echoes of the "doctors' plot" were heard at the trial of Anatoli Shcharansky, a Jewish dissident accused of spying for the United States.

POPULATION

In 1959, the Soviet Union conducted a general census. Published figures indicated there were some 2,267,000 Jews in the USSR, representing about 1.1 per cent of the total population. As a result of industrialization and the Nazi occupation the number of Jews in the historic regions of Jewish concentration, the Ukraine and Belorussia, had decreased substantially. At the same time, the number of Jews in the RSFSR (Russian Soviet Federated Socialist Republic), both in Russia proper and its constituent parts, had increased. There were even Jewish centers in the Asiatic regions of the Soviet Union consisting not only of local Jews but also of Ashkenazic Jews from Russia and Poland. (According to the census there were some 300,000 Jews in these areas.) Of the total Jewish population, 2,161,702 were residing in cities, and only 106,112 in rural areas. Even taking into account the Jewish autonomous region of Birobidzhan, created in 1928, with its population of some 14,000 to 15,000, it was clear that the attempted "agrarianization" of Russian Jews had proved to be a fiasco.

The next Soviet census, that of 1970, indicated a total Jewish population of 2,151,000, or some 117,000 less than in 1959. This five per cent decrease cannot be explained on demographic grounds, and the figure is, in fact, suspect. According to the data, the decrease occurred in the Slavic areas of the country. In 1970, Soviet citizens were permitted to choose the nationality under which they wished to be registered (Russian, Ukrainian, Belorussian, etc.), and it is quite possible that Kremlin authorities, interested in preserving the Slavic plurality in the country, encouraged certain groups to "pass." The Jews were the only group that showed a population loss. A.M. Maksimov, the Soviet statistician, argued that the decrease resulted from the "fusion of the nations which, under the conditions of a socialist society, has the character of friendship and bears no resemblance to assimilation in bourgeois society."[3]

It is odd that some scholars have uncritically accepted the 1970 census figure on the assumption that assimilation and the wish to conceal Jewish identity might account for the unprecedented drop in Jewish population betwen 1959 and 1970. Some have proposed complex theories—dividing Soviet Jews into various groups (halachic, "passport," assimilated, and others)—for arriving at a proper figure. These are interesting theories, but they call for caution in their application since, if we were to adopt them for statistical purposes, it would be necessary to change our estimates of the Jewish population in the United States, England, and other countries where there would be, for example, no "passport" Jews, but certainly a division between assimilated Jews and others. If we accept Soviet population figures, we may one day face the grave situation of finding only a small number of "statistical" Jews remaining in the Soviet Union. Soviet authorities will then claim that Jews no longer constitute a significant minority there.

A balanced estimate, taking into account the Jewish family structure and allowing for those Jews who have left the country, would put the Jewish population of the Soviet Union in 1977 at 2,678,000. Recent Soviet emigrés have spoken of three to four million Jews residing in the USSR, but this is an exaggeration. We shall have to wait for better times, when statistics coming out of Moscow are more open and honest, to arrive at a more precise figure on the number of Jews in the Soviet Union.[4]

While it is true that the Jewish community in the Soviet Union is not homogeneous, there is no need, for our purposes, to divide Soviet Jews into different sub-groups, i.e., Ukrainian, Baltic, Oriental, etc. Under present circumstances, the future of Jews everywhere in the Soviet Union will be determined by what happens in Moscow, Kiev, Minsk, and a few other central Soviet cities where groups of Jewish intellectuals are concentrated.

RELIGION

Maintaining a religious life in the Soviet Union is very difficult. The official atheistic outlook of the state works against free religious observance. Jews are particularly handicapped because the Jewish religion is intimately

---

[3] *Istoria SSSR* (Moscow), No. 5, 1971.

[4] For an exchange of views on the subject of the Soviet Jewish population, see AJYB, Vol. 77, 1977, pp. 468–476. See also Salo W. Baron, *The Russian Jew Under Tsars and Soviets,* 2nd ed. (New York, 1976), p. 296. In 1977, *Sovetish Heymland* printed a piece about the *American Jewish Year Book* accepting without comment the latter's population figure for the Soviet Union in 1975—2,680,000.

linked to Jewish national life. Soviet policy affecting the one has a direct impact on the other.

Religious life in the Soviet Union is regulated in the main by the law of April 8, 1929, which established the status of voluntary societies desiring to maintain religious facilities for their members. These societies, called *dvadsatkas*, are composed of 20 members who, with the permission of the authorities, may rent a building for the conduct of religious worship, burial services, and other religious rites. These societies are not permitted to maintain educational facilities for children. They may not print prayer books or produce prayer shawls, phylacteries, or other articles needed for the observance of Jewish ritual without permission of the authorities.

The *dvadsatkas* are certainly not an adequate substitute for the *Kehillah*. In retrospect, it is clear that the Soviet government would not permit the existence of any institutions or agencies which might indicate the formal existence of a Jewish minority. In this regard the Soviet Union is an exception to the other Communist nations of Eastern Europe. Everywhere but in Russia there is a Jewish communal structure, consisting of both religious and secular institutions, which is officially recognized. In Hungary, there is even a rabbinical seminary which conducts educational programs and carries out Jewish historical research.

The 1936 Soviet Constitution guaranteed freedom of religion to everyone in the USSR. The reality, however, has been quite different. Moreover, while there are limitations on the free exercise of religion with respect to all denominations, those placed on the Jewish religion are particularly restrictive. Without synagogues, religious articles, and rabbinic education, Jewish religious life in the Soviet Union has deteriorated to a very great extent.

Not long after the death of Stalin, the Soviet press reported that "special courts" in Kishinev were conducting trials of religious Jews accused of perpetuating "superstition," "ancient rites," and other "criminal" acts. The trials, which violated the Soviet constitutional guarantee of freedom of worship, made pariahs of the accused. Soviet authorities did everything in their power to hinder the observance of Jewish religious law. Jewish employees of Soviet factories, shops, and offices were not able to observe the Sabbath. Such observance could result in exclusion from school and employment. Recent Jewish emigrés from the USSR have reported that numbers of Soviet Jews, particularly Lubavitcher Hasidim, are leading Marrano-like lives, adjusting to difficult conditions by taking employment as night watchmen, avoiding their bosses, or bribing them to close their eyes to observance of the Sabbath and other religious practices.

A small number of synagogues survived both the Stalinist terror and the Nazi onslaught. They were old and dilapidated. Under Khrushchev, the closing of synagogues took on a mass character in the Ukraine, the Caucasus, Siberia, Lithuania, Belorussia, Moldavia, and Russia proper.[5] Synagogues were closed under various pretexts, with buildings being turned into Red Army clubs, Komsomol meeting halls, and even warehouses. These actions were accompanied by press campaigns in which, for the benefit of the non-Jewish population, it was repeatedly emphasized that Jewish houses of worship are centers for drunkards and criminals.

There is great uncertainty as to the number of functioning synagogues in the Soviet Union today. The governmental Committee for Religious Affairs reported in 1960 that there were 400 synagogues in the Soviet Union, a figure officially furnished to the United Nations as well. In the same year, however, *Mission Today,* the bulletin of the Soviet embassy in Vienna, indicated that there were 150 synagogues. In 1965, Solomon Rabinovitch, a Soviet propagandist on Jewish affairs, spoke of 97 synagogues. Rabbi Juda Leib Levin of Moscow, during his visit to the United States and Canada in 1968, reported that there were some 100 Jewish houses of worship. As recently as October 1974, the synagogue of Tomlino, not far from Moscow, was closed because, according to the authorities, it was not properly registered. Unofficial sources indicated there were 62 synagogues in 1975. The number presently functioning is unknown. Recent official statements have referred to "several tens," which, if taken to mean 50, would indicate that there is one Jewish house of prayer for every 50,000 Jews in the Soviet Union today. Soviet authorities have acknowledged the existence of some 300 *minyanim,* prayer groups meeting in private homes. The situation with respect to the *minyanim,* however, is beset with problems. In many cases, participants have been brought to trial for violating laws regulating religious organizations.

Soviet authorities are well aware of the significance of the synagogue for Jewish life, and from time to time launch fierce attacks against those who are active in synagogal affairs. In 1960, there was a wave of arrests of lay leaders of Jewish congregations on trumped-up charges of espionage and "connections with the embassy of one of the capitalist states." In 1961, three prominent Jews connected with the synagogue in Leningrad, T.R. Pechersky, E.S. Dinkin, and T.A. Kaganov, were sentenced to long prison terms on similar charges. Three Moscow religious leaders—Roshal, Goldberg, and another whose name could not be ascertained—were sentenced to three years' imprisonment. Individuals holding positions with synagogues in Kiev, Minsk, Vilna, Tashkent, and Riga were removed from their posts. The arrests created a stir of protest in the West. In succeeding years

---

[5]Synagogues were closed in such large cities as Zhitomir, Kovno, Saratov, Kazan, Tula, Kremenchug, Poltava, Chernovits, Lvov, and Orenburg.

the authorities abandoned this campaign of mass repression, and some of those who had been arrested were permitted to leave for Israel. Action continued to be taken, however, against individuals who, for one reason or another, displeased the authorities. In 1978, Solomon Kleinman was "relieved" of his position as chairman of the Moscow synagogue. Iakov Mikelberg, a former vice-chairman, took his place. It was reported that one of the reasons for Kleinman's removal as chairman was his desire to centralize Jewish religious affairs around the Moscow synagogue, thus making himself a spokesman for Soviet Jewry. Such plans were not favorably regarded by the Kremlin.

In 1977, Rabbi Pinchas Teitz of Elizabeth, New Jersey reported that the Moscow synagogue had undertaken some important initiatives, including the establishment of a Family Affairs Committee to deal with the complex problems of broken Jewish families. In 1976, at a meeting in Budapest of Jewish communal leaders from Hungary, Rumania, Yugoslavia, Poland, and Russia, it was reported that the Moscow synagogue had requested permission to send an observer to the World Jewish Congress. Nothing further, however, was heard about this request. A Soviet Jewish delegation under the late Rabbi Levin was permitted to go to Belgrade in 1970 to attend the birthday celebration for Lavoslav Kadelburg, president of the Federation of Jewish Communities there. In 1977, one Canadian and three American rabbis participated in the celebration of the 70th birthday of Solomon Kleinman of the Moscow synagogue; Leonid Shcherbakov represented the governmental Council for Religious Cults at the banquet. It is to be hoped that these infrequent celebrations are a portent of better things to come.

The radical decline in the number of synagogues has created a serious situation not only for believing Jews, but also for Jewish secularists. There is no Jewish organization, agency, or school in the Soviet Union that can serve as a center of Jewish life. The only possible center is the synagogue, and its importance cannot be overemphasized.

Jews are a unique group in the Soviet Union in their lack of a central religious organization. The Russian Orthodox Church, which enjoys a special status, is well-organized, and its hierarchy engages in far-reaching political and propagandist moves. Russian Orthodox leaders are frequent visitors to the United States and attend religious conclaves in Europe and Israel. The Georgian Orthodox Church is administered by the Patriarch Catholicos in Tbilisi. The Armenian Gregorian Church is headed by the Supreme Patriarch in Erevan, who maintains a liaison with coreligionists abroad. Groups as diverse as Baptists and Buddhists have central coordinating bodies. Moslems in the Soviet Union have central organs in the European areas of the Soviet Union, as well as in Siberia, Central Asia,

Kazakhstan, the northern Caucusus, and Transcaucasia. On occasion, Moslems have visited Mecca and Medina. The privileges enjoyed by these groups are, of course, of only relative advantage; all, to varying degrees, are controlled by the State and have little leeway in the pursuit of their activities. Nevertheless, Soviet Jews are in a special situation.

One of the most crucial problems facing Soviet Jewry is the almost total lack of trained religious personnel—rabbis, *mohalim* (circumcisers), cantors, and *shohatim* (slaughterers). Since the Bolsheviks came to power, the number of rabbis receiving ordination has been continually decreasing, and the situation is even more serious with respect to *mohalim*. Since the October revolution there has been virtually no institution for the training of *mohalim*, with the result that Soviet Jews have been largely unable to perform circumcisions.

We know from reliable sources that there were 40 rabbis in the Soviet Union in 1965, including a number who had been trained in Poland and Lithuania. Unofficial reports indicate there were five rabbis in the Soviet Union in 1977; two in the Ashkenazic areas and three in the non-Ashkenazic regions. Among the rabbis who enjoyed recognition during the period under review were Solomon Shlifer of Moscow, Juda Leib Levin of Moscow, Nuta Olevsky of the Marino-Roshchinskaia synagogue in Moscow, Chaim Lubanov of Leningrad, Abraham Panich of Kiev, Juda Menachem Rabinovich of Vilna, Shmuel Davidashvili of Tiflis, M. Openstein of Kuibishev, J.N. Alaiev of Samarkand, G. Mizrachi of Bacu, and the present rabbi of Moscow, Iakov Fishman.

During the period under review, Hasidim, particularly those of the Lubavitcher persuasion, played an important role in maintaining Jewish religious life. Rabbi Josef-Itchak, who became the Lubavitcher Rebbe in 1920, provided a model in this regard, in that he pursued many efforts in the areas of Jewish religious education and Jewish welfare, despite the dangers involved. The last remaining hasidic rebbe in the Soviet Union, A. Tversky, of the Skvir dynasty, left for Israel in 1964.

During the period of liberalization that followed Stalin's death, the Moscow rabbinate asked permission to establish a yeshiva in Moscow. In 1957, after repeated requests, Rabbi Shlifer of Moscow received such permission; the yeshiva was to be housed in, and supervised by, the Moscow synagogue. This was a significant departure from Soviet practice, and the Yeshiva Kol Iakov was greeted with enthusiasm by Jews both in and outside the USSR. Rabbi Shlifer, the first head of the yeshiva, died soon after it was opened. He was replaced by Rabbi Juda Leib Levin, who remained in the post up to his death in 1971. The yeshiva had a small but competent staff, including, at different times, Rabbis Shimon Trebnik, Chaim Katz, and Jacob Kamenetsky. Rabbi Fishman, who had been ordained under Rabbi Levin, and who had served as a rabbi in Perm, took over the teaching duties in 1971. Itsik Hurvits served as administrative head.

The yeshiva began its work with great hopes for the future. Initially there were 35 students. Soon, however, the authorities began to harass students, refusing to renew residence permits of those from Soviet Asia. Enrollment dropped to 20 in 1960, 11 in 1961, 6 in 1962, and 4 in 1965. Within a short time, the yeshiva had practically ceased to function except for an occasional class attended by a small number of elderly Jews. In 1970, there were reports that 19 new students would enter the yeshiva, but nothing came of this. In the meantime, some teachers had emigrated to Israel, and others had left the yeshiva for other reasons. In 1974, Rabbi Fishman informed Chief Rabbi Shlomo Goren of Israel that the yeshiva had resumed its efforts with some 18 adult and 10 young students in attendance. In 1976, on a visit to New York, Rabbi Fishman made reference to 10 students. In 1977, the enrollment was down to eight. Quite clearly, the yeshiva was in no position to train the needed rabbis.

With the permission of the authorities, three young men from the USSR went to Budapest to study at the neological (Conservative) rabbinic institution there. One student was also training at Yeshiva University in New York through an arrangement with the American Appeal-to-Conscience Foundation, which covered the tuition fees and living expenses of the student.

A rabbi proposed by a *dvadsatka* must be acceptable to the authorities. Given this situation, some Soviet Jewish dissidents, and some Jewish   activists in the West, have expressed a lack of confidence in the few rabbis and chairmen of synagogues now laboring under great difficulties in the Soviet Union. When Rabbi Levin of Moscow spoke at New York's Hunter College in 1968, the old man, clearly not free to express himself candidly, was received with catcalls and hostile demonstrations by many in his audience. It is, of course, true that all religious institutions in the Soviet Union are strictly supervised and must accept clearly defined limitations in order to function. The alternative, however, would be no synagogues at all. Observers abroad must be careful about expressing opinions on this very grave matter and would be wise to refrain from criticizing individuals in Russia because they have succeeded in maintaining no more than a skeletal Jewish religious life. There is deep interest in conserving, under any conditions, a Jewish religious framework in the Soviet Union, in the hope that one day it will assume greater strength.

Soviet Jews are severely handicapped in practicing their religion because they have hardly any prayer books, prayer shawls, phylacteries, or *mezuzot*.[6] In the mid-1960's, Rabbi Shlifer was permitted to print 10,000 copies of a standard prayer book. For the most part, religious items are only available on the black market at very high prices. Religious articles cannot be purchased in state shops, and the synagogues encounter great difficulty in distributing whatever small quantities they are able to obtain. Soviet authorities, suspicious of contacts between Russians and foreigners, have taken strict measures to prevent Jews from receiving gifts from tourists. In 1959, Soviet postal authorities returned to Israel parcels of religious items sent to the Soviet Union by the rabbinate of Israel. In February 1962, Rabbi Levin advised the members of his synagogue not to accept gifts from foreign visitors. In August 1963, *Izvestia* carried an article criticizing an American rabbi who, the paper claimed, distributed more than 800 prayer books and other religious articles.

In 1968, a new prayer book, *Sidur Ha'Shalom* (Prayer Book of Peace), edited by Rabbi Levin and containing prayers for festivals and other special occasions, was published by the Moscow synagogue. A religious calendar containing a Russian translation of the *Kaddish* was also issued by the Moscow synagogue. In 1977, Soviet authorities permitted the New York-based Appeal-to-Conscience Foundation to ship 10,000 copies of the Pentateuch to Moscow. In the same year, Chief Rabbi Rosen of Rumania sent 300 prayer shawls and a quantity of *mezuzot* to the Soviet Union. Rabbi Pinchas Teitz of Elizabeth, New Jersey sent to Moscow 16 boxes containing prayer books for Rosh Hashana and a large package containing 550 sets of *etrogim* (citrons) and *lulavim* (palm branches) for *Sukkot*.

Under Khrushchev, Soviet authorities, for the first time, began to interfere with the celebration of Passover.[7] In 1959, 1960, and 1961, the preparation of matzot was prohibited in Kiev, Odessa, Rostov, Kharkov, Kishinev, and Riga, although it was permitted in Moscow, Leningrad, and Tbilisi. In 1963, bakeries that had been set up by various synagogues were shut down, and the state bakeries, under various pretexts, refused to prepare *matzot*. At the same time, gifts of *matzot* from abroad to private individuals were not delivered by postal officials, and many Soviet newspapers published letters protesting "unneeded *matzot*." In July 1963, Emil Katz, Wolf Bogomolsky, Claudia Bliachman, and Malka Brio were brought to trial in Mos-

---

[6]We do not know how many religiously observant Jews there are in the Soviet Union. *Sovetish Heymland*, No. 4, 1977, cites a figure of 3 to 6 per cent, representing about 25,000 to 50,000 people, in the Ukraine. No source is given for this estimate, and it must be assumed to be a guess. See AJYB, Vol. 62, 1961, pp. 285–286; *Vestnik Izrailia* (Tel Aviv), May–June 1960; and Solomon Rabinovich, *Yidn n Soviet Farband* (Moscow, 1960).

[7]From the early days of the Bolshevik regime, the observance of Passover was ridiculed by the Bezbozhniki, the official state agency charged with spreading anti-religious propaganda. Observant Jews, however, were always able to obtain flour for the preparation of *matzot*.

cow for baking *matzot* for "profit and speculation." Three of the accused
were sentenced to prison terms; the fourth, an 82-year-old invalid, was
released because of his age. A press campaign linked *matzot* with the
Exodus and, thereby, with the "worst enemies" of Communism—Israel and
Zionism.

Toward the end of 1964 (Khrushchev was now out of power), local
administrations relaxed the prohibition against *matzot*-baking, and from
that time on there has been little difficulty in this respect. While restrictions against the importation of flour products converted into bread
have made it impossible for Jews to receive *matzot* from abroad, the authorities are now providing observant Jews, at least in the large cities,
with sufficient quantities. Mikhail Tendetny, chairman of the Moscow
synagogue, stated that sufficient quantities were being prepared for the
1975 Passover. In 1977, the authorities allocated 160 tons of flour for
Moscow, 75 tons each for Kiev and Leningrad, and 30 tons each for
Vilna and Riga. In 1978, Solomon Kleinman, then chairman of the
Moscow synagogue, reported that there would be more *matzot* available
than in the previous year. The situation in the small provincial cities,
however, is still far from satisfactory.

During the 1960's and into the 1970's, Soviet authorities, using various
pretexts, closed Jewish cemeteries in a number of cities. They also refused
to allocate to Jewish families parcels of land to be consecrated for burial
purposes. Problems involving burials arose in Minsk, Kiev, Leningrad, and
Moscow, and many Jewish families were forced to cremate the bodies of
their relatives.

Even during the worst period of Stalinist terror, strong feelings of Jewishness persisted among the Jewish population. Under Khrushchev and Brezhnev, a new religious awareness has emerged among younger Jews, notwithstanding their lack of knowledge of Jewish religious tradition. This
awareness has manifested itself in a variety of ways and represents not only
a quest for faith, but also a reassertion of Jewish national identity. At the
same time, a negative phenomenon has appeared—the attraction of Jews,
particularly among the intelligentsia, to Russian Orthodoxy. It is a sad fact
of life in the Soviet Union that individuals searching for religious meaning
have found it much easier to obtain books about Christianity than about
Judaism. Converted Jews include not only persons who have accepted
Christianity as a private act of faith, but some who have become leaders and
proselytizers of their new religion; some have even brought their new faith
to Israel and the United States.[8]

---

[8]The Russian emigré press, including *Vestnik* of Paris and *Novoye Hasskoe Slovo* of New
York, has noted the trend toward conversion. Among the prominent converts are: Lev Regel-
son, a Moscow physicist, who, along with Father Gleb Iakunin, protested to the Fifth Assem-

CULTURE

After World War II it became apparent that Soviet authorities would not permit a restoration of Jewish cultural life. Those Jews who undertook initiatives in this direction met with frustration and failure. For example, Chaim Kacherginsky, a Yiddish writer who had served in a partisan unit, attempted to renew Jewish activities in Vilna, but the authorities rejected his proposal to publish either a Yiddish newspaper or a periodical. While he succeeded in establishing a Yiddish-language school that went up to the third or fourth grade, he was not permitted to add other grades. He appealed to Solomon Michoels and Itsik Fefer of the Jewish Anti-Fascist Committee, who in turn took up the matter with Lazar Kaganovich, then a member of the Politburo and a close associate of Stalin, but these demarches elicited no response. An appeal to the Central Committee of the Party in Moscow was unsuccessful. Kacherginsky was informed that there was no need for a full-fledged Yiddish-language school in either Vilna or Kovno, since Jewish children could enter Russian or Lithuanian schools. Soon the school was closed completely.[9]

The last Jewish social organization in the USSR, the Jewish Anti-Fascist Committee, which had been created during World War II for propaganda purposes, was disbanded in 1948; most of its leaders were murdered or sent to prison camps. Over the next eight years, Yiddish disappeared as one of the official languages of the Soviet Union. Hundreds of Jewish intellectuals and officials vanished—victims of what Soviet authorities euphemistically called the "cult of personality." Some, including David Bergelson, Peretz Markish, Itsik Fefer, and Leib Kvitko, were shot in August 1952, only months before the death of Stalin.

After the death of Stalin there were reports that as part of the general policy of liberalization there would be changes with respect to Jewish cultural life. It was said that a Yiddish theater would be reestablished in Moscow, continuing the work of the great actor Michoels, who was murdered by the secret police in 1948. It was also reported—and Jewish fellow-travelers in Paris and New York gave the report wide coverage in their publications—that in addition to a Yiddish periodical, a Yiddish newspaper would be issued in Moscow. Mikhail Suslov and Boris Ponomarev, high Party officials, told a delegation of the Canadian Communist Party that

bly of the World Council of Churches in Nairobi about Soviet harassment of the Orthodox Church; Natalia Gorbanevskaia, a poet now living in Paris; Father Men, a well-known Orthodox priest, in Moscow; Nadezhda Mandelstam, the celebrated author of *Hope Against Hope;* Aleksandr Galich, a poet who died recently in Paris; and Melik Agurskii, the son of the former Evsektsia leader, now living in Israel.

[9]Kacherginsky's efforts are described in J. Lestshchinsky, *Forward* (New York), May 2, 1948.

Jewish cultural endeavors would soon be normalized. There were even reports that a special commission was preparing to revive *Emes,* the leading Yiddish newspaper. Zalman Wendroff, a Yiddish writer, reported that a memorandum had been presented to the Central Committee of the Communist Party listing the steps to be taken to reestablish Jewish cultural endeavors. All of these statements and reports proved completely hollow. Khrushchev continued his predecessor's policy of forced assimilation. For a long time this policy was covered up by a number of Jewish journalists and writers in the West who should have known better, but apparently could not shed their pro-Soviet illusions.[10]

Between 1946 and 1959, a period that included six years under Khrushchev, no Yiddish books were published in the Soviet Union. During the next 18 years some 60 Yiddish books appeared.[11] Since 1972, the authoritative *People's Economy* has not listed Yiddish books among those published in the Soviet Union; books in some 89 other languages are listed. M. Isaev, in his *National Languages in the USSR* (1977), devoted two sentences to the Yiddish language. While Yiddish writers were being translated into Russian, Ukrainian, and other languages, the use of Yiddish was obviously being discouraged, since it represented a form of Jewish continuity unacceptable to Soviet authorities.[12] Hebrew was altogether forbidden.

In the entire Soviet Union there is only one Yiddish newspaper, the *Birobidzhaner Stern,* issued five days a week under the editorship of Nokhum Kortshminskii. This newspaper carries little news of Jewish interest. It was only in 1961, some eight years into the Khrushchev era, that a Yiddish periodical, *Sovetish Heymland,* appeared. Its editor is Aron Vergelis, a Yiddish poet who climbed the bureaucratic ladder to become the top *apparatchik* of the Soviet Union. Vergelis is a strict follower of the Party line; he knows what may be published. In 1964, replying to Bertrand Russell's inquiry as to why Jewish cultural institutions had not been

---

[10]For details see Leon Shapiro's *Russian Jewry, 1917–1967* (New York, 1969), and the same author's outline of events in the new edition of Simon Dubnow's *History of the Jews in Russia and Poland* (New York, 1975). See also Salo Baron, *The Russian Jews Under the Tsars and the Soviets* (New York, 1976).

[11]One Yiddish book appeared in 1960; two in 1961; one in 1962; two in 1964; four in 1965; four in 1966; four in 1967; two in 1968; nine in 1969; two in 1970; three in 1971; three in 1972; ten in 1973–74; ten in 1975–76. (There may be discrepancies in these figures when compared with official lists, since some titles appeared after substantial delays but were dated as of the year they went to the printer.)

During the same period substantial publication activities were promoted among the small nationality groups of the Soviet Union. In 1962, for example, 34 books were issued in the language of the Udmurts, a people numbering some 600,000; 49 in the language of the Maris (500,000 population), and 116 in the language of the Bashkirs (1,000,000 population).

[12]Iliia Gordon reported in *Literaturnaia Gazeta* (1976) that there were some 466 titles by Yiddish writers available in 15 Soviet languages in some 45,000,000 copies.

reestablished in the Soviet Union, Vergelis stated that Soviet Jews had no need for "what is called cultural autonomy." He added that interest in Jewish culture had substantially diminished, and that it was not possible to increase it artificially. In 1966, Vergelis, on a trip to London, reported his intention to add a Russian-language section in his periodical. This never came about. Only in 1977 did *Sovetish Heymland* begin to include brief summaries of items in Russian and English for the benefit of those who do not read Yiddish.

Over the years *Sovetish Heymland* has broadened its content, and it occasionally dares to introduce items of Jewish news from the United States, Israel, and other foreign countries. It has taken note of the birthdays of Gladstein, Bikel, and Weinrich, and has even published an interview with the widow of Bialik. In August 1966, it featured an article by Shmuel Gordon arguing that Jews retained a distinctive character among the other nationality groups of the Soviet Union. Since the latter half of 1977, the magazine has been publishing, in installments, a manual for those wishing to learn Yiddish. For all its shortcomings, *Sovetish Heymland* is important because it affords at least some form of Jewish self-expression. The periodical has a circulation of 20,000 to 25,000.

According to *Sovetish Heymland,* there are some 100 Yiddish writers in the Soviet Union. Among them are younger men and women who, despite the difficulties presented by the unfavorable climate, choose to write in Yiddish. A number of older Yiddish writers, including Motl Saktsier, Eli Shechtman, Yankl Yakir, Meshulem Surkis, Meir Baratz, and Joseph Kerler, have left for Israel.

It is not our task to evaluate Soviet Yiddish writing. Suffice it to say that it is very much in the mode of "socialist realism." It is of interest that while Russian letters has produced a number of highly talented dissenters, Yiddish literature has not; there is no hint of underground Yiddish writing. In published works there is little mention of the Holocaust or the evils of the Stalin era. One might expect that some 25 years after they were murdered by Stalin, someone would remember in print what happened to Bergelson, Markish, Kvitko, and the others.

It is clear that Kremlin leaders have a phobia about Jewish books. In December 1977, *Sovetskaia Kultura* carried an article by E. Evseev describing the Jewish exhibits at the Moscow International Book Fair; it bore the title "Ideological Saboteurs." Apparently, in Evseev's view, books of Jewish interest are automatically subversive.

In 1978, for the first time since World War II, Kremlin officials authorized the establishment of a professional Yiddish theater in the Soviet Union. It was announced that a Jewish chamber theater, under the direction of Iurii Sherling, was rehearsing in Moscow an opera depicting the life of a Jewish family at the beginning of the 20th century. Sherling is a director who has been active in Moscow's Maiakovski Drama Theater. Some 30 young actors and singers were to participate in the production, which was to be given in both Yiddish and Russian.

Despite official discouragement, large numbers of amateur Yiddish theater and musical groups have functioned in the Soviet Union since the 1950's. When older actors, singers, and musicians initiated small circles specializing in Yiddish repertoire, younger men and women, who were interested in Jewish cultural expression, joined these efforts. Gradually, small amateur groups sprang up in Vilna, Kovno, Riga, Kishinev, Chernovits, Kiev, Leningrad, and Moscow, under the formal sponsorship of various local Soviet cultural agencies. In 1957, these groups gave 3,000 performances. In 1961, some 300,000 persons attended various programs of Yiddish repertoire. While these Jewish amateur endeavors were part of a wide system comprising similar groups performing in various other national languages, it was obvious that the authorities were not happy about the Yiddish groups; they were given no mention in the Soviet press. In Warsaw, however, the Communist Yiddish newspaper *Folksztyme* reported that Yiddish plays and recitals had become the most significant aspect of Soviet Jewish cultural life.

The best-known of the Yiddish amateur groups is the Vilna Dramatic Ensemble, which was formed in 1956. In 1977, notwithstanding the emigration of some of its members, the group, directed by Iudl Kats and Boris Landau, maintained a high level of activity; it had a vocal group, under Emil Kanevski; a jazz group, under Iasha Magid; and a dance ensemble headed by Nikolaii Margolis and Raisa Svichova. The Moscow Yiddish Drama Ensemble, under the direction of Felix Berman and Iosef Riklin, has presented programs in Rostov, Piatigorsk, Novosibirsk, and other cities. The Kovno Yiddish Drama Ensemble, under the direction of the veteran actor Iakov Betser, had 50 members in 1976. The Birobidzhan Yiddish Folk Theater, under Berta Shilman, has a dance group and orchestra. Other amateur groups include the Leningrad Drama Ensemble, the Tallin Yiddish Drama Ensemble, the Kishinev Studio of Yiddish Drama, and the Chernovits Ensemble. All performed old and new Yiddish repertoire, including works by Sholem Aleichem, Goldfaden, and Peretz, as well as modern Soviet Yiddish writers. The Vilna group even presented a Yiddish version of *Fiddler on the Roof.*[13]

---

[13]In many cities there were actors and musicians working alone or in groups: Nakhama Lifshits, Mikhail Aleksandrovich, Sidi Tal, Anna Guzik, Dina Roitkop, Zina Privoenskaia, Zinovii Shulman, Beniamin Chaitovskii, Lea Kolina, Sonia Binik, Mark Goldin, Polina Einbinder, Sofia Saitan, Anna Sheveleva, and Marina Gordon. Some of these performers have passed away; others have gone to Israel, the United States, and other countries.

There are many painters and sculptors in the Soviet Union working on Jewish themes, and some of them have had their works exhibited in various cities.[14] Gershon Kravtsov, who has concentrated on book illustration, had a special exhibit in Moscow. In recent years *Sovetish Heymland* has from time to time devoted space to artists working on Jewish themes.

Despite a hostile atmosphere, Soviet Jews are clearly striving to sustain some semblance of Jewish cultural life.

ANTI-JEWISH POLICIES

The late Solomon Schwarz argued that antisemitism was revived in the Soviet Union in the late 1920's after having been nearly extinguished in the immediate post-revolutionary period. The facts do not corroborate this view. Antisemitism has been endemic in Russia under both the Tsars and the Soviets. Stalin subjected the Jews to terror, while under Khrushchev they were gradually placed in a "special" category, as they had been in the time of the Tsars. No longer "Christ-killers," they were now regarded as a "rootless" element, plotting with Russia's enemies in the West and engaging in Zionist conspiracies. After Khrushchev's ouster, his successors followed his policy with respect to Jews. Indeed, Brezhnev and his colleagues took the policy for granted.

Ilya Ehrenburg, the writer and staunch advocate of Jewish assimilation, was forced to take note of the growing antisemitism in the Soviet Union. In a series of articles published in *Novy Mir* (1959), he warned the Russian intelligentsia in a roundabout fashion about the dangers of antisemitism. His novels *The Storm* and *The Thaw* reflected the problematic Jewish condition. He was more aware than others of the existence of anti-Jewish bias, having been attached during World War II to the Red Army, where antisemitism was quite widespread. Other writers of Jewish origin, including Margareta Aliger and Pavel Antokolskii, touched upon the new Jewish situation in their works.

During the transition period that followed the end of World War II, it became obvious that anti-Jewish bias had permeated all sectors of Soviet

---

[14]Among the painters and sculptors are Solomon Gershov, Meir Axelrod, S. Kaufman, Aron Futerman, Aleksandr Gluskin, Tanchum Kaplan, Viktor Midler, Shlome Iudovich, Leib Zevin, Robert Falk, Shmuel Kozin, Boris Valit, Mark Klionskii, Max Gelman, Joseph Chaikov, Shaia Bronstein, Aleksandr Tishler, Nohem Alpert, Zinovii Tolkachev, Hersh Inger, Shlome Teilingater, Mikhail Gurevich, Isroel Silberman, I. Mastbaum, E. Kogan, Oleg Fired, and Moishe Veinman. Some of these artists are no longer alive; others have emigrated to the West.

society. The government took no measures against increased overt anti-semitism, and in many ways encouraged it for its own purposes. The country had been liberated from the Nazis, but in many areas anti-Bolshevik bands which had collaborated with the Germans during the war were still causing trouble. The authorities were trying to arrive at an acceptable arrangement with the rightist Ukrainian extremists who, under Hitler, had participated in anti-Jewish excesses. Thus, Jews encountered difficulties in attempting to return to their homes in the Ukraine. Khrushchev, who was "boss" of the Ukraine at that time, also decided to conciliate the Ukrainians by not reappointing Jewish officials to high posts. The local population interpreted these moves as clearly anti-Jewish measures and understood that there was no longer a need to conceal their own hostile feelings toward Jews.

Khrushchev, as was noted above, was one of the framers of the Jewish policy under Stalin. He was frank about his opinion of Jews.[15] Speaking to a French Socialist delegation in May 1956, he stated: "At the beginning of the revolution the Jews were more educated than the average Russian . . . Since then we have created new cadres . . . and now if the Jews were to occupy first place, it would spread discontent among the inhabitants who have roots in the country." For Khrushchev, Jews could not be considered as having "roots" in Russia. When the poet Evgenii Evtuchenko, scandalized by the absence of a monument at the site of the Nazi massacre of Kiev's Jews, wrote his celebrated poem "Babii Iar," Khrushchev, at a meeting of Soviet writers in 1962, attacked the poet for focusing on Jewish victims, and accused him of lying about antisemitism in the Soviet Union. The attack on Evtuchenko was no mere temperamental outburst; it was an effort to eradicate the memory of Babii Iar. Shostakovitch's "Thirteenth Symphony," which used the text of Evtuchenko's poem, was harshly criticized by Khrushchev at a meeting of the Ideological Commission of the Party and was removed from the repertoire.

Elimination of Jews from positions of responsibility in Soviet society came about gradually. In the country at large the process took a long time; within the Party it was easier. With the liquidation of the so-called anti-Party group in 1957, Lazar Kaganovich, the last Jewish member of the Politburo, was ousted. Although the "anti-Party" group had no connection with Jewish affairs, Kaganovich's ouster was symbolic. It was the end of a Jewish presence among the Party leadership. Today there are only three

---

[15]Khrushchev reportedly used antisemitic expressions in speaking about Polish Jewish Communists during his visit to Warsaw to attend the funeral of Boleslav Bierut. He is said to have asked his Polish friends about the number of "Rabinoviches" still occupying responsible positions. See *Bulletin Interieur de l'Information* (Paris), November 5, 1965, and *Réalités* (Paris), March 1957.

Jews who hold positions of responsibility: Beniamin Dymshits, who serves as Vice Prime Minister, and Aleksandr Chaikovsky and Lev Volodarskii, who are members of the Party's Central Committee. Jews have also disappeared from secondary Party positions, such as regional and territorial secretaryships. (Lev Shapiro, a Jew, is the Party secretary in the Jewish autonomous region of Birobidzhan.) There are no Jews in top policy-making positions in the Army or Foreign Office.[16] Jewish executives in Soviet institutions have difficulty gaining promotions, and are often forced to take early retirement to give their non-Jewish colleagues "a chance." Finally, a quota system for Jews has been introduced in many professions.

An examination of Jewish representation in the various soviets provides an illuminating case study of how Jews have been "put in their place" in the Soviet Union. In 1937, during the worst period of Stalin's terror, there were 47 Jews among Supreme Soviet deputies; 32 among the 569 deputies of the Soviet of the Union, and 15 among the 574 of the Soviet of the Nationalities. In 1958, under Khrushchev, there were five Jews among the 1,384 deputies in both chambers, two in the Soviet of the Union and three in the Soviet of the Nationalities. The same numbers and the same distribution obtained in 1962. This figure of five to six Jewish deputies, obviously based on a quota, has remained fixed. In 1974, there were six Jews among the 1,517 deputies; two among the 767 in the Soviet of the Union, and four among the 750 in the Soviet of the Nationalities. Even more significant are the figures for the soviets of the constituent and autonomous republics. In 1961, under Khrushchev, there were only 13 Jews among 5,761 members of the soviets of the constituent republics, and only 11 among 2,848 members of the soviets of the autonomous republics. In 1963, of a total of 1,958,566 deputies of all local soviets, there were 7,623 Jews.

Soviet Jews are concentrated in certain specific areas of activity. They are widely represented in economic planning, accounting, and sales and merchandising. Many are in science, medicine, and technology. In 1960, there were 20 Jewish members in the Academy of Medicine, and 57 in the Academy of Sciences. Among scholars receiving the Lenin Prize in 1964 were 13 Jews; in 1968 there were 30. These were individuals who had made their careers some time ago. Since 1968, the proportion of Jews among prize-winners has been declining, despite the great reservoir of Jewish talent.

There has been a steady decline in the proportion of Jewish students in universities and other institutions of higher learning. In 1960, Jewish students numbered 77,176 (3.2 per cent); in 1965, 94,600 (2.5 per cent); and

---

[16]In the early 1970's, a Jewish naval officer in Leningrad was told by his superior that he could not expect normal advancement because this would mean placing a Jew in a "sensitive" position.

in 1972, 88,500 (1.9 per cent). The decline continued in 1974 and 1975. There is no doubt that a *numerus clausus* has been introduced in the universities, particularly in the prestigious schools of higher learning in Moscow, Leningrad, Kiev, and Kharkov, and in some specialized institutions providing courses in foreign affairs, journalism, and the like.[17] There are no discriminatory laws on the books, but the authorities have devised ways of excluding Jewish students, even those with excellent credentials.[18] Some university professors are openly antisemitic, but there is no one to whom Jewish students can complain. Jews admitted to universities are often denied normal advancement in accordance with their academic standing.

In 1961 and 1962, special legislation was enacted to fight economic crimes. At first, the new decree prescribed imprisonment for acts considered harmful to the Soviet economy. Soon, however, capital punishment was introduced and made retroactive for those already imprisoned. The new legislation was intended to combat widespread malfeasance and pilfering in state enterprises. Since a relatively large number of Jews worked in these enterprises, the economic trials took on a clearly anti-Jewish character. In the proceedings, special attention was directed to Jewish surnames or other indications of the Jewish origin of the defendants. It was a repetition, on a smaller scale, of the methods used in preparation for the "doctors' plot" trials.

The first trial for economic crimes, held in Moscow in 1961, involved two Jewish defendants, Rokotov and Faibishevich. During the next two years at least 56 such trials took place, with 111 defendants (60 per cent of them Jewish) being sentenced to death. An examination of the trials reveals that Jewish defendants were punished much more harshly than non-Jewish ones. Contrary to usual practice, details of the cases were publicized in newspapers and other media long before the opening of the trials, exposing the defendants to ridicule and contempt not only for the crimes they had allegedly committed, but also for their Jewishness.

In 1963, Bertrand Russell wrote to Khrushchev protesting the cruelty of the trials and the disproportionate number of death sentences meted out to

---

[17]An open letter addressed by G. Svirsky to V. Mishin of Gorky University, published in *samizdat,* is to the point here. Mishin had published a study, *Social Progress* (1970), in which he suggested that the Soviet Union adopt a policy of "national equalization" in education. Mishin objected to the fact that the percentage of students of Armenian or Georgian origin was only twice as large as their proportion in the population, while the ratio of Jewish students was seven times as large. Svirsky pointed out that if Mishin's formula were adopted, the number of Jewish students would represent 1.1 per cent of the total, indicating a return to the *numerus clausus* that had existed under the Tsars. He called Mishin's proposal a formula for intellectual genocide.

[18]A Jewish candidate may be subjected to several hours of preliminary examination in mathematics, instead of the usual one hour.

Jews. Russell, supported by Linus Pauling, François Mauriac, Albert Schweitzer, and many other Western intellectuals, charged that the trials manifested a rabid antisemitism. Khrushchev denied the charge. The trials continued after Khrushchev's ouster in 1964, but beginning some time in 1966, mention of economic crimes began to disappear from the Soviet press. There is no doubt that the actual number of trials for economic crimes was much larger than we have indicated, since many took place in the various republics and, due to language barriers, probably did not come to the attention of outside observers.[19]

During the 1960's and 1970's, anti-Jewish writings became widespread in the USSR. While such writings were not new, they first acquired respectability during the Khrushchev era. Anti-Jewish writings continued to appear after Khrushchev's departure from office, and under Brezhnev became an accepted part of Soviet literary production. Between 1960 and 1978, 90 such books were published in various languages. It must be kept in mind that there is no private publishing in the Soviet Union, and that every antisemitic book has been reviewed and approved by an appropriate state organ.

In 1961, the Ukrainian Academy of Sciences published Trofim Kichko's *Judaism Without Embellishment*. Kichko's thesis is that the Bible and Talmud preach hatred for non-Jews, and that Jews are swindlers and exploiters. The book's cover, modeled on Nazi propaganda, shows a hook-nosed Jew wearing a prayer shawl, his hands dripping with blood. Several works, among them F. Maiaski's *Contemporary Judaism and Zionism* (1964), Iurii Ivanov's *Caution Zionism* (1970), and V. Bolshakov's *Zionism in the Service of Anti-Communism* (n.d.), have attempted to show the similarities between Zionism and Naziism. Evgenii Evseev's *Fascism Under the Blue Star* charges Zionists with conducting a conscious policy of genocide. According to Evseev, Zionists dominate the world and have participated in mass killings, including the slaughter at Babii Iar. Evseev's book was published in 1971 by Komsomol, the Communist youth organization, with a printing of 75,000 copies. In some places, particularly the Ukraine, local writers have dealt with the subject of the "special Jewish character," making use of the propaganda of the Tsarist "Black Hundreds." These works provoked Aron Vergelis, the editor of *Sovetish Heymland,* to publish a two-part article, aptly titled "Not Only Ignorance," pointing out the dangers of the anti-Jewish propaganda contained in them. Vergelis strongly condemned the authors, accusing them of falsification and distortion. Finally, mention should be made of such anti-Jewish novels as I. Shevtov's *In the Name of the Father and the Son* (1970) and Iurii Kolesnikov's *The*

---

[19]See Solomon Schwartz, *Evreii v Sov Soiuze,* (New York, 1966).

Promised Land (1972). Shevtov's novel, which can only be described as a romantic version of "The Protocols of the Elders of Zion," was well received by the press, and enjoyed a success among young readers.

At times, Soviet anti-Jewish propaganda takes on a paranoid quality. Thus, the official "White Book" on the invasion of Czechoslovakia, published in several languages, repeats the accusation that the changes introduced in Prague by Dubchek were connected with international Zionism. *Zionism: Theory and Practice* (1973), published by the Academy of Sciences, emphasizes the links between Jewish banking families, and their central role in promoting international Zionism. T. Solodar's *The Wild Wormwood* (1977) presents a grotesque caricature of the Jewish religion. It is ironic that the old Russian "Protocols" have been resurrected and are being used by Marxist "scholars" in the Soviet Union.

The Soviet press engages in systematic anti-Jewish propaganda depicting Jews as conspirators working against the Soviet state. Newspaper articles use anti-Jewish stereotypes and appeal to the worst instincts of readers. Such articles, many of which are on a par with Nazi propaganda, appear in *Pravda, Isvestia, Ogonek, Komsomolskaia Pravda, Pravda Ukrainy, Zvezda, Nedelia, Sovetskaia Rossia,* and other newspapers and periodicals. On September 19, 1972, the Soviet news agency *Novosti* published an article linking the "evils" of Zionism with Jewish religious teachings. When the article was reprinted in *USSR,* the bulletin of the Soviet embassy in Paris, a stir was created among Western Communists. The International League Against Anti-Semitism in Paris brought a civil suit against *Novosti,* and on March 26, 1973, a French court found the managing editor of *USSR* guilty of defamation and incitement to racial hatred.[20]

Anti-Jewish propaganda extends also to radio broadcasts and lecture series. An important current "authority" on the Jewish question is Valerii Emelianov, an economist and university professor. In his lectures he speaks of a Jewish-Masonic plot to dominate the world. In January 1977, Soviet television presented an hour-long documentary film, *The Buyers of Souls,* which was replete with caricatures of Jewish money men and Jews conspiring with foreign governments.

One final aspect of Soviet anti-Jewish propaganda that should be noted is the silent treatment accorded the Jewish past. Soviet social scientists are engaged in a deliberate attempt to obliterate the very history of Russian Jewry. The first edition (1932) of the *Great Soviet Encyclopedia* devoted 160 columns to "The Jews," while the most recent edition contains only two columns. The latest editions of textbooks on ancient and medieval history devote two or three lines to the Jews. It is worth noting in this context

---

[20]See AJYB, Vol. 75, 1974–75, p. 500.

that while very little work in the field of Semitic and Hebraic studies is maintained at university level, the Near-Eastern division of the Leningrad Institute for Oriental Research commemorated in 1975 the 100th anniversary of the death of the Karaite scholar Avram Firkovich. Since Karaites are not viewed as Jews by the authorities, their history is treated with respect.

The policy of disregarding Jewish aspects of the Holocaust, inaugurated under Stalin and Khrushchev, continues under Brezhnev. The USSR is the only country in Eastern Europe without a monument dedicated specifically to the Jewish victims of the Holocaust. Repeatedly, Soviet police have prevented Jews from placing wreaths at the site of the massacre at Babii Iar.

The irony of Soviet anti-Jewish policy is that it makes the assimilation of Jews, which continues to be the stated policy of the regime, impossible. It may well be, therefore, that the future will witness the emergence of two Marrano-like Jewish communities in the Soviet Union—one consisting of Jews who wish to live Jewishly, and the other made up of Jewish Communists (in 1976 there were 299,744 dues-paying Jewish members of the Party) unable to find a place for themselves in Soviet society.

JEWISH DISSIDENCE

Stalin's death accelerated changes in the Soviet Union. Khrushchev's "liberalization" made for a somewhat more open climate that encouraged, for the first time in decades, the emergence of political dissent—a dissent which began to be manifested in the middle 1960's.[21] In 1965, the writers Andreii Siniavskii and Juli Daniel were arrested for publishing their books abroad under pen names. Following the invasion of Czechoslovakia in 1968, Pavel Litvinov and others demonstrated openly against the Soviet action. A leading Soviet physicist, Andreii Sakharov, made a plea for intellectual freedom. In a widely-circulated essay, "Thoughts about Progress, Peaceful Coexistence, and Intellectual Freedom," he denounced Soviet censorship. An illegal Soviet periodical, *Chronicle of Current Events,* focused on issues of concern to the dissidents. The authorities tried to stop the movement by various means; some dissidents were exiled, and others were forced to go abroad after

---

[21]There are a number of discernible trends among the dissidents: neo-Communists who want to return to Leninist tradition; human rights advocates; neo-Slavophiles; Christian socialists influenced by the thinking of Nicholas Berdiaev; democratic-socialists; and various nationality groups.

serving prison sentences.[22] From the beginning, Jewish intellectuals played an important role in the dissident movement.

Even more remarkable than the emergence of a general movement of dissent was the development of a specifically Jewish dissident movement. For the first time in decades, Jews in various Soviet cities began establishing liaison with one another; their aim was to leave the Soviet Union. The creation of the State of Israel and the Six-Day War of 1967 had a significant impact in increasing the resistance of Jews to ethnic and cultural assimilation. While there was some contact between the Jewish dissident movement and other dissident groups, the Jews chose to act on their own politically. There was a nearly exclusive emphasis on emigration; the motto of the Jewish dissidents was "Let my people go." They did not seek to bring about changes in Soviet society, or to revitalize Jewish life there. Jewish dissidents wanted to be "repatriated" to their "homeland," Israel. Among these dissidents, Vladimir Slepak, Veniamin Levich, Anatolli Shcharanski, and others who were refused exit visas became well known in the West.[23]

Many Jewish dissidents have struggled to lead a Jewish life in the Soviet Union while awaiting emigration. Groups of young Jews have organized small circles for the study of the Hebrew language and Jewish history, and for the celebration of festivals. Jewish scientists who have been refused exit visas have organized seminars dealing with their areas of specialization and with Jewish subjects. Some Jews have defied the authorities by organizing protests and sit-ins (including a sit-in at the offices of the Supreme Soviet), by submitting petitions to Soviet leaders, and by appealing to world public opinion.[24] Some Jewish dissidents have publicly renounced their Soviet citizenship, declaring themselves to be Israeli citizens, and demanding the right to emigrate. On Jewish festivals, large crowds have gathered in silent protest outside various synagogues.

---

[22]Among those forced to leave the Soviet Union were Aleksandr Esenin-Volpin, Valerii Chalidze, Zhores Medvedev, Iosif Brodsky, Andreii Siniavskii, Pavel Litvinov, Aleksandr Solzhenitsyn, Andreii Amalrik, Vladimir Bukovskii, Leonid Pliushch, Vladimir Maksimov, Viktor Nekrasov, General Grigorenko, Ernest Neizvestnyi, Mstislav Rostropovich, Galina Vishnevskaia, and Valentin Turchin.

[23]It is important to distinguish between Jewish dissidents, most of whom are of right-wing Zionist orientation, and the larger Jewish emigration movement, which is essentially motivated by non-political considerations.

[24]Among the petitioners were 26 Jewish intellectuals in Lithuania, including Party members, who called the attention of the Central Committee of the Party to the anti-Jewish writings being published by the Soviet press. In another petition, some 900 Jews complained that there was "no Jewish culture in the Soviet Union" and no possibility of living a Jewish life there, and requested permission to go to Israel. Some 100 Jewish protesters in Moscow presented a list of grievances to officials of the Central Committee. More than 150 Jewish activists from eight different cities protested at the Soviet Presidium against the refusal of the authorities to grant them exit visas.

Soviet authorities have employed severe measures against the Jewish dissidents. They have prevented Jewish travelers from coming to Moscow to discuss plans for emigration. They have disconnected telephones to prevent communication between dissidents and their supporters at home and abroad. Many Jewish dissidents have been arrested and sentenced to prison terms. The case of Boris Kochubievskii of Kiev received wide publicity in both the Soviet Union and the West in 1969. In 1970 in Leningrad, there was a celebrated trial involving 12 individuals accused of attempting to hijack a Soviet airliner at Smolny Airport in order to fly it to Sweden. Eight of the defendants—Joseph Mandelevich, Urii Fedorov, Aleksandr Murzhenko, Leib Chanokh, Anatolii Altman, Boris Penson, Israel Zalmanson, and Mendel Bodnia—were sentenced to prison terms of 4 to 14 years. Under pressure from the West, death sentences pronounced on two other defendants, Mark Dymshits and Edward Kuznetsov, were commuted to 15 years in prison. Wolf Zalmanson, an army officer, was court-martialed and sentenced to ten years. At another trial in Leningrad, nine Jewish defendants—Gila Butman, Mikhail Kornblit, Lassal Kaminskii, Lev Iagman, Vladimir Mogilever, Solomon Dreizner, Viktor Boguslavskii, Lev Kornblit, and Viktor Shtillman—were charged with belonging to an Israel-directed Zionist organization, and with distributing an illegal *samizdat* publication, *Iton.* The defendants were sentenced to prison terms of one to ten years. In 1975, Mikhail Shtern, a Jewish doctor in Vinnitsa whose children had applied for an exit visa, was brought to trial on trumped-up charges of bribery and given a harsh prison sentence. Other trials took place in Kishinev, Vinnitsa, Sverdlovsk, Kiev, Odessa, Riga, and Rostov.

In an attempt to discourage the emigration of individuals with an advanced education, a special education tax was introduced in August 1972. Soviet citizens obtaining exit visas were required to reimburse the state for the costs of their education at the rate of 5,400 rubles for a diploma equivalent to a B.A., and 19,000 rubles for a candidate degree equivalent to a European doctorate. In 1971, after vigorous protest in both the USSR and the West, the tax law was abrogated.

Soviet officials were not in a position, short of returning to Stalinist methods of mass repression, to put an end to the dissident movement. Thus, despite the hostile attitude of the authorities, the number of Jews expressing a desire to go to Israel increased, and Jewish emigration assumed substantial proportions. Small groups left in 1968 and 1969. In 1970, 1,000 left; in 1971, 14,000; in 1972, 33,000; in 1973, 35,000; in 1974, 20,000; in 1975, 13,000; in 1976, 15,000; and in 1977, 16,000. All told, 147,000 Jews emigrated in the period between 1968 and 1977. At first, the vast bulk of the emigrants went to Israel. As time passed, however, more and more of them chose to go to the United States, Canada, and other Western countries. By

1976, the figure for those emigrants choosing not to go to Israel had reached 50 per cent. This situation provoked an intense debate in Israel and the West, with some advocating that measures be taken against emigrants choosing to go to the West. As of this writing, common sense has prevailed, and Soviet Jewish emigrants are free to choose the country to which they will go.

Throughout the period under review there were protests in the free world on behalf of Soviet Jews, particularly the "refusniks," i.e., those refused exit permits. In the United States, the National Conference on Soviet Jewry, the New York Conference on Soviet Jewry, and the Student Struggle for Soviet Jewry were in the forefront of these activities. Many non-Jews, including writers, scientists, and clergymen, joined in these efforts. In February 1971, the World Conference on Soviet Jewry was held in Brussels, with 800 delegates from 38 countries attending. In February 1976, 1,200 leading representatives of Jewish organizations from 32 countries met for a second time in Brussels.

Stimulated by interested Jewish groups, U.S. Senator Henry M. Jackson, supported by 74 other United States senators, introduced an amendment to a 1973 trade agreement granting most-favored-nation status to the Soviet Union. The Jackson amendment sought to block the agreement if Soviet authorities did not stop harassing Jewish would-be emigrants. In Moscow the Jackson amendment was openly supported by Andrei Sakharov, but was opposed by another leading dissident, the historian Roy Madvedev. Moscow rejected the proposed amendment as an attempt to interfere in its internal affairs.

Jewish emigration from the USSR continues, with would-be emigrants basing their demands for exit visas, in part, on the 1973 Helsinki accord, which called for an increase in "human contacts" and the solution of "humanitarian problems." Groups have been established in various countries to monitor compliance with the Helsinki agreement. According to Amnesty International, 230 individuals in the Soviet Union have been jailed, deported, or committed to a mental clinic, in contravention to the Helsinki provisions. Many members of Helsinki monitoring groups in various Soviet cities have been arrested and convicted. In 1977, one such individual, Anatolii Shcharanskii, who was also active in the Jewish dissident movement and was among the "refusniks," was charged with espionage on behalf of the United States. Shcharanskii's trial, with strong anti-Jewish overtones, provoked a wave of protest in the West. President Jimmy Carter officially denied any connection between Shcharanskii and the CIA. Nevertheless, the defendant was given a heavy prison sentence.

We do not know the rationale behind Soviet policy with respect to Jewish emigration. Free emigration is an anomaly in the Soviet Union, since it implies a desire to leave the Soviet "paradise" for a "lower capitalist order." Soviet authorities must also reckon with the possibility that other groups will follow the example of the Jews. Indeed, some have already done so—the Volga Germans, the Dukhobors, and others. Among other factors which may play a role in Soviet emigration policy are the desire to get rid of Jewish activists and thus deprive the Jewish community of politically dangerous leadership; the desire to remove Jews from sensitive border areas; the desire to placate fiercely nationalistic local populations; and the desire to eliminate a minority group which, according to Soviet theory, should "die out," but which apparently is unwilling to do so.

Only brief reference need be made to Soviet-Israel relations. When Israel became a nation, Kremlin leaders—counting on the support of the large number of Russian Jews there—assumed that they would be able to use it as a base for penetration of the Middle East. Israel, however, was unwilling to serve Soviet interests. The Soviets then opted for the Arabs. Soviet policy toward Israel soon took on a clearly antisemitic character, and over the years anti-Zionist and anti-Israeli propaganda has proceeded unabated. The Soviet Union was one of the countries that voted in favor of the 1975 resolution adopted by the General Assembly of the United Nations equating Zionism with racism and racial discrimination.

CONCLUSION

Looking back, it is possible to delineate three stages in the development of anti-Jewish bias in the USSR. Under Stalin, it took the form of violent and repressive acts culminating in the annihilation of Jewish intellectuals and the "doctors' plot"; under Khrushchev, it took the form of widespread discrimination, sometimes disguised and sometimes open, in all areas of social life; under Brezhnev, the Khrushchev policy has become routinized and pervasive, signifying a return to the type of situation existing during the time of the antisemitic Tsarist "Black Hundreds."

Soviet society has lost its ideological foundation; little or no value is attached to Party policy pronouncements. The society is sick with alcoholism, and crime, particularly among 14- to 18-year-olds, is on the increase. At the same time, it is a conservative society that is unable to change or to find innovative means for the solution of its problems. Under these conditions, Jews serve as a convenient scapegoat.

We must be careful in making statements about the future of Soviet Jewry. Still, it is possible to point to a number of factors which will almost certainly play a role in determining what happens to the Jews in the Soviet Union.

Much depends on who will succeed the present leaders of the Politburo, most of whose members are over 70 years of age and whose leading man, Brezhnev, is apparently very ill. Will it be the heirs of Stalin or some other group? In the long run, a change at the top will have an impact on the Jewish situation;[25] a change in leadership will affect the minorities in the Soviet Union, including the Jews.

There is no doubt that Soviet Jews are threatened with assimilation. Jewish history indicates, however, that assimilation is not a simple process. A community of 2,700,000 Jews, with a great heritage, is not likely to disappear without resistance. The events taking place in the Soviet Union today are, in fact, an expression of such resistance. While at the present time Jewish dissidence is oriented mainly toward emigration, in the future it may well take another direction. Judging by present conditions in both Russia and the West, it is difficult to envision a mass exodus of Soviet Jews. Recognition of this fact should help put the emigration issue into proper perspective. Despite its importance, it should not monopolize the attention and efforts of those seeking to help Soviet Jews. Attempts should be made to strengthen Jewish life in the Soviet Union.

---

[25]See T.R. Rigby, "The Soviet Regional Leadership—the Brezhnev Generation," *Slavic Review,* March 1978, pp. 1–24. See also AJYB, Vol. 78, 1978, pp. 426–427.

Review
of
the
Year

UNITED STATES
OTHER COUNTRIES

Civic and Political

Intergroup Relations

$\mathbf{P}$OLITICAL COMMENTATORS felt that Americans were moving to the right politically in 1977. There was a good deal of talk about the "New Conservatism," which sought to draw the line somewhere on public spending, and which insisted on a cost-benefit approach to social programs. The "New Conservatism" affirmed the need for equal opportunity for Blacks and women, but strongly opposed quotas. All this, of course, had important implications for intergroup relations.

Race and Ethnicity

BAKKE CASE

There was agreement among legal scholars and intergroup relations specialists that the Bakke case was one of the most important civil-rights issues to come before the United States Supreme Court in this century.

Alan Bakke sued the University of California's Davis Medical School for denying him admission. Bakke argued that he had been discriminated against on grounds of race, since the medical school had accepted minority group students with lower grades. The university did in fact have a special program which applied separate and lower standards to Blacks, and set aside a quota of 16 seats out of 100 for minority students. The California Supreme Court, in September 1976, decided by a six-to-one vote that the special admissions program was in violation of the equal protection clause of the Fourteenth Amendment. The Regents of the University of California appealed to the United States Supreme Court, which heard arguments on the case in October 1977.

Jewish groups, reflecting the Jewish community's fear of quotas and support of the merit system, came out in favor of Bakke. They argued, as a joint press release issued by the American Jewish Committee and American Jewish Congress put it, "that the use of racial quotas as advocated by the University of California would sacrifice the basic principles of racial equality for expediency and short-term advantage . . . and [would be] profoundly damaging to the fabric of the American society." Black groups and others arguing against Bakke's admission asserted that if he prevailed, Black gains in college admissions and hiring would be permanently reversed. In a September 9 telegram to President Carter, a coalition of 15 prominent Black leaders urged him to intervene directly in the writing of the Justice Department brief in the case. The telegram warned that any brief taking the side of Bakke would "sabotage Black advances and frustrate minorities who look to your administration for help."

In the months preceding the scheduled hearing of arguments before the Supreme Court, expressions of concern by pro- and anti-Bakke forces grew in intensity. Supreme Court officials noted that the Bakke case generated more legal briefs from interested parties than any other case argued before the high court in more than 20 years. In total, 58 amicus briefs were filed on behalf of 162 organizations and individuals, and the United States Government; 41 of the briefs supported the University of California; 16 argued that Bakke's constitutional rights had been violated; the U.S. Government brief, reflecting much internal debate and external pressure, argued that racial factors may be taken into account in attempting to compensate for the effect of previous discrimination, but evaded the question of the constitutionality of quotas *per se.*

The Bakke case created a strange tangle of alliances. Pro-Bakke briefs were filed by, among others, the American Jewish Committee, the Sons of Italy, and the Polish American Affairs Council. Among those opposing Bakke were the Japanese American Citizens League, various Black organizations, and the American Civil Liberties Union. The "liberal" American Federation of Teachers and the "conservative" Young Americans for Freedom supported Bakke. The "liberal" National Association for the Advancement of Colored People and the "conservative" American Bar Association sided with the University of California.

In a column appearing in the Black-oriented *Amsterdam News,* Clayton Jones, a New York lawyer, attacked the Jewish community for supporting Bakke. "Organized Jewry," Jones wrote, "has taken the position that affirmative action to remove the vestiges of 400 years of white racism is acceptable, but that preferential treatment to achieve a specific goal is somehow un-American." Pointing to the creation of the State of Israel, Jones argued that Jews were in fact "the greatest beneficiaries of preferential treatment in the history of mankind."

Not all Black leaders shared the view of those who argued that the future of Blacks in America depended on the results of the Bakke decision. Civil-rights activist Bayard Rustin saw this claim as "greatly exaggerated." Rustin insisted that the issue was not affirmative action, but quotas. "Most affirmative action programs," he maintained, "do not rely on rigid numerical quotas, and this has not prevented them from helping to place thousands of Blacks in jobs and college programs." Taking cognizance of the developing polarization over the Bakke case, he warned Blacks that by overestimating the significance of the case, they were "setting up a situation which will encourage people to lash back at those such as Jewish groups and some labor unions who oppose the civil rights position on this issue, but who may be solid allies in the struggle for economic change."

It seemed inevitable that the Bakke case, whatever its ultimate outcome, would leave a residue of bitterness. Writing in the *Nation,* Paul Delaney stressed that Blacks and other minorities saw the case as proving "that white liberals were unreliable as allies." Naomi Levine, executive director of the American Jewish Congress, observed that "the civil rights movement has been torn over the issue of quotas. . . ." Hoping to stave off a crisis in race relations, the 79 organizations belonging to the Leadership Conference on Civil Rights pledged to "work together in the future as we have in the past to secure civil rights for all our citizens."

AFFIRMATIVE ACTION

The debate and controversy surrounding the Bakke case heightened public consciousness of the Government's commitment to affirmative action. Quite often, however, the discussion was marred by a blurring of the distinction between affirmative action and quotas. Major Jewish organizations made strenuous efforts to explain the difference between the two, stressing that they favored affirmative action but opposed racial and ethnic quotas as a means of compensating for past discrimination against minorities.

The Government's commitment to affirmative action was enunciated by Vice-President Walter Mondale, who pledged that the Carter Administration would "not turn its back on 200 years of discrimination against minority groups in this land. We think [affirmative action] is an essential and positive tool to overcome past denial." Despite the Government's position, poll data compiled by the Gallup organization indicated that the overwhelming majority of Americans regarded affirmative action as nothing more than reverse discrimination, and were opposed to it. A Gallup poll revealed that eight out of ten people believed that ability, as determined by examination, should be the main criterion in selecting students for college admission. Seymour Lipset and William Schneider, in reviewing 30 years of poll data on the subject, concluded that the majority of Americans rejected the concept of preferential treatment in hiring or university admissions. They noted, however, that most Americans, while insisting on strict adherence to merit standards, were willing to accept programs that helped disadvantaged groups to meet those standards.

Where government programs were viewed as *de facto* quotas or reverse discrimination, Americans, in increasing numbers, took to the courts to prevent their implementation. Thus, the Association of General Contractors, a national trade association of construction companies, sought in October 1977 an injunction against a government requirement that ten per cent of a $4-billion public works project be given to minority contractors. A number of white male applicants for university teaching positions legally contested affirmative action programs which favored women and minorities. Steelworkers in Louisiana, firemen in Pittsburgh, and teachers in Detroit filed suits on similar grounds.

Taking cognizance of the growing number of lawsuits challenging affirmative action programs, the U.S. Equal Employment Opportunity Commission (EEOC) released a proposed set of guidelines designed to protect companies from lawsuits charging reverse discrimination. The guidelines, applicable to both private and governmental employers, advised that "the remedial and/or affirmative action programs may be race, color, sex, and ethnic conscious and may include goals and timetables, ratios, and other numerical remedies." The American Jewish Committee, the American Jewish Congress and the Anti-Defamation League of B'nai B'rith urged the EEOC to revise the guidelines, claiming that they "encouraged employers to hire and promote preferentially," and failed "to prohibit the hiring or promotion of persons less qualified over those better qualified for reasons of race, ethnicity, or sex."

BLACKS

Roger Wilkins, a prominent Black spokesman, writing at the end of 1977, stated that the "mood of informed segments of Black America is grim this Christmas season." Citing a recent discussion among Black journalists, he reported that they were "uniformly gloomy about racial developments in 1977, and pessimistic about prospects for 1978 because of the high rate of Black unemployment both among adults and particularly among Black teenagers, and the lack of response to Black concerns by the Carter Administration." Herbert Hill, former national labor director for the NAACP, was even more grim. Speaking in Washington, D.C. on December 5, Hill asserted that a "counterrevolution against the civil rights of Blacks" was under way, and warned of an impending "explosion in the ghettos."

U.S. News & World Report, citing figures released by the United States Department of Labor, noted that the gap between Black and white unemployment rates had widened in 1977; the unemployment rate for whites was 6.1 per cent, while that for Blacks was 15 per cent. Unemployment among Black teenagers was a staggering 40 per cent. On the other hand, data revealed that the proportion of Black families with income over $15,000 had increased twice as fast as that of whites. The U.S. Civil Service Commission reported that the number of Blacks and other minorities in high-paying Federal jobs was increasing rapidly. Minorities now constituted 7.1 per cent of the top civil servants, in contrast to 5.5 per cent in 1973.

The Carnegie Council on Policy Studies in Higher Education and the National Association of State, University, and Land Grant Colleges, reported in October that the percentage of Blacks enrolled in the nation's colleges, universities, and professional schools continued to rise. It was noted that 41 per cent of those Blacks who sought entrance to medical schools were admitted, as against 37 per cent of whites.

School desegregation problems persisted in the larger cities of the North. A study by Diane Ravitch, a Columbia University historian, revealed that minority group children outnumbered whites in all but eight of the country's largest cities, and that the trend was continuing. In New York City, public schools were 67 per cent non-white; in Chicago, 70 per cent; in Detroit, 81 per cent; and in Washington, D.C., 96 per cent. William L. Taylor, director of the Center for National Policy Review, observed that "we are getting into the problem of whole school districts that are racially isolated."

Given the overwhelming support which Blacks gave Jimmy Carter in the 1976 elections, Black leaders assumed that they would have ready access to the White House. More importantly, they anticipated that the new president would be responsive to their political agenda. Yet, while the doors of the White House were open to them, Black leaders were disappointed by what they perceived as a lack of tangible results. The Congressional Black Caucus complained that no Black other than UN Ambassador Andrew Young was close to President Carter; that the President was unenthusiastic about their number one legislative priority, the Humphrey-Hawkins Full Employment Bill; and that Carter had little or no interest in such matters as welfare reform, tax revision, and national health insurance. Vernon Jordan, executive director of the Urban League, sharply criticized the President. In a July 21 press interview, Jordan declared: "We expected Mr. Carter to be working as hard to meet the needs of minorities and the poor as he did to get our vote. But so far, we have been disappointed."

Blacks continued to place heavy emphasis on electoral politics, and with increasing success. For the first time in 75 years, a Black, John D. Bryant, was elected to Boston's School Committee. Bryant's victory was particularly impressive given the bitter struggle that had taken place in Boston over court-ordered bussing. According to data compiled by the Washington-based Joint Center for Political Studies, Blacks registered other impressive political gains. The Center reported that there were 4,311 Black elected officials nationwide, including 295 in Mississippi, 281 in Illinois, 276 in Louisiana, 235 in Michigan, 225 in Georgia, 221 in North Carolina, 218 in Arkansas, and 201 in Alabama. There were four Black elected state officials, and 163 Black mayors. In the past decade, there had been an 81-per-cent increase in Black state senators and a 74-per-cent increase in Black state representatives.

While the Bakke case led to strains in Black-Jewish relations, there were positive developments as well. The Black Americans to Support Israel Committee (BASIC), under the leadership of Bayard Rustin, played an important role in informing the Black community about developments in Israel. The *Chicago Daily Defender,* a leading Black newspaper, praised Israel for her relations with Black Africa.

In Chicago, a group of prominent Jews and Blacks, led by Rabbi Robert J. Marx and the Reverend Jesse Jackson, met in August to form an organization which would address itself to the concerns of both communities. The Chicago chapter of the American Jewish Committee sponsored a law career seminar at Malcolm X College for 80 minority students. The presidents of the American Jewish Committee and the American Jewish Congress publicly urged increased efforts at the junior and senior high school level to help Blacks prepare for medical and other professional careers.

ALIENS

The problem of illegal aliens entering and remaining in the United States continued to be a divisive issue on the American scene. While estimates varied, the Immigration and Naturalization Service of the Justice Department estimated the number of illegal aliens in the country at six to eight million.

Organized labor opposed the influx of illegal aliens, as the latter were a source of cheap labor. For the very same reason, agricultural interests looked with favor on the aliens. State Department officials were fearful that stringent measures to halt the flow of aliens would worsen relations with Mexico and other Latin American countries. Various religious groups demanded amnesty for those aliens already residing in the United States. Bishop Rene Gracida, chairman of the Catholic Bishops Committee on Migration, asserted that the influx of aliens had "prompted a series of repressive measures," including "raids" on Hispanic communities. Other active opponents of restrictions on aliens were the Christian Community Service Agency in Miami, the National Council of Churches, and the Episcopal Church's National Commission on Hispanic Affairs.

President Carter sent his proposals on how to deal with the problem of illegal aliens to Congress on August 4. The proposals contained three major legislative ingredients: the use of injunctions and civil fines against employers who knowingly hired illegal aliens; intensified border patrols; and an adjustment in the status of those illegal aliens living in the United States, so that they might stay here. As the *Congressional Quarterly* noted, President Carter "took the middle ground on the controversial issue of employer sanctions and opted for an interim solution to the wrenching problem of those illegal aliens who already have established some degree of 'equity' in U.S. society." The Administration's recommendations failed to produce any legislation in the first session of the 95th Congress.

WOMEN

Ten years after the Women's Movement first emerged, feminist Betty Friedan observed that its impact was felt "everywhere—in sports, churches, offices and homes." Isabel Sawhill, director of the National Commission for Manpower Policy, stated that in 1977, women had much higher aspirations and were experiencing upward mobility.

The National Women's Conference, held in November, was a major event. The Conference, an outgrowth of International Women's Year, was sponsored by the United Nations and financed by a $5 million Congressional appropriation. More than 2,000 women gathered in Houston, Texas to assess the status of women and make recommendations to the President and the Congress "for the elimination of barriers that still prevent women's full participation in all areas and aspects of American life." Prior to the Conference, a 45-member National Commission, appointed by President Carter, considered some 100 proposals, with the aim of formulating a national plan of action. At the Conference itself, delegates voiced approval of, among other things, the Equal Rights Amendment; abortion on demand; federal and state funding for poor women seeking abortions; a national health insurance plan with special provisions for women; Social Security payments for housewives; the banning of employment, housing, and credit card discrimination against lesbians; federal and state funding for victims of child abuse; and funds for programs in rape prevention. By far, the most controversial resolutions were those relating to abortion and lesbianism. The only resolution that failed to pass was one calling for the establishment of a federal Women's Department to be headed by a Cabinet officer.

The prospect of legislative enactment of the Women's Agenda that emerged from the Conference was by no means certain. A coalition of political and religious conservatives, which sponsored a counter rally at Houston at the same time that the National Women's Conference was held, vowed to do everything in its power to prevent its adoption. Agudath Israel of America, an Orthodox Jewish group, called upon the Government to stop financing "feminist goals," and condemned the Houston conference for "adopting a broad range of resolutions which are contrary to the accepted moral values of our society."

The proposed Equal Rights Amendment to the Constitution, which passed both houses of the Congress by wide margins in 1972, appeared to be running into considerable difficulty. A resolution accompanying the amendment had set a seven-year deadline (March 22, 1979) for ratification by three-fourths of the states. At the end of 1977, 35 state legislatures, three short of the 38 required for enactment, had approved the amendment. To the consternation of ERA supporters, the momentum for enactment seemed to be dissipating. Fearing that ratification in three more states would not be achieved by the mandated deadline, supporters of the amendment sought a resolution by the Congress extending the deadline to 1986. Legal scholars hotly debated whether or not the Congress had the right to extend the date for ratification, and whether the extension would require a simple majority vote or a two-thirds vote by the House and Senate.

Religion

CATHOLIC-JEWISH RELATIONS

Despite differences over issues such as abortion and aid to public schools, Catholic-Jewish relations continued to be harmonious. Typifying the spirit of understanding between the two faiths was the offering of prayers in all Catholic churches in the Los Angeles diocese during the Jewish High Holy Day period. New York City's St. Patrick's Cathedral and Temple Emanu-El broke new ground when they exchanged senior clergymen; the clergy of St. Patrick's delivered five lectures on the "Essence of Catholicism" at the adult education classes of Temple Emanu-El, and the Temple's rabbis gave five talks on the "Essence of Judaism" at St. Patrick's.

The American Catholic Bishops' Committee on the Liturgy recommended that the "Reproaches," a hymn offensive to Jews, be omitted from the Good Friday ritual. Rabbi Marc Tanenbaum, director of the Interreligious Affairs Department of the American Jewish Committee, in a letter to Archbishop John R. Quinn, stated that the recommendation constituted "a significant act of spiritual liberation whose fruits ultimately will be a weakening of the roots of anti-Judaism and a fostering of mutual respect . . . between Catholics and Jews." Dr. Eugene Fisher, director of the Secretariat for Catholic-Jewish Relations of the National Conference of Catholic Bishops, noted the significant progress that had been made since the second Vatican Council regarding the way in which Catholic textbooks described Jews and Judaism.

Participants in Catholic-Jewish dialogues did, however, encounter some problems. John Sheerin of the United States Catholic Conference observed that the deicide issue was still a matter of concern for Jews, as was the notion held by many Catholics that Judaism had "lost all reason for existence after Christ established the Church." Jews were also troubled, Sheerin stated, by the "lack of Christian interest in Israel, Catholic silence during Hitler's campaign to exterminate the Jews, and anti-Semitic insinuation in liturgical texts."

PROTESTANT-JEWISH RELATIONS

New ground was broken in Protestant-Jewish relations when officials of the Southern Baptist Convention held a three-day dialogue with Jewish religious and communal leaders at Southern Methodist University. The 900,000-member Southern Presbyterian Church adopted a revised "Book of Confessions," which included a statement reflecting increased sensitivity to Jews, Judaism, and the Jewish background of Christianity. In a public statement, the Southern Presbyterian leadership declared: "We Christians have rejected Jews throughout our history with shameful prejudice and cruelty. God calls us to dialogue and cooperation that do not ignore our real disagreement yet proceed in mutual respect and love."

There were, however, some discordant notes in Protestant-Jewish relations. The Anti-Defamation League accused the National Council of Churches (NCC) of "pronounced anti-Israel prejudice" and "insensitivity" to Jewish concerns. The charges were vigorously denied by Dr. William L. Weiler, executive director of the NCC's Office on Christian-Jewish relations. Weiler asserted that a 1974 resolution adopted by the NCC Executive Committee simultaneously affirmed "the right of Israel to exist as a free nation within secure borders," and "the right of the Palestinian people to self-determination and a national entity."

EVANGELICALS

An estimated 45.5 million churchgoers loosely described as "Evangelicals" continued to be an important force on the religious scene. Rice University sociologist William Martin observed that "the Evangelicals have become the most active and vital aspect of American religion today." The Evangelical movement, which cut across denominational lines and included both Fundamentalists and Pentecostalists, stressed the need for a conscious personal commitment to Christ, and affirmed the authority of the Bible in all matters. The Evangelicals used every means at their disposal, including television and radio programs, Congressional prayer meetings, and testimonials by prominent athletes, to get their message across to the public.

Encouraged by success on the American scene, a group of business, professional, and political figures announced a worldwide Evangelical campaign. William Bright, a key figure in the endeavor, had been the head of the Campus Crusade for Christ for several years, and had been involved in 1976 in a well-publicized political endeavor to elect "born-again" Christians to public office. Bright's role in the Evangelical campaign gave rise to fears by some that he and other ultra-conservative Evangelicals were attempting to "Christianize" America.

There were increasing signs of an ecumenical link between the Evangelicals and the American Jewish community. Billy Graham, one of the most influential Evangelicals in the United States, addressed the American Jewish Committee's National Executive Council meeting in Atlanta, on October 30, and affirmed his support for the State of Israel, which he regarded as a fulfillment of Biblical prophecy. Support for Israel was also expressed in an advertisement which appeared in the New York *Times* and the Washington *Post* on November 1. The advertisement, signed by 15 individuals prominent in the Evangelical movement, affirmed the right of Israel to exist as a free and independent nation, and expressed concern over the "erosion of American Government support for Israel."

CHRISTIAN YELLOW PAGES

The Christian Yellow Pages and the Christian Business Directory aroused significant controversy. Both directories solicited and accepted advertising only from people willing to sign an oath that they were "born-again" Christians. Early in 1977, the Anti-Defamation League reported that the Christian Yellow Pages and Christian Business Directory had appeared in 19 cities. By September, the directories were circulating in 57 cities.

As the Christian Yellow Pages and Christian Business Directory came into wider circulation, criticism of them mounted. The official newspaper of the Archdiocese of San Francisco asserted that the directories were "encouraging rank discrimination, not only against Jews and other non-Christians, but also Catholics and some Protestant denominations which do not accept the 'born again' concept of relationship with Christ." The Southern Presbyterian Church called upon its membership to ignore the directories, asserting that they were "divisive among Christians" and "discriminatory in relation to the Jewish community." In August, units of the Anti-Defamation League in San Francisco, Los Angeles, and San Diego filed suit against the Christian Yellow Pages and the Christian Business Directory on the grounds that they violated several California statutes dealing with unfair business competition and religious discrimination.

RELIGIOUS SYNCRETISM

Observers of the religious scene in America took note of an emerging phenomenon—the blending of disparate faiths with the aim of promoting interreligious understanding, or even creating a new universal religion. New York *Times* religion editor Kenneth Briggs, in a report on this phenomenon, indicated that "it is no longer unusual to find Catholic monks practicing Zen Buddhism," and that "hundreds of churches annually hold a seder service each year at the Jewish Passover." Two Long Island Lutheran churches which incorporated Jewish rituals into their regular service were suspended by Lutheran authorities on grounds of "subordinating the Christian Gospel to Jewish religious and social customs." The *Christian Science Monitor,* quoting unidentified "leading ecumenists," reported on an emerging "new stage" of church unity in which doctrinal differences were minimized. It noted that 19 major American denominations, with a combined membership of 23 million, were exploring the possibility of forming a union under the auspices of the Princeton-based Consultation on Church Union.

PROSELYTIZERS

Efforts to convert Jews to Christianity appeared to increase. Various proselytizing groups utilized converted Jews to carry out their mission in some 40 states. "Hebrew-Christians" groups, including the American Board of Missions to the Jews, Beth Yehoshua, and Jews for Jesus, began to utilize sophisticated media and marketing techniques, purchasing full-page advertisements in metropolitan dailies, and radio and television time. Statistics on the number of conversions were impossible to obtain.

The Unification Church and its leader Sun Myung Moon continued to be a source of controversy. The news media carried stories about Moon's extensive financial holdings, his alleged ties to South Korean intelligence agencies, and the claims of anguished parents who insisted that their children were virtual captives of the Unification Church. Leaders of three major Protestant, Catholic and Jewish organizations denounced the Unification Church as a "fecund breeding ground" for antisemitic, anti-Christian, and anti-democratic beliefs.

Both the Hare Krishna sect and the Children of God movement came into increasing conflict with established Christian churches and civil authorities over charges of duress in their proselytizing efforts. The Federal Bureau of Investigation had more than a dozen cases under investigation involving alleged assaults or kidnappings by Hare Krishna and Children of God members, and at least six state legislatures contemplated resolutions to limit or investigate their activities.

Extremism

NAZIS

A small, fragmented, politically insignificant American Nazi movement generated a tremendous amount of publicity in 1977. Adopting a tactic successfully utilized by Great Britain's neo-Nazi National Front—confrontation in racially sensitive areas—the Chicago-based National Socialist Party of America (one of the seven or eight Nazi groups claiming national membership) announced early in 1977 its intention to demonstrate in Skokie, Illinois, on Hitler's birthday. Skokie was chosen because approximately half its population of 70,000 is Jewish; 7,000 Holocaust survivors live there. From April through July, a series of legal maneuvers by Skokie officials to enjoin the march proceeded through state and federal courts. At the same time, town officials enacted ordinances requiring all permit applicants to obtain $350,000 worth of insurance, prohibiting the dissemination of material which incited racial or religious hatred, and banning public demonstrations by members of political parties wearing military-style uniforms. During the entire period, the news media provided extensive coverage of the events.

Adding to the public's interest in the Skokie affair was the prominent role played by the American Civil Liberties Union (ACLU), which defended the Nazis in court. The ACLU's involvement on behalf of the Chicago Nazis resulted in the immediate loss of more than 2,000 members. ACLU officials met with representatives of national Jewish organizations in an attempt to explain their motivation in defending the Nazis' right to march in full uniform. The ACLU argued that it was defending the First Amendment, and not the Nazis. Editorial comment was widespread, with the overwhelming majority of newspapers defending the Nazis' right to march.

As the case worked its way through the courts, resentment against the Nazis' contemplated march mounted in the American Jewish community. The large concentration camp survivor element in Skokie viewed the march as indicative of a revived Nazi movement. By the end of the year, while the matter was still before the courts, the Jews of Skokie, and Jewish groups all over America, were devising plans for a massive counter-demonstration if the Nazis, in the end, received the necessary permits to march.

Despite the fears of many that the situation in Skokie was indicative of a resurgent Nazi movement, an exhaustive study by the American Jewish Committee revealed that total Nazi membership in the United States was no more than 1,500 to 2,000. While there were many local Nazi groups, those claiming national membership were the National Socialist White People's Party (Arlington, Va.); the National Socialist

Party of America (Chicago); the National Socialist Movement (Cincinnati); the White Power Movement (Reedy, W. Va.); the NSDAP-Overseas Branch (Lincoln, Neb.); the National Socialist White Workers Party (San Francisco); the National Socialist League (Los Angeles); and the National Socialist Liberation Front (Los Angeles). In its assessment of the Nazi movement in America, the report concluded: "If, as the desperate Nazi groups maintain, their ultimate objective is to become the dominant political power, they manifest an abysmal ignorance of what motivates the American electorate. American Nazism has failed to develop a motivating philosophy, much less attract a political figure of stature to its cause."

During 1977, minor skirmishes between demonstrating Nazis and enraged citizens occurred in Milwaukee, St. Louis, and Oakland, California. In late March, a San Francisco-based Nazi unit opened a bookstore in an area with a large concentration of Holocaust survivors. The store was fire-bombed. In retaliation, local Nazis smashed the windows of Temple B'nai Emunah.

KLANS

The ability of David Duke, the intelligent, articulate, 27-year-old Grand Wizard of the Knights of the Ku Klux Klan, to attract media attention gave rise to speculation about a resurgence of the klans. Duke appeared on more than 600 radio and television programs all over the country, and was profiled in several national news magazines.

Several incidents helped focus attention on the klans. The Anti-Defamation League reported that it had uncovered the existence of a 50-member klan unit in the Far Rockaway section of Queens, which was the first manifestation of klan activity in the Metropolitan New York area since the 1920's. Police sources claimed that the report was greatly exaggerated. At a klan rally in Plains, Ga., President Carter's hometown, a man drove his automobile into the assembled crowd, injuring some 30 people, including klansmen and innocent bystanders. Klansmen battled with police on the steps of the state capitol building in Columbus, Ohio.

Estimates of actual klan membership varied. The Anti-Defamation League spoke of 8,000 klansmen—indicating a 60 per cent growth in national membership over the past two years. The *Wall Street Journal,* attributing its information to unidentified law enforcement agencies, reported the number of "hard core, dues-paying, robe-wearing klansmen" at 1,000.

The klan, like the neo-Nazi movement, was beset with feuds and rivalries. Approximately a dozen klans were operative in varying degrees during 1977. Among those claiming national membership, in addition to Duke's Knights of the Ku Klux Klan, were the United Klans of America, led by Robert Shelton; the Invisible Empire, Knights of the Ku Klux Klan, led by Bill Wilkinson; and the National Knights of the Ku Klux Klan, led by James Venable. Other klans, essentially statewide in scope, were the United Klans of Florida; the South Carolina Invisible Klan Empire; the Maryland Knights of the Ku Klux Klan; the Independent

Northern Klans (New York); the New Order of the Knights of the Ku Klux Klan (Missouri); the Independent Knights of the Ku Klux Klan of North Carolina; and the National Knights of the Ku Klux Klan (West Virginia).

HANAFIS

A major antisemitic incident, which became front-page news, occurred on March 9 in Washington, D.C., when seven members of the Hanafi Muslim sect occupied several floors of the national headquarters of B'nai B'rith. (Other Hanafis took over the Islamic Center on Embassy Row and a municipal building. A newsman covering the story at the latter site was shot dead.) The Hanafis, who threatened to kill their Jewish hostages, railed against Jewish control of the courts and the media. The crisis finally ended two days later, when police and F.B.I. negotiators, materially aided by Ambassadors Ghorbal of Egypt, Yaquib-Khan of Pakistan, and Zahedi of Iran —all Muslims—persuaded the Hanafis to surrender. Hamaas Khaalis, the Hanafi leader, and his followers were convicted of armed kidnapping and other crimes, and were given lengthy prison sentences.

In the aftermath of the siege and surrender, the Washington *Post* ran a feature article about the Hanafis which carried the title "Hanafi Muslim Blames 'Zionist Jews' for Group's Plight." The story, based on uncritical interviews with several members of the sect, quoted them as charging "Zionist Jews" with having attempted to destroy the Islamic faith throughout history. On April 14, the Jewish Community Council of Greater Washington condemned "the hatred spewed into our community by Hanafi pronouncements" and expressed shock at the "excessive space devoted by the Washington *Post* to totally unfounded allegations."

MILTON ELLERIN

The United States, Israel, and the Middle East

Duration CONFIRMATION HEARINGS on January 11, 1977, Secretary of State-designate Cyrus Vance told the Senate Foreign Relations Committee that resolving the Arab-Israel conflict would be "very high" on the agenda of the new Carter Administration. In the following months, the Administration pressed ahead with efforts to go beyond the bilateral disengagement agreements that the United States had helped Israel conclude with Egypt and Syria after the Yom Kippur War, and to achieve a comprehensive settlement between Israel and all its neighbors.

Carter Presses for Comprehensive Settlement

Both in aim and method, the Carter Administration differed from its immediate predecessor. Whereas the Kissinger diplomacy had been marked by secrecy, President Jimmy Carter took the lead in opening and encouraging public debate on the fundamental points at issue. Moreover, in place of the pragmatic step-by-step approach undertaken by the Nixon and Ford administrations, Carter decided to tackle all the issues at once and set as his goal the swift reconvening of the Geneva Conference as the framework for comprehensive peace talks. The Geneva Conference had last met briefly in the winter of 1973; its role then had been limited to the essentially ceremonial one of endorsing the already concluded Egyptian-Israeli disengagement agreement.

At his first press conference on January 31, Secretary Vance argued that it was "critically important" that the Geneva Conference be convened during 1977, and warned that delay would permit "all kinds of disruptive factors" to emerge. In this assessment, he echoed the views expressed to him by the ambassadors of Egypt, Lebanon, Syria, Saudi Arabia, and Kuwait, with whom he had met earlier in the month. The prospects for progress toward a comprehensive settlement were now more favorable than they had been in the past, Vance said, citing the apparent end of the Lebanese civil war, the "greater cohesion among the forces of moderation in the area," and the indicated willingness of "all the parties" to go to Geneva promptly. Vance had also met with Israeli Ambassador Simcha Dinitz, who had conveyed his government's readiness to cooperate in peace efforts. This optimistic assessment was made two weeks before Vance's first trip to the Middle East, where he was to learn that the substantive differences separating Israel and the Arab states —as well as the underlying inter-Arab rivalries—were far more profound than he had anticipated. Even such seemingly procedural questions as the nature of Palestinian representation at Geneva and the Russian role as co-chairman of the Conference were to arouse intense and bitter controversy.

The activist role undertaken by the Carter Administration in the Middle East had long been advocated by Zbigniew Brzezinski, who was appointed by the President as his national security adviser. Brzezinski had become Carter's mentor in foreign affairs when the then Governor of Georgia had been invited to serve on the Trilateral Commission—a Rockefeller-funded project of which Brzezinski was the director. Never hesitant to express his views, Brzezinski had first set forth "A Plan for Peace in the Middle East: Separating Security from Territory," in an article published in *The New Leader* on January 7, 1974; it proved to be a blueprint for the Carter program as it gradually unfolded. The attainment of peace, Brzezinski wrote, "requires American pressure on both parties to the dispute—and determined pressure." The Israelis, for their part, "must yield political control over the Arab lands and peoples held since 1967—following certain minor rectifications, perhaps, . . ." while the Arabs had to agree to demilitarized zones, a UN peace-keeping force, and other safeguards written into "a peace treaty normalizing Israel-Arab relations." The best solution for the West Bank, Brzezinski wrote, would be the creation of an "autonomous Palestinian-Arab state, linked to Jordan in a federal union." The Gaza Strip would probably also be part of this state. "At the same time, all Israeli settlements established on the West Bank after 1967 would be disbanded." Other supplementary components were to be a formal United States guarantee for Israel and a Middle East economic development plan.

Brzezinski pointed out that the extent of Washington's leverage on Israel had been illustrated by Israel's extraordinary dependence on American arms supplied during the Yom Kippur War. "The United States should not hesitate to use that influence to the fullest," for a settlement of the Arab-Israel conflict was in the American national interest. U.S. intervention "is urgently required," he wrote, to prevent jeopardizing important American assets in the region and the strengthening of Soviet influence. "What is more, so long as there is no agreement, the Arab oil embargo will wreak havoc within the international economy, and America's primary links, namely those with Europe and Japan, will be severely strained." Although Brzezinski's dire prediction proved false, since the Arab oil embargo was lifted a few months later despite the absence of a comprehensive Arab-Israel settlement (AJYB, 1974–75, Vol. 75, pp. 136–37), his preoccupation with "the importance of oil in world affairs" did not diminish in subsequent years and was to remain a key influence on the Carter Administration's Middle East policy.

Brzezinski and William Quandt, whom he appointed as his Middle East deputy on the National Security Council, had also served on the Rockefeller-funded Brookings Middle East Study Group, which completed its report, "Toward Peace in the Middle East," at the end of 1975. Although less explicit on some points and more circumspect in its call for American pressure, the report endorsed the basic Brzezinski idea of a comprehensive settlement to be implemented in stages with active American participation in the process. The signers of the report, including Middle East scholars and several prominent individuals from both the Jewish and Arab American communities, stated: "We believe that, in exchange for the assured establishment of peaceful relations with its neighbors and suitable security arrangements, Israel should and would agree to withdraw to the June 5, 1967 lines, with only such modifications as might be mutually accepted."

The Brookings report was presented to and read by President Carter. It was also read by the Israeli Government, which was not pleased by the above formulation and some other aspects of the report. It is therefore not surprising that the Carter Administration and the Israeli Government soon found themselves at odds on various aspects of Middle East policy. While these differences became more visible and extensive after the election in May of Prime Minister Menachem Begin, differences had already begun to emerge between the Carter Administration and the outgoing Labor Party.

Following Vance's return from his fact-finding mission to Israel, the four neighboring Arab states, and Saudi Arabia, President Carter announced on February 16 that he would meet personally with Arab and Israeli leaders before the end of May, in order to obtain a "clearer picture" of the Middle East scene. Only then, Carter indicated to the press, would the Administration determine its proper role in promoting an Arab-Israeli settlement. In actuality, however, the President did not wait until June to publicly express his views.

U.S.-Israel Disagreements

The Administration took several actions which displeased Israel. On February 17, President Carter cancelled the pending sale of 250 CBU-72 cluster bombs which had been promised to Israel by the previous administration. The official reasons for the cancellation were that the United States was reviewing its entire arms sale policy and that President Carter regarded the cluster bombs as weapons of such an extreme nature that the U.S. should not sell them. Prime Minister Yitzhak Rabin told a radio interviewer that during his visit to Washington in March he would try to reverse Carter's decision.

Even more distressing to the Israelis was the Administration's decision to block the pending sale of Israeli-made Kfir C-2 fighter bombers to Ecuador. The U.S. had the right to veto the sale, since the planes contained American-made engines. The Israelis regarded the loss of the $200-million sale as a serious blow to Israel's aircraft industry, and to the country's efforts to achieve economic self-sufficiency. Secretary Vance denied that the U.S. decision was intended to put pressure on Israel, and said it was part of a general policy to restrain the Latin American arms race. But when, at hearings on February 24, Senator Dennis DeConcini (D-Ariz.) of the Senate Appropriations Subcommittee on Foreign Operations pointed out to Vance that Ecuador would now turn to France or the Soviet Union to obtain similar aircraft, Vance responded that the American decision was "firm and final," notwithstanding the possibility that others would fill the gap.

The Israelis were also annoyed by the State Department's public rebuke to Israel over its oil drilling in the Gulf of Suez, released on the eve of Vance's arrival in

Israel, and by officially inspired leaks of reports that Israel had illegally obtained American uranium to develop its nuclear weapons capability.

There was still some question in Israel, however, whether these actions were explicitly ordered by President Carter or whether they reflected the decisions of middle-level State and Defense Department bureaucrats who were pushing for a more "even-handed" American policy in the Middle East. Indeed, not all the early Carter Administration signals were anti-Israel. On the positive side, the Carter Administration increased by $285 million the economic assistance for Israel contained in the Ford Administration's proposal for fiscal 1978. The new Administration also turned down the visa application of Sabri Jiryis, the Palestine Liberation Organization's (PLO) Israeli affairs expert, who had been invited to attend an American Friends Service Committee conference near Washington in February. The official reason for the denial was that Jiryis' Sudanese passport and original visa application contained false information. The main reason for the rejection, however, was that the State Department felt that approval of the visit on the eve of Vance's trip to the Middle East would be interpreted as a significant gesture of American recognition of the PLO.

In a statement in Israel after meeting with Prime Minister Rabin on February 16, and again in an interview on CBS' *Face the Nation* on February 27, Vance ruled out PLO participation in a reconvened Geneva conference until the organization recognized Israel's right to exist, accepted UN Security Council Resolutions 242 and 338, and revised its national covenant, which specifically called for Israel's elimination. Asked if the U.S. would then recognize the PLO, Vance hedged and said that this would create "a new situation and we'll have to take a look at it."

Regarding the American role in a reconvened Geneva conference, which Vance said the Arab states and Israel had agreed to attend later in the year, the Secretary of State stressed that the United States should act as a "catalyst" in the negotiating process, but should not come up with a U.S. plan for an overall settlement. This would "hinder" rather than "help," he said.

Carter Outlines Peace Proposal

President Carter did not seem to heed his Secretary of State's advice. In welcoming Prime Minister Rabin to the White House on March 7, Carter reaffirmed the American commitment to Israel and stated that the American objective was permanent peace "so that Israel might have defensible borders, so that peace commitments would never be violated." The phrase "defensible borders" was immediately seized upon by reporters as reflecting a significant pro-Israel shift, since the term had been used by the Israelis to justify considerable territorial changes from the pre-1967 lines which the Israelis regarded as vulnerable and inherently indefensible. The Arabs, for their part, demanded that Israel withdraw from all the territories occupied in the June 1967 war. State Department officials tried to explain that the President's choice of words did not signify a change in American policy.

At a press conference on March 9—to the consternation of Israelis, Arabs, and diplomatic observers—President Carter elaborated his ideas for peace, ideas which bore a striking resemblance to the Brookings Report and the plan that Brzezinski had first proposed three years earlier. Carter dismissed the defensible borders phrase as "just semantics" and proceeded to distinguish between defense lines and "permanent and recognized borders where sovereignty is legal as mutually agreed." He went on to suggest that "there may be extensions of Israeli defense capability beyond the permanent and recognized borders." The components of this defense capability might include Israeli forces, outposts, and electronic monitoring stations as in the Sinai Agreement, and possibly international forces and demilitarized zones. He saw such an arrangement as lasting for an interim period of between two and "eight years or more," during which there would develop "a mutual demonstration of friendship" and an end to the state of war. The President asserted that the United States and Israel shared the same conception of peace, which included not simply an end of belligerence, but also Arab recognition of Israel's "right to exist in peace, the opening up of borders with free trade, tourist travel, cultural exchange between Israel and her neighbors." Peace would involve "substantial withdrawal" of Israeli forces, although there might be "some minor adjustments in the 1967 borders." In response to a follow-up question, he reiterated that there might be "minor adjustments to the pre-1967 borders," but that this was a matter for Israel and her neighbors to decide. He did not wish to define the exact delineation of borders, noting that he had not yet had a chance to meet with Arab leaders to get their views. In addition to peace and defined borders, the third component in a settlement, he said, was "dealing with the Palestinian question." Carter concluded by insisting that he was not trying to lay down the final terms of a settlement, saying, "I don't know what an ultimate settlement will be."

The Israelis, while pleased with the President's definition of peace, were disturbed by his repeated reference to minor adjustments. They believed that the President had seriously undermined their bargaining position, since the Arabs were certainly not going to accept anything less than what the United States, Israel's major supporter in the international arena, believed that Israel should yield. When Secretary of State William Rogers had made public a similar proposal in 1969, it was shelved after encountering strong Israeli and Arab objections. It was easier to ignore the Rogers plan since it never was formally endorsed by President Nixon. But now President Carter had put his personal prestige behind a Middle East peace plan.

Carter contended that it was healthy for the points at issue to be "freely and openly debated within our own country and within the countries involved." In response to a question at a town meeting in Clinton, Mass. on March 16, Carter declared that the establishment of Israel was "one of the finest acts of the world nations that has ever occurred." He then went on to define his vision of peace. After reiterating his earlier definition of real peace and the need for agreement on permanent borders to be negotiated between the Arab countries and Israel, the President elaborated upon the Palestinian component in a comprehensive settlement. He noted that the Palestinians continued to claim that Israel had no right to exist and that they "have never yet given up their publicly professed commitment to destroy Israel. That has to be overcome." The President continued, "There has to be a homeland provided for the Palestinian refugees who have suffered for many, many years. And the exact way to solve the Palestinian problem is one that first of all addresses itself right now to the Arab countries and then, secondly, to the Arab countries negotiating with Israel." On the plane back to Washington, Carter amplified his reference to a Palestinian homeland by saying that some provision had "to be made for the Palestinians, in the framework of the nation of Jordan or by some other means."

Although he had made similar comments before he became President, the Israelis were considerably upset, and the Arabs pleased, by the acknowledgement for the first time by an American president in recent years that the Palestinians should be regarded as a group entitled to a homeland, and not merely as individual refugees entitled to repatriation or compensation and resettlement. For the Israelis in particular the term "homeland" had nationalistic connotations, since it was the concept of the Jewish national home, incorporated into the Balfour Declaration and the League of Nations Palestine Mandate, that served as the basis for the eventual creation of the Jewish state in 1948. Moreover, the President seemed to be implicitly acknowledging that the PLO spoke for all Palestinians when he said that "the Palestinians" had not given up their objective to destroy Israel, ignoring the fact that there were a considerable number of Palestinian Arabs on the West Bank and elsewhere who were prepared to coexist with Israel.

In his Clinton remarks, the President also emphasized that if there were no progress toward peace, a major war might erupt in the Middle East "which could quickly spread to all the other nations in the world." While the United States could survive an oil embargo, he said, "many countries depend completely on oil from the Middle East for their life." Because this was such a crucial area of the world, Carter said, he would be "devoting a major part of my own time on foreign policy between now and next Fall, trying to provide for a forum within which they can discuss their problems and, hopefully, let them seek out among themselves some permanent solution."

U.S. Attitude to the PLO

The Carter Administration was, in fact, engaged at the time in behind-the-scenes efforts to get the PLO to modify its public position in the hope of bringing a reborn, peace-loving PLO into the Geneva negotiating process.

At the start of 1977 rumors were rife that the PLO was ready to moderate its position and adopt a more realistic posture toward coexistence with Israel. Palestinian "spokesmen" visiting the United States and Western Europe reinforced the idea that the PLO leadership was going through an agonizing reappraisal. One reason frequently cited was the military setback suffered by the extremist Palestinians in their confrontation with Syrian forces in Lebanon. Another was the apparent determination of the Arab confrontation states of Egypt, Jordan, and Syria, with the powerful backing of Saudi Arabia, to embark upon a "peace initiative" leading to a Geneva conference, in which they would press for establishment of a mini-Palestinian state to be carved out of the West Bank and Gaza Strip. Faced with the choice of accepting coexistence with Israel or being frozen out of the negotiations altogether, the PLO leadership was allegedly being prodded by the Arab states to scale down its ambitions.

United Nations Secretary General Kurt Waldheim reported on February 16, after completing a trip to the Middle East, that PLO leader Yasir Arafat now appeared to be "more flexible." Waldheim concluded that an evolutionary process was underway in the PLO, leading the group away from insistence on a secular, democratic state embracing all of Palestine including Israel, and toward acceptance of a "smaller solution." The UN chief suggested that Israel and the PLO might come to "mutually recognize each other" during negotiations, although Israeli officials had clearly ruled out any PLO participation in Geneva. Waldheim explained that it was not feasible to meet the goal set by the General Assembly in a resolution calling for the start of the Geneva Conference by March 31, even though both the Arab states and Israel had indicated "a very clear and visible interest" in negotiations. A major test of PLO intentions, Waldheim said, would come in the forthcoming meeting of the Palestine National Council (PNC) scheduled to begin in Cairo on March 12.

After talking with Secretary of State Vance in Cairo on February 17, Egyptian President Anwar Sadat told reporters that he was urging Jordan and the Palestinians to forge an "open and declared" link, preferably in the form of a confederation, "even before the Geneva Conference meets." Sadat did not spell out how this was to be accomplished. His main concern was to prevent the Palestinian issue from blocking the resumption of Geneva talks. He hoped that if the Palestinians were incorporated within a Jordanian framework, this would overcome American and Israeli opposition to dealing with the Palestinians as officials of the PLO. Moreover, senior Egyptian officials had conferred with Arafat earlier in the day, leading Vance to say that he had "the feeling" that the Egyptians were exerting pressure on the PLO to amend its covenant so as to acknowledge Israel's existence.

Jordan's King Hussein had already proposed a confederation under his leadership as far back as 1972, but had shelved the idea after the Arab summit conference in Rabat in 1974 declared the PLO to be the Palestinians' sole legitimate representative. After meeting with Sadat in mid-January 1977, Hussein reiterated his desire for the "establishment of the closest relations" between Jordan and a West Bank Palestinian state, but significantly omitted reference to the PLO. Hussein agreed finally to meet with Arafat in Cairo during an Arab-African conference on March 8. They agreed "in principle" on the need for a strong link between Jordan and a projected Palestinian state, but no details were revealed as to the nature and extent of the cooperation, nor was there any indication as to how quickly the proposed link was to be established. In fact, many in the PLO opposed any real cooperation with King Hussein, and the Jordanian monarch remained wary of the PLO's intentions. Nothing tangible came out of the Hussein-Arafat meeting, and Jordan played a cautious waiting game throughout the period under review.

The United States Government was also trying to bring about a change in the intransigent official Palestinian position. It was no accident that President Carter, for the first time, gave official governmental backing to the concept of a Palestinian "homeland" in his Clinton remarks on March 16, while the Palestine National Council was meeting in Cairo. Arafat, when told by reporters of the President's remarks, termed Carter's reference to a Palestinian homeland as "a very important note" and as a "progressive step," because it meant that Carter "has finally put his hand on the heart of the problem of the Middle East crisis." In an interview with CBS, Arafat expressed the hope that the President's statement signified "a first step towards a better understanding of the Palestinian cause by the American people," and added that he personally trusted President Carter and was prepared to cooperate with him. Arafat's assessment was, however, immediately challenged by others at the PNC session. Taisir Kubbaa, representative of the rejectionist Popular Front for the Liberation of Palestine, declared: "We do not agree with Arafat. Carter is our main enemy; Israel is only a tool. We reject cooperation with our main enemy."

The Carter Administration sent a second signal to the PLO the following day, on March 17, when the PLO observer to the United Nations, Hassan Abdel Rahman, was invited to hear the President's address to the General Assembly and to attend the following champagne reception, at which the President shook hands with him. Arafat termed the gesture a "very important signal." In response to protests by Israeli officials and American Jewish leaders at this obvious departure from the long-standing American policy of rejecting any official contacts with the PLO so long as it had not abandoned its commitment to Israel's destruction, State Department officials tried to minimize the significance of the action by placing the responsibility for the invitation on the UN Secretary-General, who was the host. The White House also tried to limit the publicity impact of the event by asking that photographers be barred from the reception. Nevertheless, the prevailing view was that the President's action was intentional and of symbolic significance.

The official 15-point political declaration adopted by the PNC in Cairo on March 20 proved disappointing to the Carter Administration, for it did not change the PLO Covenant or express any readiness to coexist with Israel. A State Department comment noted that since the Cairo conference decisions did not alter the PLO's refusal to accept Israel, they would "not contribute" to a resolution of the Middle East conflict.

Some press reports, quoting unnamed Western diplomats in Cairo, found "positive" and "constructive" elements in the declaration. They were apparently reflecting the optimistic briefings by Egyptian officials, who also inspired the official Egyptian newspaper *Al Goumhouriah* to carry, on March 22, a front-page, red banner headline declaring, "The Palestine Liberation Organization is willing to go to Geneva." However, a close look at the actual PLO declaration made it quite clear that the kind of conference and the outcome envisaged were not what President Carter had outlined in his three-point program for peace.

The hard line adopted by the PNC in Cairo, despite the control of the meetings by the reputedly more "moderate" wing of the PLO, was in sharp contrast to the optimistic forecasts. The lengthy official PNC declaration refused even to mention the word "Israel." The declaration began by affirming that the Palestine issue was the essence of "the Arab-Zionist conflict." It asked all states to cut off all assistance to and cooperation with what it termed "the racist Zionist regime." The PNC called for escalation of armed struggle, rejected "all kinds of American capitulationist settlements and liquidationist projects," threatened to abort the American peace effort, and called on all Arab states to "strengthen the Palestinian revolution in order to cope with the imperialist and Zionist designs."

Although the PNC did not formally modify the covenant calling for Israel's dissolution, and the 15-point political declaration retained much of the militant anti-Israel rhetoric, it still was not extreme enough for George Habash's Marxist Popular Front for the Liberation of Palestine. The PFLP was annoyed that the PNC had not reaffirmed the 1974 program calling for the revolutionary masses to overthrow King Hussein. The Popular Front rejected the new PLO policy of cooperating with the Arab regimes, since the PFLP contended that "Sadat, Assad, and Hussein are fully within the U.S. orbit." Accordingly, the PFLP declined to occupy its seat on the new PLO executive committee.

Said Hammami, the PLO's representative in London who had long taken a more pragmatic public line toward Israel, made a virtue of necessity and contended that the exclusion of the extremist PFLP from the new executive committee "was the most significant political decision" of the Cairo Council session. Others pointed out that the executive committee, which was largely dominated by Arafat's *al-Fatah*, was now empowered to decide about PLO participation in a Geneva conference, whereas prior to the Cairo conference such a decision required a new special session of the PNC. It was this new fact that prompted the Carter Administration to continue its efforts during the year to induce the PLO to modify its public posture sufficiently to bring it into the Geneva negotiations. Brzezinski, in particular, had not yet changed his own view, expressed in an article in *Foreign Policy*'s Summer 1975 issue, that to tackle "the central problem in the Middle East conflict," the relationship between Israel and the Palestinians, "almost certainly means, in practice, the PLO."

While Hammami was indicating that a Palestinian state would coexist with Israel, Farouk Kaddoumi, head of the PLO's political department, made it clear that the organization's shift was tactical and did not reflect a change in ultimate aims: "We are prepared to be flexible and to agree to the establishment of a state on part of our land, but we will never recognize the state of Israel." As-Saiqa leader Zuhair Mohsen, who was also a member of the executive committee and head of the PLO's military department, was even more explicit: "Our sole aim in establishing the West Bank Palestinian state is to support our demand for the rest of Palestine." It was these militant assertions that convinced other rejectionist organizations, such as the Arab Liberation Front and the Popular Front for the Liberation of Palestine-General Command, to vote for the Cairo declaration and to join the new executive committee.

Sadat-Carter Talks

During Sadat's visit to Washington in April, he emphasized to President Carter that the Palestinian question was "the core and crux" of the Arab-Israel dispute. In a toast at a White House dinner on April 4, he praised Carter for coming "very close to the proper remedy" in his remarks about the need for a homeland where, Sadat said, "they could establish a state." On his arrival in Washington, Sadat had spoken of the need for establishment of "a political entity" where the Palestinians could "at long last be a community of citizens, not a group of refugees." In other remarks as well, Sadat seemed to be vacillating between calling for a Palestinian state, which implied sovereign independence, and a more limited autonomy for the Palestinians within the larger framework of a confederation with Jordan. Sadat seemed less concerned with details than with finding some formula that would get the negotiating process started.

Sadat was also eager to obtain additional American financial help to meet Egypt's increasingly serious economic problems, which had been highlighted by rioting in January following the Government's institution of an austerity program cutting back food subsidies. Moreover, Sadat was anxious to get the United States to become a major source of equipment for Egypt's armed forces. During his April visit, Sadat said he wanted some 200 F-5E fighters, as well as anti-tank weapons. Sadat insisted that he wanted the planes not to launch a new attack against Israel, but to deal with the threat of growing Soviet penetration of Africa. He drew an alarming picture of Soviet and Cuban activities in Africa that he said threatened not only Egypt but also the Sudan and Zaire as a result of Soviet involvement in Libya, Ethiopia, Angola, and Mozambique. At the end of the visit, the White House announced that "no commitments" were made in regard to Sadat's specific arms requests, but "Egypt's importance on the continent" was noted, and the two countries agreed to maintain "close, continuing discussions on developments in Africa."

During the Washington visit, President Carter apparently had some influence on Sadat's views as to the nature of the peace to be achieved with Israel. Earlier, Sadat had said that the most that could be expected was an end to the state of belligerence, with any normalization of relations having to wait for the next generation, because of the deep-seated nature of Arab-Israel hatred and mistrust. At a press conference at the end of his three-day April visit, Sadat responded to a question as to whether signing a Geneva agreement would lead to normalization by saying, "For sure, it will be normalization." He added, however, that Egypt should not be pressed to include such normalization as trade within the text of the final agreement. Carter Administration officials let it be known that Sadat had told the President that normalization could occur within about five years of a peace agreement.

Hussein-Carter Meeting

Sadat was followed to Washington later in April by King Hussein, and discussions centered on the thorny question of Palestinian representation in a Geneva conference. While Arafat had reportedly been insisting on a separate Palestinian delegation, Hussein favored the idea of a single Arab delegation including Palestinians. At the conclusion of two days of talks at the White House, on April 26, Hussein told reporters that "Geneva would be a disaster without prior planning and without a realistic appraisal of all the difficulties and possibilities" in advance of the conference. He called on Israel to make "a gamble for peace" by agreeing to withdrawal to the pre-1967 lines.

Carter echoed Hussein's caution and suggested that it might be better not to reconvene the Geneva Middle East Peace Conference unless there were "some strong possibility for substantial achievement." However, as the months passed and procedural issues remained unresolved, the Carter Administration, in its eagerness to demonstrate visible progress, began to press for a Geneva conference, notwithstanding the cautious advice Carter seemed to have accepted from Hussein.

Assad-Carter Meeting

President Hafez al-Assad of Syria was the next in the series of Arab leaders scheduled to meet with President Carter. But while Hussein had long been in the Western camp—indeed, an embarrassing revelation of CIA payments made over the years to the King had appeared in the *Washington Post* on the day of Vance's arrival in Amman in February—and President Sadat had in recent years been sharply feuding with the Russians, Assad was anxious to maintain his ties with Moscow. As a sign of his independence from the United States, Assad did not join the procession of Middle Eastern leaders to the White House. President Carter agreed to meet with Assad in Geneva at the conclusion of Carter's participation in a Western summit conference in London.

Assad and Carter met in Geneva on May 9 for three-and-a-half hours. They went into detail on the possibility of demilitarized zones and other security arrangements for the Golan Heights, in keeping with Brzezinski's thesis that Israel's security could be assured by means other than extension of Israeli sovereignty over territory occupied in the 1967 war. The talks were described by Brzezinski as "extremely valuable, very informative, very friendly." At their conclusion, Carter praised Assad for demonstrating his "good will" and included Assad as among the "strong and moderate leaders" in the Middle East seeking peace. Assad, in turn, expressed appreciation for President Carter's "sincerity" and agreed that a Middle East conference in Geneva "should be well prepared." Carter's expressions, he said, had created an encouraging atmosphere of faith and optimism.

After the meeting with Assad, Carter reiterated to reporters that the components of peace must include "a resolution of the Palestine problem and a homeland for the Palestinians." Israeli authorities were troubled by Carter's praise for Assad as a moderate, and by the Administration's implication that defensible borders could be achieved through demilitarization—a view that was greeted with skepticism in Jerusalem, in view of the long record of Syrian violations of the demilitarized zones that had been created as part of the 1949 Syrian-Israeli Armistice Agreement. The Israelis were also distressed by Carter's failure to declare that a Palestinian home-land should be linked to Jordan. Carter did not allay these Israeli fears in a press conference a few days later, on May 12, when he stated that "the exact definition of where that homeland might be, the degree of independence of the Palestinian entity, its relationship with Jordan, or perhaps Syria and others, the geographical boundaries of it, all have to be worked out by the parties involved."

Carter also indicated that he believed there was "a chance that the Palestinians might make moves to recognize the right of Israel to exist," and that this would remove a major obstacle to progress. He recalled that the United States, "before I became President," had promised Israel that Washington would not recognize the PLO by direct conversations or negotiations, "as long as the PLO continued to espouse the commitment that Israel had to be destroyed." Carter said that "we are trying to add our efforts" to bring about a change in the PLO position. The Israelis concluded that the United States was eager to involve the PLO in the negotiations, and Jerusalem feared that Carter had bought the Arab thesis that a Palestinian state on the West Bank and Gaza would not pose an inherent threat to Israel, and that some gesture by the PLO toward coexistence with Israel would be enough to justify American contacts with the PLO.

Secretary Vance had tried to reassure the Israelis in a meeting with Foreign Minister Yigal Allon in London the previous day, May 11, that the American position on the PLO had not fundamentally changed, that the United States would not make public any peace plan before giving the parties a chance to react to it, and that the U.S. would continue to supply Israel with needed arms, together with "advanced technology." The latter had become an issue after the Carter Administra-tion announced a new arms transfer policy, which would have excluded Israel from the list of countries, such as NATO members, with whom the United States was prepared to enter into co-production agreements for advanced weapons. (AJYB, 1978, [Vol. 78], pp. 103–104.)

Israeli Apprehension Over U.S. Policy

Despite the official disclaimers, in early May, apprehension was growing in Israel, and within the American Jewish community, that the Carter Administration was setting the stage for an imposed settlement in the Middle East. United Nations

Ambassador Andrew Young said that the United States would put forward "some formulations" of its own to break the stalemate. President Carter himself told three European journalists that he would not hesitate, if he saw a fair and equitable solution, "to use the full strength of our own country and its persuasive powers to bring those nations to agreement." Secretary Vance also told the press that once the initial round of consultations with Middle East leaders was completed, the United States would make "suggestions on all the core issues." He dismissed as a matter of semantics a reporter's question as to whether these suggestions would amount to a comprehensive peace plan. The popular New York *Daily News* interpreted Vance's remarks as indicating that he intended to take a "made in the U.S.A. peace plan" to the area on his next visit. "We hope the Carter Administration knows what it is doing," the *News* editorialized on May 6, noting that the Carter approach "represents a significant departure from past policy, which was to cast the country solely in the role of honest broker between Israel and its Arab foes." The *News* warned that "one false step and we could not only damage the prospects for successful negotiations, but destroy our usefulness as trusted middleman as well."

The Administration also seemed oblivious to the consequences of its actions upon the Israeli public's thinking. After Prime Minister Rabin had been replaced by Defense Minister Shimon Peres as leader of the ruling Labor Party, the Carter Administration continued to assume that Labor would win in the May 17 elections and that the timetable for Geneva would at most be delayed by a few weeks, to give the new Israeli leader a chance to meet with President Carter. The Carter Administration was completely unprepared for the results of the May elections, which led to the defeat of Labor and the formation of a government led by Menachem Begin of the opposition Likud Party. (See Louvish, pp. 260–266 for details.)

While it is true that Labor's defeat after 29 years of continuous rule was due primarily to domestic factors, a credible case could be made for the argument that at least some of the strength gained by Likud was due to a popular feeling that in the impending peace negotiations the country needed tough new leadership that was prepared to stand up to American pressure. One of the major campaign arguments of the Labor Party had been that it had experience in dealing with America, and that it had successfully developed and nurtured the special relationship with the United States. Prime Minister Rabin had been Israel's ambassador in Washington for some five years, and it was under the Labor governments that Israel had achieved unprecedented levels of American economic and military aid. The reported failure of Rabin to influence the Carter policy during his trip to Washington, signaled by the refusal of the Carter Administration to lift the ban of Kfir sales to Ecuador, the unveiling of the Palestinian homeland plan, the call for Israeli withdrawal to the 1967 lines with only minor changes, and the continuing American flirtation with the PLO, all undermined the credibility of the Labor Party's claim to influence upon official Washington's thinking.

Soviet Mideast Policy

While the Carter Administration was gathering most of the headlines in its quest for a resumed Geneva conference, the Soviet Union was also actively working to assure itself a place in the formal negotiations. Moscow was still smarting from the ignominy of being frozen out of the disengagement agreements that Dr. Kissinger had brought about between Israel and Egypt and Syria. The Carter approach appeared to be more receptive to a Soviet role. In a major address on March 21, Soviet party chief Brezhnev spoke in favor of "concerted actions" by the Soviet Union and the United States to achieve a just and lasting Middle East settlement. There were certain nuances in the speech that were considered mildly encouraging by Israel, such as Brezhnev's acknowledgment that the drawing up of detailed peace terms was "primarily a matter for the opposing sides themselves," that withdrawal could be carried out in stages, spaced over several months, that all states in the area had the right to "independent existence and security," and that from the moment of the completion of Israeli troop withdrawal "the state of war between the Arab states participating in the conflict and Israel will be ended and relations of peace established." The Soviet leader also favored the establishment of demilitarized zones and the possibility of a UN emergency force or UN observers. On the Palestinian question, Brezhnev declared: "It goes without saying that the inalienable rights of the Palestinian Arab people should be insured, including its right to self-determination, to the creation of its own state." In Jerusalem there was speculation that Moscow might be moving to a resumption of diplomatic relations with Israel, which the Soviet Union had broken in the wake of the 1967 war. But the hopes for a rapprochement between Moscow and Jerusalem were soon to be dashed.

On April 4, Yasir Arafat arrived on an official visit to Moscow and, for the first time, was publicly received by Brezhnev. On April 7, a joint statement was issued in which Brezhnev confirmed that the Soviet Union was striving for a comprehensive Middle East settlement, "a pillar of which must be the guaranteeing of the legitimate national rights of the Palestinian Arab people, their right to self-determination and their right to create an independent Palestinian state." The Soviet Union, the statement continued, "constantly and firmly supports the participation of PLO representatives in the Geneva Conference." Arafat emphasized that the Palestinian resistance movement would continue to struggle "against the intrigues of imperialism and reaction" and pledged to "strengthen its ties of friendship and cooperation with the Soviet Union and all the other socialist community countries." Arafat expressed his profound gratitude to the Soviet Union for its "consistent and all-round support."

The Soviet leadership in early 1977 also received Libya's Muammer Qaddafi and Iraq's Saddam Hussein. During the year, the Soviet Union significantly increased its military arms supply to both countries, according to CIA and other Western intelligence sources. This raised questions as to the sincerity of the Soviet Union's quest for a genuine Middle East settlement, since Iraq and Libya were vehemently opposed to peace with Israel. Syrian President Assad also was promised increased military aid when he visited Moscow in April.

Saudi Position

Saudi Arabia was also busy trying to convince the world that the PLO was moderating its position. Crown Prince Fahd told American journalists in Jidda on May 10 that he believed "the leaders of the Palestinian people will be willing to accept any peaceful solution to the problem, if that peaceful solution includes the establishment of a Palestinian state on the West Bank and the Gaza Strip." Fahd stressed that it was imperative to find a solution during 1977; otherwise, "disturbances and tensions" would rise and a renewal of conflict was possible. Foreign Minister Prince Saud al Faisal similarly asserted that failure to reach a solution would lead to "an international catastrophe." Nevertheless, both Fahd and Saud, as well as Petroleum and Mineral Resources Minister Sheikh Zaki Yamani, insisted that neither the pricing nor the production level of Saudi oil would be used as a means to force a solution.

Following the Begin victory in Israel, Egyptian Foreign Minister Ismail Fahmi raised the prospect of a new Arab oil embargo in a meeting with reporters on May 22. Oil, he said, "is one of the Arabs' principal weapons, and there should be no doubt that it will be used automatically if Israel persists in its aggression against occupied Arab lands." However, after Saudi Crown Prince Fahd completed two days of talks at the White House on May 25, President Carter said that he had been assured by Fahd that the threat of an embargo was a "completely false report." Carter added that he found "no disturbing differences" about the Middle East in his talks with the Saudi leader and that Fahd had assured him that the Saudis were prepared to live in peace with Israel. Fahd again emphasized the Palestinian issue as the core of the Middle East problem, and Saudi officials privately expressed confidence that President Carter would soon endorse a West Bank-Gaza state. Carter emphasized the vast economic interests that linked the Saudis and Americans, noting that the Saudis had invested about $60 billion in the United States and were "one of our largest customers," buying $3.5 billion in American goods annually, with that figure expected to grow. This "very important" relationship, Carter said, "helps to tie us together in dealing with political problems which we face in a mutual way." A $100-million, joint Saudi-American solar-energy research program was announced during the visit. Fahd declined to speculate on what effect the Begin election would have on peace prospects, but asked Carter to urge the Israelis not to close the door on a settlement "that would provide a just and lasting peace."

U.S. Reaction to Begin Victory

Two days after his election, Menachem Begin visited the Gush Emunim (Bloc of the Faithful) Jewish settlement of Elon Moreh in the West Bank area of Camp

Kaddum to dedicate a synagogue. In his remarks, he declared that in the next few months "there will be many Elon Morehs." The Labor government had refused to grant official recognition to the privately established settlement, since it wished to see settlements only in strategically important areas and not near Arab population centers. In response to a reporter's question as to whether he intended to annex the West Bank, Begin pointed out that since the area of Judea and Samaria was an integral part of the sovereign Jewish land of Israel, he regarded the area as "liberated" and not annexed. The Likud had run on a platform declaring that there would be no foreign rule in the area west of the Jordan River.

These statements and actions, which seemed to reject the concept of territorial compromise advocated by the previous Labor government, aroused deep concern in the United States. In an address at Notre Dame University on May 22, President Carter inserted a sentence declaring: "We expect Israel and her neighbors to continue to be bound" by the obligations undertaken in UN Security Council Resolutions 242 and 338. In his press conference on May 26, the President reiterated that "withdrawal from West Bank territories—either partially or in their entirety" was envisaged in any ultimate settlement. He refrained from drawing any exact lines, he said, since this was for the parties to work out.

Carter was asked whether he thought Begin's views would constitute an obstacle to peace. The President responded that he did not think this would be an insuperable problem, noting that Begin would have to reconcile conflicting interests to form a cabinet. Carter also expressed confidence that Begin's views would be modified "when I meet him personally, and when he meets with the Congressional leaders and with the Jewish Americans who are very deeply interested in this and see the purpose of our own country."

The President's remarks foreshadowed intensive efforts by both the Carter Administration and the Begin Government to enlist support within the American Jewish community for their respective approaches to a Middle East settlement. American Jews became increasingly uneasy at the prospect that in a confrontation between the two governments they would be forced to choose sides. Matters were not helped by intimations in some Jewish circles that any dissent from the Begin policies was a betrayal of Israel, and by veiled hints by Administration advocates that opposition to the Carter policy by special interest groups was against the U.S. national interest.

In a major speech on June 17 before the World Affairs Council in San Francisco, Vice-President Walter F. Mondale sought to explain the Administration's policy and to reassure the Jewish community. He underscored the United States' "unique and profound relationship" with Israel since its creation. "Our sense of shared values and purposes," he said, means that for Americans "the question of Israel's survival is not a political question, but rather stands as a moral imperative of our foreign policy." Mondale also stressed the need for direct negotiations between the Arab states and Israel, and reasserted that the Carter Administration did "not intend to use military aid as pressure on Israel." He conceded that there might be differences over military aid, but insisted that these would only be on military or economic grounds, but not on political grounds. Differences over diplomatic strategy would be worked out on the political level, but would not alter the American commitment to Israel's military security. He added that the U.S. realized that "peace cannot be imposed from the outside, and we do not intend to present the parties with a plan or a timetable or a map." At the same time, Mondale reiterated the Administration's optimistic view that all the Arab leaders with whom Carter met had a "great desire for peace." Moreover, Mondale elaborated on the Brzezinski thesis that security arrangements would be separated from recognized boundaries and, in this way, Israel could return "to approximately the borders that existed prior to the war of 1967." On the Palestinian question, he endorsed the possibility of some arrangement "for a Palestinian homeland or entity—preferably in association with Jordan." Such an association would enhance the viability of the concept and the security of the region, he said in the name of the President. But then he quickly added that "the specifics are for the parties to decide."

Criticism of Carter Policy

The Mondale speech failed to reassure the Israelis, and was criticized in the United States. Senator Jacob K. Javits (R-N.Y.), a ranking member of the Foreign Relations Committee, said the Carter proposals might undercut the possibility of a successful U.S. role as mediator. The "persistent public advocacy" by the Carter Administration of Israeli withdrawal to "approximately" the June 1967 lines and the establishment of a Palestinian entity prior to any negotiations between Arab and Israeli leaders, Javits warned, "can only continue to feed Arab illusions that President Carter will deliver to them what they have been unable to deliver to themselves" by other means, including war. To be "as specific as Vice-President Mondale's blueprint of the Administration's position, in advance of Geneva, has raised both Arab expectations and Israeli fears, thereby inviting failure."

On June 27, shortly before Prime Minister Begin's arrival in Washington, the State Department issued a statement on the Administration's Middle East policy pointedly emphasizing consistent American support for the principles in UN Security Council Resolution 242 and their application through negotiations as called for in Resolution 338. In an attempt to allay the criticism of the Carter policy, the State Department statement stressed that the United States "was not asking for any one-sided concessions from anyone," adding that the Arabs would have to agree to a durable peace with satisfactory security arrangements and normalization of relations with Israel. The new point in the statement, however, was its emphasis that the United States considered that Resolution 242 "means withdrawal from all three fronts in the Middle East dispute—that is, Sinai, Golan, West Bank and Gaza—the exact borders and security arrangements being agreed in negotiations." Such negotiations, the State Department stressed, "must start without any preconditions from any side." To automatically exclude any territories from negotiation "strikes us as contradictory to the principle of negotiations without preconditions." This was taken by the Israelis as a pointed criticism of Prime Minister Begin's declarations that the withdrawal provisions of Resolution 242 did not apply to Judea and Samaria (the West Bank), since these areas were not taken by Israel from any legitimate foreign sovereign, but had been liberated from the illegal Jordanian occupation of 1948.

In an effort to avoid an immediate confrontation with the U.S. on this matter, the new Israeli government's Basic Policy Guidelines, adopted on June 20, declared that although the Knesset had empowered the Cabinet to apply by administrative order "the law, judiciary and administration of the state to all territory of the Land of Israel" (presumably including the West Bank and Gaza), the Government would not invoke this authority "so long as negotiations are being conducted on a peace treaty between Israel and its neighbors." The Government also promised to bring this matter up for special debate and approval by the Knesset before taking such action. This compromise language was reportedly adopted upon the urging of Foreign Minister Moshe Dayan.

President Carter was also anxious to avoid a confrontation. Concerned by the mounting criticism in the Jewish community of his Middle East policy, he invited Rabbi Alexander M. Schindler, chairman of the Conference of Major American Jewish Organizations, and some 40 other American Jewish leaders to the White House on July 6. He emphasized that the definition of peace that he was urging the Arab leaders to accept included full diplomatic relations with Israel at the ambassadorial level, trade, tourism, and cultural exchanges. He was much more explicit than he had been in public in expressing opposition to a fully independent Palestinian state. He was quoted by one of the participants at the closed-door session as saying: "We see any kind of Palestinian entity as tied to Jordan. Anything else would be a distinct threat to peace; it could easily be used by Qaddafi or the Soviets as a threat to peace. We don't envisage an independent state at all." Carter added that several of the Arab leaders with whom he met shared his view. He did not cite them by name, but on July 10, after meeting in Alexandria, President Sadat and King Hussein agreed to secure a Palestinian role in the Geneva talks by establishing an "explicit link between Jordan and the Palestinians" on the West Bank.

There were different assessments of the White House Jewish meeting. Rabbi Schindler characterized it as "a very fruitful, helpful and frank discussion," adding that the group was particularly pleased by the President's definition of peace, and "reassured" by Carter's statements that there was no deviation in his support of Israel expressed during the Presidential campaign. Rabbi William Berkowitz, president of Bnai Zion, disagreed. He believed that Carter had "still left many gaps and doubts and unanswered questions about American policy vis-à-vis Israel." He came away from the "inconclusive, unclear and fuzzy" meeting with the impression that the Administration believed peace required Israel to withdraw to the pre-1967 borders. Berkowitz asserted that there was a continuing erosion of support for Carter among "average Jewish voters," and while some in the Jewish community "may have been convinced, many are still skeptical" regarding Carter's policy toward Israel.

Carter-Begin Meeting

The widely-predicted American-Israeli confrontation was avoided during the White House meetings on July 19 and 20, as both leaders agreed to concentrate on the procedural steps necessary to bring about negotiations. Commenting on the Israeli elections, Carter noted that Begin represented a nation which demonstrated "the importance of a true democracy where people in an absolutely unconstrained expression of individual preference in open elections can decide who their leader will be." The President added that he was "very proud" of Prime Minister Begin's attitude that all issues were negotiable, and encouraged by Begin's statements that he hoped that talks with Sadat, Hussein, and Assad could commence in Geneva in October.

At a press conference in Washington, Begin described his proposals for a framework for direct negotiations, in accordance with Security Council Resolution 338, adding that the government of Israel "acknowledges that Resolution 338 includes and makes reference to Security Council Resolution 242." Israel would negotiate with the accredited delegates of Egypt, Syria, and Jordan—as well as Lebanon, if the latter wished to join. The negotiations were to be free and with no prior commitments by either side. Israel proposed a format of separate bilateral commissions composed of Israel and each of her neighbors. Begin categorically rejected the participation of the PLO as a separate delegation or as part of another Arab delegation, since the PLO's "design is to destroy our country and to destroy our people." However, Israel would not object to the participation of individual Palestinian Arabs within the Jordanian delegation. Should the Arab states insist on the participation of the PLO, which would make it impossible to reconvene a full-fledged Geneva conference, Begin said, then Israel suggested two alternatives: either the United States should use its good offices to establish three or four mixed commissions for separate bilateral talks on the model of the Rhodes negotiations which led to the 1949 series of Armistice Agreements; or the United States should revive the 1972 idea of proximity talks by which the American delegate would initially shuttle between the representatives of Israel and one or more Arab states meeting in New York or another city, with the U.S. using its good offices to bring them together.

Controversy Over Settlement Policy

Upon Begin's return to Israel, the Cabinet Committee on Settlements gave official recognition to three Gush Emunim civilian settlements in the heart of the West Bank which the previous Labor government had refused to legalize. At his press conference two days later, President Carter said that he had let Prime Minister

Begin know "very strongly" that creation of new settlements would cause "deep concern" to the American Government. Carter added that Israeli settlements in occupied territory had "always been characterized by our government, by me and my predecessors, as an illegal action." Carter said that he had not specifically discussed the question of legalizing existing settlements with Begin, and that the Israeli leader had not given him any prior notice.

On August 14, the Israeli Government announced that it was extending economic and social services to the inhabitants of the West Bank and Gaza, to grant them rights equal to those enjoyed by residents of Israel. The following day, Begin explained that the move was "by no means the beginning of annexation, but was motivated solely by a desire to improve the lot of the Arabs under Israeli rule." On August 17, the Government approved the establishment of three new settlements on the West Bank. The State Department responded with a strongly worded statement, approved by President Carter, reiterating that these "unilateral illegal acts in territories presently under Israeli occupation create obstacles to constructive negotiations." A second statement, while noting the "humanitarian aims" of Israel's extension of economic and social services in the West Bank and Gaza, pointed out that "the action creates an impression of permanence of Israeli occupation . . . that is not helpful." Israeli spokesmen countered by pointing out that the three new settlements were all in close proximity to the 1949 Armistice Demarcation Lines and thus fell within the category of minor modifications that the United States had sanctioned. Moreover, the three settlements had been approved in principle by the previous Labor government, since they could be justified by the need for "secure" boundaries and thus fit into the Allon Plan formula.

Jewish Community Reaction to Begin

Begin's election, his more active settlement policy, and his outspoken opposition to territorial compromise on the West Bank aroused misgivings among many American Jews. Rabbi Schindler and the leaders of such intergroup relations organizations as the American Jewish Committee, the American Jewish Congress, and the Anti-Defamation League of B'nai B'rith spoke privately with Begin and other members of his government to convey their concern over the difficulties they were encountering in explaining certain Israeli policies and tactics to the American public. However, these misgivings were rarely given public expression during the period under review. There was a general feeling that the new government in Israel should be given a chance to prove itself, especially since it was premature to judge whether Begin's seemingly tough stance represented an inflexible ideological commitment, or was a diplomatic bargaining position that might be modified in the course of negotiations with the Arab states. Moreover, in view of the mounting pressure on Israel in the international arena and the activist policy being followed by the Carter Administration, there was widespread concern within the Jewish community that any public criticism of the Begin Government would be seized upon by elements unfriendly to Israel and used to justify their own criticism of Israeli policies. Finally, there was a widespread feeling among the Jewish masses that American Jews should be supportive of whatever government had been democratically elected in Israel, especially in questions affecting Israel's security.

It is noteworthy that even *Breira* refrained from publicly criticizing the Begin Government. *Breira* (Alternative), founded in 1973, had been vocal in its criticism of the Israeli Government for its handling of the Arab-Israel conflict. Although *Breira* never achieved a membership of more than 1,500, its ability to attract some individuals prominent in the rabbinate, on campuses and in the Jewish institutional world, and the public relations skills of some of its spokesmen, had enabled *Breira* to get considerable press coverage for its views. *Breira* encountered intensive criticism in early 1977 from several Anglo-Jewish publications, which attacked not only the substance of its positions, but impugned the motives of its advocates. Most of the criticism had focused on *Breira's* advocacy of the creation of an independent Palestinian state in the West Bank and Gaza Strip, and the call for negotiations by Israel with any Palestinians who had renounced terrorism and accepted Israel's right to exist.

Vance's Second Middle East Trip

On August 1, Secretary of State Vance opened the second round of his Middle East travels with a meeting with President Sadat in Alexandria. The Egyptian leader proposed that in preparation for a full-fledged Geneva conference the foreign ministers of the Arab states and Israel meet in New York or Washington in mid-September as a working group. This was seen as a way to bypass the problem of PLO participation in the initial stages. He indicated that he had no objection to the Israeli and Egyptian representatives sitting together. Vance welcomed the idea, saying that the better prepared a Geneva conference was, the greater its chances of success. However, Vance said, it was up to the Arabs to decide if they favored the idea. The Syrians promptly announced that they rejected the working group proposal, and President Assad emphasized that there would be no direct or indirect meetings between the Syrian Foreign Minister and Israeli officials at the UN.

After meeting with Lebanese President Elias Sarkis in Beirut on August 3, Vance announced that the Carter Administration would ask Congress to approve $100 million in military credits over the next three years to help Lebanon build up a 3,000-man militia for domestic security. The continuation of factional strife and the absence of Lebanese central government control in the south led to frequent clashes between Christian and Moslem villagers, and to guerrilla raids by Palestinian militants. Earlier in the year, the U.S. had several times exerted behind-the-scenes diplomatic efforts to dissuade Israel and Syria from becoming directly involved with their own forces in the southern region bordering on Israel.

On Vance's stop in Amman, King Hussein said Jordan "could not afford a failure" in a Geneva conference, and indicated that he was reluctant to commit Jordan to attend unless there was "some understanding of the principles on which we are going to base our talks" in Geneva.

During Vance's visit to Taif, the Saudi summer capital, the Saudis informed him that the PLO was moving toward accepting UN Resolution 242 if the United States made an appropriate reciprocal gesture to open a direct dialogue with the Palestinian group. The United States Government had already been in indirect contact with the PLO through meetings of congressmen, such as Lee Hamilton (D-Ind.), chairman of the House International Affairs Subcommittee on Europe and the Middle East, who had met with Arafat in Cairo in mid-July. Hamilton reported that he gained the impression that the PLO leader "accepts Israel" and would accept a Palestinian "mini-state," although Arafat did not say so explicitly.

According to highly placed Palestinian sources, Arafat had informed the Saudis that *al-Fatah,* the main Palestinian guerrilla group which he headed, would acquiesce in 242 if the resolution were "interpreted" as recognizing the right to create a Palestinian state. In transmitting the message to Secretary Vance, the Saudis reportedly modified it to read "independent homeland" instead of "state," presumably to make it appear more congruent with the Carter position.

The Carter Administration appeared at this time to be scaling down its requirements for opening discussions with the PLO. In an interview with *Time* magazine, published August 8, President Carter was asked whether Begin had said he would drop his opposition to any PLO participation in the Geneva Conference, if the PLO were to accept the principle of the existence of Israel. Carter said that Begin had objected to any identifiable PLO members attending such a conference because the PLO was publicly committed to Israel's destruction. The President went on to state: "I cannot speak for Mr. Begin, [but] if the Palestinian leaders adopted that position [acceptance of Israel's existence] or espoused the U.S. Resolutions 242 and 338 as a basis for negotiations at Geneva, we would immediately commence plans to begin talks with the Palestinian leaders." In an informal news conference in Plains, Georgia on August 8, the President reiterated his remarks to *Time,* and then noted that the PLO might add a unilateral statement to its acceptance of 242 to the effect that the Palestinians "have additional status other than as just refugees." Adding such a proviso, Carter said, "would suit us okay."

Speaking to newsmen in Taif, Secretary Vance said that he had been informed that the PLO was contemplating a change in its position, but noted that he had seen nothing concrete as yet. "If the PLO were to accept 242," Vance said, "they would be accepting the principle that they recognize the right of Israel to exist in a state of peace, within secure and recognized boundaries." Vance added: "That, in my judgment, would revoke the Covenant." This was a departure from Vance's earlier position, enunciated during his February trip, in which he had reiterated the traditional American position that the PLO would have to accept Israel's right to exist, recognize 242 and 338, and explicitly renounce or formally amend its National Covenant before the United States would agree to deal with the organization.

In Israel, on August 13, Vance reportedly stated to a group of West Bank Arab dignitaries who had been brought together by Foreign Minister Dayan, that the United States considered a transition period under United Nations trusteeship as the most reasonable solution of the issue of a Palestinian homeland. Several West Bank mayors, who refused to meet with Vance, stressed their support for the PLO. Another group of West Bankers who did attend the Dayan reception for Vance asserted that the Arabs actually living in the area should have the right of self-determination.

On August 26, the PLO Central Council issued a hard-line statement condemning "all the United States and Zionist maneuvers" as plots aimed at liquidating the Palestinian cause. The statement again rejected UN Resolution 242. The PLO Council warned the "cowards" living "in occupied Palestine" against cooperating with the plans of the Zionist enemy, further warned against "giving credence to imperialist and Zionist promises," and urged instead a renewal of militancy and "confrontation." President Carter termed the statement "an obstacle in the way of our efforts to convene a peace conference."

Palestinian Representation Issue

On September 12, on the eve of Secretary Vance's scheduled series of meetings with the Israeli and Arab foreign ministers attending the UN General Assembly, the State Department issued a new policy statement on the Middle East. After reiterating that all participants at a renewed Geneva conference should adhere to the terms of Resolutions 242 and 338, the statement placed special emphasis on settling the question of "the status of the Palestinians" in a comprehensive Arab-Israeli agreement. Toward this end, the statement went on, "the Palestinians must be involved in the peacemaking process. Their representatives will have to be at Geneva for the Palestinian question to be solved." The statement did not make explicit reference to the PLO nor to the form of Palestinian representation. Nevertheless, PLO leader Arafat welcomed it as "a positive step." Secretary Vance, on September 14, said that the two alternatives which seemed most promising were Palestinians within a Jordanian delegation or Palestinians within a single pan-Arab delegation.

The always outspoken American Ambassador to the United Nations, Andrew Young, declared on September 18 that the PLO would have to be brought into the negotiations. "You're not going to have peace in the Middle East until the people who are doing the fighting are somehow brought to the table," he said, adding, however, that the PLO must first recognize "Israel's right to exist." He also recommended the holding of a plebiscite to determine if the PLO "is truly representative of the aspirations of the entire Palestinian people."

Following meetings between Foreign Minister Dayan and Secretary Vance, the Israeli Cabinet, on September 25, approved a proposal calling for a single unified Arab delegation, including Palestinians, to attend the opening session of a Geneva conference. The Palestinian Arabs, whom the Cabinet referred to as the "Arabs of Eretz Israel," could not be known officials of the PLO, although they might be sympathizers of the organization. Moreover, Israel would not negotiate with the unified delegation as such; once the ceremonial session was over, the Arabs would have to be split into separate national delegations to negotiate peace agreements with Israel. The Cabinet decision left unclear whether the Palestinians would then become part of the Jordanian delegation, or could also be members of the Egyptian and possibly Syrian delegations as well.

The PLO gave a noncommittal response. A PLO spokesman in Beirut reiterated that the PLO was the "sole legitimate" representative of the Palestinian people, adding that after the PLO received "a formal invitation to Geneva," then the organization would "consider the details of Palestinian representation there."

At this news conference on September 29, President Carter also emphasized the need for "adequate Palestinian representation" at a peace conference. He reasserted the recent American position that the United States Government would "begin to meet with and work with the PLO" as soon as they accepted UN Resolution 242 as a basis for negotiations, even with the qualifying comment that they regarded the resolution as inadequately meeting Palestinian interests. Asked whether the United States regarded the PLO as a representative of the Palestinians, the President replied: "Obviously they don't represent a nation. It is a group that represents certainly a substantial part of the Palestinians. I certainly don't think they're the exclusive representatives of the Palestinians. Obviously there are mayors, for instance, and local officials in the West Bank area who represent Palestinians. They may or may not be members of the PLO."

Soviet-American Joint Efforts

At his September 29 press conference, Carter noted that "a further complicating factor" in preparing for Geneva was that the Soviet Union was a co-chairman. Therefore, in the call for the conference and in the negotiations preceding the format of the conference "we have to deal with the Soviet Union as well." Intensive Soviet-American discussions, which had begun in August with a meeting between Secretary Vance and the Soviet Ambassador in Washington, Anatoly F. Dobrinin, were capped by a 90-minute meeting between Vance and Soviet Foreign Minister Andrei A. Gromyko in New York on September 30. On the following day, a joint Soviet-American statement on the Middle East was issued.

The statement began by declaring their agreement on the urgent necessity of achieving a just and lasting comprehensive settlement of the Arab-Israeli conflict. Noting that some procedural and organizational problems remained, they pledged through joint efforts and their contacts with the parties to facilitate the resumption of the Geneva Conference "not later than December 1977." The statement said that the questions to be resolved in a comprehensive settlement included "such key issues as withdrawal of Israeli armed forces from territories occupied in the 1967 conflict; the resolution of the Palestinian question, including insuring the legitimate rights of the Palestinian people; termination of the state of war and establishment of normal peaceful relations on the basis of mutual recognition of the principles of sovereignty, territorial integrity, and political independence."

The joint statement aroused a storm of controversy within the Congress, which had not been informed in advance, among the general American public, and in the Middle East. State Department officials explained that since the Russians were going to be at Geneva in any case, Secretary Vance believed it useful to develop a "common denominator" of agreed principles with them. The American negotiators claimed, moreover, to have won certain concessions from the Russians in the process of hammering out the joint statement. For instance, the Russians no longer demanded Israeli withdrawal from "all" or from "the" territories, and the Russians now endorsed the goal of normal peaceful relations and not merely an end of the state of belligerence.

On the Palestinian question, the statement omitted explicit reference to the Palestine Liberation Organization. However, it called for participation in the Geneva Peace Conference "of representatives of all the parties involved in the conflict, including those of the Palestinian people." The Israeli Government was also distressed by the fact that the United States, for the first time, agreed to support "the legitimate *rights* of the Palestinian people," whereas in the past the United States had limited herself to endorsing the legitimate *interests* of the Palestinians. State Department officials countered that they had won a concession from the Russians on this point as well, since in the past the Soviet Union had spoken of the legitimate *national* rights of the Palestinians. State Department officials also noted that the American position went no further than that of the nine-member European Economic Community, which on June 29, 1977 had adopted a statement affirming their belief that a solution of the Middle East conflict was possible "only if the legitimate right of the Palestinian people to give effective expression to its national identity" were translated into "a homeland for the Palestinian people."

From the Israeli perspective, however, the net result of all the Soviet-American semantic bargaining was to erode the solemn United States commitment to Israel on Palestinian participation in Geneva that had been given by former Secretary of State Kissinger to Israeli Foreign Minister Allon as part of the September 1, 1975 Sinai II Agreement (AJYB, 1977 [Vol. 77], pp. 91–92).

Most distressing to Israel was the fact that the joint Soviet-American statement made no explicit reference to either Resolution 242 or 338. The American explanation was that the Soviet Union had begun by asking for explicit endorsement of General Assembly resolutions that spelled out Palestinian rights, and the compromise solution was to drop reference to any United Nations resolutions. But seen in the context of the Carter Administration's efforts to bring the PLO into the Geneva negotiations, the joint statement could be regarded as a face-saving device designed to enable the PLO to come to Geneva without having explicitly to endorse Resolution 242.

The American Jewish community was shocked and outraged by the joint Soviet-American statement. In a telegram to Secretary Vance, Rabbi Schindler of the President's Conference said the joint statement appeared to be "an abandonment of America's historic commitment to the security and survival of Israel" and "a shocking about-face" of the President's public pledges to support a negotiated settlement within the framework of Resolution 242. The joint statement initiated a wave of protest in the Jewish community that had been building over the months.

In the aftermath of the October 1 statement, the White House was, in fact, flooded with thousands of irate phone calls, telegrams, and letters. According to Washington observers, the vehemence and volume of the protest surprised the Administration, which had not foreseen the domestic consequences of the joint statement. Some of the political consequences, however, were immediately apparent to Los Angeles Democratic Party leaders, who reported that many normally stalwart Jewish supporters were refusing to buy tickets for a $1,000-a-plate, Democratic fund-raising dinner scheduled for October 22. "I have never seen them as upset by anything as they are now," Hershey Gold, a veteran Democratic fund-raiser, told the Los Angeles *Times.* State Department spokesman Hodding Carter III tried to mollify the opposition, saying that Palestinian rights were not to "be purchased at the expense of Israel" and that PLO endorsement of the joint statement would not in itself constitute "acceptance of our terms for talking to" the PLO.

The Israeli and American Jewish critics were joined by many prominent Americans, such as labor leader George Meany, who questioned the Administration's wisdom in enhancing the Soviet Union's role in the Middle East in the absence of any evidence that Moscow truly shared Washington's basic objectives of peace and stability in the area. The statement explicitly mentioned that in addition to demilitarized zones and the agreed stationing therein of UN troops or observers, "international guarantees of such borders as well as of the observance of the terms of the settlement can be established, should the parties so desire." The statement added that "the United States and the Soviet Union are ready to participate in these guarantees, subject to their constitutional processes."

Among members of Congress and their constituents, this raised the spectre of Syria or a PLO-dominated Palestinian entity calling in Soviet troops or "volunteers" to enforce its interpretation of its rights. The result could be open confrontation between Soviet and American forces. Or, if a post-Vietnam mood meant that an American Congress would block any firm response, the Russians or their Cuban surrogates could have the field to themselves, since Moscow was not subject to the same constraints in its "constitutional processes."

Senator Henry M. Jackson (D-Wash.) called the joint statement "a step in the wrong direction," noting that not only the Israelis were unhappy about reintroducing the Russians. "The American people must certainly raise the question: 'Why bring the Russians in at a time when the Egyptians have been throwing them out?' "

the Senator said. Jackson was also angered by the Administration's failure to consult Congress about the proposals for joint Soviet-American guarantees of the Arab-Israel borders, pointing out that this "could mean the positioning of Russian and American troops" in the area, which was a mistaken policy since it would "raise issues of confrontation." Senator Robert J. Dole (R-Kans.) said the statement was an "abdication of Mideast leadership by President Carter." Senator Daniel P. Moynihan (D-N.Y.) charged that the joint statement was a sign of "escalating diplomatic pressure against Israel."

National Security Adviser Brzezinski took a more optimistic view. In an interview on Canadian television, Brzezinski said that the Soviet Union "realizes that the situation of continued conflict in the Middle East does not enhance its interests. It jeopardizes them locally and in terms of their relations with us." He expressed optimism that the Geneva Conference would be reconvened before the end of the year, and brushed aside Israeli objections. He expected Israel to attend the Conference, he said, since it did not want to be isolated and left out of the peace-making process. He also left no doubt that the United States was prepared to prod Israel to attend. "I think the point to bear in mind is that the United States is not just an interested bystander, not even just a benevolent mediator," he said. Since the United States "has a direct interest in obtaining a resolution of the conflict," he emphasized, "the U.S. has a legitimate right to exercise its own leverage" to obtain a settlement. "And that's exactly what we will be doing."

President Carter used a softer tone in his address to the UN General Assembly on October 4. "We do not intend to impose from the outside a settlement on the nations of the Middle East," the President said. He also reaffirmed the elements of peace outlined earlier and explicitly mentioned that the "basis for peace" was provided in Security Council Resolutions 242 and 338, adding that negotiations in good faith by all the parties were needed to give substance to peace. While declaring that the American commitment "to Israel's security is unquestionable," he again asserted that "the legitimate rights of the Palestinians must be recognized."

U.S.-Israel Working Paper

The Israeli Government made it clear that it regarded the Soviet-American joint statement as an unacceptable basis for negotiations. Foreign Minister Dayan carried with him a draft statement explaining why his government would not participate in the Geneva talks, as he began six hours of intensive discussions with President Carter and Secretary Vance on the night of October 4–5. Early in the morning, agreement was reached on a joint statement declaring that the United States and Israel agreed that Resolutions 242 and 338 "remain the agreed basis" for Geneva, and that "all the understandings and agreements between them on this subject remain in force." The statement also specified that "acceptance of the joint U.S.-U.S.S.R. statement of October 1, 1977 by the parties is not a prerequisite for the reconvening and conduct of the Geneva Conference." This formulation enabled Israel to maintain that it regarded the Soviet-American statement as null and void, while the United States could say that it regarded the statement as valid. Dayan, Carter, and Vance also developed a working paper for resolving the procedural obstacles to Geneva, which Dayan was to submit to his government and Vance would present to the other parties.

On October 11, the Israeli Cabinet approved the "working paper," which provided that the Arab parties would be represented by a unified Arab delegation, "which will include Palestinian Arabs." After the opening session, the Conference would split into several working groups. The negotiation and conclusion of peace treaties would be by bilateral groups constituted on a geographic basis, i.e., Egypt-Israel, Jordan-Israel, Syria-Israel, and Lebanon-Israel, whenever Lebanon chose to join. West Bank and Gaza issues were to be discussed in a separate working group to consist of Israel, Jordan, Egypt, and the Palestinian Arabs. Solution of the problem "of the Arab refugees and of the Jewish refugees [would] be discussed in accordance with terms to be agreed upon." While American spokesmen had previously acknowledged that the reference in Resolution 242 to "a just settlement of the refugee problem" could apply to Jewish as well as to Arab refugees, the working paper marked the first time that the Jewish refugees from Arab countries were explicitly placed on a par with the Palestinian Arab refugees in a high-level American document. The working paper reiterated that 242 and 338 were the agreed basis for the Geneva talks, and that "all the initial terms of reference" of the Geneva Conference would remain in force, except as modified by agreement of the parties. Under these terms, Israel obtained the right to veto the participation by any additional state or other party, such as the PLO, in the negotiations. The working paper did not specify how the Palestinian Arabs to participate in Geneva were to be selected.

President Carter welcomed the Israeli Cabinet's approval of the working paper, and in an interview with news editors on October 14 again reassured Israel that any agreement would have to be voluntarily accepted and that he did not favor an independent Palestinian state.

Egyptian President Sadat suggested that the Palestinians might be represented in Geneva by noted American professors of Palestinian origin. Although several such persons were known to be close to the PLO ideologically, they had never participated in any terrorist actions and were, therefore, presumably acceptable to Israel. The Saudis, however, took a tougher line. Saudi Foreign Minister Prince Saud al-Faisal told the National Press Club in Washington, on October 26, that the PLO was "undeniably the legitimate representative of the Palestinian people." He also indicated uneasiness at the American eagerness to have the Geneva Conference begin as soon as procedural details had been arranged, without agreement on basic principles. While Prince Saud spoke of the need for a "peaceful settlement," he never explicitly endorsed Arab peace with Israel. In contrast to his relatively moderate tone in Washington, the Saudi foreign minister was quoted in an interview in the

Beirut newspaper *an-Nahar* as declaring that in case of a renewal of Arab-Israeli conflict, "not only will Saudi Arabia sacrifice its oil and financial resources, but also the blood of its sons."

Damascus was adopting an equally hard line. Syrian Defense Minister Mustafa Tlas declared on Damascus radio on October 7 that Israel's creation constituted an unprecedented act of aggression against the Arab nation, and this made it incumbent to wage a continuous struggle against the Zionists and their imperialist allies. "In revolutionary Syria, we will never extend our hand to shake the treacherous and criminal hand stained with the blood of our martyrs," he declared. The official newspaper of Syria's ruling Ba'ath Party announced on October 22 that "Syria is now taking the line of direct military confrontation with Israel," since the dangers of the "military option are considerably less than the dangers of submitting to ambiguous settlements that bestow legitimacy on Zionist occupation." Meanwhile, the PLO continued its unwillingness to send an unambiguous signal of readiness to abandon its objective of Israel's dissolution.

The Sadat Initiative

On November 9, President Sadat delivered a lengthy address at the opening of the fall session of the People's Assembly in Cairo. He reviewed the activities to prepare for resumption of the Geneva Conference, and noted his personal efforts to coordinate the Egyptian position with the leaders of Saudi Arabia, Syria, Jordan, and the PLO. He pointed out that he had met earlier in the day with Yasir Arafat, "a dear brother and a splendid comrade in struggle."

After tracing the procedural wrangles over the details of the working paper, Sadat expressed his disdain for procedural details. He said that the Israelis were raising procedural obstacles so that the Arabs should "have a nervous breakdown" or "suffer a fit" and declare that they were not going to Geneva. This would put the onus on the Arabs for the failure of peace. Sadat said he would unmask the Israeli tactic, saying, "I agree to any procedural process." He was determined to go to Geneva, he said, because "neither Israel nor the powers of the world can dissuade me from what I want—the Arab territory occupied in 1967 and the rights of the Palestinian people, including their right to establish their state."

Noting that his speech was being broadcast for all the Egyptian people and the Arab nation to hear, Sadat then dropped his bombshell: "I am ready to go to the ends of the earth if this will prevent a soldier or an officer of my sons from being wounded—not being killed, but wounded. Israel will be astonished when it hears me saying now before you that I am ready to go to their house, to the Knesset itself and to talk to them."

Prime Minister Begin responded the following day, welcoming Sadat's offer and declaring that the Egyptian leader would be received with all honor when he came to Israel. An official invitation was extended by the Knesset, and was transmitted to Sadat via the American ambassadors in Tel Aviv and Cairo. (For details of the Sadat visit to Israel, see Louvish, pp. 271–274.)

The dramatic Sadat initiative took American officials by surprise, even though President Carter had earlier in the year tried to encourage some direct contact between Sadat and Begin. American officials were at first privately skeptical that anything would result from the Sadat visit, and were fearful that his "high risk" undertaking would further divide the Arab world and scuttle the chances for the Geneva Conference that the United States had been laboring so intensively to bring about. Aside from these policy considerations there was apparently also a certain measure of pique at having been upstaged by the Egyptian president. Indeed, there was some evidence that Sadat's action was prompted by dissatisfaction with American policy—particularly the re-introduction of the Russians, after Sadat had worked hard to eliminate them from Egypt, and the American efforts to satisfy the difficult demands of the fence-sitting Syrians—which had convinced Sadat that the Geneva Conference would never get started unless he took matters into his own hands.

Whatever the reasons, for several crucial days while opposition was mounting in the Arab world, the United States Government refrained from publicly endorsing the Egyptian move. It was only on November 16 that President Carter declared that Sadat's "unprecedented" decision was "very courageous" and "a step in the right direction." The Administration did not relinquish its hopes for a Geneva conference, and was careful to avoid any impression that it favored the idea of a separate Egyptian-Israeli agreement. This was implicit in Carter's comment that he believed that Sadat's visit to Jerusalem "will be a constructive step toward a general conference that will let the hopes for Middle Eastern peace come closer to realization."

Despite Egyptian and American assertions that Sadat was not seeking a separate peace and was presenting all the Arab and Palestinian demands to Israel, virulent opposition to Sadat was mounting in the Arab world. The position of the rejectionists, such as Libya and Iraq, could have been predicted. However, the United States was particularly concerned about the prominent anti-Sadat stand taken by the Syrians, who were ostensibly committed to a peaceful solution. A personal visit by Sadat to Damascus on November 16 failed to convince Assad to endorse the pending Egyptian trip to Jerusalem. On the contrary, Damascus proclaimed a day of national mourning, and Syrian official statements labelled Sadat a "traitor," a "dupe," and a "capitulationist."

President Carter was only mildly critical of the Syrian position in an ABC news interview on November 20. He explained that the Syrians had been the most difficult because they were in the most difficult position, since they were no match for Egypt or Israel in military strength. "But they are the tie between the moderate Arab world and the Arab world that still is perhaps most radical." Carter added that he believed Assad, whom he recalled meeting in Geneva, "genuinely wants peace," but "he has become kind of a spokesman in a strange way for some of the more radical Arab leaders" who did not want to move toward recognition of Israel. Carter expressed the hope that the Sadat visit might break the Arab psychological barrier against recognizing Israel, adding that it was "obvious that President Assad doesn't want to see Syria left out of the future negotiations." The Syrians feared a separate bilateral Egyptian-Israeli peace treaty. Since neither he (Carter) nor Sadat nor Begin wanted a separate peace, the President expressed confidence that a Geneva conference would become possible once the rest of the Arabs were reassured that there was no danger of their "being abandoned by the strong nation of Egypt."

On his trip to the Middle East in early December, the Secretary of State extracted public declarations from Sadat and Begin affirming that they were not planning a separate deal. Nevertheless, the United States proved unable to convince any of the other Arab states, including the ostensibly moderate pro-Western Jordanians and Saudis, to participate in the conference that Sadat sought to convene in Cairo. Morocco and the Sudan, both friendly to Sadat and geographically removed from the Arab-Israeli conflict, were the only Arab League members openly to support the Egyptian initiative. A rejectionist summit was convened by Colonel Qaddafi in Tripoli. The Iraqis, perennially feuding with Syria, left the conference before the end, because it was not sufficiently militant for them. The other participants from Syria, Libya, South Yemen, Algeria, the PLO, and the Popular Front for the Liberation of Palestine issued a declaration terming the Sadat initiative "high treason" and decided on the "freezing of political and diplomatic relations" with Cairo. Israel was referred to only as "occupied Palestine," and Sadat was lambasted for allying himself with the "Zionist-imperialist enemy." In addition, the Palestinian groups issued their own communiqué rejecting "all international conferences based on UN Resolutions 242 and 338, including Geneva."

Egypt responded by breaking diplomatic relations with the five Arab states that had attended the Tripoli conference. Sadat also recalled the Egyptian ambassador from Moscow, blaming the Russians for the divisions in the Arab world and for instigating the "rubbish" at the Tripoli conference through their "vicious" policy.

The United States took a more restrained public stance toward the Russians, despite Moscow statements accusing the U.S. of conspiring with Egypt and Israel to foil the Geneva Conference. Vance said on December 6 that some recent Soviet statements "have not been helpful," and raised questions about "what their ultimate objectives are." Undersecretary of State Philip C. Habib was dispatched to Moscow to urge Soviet authorities to cool their opposition to the Sadat initiative, and to ask the Russians to influence the Syrians in not joining the rejectionists. Habib returned to Washington empty-handed.

This resulted in a revision of the American policy of cooperation with Moscow signaled in the October 1 joint statement. National Security Adviser Brzezinski outlined the new American approach on ABC's *Issues and Answers* on December 11. In an attempt to fit the new realities created by the Sadat initiative into a conceptual framework, Brzezinski spoke of three concentric circles. Beginning with the inner circle of an Egyptian-Israeli settlement, U.S. policy would move outward to the intermediate circle and seek an accord among Israel, "the moderate Palestinians," and Jordan regarding the West Bank. Finally, the United States would move to encourage an Israeli-Syrian agreement as part of a comprehensive settlement. This could be confirmed with Soviet participation at a Geneva conference, with possible American and Soviet guarantees of the overall settlement. The Russians were thus being relegated once again to a subsidiary role at a later stage in the negotiations. As for the United States, Washington officials made it clear that the Carter Administration would not adopt a "passive posture," but intended actively "to engage in shaping the process" of peace negotiations.

Prime Minister Begin flew to Washington in mid-December to present his peace plan to the President before conveying it to Sadat in Ismailia on December 25. President Carter termed the Israeli proposals "constructive" and a "fair basis for negotiation." However, Begin was privately told by American officials that the plan was unlikely to be accepted by Sadat in its initial form. Following the Ismailia meeting, the State Department issued a statement saying the United States was "pleased" that the two sides had agreed to continue the substantive discussions through the establishment of a military committee to meet in Cairo and a political committee to meet in Jerusalem. "Establishing a negotiating framework for a comprehensive settlement will be one of the important items on the agenda in the weeks ahead," the statement concluded.

Not only did the United States continue to support the idea of a comprehensive settlement, but it was careful to distance itself from the Begin proposals. Accompanying President Carter on his end-of-the-year trip to Europe, Asia, and the Middle East, Secretary Vance emphasized to reporters, while in Warsaw on December 29, that although the Carter Administration believed Israel's proposals for the West Bank were an appropriate start for negotiations, the United States had not endorsed the plan. During the following months, the United States was to exert influence on Israel to "be more forthcoming" regarding a statement of principles on the future status of the West Bank and the ultimate role of the Palestinians.

GEORGE E. GRUEN

The Belgrade Conference

Background

THE FIRST OFFICIAL MEETING arranged in compliance with the follow-up provisions of the 1975 Helsinki Final Act (technically, the Final Act of the Conference on Security and Cooperation in Europe) was held in Belgrade over a period of 27 weeks, from October 4, 1977 to March 10, 1978 (see AJYB, 1978 [Vol. 78], pp. 121–145). Two days before the close of the conference, the 35 participating nations (the NATO allies, the Warsaw Pact countries, Finland, Switzerland, Yugoslavia, and the Holy See) adopted a final document reflecting the inconclusive character of the proceedings.

The signers of the Final Act had committed themselves to implementing its provisions unilaterally, bilaterally, and multilaterally. On the multilateral level, they had agreed to work toward "the deepening of mutual relations, the improvement of security, . . . and the development of the process of détente in the future." A "thorough exchange of views on the implementation" of the various provisions was called for in the accord. Toward this end, it was agreed that periodic follow-up meetings would be held, with the first taking place in Belgrade in 1977. The Belgrade Conference was to be governed by the same procedures that applied at Helsinki; each nation was to have an equal voice, and decisions were to be reached by consensus.

A group of American and West European legal experts meeting in Strasbourg, France in June 1977 agreed that the Final Act, while not a treaty, did have important implications for international law. The Final Act, in their view, legitimated peaceful political action among the signatory nations in seeking information from one another about implementation of the Helsinki accord, and in demanding compliance with its provisions. This applied with particular force to Principle 7 and Basket 3, the human rights provisions.

Both the Communist and the Western nations came to Belgrade with specific objectives in mind. The former, having rendered themselves vulnerable by their human rights commitments at Helsinki, sought to avoid being placed "in the dock" at Belgrade. Toward this end, the Soviet Union employed a variety of tactics, including charging Western critics with interfering in Soviet affairs, threatening to retaliate with counter-charges of Western human rights violations, and diverting attention from the question of past compliance by focusing on proposals for future activities in other areas, such as energy, environment, and transport. On April 25, 1977, *Tass,* the official Soviet news agency, editorialized that the Conference "must be oriented to the future . . . Proposals by some Western politicians and press organs to amend or make more specific the wording of individual concrete formulations of the Final Act containing important accords, whether concerning measures toward stronger trust or in questions of humanitarian cooperation, are without substance. The Belgrade meeting is not empowered to revise even a single letter in the Final Act."

The Western nations, for their part, were determined to press for a reaffirmation of the Helsinki human rights commitment, and for a detailed review of compliance—while avoiding confrontation, if possible. They also sought to secure agreement for yet another review meeting. The United States, reflecting congressional sentiment and public expectations, inclined to a tougher stance regarding Communist violations than did other Western nations. In an interview in February 1977, Arthur Goldberg, the head of the United States delegation to the Belgrade Conference, stated that the U.S. "had to speak out honestly to maintain its credibility" and to give "hope to dissenters in Prague and the Soviet Union . . ." Britain, France, and West Germany generally preferred a more cautious approach, with public exchanges limited to generalities, and particular cases dealt with behind the scenes. This was also the view of the neutral and non-aligned nations.

Dissident groups in Eastern Europe, acting on the basis of Principle 7, which confirmed "the right of the individual to know and act upon his rights and duties," undertook to monitor their governments' compliance with the Helsinki accord. They did so in the hope of influencing world public opinion, which, in turn, might be brought to bear on the various Communist regimes. One of the most active of these groups was the Moscow-based Group to Promote the Observance of the Helsinki Agreement in the USSR, whose members, in an appeal dated November 21, 1977, called upon the Western nations to "be absolutely firm and decisive" in dealing with Soviet human rights violations. Similar appeals were made by three other Soviet dissident groups—the Christian Committee to Defend the Rights of Believers in the USSR, the Working Commission to Investigate the Abuse of Psychiatry for Political Purposes, and the Free Adventists. Soviet authorities responded to the activities of the monitoring groups by arresting their leaders. Twenty human rights activists were taken into custody; two others, travelling abroad on Soviet passports, were stripped of their citizenship and denied the right to return.

In Czechoslovakia, in October 1977, representatives of Charter 77, a dissident group, issued a statement calling on President Gustav Husak to honor the Final Act. They called attention to the harassment of Charter 77 members, and to various other human rights violations. In Poland, in June 1977, a Worker's Defense Committee appealed to the Belgrade participants to act against the arrest of Committee members and other human rights violations. In Rumania, several individuals signed an appeal to Belgrade delegates calling for an investigation of the human rights situation in their country.

The Steering Committee of the World Conference on Soviet Jewry undertook, in preparation for the Belgrade Conference, to survey the situation of Soviet Jewry in the light of the provisions of the Final Act. The survey, published under the title of "Soviet Jewry and the Implementation of the Helsinki Final Act," pointed to gross violations of human rights by the Soviet government. In the United States, the National Conference on Soviet Jewry and other Jewish organizations presented their views and suggestions to the State Department and U.S. Executive-Congressional Helsinki Commission. In November 1977, a delegation of the U.S. National Interreligious Task Force on Soviet Jewry traveled to Belgrade to meet with members of various delegations, including those of the United States, the Netherlands, Great Britain, Hungary, and the Vatican. The delegation intervened on behalf of both Jews and Christians, emphasizing, among other things, the need for specificity in any discussion of the issues of emigration and religious freedom.

In June 1977, the Yugoslav government expelled a group of Jewish women (the "35 Group") who had come to Belgrade from 13 Western countries to demonstrate for the rights of Soviet Jews. The demonstrators were prevented from handing out leaflets accusing the Soviet Union of non-compliance with the Helsinki human rights provisions. Five groups of West European parliamentarians of various political orientations visited Belgrade during the course of the Conference to lobby on behalf of Soviet Jews. During the early days of the Conference, a group of more than 100 Jewish activists from nine Soviet cities released a public letter charging Soviet authorities with numerous violations of the Final Act, and pointing to an official antisemitic policy.

The Conference Proceedings

REVIEW OF PAST COMPLIANCE

A contentious atmosphere surrounded the Belgrade Conference from the outset. Arthur Goldberg, in his opening statement, indicated that not enough progress had been made in fulfilling the Helsinki accord. He pointed to shortcomings in several areas, including the jamming of broadcasts, the failure to reunite divided families, the persecution of dissidents, and the harassment of monitoring groups. The Soviet delegate responded with a vigorous defense of his country's human rights record, and warned of the dire consequences for the Conference if confrontation became the order of the day. As the Conference unfolded, the United States and Soviet Union clashed repeatedly over the question of how specific the review of the human rights situation should be. The Soviet Union insisted throughout that a discussion of particulars was precluded by the principle of nonintervention. The U.S. and other Western nations, with varying degrees of conviction, insisted that a serious review had to deal with specifics.

The review of the Final Act proceeded paragraph by paragraph, beginning with the Declaration on Principles Guiding Relations Between Participating States. The Soviet Union, as expected, stressed Principles 1, 3, and 6, relating to sovereignty, the inviolability of frontiers, and nonintervention. The Western nations, for their part, emphasized Principle 7, dealing with "respect for human rights and fundamental freedoms, including the freedom of thought, conscience, religion, or belief." The debate on Principle 7 was the most acrimonious, with the U.S. insisting that governmental respect for it was a precondition for meaningful détente. In this connection, Arthur Goldberg cited by name three leading Soviet dissidents—Anatoly Shcharansky, Yuri Orlov, and Aleksandr Ginzburg—who had been arrested on charges of anti-Soviet activity, as well as several Czechs tried for belonging to Charter 77.

The review of Basket 3, "Cooperation in Humanitarian and Other Fields," with its four sections on contacts, information, culture, and education, evoked considerable controversy. The Soviet Union and other East European nations praised their own records of implementation in regard to human contacts, offering statistical evidence on the number of inter-governmental agreements signed. The Western nations, especially the United States, focused on the plight of individuals, with reference to such matters as obstacles to family reunification, the denial of visas on grounds of state security, and the harassment of applicants for exit visas.

Two forceful statements on "contacts" were made by U.S. delegates Sol C. Chaikin and Professor Joyce Hughes. Both accused the Soviet Union of violating the Universal Postal Convention by failing to deliver George Meany's invitation to Andrei Sakharov to address the AFL-CIO annual convention in Los Angeles. They also pointed to impediments placed in the way of Sakharov's New York publisher, Random House, when the latter attempted to correspond with him directly. The Soviet delegates countered the charges by asserting that U.S. customs and postal officials opened many thousand pieces of mail each year.

The discussion on "information" highlighted fundamental differences in East-West philosophy. The Communist delegates emphasized that journalists and other disseminators of information were obligated by the Final Act to contribute to developing mutual understanding and improved relations among the participating states, and that governments had the right to make them conform to this purpose. The Western delegates stated that their countries did not wish to control the dissemination of information, and that the free flow of information, in itself, contributed to understanding. The Soviet delegate attacked Radio Liberty and Radio Free Europe for interfering in the internal affairs of the Communist bloc nations, while the U.S. protested the expulsion and harassment of American journalists.

In discussing "culture and education," the Communist delegates cited statistics showing that the nations of Eastern Europe imported more books, films, and other cultural materials from the West than vice versa. Western delegates replied that in their countries cultural activities were not controlled by the government, and that imported cultural material had to compete with domestic works. The U.S. called for fuller opportunities for exchange scholars and researchers to have access to archives and other facilities. They also criticized the obstacles that were placed in the way of collaboration between Eastern and Western scientists.

NEW PROPOSALS

In addition to reviewing past compliance with the Helsinki provisions, the Western and Eastern bloc nations put forward proposals involving both matters of principle and specific undertakings. Some of the proposals were intended for inclusion in the final document, while others were suggested for adoption as separate resolutions.

While the Western proposals touched upon military or other matters related to Baskets 1 and 2, they were concerned primarily with the human rights and humanitarian issues connected with Principle 7 and Basket 3. One proposal affirmed the right of private organizations and individuals to monitor governmental compliance with the Final Act. Another called upon the Helsinki signers to guarantee "freedom of thought, conscience, religion, or belief." Among the many proposals dealing with ways of facilitating contacts between people were those calling for reduced costs for transnational family visits, limits on travel document fees, the issuance of passports that would be valid for five years of unrestricted travel, and speedy consideration of family reunification applications.

With respect to information gathering and dissemination, the Western nations proposed, among other things, that foreign journalists be permitted to import reference material needed for the practice of their profession; that they "not be expelled, or otherwise acted against, as a result of news or opinions published or broadcast in the media they represent"; and that foreign press associations be established "to facilitate cooperation among journalist members, and between them and the authorities of the host country, for the purpose of a better exercise of their profession."

The Communist bloc proposals were in a quite different vein, carefully avoiding human rights issues. Thus, the Soviet Union and its allies called for special conferences on energy, the environment, transportation, and the restoration of historical and cultural monuments. Bulgaria proposed exchanges and contacts among manual workers, meetings on youth issues, and wider cooperation in the area of sports. Rumania called for a freeze on military budgets, and various pan-European youth activities. Czechoslovakia called for a prohibition against the abuse of the mass information media for "propaganda in favor of war, violence, and hatred among people."

ARAB-ISRAEL DISPUTE

The Final Act had declared the intention of the signatory nations "to promote the development of good, neighborly relations with the non-participating Mediterranean states." Malta, with the support of Yugoslavia and Cyprus, sought an active role for the non-European Mediterranean nations in the Belgrade Conference, and looked toward the discussion of political and security issues related to the area. The U.S. and other Western nations, anxious to keep the Arab-Israel dispute from coming up as a subject of discussion, insisted on limiting their participation. However, a number of Arab states which had received observer status used the opportunity to attack Israel. Egypt, Syria, Algeria, and Lebanon introduced the usual anti-Israel themes and rhetoric. The PLO, through its office in Belgrade, lobbied with delegations to encourage the discussion of Mediterranean political issues. They also tried to obtain authorization to address the Conference directly, but a Soviet supporting motion was blocked by Western delegations. Israel, also an observer at Belgrade, spoke of the help it could provide in the areas of agriculture, science, and tourism, and focused on Soviet harassment of Jews seeking to emigrate.

THE FINAL DOCUMENT

As the Conference moved toward an inconclusive culmination, some observers, such as the Yugoslav dissident writer Mihajlo Mihajlov, argued that it would be better to adopt no final document than to adopt one that made no reference to human rights. In a public plea to the Conference delegates, Mihajlov argued: "The abdication regarding strict defense of human rights would mean an end to détente, reinforcement of totalitarianism, and the first step toward European war . . . It would be better to dissolve the Helsinki agreement than for the world to lose faith in all agreements and declarations . . ." This view, however, did not prevail.

Soviet obstructionism and the rule of consensus made it inevitable that the final document, based on a Danish draft, would disappoint Western expectations. Not only did it add nothing to the text of the Final Act with regard to human rights, but it did not even reiterate any of the human rights principles or undertakings already contained in that document. At most, it did so indirectly, in emphasizing the dependence of détente on implementation of the Final Act, and in repeating the "resolve" of the participating states "to implement fully, unilaterally, bilaterally and multilaterally all the provisions of the Final Act." The final document noted that the exchange of views at Belgrade was an important contribution to achieving the aims of the Helsinki accord, even though views differed as to the degree of implementation achieved so far. It noted the resolve of the participating states to hold further meetings, with the next one scheduled for Madrid in November 1980. Note was also taken of the decision to hold a series of sessions to deal with such matters as the peaceful settlement of disputes (Bonn, June 1978); scientific cooperation

(Montreux, October 1978); and economic, scientific and cultural cooperation in the Mediterranean area (Malta, February 1979).

The White House reacted to the final document with the following statement: "We regret that the Soviet Union failed to permit the conference to proceed to its proper conclusion. We intend to press the Soviet Union to fulfill its commitment to respect human rights." Arthur Goldberg, in his final plenary statement, declared that the United States was determined to pursue the many ideas proposed in vain for inclusion in the final document. In the weeks following the Belgrade Conference, the United States made clear its intention to continue to utilize the Final Act as a yardstick and goad in its relationships with the East European countries, particularly the Soviet Union. Thus, on June 6, the U.S. Helsinki Commission released a study of the treatment of 22 Soviet dissidents, members of Helsinki monitoring groups, who since February 1977 had been imprisoned, stripped of their citizenship, and in other ways punished on various criminal charges. The study pointed out that Soviet authorities had broken their own laws by conducting improper searches, prolonging pre-trial detentions, and denying the defendants their procedural rights.

Evaluations

Opinions in the West varied as to the significance of the Belgrade Conference. If the test of success was a Soviet acknowledgment of wrongdoing, then the Conference was clearly a failure. Pessimists were confirmed in their view by the crackdown on dissidents in the Soviet Union and other East European countries. Some Western and neutral observers attributed the failure of the Belgrade Conference to achieve more to the tactics of the American delegation, which they viewed as too polemical and intended for public applause back home rather than solid accomplishment at the Conference. Other observers maintained that the outcome of the Conference was a foregone conclusion once Soviet authorities recognized the seriousness of their error in agreeing to the Helsinki accord. In this view, Belgrade simply highlighted the fundamental differences between Communist and Western human rights philosophies, and no refinements in U.S. or Western tactics could have yielded a more favorable outcome.

Optimistic commentators saw as a major success the fact that human rights had been the central issue at the Belgrade Conference, and that the Soviet Union and its allies had been subjected to continuing and particularized criticism on this score. The optimists also argued that the events of the months preceding the Conference had to be taken into account in evaluating the Belgrade meeting. During this period Western and Communist governments had assembled an unprecedented mass of documentation on human rights, and private groups had been encouraged to undertake protest activities. Finally, the optimists maintained that the Belgrade participants had affirmed either explicitly or implicitly a number of important principles: that human rights are a matter of legitimate international concern; that human rights are an important aspect of the agenda of East-West diplomacy; that détente and peace depend on the just conduct of nations toward each other and their own citizens; and that the human rights provisions of the Final Act cannot be ignored, while other aspects of the agreement are honored.

SIDNEY LISKOFSKY

Communal

DOMESTIC AFFAIRS

Affirmative Action

The American Jewish Committee (AJ-Committee) restated its pledge to support programs to upgrade "those who have been historically disadvantaged or discriminated against by reason of race, religion, or sex." It rejected the concept of quotas as being "contrary to the best interests of all Americans, including the disadvantaged," and spelled out details for fair and effective affirmative action programs (May 12).

The American Jewish Congress (AJCongress) published an analysis of 20 civil rights decisions affecting the Jewish community, and called on all groups to work for racial justice (June 7).

Seven organizations—Agudath Israel of America, AJCommittee, AJCongress, Anti-Defamation League of B'nai B'rith (ADL), Jewish Labor Committee, Jewish War Veterans, and National Council of Jewish Women—wrote to U.S. Secretary of Health, Education, and Welfare Joseph A. Califano, Jr., urging him to

*Compiled mainly from press releases issued by organizations in 1977. References to items may be found in Index under the various agencies.

develop guidelines for the elimination of discrimination in employment and education. A copy of the letter was sent to President Jimmy Carter with the request that he declare a policy which "vigorously pursues legitimate aims of affirmative action while eschewing any taint of a quota system" (August 11).

Bakke Case

Several organizations—ADL, AJCommittee, AJCongress, National Jewish Commission on Law and Public Affairs (COLPA), and Jewish Labor Committee—submitted *amici curiae* briefs on behalf of Allan Bakke, who had sued the University of California Medical School at Davis for denying him entrance while admitting minority students with lower scores. These groups argued that a Supreme Court decision prohibiting university preferential admissions programs based on race would encourage the development of non-discriminatory admissions procedures (August 8, 10).

ADL (September 19) and AJCommittee (September 26) criticized a Justice Department brief supporting the University of California as condoning the use of racial quotas in school admissions. AJCommittee and AJCongress issued a joint statement recommending a strong affirmative action program beginning at the junior high school level "to correct Black underrepresentation among qualified candidates" (December 30).

AJCongress, AJCommittee, and ADL joined 76 national organizations in a pledge to work together for full civil rights for everyone, in spite of the controversy which had arisen over the Bakke case (November 8).

New York City Quotas

The New York Metropolitan Council of the American Jewish Congress disputed the Federal Office for Civil Rights (OCR), which had charged the New York City school system with discrimination against minority teachers. AJCongress accused the agency of being "ignorant of recent New York City school history and the legislation it produced" (January 9). Later in the year, AJCongress protested against OCR's threat to withdraw funds from New York schools unless they acceded to racial quotas in hiring (September 11). ADL termed OCR's plan to assign New York City teachers by ethnic and racial background "unconstitutional and undemocratic" (October 27).

ADL reported the settlement of a class action suit requiring the City College Center for Biomedical Education to admit or recompense students rejected from a 1974 program because of reverse discrimination (June 24).

Ethnicity

ADL published the proceedings of a conference on "Pluralism in a Democratic Society," with the aim of helping school officials to develop understanding and respect for cultural differences (January 26). ADL produced a film, "Free to Be?", exploring ethnic and religious differences (June 30).

AJCommittee's Institute on Pluralism and Group Identity published a selective bibliography and literature review in the area of mental health and ethnicity. Its purpose was to point out the importance of ethnic identity, thus providing federal agencies with a new perspective for dealing with various social problems (May 15).

Urban Problems

Several Orthodox groups, including Agudath Israel of America, the National Council of Young Israel, Torah Umesorah, and the Union of Orthodox Jewish Congregations (UOJC), formed People Against Crime, in an effort to make New York City streets safer through tougher laws (April 21). UOJC called on the Mayor and the New York City Police Department to do something about the inadequate police protection prevailing in Orthodox Jewish communities in Brooklyn (June 28).

AJCongress' Black-Jewish Information Center urged businessmen in high-crime areas to look into the Federal Crime Insurance Program offering low-cost protection against property loss resulting from burglary (May 20).

AJCommittee's New York City chapter assisted in a special project to aid small merchants whose businesses had been destroyed in the looting that followed a power blackout (July 21).

The Metropolitan New York Coordinating Council on Jewish Poverty reported that efforts by local Jewish religious, educational, social service and fraternal organizations in the Washington Heights-Inwood section of the City had met with success in preserving and upgrading the quality of life of the Jewish community there (July 21).

AJCongress' New York Metropolitan Council urged the New York City Council to take action against banks refusing mortgage loans to poor people and members of minority groups (June 11).

Welfare and Social Security

AJCongress issued a study of President Carter's proposed changes in the Social Security system, explaining how citizens would be affected, and describing existing benefits and their limitations (January 11).

AJCongress filed a brief with the New York State Court of Appeals challenging a state law prohibiting home relief payments for minors in certain cases. It testified before the New York State Assembly committees on health and welfare that the cuts in public assistance grants and Medicaid proposed by Governor Hugh Carey would have a "disastrous impact on the neediest members of our society" (February 24).

AJCommittee urged the Carter Administration to act more boldly in the area of welfare reform (May 14). It supported the President's proposed restructuring of the welfare system and recommended that a national health-care system and the Social Security system be incorporated into the President's plan (August 11).

Employment

National Full Employment Week received the support of AJCongress, whose members were urged to organize rallies and demonstrations (July 27), and AJCommittee, which called for comprehensive full employment legislation (August 16). The Jewish Labor Committee encouraged support of the Full Employment Action Council's national job program (July-August).

AJCongress announced that, through its affiliated Experience Reserve Bank, it was launching a one-year program to help qualified business persons from minority communities in California buy established businesses; management and technical assistance would be provided (October 21).

Energy

AJCommittee endorsed President Carter's proposal for a Federal Energy Department (March 9), sponsored a joint meeting with 36 voluntary organizations to publicize the need for mass support of the President's energy program (April 21), called on Congress to enact a balanced energy package as speedily as possible (October 24), and stated its preference for the de-regulation of newly found natural gas (October 28).

The National Jewish Community Relations Advisory Council, coordinating body of nine major Jewish organizations, urged its constituent groups to form coalitions with other national groups "for an effective energy program" (August 5).

AJCongress proposed an energy-action program which called for, among other things, reduced consumption of imported oil and the achievement of energy self-sufficiency (August 26).

Aged

AJCommittee submitted a brief to the New York State Supreme Court arguing that elderly people eligible for Supplemental Security Income (SSI) should also be eligible for Medicaid assistance (January 5). The court affirmed this position.

AJCongress filed an *amicus* brief with the New York State Supreme Court contesting a state law prohibiting home relief payments for recipients of SSI (May 25). AJCommittee joined those seeking to overturn a New York law preventing needy persons over 65 from receiving home relief benefits. A court decision granting these benefits was handed down on December 27.

AJCongress' Northern California division received a grant from the State to provide for five ACTION-VISTA volunteers to work in projects for needy senior citizens in San Francisco (March 30).

AJCongress charged that New York State's system of handling nursing-home abuse failed to deal properly with patient complaints and the hardships of the sick and elderly (April 11).

The National Jewish Welfare Board (JWB) announced that its Florence Heller Research Center had received a grant of $30,000 to conduct a three-year project on health and physical fitness for the elderly (April 12).

AJCommittee, together with the National Council of the Churches of Christ, U.S. Catholic Conference, and Columbia University Graduate School of Journalism, sponsored a meeting on "Images of Old Age in the American Media." President Carter's counsellor on the aging spoke of the difference between the media image of the Social Security system and its actual provisions (December 8).

Abortion

The Union of Orthodox Jewish Congregations of America praised the U.S. Supreme Court for not compelling the government to subsidize abortions through Medicaid. AJCongress saw the denial of government funds for abortion as "crude discrimination against the poor" (April 26). It criticized President Carter for statements justifying the Supreme Court decision (April 26, June 27).

Electoral College

Two groups reacted negatively to President Carter's proposal to abolish the Electoral College. AJCongress saw the revision of the present electoral system as a threat to democracy. AJCommittee cautioned that the proposed change could eliminate the political voice of labor and ethnic minorities (April).

INTERFAITH ACTIVITIES

Relations with Church Groups

ADL expressed deep concern over the National Council of Churches' "record of insensitivity" to Jewish concerns, particularly its "pronounced anti-Israel prejudice" (February 18).

Meeting with Vatican bodies in Italy, representatives of ADL, AJCommittee, the World Jewish Congress, the Synagogue Council of America, and the Israel Interfaith Committee discussed Catholic-Jewish relations, especially the matter of proselytism (March 27–30).

AJCommittee hailed a recommendation by the American Catholic Bishops Committee on Liturgy to omit from the Good Friday ritual a hymn containing offensive references to Jews (April 1). AJCommittee's Interreligious Affairs Department published a report, prepared in conjunction with the National Conference of Catholic Bishops, on religious texts used in Catholic schools. The report noted the slow but steady removal of offensive Jewish stereotypes (May 11).

The Union of American Hebrew Congregations, in cooperation with the Central Conference of American Rabbis and the University of Chicago, held a four-day convocation for Christian and Jewish scholars to consider changing religious trends in the western world (April 17–20).

ADL applauded the resolution of the General Assembly of the Presbyterian Church denouncing the Christian Yellow Pages and similar "buy Christian" directories (June 24).

ADL issued two volumes, *Jewish Philosophical Polemics Against Christianity in the Middle Ages* and *Stepping Stones to Further Jewish-Christian Relations* (July 19).

AJCommittee praised the United Presbyterian Church's 189th General Assembly for rejecting a resolution calling for U.S. Government recognition of the Palestine Liberation Organization (June 30). AJCommittee and the Texas Baptist Convention co-sponsored a three-day dialogue on issues of mutual concern (December 5–7).

The Synagogue Council of America participated in the second meeting of the Interreligious Peace Colloquium in Lisbon. The session focused on ways in which the major faiths could cooperate to meet pressing human needs (November).

Humanitarian Concerns

AJCongress urged President Carter to promulgate "a broadly framed amnesty for those who resisted this country's participation in the Vietnam War" (January 23).

ADL and AJCommittee praised the Carter Administration's commitment to human rights and support of Andrei Sakharov, dissident Soviet physicist (February 2). AJCongress (April 2) and AJCommittee (May 2) applauded President Carter's statement that foreign policy must be based on social justice and human dignity. AJCommittee's annual meeting issued a statement on human rights, and called upon the U.S.

delegation to the Belgrade Conference to work to ensure freedom of emigration and other guarantees of individual and group rights (October 30). ADL expressed solidarity with Soviet dissidents Anatoly Shcharansky and Andrei Sakharov (November 31).

The National Interreligious Task Force pressed for human rights and religious liberty in the Soviet Union at the Conference on European Security in Belgrade. It made a similar appeal to Vatican officials (November 18).

AJCongress called on the Carter Administration to grant haven to 249 Indochinese refugees living on a tanker off the coast of Singapore (June 22). AJCongress and the Union of Orthodox Jewish Congregations praised the Israeli government's offer of asylum to 16 Indochinese refugees rescued by an Israeli freighter in the South China Sea (June 24). ADL lauded President Carter's decision to grant emergency admission to 15,000 Indochinese refugees (July 20).

The Synagogue Council of America adopted a resolution appealing to the governments of South Africa and Rhodesia to work toward "policies based on human dignity, justice, and racial conciliation . . ." (October 7). AJCommittee's annual meeting deplored South Africa's apartheid policy and repressive measures against Blacks, and urged the South African government to reduce and ultimately eliminate "legal and de facto discrimination against its non-white population" (October 30).

Church-State Issues

AJCongress hailed a New Jersey Court of Appeals decision outlawing religious practices in public schools (March 29). It urged New York Governor Hugh Carey to veto two measures that would revive Sunday blue laws, arguing that the State has no right to "compel adherence by all persons" to Sunday observance (July 28). AJCongress joined with 12 New Jersey civic and religious organizations in challenging a state law providing tax deductions for tuition in parochial schools (November 8).

The Union of Orthodox Jewish Congregations of America criticized a Supreme Court decision that employers need not make special arrangements for people who observe Saturday as the Sabbath, if such arrangements create overtime pay costs or violate employee seniority privileges. It called upon Congress to "pass remedial legislation to further guarantee the employment rights of the Sabbath observer" (July 6).

The Union of Orthodox Jewish Congregations of America hailed the decision of the trustees of the State University of New York to suspend classes on Rosh Hashanah and Yom Kippur (July 5). ADL praised the U.S. Department of Labor for issuing a reminder to federal contractors that "as the Jewish High Holy Days approach . . . employers should take positive steps to accommodate the needs of those who must be away from work for religious observances" (September 8).

AJCongress filed an *amicus* brief defending the right of Congregation Beit-Havurah in Norwalk, Connecticut to worship in a farmhouse also used for sleeping quarters. A Norwalk zoning law prohibited use of the house in this manner (March 30). AJCongress joined nine religious and civic organizations in challenging a Tennessee statute which barred clergymen from holding public office (August 1).

DISCRIMINATION AND ANTISEMITISM

Employment

AJCommittee, reporting success in its executive suite program, commended eight major corporations for efforts "to recruit and promote Jewish personnel in management positions on the basis of merit" (May 14). It made public a report by its Philadelphia chapter on a substantial increase in the number of Jews in managerial positions in the area (June 15). AJCommittee hailed the first-year results of an affirmative-action program under government auspices, involving the hiring and promotion of Jews for executive positions with a major national insurance company (December 3).

"Buy Christian"

ADL reported that over a million copies of the "Christian Yellow Pages" and the "Christian Business Directory" had been distributed in 18 cities (March 3). It filed suit against the publishers, charging them with religious discrimination (August 25).

Nazism

ADL reported that The Hoax of the Twentieth Century, a book by Northwestern University professor Arthur R. Butz, claiming that the Holocaust never happened, was published by the neo-fascist National Front Press in England, and promoted by the American Nazi Party (February 3).

The Synagogue Council of America and AJCongress announced that protests by several American and Canadian groups had succeeded in preventing the admission of Ferenc Fiala, former official of the Nazi-puppet regime in Hungary, to the United States for a lecture tour (March 21). The Congress expressed satisfaction that the U.S. Immigration and Naturalization Service had cancelled the stay of deportation against Croatian war criminal Andrija Artukovic (May 6).

AJCommittee, at its annual meeting, heard U.S. Representative Elizabeth Holtzman call on Congress to investigate why the Immigration and Nationalization Service had failed to deal with cases of Nazi war criminals living in the United States (May 15). It issued a report claiming that U.S. Nazi groups constituted no serious danger to American political institutions, despite increased activity on their part, and took under advisement the question of Nazi rights under the first amendment (October 30).

ISRAEL AND THE MIDDLE EAST

U.S. Middle East Policy

AJCommittee urged the Carter Administration to "hold fast to policies that will ensure Israel's survival" (February 14). AJCongress' national women's division warned that "any accommodations Israel may be called upon to make must be assessed with great care and circumspection" (April 27). The president of the Union of American Hebrew Congregations alleged that statements by President Carter represented a "disengagement from the traditional American position calling for direct negotiations without pre-conditions" (June 13). The Union of Orthodox Jewish Congregations detected a "dangerous drift in United States Middle East policy" and criticized the President's remarks about a Palestinian homeland (June 16). The president of the Central Conference of American Rabbis called on President Carter to "hold fast to his pre-election affirmations regarding the State of Israel" (June 20). ADL criticized the U.S.-Soviet joint declaration of principles for the Geneva Peace Conference, deploring the "reintrusion of Soviet influence in an area that was comparatively well rid of it" (October 3). AJCommittee's National Executive Council warned that "a crisis of confidence in the administration's Middle Eastern policy has arisen among American friends of Israel" (October 30). ADL expressed concern about the role of the Arab oil weapon in shaping U.S. Middle East policy (November 17).

Likud Victory

Prior to the election in Israel, AJCongress restated its commitment "to the idea of a Jewish state and to the security of the people of that state" regardless of "any individual political leader or political party" (April 11). Following the victory of Menachem Begin, AJCongress expressed confidence in continued consultation and exchange between Israeli and American Jewish leaders (May 18). The Union of Orthodox Jewish Congregations of America lauded Israel's democratic system of government and likened the economic philosophy of the Likud to the American free enterprise system (May 20). The American Zionist Federation called for support of the new government and its peace efforts (June 23).

Sadat Visit

AJCommittee saw in Egyptian President Anwar Sadat's trip to Israel a model for "face-to-face discussions among all parties to the dispute of the Middle East" (November 18). The American Zionist Federation called the Sadat-Begin meeting the beginning of a "new era in Middle East diplomacy . . . an era in which Jew and Arab face each other openly" (November 21). AJCongress warned that the "euphoria" of the meeting must be replaced by "sober evolution of events" (November 21). Hadassah supported the peace plan put forward by Israeli Prime Minister Begin (December 22).

United Nations

AJCommittee urged Jews not to abandon the UN, but to work for its improvement (May 13).

AJCongress hailed U.S. withdrawal from the International Labor Organization because of the "continued exploitation of that body's processes and procedures for anti-democratic political purposes" (January 12).

The Union of American Hebrew Congregations asked President Carter and UN Ambassador Andrew Young to assume the "moral initiative" in reversing the anti-Zionist resolution passed by the General Assembly (September).

Palestine Liberation Organization

ADL charged that a PLO official, formerly ordered to leave the United States because of passport fraud, had returned to open a propaganda office in Washington (January 7). AJCongress expressed regret that President Carter had agreed to meet with PLO representatives at a UN reception (March 16), and protested the issuance of a visa permitting the PLO official to "roam the country at will" (October 31).

ADL accused the American Friends Service Committee (AFSC), which had invited a PLO official to a Middle East conference, of being a "mouthpiece for the propaganda line" of the PLO. Hadassah, in a letter to the AFSC president, explained that Jewish organizations perceived AFSC as "antisemitic, anti-Israel, pro-Arab, pro-Palestinian, and pro-PLO," because it fosters PLO activity despite that group's avowed aim to destroy the Jewish State. AJCongress stated that AFSC had been "misled by Arab propaganda" into pressuring Israel to negotiate with the terrorist PLO (February).

Terrorism

Virtually all Jewish organizations condemned the release of Palestinian terrorist Abu Daoud by the French government, accusing it of cowardice and expediency. AJCongress announced cancellation of a membership travel program to France (January 14).

AJCongress praised the ambassadors of Egypt, Iran, and Pakistan for their intercession on behalf of Jewish and other hostages held by Moslem terrorists in three Washington buildings (March 11). AJCommittee urged stronger legal measures against terrorists who took innocent hostages for political purposes (March 17).

Following the terrorist highjacking of a Lufthansa plane, AJCongress called upon the Carter Administration and civil aviation authorities to boycott all countries giving sanctuary or support to air highjackers (October 24). AJCommittee's National Executive Council condemned Algeria, Libya, and Uganda for granting asylum to highjackers, and urged a suspension of air service to all countries abetting such terrorists (October 30).

Arab Boycott

Three organizations (AJCommittee, AJCongress, and ADL) reported that an analysis of boycott-related reports filed with the Department of Commerce indicated that 87 per cent of American firms doing business in Arab countries complied with the boycott (January 6). An AJCongress study revealed a similar high degree of compliance among the largest American corporations (February 1). Upon pressure from AJCongress, eight major corporations formally agreed not to take part in the boycott (April 21).

AJCommittee, AJCongress, and ADL opposed the Justice Department's proposed settlement of an antitrust action against the Bechtel Corporation, claiming it failed to prohibit Bechtel's "participation in, and implementation of, the Arab boycott of U.S. firms" (April 6).

ADL representatives met with leaders of the Business Roundtable (executives of 170 major corporations) to consider the feasibility of drafting a joint statement of principles with regard to federal foreign boycott legislation (March 4).

Spokesmen for several Jewish organizations testified before the House Committee on International Relations, endorsing the Bingham-Rosenthal Bill against the Arab boycott (March 8), and before the Senate Subcommittee on International Finance, endorsing the Williams-Proxmire proposal (May 3).

Various Jewish groups witnessed the signing of the first anti-boycott law by President Carter (June 22). AJCommittee, AJCongress, and ADL called on Secretary of Commerce Juanita Kreps to enforce the new federal anti-boycott law, and to plug potential loopholes in the measure (August 24). They

criticized proposed Commerce Department regulations as subverting the "thrust and purpose of the anti-boycott statute" (November 16).

AJCongress filed a complaint with the New York State Division of Human Rights against Morgan Guaranty Trust and Citibank for "unlawful discrimination" in violation of the state anti-boycott law (January 14).

AJCommittee and ADL exhorted the New York State Division of Human Rights to stop the U.S.-Arab Chamber of Commerce from engaging in acts that encouraged the Arab economic boycott of Israel (May 5). In response, the Division charged Chemical Bank with "discriminatory practice" in compliance with the Arab boycott (May 10).

AJCongress labeled as "grossly inaccurate" reports that the New York anti-boycott law was harming the state's economy (February 10, June 13).

AJCommittee's New York chapter and AJCongress urged the City Council to adopt pending legislation that would prohibit the granting of municipal contracts to suppliers participating in illegal international boycotts (August 31).

ADL hailed a federal government ban on anti-Jewish discrimination by U.S. firms hiring for overseas work (February 2). In response to a complaint by ADL, the U.S. Department of Commerce ordered the withdrawal of a discriminatory advertisement for employment in Saudi Arabia which had been publicized by the U.S. Merchant Marine Academy (October 13). AJCongress asserted that the federal government was a "silent partner" in Saudi Arabia's "religious bigotry against Jews" because, in pursuing economic cooperation with that country, it participated in "discriminatory arrangements" (October 13).

AJCommittee criticized Harper and Row for publishing a *Businessman's Guide to the Middle East* with the name of Israel omitted from the central map (October 13).

ADL and AJCommittee accused the French government of endorsing the Arab boycott through an executive order excluding Israel from a law against discrimination in commerce (August 5,9).

THE INTERNATIONAL SCENE

Soviet Jewry

The Synagogue Council of America adopted a resolution reaffirming the obligation of the Jewish community to assist all Jews who emigrate from the Soviet Union.

The Workmen's Circle, American ORT, and the Jewish Labor Committee participated in a Solidarity Day march sponsored by the New York Conference on Soviet Jewry (May 1). Representatives of Jewish groups joined the solidarity program sponsored by the National Conference on Soviet Jewry in Washington, D.C. (June 12).

AJCommittee's National Executive Council expressed deep concern over the Soviet Union's continued harassment of Jewish activists, suppression of Jewish religious and cultural life, and denial of the right to emigrate (October 30).

European Jewry

AJCommittee denounced the Czechoslovak government for its allegation that the signers of the "Charter 77" human-rights manifesto were Zionists involved in a "fight against Socialist Czechoslovakia" (April 26).

ADL labeled the appointment of a former SS officer to the West German Parliament "an offensive and insensitive act of deep concern" (July 1).

ADL heard a report from Chief Rabbi Moses Rosen of Rumania on the strengthened relations between Israel and his country. He described the Rumanian Jewish community as "thriving" and "vibrant" (November 10).

The World Zionist Organization-American Section announced that the first official delegation of Polish Jews residing in the United States visited Poland at the invitation of the Government. The group presented a memorandum requesting action to preserve and commemorate the Polish Jewish heritage (December 12).

Jews in Arab Countries

The Union of American Hebrew Congregations was instrumental in the shipment of 2,500 pounds of matzohs to the

400 Jews living in Alexandria and Cairo, Egypt (February 20).

AJCommittee's Foreign Affairs Department issued an update on the situation of the 5,000 Jews living in Syria. It reported that while many restrictions and abuses had been eliminated, Jews were still under a measure of restraint. The ban on emigration remained in force (May).

The World Organization of Jews from Arab Countries described Egyptian President Anwar Sadat's invitation to Jews to return to that country as "nothing but hypocrisy intended to mislead public opinion." It pointed out that only five per cent of Egyptian Jews had held Egyptian citizenship (July 28).

Latin America

AJCommittee announced the closing of its Buenos Aires office because of death threats received by the office's director (July 7).

ADL reported that three members of the Deutsch family, kidnapped on August 27 and detained by government authorities, had been released. Two other family members remained in custody (October 27).

AJCommittee's National Executive Council reaffirmed its solidarity with the Jewish community of Argentina, and called on the United States to assure the Argentine government that "restoring basic freedoms . . . will have a direct impact on Argentine-American relations . . ." (October 30).

The ADL Director of Latin American Affairs added his voice to an inter-faith appeal to Argentine President Jorge Rafael Videla for a holy day amnesty for "prisoners of conscience now being detained without charge in government facilities" (December 20).

AJCommittee urged Videla to free newspaper editor Jacobo Timerman, and permit him and his family to leave the country (December 21).

Fourteen leaders of American Jewish organizations met with Mexican President José Lopez Portillo to assure him that a number of Mexico's votes in the United Nations had "done much to ease past strains" (February 17).

AJCommittee hailed the fifth Jewish-Catholic meeting held in San José, Costa Rica as "an important event that holds great promise for future cooperation" (April 25).

AJCommittee urged Congress to ratify the Panama Canal Treaty, asserting that such a step would have a "positive impact on U.S. relationships with Latin America" (September 2).

JEWISH IDENTITY, RELIGION, AND CULTURE

Youth

ADL conducted a survey of 200 rabbis in 136 American cities regarding missionary activities. It found that while attempts by religious cults to convert young Jews had largely failed, missionary activities continued, causing strong anxiety among parents (March 16). AJ-Committee devoted a session of its annual meeting to the impact of cults on Jewish young people (May 13). The Union of American Hebrew Congregations listed the cult problem high on its conference agenda (November 18–22). Its rabbinical affiliate, the Central Conference of American Rabbis, had previously considered the question of "Methods and Techniques in Dealing with Cults" (June 23).

The North American Jewish Students' Network published *A Guide to Jewish Student Groups,* [Vol. IV], describing more than 350 Jewish campus and high-school groups (September).

Family

JWB's National Conference on Jewish Camping focused on the theme, "The Changing Life-Styles, Values, and Relationships in the Jewish Family" (January 16–20).

The Tarbuth Foundation, in cooperation with local Jewish federations, sponsored a series of family weekends in cities throughout New England, dealing with such matters as divorce, the single-parent family, and the aged (April 28).

At its annual meeting, the Union of Orthodox Jewish Congregations of America dealt with the problems of intermarriage and assimilation as threats to Jewish family life and continuity (May 15).

The Women's League for Conservative Judaism conducted a two-day conference on the Jewish family, and held a follow-up conference evaluating action

programs in this area in the light of "rapidly-changing social, cultural, and behavioral mores and values" (September 19).

At the Union of American Hebrew Congregations' biennial General Assembly, it was agreed to develop special synagogue programs to meet the needs of increasing numbers of singles and single-parent families (November 23).

Women

The *United Synagogue Review,* reflecting the views of Conservative Judaism, devoted three of its issues to discussions of women in Jewish law, as synagogue presidents, and as future rabbis (March 17).

The Central Conference of American Rabbis launched a program to make Reform congregations aware of the growing number of women rabbis seeking pulpits (October 11).

The Jewish Theological Seminary named a Commission for the Study of Women in the Rabbinate to prepare recommendations for the 1979 Rabbinical Assembly convention (November 10).

Hadassah and AJCongress' National Women's Division sent delegations to the National Women's Conference in Houston (November 18–21).

Hadassah (February 24) and AJCommittee (October 29) declared their support of the Equal Rights Amendment, and urged members to work actively for its passage.

Religion

Agudath Israel of America held an All-European Conference in Antwerp at which delegates from branches in England, Switzerland, Belgium, France, Austria, Holland, and Denmark made plans to strengthen religious observance and raise standards of Torah study in European countries (January 6–9).

JWB shipped Passover supplies to U.S. Jewish military personnel and hospitalized veterans throughout the world (February 28), and arranged High Holy Day services at all military bases where Jews were stationed (August 1).

The Union of Orthodox Jewish Congregations of America reported that over 1,000 newly-settled Russian Jews participated in its special Passover seder program in New York and Israel (April 25).

The Union of American Hebrew Congregations' biennial General Assembly considered the theme "Judaism in a Secular Age" and dealt with problems of synagogue administration, education, worship, social action, and interreligious affairs (November 18–22).

Jewish Education

Agudath Israel of America reported the success of its adult Torah home-study program. (January 5).

The Women's League for Conservative Judaism and the Jewish Theological Seminary of America sponsored a series of weekly lectures on biblical texts and Jewish thought. The program was designed for women who wanted "to move toward a deeper understanding of the meaning of Jewish existence and the Jewish mission" (February 2).

AJCommittee's National Executive Council issued a statement urging the intensification of efforts to promote Jewish education, particularly in the area of day schools (October 28). It also announced the publication of a series of discussion guides on subjects of concern to the Jewish community (January 5).

AJCommittee's Academy for Jewish Studies Without Walls conducted a five-day seminar on a biblical theme at Brandeis University (July 11–14). It also sponsored a two-week television series on Jewish history, tradition, and culture, broadcast nationally by NBC (February 28–March 11).

JWB's National Conference on Jewish Camping conducted workshops on Jewish subjects to "deepen the Jewish knowledge and commitment of camp executives" (January 6–11).

The North American Jewish Students' Network sponsored a second Conference on Alternatives in Jewish Education (August 24–29).

The World Zionist Organization-American Section sponsored its seventh annual *Yediat Israel* examination (April 17). Its Commission on the Teaching of Zionism and Israel initiated a pilot program to strengthen and enrich the teaching of these subjects in Jewish schools throughout the country (December 15).

The Yivo Institute for Jewish Research, at its 51st annual conference, heard scholars speak on Yiddish culture, Jews and Russian culture, and New York Jewry (April 24–27).

The World Zionist Organization–American Section reported that 120 contestants from 45 different communities met in New York City to compete for selection as representatives to the 1978 International Bible Contest in Jerusalem (May 15).

The Tarbuth Foundation for the Advancement of Hebrew Culture inaugurated three new television series on Jewish historical and artistic themes for cable TV in New York City (November 14).

Holocaust Programs

ADL sponsored a poster exhibition entitled "The Holocaust: 1933–1945," at the Jewish Museum (April 14–24).

The Workmen's Circle held a public ceremony in commemoration of the Holocaust at which a bronze sculpture by Natan Rapoport symbolizing the martyrdom of victims of the Holocaust was unveiled (April 19).

ADL established a Holocaust Information Center to house audio-visual and teaching materials on the Holocaust (July 29). ADL sponsored a conference for 200 educators on teaching the Holocaust in American secondary schools (October 9–11). Its New York Regional Board hailed a curriculum guide on the Holocaust for the City's schools as a way of helping students "understand the background and concerns of the Jewish people" (November 16).

JWB, in cooperation with local agencies and other national groups, instituted community projects to commemorate the Holocaust in St. Louis, St. Paul, Buffalo, and other cities (October).

Jewish Culture

The Jewish Museum was selected by the National Endowment for the Humanities to participate in its Challenge Grant Program. The funds received were to be used to meet operating costs and improve the facilities (June 20).

The Tarbuth Foundation for the Advancement of Hebrew Culture, in cooperation with the Oxford (England) Center for Postgraduate Hebrew Studies, conducted the first International Conference on Jewish Art in Oxford. The conferees urged Jewish communities everywhere to seek landmark preservation of Jewish historical sites (August 31).

AJCongress received a grant of $560,000 under the Federal Comprehensive Employment and Training Act (CETA) to hire 50 artists for a variety of year-long programs involving Jewish themes (November 17).

The Jewish Theological Seminary of America library acquired a unique collection of more than 2,000 manuscripts and books relating to Jewish music (January 13).

JWB sponsored "Here is Israel," a multi-media production (September–December), as well as tours by the Haifa Municipal Theater (February 20–April 16) and the Nesher puppets (September). The organization's Book Council announced publication of Volume 35 of the *Jewish Book Annual,* a trilingual annual of Jewish literary achievement (October 17). It's Music Council held its 33rd annual Jewish Music Festival, at which the theme was "Music of Jewish

Resistance and Survival" (March 4–April 2). It also sponsored an all-day conference on "Jewish Music in America: Status and Directions" (June 19).

Israel Programs

The World Zionist Organization–American Section issued the 12th edition of its annual *Guide to Israel Programs,* listing almost 200 programs, from brief study tours to six-month work programs and academic courses at the high-school, yeshiva, and university levels (March 18).

More than 100 students participated in year-long high school programs sponsored by the World Zionist Organization's Department of Education and Culture and the American Zionist Youth Foundation (August 28). The World Zionist Organization's Torah Education Department arranged for more than 160 yeshiva students to study in Israel (February 14). American Zionist Youth Foundation sponsored a semester of study at Tel Aviv University for 15 students (February 27). The World Zionist Organization's Department of Education and Culture conducted a year-long program for 33 college students at Hayim Greenberg College in Jerusalem (September 6).

The American Zionist Youth Foundation arranged for 85 volunteers to participate in two six-month work and study programs in Israel (February 3). It also sent 70 college graduates to Israel for a year of social service, as part of its Sherut La'am program (July 18, October 28).

The American Zionist Youth Foundation conducted a leadership-training program for high-school graduates, consisting of a year's study and work on a kibbutz or moshav (September 6). It also sponsored a folk-dance seminar, and an Israel Summer Sports Program, combining a tour of Israel and participation in the Maccabiah Games (January 12).

Hadassah announced plans to open a fifth Youth Aliyah Center to serve as an all-day facility offering remedial instruction, recreation, guidance, and vocational training for teen-agers (August 21).

JWB participated in the First World Conference of Jewish Community Centers held in Jerusalem (May 3–8). It opened permanent headquarters there in November, and initiated programs aimed at increasing study, volunteerism, and travel in Israel (November 25).

Special tours of Israel included the American Zionist Federation's ten-day tour for 30 journalists (March 6) and three-week work and study mission for 24 nuns, priests, and lay Catholics (June 28); ADL's two-week study seminar for 20 professional staff members (March 14); and AJCongress' 13th annual American-Israel Dialogue in Jerusalem, bringing together 35 jurists and rabbis from the United States and Israel (July 5–8).

Leadership Training

AJCommittee established the Hilda Katz Blaustein Leadership Development Program for the training of competent and committed leaders on the local and national levels (May 13).

JWB, which instituted a leadership development program in 1976, conducted a seminar in Atlanta, Georgia to train leaders for that community (May).

The National Federation of Temple Youth produced a documentary film depicting the training of future lay and rabbinic leaders for Reform Judaism (May 22).

The Union of Orthodox Jewish Congregations of America conducted its second national Orthodox Leadership Conference on Public Affairs to explore the problems and prospects of the urban Orthodox community (November 23–24).

GERALDINE ROSENFIELD

Demographic

Jewish Population in the United States, 1978

THE ESTIMATE of the United States "Jewish Population"* for 1978 is 5,781,000, virtually the same as that reported in 1977 (5,776,000); however, certain regional shifts are evident. In 1978, Jews residing in the Northeast and North Central States comprise 70.9 per cent of the total; in 1977 the figure was 72.2 per cent. The South and West account for 29.1 per cent of the total Jewish population in 1978; in 1977 these regions contained 27.8 per cent of the whole. The two states showing the greatest increase in the South and West, respectively, are Florida and California. A revised upward estimate for the Washington, D.C. area raises the figures for the District of Columbia, Virginia, and Maryland.

Local Jewish federations serve as the primary source for the community estimates shown in Table 3. Cities marked with an asterisk provided such estimates either in 1978 or 1977.

In the past, estimates for non-federated communities were based on data obtained from the national United Jewish Appeal's field staff. UJA, however, has not been updating these data. In an effort to verify the figures which have been published in the AJYB, questionnaires were sent to synagogues in those areas where population changes were thought likely to have occurred. Such changes, where reported, are included in this year's table. The process of verifying the estimates for all non-federated communities will be completed next year.

The state totals shown in Table 1 are the sum of the individual community estimates, excluding duplicate listings and out-of-state figures where a community extends across state boundaries. Also included are communities with less than 100 Jews (not shown in Table 3).

The estimates reported in Table 3 take into account the fund-raising and service areas of the federations located in the cities listed. These areas are often larger than the political boundaries of the cities, but are usually smaller than what the Census Bureau defines as a metropolitan area. In most cases, federation fund-raising and

---

*Represents the number of individuals in households in which one or more Jews reside, and therefore includes non-Jews living in such households as a result of intermarriage, etc. For a discussion of this, see AJYB, 1974–75, Vol. 75, pp. 296–297.

service areas come closest to the Census definition of an urban area, encompassing the city itself and the more densely populated surrounding areas. Further information with regard to the areas covered is provided in footnotes.

While national, regional, and state totals are presented, it should be emphasized that they are only estimates. There is a good deal of variation with regard to the accuracy of the figures. Some communities have conducted recent population studies, and their totals may be considered relatively close to what a current census would reveal. Other communities rely on estimates based on federation contributor lists and certain assumptions with regard to unaffiliated Jews. It is likely that communities experiencing Jewish population growth will take note of it in population estimates more quickly than communities suffering Jewish population loss.

New York City is a special case in that a change in its population estimate could seriously affect the national total. The figure cited is that given in the 1970 National Jewish Population Study.

Annual Census Bureau reports on changes in general population levels are based on birthrates, deathrates, and net migration figures. None of these elements is available for a discussion of shifts in Jewish population. Since there is no question on religion in the U.S. Decennial Census, this source provides no data for Jewish population estimates. The 1970 National Jewish Population Study arrived at a total population estimate quite close to the one published that year in the AJYB. The NJPS found that the number of Jews in the United States had leveled off; it predicted no significant shift within the next decade. The estimates carried in recent AJYB volumes do not contradict this projection.

ALVIN CHENKIN
MAYNARD MIRAN

APPENDIX

TABLE 1. JEWISH POPULATION IN THE UNITED STATES, 1978

State	Estimated Jewish Population	Total Population*	Estimated Jewish Per Cent of Total
Alabama	8,825	3,690,000	0.2
Alaska	720	407,000	0.2
Arizona	33,180	2,296,000	1.4
Arkansas	3,280	2,144,000	0.2
California	688,555	21,896,000	3.1
Colorado	31,830	2,619,000	1.2
Connecticut	99,615	3,108,000	3.2
Delaware	9,500	582,000	1.6
District of Columbia	40,000	690,000	5.8
Florida	391,280	8,452,000	4.6
Georgia	30,680	5,048,000	0.6
Hawaii	1,500	895,000	0.2
Idaho	500	857,000	0.1
Illinois	267,175	11,245,000	2.4
Indiana	24,345	5,330,000	0.5
Iowa	7,745	2,879,000	0.3
Kansas	10,325	2,326,000	0.4
Kentucky	11,385	3,458,000	0.3
Louisiana	16,040	3,921,000	0.4
Maine	7,600	1,085,000	0.7
Maryland	185,745	4,139,000	4.5
Massachusetts	253,400	5,782,000	4.4
Michigan	90,145	9,129,000	1.0
Minnesota	34,480	3,975,000	0.9
Mississippi	3,395	2,389,000	0.1
Missouri	72,770	4,801,000	1.5
Montana	495	761,000	0.1
Nebraska	8,155	1,561,000	0.5
Nevada	13,880	633,000	2.2
New Hampshire	4,690	849,000	0.6
New Jersey	442,480	7,329,000	6.0
New Mexico	5,155	1,190,000	0.4
New York	2,143,485	17,924,000	12.0

State	Estimated Jewish Population	Total Population*	Estimated Jewish Per Cent of Total
North Carolina	12,580	5,525,000	0.2
North Dakota	1,085	653,000	0.2
Ohio	158,500	10,701,000	1.5
Oklahoma	6,040	2,811,000	0.2
Oregon	10,800	2,376,000	0.5
Pennsylvania	418,440	11,785,000	3.6
Rhode Island	22,000	935,000	2.4
South Carolina	8,090	2,876,000	0.3
South Dakota	690	689,000	0.1
Tennessee	17,070	4,299,000	0.4
Texas	70,275	12,830,000	0.5
Utah	2,300	1,268,000	0.2
Vermont	2,465	483,000	0.5
Virginia	58,715	5,135,000	1.1
Washington	15,385	3,658,000	0.4
West Virginia	3,840	1,859,000	0.2
Wisconsin	30,020	4,651,000	0.6
Wyoming	310	406,000	0.1
U.S. TOTAL	5,780,960	216,332,000	2.7

N.B. Details may not add to totals because of rounding.

*July 1, 1977, resident population. Total population, including Armed Forces overseas was 216,817,000. Total civilian population was 214,685,000. (Sources: U.S. Department of Commerce, Bureau of the Census, *Current Population Reports,* Series P. 25, No. 711 and No. 727.)

TABLE 2. DISTRIBUTION OF U.S. JEWISH POPULATION BY REGIONS, 1978

Region	Total Population	Per Cent Distribution	Jewish Population	Per Cent Distribution
Northeast:	49,280,000	22.8	3,394,175	58.7
New England	12,242,000	5.7	389,770	6.7
Middle Atlantic	37,038,000	17.1	3,004,405	52.0
North Central:	57,941,000	26.8	705,435	12.2
East North Central	41,057,000	19.0	570,185	9.9
West North Central	16,884,000	7.8	135,250	2.3
South:	69,849,000	32.3	876,740	15.2
South Atlantic	34,305,000	15.9	740,430	12.8
East South Central	13,837,000	6.4	40,675	0.7
West South Central	21,707,000	10.0	95,635	1.7
West:	39,263,000	18.1	804,610	13.9
Mountain	10,031,000	4.6	87,650	1.5
Pacific	29,232,000	13.5	716,960	12.4
TOTALS.	216,332,000	100.0	5,780,960	100.0

N.B. Details may not add to totals because of rounding.

TABLE 3. COMMUNITIES WITH JEWISH POPULATIONS OF 100 OR MORE, 1978
(ESTIMATED)

State and City	Jewish Population	State and City	Jewish Population	State and City	Jewish Population
ALABAMA		Lancaster (incl. in Antelope Valley)		**COLORADO**	
*Anniston	100	*Long Beach	12,500	*Colorado Springs	1,000
*Birmingham	4,000	*Los Angeles Metropolitan		*Denver	30,000
Dothan	265	Area	455,000	Pueblo	375
*Gadsden	180	Merced	100		
Huntsville	650	Modesto	260		
*Mobile	1,200	*Monterey	1,500		
*Montgomery	1,625	*Oakland (incl. in Alameda		**CONNECTICUT**	
Selma	210	& Contra Costa Counties)		*Bridgeport	14,500
Tri-Cities[a]	120			Bristol	250
Tuscaloosa	315	Ontario (incl. in Pomona Valley)		Colchester	525
		*Orange County	35,000	*Danbury (incl. New Milford)	3,000
ALASKA		*Palm Springs	4,500	*Greenwich	2,200
Anchorage	420	*Pasadena (also incl. in Los Angeles Metropolitan		*Hartford (incl. New Britain)	23,500
Fairbanks	210	Area)	2,000	Lebanon	175
		Petaluma	320	Lower Middlesex County[d]	125
ARIZONA		*Pomona Valley[c]	3,500	*Manchester	1,200
*Phoenix	25,000	*Riverside	1,200	*Meriden	1,400
*Tucson	8,000	*Sacramento	5,700	*Middletown	1,300
		Salinas	240	*Milford	500
ARKANSAS		San Bernardino	1,900	*Moodus	150
*Ft. Smith	160	*San Diego	23,000	*New Haven	20,000
Hot Springs	600	*San Francisco	75,000	*New London	4,500
*Little Rock	1,740	*San Jose	14,500	*Newtown	375
*Pine Bluff	175	*San Pedro	300	*Norwalk	4,000
Southeast Arkansas[b]	140	*Santa Barbara	3,800	*Norwich	2,500
Wynne-Forest City	110	*Santa Cruz	1,000	Putnam	110
		*Santa Maria	200	Rockville	525
CALIFORNIA		Santa Monica	8,000	*Stamford	11,000
*Alameda & Contra Costa Counties	28,000	*Santa Rosa	750	Torrington	400
*Antelope Valley	350	Stockton	1,050	*Valley Area[e]	700
Bakersfield (incl. in Kern County)		*Sun City	800	Wallingford	440
El Centro	125	Tulare and Kings County	155	*Waterbury	2,800
Elsinore	250	Vallejo	400	Westport	2,800
Fontana	165	*Ventura County	5,000	*Willimantic	400
*Fresno	2,200			Winsted	110
Kern County	850				

State and City	Jewish Population

DELAWARE
*Wilmington (incl. rest of state) 9,500

DISTRICT OF COLUMBIA
*Greater Washingtonᶠ 160,000

FLORIDA
*Brevard County . . 2,250
Daytona Beach . . 1,200
*Fort Lauderdale . 50,000
Fort Myers 300
Fort Pierce 270
Gainesville 700
*Hollywood . . . 30,000
*Jacksonville . . . 6,000
Key West 170
*Lakeland 800
Lehigh Acres . . . 125
*Miami 225,000
*Orlando 10,000
*Palm Beach
County 40,000
*Pensacola 725
Port Charlotte . . . 150
*Sarasota 5,400
St. Augustine . . . 100
*St. Petersburg (incl. Clearwater) 10,000
*Tallahassee 1,000
*Tampa 7,000

GEORGIA
Albany 525
*Athens 250
*Atlanta 22,000
*Augusta 1,500
Brunswick 120
*Columbus 1,000
Dalton 235

Fitzgerald-Cordele . 125
Macon 785
*Savannah 2,600
*Valdosta 145

HAWAII
Honolulu 1,500

IDAHO
Boise 120

ILLINOIS
Aurora 400
*Bloomington 125
*Champaign-
Urbana 1,000
*Chicago Metropolitan
Area 253,000
Danville 240
Decatur 450
East St. Louis (incl. in So. Ill.)
*Elgin 700
*Galesburg 130
*Joliet 800
*Kankakee 260
*Peoria 2,000
*Quad Citiesᵍ . . . 3,000
Quincy 200
Rock Island (incl. in Quad Cities)
*Rockford 1,025
*Southern Illinoisʰ . 2,000
*Springfield 1,150
Sterling-Dixon . . . 110
*Waukegan 1,200

INDIANA
Anderson 105
Bloomington 300
*Elkhart 160
*Evansville 1,200
*Ft. Wayne 1,350

*Gary (incl. in Northwest Indiana - Calumet Region)
*Indianapolis . . . 11,000
Lafayette 600
Marion 170
Michigan City 400
Muncie 175
*Northwest Indiana-Calumet Regionⁱ . . . 5,000
Richmond 110
Shelbyville 140
*South Bend 2,600
*Terre Haute 450

IOWA
Cedar Rapids 330
Council Bluffs 245
Davenport (incl. in Quad Cities, Ill.)
*Des Moines 3,300
Dubuque 105
Fort Dodge 115
Mason City 110
Muscatine 120
Ottumwa 150
*Sioux City 1,090
Waterloo 435

KANSAS
Topeka 500
*Wichita 1,200

KENTUCKY
*Lexington 1,400
*Louisville 9,200
Paducah 175

LOUISIANA
*Alexandria 760
*Baton Rouge . . . 1,100
Lafayette 600
*Lake Charles 250

State and City	Jewish Population	State and City	Jewish Population	State and City	Jewish Population
*Monroe	300	*Haverhill	1,600	*Saginaw	550
*New Orleans	10,600	Holyoke	1,100	*South Haven	100
*Shreveport	1,600	*Hyannis	245		
		*Lawrence	2,550	**MINNESOTA**	
MAINE		Leominster	1,525	Austin	125
Augusta	215	Lowell	2,000	*Duluth	1,000
*Bangor	1,500	*Lynn (incl.		Hibbing	155
Biddeford-Saco	375	Peabody)	19,000	*Minneapolis	22,090
Calais	135	Medway	140	*Rochester	240
*Lewiston-Auburn	1,000	Milford	245	*St. Paul	9,750
*Portland	3,500	Mills	105	*Virginia	100
*Waterville	300	*New Bedford	3,100		
		Newburyport	280	**MISSISSIPPI**	
MARYLAND		North Berkshire	675	*Clarksdale	160
*Annapolis	2,000	Northampton	350	*Cleveland	180
*Baltimore	92,000	*Peabody	2,600	*Greenville	500
Cumberland	250	*Pittsfield	1,685	*Greenwood	100
Easton Park		*Plymouth	500	*Hattiesburg	180
Areaʲ	100	*Salem	1,150	*Jackson	750
Frederick	400	Southbridge	105	*Meridian	135
*Hagerstown	275	*Springfield	11,000	Natchez	140
Hartford County	420	Taunton	1,200	Vicksburg	260
*Montgomery		Webster	125		
Countyʳ	70,000	*Worcester	10,000	**MISSOURI**	
*Prince Georges				*Columbia	350
Countyʳ	20,000	**MICHIGAN**		*Joplin	115
*Salisbury	300	*Ann Arbor (incl. all		*Kansas City	19,000
		Washtenaw		Kennett	110
MASSACHUSETTS		County)	3,000	Springfield	230
*Amherst	750	Battle Creek	245	*St. Joseph	490
*Athol	110	*Bay City	650	*St. Louis	60,000
*Attleboro	200	*Benton Harbor	650		
*Beverly	1,000	*Detroit	80,000	**MONTANA**	
*Boston (incl.		*Flint	2,395	*Billings	160
Brockton)	170,000	Grand Rapids	1,500		
*Brockton	5,200	Iron County	160	**NEBRASKA**	
*Fall River	3,000	Iron Mountain	105	*Lincoln	1,050
*Fitchburg	300	*Jackson	375	*Omaha	6,500
*Framingham	16,000	*Kalamazoo	650		
*Gardner	100	*Lansing	1,800	**NEVADA**	
*Gloucester	400	Marquette County	175	*Las Vegas	13,500
Great Barrington	105	Mt. Clemens	420	Reno	380
Greenfield	250	Muskegon	525		

State and City	Jewish Population	State and City	Jewish Population	State and City	Jewish Population
NEW HAMPSHIRE		*North Jersey^q . . .33,500		*Buffalo 22,000	
*Claremont 130		*Northern Middlesex		Canandaigua 135	
*Concord 350		County^r 17,500		*Catskill 200	
*Dover 425		*Ocean County . .12,000		Corning 125	
Keene 105		*Passaic-Clifton . . .7,800		Cortland 440	
Laconia 160		Paterson (incl. in North		Dunkirk 200	
*Manchester 2,000		Jersey)		*Ellenville 1,450	
*Nashua 450		Paulsboro 165		*Elmira 1,400	
*Portsmouth 700		Perth Amboy (incl. in		*Geneva 300	
		North Middlesex		*Glens Falls 360	
NEW JERSEY		County)		*Gloversville 535	
*Atlantic City (incl. Atlan-		Plainfield (incl. in Union		Herkimer 185	
tic County) . .11,800		County)		*Highland Falls . . .105	
Bayonne 8,500		*Princeton 2,600		Hudson 470	
*Bergen County^k .100,000		*Raritan Valley^s . .18,000		*Ithaca 1,000	
*Bridgeton 375		Salem 230		Jamestown 185	
*Camden^i 26,000		*Somerset County^t .6,000		*Kingston 2,400	
*Carteret 300		Somerville (incl. in Somer-		Liberty 2,100	
Elizabeth (incl. in Union		set County)		Loch Sheldrake-	
County)		Toms River (incl. in		Hurleyville 750	
*Englewood (also incl. in		Ocean County)		Monroe 400	
Bergen County) 10,000		*Trenton 7,200		*Monticello 2,400	
*Essex County^m . .95,000		*Union County . .39,500		Mountaindale 150	
Flemington 875		*Vineland^u 3,335		Greater New	
Gloucester County^n .165		*Wildwood 425		York 1,998,000	
Hoboken 500		Willingboro (incl. in Cam-		New York	
*Jersey City 8,000		den)		City 1,228,000	
Metuchen (incl. in North				Manhattan .171,000	
Middlesex County)		NEW MEXICO		Brooklyn . .514,000	
Millville 240		*Albuquerque 4,500		Bronx . . .143,000	
*Monmouth		Las Cruces 100		Queens . . .379,000	
County 30,000		Santa Fe 300		Staten Island 21,000	
*Morris-Sussex				Nassau-Suffolk 605,000	
Counties^o 15,000		NEW YORK		Westchester .165,000	
Morristown (incl. in Mor-		*Albany 13,500		New Paltz 150	
ris County)		Amenia 140		Newark 220	
*Mt. Holly 300		Amsterdam 595		*Newburgh-	
Newark (incl. in Essex		*Auburn 315		Middletown 4,900	
County)		*Batavia 165		*Niagara Falls . . .1,000	
New Brunswick (incl. in		Beacon 315		Norwich 120	
Raritan Valley)		*Binghamton (incl. all		*Olean 140	
North Hudson		Broome County) 4,000		*Oneonta 175	
County^p 7,000		Brewster 175		Oswego 100	

State and City	Jewish Population
Parksville	140
Pawling	105
*Plattsburg	275
Port Jervis	560
*Potsdam	175
*Poughkeepsie	4,900
*Rochester	21,500
Rockland County	25,000
*Rome	205
*Saratoga Springs	500
*Schenectady	5,400
Sharon Springs	165
South Fallsburg	1,100
*Syracuse	11,000
*Troy	1,200
*Utica	2,500
Walden	200
Warwick	100
Watertown	250
White Lake	425
Woodbourne	200
Woodridge	300

NORTH CAROLINA

State and City	Jewish Population
*Asheville	1,000
*Chapel Hill-Durham	1,650
*Charlotte	3,000
*Fayetteville (incl. all Cumberland County)	500
*Gastonia	220
Goldsboro	120
Greensboro (incl. in N.C. Triad)	
High Point (incl. in N.C. Triad)	
*North Carolina Triad[v]	2,700
*Raleigh	1,375
Rocky Mount	110
Whiteville Zone[w]	330
*Wilmington	500
Winston-Salem (incl. in N.C. Triad)	

NORTH DAKOTA

State and City	Jewish Population
*Fargo	500
Grand Forks	100

OHIO

State and City	Jewish Population
*Akron	6,500
Ashtabula	160
*Canton	2,710
*Cincinnati	30,000
*Cleveland	80,000
*Columbus	13,000
*Dayton	6,000
East Liverpool	290
*Elyria	275
Hamilton	560
*Lima	290
Lorain	1,000
*Mansfield	600
*Marion	150
*Middletown	140
New Philadelphia	140
Newark	105
Piqua	120
Portsmouth	120
*Sandusky	150
*Springfield	340
*Steubenville	405
*Toledo	7,500
*Warren	500
*Wooster	200
Youngstown	5,400
Zanesville	350

OKLAHOMA

State and City	Jewish Population
Muskogee	120
*Oklahoma City	2,000
Oklahoma City Zone[x]	190
*Tulsa	2,600

OREGON

State and City	Jewish Population
Corvallis	140
*Eugene	1,500
*Portland	8,700
Salem	200

PENNSYLVANIA

State and City	Jewish Population
Aliquippa	400
*Allentown	4,980
*Altoona	1,200
Ambridge	250
Beaver	115
*Beaver Falls	350
Berwick	120
*Bethlehem	960
Braddock	250
*Bradford	150
Brownville	150
*Butler	340
Carbon County	125
*Carnegie	100
Central Bucks County	400
*Chambersburg	340
Chester	2,100
Coatesville	305
Connellsville	110
Donora	100
*Easton	1,300
Ellwood City	110
*Erie	940
Farrell	150
Greensburg	300
*Harrisburg	4,750
*Hazleton	800
Homestead	300
*Indiana	135
*Johnstown	600
Kittanning	175

State and City	Jewish Population
*Lancaster	1,900
*Lebanon	425
Lock Haven	140
*Lower Bucks County[y]	18,000
McKeesport	2,100
Monessen	100
Mt. Carmel	100
Mt. Pleasant	120
New Castle	400
New Kensington	475
Norristown	2,000
North Penn	200
*Oil City	165
Oxford-Kennett Square	180
*Philadelphia Metropolitan Area	295,000
Phoenixville	300
*Pittsburgh	51,000
*Pottstown	700
Pottsville	500
*Reading	2,800
Sayre	100
*Scranton	4,190
Sharon	470
Shenandoah	230
*State College	450
Stroudsburg	410
Sunbury	160
*Uniontown	290
Upper Beaver	500
*Washington	325
Wayne County	210
West Chester	300
*Wilkes-Barre	4,300
Williamsport	770
*York	1,600

RHODE ISLAND
*Providence (incl. rest of state) 22,000

State and City	Jewish Population
SOUTH CAROLINA	
*Charleston	3,200
*Columbia	2,150
Florence	370
Greenville	600
Orangeburg County	105
*Spartanburg	295
Sumter	190
SOUTH DAKOTA	
*Sioux Falls	135
TENNESSEE	
*Chattanooga	2,250
Johnson City[z]	210
*Knoxville	1,350
*Memphis	9,000
*Nashville	3,700
Oak Ridge	240
TEXAS	
*Amarillo	300
*Austin	2,000
Baytown	300
*Beaumont	385
Brownsville	160
*Corpus Christi	1,020
*Dallas	20,000
De Witt County[aa]	150
*El Paso	4,500
*Ft. Worth	2,800
*Galveston	645
*Houston	27,000
Kilgore	110
*Laredo	420
*Longview	185
*Lubbock	350
*McAllen	295
*North Texas Zone[bb]	100
Odessa	150
Port Arthur	260
*San Antonio	6,500

State and City	Jewish Population
Texarkana	100
*Tyler	500
*Waco	700
*Wharton	170
UTAH	
Ogden	100
*Salt Lake City	2,200
VERMONT	
Bennington	120
*Burlington	1,800
*Rutland	350
*St. Johnsbury	100
VIRGINIA	
*Alexandria (incl. Falls Church, Arlington County and urbanized Fairfax County)[f]	30,000
Arlington (incl. in Alexandria)	
*Danville	180
Fredericksburg	140
Hampton (incl. in Newport News)	
*Harrisonburg	115
Hopewell	140
*Lynchburg	275
Martinsville	135
*Newport News (incl. Hampton)	3,000
*Norfolk (incl. Virginia Beach)	11,000
*Petersburg	600
*Portsmouth (incl. Suffolk)	1,150
*Richmond	10,000
*Roanoke	800
Williamsburg	120
*Winchester	110

State and City	Jewish Population	State and City	Jewish Population	State and City	Jewish Population
WASHINGTON		*Morgantown	200	*Madison	3,000
Bellingham	120	*Parkersburg	155	Manitowoc	175
Bremerton (incl. in		Weirton	150	*Milwaukee	23,900
Seattle)		*Wheeling	650	Oshkosh	120
*Seattle	13,000			*Racine	405
*Spokane	800	WISCONSIN		*Sheboygan	200
*Tacoma	750	*Appleton	325	*Superior	165
WEST VIRGINIA		*Beloit	120	Waukes	135
*Bluefield-Princeton	190	*Eau Claire	120	*Wausau	155
*Charleston	1,150	*Fond du Lac	100		
*Clarksburg	205	Green Bay	440	WYOMING	
Huntington	350	*Kenosha	250	*Cheyenne	255

*Denotes estimate submitted within two-year period.

ªFlorence, Sheffield, Tuscumbia.

ᵇTowns in Chicot, Desha, Drew Counties.

ᶜIncludes Alta Loma, Chino, Claremont, Cucamonga, La Verne, Montclair, Ontario, Pomona, San Dimas, Upland.

ᵈCenterbrook, Chester, Clinton, Deep River, Essex, Killingworth, Old Lyme, Old Saybrook, Seabrook, Westbrook.

ᵉAnsonia, Derby-Shelton, Oxford, Seymour.

ᶠGreater Washington includes urbanized portions of Montgomery and Prince Georges Counties, Maryland, Arlington County, Fairfax County (organized portion); Falls Church, Alexandria, Virginia.

ᵍRock Island, Moline (Illinois); Davenport, Bettendorf (Iowa).

ʰTowns in Alexander, Bond, Clay, Clinton, Crawford, Edwards, Effingham, Fayette, Franklin, Gallatin, Hamilton, Hardin, Jackson, Jasper, Jefferson, Jersey, Johnson, Lawrence, Mascoupin, Madison, Marion, Massac, Montgomery, Perry, Pope, Pulaski, Randolph, Richland, St. Clair, Saline, Union, Wabash, Washington, Wayne, White, Williamson Counties.

ⁱIncludes Crown Point, East Chicago, Gary, Hammond, Munster, Valparaiso, Whiting, and the Greater Calumet region.

ʲTowns in Caroline, Kent, Queen Annes, Talbot Counties.

ᵏAllendale, Elmwood Park, Fair Lawn, Franklin Lakes, Oakland, Midland Park, Rochelle Park, Saddle Brook, Wykoff also included in North Jersey estimate.

ˡIncludes Camden and Burlington Counties.

ᵐIncludes contiguous areas in Hudson, Morris, Somerset, and Union Counties.

ⁿIncludes Clayton, Paulsboro, Woodbury. Excludes Newfield; see Vineland.

ᵒSee footnote (m).

ᵖIncludes Guttenberg, Hudson Heights, North Bergen, North Hudson, Secaucus, Union City, Weehawken, West New York, Woodcliff.

�q Includes Paterson, Wayne, Hawthorne in Passaic County, and nine towns in Bergen County. See footnote (k).

ʳIncludes Perth Amboy, Metuchen, Edison Township (part), Woodbridge.

'Includes in Middlesex County, Cranbury, Dunellen, East Brunswick, Edison Township (part), Jamesburg, Matawan, Middlesex, Monmouth Junction, Old Bridge, Parlin, Piscataway, South River, Spottswood; in Somerset County, Kendall Park, Somerset; in Mercer County, Hightstown.

'Excludes Kendall Park and Somerset, which are included in Raritan Valley.

"Includes in Cumberland County, Norma, Rosenheim, Vineland; in Salem County, Elmer; in Gloucester County, Clayton, Newfield; in Cape May County, Woodbine.

'Greensboro, High Point, Winston-Salem.

"Burgaw, Clinton, Dunn, Elizabethtown, Fairmont, Jacksonville, Lumberton, Tabor City, Wallace, Warsaw; and Dillon, Loris, Marion, Mullins, S.C.

ˣTowns in Alfalfa, Beckham, Cadelo, Canadian, Cleveland, Custer, Jackson, Kingfisher, Kiowa, Lincoln, Logan, Oklahoma, Payne, Roger Mills, Tillman, Washita Counties.

ʸBensalem Township, Bristol, Langhorne, Levittown, New Hope, Newtown, Penndel, Warington, Yardley.

ᶻIncludes Kingsport and Bristol (including the portion of Bristol in Virginia).

ᵃᵃIncludes communities also in Colorado, Fayette, Gonzales, and La Vaca Counties.

ᵇᵇDenison, Gainesville, Greenville, Paris, Sherman, and Durant (Oklahoma).

Canada

Domestic Affairs

ON OCTOBER 17, the House of Commons opened its doors for the first time to the electronic news media. At a cost of $5 million, Canada bought itself non-stop, unedited radio and television coverage of everything that was said in the House. In a unique way, Canadians were able to watch their political leaders and elected representatives at work. The actual substance of the discussions, however, was largely discouraging. The bad news about the economy in 1977 was stunning. Almost no one talked anymore about great times being ahead.

During 1977, the national unemployment rate stood at 8.4 per cent, the highest since the depression of the 1930's. Inflation accelerated, and the real income of workers fell. The Canadian dollar was devalued by more than 10 per cent, and Canada borrowed large amounts of money abroad to repay the interest on previous foreign loans. The federal government's $8.5 billion financial deficit was at a record level and promised to go even higher in the next year.

Particularly disturbing was the news that major natural resource exporters, such as Inco and Falconbridge, were cutting Canadian production and laying off Canadian workers. With oil reserves also dwindling, Canada was losing the "resource security blanket" on which politicians and bureaucrats in Ottawa had long relied to carry Canada through hard times.

During 1977, the spectre of a dismembered Canada continued to trouble the nation. More money, as well as people, left the province of Quebec, although exact figures were difficult to determine. There was hope that there would be sufficient time to work out a new arrangement that would please both Quebec and the other provinces before the 1979 referendum that Prime Minister René Levesque of Quebec had promised. Some widely-suggested concessions included granting Quebec a role in immigration and communications, and a voice in appointments to the Senate and Supreme Court. Some Canadian politicians and economists suggested a constitutional restructuring of the country to concede the existence of *deux nations.* In November 1977, Premier Levesque visited Paris and was accorded all the honors normally given to a head of state.

Newspaper headlines during the year were dominated by stories of wrongdoing attributed to the Royal Canadian Mounted Police. Two government-appointed commissions investigated the undercover methods of the agency's intelligence branch. The Mounted Police were accused of illegal break-ins, thefts, tampering with the mail, and international espionage.

Many Canadians continued to express confidence in the Mounted Police. There was no doubt, however, that the stock of the Mounties, one of the nation's enduring symbols, reached its lowest point in history. The unfolding drama, while providing the public with inside glimpses of police intelligence work, raised grave moral questions. Prime Minister Pierre Elliott Trudeau took the position that any laws jeopardizing national security had to be changed, and that the Mounties should not be held accountable for any illegal activities carried out in the name of national security.

Foreign Relations

Relations between Canada and the United States improved greatly during the year. There was a widespread feeling that the insecurity bred by the Parti Québécois victory in the Quebec elections had led many English-speaking Canadians to regard Americans as their allies in the fight to keep Canada a united nation. Prof. Louis Balthazar of Laval University in Quebec City wrote: "The Parti Québécois government has contributed to the creation of a completely new climate for Canadian-American relations as a whole, a climate that is likely to result in the links between Canadians and Americans being strengthened, and to the drawing of a veil over old quarrels."

The two countries signed a pipeline agreement to assure the uninterrupted flow of oil and natural gas across each other's territory. The United States government also opted for the construction of a pipeline through Canada to carry natural gas from Alaska to the lower 48 states. If approved by the Canadian Parliament, the project would be the largest private venture ever undertaken.

The United States agreed to hold off on those portions of the Garrison diversion project in North Dakota that Canada contended would cause flooding and pollution in Manitoba. At the beginning of the year, the project—a $550 million irrigation scheme—was considered to be the most important issue outstanding between the two countries.

On January 1, Canada extended its fishing limit to 200 miles; on March 1, the United States did the same. The extension brought up problems of maritime boundaries, with all that this implied for the future development of underwater minerals. The two countries quickly agreed to an interim arrangement that would allow orderly maritime commerce until a permanent agreement could be negotiated.

In 1977, Canada registered a success in the raising of the St. Lawrence Seaway tolls, which the United States had opposed. One issue that was being pursued aggressively by the Canadian government was a clause in the United States Tax Reform Act (which took effect at the beginning of 1977) that disallowed as a tax write-off the costs of United States citizens attending conventions in other countries,

Canada included. There was considerable sympathy in the United States Congress for Canada's case, since it was estimated that Canadian hotels experienced a direct loss of $35 million in the first seven months of the year through cancellations due to the act. At the same time, Canada had a deficit of $781 million in its travel account with the United States in the first six months of the year.

Intergroup Relations

There was growing concern over manifestations of racism in major Canadian cities. An Ontario Task Force on Human Relations reported in 1977 that Canadians were living in an ever more diverse and heterogeneous society. In 1951, 19 per cent of Toronto's residents had been born outside the country. By 1971, as the population doubled, the number of foreign born had jumped to 37 per cent. In the last six years, Toronto had attracted 31 per cent of Canada's immigrants, and by 1976 close to 60 per cent of the new arrivals were members of visible minorities—Asians, West Indians, and Africans. The report indicated that "there is in Toronto a body of racist opinion and a broad spectrum of racist attitudes which [manifest themselves] as ethnic jokes, harassment and name-calling." The situation was undoubtedly quite similar in Montreal.

A public opinion poll conducted by the Data Laboratories Research Consultants of Montreal for *Weekend Magazine* showed that 88 per cent of Canadians believed in some kind of supreme being or cosmic force, and that 73 per cent had very strong or somewhat strong religious beliefs. Only 5 per cent had no religious affiliation at all. The overwhelming majority of Canadians were professed Christians: 46 per cent Protestant; 41 per cent Roman Catholic.

JEWISH COMMUNITY

Demography

The Jewish population of Canada in 1977 was estimated at 305,000. Leading Jewish centers were Toronto (115,000); Montreal (115,000); Winnipeg (20,000); Vancouver (12,000); and Ottawa (7,500).

A survey conducted by the Jewish Camp Council (JCC), a United Jewish Appeal (UJA) beneficiary agency, found that 24 per cent of the campers came from single-parent homes. JCC operated four camps in Ontario. "We were aware that the single-parent families were on the increase," said JCC executive director John Bernstein, "but this ratio of one in four really astounded us. We're beginning to catch up with the rest of the community." As a direct result of this finding, the Social Planning Committee of the Toronto Jewish Congress (TJC) decided to focus its attention on single-parent families, as well as on the steadily increasing number of singles in the Jewish community. An in-depth study was planned to determine what supportive services were needed.

In a submission to the Quebec provincial government, the Canadian Jewish Congress (CJC) indicated that 18 per cent of the Jewish community of Montreal, or some 20,000 individuals, were living at or below poverty level. Many of these people were over 65 years of age, and a variety of services were required for them. It was noted that the government had not yet given approval for two additional floors to the Maimonides Hospital and Home for the Aged. The situation was so drastic that the Jewish community was paying $350,000 a year to private nursing homes for the care of 53 indigent old people.

A report by Jean Lee of the Toronto Jewish Family and Child Service estimated that about 13,000 people, or 13 per cent of Toronto's Jewish population, were living at or below poverty level.

Immigration

A new Canadian immigration act enshrined in law for the first time such fundamental principles as non-discrimination, family reunification, humanitarian concern for refugees, and the promotion of Canada's economic, social, demographic, and cultural goals.

Under the new act, the sponsored dependent category was replaced by the family class. Canadian citizens would now be able to sponsor the immigration of a wider range of relatives, including parents under the age of 60. It was anticipated that relatives now eligible for nomination by Canadian citizens would receive the same kind of preference they enjoyed under the previous regulations. The act contained guidelines intended to protect Canada against terrorists and organized crime. It confirmed the obligations Canada had assumed as a party to the United Nations' Convention and Protocol on Refugees, provided for special selection standards for refugees, and gave persons who claimed refugee status new protection under the law.

In 1976, the Jewish Immigrant Aid Services (JIAS) had handled 315 new families, as compared with 456 in 1975. The number of immigrant families from the Soviet Union dropped from 324 to 186.

A two-day conference in Montreal brought together 40 professionals from across the country to discuss problems relating to Jewish immigration and the integration of newcomers. It was noted that more Russian immigrants were anxious to settle on the prairies, far from Montreal and Toronto, where Jewish immigrants had made their homes ever since the first Jews came to Canada in the 18th century. Social workers in the Canadian west had been swamped with clients that they were too inexperienced to handle.

Final statistics for 1977 were expected to show that the number of Israelis emigrating to Canada was down only slightly from the 1975 peak of 1,668. The population flow between the two countries was now almost entirely one way. In 1976, as in 1975, fewer than 300 Canadians had emigrated to Israel.

Communal Activities

The 18th Plenary Assembly of the Canadian Jewish Congress was held in May at the Queen Elizabeth Hotel in Montreal. The number of registered delegates and alternates came to 1,015. Several hundred persons attended as observers. Elected to office were Rabbi W. Gunther Plaut, president, and David Satok, chairman of the national executive. It was announced that Steve Ain would become national executive director, and that Alan Rose would serve as executive vice-president.

Uppermost in the minds of the delegates was the question of the future of Quebec Jewry in the wake of the victory of the separatists in that province. Significantly, one of the 24 resolutions adopted called for increased efforts by CJC to protect civil rights.

A joint research project of the Allied Jewish Community Services (AJCS) and the CJC to determine the future of the Jews in Quebec was unveiled at the convention. Called the Quebec Policy Research Institute, the project aimed at ascertaining how many Jews were leaving the province and why. In addition, it was to study legislation which seriously affected Jews in such areas as education, health, welfare services, business, and the professions. The study was headed by McGill University law professor Irwin Cotler; Jack Kantrowitz was named coordinator of research. A committee of 15 lay people—five from AJCS, five from CJC, and five from the community at large—was to supervise the project.

A gloomy picture of the Jewish community, in which nearly every organization was in dire financial straits, was painted by Milton Harris, president of the Toronto Jewish Congress, at the second annual meeting of the organization in March. Harris made several five-year projections based on the rate of increased income from 1975 to 1976 in the UJA drive, and the rate of increased expenditures in local and national programs. In 1982, he maintained, UJA would raise $20.5 million as compared with $18.9 million in 1976, a rise of 1.5 per cent. Local and national program expenditures during the same period would go from $5.6 million to $10.8 million, a 93 per cent increase. The United Israel Appeal (UIA) allocations would decrease 33 per cent, from about $12 million to $8 million.

Allocations totalling $5,901,900 for Canadian Jewish welfare and educational services were approved by the executive of TJC, which disburses funds raised by UJA. The allocations, which covered the fiscal period July 1, 1977 to June 30, 1978, were only 4.4 per cent higher than the previous year. Ronald Appleby, chairman of TJC's Budget and Finance Committee, called it an austerity budget "which reflects the fact that the 1977 UJA campaign did not raise sufficient funds and thus limited the community's ability to fund all the needs to the extent we would have liked."

The budget allocations for Jewish education totalled $3,097,281, an increase of 5.8 per cent over the previous year. Local social service agencies would receive $1,134,409, an increase of 1.6 per cent. National agencies (CJC, JIAS, and UJRA)

were allocated $1,342,105, an increase of 1.4 per cent. The TJC administrative
budget of $378,450 represented an increase of 4 per cent.

Community Relations

The Canada Israel Committee (sponsored by the Canadian Zionist Federation,
CJC, and B'nai Brith) protested the use of public funds by the Quebec arm of the
Canadian University Service Overseas for the distribution of Arab League propaganda, and for printing of anti-Israel pamphlets and articles in its monthly magazine.

The Quebec Jewish community felt anxious at the candidacy of Roger Delorme
for Parliament. Delorme, a Montreal television broadcaster, had made frequent
anti-Zionist and antisemitic remarks. CJC deplored as inadequate a statement by
Joe Clark, leader of the Federal Progressive Conservative Party, that Delorme
would abide by the party's policies on Israel despite his own publicly stated anti-
Zionist views. Jews in Quebec and elsewhere who were members or backers of the
Conservative Party were embarrassed by the turn of events. Delorme, however, was
defeated in the election.

Three synagogues in western Ontario were vandalized during the election campaign. In each instance, an anti-Israel message was scrawled on the walls of the
building. Gerald Klein, president of the London (Ontario) Jewish Community
Council, declared that the "acts of vandalism have serious racial overtones. All
kinds of people have been living in London for generations in friendship and peace,
and vandalism against a house of worship is against all the principles on which our
society is based." The London *Free Press* editorialized that "sooner or later, the kind
of people who throw paint on a synagogue and leave hate literature at its doors are
bound to expose themselves. An alert community may then be able to identify,
arrest, and convict such people of a crime which has no place in our democratic
Judaeo-Christian society . . ."

In December, three self-proclaimed neo-Nazis went on trial in Toronto for,
among other things, distributing antisemitic propaganda, painting swastikas on
synagogues, and conspiring to throw smoke bombs in a stadium where Israeli
athletes were competing. The accused—36-year-old Don Andrews, 20-year-old
Dawyd Zarytshansky, and 29-year-old Wayne Elliot—faced an array of charges
including arson, malicious damage, conspiracy, and possession of explosives. At
year's end the trial was continuing.

A dispute between the Montreal Symphony Orchestra and the Musicians' Guild
had as one of its central issues the demand of the Guild that no performances be
scheduled on either Yom Kippur or Easter Sunday. The director general of the
Orchestra stated in a written communication: "I reiterate our promise that we will
do the utmost to avoid scheduling, in future years, concerts on the Day of Atone-
ment."

A number of changes in the Ontario Human Rights Code were suggested by the Ontario Human Rights Commission. Included were recommendations for legislation, within Provincial jurisdiction, counteracting the Arab boycott. The Commission also advocated the permissibility of "class-action complaints from individuals who believe that they have suffered discrimination as a group." It asked for provisions to "require all police, high school, and elementary students and some university students to take mandatory human rights courses." In support of these recommendations, the Commission noted that "Ontario is becoming more complex, creating an increasing scope for inter-group tension, racial abuse, violence of the mind and body and various forms of hate literature."

Zionism and Israel

In October, the Toronto Zionist Council observed its 70th anniversary, and was hailed in the community for its efforts on behalf of Zionism and Israel over the years.

The Canadian Reform movement established Kadima, potentially the largest national Zionist organization. A drive for membership in Reform congregations over the 1977 High Holy Days resulted in close to 3,000 adherents. Formed, in part, as a reaction to trends in Israel questioning the legitimacy of liberal Judaism, Kadima became a bona fide member of the Canadian Zionist Federation and was seeking representation at the World Zionist Congress. There were indications that the Conservative movement was considering a similar plan.

Phil Granovsky, national president of UIA, accused the Jewish Agency and the Israeli government of not paying sufficient attention to the Canadian Jewish community. At a meeting of the Agency's board of governors in Jerusalem, Granovsky declared: "Canada is now the second largest producer of cash after the United States. It is my firm conviction that our campaign . . . does not receive the attention from Jerusalem that is warranted." In July, at a meeting of the Jewish Agency assembly in Jerusalem, Granovsky was elected chairman of Keren-Hayesod United Israel Appeal, the worldwide fund-raising body. This was the highest post in the international Jewish field ever attained by a Canadian.

The Canada Israel Committee took the government to task for its voting record at the United Nations, charging that the government "unnecessarily bent over backwards to be "evenhanded" in the Arab-Israel dispute. It was suggested that the Canadian government's lessened support for Israel in the United Nations was due to significant changes in the world economic landscape, the increased prestige accorded the Palestine Liberation Organization by the international community, and the passage by the United Nations of 50 anti-Zionist resolutions in the past five years.

A new project of the Hadassah-Wizo Organization of Canada was announced at the 27th biennial convention in Jerusalem. It involved the restoration of the old Tel Aviv Museum from which Israel's independence had been proclaimed. To be renamed the Hall of Independence, the building would house the scroll of independence, documentary material, photographs, and a recording of David Ben-Gurion's speech proclaiming the founding of the state.

Despite an estimated 10 to 15 per cent decline in population in the communities it served, UIA of Ontario raised the same amount of money as the year before.

Arab Boycott

In December, leaders of major Jewish organizations expressed dissatisfaction with the Canadian government's policy toward the Arab boycott. Trade Minister Jack Horner and External Affairs Minister Don Jamieson reported in the House of Commons that although the government had not changed its policy of opposing the boycott, there were problems in making public a list of those Canadian firms that the government knew to have been asked to include boycott clauses in their sales contracts.

According to the *Financial Post,* Canada was sixth on the list of countries most often blacklisted by the Arab boycott, and 243 Canadian companies and organizations were on the boycott list. Canadian exports to the Middle East totalled $600 million in 1975, compared to $130 million in 1971.

Soviet Jewry

During the year, a variety of activities on behalf of Russian Jewry took place throughout the country. Five hundred people attended a "Call to Action" meeting for Soviet Jewry held at the Shaarei Shomayim Synagogue in Toronto on March 30, and sponsored by the Canadian Committee for Soviet Jewry (CCSJ). The audience was asked to participate in sending protest postcards to Soviet party chief Leonid Brezhnev, mailing a small packet of matzot to the Russian ambassador in Ottawa, and providing information on prisoner of conscience Anatoly Shcharansky to members of Parliament. Hundreds of items were mailed. CCSJ acknowledged the assistance of the Toronto Action Committee for Soviet Jewry, the Toronto Group of 35, and the Youth Council for Soviet Jewry.

Coinciding with a November 7 celebration held at the Soviet consulate in Montreal to mark the 60th anniversary of the Bolshevik Revolution, a demonstration for Soviet Jewry in general, and Anatoly Shcharansky in particular, was arranged by the Montreal Group of 35. Taking part in the demonstration was Shcharansky's wife. During her visit, Mrs. Shcharansky spoke at a special assembly and participated in demonstrations held in Montreal and Ottawa.

On December 4, about 350 persons attended a Chanukah ceremony in front of the Court House in Vancouver, arranged as part of the worldwide observance of Solidarity Week for Soviet Jewry. In Toronto, a candle-lighting ceremony took place on the lawn of Beth Tzedec Synagogue, where a menorah was specially erected by the Toronto Committee for Soviet Jewry. The Solidarity Week was dedicated to the cause of Anatoly Shcharansky.

CCSJ maintained almost weekly telephone contacts with three Jewish activists in Moscow: Vladimir Prestin, Pavel Abramovitch, and Viktor Yelistratov. All three men had been out of work since applying for exit visas some years ago.

A panel discussion, dealing mainly with the civil and human rights of Soviet Jews, took place in Toronto on February 5. The seminar was part of the mid-winter meeting of the Canadian Bar Association and was sponsored by its civil liberties section for Association members and guests.

Holocaust Observances

Over 1,500 people attended the annual Yom Hashoa commemoration, which was held on April 14 at the Beth Tzedec Synagogue in Toronto. The speaker was Dr. Howard Roiter of the University of Montreal. A pictorial display by Yad Vashem was on view in the foyer of the synagogue.

More than 600 persons were present at a Yiddish lecture, and over 250 persons at a French lecture, given by Leopold Treeper on June 20 and 21, respectively, under the sponsorship of the Holocaust Memorial Committee of CJC and several Montreal organizations.

A memorial service to commemorate the Holocaust victims took place at the Bnai Abraham Synagogue in Winnipeg on the evening of April 14. The following day the anniversary of the Warsaw Ghetto uprising was commemorated in front of the YMHA community center, with civic, provincial, and federal government representatives participating. During the ceremony a proclamation was read designating April 15–22 Holocaust Memorial Week.

Hamilton Jewry viewed an exhibition entitled "The Holocaust and Resistance," and participated in a mass rally which was followed by group discussions.

Religion

During 1977, leading rabbis, in comments and letters to the *Canadian Jewish News,* expressed the view that the relationship between the Orthodox, Conservative, and Reform branches of Judaism in Toronto was slowly deteriorating, with the political and religious debate in Israel serving as the catalyst. Rabbi Herbert Feder of Conservative Congregation Beth Tikvah declared: "Orthodoxy has been increasingly boycotting meaningful dialogue with the Conservative and Reform. This is fruitless and sabotages our necessary kinship. A decade ago," he added, "communication was not ruled out. Now we no longer meet. There is certainly no arena in which individual rabbinic spokesmen talk as human beings. And that's a disgrace."

The formation of Kadimah, a Reform Zionist organization, was the subject of dispute. Rabbi David Schochet (Lubavitch) stated that the formation of Kadimah was an "unforgivable move. It has been organized to counteract religious influence in Israel." Rabbi Gunther Plaut of Holy Blossom Temple (Reform) countered Schochet's statement by remarking: "If they are willing to dissolve Mizrachi then we will dissolve Kadimah. If Israel adopts a restrictive interpretation of what constitutes proper religious practice, that will bring about alienation in the Diaspora."

At the biennial convention of the Canadian Council of Liberal Congregations in Hamilton, Rabbi Gunther Plaut declared that the entire matter of religious divorce for Reform Jews must be reconsidered. He predicted the polarization of Jewish points of view into two main camps, the Orthodox and the non-Orthodox. "By definition," he argued, "this means that we will move closer to Conservatives and they to us. We ought to welcome this new alliance. We both need it."

The theme of the convention was "Prospect and Retrospect." In his keynote address, Rabbi Bernard Baskin of Temple Anshe Sholom (Reform), the host congregation, set the tone when, following an analysis of the philosophy of Reform Judaism, he said that "the trend is unmistakable. The direction is toward tradition."

In March, over 50 religious and lay leaders, Jewish and Christian, attended a luncheon meeting at the Samuel Bronfman House in Montreal, arranged by the national religious department of CJC, in association with the Canadian Council of Christians and Jews and the Montreal Committee for Catholic-Jewish Relations. The meeting was addressed by Marcel Dubois, a renowned Catholic theologian and leader of the interfaith movement in Israel, on the subject "The Christian Outlook on Israel." During his stay in Montreal, Dubois addressed a number of other Jewish and Christian gatherings.

Jews and Christians from across Canada met in Ottawa at an interfaith colloquium to consider the quality of life in the country. This was the first joint undertaking of official Catholic, Protestant, and Jewish bodies. The colloquium, "The Quality and Sanctity of Life," was sponsored by the Canadian Council of Churches, the Canadian Catholic Conference, CJC, and the Canadian Council of Christians and Jews.

A new independent Jewish organization designed to foster interest in Judaism, the Association for the Living Jewish Spirit was formed in Toronto. Rabbi Reuben Slonim served as chairman of the Leadership Committee. According to Felix Eckstein, secretary-treasurer, the purpose of the new group was to offer members insight into the meaning of Judaism and the task and destiny of the Jewish people.

Jewish Education

In a sharp reversal of tradition, TJC called for Ontario government funding for Jewish day schools and for all independent schools in the province. A resolution approved by the TJC executive declared: "Because of the rising costs and growing deficits in our Jewish day schools and the growth of enrollment in them, . . . the Toronto Jewish Congress deems it essential to continue attempts to obtain funding from government sources."

During 1977, the Jewish school system was plagued by unprecedented deficits, resulting in a 10 per cent across-the-board tuition increase. Projections indicated that TJC would have to allocate close to $3 million in subsidies for education during the year, with some $325,000 of that directed to the administrative arm, the Board of Jewish Education. Presenting the financial report of the Toronto Associated Hebrew Schools, budget chairman Ron Heller indicated that the schools, facing an accumulated deficit just short of $1 million, were "to all intents and purposes bankrupt." The Eitz Chaim School showed a deficit for the year of $600,000 in accumulated debts. The Associated Hebrew Schools and the Eitz Chaim School accounted for some 2,200 students, well over one-third of the entire day school enrollment.

Negotiations over the experimental plan to integrate the Associated Hebrew Schools' junior high school into the public system in North York were stalemated. Minister of Education Thomas Wells reiterated his opposition to public funds being given to any school where religious courses were compulsory. Late in the year the North York Board of Education decided to test in the Supreme Court of Canada the legality of integrating a Jewish school into the public system.

In Quebec, Jewish day schools were under pressure to increase the hours of French instruction from the present 8 hours a week to 14 or 15 hours. Carl Laxer, chairman of the Association of Jewish Day Schools (AJDS), complained that "more French instruction will reduce the time available for Jewish studies." In November, AJDS received a letter from Education Minister Jacques Yvan Morin offering 60 rather than 80 per cent funding to almost all of the schools. The previous year, the day schools had received a total of $1.8 million from the government.

Joe Ain, president of Allied Jewish Community Services, explained what he called "the financial facts of life about Jewish education." He stated:

> Jewish schools in Montreal are funded in four ways: school fees, the schools' own campaigns, allocations from Combined Jewish Appeal (AJCS), and provincial per capita grants. Government grants total more than $6 million and, should a situation develop whereby some or all of the government funds were to be discontinued, the schools would be compelled to devise other fiscal resources. Allied Jewish Community Services, through its Combined Jewish Appeal which now supplied $500,000 directly to day schools, will have to make additional grants to schools as one of several means of meeting whatever financial problem may arise.

The future of the 22 Jewish pre-schools in the Montreal area was put in doubt following the January implementation of new regulations governing the operation of day care centers and nursery schools. The new ruling transferred jurisdiction over these schools from the Social Affairs Ministry to the Education Department. Opponents claimed that the new regulations would so alter the structure of the pre-schools that they would cease to exist.

École Maimonide, a day school maintained by the Sephardic community, rejected a Ministry of Education proposal for a new classification. The Ministry suggested an "ethnic public" status, which would provide the school with 100 per cent subsidization, while placing hiring, curriculum, and teacher evaluation in the hands of a public school commission. Jean-Claude Lasry, the school's president, declared: "I'd rather close the school and hold classes in a shopping centre than accept the proposal as it now reads. The only thing that would remain of the school as we know it now would be its name."

Jewish Culture

The National Library of Canada received what was believed to be its largest single gift—a $2 million collection of Hebrew books and manuscripts belonging to Jacob M. Lowy of Montreal. The collection included Hebrew and Latin incunabula, Talmud editions, a Flavius Josephus collection, rare Bibles, and Hebrew books dating from the 16th to the 19th centuries. The collection was to be kept intact under the name of the "Jacob M. Lowy Collection" and housed in the main building of the National Library. Its quarters would allow space for scholars to do research.

In June, a $6.5 million complex housing the Koffler Center of the Arts, the Leah Posluns Theatre, and the physical education wing of the YM-YWHA was officially opened. The Koffler Center was hailed as one of the three major "Y"-linked Jewish cultural centers in North America.

The Jewish Historical Society of Canada issued the first edition of its semiannual journal. The editor was Rabbi Jonathan Plaut of Windsor; contributing editor was Dr. Stephen Speisman of Toronto, director of Canadian Jewish Congress, Central Region archives.

The Jewish Book Month observance in Montreal was attended by an estimated 1,200 persons. The opening lecture was given by Chaim Potok. Activities for Jewish Book Month in Montreal included lectures, the publication of essays and poetry by students, and the exhibition of books of Jewish content in many university and public libraries across the city.

The first Toronto Book Fair was well publicized and attended. Speakers included Irving Howe, Lucy Dawidowicz, Howard Blum, Zalman Abramov, Chaim Grade, Matti Meged, and Danny Siegel. Arrangers of the fair were the Jewish Public Library, TJC, the YM-YWHA, and the Federation of Jewish Women's Organizations.

An estimated 10,000 people attended the Yiddish Music and Theatre Festival, sponsored by the National Committee on Yiddish, at Hampstead Park in Montreal in August, 1977. The CBC Festival Chamber Orchestra, conducted by Victor Feldbrill, presented a concert in observance of Toronto's Jewish Music Festival at Beth Tzedec Synagogue. The orchestra, conducted by Boris Brott, participated in a concert held at the Beth Tikvah Synagogue. Included was the composition "From the Diary of Anne Frank" by Oskar Morawetz. A number of Jewish choirs in Toronto presented an "Evening of Jewish Choral Music" at the Beth Emeth Bais Yehuda Synagogue. A new composition by Srul I. Glick was featured.

A Jewish Cultural Council was set up in Toronto by TJC as an extension of its Educational and Cultural Committee. The aim of the Council was the encouragement of Jewish cultural arts and informal Jewish education. Representation on the Council was open to all synagogues, community agencies, and organizations.

An unusual attempt to bring together scholars in the fields of literature, rabbinic studies, and biblical history took place at a symposium in Ottawa on "Biblical Literature: Rabbinic and Modern Perspectives." Close to 50 people from throughout North America and Israel attended the three-day symposium co-sponsored by the Ottawa Jewish Community Council and Carleton University.

Publications

The Abramsky Variations by Morley Torgov deals, in a manner both serious and amusing, with three generations of a Canadian Jewish family in search of meaning and identity.

Matt Cohen's sixth novel, *The Colours of War,* explores the intricate relationships between fathers and sons, husbands and wives, against the background of rural Ontario.

The Governor General's Award for Poetry was presented to Joe Rosenblatt of Toronto for his collection *Top Soil: Selected Poems.* Rosenblatt was editor of *Jewish Dialogue,* a Toronto-based literary periodical which publishes short stories and poems. Also honored was Miriam Waddington for her collection of poems *The Price of Gold.* Myra Paperny of Calgary was among the winners of the Canada Council Children's Literature Prize.

Spanning the Generations by Evelyn Kallen is a study of Jewish identity, based, in part, on a doctoral dissertation done for the department of anthropology at the University of Toronto.

The Summer 1977 issue of *Jewish Dialogue* was given over entirely to "Lost Boryslaw, Memories of a Galician Youth." The recollections were those of Meilech Schiff, an 85-year-old Montreal resident and retired carpenter.

Wayne Edmonstone wrote *The Making of a Critic,* about Nathan Cohen, the highly regarded late drama critic of the Toronto *Star.*

Nachman Shemen's *Sanctity in Jewish Family Life* was written in Yiddish and published in Israel.

In *Past Redemptions* David Birkan of Toronto deals in sonnet form with the traditional 54 portions of the Pentateuch, striving to find contemporary relevance in biblical events and personalities.

Out of Place by poet Eli Mandel focuses on the quest for Jewish origins in the small communities of the Canadian prairies.

The Noise of Singing and *Dark Caves* by Abraham Ram are short novels about Montreal Jewish life and a perplexed academic, Moe Tabb.

The 18th Plenary Assembly of CJC recognized the importance of Yiddish literature in Canada. It was pointed out that three writers—the late Melech Ravitch, Rachel Korn, and Yehuda Elbarg—received the highly coveted Itzik Manger Prize in Israel. Among Yiddish writers who received awards from the J.J. Segal Fund in Montreal over the years were S. Dunsky, Y. Elberg, M. Husid, the late Melech Ravitch, Chava Rosenfarb, M. M. Shafir and J. Zipper.

Personalia

Philip G. Givens, a former president of the Zionist Organization of Canada, was appointed Judge of the Ontario Provincial Court and member of the Metropolitan Toronto Police Commission. Willie Rudy was re-elected to a third term as Mayor of Ste. Sophie, Quebec.

Jewish Canadians awarded the Order of Canada included: David Golden of Ottawa; Sol Kanee of Winnipeg, former president of CJC and former director of the Bank of Canada; Sam Steinberg, of Montreal, head of a grocery chain bearing the family name; G. Sydney Halter, Q.C. of Winnipeg, the first Football League Commissioner, known as "the Czar of Canadian football"; Louis Applebaum of Toronto, well-known composer and musicologist; Muriel Kovitz, chancellor of the University of Calgary; Murray Koffler, of Toronto, pharmacist, hotel-owner and patron of the Weizmann Institute, Mount Sinai Hospital, the YMHA Arts Centre in Toronto, and other institutions.

As a result of the spring 1977 election, the number of Jewish MP's in the Ontario legislature was reduced by two. This was accounted for by the pre-election withdrawal of two Toronto Liberals, Vern Singer and Philip Givens, the defeat of Liberal-turned-Conservative Marvin Shore in London, and the election of David Rotenberg in Singer's former riding. The other three Jewish members of the legislature sat in the previous assembly. They were Larry Grossman of St. Andrews-St. Patrick; Liberal leader Stuart Smith of Hamilton West; and New Democrat leader Stephen Lewis of Scarboro West. Lewis resigned his position as leader of the NDP, although he continued to hold his seat in the Legislature.

In the provincial election in Manitoba, 5 Jewish MP's were elected. They were Sidney Spivak, the former leader of the Conservative Party, who was made minister without portfolio; Saul Cherniak; Sidney Green; Saul Miller; and Abe Kovnats.

Norman Vickar of Melfort, Saskatchewan, was named Minister of Industry and Commerce of the government of Saskatchewan, thus becoming the first Jewish cabinet minister in the history of that province. Sydney M. Harris, past president of the Canadian Jewish Congress and chairman of the board of governors, was appointed a provincial court judge. Named Dean of Arts and Sciences of the University of Toronto was economist Arthur Kruger. He was the first Jew to hold this post. He served as the first dean of Woodsworth College, the University of Toronto's School of Continuing Education. Allan Gotlieb, deputy minister of Manpower and Immigration for several years, was appointed Undersecretary of State for External Affairs, the second highest post in the ministry.

Victor Kugler was awarded the $10,000 Nicholas and Hedy Munk Brotherhood Prize. Channeled through the Canadian Council of Christians and Jews, the prize was given to him for providing shelter to the Otto Frank family in Amsterdam when such an act meant risking execution by the Nazis.

Retiring from their long held rabbinical posts were Rabbi W. Gunther Plaut of Toronto's Holy Blossom Temple; Rabbi Samuel S. Stollman, spiritual leader of Shaar Hashomayim, Windsor, Ontario; and Rabbi Israel Freedman of St. Catharines, Ontario. Dr. Ernest Klein, world-renowned etymologist, received honorary degrees from Guelph and McMaster Universities in Ontario on consecutive days in May. Shmuel Ovnat, Israel's consul general in Toronto for the past five years, left to take up his new ambassadorial post in Burma. Montreal-born Martin Park was appointed the new executive director of the Toronto YM-YWHA. He succeeded David Andrews, who served as director for 25 years. Andrews, in turn, assumed the new post of executive vice-president.

Among Canadian personalities who died in 1977 were: Moishe Myerson, veteran community worker, deeply devoted to a variety of Jewish causes; Michael Garber (75) of Toronto, former president of both the Zionist Organization of Canada and CJC; Sara Gittel Salsberg (94), active in support of Jewish education, and a matriarch of Toronto's Polish Jews; Selma-Marguerite Marguilies (95), of Montreal, a founder of the Women's International Zionist Organization (WIZO) in 1917 and of Ayanot, the first agricultural school for girls in Palestine; Alan Mills (63), Canadian folk singer and actor; Esther Volpe (82), active in women's groups for over six decades; Dr. Abraham I. Willinsky (91), one of the pioneer Jewish doctors in Toronto, and chief urologist at the Toronto Western Hospital until 1946; and David Green (82) of Toronto, who served as president of the Hebrew National Association for many years.

BERNARD BASKIN

Latin America

Argentina

Domestic Affairs

AT THE END OF 1977, Argentina was a somber nation, still struggling to achieve order and stability. Extreme left- and right-wing terrorism had not been fully contained, although bombings and shoot-outs were far less common. Liberal Argentines were troubled by the fact that some extreme right-wing para-military and para-police forces continued to act with impunity. As the Buenos Aires *Herald* expressed it:

> It is ridiculous to pretend that there is only left-wing subversion in Argentina. Today the evidence suggests that while left-wing terrorism is on its last legs, right-wing extremists are more active than they have ever been . . . There is also evidence that Nazi symbols have been used by some members of the security forces, who have told prisoners that they admire Hitler and Nazi war criminals . . . It does not really matter whether the terrorism comes from the extreme left or the extreme right . . . The important thing is to wipe out all violence. This has not been possible up to now, because the government has not chosen to condemn excesses . . . and because the whole unpleasant subject has been hidden in a fog of fear.

The United States government reduced military aid to Argentina in February because of violations of human rights. U.S. Secretary of State Cyrus Vance, during his one-day visit to Buenos Aires at the end of November, brought a list of some 7,500 people whose American relatives had appealed to the United States government for help in tracing their whereabouts. At a press conference on November 30, Foreign Minister Vice-Admiral Oscar A. Montes stated that "the list is unofficial, and not sponsored by the U.S. government. It was turned over by the Embassy in a gesture of cooperation with our authorities." The new United States Ambassador to Argentina, Raúl H. Castro, said that the list was given to President Carter by three human rights groups. While acknowledging a marked decrease in the rate of disappearance, Castro indicated that the United States would welcome the publication of a list revealing the names of those arrested, the charges made against them, and the circumstances surrounding their arrests.

On May 7, the 25th Plenary Assembly of the National Conference of Bishops expressed anxiety over the wave of kidnappings and disappearances. The Conference document stated that "no notion of collective security, however important, could infringe upon human rights." With regard to those priests and nuns who had disappeared, the document noted that the Church had its own disciplinary system, and could not accept the light manner in which priests and bishops were sometimes linked with ideologies which are at variance with the Catholic faith.

On December 8, a petition signed by almost 1,000 people was published in *La Nación.* Immediately thereafter, 24 of the signers were arrested by men claiming to be police. The majority were seized by men in civilian clothes, who arrived in unmarked cars outside the Buenos Aires Holy Cross Church. One woman of a group of some 100 who demonstrated weekly throughout the year stated to the press on December 13: "All we want to know is what we ask in the petition: are our missing relatives alive or dead, and where are they?"

The Jewish community showed great concern over the fate of Jacobo Timerman, editor of the liberal daily *La Opinion,* and perhaps Argentina's foremost journalist. On April 15, Timerman was removed from his home and placed under arrest. Although a military court asserted in unequivocal terms that Timerman had no connection whatsoever with subversive activities, at the end of the year he was still being held by the military authorities. A writ of habeas corpus lodged on behalf of Timerman by his wife was turned down by the Court of Criminal Appeals. The charges against him had in no way been clarified. On November 17, at a meeting of the Delegación de Asociaciones Israelitas Argentinas (DAIA), the organization's president, Nehemias Resnizky, expressed the "deep concern of the Jewish community of Argentina over the decision of the military authorities to hold Mr. Timerman under the terms of the Acta Institucional." International Jewish efforts to secure Timerman's release proved fruitless.

Argentine Jewry also evidenced considerable uneasiness over the so-called Graiver affair. In August 1976, David Graiver, a financier who headed the Banque de l'Amérique du Sud of Brussels, was reported dead in a plane crash in Mexico at the age of 32. According to published accounts, Gravier created a fictitious Panamanian company called "New Loring, Inc." and swindled investors, mainly Mexicans, out of more than $20 million. In July, the *Wall Street Journal,* Montevideo's *La Mañana,* and Mexico City's *El Sol* published full reports about the matter. According to *El Sol,* Gravier was assassinated by unnamed extremists, and, at the time of his death, was involved in a conspiracy to launder vast sums of money for the Montoneros (Peronist left-wing extremists). On December 10, the Argentine press reported that Graiver's father, brother, and wife were sentenced to 15 years in prison for having acted as financial agents of the Montoneros. Many people remained skeptical about the claim that Graiver and his family were involved with political extremists. The publicity concerning the case had definite antisemitic overtones.

Planning Minister General Ramón Genaro Diaz Bessone stated at the end of November that the political organizations active on March 24, 1976 (the date of the coup d'état), would not play a role in determining Argentina's future. In the same month, Interior Minister Albano Hargindaguy made it clear that there would be no national elections until 1987, at the earliest. On November 30, the Buenos Aires *Herald* stated: "These announcements should have caused panic among the leadership of the country's political movements. But they did not. To say the least, it is difficult for liberal Argentines to imagine the coming decade under a military dictatorship, benign as it may prove to be."

In October, President Jorge Rafael Videla, at the urging of Jewish groups, instructed Justice Minister Julio Gómez to prepare a law against racial and religious prejudice. The draft of the legislation was sent to the skeleton parliament, the Legislative Advisory Commission. Reports stated that the law was meant to be comprehensive, and would, if applied effectively, outlaw propaganda and discrimination against racial, ethnic, or religious groups. At the end of the year, the law had not yet been promulgated.

In December, the defunct Peronist party reappeared and petitioned the government for the release of Isabel Martinez de Perón. The petition was signed by 100,000 people. At the end of the year, however, Mrs. Perón was still in prison. Similarly, ex-president Héctor Cámpora was still at the Mexican Embassy, where he had been granted asylum in March 1976.

Relations with Israel

In spite of ongoing terrorism and systematic attempts by antisemitic groups to intensify anti-Israel feelings in the country, Israel Ambassador Ram Nirgad met with great success in maintaining friendly relations between the governments of Israel and Argentina. He spoke many times on radio and television, and made his influence felt in Jewish communal affairs. In August, he accompanied select representatives of the Argentine Jewish community to a meeting with Prime Minister Begin and his cabinet. At the end of October, he presented a copy of the *Encyclopedia Judaica* to Argentine Education Minister Dr. Juan José Catalán.

In January, university presidents from various Latin American countries, including Argentina, participated in the planting of a peace forest in Jerusalem. At the same time, the third Argentine-Jewish mission to Israel, organized by Keren Kayemet Le'Israel, travelled there in honor of the organization's 75th anniversary. The Argentine-Israel Chamber of Commerce noted in January that Israel was 20th on the list of 130 countries maintaining commercial relations with Argentina, while Argentina was Israel's 13th principal supplier. The final figures for 1975 showed a balance of payment in favor of Argentina of over $15 million. In August, the Argentine chief of staff, General Roberto Edmundo Viola, presented a medal to the Israeli military attaché Yosef Castel before the latter's return to Israel.

Guests from Israel included the well-known Israeli chanteuse Hanna Aroni, who performed in Buenos Aires in May. In June, Gvirol Goldring, professor of experimental physics at the Weizman Institute, presented lectures to the Argentine academic community. Dr. Raúl Ghinsberg, head of the department of contagious diseases of the Israel Ministry of Public Health, addressed the 7th Latin American Congress of Microbiology in April. Leon Dulzin, treasurer of the Jewish Agency, visited Argentina later in the year, as did Eliezer Shmueli, director general of the Israel Ministry of Education.

The Argentine Ambassador to Israel, Enrique Ros, was received by DAIA and spoke in the Comunidad Bet El, prior to taking up his new post at the United Nations. The new Argentine Ambassador to Israel was Jorge Emilio Casal, who had previously served in the position.

In June, a series of meetings at the Argentine Ministry of Foreign Affairs resulted in a cultural and educational agreement between the two countries. A visit by the Israel Philharmonic Orchestra to Argentina was planned, as was Argentina's participation in the Spinoza anniversary in Israel.

The Argentine-Israeli Council of Agricultural Interchange, headed by Dr. Noe Davidovich, maintained a heavy schedule of activities.

Since the establishment of the State of Israel, some 35,000 Argentine Jews have made *aliyah*. The figure for 1977 was approximately 2,500.

Antisemitism

The Odal publishing house issued a variety of antisemitic materials at the beginning of the year. This led Nehemias Resnizky, president of DAIA, to protest to General Villareal, secretary to President Videla. Several days later, Odal publications were prohibited by the government.

A cinema in the city of Cordoba showing "Victory at Entebbe" was bombed. There was material damage, but no casualties. A bomb also exploded at the Natan Gesang School, causing further damage.

On June 28, Jacobo Kovadloff, executive director of the American Jewish Committee's office in Latin America, left Argentina, to be joined shortly thereafter by his wife and two children. He had received anonymous telephone calls, warnings, and threats of assassination. The American Jewish Committee had operated its office in Buenos Aires for 29 years. Kovadloff, a highly respected Jewish leader, was considered one of the most knowledgeable people in the country with regard to political affairs, especially matters involving human rights and antisemitic tendencies. Upon his arrival in the United States, Richard Maass, president of the American Jewish Committee, issued a statement charging that the "nature of the harassment to which Mr. Kovadloff and his family were subjected showed that this was neither a prank nor the work of a crank, but rather that security police or other government authorities were maintaining a close watch on the Kovadloff family, and that their lives were threatened." Mr. Maass indicated that he did not regard the

Jewish community as being endangered. Antisemitism, he noted, was not official government policy. At the same time, he criticized the government for being unable or unwilling to take strong measures to arrest and bring to trial those engaged in antisemitic activity. Mr. Kovadloff himself stated: "Although antisemitic episodes and publications were occurring with alarming frequency and causing justifiable concern within the Argentine Jewish community, these episodes were not representative of the feelings of the majority of the Argentine population, nor of those authorities cooperating with President Videla. Rather . . . they originated with individuals and groups of nazi-fascist mentality and ideology, who infiltrated the government in high positions."

On July 6, James Neilson wrote in the Buenos Aires *Herald:*

On June 19, I had some harsh words for three retired generals, Rodolfo Mujica, León J. Bengoa, and Juan Antonio Buasso, and for retired Admiral Horacio Justo Gomez Beret, all of whom had attended the fourth anniversary dinner of the now banned magazine *Cabildo*. *Cabildo* is an extreme right-wing publication I find abhorrent, not because of its anti-communism but because of its antisemitism. A recent editorial in it, calling on the armed forces to lay aside their scruples, and deal with the "Jewish problem" in such a way that no Jew would ever again play a major role in the nation's life, looked to me like an encitement to a pogrom on an almost Hitlerian scale.

The generals in question challenged Neilson to a duel. In reply, he argued that if "the four really value[d] their honor, . . . they [would] make it clear that they are against nazism and active persecution of the Jews."

After several months of silence, *Cabildo* reappeared as an illustrated monthly edited by Ricardo Curutchet and Juan Carlos Monedero.

In March, the executive branch of the national government passed a decree prohibiting Nazi and antisemitic publications. This was hailed by DAIA as "a most important event for Argentina in general, and Jewish life in particular." DAIA president Nehemias Resnizky pointed out that this was the first law of its kind in Latin America. Resnizky attributed its promulgation to the activity of DAIA, and the view of the executive department of the government that antisemitic literature worked against the interests of the country.

In May, DAIA had a meeting with Interior Minister General Albano Eduardo Harguindeguy, with regard to publications making Jews appear responsible for various crimes under investigation, particularly the Graiver affair. Minister Harguindeguy assured the DAIA delegation of the government's intention to suppress antisemitic groups who introduced "elements of disunity into the Argentine family." At a meeting of DAIA at the beginning of May, Nehemias Resnizky denounced the virulent antisemitism seizing major sections of the country as a result of the Graiver affair. He stated that "nobody speaks any longer of the enormous problems that are hindering the growth of Argentina . . . The Graiver case, and any other issue where Jews appear, is held up as the unique factor that explains the Argentine drama today."

Important Buenos Aires papers, such as *La Nación, La Prensa,* and the *Herald,* expressed indignation at manifestations of antisemitism, and made detailed mention of the valuable contributions of Jews to the progress and prosperity of Argentina.

In June, an important monthly magazine, *Carta Politica* ("Political Letter") devoted its cover story to "Los Judios" ("The Jews"). The article caused great anxiety in the Jewish community, due to its underlying message that Argentine Jews had better assimilate. It stated quite clearly that there was no room in Argentina for genuine pluralism. Father Jorge Mejia, editor of the prestigious Catholic weekly *Criterio,* responded by attacking the antisemitic bias of *Carta Politica* and pointing out the many factual errors contained in the article.

It was the considered opinion of many analysts that, despite the government's repeated protests that it was not antisemitic, there were powerful antisemitic forces at work in the country. The almost exclusive emphasis on Jewish names such as Graiver, Gelbard, Broner, and Timerman made it appear as though only Jews were involved in subversive activity, economic crimes, etc.

There was no doubt that Jews received especially harsh treatment in the country's prisons and detention centers. Zionism was a hated term, and Jewish prisoners were questioned about Israel's plan to invade Argentina, as well as the headquarters of the "Elders of Zion."

JEWISH COMMUNITY

Demography

Demographic studies by Hebrew University and Tel Aviv University indicated that the Jewish population of Argentina was approximately 300,000. The vast majority of Jews continued to live in Buenos Aires, with sizeable communities in the provinces of Rosario, Córdoba, Santa Fé, La Plata, Tucumán, Mendoza and Bahía Blanca.

Communal Organizations

The Asociación Mutual Argentina (AMIA), a 35,000-member Ashkenazi group, continued to be the largest Jewish organization in the country. The 1977 budget of AMIA was set at $6.5 million. Ninety-three per cent of this amount was expected to come from AMIA's four cemeteries, the only Ashkenazic burial grounds in Buenos Aires. However, as AMIA President Mario H. Gorenstein indicated, since more and more Jews were being buried in non-Jewish cemeteries, the organization's membership was declining.

The Delegación de Asociaciones Israelitas Argentinas (DAIA) was the representative body of Argentine Jewry before the national government and the press. *Informativo,* published by DAIA, was almost completely devoted to anti-defamation material.

The third principal organization of Argentine Jewry was the Organización Sionista Argentina (OSA). Segismundo Dresner continued to serve as president. In November, OSA held elections throughout the country. Out of a total of 22,000 members, 6,220 voted. The results were as follows: Labor Zionist, 1,813; Likud, 1,689; Mizrachi, 928. All other movements received considerably fewer votes.

Jews of Turkish and Balkan origin, and from the island of Rhodes, were organized into the Asociación Comunidad Israelita Sefaradi de Buenos Aires (ACIS). The Congregación Israelita Latina united Moroccan Jews, while those of Syrian and Lebanese origin formed the Asociación Israelita Sefaradí Argentina (AISA). Separate Sephardic cemeteries were maintained.

The Jewish community sponsored other important institutions, among them the newly formed Federation of Sports Clubs, composed of Sociedad Hebraica Argentina, Hakoach, Club Atletico Sefaradí Argentina, and Macabi. Social service and public health institutions included the Hospital Israelita Ezra, Hogar Israelita Argentino para Ancionos y Niños, Clinica Sefaradí, Comedores Populares Israelitas Argentinos, Liga Israelita Contra la Tuberculosis, and Hogar de Ancianos Adolfo Hirsch. Most of these institutions suffered from a lack of funding. Also active on the Jewish scene were: Confederación Juvenil Judeo Argentina, a union of Jewish youth groups; the Latin American section of the World Jewish Congress; Organización Sionista Femenina Argentina (OSFA), an affiliate of WIZO; Sheerit Hapleita, an organization of concentration camp survivors; Horim, the parent-teachers association of Jewish schools; B'nai B'rith; Keren Kayemet; and Keren Hayesod. There were over 100 Jewish organizations in greater Buenos Aires alone.

Communal Activities

Due to the instability of Argentine politics, DAIA had one of its most active years, intervening numerous times with the government, the press and international bodies. At the beginning of the year, a DAIA delegation met with the French ambassador, François de la Corce, to express the Jewish community's extreme displeasure at the release of the Arab terrorist Abud Daoud. DAIA received letters of greeting to the Jewish community from President Videla and Admiral Emilio Massera, the commander-in-chief of the navy. In April, the 34th anniversary of the Warsaw Ghetto uprising was observed at a mass rally sponsored by AMIA, OSA, DAIA, and Sheerit Hapleita.

In March, Tenuat Aliyah held its 8th convention. The Argentine Zionist Federation held its annual convention in April. In May, OSFA offered a course on the history of Zionism. It also organized excursions to Israel for Independence Day and Rosh Hashanah. In August, the Labor Zionists conducted their annual convention and elected Simon Edenburg as president. The 29th anniversary of the State of Israel was celebrated by every major Jewish organization.

Mundo Israelita, the organ of the Labor Zionist party, and Argentine Jewry's only Spanish language weekly, celebrated its 54th anniversary in June. Naval Captain Carlos P. Carpintero, secretary of Public Information, sent a message of congratulations to the editor, Gregorio Fainguersch. Many Jewish intellectuals, however, criticized *Mundo Israelita* for its complete silence on the question of human rights.

El Comite pro Derechos de los Judios en la Union Sovietica, an organization involved in Soviet Jewry activities, sponsored ceremonies marking the 25th anniversary of the assassination, under Stalin, of Jewish poets and writers. It also published, with the aid of the American Jewish Committee office, *Samizdat Judio*, a 262-page volume devoted to Soviet Jewish underground writing; the volume was edited by Simcha Sneh.

In October, 300 delegates, including 150 from the interior, attended the tenth national convention of the Waad Ha'kehillot. *Mundo Israelita* stated that the religious problem "was by far the most irritating subject of the entire convention." AMIA Chief Rabbi Shlomo Ben Hamu refused to participate in deliberations with any non-orthodox rabbi. Tobias Kamenszain, chairman of the session, warned about the dangers of a religious monopoly by the Orthodox. Marc Turkow maintained that the community was facing a possible "Kulturkampf." AMIA president Mario Gorenstein closed the session by stating: "We will maintain the chief rabbinate and its orientation, but . . . no one has the right to limit the varied practices and currents which other sectors of Jews may choose to embrace. Those who believe that we will be indifferent in the face of this intolerance are completely mistaken."

Marc Turkow spoke about the tremendous divide existing between Ashkenazic and Sephardic Jewry. He maintained, however, that the chief problem facing Argentine Jewry was the "phenomenon of colossal Jewish ignorance." He proposed the creation of a commission to study the possible formation of a new umbrella organization for Argentine Jewry, and stressed the critical need for rabbinical leaders who could relate to the younger generation. Gregorio Makowski of Resistencia pleaded for enlightened leadership capable of charting a course for the future, and urged that the Jewish community be open to all. Simon Liberman of Santa Fé found it "extremely depressing to speak at a convention at which the majority of the seats [were] empty," and "younger colleagues conspicuously absent." More generally, he warned his listeners of the "terrifying disintegration of Jewish life taking place."

In October, a seminar on geriatric problems was held under the auspices of the United Community Fund and the Argentine Council of Jewish Women. The Hogar Israelita para Ancianos y Niños celebrated its 62nd anniversary at the end of November. The Latin American Jewish Congress held its 14th plenary convention at the beginning of December in Buenos Aires. Marc Turkow, the veteran Jewish leader who acted as the executive director of the Congress' Latin American section, retired at the end of the year.

Jewish Education

In January, Rabbi Mordechai Edery (Conservative) resigned from the directorate of the Midrasha Ha-ivrit, a position he had held for 12 years, in order to devote himself to his tasks as vice-rector of the Seminario Rabínico Latinoamericano (Conservative) and co-rabbi of the Comunidad Bet El (Conservative). On January 8, *Mundo Israelita* stated: "The preparation of Jewish teachers for schools in the interior must be the number one priority of the Jewish community in Buenos Aires." During January and February, the Wa'ad Ha-hinnukh of AMIA, directed by Jaime Barylko, held seminars in the seaside resort of Necochea for administrators of the Jewish school system. A statistical study published by the Wa'ad Ha-hinnukh indicated a 15.7 per cent drop in the enrollment of Jewish primary and secondary school pupils in greater Buenos Aires. On the secondary level the drop-out rate was 49.8 per cent. There were 31 kindergarten and primary schools in Buenos Aires, and 15 in surrounding areas. In July, Rabbi Reuben Nisenbom (Conservative) returned from Bogotá, Colombia to become a professor at the Seminario Rabínico Latinoamericano. At the beginning of November, Argentine ORT conducted its annual science fair. In the same month, the Sephardic community opened a new kindergarten, "Toranit."

Dozens of Jewish teachers left their positions because of insufficient salaries. There were virtually no male Hebrew teachers, as it proved impossible to maintain a family on the salaries offered. The Jewish press, Jewish communal leaders, and even officials of the education system repeatedly complained about the failure of Jewish education to strengthen Jewish identity.

Jacob Rubel was director of the local center for Jewish studies established under the auspices of Tel Aviv University and the Jewish Agency. Some 80 students enrolled in courses offered there. The Israel Ministry of Education and Culture extended recognition to graduates of Bet Midrash Lemorim Datiim, the religious normal school of Buenos Aires.

Religion

A lack of religious vitality and dynamism was evidenced in the estimated number of Jews present in the 50-odd synagogues of greater Buenos Aires during Rosh Hashanah. By the most generous count, some 13,000 Jews out of a total of 225,000 attended services. On Yom Kippur, the figure increased by some 10,000.

In March, cornerstone ceremonies were held for the new building of the Orthodox Kolel, Rabino Marcos Guertzenstein. In November, Rabbi Reuben Nisenbom joined Rabbis Marshall T. Meyer and Mordecai Edery in the rabbinate of the Comunidad Bet El, which had hosted some 4,000 Jews on the High Holy Days. In December, groundbreaking ceremonies were conducted for the Seminario Rabínico Latinoamericano. Both DAIA and the Seminario gave farewell dinners for Father Jorge Mejia, professor of Bible and editor of the Catholic weekly *Criterio,* before he left for the Vatican to assume the position of secretary for Jewish-Christian relations.

The Isidoro Mazel religious school gave its annual award to Abraham Berg, president of the committee for construction of the Marcos Guertzenstein yeshiva. The Instituto Superior de Estudios Religiosos (Higher Institute for Religious Studies) of the Seminario Rabínico Latinoamericano was active in ecumenical affairs. Rabbi Robert Graetz (Reform), local director of the World Union of Progressive Judaism, left the Comunidad Lamroth Hakol to devote his full attention to Temple Emanu-El. Rabbi Shlomo Ben Hamu was designated as interim chief rabbi of AMIA. Due to the instability of the political situation, and terrorist activity in the Province of Córdoba, Camp Ramah Argentina of the Comunidad Bet El did not open in 1977.

Publications

The only Jewish weekly in Spanish was *Mundo Israelita,* which celebrated its 54th anniversary; the only Yiddish daily was *Di Presse,* which completed its 60th year of publication. Other periodicals included the quarterly *Majshavot,* published by the World Council of Synagogues and the Seminario Rabínico Latinoamericano; the German language weekly *Jüdisches Wochenblatt;* the Yiddish *Davka;* the Mapam fortnightly *Nueva Sion;* and the Spanish language fortnightly *La Luz.* The Sociedad Hebraica Argentina's *Davar* published a special edition in honor of its 50th anniversary.

Several books of Jewish interest appeared during the year. In March, the second edition of Marcos Aguinis' novel *Refugiados* ("Refugees") was published. DAIA edited another book by the same author on the Argentine naval hero Almirante Guillermo Brown. The book was presented to leading figures of the Argentine navy at a special ceremony in November. In May, Simja Shen published a book of 12 short stories dealing with the Holocaust and other Jewish themes.

Abraham Weiss, editor of Acervo Cultural publishing house, continued the publication of a bilingual edition of the Talmud. He had already published the complete works of Josephus and Philo of Alexandria. Five volumes of Baruch Spinoza's writings were also published during the year.

Jaime Barylko's *An Introduction to Judaism,* published by Flaischman and Fischbein, appeared in November. In the same month, Simon Dubnow's *History of Hasidism* was reissued by Sigal Publishing. YIVO continued its important series, *Musterwerk fun dee Idisher Literatur,* under the editorship of Samuel Rollansky. Editorial Yehuda commenced publication of a bilingual Tanach with a translation of Rashi's commentary. The Biblioteca Popular Judía, sponsored by the Latin American Jewish Congress, celebrated the appearance of its 200th Judaica booklet, 27 of which had been prepared by Dr. Jaime Barylko.

Personalia

Betzalel Baler, Yiddish author and journalist, leader in the Comunidad Bet El, died in Buenos Aires in February, at the age of 84. Dr. Otto Kauders, renowned international lawyer, active in the Seminario Rabínico Latinoamericano, who lived in Buenos Aires from 1940 to 1976, died in Denver, Colorado on March 6, at the age of 67. León Bernstein, commercial director of Paidos Publishing, past president of Comunidad Bet El, past secretary of AMIA, active in the Seminario Rabínico Latinoamericano, died in Madrid in May, at the age of 64. Naum Radzichowski, secretary general of the Zionist Labor Party, ex-president of the Argentine Zionist Organization, member of the Jewish Agency, ex-secretary and ex-vice-president of AMIA, died in Buenos Aires in July, at the age of 57. Joseph Buttenwieser, born in Hamburg, Germany, leader of Comunidad Bet El and Seminario Rabínico Latinoamericano, who came to Buenos Aires in 1950, died on August 9, at the age of 78. Paloma Efron, leading Argentine chanteuse, actress, and television figure, active in Zionist affairs, died in Buenos Aires on September 1, at the age of 63. José Ber Gelbard, Argentine industrialist, Peronist leader and ex-minister of finance, died in Washington D.C. on October 4. Jak Spolski, active in AMIA, Hospital Israelita and Keren Hayesod, as well as the Jerusalem synagogue and school, died in Buenos Aires in November, at the age of 74.

NAOMI MEYER

Western Europe

Great Britain

Domestic Affairs

Events in great britain in 1976 and 1977 were dominated by economic developments, both favorable and unfavorable. At the end of the period, the country was in a decidedly optimistic mood, although it was doubtful whether the basic problems of productivity had been solved.

Nineteen seventy-six began promisingly enough with a gradual fall in the minimum lending rate from 11 to 9 per cent. In March, however, events took a turn for the worse. The government's general economic strategy was rejected in Parliament by 28 votes. The lending rate rose from 9 per cent in March to 15 per cent in October. The value of the pound sterling fell from $2.02 to $1.70, and did not start to recover until the government announced budget cuts in July and December. These cuts paved the way for a loan from the International Monetary Fund amounting to £2,300 million. The economy was also bolstered by a loan of £1,765 million from the Bank of International Settlements and a loan of £873 million from a number of British, West German, and American banks.

The ruling Labor Party dealt with the early phases of Britain's economic difficulties under the leadership of James Callaghan, who on March 16, 1976 replaced Prime Minister Harold Wilson. Callaghan had to contend with Labor's growing unpopularity. In May 1976, the Conservatives made substantial gains in local government elections; in June and July, the Labor majority was further reduced; in November, Labor lost two additional seats to the Conservatives; in December, the Opposition made more gains. Labor's losses were partially offset when a pact was made with the Liberals in March 1977.

The economic news continued to be mixed. The lending rate, which had reached 14 per cent at the end of December 1976, fell to seven per cent by November 1977. The rate of inflation at the end of 1977 stood at a low 13 per cent. Most importantly, as oil began to flow from wells in the North Sea, Great Britain enjoyed a balance of payments surplus, with reserves reaching a record level of more than $20,000 million. However, unemployment was rampant (1.5 million people), and there was a rash of strikes.

Overall, in the second half of 1976 and in the first half of 1977, Great Britain's position in the international economy advanced, while the second half of 1977 witnessed a substantial improvement in the standard of living. A sense of well-being came to the fore, and was augmented by the celebration of the Queen's Silver Jubilee. The standing of the Labor Government correspondingly improved.

Intergroup Relations

Despite the introduction in June 1977 of an amended Race Relations Act, which made the fomenting of racial hatred a criminal offense, the extreme right-wing National Front continued to grow. Aided by unemployment and the general frustration engendered by Britain's economic problems, the National Front put forward large numbers of candidates in local government elections and parliamentary by-elections, and sometimes succeeded in beating Liberal candidates for third place. In the May 1977 Greater London Council elections, the National Front contested all but one of 92 seats, and polled 119,000 votes—more than its total in the 1974 parliamentary elections throughout Britain. The National Front won no seats, but pushed the Liberals into fourth place in 32 constituencies.

An Essex University report concluded that the National Front had become a significant factor on the British scene, and was making rapid gains. In May 1977, the Board of Deputies joined Asian and West Indian organizations in a campaign to stem the growth of the National Front.

All the major political parties expressed opposition to racism. In September 1976, the Liberal Party assembly adopted a program of action against increasing racism and fascism in Britain. In October of the same year, the Conservative Party adopted a resolution calling for restrictions on immigration, but stressing that all those entering the country should be treated as equal and welcome members of British society. In December 1977, the Labor Party, in conjunction with the Trade Union Council, announced that it was stepping up a nationwide campaign against racism; its theme was, "The National Front is a Nazi Front." In December, an all-party Joint Committee Against Racism was established by the Board of Deputies and immigrant groups.

Violence at National Front marches in London in April and August 1977 led to the banning of a march planned for Manchester in October. In January 1978, 90 Labor MPs signed a motion calling for the dismissal of a judge who had acquitted former National Front Chairman John Kingsley Read of inciting racial hatred.

Foreign Relations

Great Britain's foreign relations were dominated by a concern over events in Rhodesia. In February 1976, Lord Greenhill, former head of the diplomatic service, flew to Salisbury to determine whether there was any possibility that British influence might help promote a settlement. In September of that year, a conference of Black and white Rhodesian leaders was held in Geneva to discuss the form an interim government might take. The meeting ended without success. In May 1977, the initiative passed to an Anglo-American consultative group which met with Premier Ian Smith, Black nationalist spokesmen, and the leaders of neighboring African countries. This also produced no immediate results, but had the advantage of involving the United States in British endeavors. Toward the end of 1977, Premier Smith took steps to reach an agreement with moderate Black leaders on majority rule.

Relations with Israel

In June 1976, for the first time, an Israeli head of state (Ephraim Katzir) was entertained by the Queen of England. In December 1977, Great Britain officially welcomed Prime Minister Menachem Begin, thus ending British ostracism of the former Irgun Zvai Leumi leader, while continuing to affirm that she would "sustain Israel on the difficult road to a lasting peace and not support any settlement which jeopardize[d] her existence or security." At the same time, Prime Minister James Callaghan, in an October 1977 address to the Board of Deputies, indicated British support for the establishment of a Palestinian "homeland of some kind," provided it did not present an "unacceptable threat to Israel's security."

In the wake of President Anwar Sadat's peace initiative, Begin asked Callaghan to urge his partners in the European Economic Community to give the Israeli-Egyptian negotiations a chance to succeed without interference. Following his meeting with Begin, Callaghan voiced satisfaction that both Begin and Sadat "recognize the need for a comprehensive settlement." In December 1977, Britain, like the United States, voiced approval of the proposals presented by Prime Minister Begin to President Sadat.

Despite assurances in February 1976 that Britain would not supply the Middle East with arms which might provoke a new Arab-Israeli war or hinder a peace settlement, British Defense Secretary Fred Mulley, in September 1977, signed a £500 million contract designed to strengthen the Saudi Arabian air force. In January 1978, Mulley also signed, with the member countries of the Arab Organization for Industrialization, a "memorandum" calling for the supply of military equipment. The Defense Ministry stated that the new agreement "should help to establish a leading position for Britain's defense industries with the AOI countries and, through them, with the Arab world generally."

A poll commissioned by the Council for the Advancement of Arab-British Understanding and published in September 1977, showed that 70 per cent of the population were sympathetic to the Jewish people, but that 43 per cent were opposed to Zionism. In the conflict over Palestine, 29 per cent said their sympathies were mainly with the Israelis, while nine per cent sided with the Palestinians. Seventy-six per cent of those polled felt that the Arabs should agree to recognize Israel. These results confirmed a trend observed by the Institute of Jewish Affairs in a survey of British public opinion polls conducted between the Six-Day War and August 1976.

The study had noted a lessening of sympathy for Israel (from 46 to 36 per cent) and a slight rise in support for the Arabs (from four to seven per cent).

Prime Minister James Callaghan, who had four Jews serving in his cabinet, assured the Labor Friends of Israel in October 1977, that "our country's devotion to Israel transcends governments. And this remains the policy of Her Majesty's Government whatever government may be in office in Israel." Michael Fidler, director of the Conservative Friends of Israel, reacted to Likud's election victory by stating: "Conservatives are naturally gratified that Conservative opinion has proved its electoral validity. However, so far as the Conservative Friends are concerned, their prime objective is friendship with the people and the State of Israel rather than with any political party." Lord Carrington, Conservative peer leader, assured the group, which claimed the support of 110 MPs, that "the next Conservative government will be committed not only to Israel's survival, but also to the achievement of a just and fair solution" of the Arab-Israel conflict. In April 1977, Jeremy Thorpe, principal Liberal Party spokesman on foreign affairs, described the Young Liberals position on the Israel-Arab conflict as "lunatic." The group, at its annual conference, had voiced approval of the United Nations' resolution equating Zionism with racism, and expressed support for the Palestine Liberation Organization (PLO). Pro-Palestinian Michael Steed was elected Liberal Party president in October.

In November 1977, the Council for the Advancement of Arab-British Understanding, while saluting President Sadat's "personal courage" in going to Jerusalem, reiterated its long-held position on the Palestinians, urging the foreign secretary to "establish contact with the PLO leadership and assure them that Britain recognizes and esteems the way in which they have moved . . . towards acceptance of the need for peaceful co-existence between Israelis and Palestinians . . ." Both Zionist and pro-Arab elements in the House of Commons signed a motion welcoming Sadat's visit to Israel and congratulating both Sadat and Begin "for the new hope they have given to the world . . ."

Continual purchases by Middle East investors of British property, including London's Dorchester Hotel, popular venue for Jewish functions, aroused comment throughout the period. Exhibitions on "Palestine" and "Moslem Jerusalem" formed part of a four-month "Festival of Islam" in Spring 1976. In July 1977, Foreign Secretary David Owen opened a new Arab-British Center in London.

Britain gave only belated and reserved approval to the Israeli rescue raid at Entebbe in July 1976. Labor and Conservative members of Parliament, however, introduced motions congratulating the Israeli Government on "brilliantly and bravely confounding an act of air piracy." They also voiced condemnation of Ugandan President Idi Amin "for aiding and arming international terrorists."

In January 1977, Britain signed the European Convention on the Suppression of Terrorism. This came in the wake of the release of Arab terrorist Abu Daoud by a French court. Nonetheless, in August 1977, a senior British diplomat (James Craig, the British ambassador to Syria) met openly, for the first time, with a PLO official. The Foreign Office stated, however, that Britain had not changed its policy of refusing to recognize the PLO "until it recognized the right of the State of Israel to exist."

The National Union of Students voted in December 1977 to amend its constitution to permit the suspension of student unions denying democratic rights to individual students. This came at the end of a two-year anti-Jewish campaign conducted by Arab and radical students on university campuses throughout Britain. Motions equating Zionism with racism, or condemning Israel as a racist state, were frequently passed by student unions. Attempts were made to expel Zionist groups from the National Union of Students.

Jewish student responses to this campaign of vilification ranged from attempts to defeat anti-Israel motions to appeals to the courts and the Commission for Racial Equality. In November 1977, the Zionist Federation (ZF) stated: "It is the responsibility of the Jewish community as a whole and the Zionist movement in particular to seek every opportunity to aid the students in their battle, and to ensure that adequate funds and other resources are made available to the Union of Jewish Students." In August, the Zionist Federation, in cooperation with other organizations, had established an Academics for Israel Committee, and in September had sponsored, together with the B'nai B'rith Hillel Foundation, Union of Jewish Students, Board of Deputies, and Britain/Israel Public Affairs Committee, a "Campus Confrontation" conference.

In September 1977, the Israel Embassy in London accused the *Sunday Times* of conducting a "crude, systematic and ugly smear campaign" to isolate Israel in world opinion. This followed a renewal of allegations of torture of Arab detainees in Israeli interrogation centers. A new independent Arab daily, *Al-Arab*, began publication in June 1977.

Arab Boycott

In July 1977, Lord Byers introduced into the House of Lords a Foreign Boycotts Bill which would, if passed, make it illegal to refuse to do business on the basis of a foreign boycott. This action followed a year of protest against the Arab boycott. In February, the Anti-Boycott Coordination Committee of the Anglo-Israel Chamber of Commerce had called on members of Parliament to urge the Government to take a more "forthright stand in defense of freedom of trade." In March, a new all-party parliamentary group was established to bring maximum pressure on the Foreign Office and the Department of Trade. In May, another campaign was launched demanding government action against the boycott.

Despite these efforts, Secretary of State for Trade Edmund Dell reiterated in Parliament in November that while he deplored the boycott, he had no intention of acting to stop it. He stated: "No figures are available for the effect of the boycott on our trade. We are keeping a close watch on the preparation of the American regulations as regards both their possible extra-territorial impact on the United

Kingdom and their potential effect on United States firms and their trading operations. But I have no present intention of introducing similar legislation."

In July 1977 a branch of the Bank Hapoalim was opened in Manchester. This step was taken as part of an all-out effort by the Israeli Government to close the gap in the trade balance between Israel and Great Britain, by persuading British businessmen to invest in Israel. In October, the UK-Israel Joint Committee, which had been established in 1976 by the British Trade Department and the Israeli Ministry of Industry, Commerce, and Tourism, noted an increase in trade between the two countries, and stated that growth prospects were good. The British delegation, however, refused to go beyond the Government's position of deploring the boycott and supplying information on it to British firms, while leaving companies free to act as they wished.

JEWISH COMMUNITY

Demography

The Jewish population of Great Britain was estimated to be 410,000. Leading Jewish population centers were London (280,000), Manchester (35,000), Leeds (18,000), and Glasgow (13,000).

Synagogue marriages declined 24 per cent in 1976, according to information gathered by the Board of Deputies. The 1976 figure of 1,397 was the lowest peacetime total in this century, and showed a faster rate of decline than the national average. Two hundred marriages performed under Reform auspices accounted for 14.5 per cent of the total, while 90 performed under Liberal auspices added up to 6.5 per cent of the whole. Of Orthodox marriages, only the ultra-orthodox sector showed an increase, rising to 97, or six per cent of the 1976 total. Other studies indicated that the ultra-orthodox also had more children than the Anglo-Jewish norm (1.7 per family).

Burials and cremations under Jewish auspices, numbering 5,068 in 1976, remained constant. One trend emerging from a comparison of marriage and death rates was the decline of provincial communities. Young people (those marrying) were likely to be found in London, where it was estimated two-thirds of Anglo-Jewry lived.

Communal Activities

An anonymous gift of £500,000 to the Central Council of Jewish Social Services financed the purchase of a North-West London Day Center slated to serve an eventual 250 Jewish Welfare Board (JWB) and Blind Society clients daily. Although JWB was forced to close its Samuel Lewis convalescent home in April 1976, because of rising costs, it opened a new North London residential home in August. This marked the end of a ten-year expansion program involving the expenditure of £14.5 million on 21 facilities. In April 1977, plans were announced for the first home to be administered by JWB for mentally-handicapped adults.

In December 1976, Prince Charles opened a £1.5 million extension to Nightingale House in Wandsworth, London, making the home, housing nearly 400 elderly Jews, the largest of its kind in the United Kingdom. In December 1977, the Duke of Edinburgh opened Edinburgh House, a new home for the aged, in Wembley, Middlesex, under Sephardic auspices.

In July 1976, Lord Hirshfield reported the establishment of the Norwood Trust to provide aid to Jewish children overseas. In May 1977, a new fund-raising organization, Norwood Aid, Ltd., was formed to support the Norwood Foundation.

In January 1976, Raymond Goldwater, chairman of the Religious Advisory Committee of Anglo-Jewish Youth, stated that aspects of the current Anglo-Jewish youth scene were "terrifying." He pointed out that only eight of the 78 full-time youth workers in the Jewish community were both professionally qualified and Jewishly knowledgeable; that 64 per cent had been in their present positions for less than two years; and that one in five vacant youth leadership positions could not be filled for lack of suitable candidates. Both in London and the provinces, no more than a quarter of Jewish youngsters were associated with any kind of Jewish or Zionist youth activity, Goldwater noted. In the wake of his comments, plans were announced for several new London youth centers.

Zionism

The final report of the Sacher committee of inquiry into the reorganization of Jewish Agency activities in Britain was published in June 1976. It described the existence of three separate Zionist educational bodies (the Department for Education and Culture, the Department for Torah Education and Culture, and the Youth and Education Department of the Jewish National Fund) as "unnecessary and perhaps wasteful," and called for the gradual replacement of Israelis by local teachers in Jewish schools.

Eric Moonman's report to the first biennial Zionist Federation meeting in July 1976 included a call for a new drive to widen and strengthen the Zionist movement within the community. Discussions were held with Reform synagogues and the Maccabi Association about affiliation with the Federation, and the Mizrachi Federation was offered "association" status. Cooperation also improved between ZF and the Joint Israel Appeal (JIA).

ZF Secretary Aubrey Litt described the year as one of "consolidation, development and expansion." He indicated that ZF was beginning to attract greater numbers of young people and intellectuals. In September, JIA launched an all-out effort to attract more workers.

In December 1977, agreement was reached in the long-standing negotiations over the distribution of slots to the Zionist Congress, which was to be held in February

1978. This eliminated the need for elections, which would have cost an estimated £100,000. Under the agreement, Herut increased its representation by 100 per cent. In addition, four parties—United Zionists, Poale Zion, Herut and Mizrachi—undertook to have students included in their delegations.

A highly successful solidarity gathering in support of Israel was held in March 1976. The gathering was sponsored jointly by the Board of Deputies, ZF, and JIA.

In December 1977, the weekly *Jewish Observer and Middle East Review,* official organ of ZF, ceased publication. It was to be replaced by a new monthly in May 1978.

There was a decline in *aliyah* from 511 people in 1975 to 352 people in 1976. This led to the transfer of responsibility for *aliyah* promotion from the Jewish Agency to ZF. In May 1976, the Jewish Agency Aliyah Department in London embarked on a study aimed at discovering why many would-be candidates either postponed or abandoned their intention to settle in Israel. At the same time, ZF stepped up its campaign by appointing a full-time officer whose sole responsibility was encouraging *aliyah*. In September 1976, ZF's national executive council decided to mount an *aliyah* promotion drive with the participation of an Israeli "flying emissary." In September 1977, Shalom Solly was appointed executive director of a newly-created National Aliyah and Volunteers Council. Solly saw the committee as working to coordinate all *aliyah* promotion in Great Britain.

Soviet Jewry

The plight of Soviet Jewry continued to be of great concern to British Jews. Chief Rabbi Immanuel Jakobovits stated in December 1976 that the hopes generated by his historic mission to the Soviet Union a year before had largely dissipated. Various groups, including the National Council for Soviet Jewry (NCSJ, launched February 1976), National Youth Council for Soviet Jewry (formed April 1976), Women's Campaign for Soviet Jewry, and Conscience '77, sought to utilize every opportunity to convey their message to Soviet authorities and the British public. Visits by Soviet Foreign Minister Andrei Gromyko in March 1976 and Soviet party leader Boris Ponomarov in November 1976, provided opportunities for continuous demonstrations which, in turn, sparked parliamentary and press criticism of Soviet policy.

Soviet Jews who had succeeded in leaving Russia visited Great Britain. During Solidarity Week, Chanukah 1977, eight such emigrants spoke at nationwide events. In April 1977, 6,000 marchers protested at the Soviet Embassy, demanding the release of Anatoly Shcharansky. In June 1977, hundreds of MPs were approached in a mass lobbying effort by NCSJ. The first conference organized by the interdenominational working group of NCSJ, held at Westminster Cathedral in May 1977, heard the Archbishop of York condemn Soviet authorities for denying Jews their rights.

Religion

The primary concern of the United Synagogue (US) continued to be adaptation to population shifts. The need to provide for newer communities growing in London's outer areas lay behind the introduction of a "regionalist" plan. The plan called for the mandatory retirement of individual rabbis in declining communities, and the use of regional ministers who would be paid by several synagogues. Similarly, there was to be a redistribution of resources. Thus, the £55,000 obtained from the sale of the Stoke Newington Synagogue in June 1976 was earmarked to meet synagogue building costs in London's periphery. Early in 1977, several synagogues in East London were closed.

An indication of US's intention to expand the scope of its activities in the new areas could be seen in a proposal to amend the Scheme of the United Synagogue Act, granting it the power to promote the establishment of schools. Debate on this proposal, one of 69 presented for the restructuring and merging of constituent and district synagogues, was in process at the end of 1977.

Chief Rabbi Immanuel Jakobovits proposed to transfer such general synagogue functions as education, youth, and culture from boards of management to new synagogue councils which would have both male and female elected representatives. "The proposal would enable women to participate fully in the activities of congregations," a statement in January 1978 said.

The first major study of a suburban Jewish community in Great Britain was begun in November under the direction of the Board of Deputies, to establish whether the facilities existing in the expanding community of Redbridge, outside London, would be adequate for the future Jewish population.

Vacancies on US's Beth Din were filled in June 1976 by the appointment of Rabbis Casriel David Kaplin and Isaac Lerner as full-time *dayanim;* in October 1977, Rabbi Zalmon J. Alony became Federation Rosh Beth Din.

Britain's 9,000-strong Sephardic community, organized into some ten or eleven congregations, also witnessed changes. At the annual meeting of the London congregation, in March 1977, it was decided to appoint Dr. Solomon Gaon (whose retirement as Haham of the congregation caused a furor in January) Haham of the Association of Sephardi Synagogues, comprising congregations in London and Manchester. The decision partly implemented a recommendation, made in April 1976 by a special long-term planning committee of the London Spanish and Portuguese Synagogues, that the Haham be an officer of the Association, elected by and serving it, rather than senior minister of a specific congregation. The Haham was also to head the Sephardic Beth Din which was under the Association's aegis.

The London Board for Shechita raised its fees in February 1977, despite concern about a sharp reduction in Kosher meat and poultry consumption, partially attributed to high prices. Causes of the fee rise were higher staff salaries and the costs involved in bringing the East Ham, London poultry abattoir up to EEC standards. In London, Kashrus Commission President, Frank Levine called for a merger of

Kashrut supervision by the Ashkenazic and Sephardic communities. A first step in this direction was taken in May 1976 when the London Board for Shechita began to share office space with the Kashrut Commission.

Jewish Education

Great concern was expressed over the state of Jewish education in Great Britain. While 25 per cent of Jewish children attended day schools, over 30 per cent received no Jewish education at all. Hillel Foundation Deputy Chairman Fred Worms, in June 1976, described the Jewish educational scene as "never worse." His suggestion that radical improvement be supported by a newly-created division of JIA devoted to fund-raising for education aroused controversy, despite the publication of figures evidencing a drop in the number of children provided for by the London Board of Jewish Religious Education, as well as a critical shortage of places in Jewish day schools. In October 1977, an Association for the Advancement of Jewish Day Schools was founded.

In December 1976, a group of Jewish educators proposed summoning Education Secretary Shirley Williams before the European Commission of Human Rights for alleged discrimination against Jewish schools, claiming that the department of education was breaking the law by failing to grant such schools sufficient aid. Professor S.J. Prais of London's City University and the National Institute of Economic and Social Research argued that the Jewish community was experiencing "gross inequality," with only 20 per cent of Jewish children of primary school age being granted state aid, as compared to 80 per cent of all Roman Catholic children. In July, Williams promised full cooperation in establishing improved Jewish educational facilities, by pooling students from different Jewish communities into a single student body, and by turning defunct secular schools into Jewish schools.

Reflecting the concern about Jewish education, the revised 1977 program of the Chief Rabbi's Jewish Educational Development Trust sought to promote state aid for established and newly-completed Jewish schools. The program also recognized the need for the Jewish community to assist synagogue schools in meeting operating costs, and called for scholarships to encourage undergraduates in the field of Jewish education, in-service training of teachers, and the use of sophisticated educational technology.

In March 1977, US joined with the B'nai B'rith Hillel Foundation and the London Jewish Students' Association in a program to provide counselling to Jewish students in 32 colleges and polytechnics in the Greater London area. In November 1977, Asher Fishman, chairman of the London Board of Jewish Religious Education, announced plans for a joint study program at Northern Polytechnic and Jews' College. In July 1976, the latter school had reported its largest graduating class (22) in 50 years. In July 1977, Dr. Irving Jacobs was appointed to its newly-established Sir Israel Brodie Chair.

Publications

The Jewish Chronicle Book Award, given in 1976 to Rabbi Lionel Blue (who, with Rabbi Jonathan Magonet, co-edited a new Reform Synagogues of Great Britain prayer book) for his *To Heaven with Scribes and Pharisees,* was enlarged in 1977 to become the Jewish Chronicle-Harold H. Wingate Literary Awards. The non-fiction prize was awarded to Chaim Bermant for *Coming Home,* an autobiography. In the fiction category the winner was David Markish for *The Beginning.*

Two considerable contributions to Anglo-Jewish history were Bill Williams' *The Making of Manchester Jewry 1740–1875* and Aubrey Newman's *The United Synagogue 1870–1970.* Varying aspects of Jewish history were presented in Magnus Magnusson's *B.C.: the Archaeology of the Bible Lands;* Joan Comay's *The Hebrew Kings;* Geza Vermes' *The Dead Sea Scrolls;* Nicholas de Lange's *Origen and the Jews;* Bernard S. Jackson's *Essays in Jewish and Comparative Legal History;* Arthur Koestler's *The Thirteenth Tribe: The Khazar Empire and its Heritage;* Robert S. Wistrich's *Revolutionary Jews from Marx to Trotsky;* Martin Gilbert's *The Jews of Russia: Their History in Maps and Photographs;* Richard Gutteridge's *Open Thy Mouth for the Dumb: The German Evangelical Church and the Jews 1879–1950;* H.J. Zimmel's *The Echo of the Nazi Holocaust in Rabbinic Literature;* Bradley Smith's *Reaching Judgement at Nuremburg;* and David Irving's *Hitler's War.*

The Arab-Israeli conflict figured prominently in a large number of works: Mohamed Sid-Ahmed's *After the Guns Fall Silent;* David Hirst's *The Gun and the Olive Branch;* Galia Golan's *Yom Kippur and After: The Soviet Union and the Middle East Crisis;* A.I. Dawisha's *Egypt in the Arab World;* David Vital's *The Origin of Zionism;* James Cameron's *The Making of Israel;* Sir Alec Kirkbride's *From the Wings: Amman Memoirs, 1947–1951;* Martin Gilbert's *Jerusalem Illustrated History Atlas* and *The Jews of Arab Lands: Their History in Maps;* Richard Deacon's *The Israeli Secret Service;* and David B. Tinnin's *Hit Team.*

Autobiographical and biographical works included Desmond Stewart's *T.E. Lawrence;* H.M. Blumberg's *Weizman, His Life and Times;* Robert Rhodes' *Victor Cazalet;* Lord Rothschild's *Meditations of a Broomstick;* Yehudi Menuhin's *Unfinished Journey;* Charles Landstone's *I Gate Crashed;* Evelyn Cowan's *Portrait of Alice;* and Lionel L. Loewe's *Basil Henriques.*

Among notable works of fiction were Dan Jacobson's *The Confessions of Josef Balsz;* Alexander Baron's *France is Dying;* Chaim Bermant's *The Second Mrs. Whitberg;* Wolf Mankowitz's *The Day of the Women and the Night of the Men: Fables;* Elaine Feinstein's *The Ecstasy of Dr. Miriam Garner;* and *New Writings from Israel,* edited by Jacob Sonntag.

A book of note dealing with religious themes was Chief Rabbi Immanuel Jakobovits' *The Timely and the Timeless: Jews, Judaism and Society in a Storm-Tossed Decade. A Bibliography of the Printed Works of James Parkes,* compiled by Sidney Sugarman and Diana Bailey and edited by David Pennie, was intended to coincide with Parkes's 80th birthday.

Personalia

British Jews who received honors in 1976 and 1977 included Reginald Freeson, minister for Housing and Construction, and Robert Edward Sheldon, financial secretary to the Treasury, who were made Privy Counsellors. Life peerages were awarded to Sir Frank Schon, chairman of the National Research Development Corporation; Sir Bernard Delfont, chairman of EMI Film and Theatre Corporation; Sir Lew Grade, chairman of the Associated Television Corporation; Sir Joseph Kagan, chairman of Kagan Textiles; Sir Max Rayne, industrialist; Sir Joseph Ellis Stone, Harold Wilson's personal physician; and Sir Arthur George Weidenfeld, publisher. Knighthoods were conferred on David Napley, president of the Law Society; Leonard Gordon Wolfson, chairman of the Wolfson Foundation; Judge Rudolph Lyons, circuit judge and recorder of Liverpool; Professor Otto Kahn-Freund, law scholar; Eric Merton Miller, chairman of the Peachey Property Corporation and treasurer of Socialist International; and Sigmund Sternberg, chairman of Commodities Research Unit. Leo Pliatzky, second permanent secretary to the Treasury, was appointed knight commander of the Order of the Bath; Lord Zuckerman became president of the Zoological Society; and Alfred John Balcombe was made a judge of the High Court.

British Jews who died in 1976 included: Sir Frank Milton, chief metropolitan magistrate, 1967–1975, in January, aged 70; Cyril Quixano Henriques, eminent Zionist, in January, aged 96; Jack Djanogly, leading British industrialist, in January; Professor Ernst Joseph Cohn, authority on German law, in January, aged 72; Alfred Scheur, Czech-born archaeologist, in February, aged 78; Maurice Jacobson, composer and pianist, in February, aged 80; Rabbi Dr. Ignaz Maybaum, leading exponent of progressive Judaism, in March, aged 79; Olga Somech Phillips, writer, historian and lecturer, in March, aged 74; Sid James, actor, in April, aged 62; Maurice Williams, philatelist, in June, aged 70; Sidney Bright, musician, in July, aged 71; Levi Gertner, leading Anglo-Jewish educator, in July, aged 68; Emil (Solly) Sachs, former South African trade union leader and opponent of racism, in July, aged 72; Harry Samuels, communal leader, in July, aged 82; Sam Keller, former fly-weight and bantam-weight boxer, in July, aged 90; Simon Rurka, joint treasurer, Federation of Synagogues, in July, aged 72; Osias Freshwater, real estate magnate, in July, aged 76; Dr. Leonard Snowman, physician and *mohel,* in August, aged 76; Mrs. Carmel Gilbert, vice-president, Federation of Women Zionists, in August; Dr. Meir Gertner, educator and Hebraist, in August, aged 71; Gina Bachauer, pianist, in August, aged 63; B.B.Lieberman, former Board of Deputies vice-president and treasurer, in August, aged 87; Harry Gaventa, former president, London Shechita Board, 1947–57, in September, aged 81; Millie Chissick, actress, in September, aged 95; Peter Ury, journalist and composer, in September, aged 55; Elazar Halevy, Hebrew educator and founding member of the Mizrachi Federation in Britain, in October; Cyril Bennett, program controller, London Weekend Television, in November, aged 48; Julius Newman, president, Jewish Deaf Association, in November, aged 85; Jacob Bornfriend, artist, in November, aged 72; Rabbi Dr. Arnost Zvi Ehrman, scholar, in December, aged 62; Sir Henry d'Avigdor-Goldsmid, politician, soldier, communal leader, in December, aged 67; Dr. Abraham Roith, psychiatrist, in December, aged 49; Edward Elkin Mocatta, bullion broker, leader in the Reform movement, in December, aged 60; Eliahu Dangoor, prominent Baghdad publisher, in December, aged 93.

Jews who died in 1977 included: Rabbi Dr. Eugene Newman, minister of London's Golders Green Synagogue for over 20 years, in January, aged 63; Hugh Goitein, professor of commercial law at Birmingham University, 1930–1962, in January, aged 80; Sydney Simon Primost, author, broadcaster, in January, aged 76; Theodore Goodman, art and music critic, in February, aged 65; Camille Rachmil Honig, Yiddish writer, in February, aged 71; Isy Geiger, musician, in February, aged 90; Alan Nabarro, communal leader, in March, aged 62; Stefanie Felsenburg, psychiatrist, in March, aged 74; Liza Fuchsova, pianist, in March, aged 63; Dr. Freddy Himmelweit, virologist, bacteriologist, in March, aged 74; Aaron Harold Levy, opthalmic surgeon, in April, aged 101; Benjamin Levin (popularly known as Issy Bonn), comedian, in April, aged 74; Dr. Ralph Jessel, deputy president, Union of Liberal and Progressive Synagogues, in April, aged 70; Ethel Moss Levy, vice-principal and principal, Evelina de Rothschild School, Jerusalem, 1925–1960, in May; Leslie Maurice, Lord Lever of Ardwick, Member of Parliament, 1950–1970, in July, aged 72; Rabbi Yitzchak Dubow, instructor, Manchester yeshiva, in July, aged over 90; Arnold Silverstone, Lord Ashdown, joint chairman, Conservative Party, since 1974, in July, aged 65; Henry Cohen, Lord Birkenhead, physician, in August, aged 77; Professor Sir Misha Black, architect and industrial designer, in August, aged 66; Dr. Eichon Hindren, pediatrician, in August, aged 69; Jack Morrison, real estate magnate, communal worker, in August, aged 75; Isidore Godfrey, musical director, D'Oyly Carte Company, 1929–68, in September, aged 76; Marco Bolan (born Mark Feld), pop star, in September, aged 29; Isaiah Shachar, Jewish scholar, in September; Charles Solomon, journalist and mathematician, in October, aged 78; Rabbi Beresh Finklestein, scholar of rabbinic literature, in October, in mid-80's; Millie Miller, Member of Parliament, in October, aged 54; Sir Michael Balcon, doyen of the British film industry, in October, aged 81; Julius Lee, professor of endocrine physiology, in November, aged 58; Leo Schafler, former deputy general secretary, Zionist Federation, in November, aged 87; Gottfried Moller, founder of Chevrat Bikkur Cholim, in November, aged 78; Jacob Braude, communal leader, author of Jewish educational surveys, in December, aged 75; Arthur Erdelyi, professor of mathematics, Edinburgh University, in December, aged 69.

LIONEL AND MIRIAM KOCHAN

France

Domestic Affairs

NINETEEN SEVENTY-SEVEN was marked by disunity and polarization in the two political camps vying for power in the March 1978 national legislative elections: the left opposition and the so-called "presidential majority." On the left, a full schism between the Socialist and Communist parties brought to an end the "common program" initiated in 1972, and entirely changed the outlook for the elections. The left coalition, which had been considered an almost sure winner after the March municipal elections, was greatly weakened. Polls indicated that the left-wing parties would receive about 52 per cent of the vote in the first round; but would, in the absence of an electoral agreement between Socialists and Communists, be defeated in the second.

Discord in the governing majority was due primarily to friction between the formerly dominant Gaullist faction and the more moderate centrist elements, or "Giscardiens." There was personal antagonism between ex-Prime Minister Jacques Chirac, subsequently elected mayor of Paris, and both Prime Minister Raymond Barre and President Valéry Giscard d'Estaing. These conflicts, however, did not result in a split; the Giscardien-Gaullist coalition held together after the defeat in the March municipal elections.

The division in the left opposition was attributable to a tactical maneuver by the Communist Party. Convinced that the problems of the French economy could not be solved through the "common program," Communist leaders felt that their participation in a left government dominated by the Socialist Party would decrease their working class support. They preferred remaining outside the government to running the risk of being the unpopular managers of a deepening crisis.

The split between the Communist and Socialist parties sent shock waves through the latter. Socialist Party leader François Mitterrand, who had believed it possible to reach an understanding with the Communists, suffered a loss of prestige and faced the prospect of having to campaign against both Prime Minister Barre and Georges Marchais, the Communist Party leader.

Foreign Relations

Leonid Brezhnev visited France in June and was received with honors. Lieutenant Colonel Ibrahim Mohammed el Hamdi, president of the Arab Republic of (North) Yemen, was in France in July. King Hussein of Jordan visited Paris in September. In the same month, Prime Minister Barre met with Soviet leaders in the Kremlin.

Marshal Tito of Yugoslavia visited France in October. Prime Minister René Levesque of Quebec Province was in France in November, as was the Shah of Iran.

In September, October, and early November, there was considerable agitation over the capture and execution of Hans Martin Schleyer, a prominent West German business leader, by the Baader-Meinhof terrorist gang. Schleyer's body was found in Mulhouse, Alsace, and it was assumed that he had been executed on French soil. The West German press criticized the French police for an alleged lack of cooperation in the search for the terrorists. On October 21, however, Prime Minister Barre visited Chancellor Helmut Schmidt in Bonn, to commend his firmness in the struggle against terrorism. Ernst Croissant, a West German lawyer who defended the Baader-Meinhof gang and was accused of complicity with the terrorists, took refuge in France, where he was arrested. His extradition to West Germany provoked a storm of protest in left-wing circles.

On January 7, the DST (Territorial Defense and Security Forces), acting on an international warrant, arrested Abu Daoud, a Palestinian Arab implicated in the killing of Israeli athletes at the Munich Olympics. Daoud had assumed an alias and come to Paris from Beirut in order to attend the funeral services for a Palestinian bookseller. As the member of a Palestinian delegation, Daoud had been received by French government officials. It was expected that he would be extradited to West Germany or Israel, but on January 11 the Chamber of Accusation of the Paris Court of Appeals decided to free him, and he was expelled from France. The reasons given for Daoud's release were both vague and specious. In fact, the French government had decided to avoid antagonizing the Arab world. In Israel, there was great bitterness; and in France, sharp protests by Jewish and pro-Israel groups.

Relations with Israel

The May 1977 Israeli elections, which brought the Likud Party to power, aroused criticism in the media. An attempt was made to portray Menachem Begin as an extreme right-wing nationalist whose accession to power would precipitate a new Middle East war. Jewish and pro-Israel circles were embarrassed by the defeat of Israel's Labor Party. The image—already quite old and a little tarnished—of a "socialist" Israel had been obliterated. Daniel Mayer, a former Socialist minister, and ex-president of the League for the Rights of Man, who for years had written a column in the Zionist magazine *La Terre Retrouvée* ("The Refound Land"), ceased doing so, declaring that his socialist convictions made it impossible for him to continue to defend Israel under the new political order.

The Flatto-Sharon affair outraged many people. Sharon, a Jewish businessman of Polish origin, holding French citizenship, had some matters to settle with French judicial authorities. He fled to Israel, and became an Israeli citizen according to the Law of Return. France requested his extradition. While his record was being examined, Sharon became a candidate, on his own list, in the Knesset elections, and ended up being elected an Israeli deputy by a very comfortable majority. The victory was, in part, a retort by the Israeli electorate to France's release of Abu Daoud.

In November, the Sadat-Begin dialogue in Jerusalem helped improve the latter's image among the French populace. The "rightest" stigma was erased, and Begin became quite popular. Jewish and Zionist opinion turned pro-Begin. On the other hand, the Government was quite reserved; unlike other heads of state, President Giscard d'Estaing was slow in congratulating Sadat and Begin on their mutual steps toward peace.

Arab Boycott

In June 1977, the French Parliament unanimously passed a law prohibiting racial or religious discrimination in commercial transactions. Two paragraphs in the law made the Arab boycott a crime. But a third, passed at the same time, contained an exemption clause rendering the first two inapplicable when a discriminatory practice was consistent with Government policy. Before two months had elapsed, the Government, in one of its "recommendations and communications" published in the *Journal Officiel,* interpreted the exemption clause to mean that a boycott was not prohibited if it affected relations with oil-producing countries. This meant that the Arab boycott against Israel could be honored. The reasons given for this virtual repeal of the adopted law referred to the purposes of an earlier law, passed in July 1976, which had been intended to restore France's balance of payments and improve the employment situation. Commenting on this about-face, the jurist Raymond Lindon wrote in the *Tribune Juive* of August 1977: "I believe there is only one dignified and sensible attitude for any Jew who is not ashamed of his Judaism: to deny his vote to those whose 'recommendations and communications' guarantee the return of the Nuremberg laws and the rebirth of the yellow star."

Antisemitism

Antisemitic groups disseminated literature denying the reality of the Holocaust. Two pamphlets, *The Auschwitz Lie* by Thies Christopherson, and *Did Six Million Really Die?* by Richard Harwood, were widely distributed in France, the first in an edition of 60,000 copies.

In an article in the October issue of *Information Juive,* Emile Touati cited a teaching manual used in "free" (Catholic) schools as an example of what Jules Isaac called "the teaching of contempt." Among other things, the manual stated that "the Hebrews were a poor and violent people [who] plundered the lands of peaceful folk," and that, "All Jews are . . . sustained by the hope that a savior will arrive who will assure their domination of the world."

Toward the end of the year, in Dijon, Jewish merchants were anonymously accused of trapping young girls and women in their shops and selling them into white slavery. As in the past, the League Against Anti-Semitism protested, the Jewish community complained, and the mayor offered some soothing words.

In the intellectual sphere, two developments were significant in terms of their antisemitic connotations. The works of Louis-Ferdinand Céline, which had hitherto not been discussed on either radio or television because of their violently antisemitic nature, were lavishly praised on both media. Céline's hatred of Jews was either ignored or minimized. An exhibit on the life and works of André Maurois at the Bibliothèque Nationale (National Library) did not mention the Jewish origins of this celebrated writer.

JEWISH COMMUNITY

Demography

The Jewish population of France was estimated to be 650,000. Paris was the leading Jewish center with a population of 300,000. Other important Jewish communities were Marseilles (65,000), Nice (20,000), Lyons (20,000), and Toulouse (18,000).

Communal Activities

The Fonds Social Juif Unifié (FSJU, United Jewish Philanthropic Fund), which collected money for domestic needs, and the Appel Unifié des Juifs de France (AUJF, United Jewish Appeal of France), which raised funds for Israel, suffered severely from the economic recession. Julien Samuel, secretary general of FSJU, who had also served as director of the magazine L'Arche (The Ark) since it began publication, retired, and was named the organization's honorary president. Samuel had been active in Jewish life for 30 years, and had played a key role in rebuilding the French Jewish community after the second World War.

On October 30, approximately 65,000 people attended "Twelve Hours for Israel," a celebration in the vast area around the Palais des Expositions de la Porte de Versailles in Paris. The FSJU leadership, fearing that elements on the left might take political advantage of a large gathering, had opposed the event. At the sixth session of FSJU's National Council in November, President Guy de Rothschild sharply criticized the rally's organizers for having bypassed the FSJU, and warned of the danger of a split in the French Jewish community.

The election of delegates to the Zionist Congress evoked little excitement. Organized Zionism had never been a potent factor on the French Jewish scene. According to official figures, 50,000 voters selected candidates from six lists. The first list was a coalition of four parties: the General Zionists, the United Zionist Federation, Mizrachi, and Herut. This bloc, which supported the Begin Government, was thought likely to win the majority of French Zionist votes. The extreme left wing of Mapam, led by singing star Herbert Pagani, was the only group that mentioned recognition of "national rights of the Arab people of Palestine."

In the religious sphere, there were two positive developments. Numerous new synagogues were established in the Paris area and in the south of France. The Lubavitch Youth Organization increased its ranks, drawing new members from non-observant and quite assimilated families.

Another youth group of a more political nature, Betar, the Zionist Revisionist youth organization, was revitalized as a result of the popularity of Menachem Begin.

Publications

Two books, written by Jews, made a sensation as part of the post-Marxist "new philosophy." They were André Glückman's *Les Maîtres-Penseurs* ("The Master Thinkers"; Grasset) and Bernard-Henri Lévy's *La Barbarie à Visage Humain* ("Barbarism with a Human Face"; Grasset).

Among literary works of Jewish interest were Claude Vigee's poems, *Délivrance du Souffle* ("Deliverance from Breath"; Flammarion). A former professor at Brandeis University who now teaches at the Hebrew University in Jerusalem, Vigee won the 1977 Paul Burckhardt Prize for European literature, awarded by the city of Basel. Another winner of an international prize for literature, this one awarded in Germany, was novelist Manès Sperber, for *Le pont inachevé* ("The Unfinished Bridge"; Calmann-Levy), a memoir continuing his *Porteur d'eau* ("Water-Carrier"). André Chouraqui, former deputy-mayor of Jerusalem, was awarded a gold medal by the Académie Française.

A selection of stories by the classic Yiddish writer, J.L. Peretz, *Métamorphose d'une Mélodie* ("Metamorphosis of a Melody"; Albin Michel) was published in a translation by Joseph Gottfarstein. A selection of poems by the Israeli Yehuda Amichai, translated by Liliane Touboul, was issued by Publications Orientalistes de France. Sociologist Albert Memmi, known for his *Portrait d'un Juif* ("Portrait of a Jew"), wrote *Le Désert* ("The Desert"; Gallimard), an oriental legend. Raymond Levy's *Schwartzenmurtz ou l'esprit de parti* ("Schwartzenmurtz or Party Spirit"; Albin Michel), a satire on Communist circles in the post-Stalinist backwash, is generously sprinkled with a mixture of Jewish humor and French wit.

Among new books on Israel were *Retour de Jérusalem* (a translation of Saul Bellow's *To Jerusalem and Back;* Flammarion) and *Sur Israël* ("On Israel"; Albin Michel), by the famous Swiss-German novelist and playwright Friedrich Dürrenmatt. In the last days of December, because of the Sadat-Begin meeting in Jerusalem, a biography of the Israeli prime minister was rushed into publication: Victor Malka's *Menahem Begin, la Bible et le Fusil* ("Menahem Begin, the Bible and the Gun"; Editions Media).

Jean Lacouture's *Léon Blum* (Seuil), while not directly concerned with the Jewishness of this French politician, does show the significance of this aspect of Blum's personality. In France's highly politicized climate, the book became a best seller.

Léon Poliakov's *L'Europe suicidaire* ("Suicidal Europe"; Calmann-Levy) was the most recent volume in his monumental history of antisemitism.

Answers by France's Chief Rabbi Jacob Kaplan to questions asked him by Pierre Pierrard resulted in *Justice pour la foi juive* ("Justice for the Jewish Faith"; Centurion). Through the events of Kaplan's own career, the book traces the history of the French Jewish community since the 1920's. André Amar, a militant French Zionist and former Jewish resistance fighter, who until very recently had been considered indifferent to religion, made a surprising turnabout in *Moïse* ("Moses"; Editions du Rocher). In *Les Juifs et le monde moderne* ("Jews and the Modern World"; Seuil), Annie Kriegel, the eminent historian and sociologist who turned from Communism to Zionism, examines the perplexities of the modern Jewish experience. *Clefs pour le Judaïsme* ("Keys to Judaism"; Seghers) by André Neher, is a didactic and dialectical introduction to Jewish humanism. *Le Récit de la disparue* ("The Story of the Woman Who Disappeared"; Gallimard) by Shmuel Trigano, deals with Jewish theology and philosophy. Trigano is at home in the world of the Kabbalah, but expresses his ideas in a modern fashion.

Personalia

Armand Lunel, a Provençal Jewish writer, died on November 3 in Monaco. Born in Aix-en-Provence in 1892, he was a novelist and chronicler of the old ghettos of the papal states of Avignon and Carpentras. In 1926, he won the Théophraste-Renaudot Prize for *Niccolo Peccavi ou l'affaire Dreyfus à Carpentras* ("Niccolo Peccavi or the Dreyfus Case in Carpentras"), and in 1976 the Académie Française Prize for his entire ouvre.

Professor Georges Friedmann died in December at the age of 71. A philosopher and sociologist, he won his greatest fame for research on assembly-line labor. After the establishment of the Jewish state, Friedmann became actively interested in Israeli affairs and made several prolonged trips to the country. One of his books, which attracted a good deal of attention, was *Fin du peuple juif?* ("The End of the Jewish People?").

ARNOLD MANDEL

Central Europe

Federal Republic of Germany

Domestic Affairs

NINETEEN SEVENTY-SEVEN was a challenging year for the federal government in Bonn. The main challenge was to safeguard domestic security and combat terrorism. In addition, the government sought to breathe new life into a stagnant economy.

Left-wing extremism dominated the news during the year. In comparison, right-wing extremism remained a marginal phenomenon, although its intensification made for added unrest, particularly among Jews and others who had been persecuted by the Nazi regime. The political leadership systematically sought to curb excesses on the left, while keeping a watchful eye on the right.

A chronology of events relating to left-wing extremism includes the following: on January 8, two terrorists opened fire on a Swiss official at a German-Swiss border crossing; on March 24, law offices in Frankfurt were bombed; on April 7, in Karlsruhe, terrorists killed Chief Federal Prosecutor Siegfried Buback; on April 28, in Stuttgart, terrorist leaders Andreas Baader, Jean-Carl Raspe, and Gudrun Ensslin were sentenced to life in prison for murder; on May 9, Hans-Joachim Klein, a wanted terrorist, revealed a plot to assassinate the presidents of the Jewish congregations in West Berlin and Frankfurt; on June 2, in Kaiserslautern, terrorists Manfred Grashof and Klaus Jüschke were given life sentences; on July 20, in Düsseldorf, terrorists Hanna Krabbe, Lutz Taufer, Karl-Heinz Dellwo, and Bernhard Rössner received life sentences; on July 30, terrorists in Oberursel shot and killed Jürgen Ponto, board chairman of the Dresdner Bank; on September 5, terrorists in Cologne kidnapped Hanns Martin Schleyer, president of the West German Confederation of Employers' Associations, killing three policemen and a chauffeur in the process; in exchange for Schleyer's release, the Rote Armee Fraktion (RAF; Red Army Faction), the most important and most fanatical German terrorist organization, demanded the release of 11 imprisoned terrorists, and the Government responded with delaying tactics, negotiating with RAF through a Swiss attorney; on September 22, in Utrecht, the Netherlands, two German terrorists, Knut Folkerts and Brigitte Mohnhaupt, killed a policeman, after which Folkers was sentenced to 20 years in prison; on October 13, in connection with the Schleyer affair, four Palestinian terrorists hijacked a German passenger plane; five days later in Mogadiscio, Somalia, German commandos stormed the hijacked plane, freeing all the hostages and killing three of the hijackers, and Baader, Raspe and Ensslin, the three RAF leaders, committed suicide; the following day Schleyer was found dead; on November 12, Ingrid Schubert, a terrorist, committed suicide in a Munich prison; on December 20, two terrorists, Christian Möller and Gabriele Kröcher-Tiedemann, were arrested in Switzerland.

Right-wing extremists also intensified their activities, which consisted of reviling democracy, extolling the Hitler regime, and white-washing Nazi crimes. With growing boldness, right-wing elements exploited the liberality of the democratic system to promote pro-Nazi and anti-democratic views in public. Law-enforcement agencies, for the most part, took only hesitant steps against them, and often displayed disquieting leniency in sentencing the culprits.

Together with these extremist tendencies, a so-called "Hitler wave" made itself unpleasantly felt. It took the form of films, records, books, pamphlets, and magazine features seeking to gloss over or even glorify the Nazi dictatorship, as well as Hitler's influence and personality. An important role in this connection was played by a documentary film, *Hitler: A Career,* based on a book by the historian Joachim C. Fest which made its debut during the summer and promptly became a box-office success. Three months after its first showing, the film had been seen by more than a million viewers in West Germany; it was also a success in Austria and Switzerland. Critics charged that the film presented a distorted view of the Nazi regime and a white-washed Hitler. They regarded it as dangerous, especially for the poorly-informed younger generation. The radical right welcomed the film.

Three young Germans in Hamburg, assisted by prominent musicians, produced a two-disc "rock opera" about Hitler, portraying him as an occult figure. According to the producers, English and American firms expressed interest in marketing the records. A growing, openly-conducted trade developed in Nazi paraphernalia, photos, and literature. The official ban on this trade was ignored; the authorities rarely intervened.

Toward the end of the year, West German toy stores offered quantities of military toys with Nazi emblems. Bundestag deputies and others vainly demanded legal measures against the manufacturers and distributors.

Records of speeches by National Socialist leaders, and Nazi songs and marches appeared in increased quantities. They were offered by both German and foreign producers, and were sold by right-wing radical enterprises, as well as by department stores and other retail outlets, reportedly with considerable success. Though the distribution of Hitler speeches and similar recordings was illegal, law-enforcement agencies hardly ever interceded. At the end of the year, Herbert Wehner, leader of the Social Democratic faction (SPD) in the Bundestag, felt compelled, in the wake of protests from abroad, to emphasize to the legislature that effective measures against such distribution of Nazi materials were urgently needed.

Organizations of Third Reich veterans held dozens of conventions. In particular, HIAG (Hilfsorganisation auf Gegenseitigkeit), the organization of former *SS* members, kept holding rallies. In more than a few instances, members of the Bundeswehr (West German armed forces) took part in such events. Ulrich Rudel, an unrepentant Nazi officer who had been awarded the Third Reich's highest military decoration, was feted at various veterans' meetings and at rallies of radical right-wing youth organizations. Rudel was lauded in the pages of the Munich weekly *Deutsche National-Zeitung,* whose editor-in-chief, Gerhard Frey, carried on a pro-Nazi, anti-democratic, anti-Israel, and anti-Jewish campaign with increasing boldness.

In July, Werner Nachmann, chairman of the board of the Zentralrat der Juden in Deutschland (Central Council of Jews in Germany), warned against the dangers of the "Hitler wave." He felt that young people were being exposed to a totally false image of Hitler, and that Hitler's responsibility for the death of millions was being deliberately ignored. Nachmann stated that the glorification of Hitler might well be followed by a new wave of antisemitism. He added that greedy profit makers and certain radical political interests stood behind the Hitler nostalgia. The Koordinierungsrat der Gesellschaften für christlich-jüdische Zusammenarbeit (Coordinating Council of the Societies for Christian-Jewish Cooperation) voiced deep concern "over the growing distribution of writings extolling National Socialism." The Bund der Verfolgten des Naziregimes und Antifaschisten (League of Nazi Persecution Victims and Anti-Fascists) demanded dissolution of all neo-Nazi organizations and confiscation of all neo-Nazi propaganda. The organization of persecution victims in Bavaria protested the *SS* veterans' rallies, viewing them not only as a danger to the democratic state, but also as a provocation against those who had fought against National Socialism. The Social Democratic Party (SPD) called on the Federal Government to act against neo-Nazi groups and the distribution of neo-Nazi literature. Antisemitic preaching, in particular, the SPD maintained, should be rigorously prosecuted. SPD chairman Willy Brandt, criticizing the rising number of nationalist war veterans' rallies and other neo-Nazi meetings, charged that the communal authorities were much less watchful of neo-Nazi dangers than they were of left-wing attacks on the democratic order.

The Federal Government did not share Brandt's concern. A spokesman averred that there was no justification for the charge that the agencies concerned were remiss in watching right-wing extremist groups. In October, the Government declared that it did not consider right-wing extremism a danger to the security of the Federal Republic, but stressed that, because of their stepped-up activities, extreme rightist movements would continue to need careful watching. The Government, it was stated, would continue to see to it that no right-wing extremists were admitted to public service positions. At the same time, Chancellor Helmut Schmidt asserted that both left- and right-wing extremism played only a minor role in the country.

An opinion survey conducted by the Elections Research Group in Mannheim found that one third of the voting public constituted potential radical-right sympathizers, a proportion that had remained constant for 10 years. Active sympathy with the Nazi regime had declined, but the rejection of such democratic essentials as the multi-party system, the division of powers, and parliamentary give-and-take held steady.

Antisemitism

Radical tendencies and occurrences could hardly be separated from antisemitic incidents, since most extremist groups also disseminated anti-Jewish ideas. The anti-Jewish manifestations of the extreme left, assuming the form of anti-Zionism, were directed mainly against Israel, and only in exceptional cases against Jews in Germany. Agitation by right-wing extremists, on the other hand, was openly aimed at Jews in general and against the Jewish minority in the Federal Republic in particular. Anti-Jewish utterances on the right, evidencing growing militancy, included demands that Jews remove themselves from Germany, and even threats of murder.

The most conspicuous anti-Jewish group in 1977 was Gary Lauck's NSDAP Foreign Organization, headquartered in Lincoln, Nebraska. Lauck succeeded in filling a growing number of young Germans with enthusiasm for his hate campaign against Jews. The German authorities were unsuccessful in stopping the activity of the NSDAP, or in putting a halt to the illegal importation from the United States of antisemitic literature. Lauck's group was most active in southwestern Germany, around Frankfurt, Hanover, and Hamburg.

Toward the end of the year, Hanover became the center of the Lauck group's agitation. Not only were Nazi and antisemitic slogans daubed on walls and anti-Jewish pamphlets distributed, but Jews were also provoked, threatened, and attacked in public. Members of the Hanover Jewish congregation received telephone threats. On several occasions, young people appeared in the streets wearing Nazi-type garb. The police arrested a number, who admitted to being members of the NSDAP. The Lower Saxony state government, however, sought to represent the events in Hanover as the acts of a few outsiders, and as politically insignificant.

Another group that publicly agitated against Jews was Erwin Schönborn's German Soldiers' Combat League. The League asserted that not one Jew had been gassed by the Germans. The group distributed its pamphlets throughout the country, even in armed forces posts, and in front of courthouses where Nazi criminals were being tried. To bring its campaign to the attention of the public at large, the group attempted to hold what it called "Auschwitz conventions" in Nuremberg and Frankfurt. Following protests by democratic organizations and victims of Nazi persecution, the municipal authorities banned these events, whereupon Schönborn arranged to replace them with meetings behind closed doors.

A publisher in southern Germany issued a book by a Catholic teacher of religion, Manfred Adler, entitled *Söhne der Finsternis— Weltmacht Zionismus* ("Sons of Darkness: The World Power of Zionism"). The book was based on the *Protocols of the Elders of Zion* and dedicated "to the victims of Zionism, in human fellowship." In July, a German edition of *The Hoax of the Twentieth Century,* by Arthur R. Butz, an American professor, was issued in West Germany and promoted by the radical right. Dr. Gerhard Frey, editor of the *Deutsche National-Zeitung,* invited Butz to Germany, where he was introduced to German sympathizers and awarded a prize. A pamphlet, *Did Six Million Really Die?,* by British author Richard E. Harwood, was also marketed by groups on the far right.

Antisemitic episodes were also noted in the armed forces. The high point was a symbolic "Jew burning" at the Bundeswehr Academy in Neubiberg in February. A number of officer candidates sang Nazi songs at a party and burned scraps of paper bearing the word "Jew." As a result of the incident, six men were discharged from the army. Previously, two officer candidates in the same academy had been discharged for right-wing extremist activities. Other Nazi episodes were reported from barracks in Nuremberg and Rheine, and from the Bundeswehr Academy in Hamburg. In November, following press criticism of right-wing extremist and anti-Jewish tendencies and manifestations in the armed forces, a spokesman for the Defense Ministry stated that antisemitism was not a problem in the Bundeswehr. At the same time, however, he deplored the fact that "no one so far has succeeded in getting the experiences and lessons of the Nazi era across to the young."

During 1977, Jewish cemeteries were desecrated in Schorten, Hamburg, Hanover, Cham, Affaltrach, Warburg-Ossendorf, Billerbeck and Havixbeck. In Hanover, a member of the Lauck group was convicted as one of the desecrators and sentenced to 15 months' detention. In April, a court in Celle sentenced four defendants to penalties ranging from nine months' imprisonment to a DM 1,000 fine for defacing the memorial at the former Bergen-Belsen concentration camp in May 1976.

Foreign Relations

In summing up the year's events in the area of foreign affairs, the Government stated that its goal had been to reduce international tensions. This policy found expression in Chancellor Schmidt's visit to Poland, and in efforts to solve the problems between the two Germanies.

Schmidt was the first German chancellor to visit the former Auschwitz extermination camp. While there, on November 23, he stated: "We have come to Auschwitz to remind ourselves and others that without knowledge of the past there is no path to the future, and no way to a new, unconstrained relationship between Germans and Poles . . . The crimes of Nazi fascism, the guilt of the German Reich under Hitler's leadership, lie at the bottom of our responsibility. We Germans of today are not guilty as individuals, but we must take upon us the political heritage of those who were guilty. In this lies our responsibility . . ."

The Middle East conflict figured large in West German foreign policy. In his address to the General Assembly of the United Nations on September 29, Foreign Minister Hans-Dietrich Genscher emphasized:

A just and lasting peace settlement must start out from Security Council Resolutions 242 and 338, and must implement the following principles: It must respect the right of all states in the region, including Israel's, to live in peace within secure and recognized boundaries. It must terminate the territorial occupation Israel has maintained since 1967. It must consider the legitimate rights of the Palestinians . . . to self-determination and effective expression of national identity. Thus, any solution must take the need of a homeland for the Palestinian people into account. The Palestinians must take part in the peace negotiations, which must not be blocked by unilateral *faits accomplis*. For this reason, the Federal Government goes on record in this forum as opposing the creation of Israeli settlements in the occupied Arab territories.

The Government welcomed the peace initiative launched by Egyptian President Anwar el-Sadat. Chancellor Schmidt, on an official visit to Cairo in late December, praised Sadat's courage and reaffirmed Bonn's view that the Palestinian people must not be denied "the right to self-determination." Both sides in the Middle East conflict, he pointed out, would "have to bend their energies to self-denial, modifying their heretofore irreconcilable postures and views enough to make a rapprochement possible." He assured President Sadat: "My government supports any steps that will bring peace nearer."

West German politicians had a number of contacts with representatives of the Palestine Liberation Organization (PLO) during the year. In November, leading members of the SPD met with PLO representative Dr. Issam Sartawi. Following criticism by Friedrich Zimmermann, a Christian Social Union (CSU) Bundestag deputy, Hans-Jürgen Wischnewski, state minister in the office of the federal chancellor, declared that the discussion had served to air the views of a "political power that is decisively relevant" to the future of the Middle East. The Bonn PLO bureau chief, Abdallah Frangi, was included in a delegation of Arab ambassadors to Bonn who were invited to Hanover by the prime minister of Lower Saxony, Ernst Albrecht of the Christian Democratic Union (CDU), to engage in discussions with politicians in that state. A few days earlier, Frangi, at a rally organized by German left-wing extremists in West Berlin, had advocated the destruction of the state of Israel.

Relations with Israel

The victory of Likud leader Menachem Begin in Israel's parliamentary election on May 17 threatened new tensions in German-Israeli relations. Though the head of CDU, Dr. Helmut Kohl, was the first West European politician to congratulate Mr. Begin on his victory, government circles worried about the future of German-Israeli relations because of Begin's well-known unfavorable attitude toward Germany in past decades. Almost without exception, the German press published critical comments and offered gloomy prognoses in regard to both relations between Germany and Israel, and resolution of the Middle East conflict. Only toward the end of the year, in the face of the Egyptian-Israeli peace initiative, did these critics arrive at a milder, if still skeptical, assessment of the Begin government and its negotiating posture.

A few weeks after Begin's victory, the German ambassador to Israel, Per Fischer, was assured in a conversation with Likud functionaries that the new Israeli government not only wished to maintain relations at the present level, but was hoping to expand them further, especially in the economic sphere. During September, Begin, for the first time, commented on German-Israeli relationships, saying they were normal. He indicated that he felt it had been a mistake to sign a restitution pact as early as 1952. Since relations between Israel and Germany were a reality, however, he made it clear that he contemplated no changes.

The first German government representative received by Prime Minister Begin was the new ambassador, Klaus Schütz, 51, who had been mayor of West Berlin from 1967 to 1977, and had been named in August to succeed Per Fischer. In presenting his credentials to President Ephraim Katzir, Schütz stated that the Federal Republic was happy that relations between the two countries had developed in a spirit of mutual trust, despite the painful past.

Bonn's posture on the Middle East question was severely criticized on several occasions by Israel as being too pro-Arab. Jerusalem signaled to Bonn that keeping silent would be a wiser course than asking political sacrifices of Israel. However, the federal government persisted in its view that the Middle East conflict touched directly upon the interests of Germany and the other states of the European Economic Community and that taking a clear position was, therefore, indispensable. A visit by Israeli Foreign Minister Moshe Dayan to Bonn in late November did not alter this posture.

Simcha Ehrlich, Israeli minister of finance, visited Bonn in early December. The Government replied negatively to Israel's request for an increase in capital assistance above the previous level of DM 140 million per year, on the grounds of budgetary strains and numerous obligations to developing countries. However, Bonn declared itself ready to guarantee German investments in Israel, and to promote further investment in the Jewish state. At the end of June, German direct investments in Israel amounted to DM 547 million; German credits to Israel totaled DM 1.65 billion.

The Federal Republic was Israel's second biggest export customer. During 1976, merchandise worth $201 million was imported from Israel, 25.3 per cent more than in 1975. Simultaneously, the Federal Republic consolidated its position as the leading importer of Israeli goods among the countries of the European Economic Community; its share of such imports amounted to 22.7 per cent. However, this positive development continued to be impaired by Israel's high deficit in her trade with West Germany; though reduced by more than 44 per cent since 1974, it remained substantial.

During the fall, Mayor Shlomo Lahat of Tel Aviv spent two weeks in West Germany. A delegation of Israel's Council of Local Municipalities, invited by its German counterpart, traveled in the Federal Republic to inform itself about communal institutions and industrial planning. A youth delegation of the Magen David Adom, invited by the German Youth Red Cross, visited the country during August. In July, a delegation of the German organization had attended an international Red Cross Youth Conference in Israel. Several groups of Israeli teachers and secondary-school students came to West Germany during the year. A number of Israeli artists presented their work to the German public, among them the painters Rafael Rila, Samuel Bak, Arie Ogen, Raphael Uzan, Yeshayahu Scheinfeld, Itzhak Roman, and Simon Karczmar. The Israeli Kibbutz Chamber Orchestra toured West Germany during the fall. A DM 25,000 International Prize for Research in Communications endowed by a German publisher, Dr. Hubert Burda, was presented in Essen, during November, to an Israeli researcher, Dr. Eliahu Katz.

In May, the Deutsch-Israelische Gesellschaft (German-Israeli Society) in Bonn elected Erik Blumenfeld of Hamburg, a CDU Bundestag deputy, as its new president. He replaced another Bundestag deputy, Heinz Westphal of the SPD. Westphal was elected a vice-president, as were Detlef Kleinert, Hans Stercken, and Walter Hesselbach. Blumenfeld had been interned in a concentration camp during the Nazi era because of his Jewish descent. His election was surrounded by controversy, touched off by the question of whether the Society was free to adopt a posture critical of Israel. A minority advocated "critical solidarity," with the right of dissenting from official Israeli policy. A majority, led by Blumenfeld, thought that such criticism of Israeli policies would not be opportune. The controversy led to a split. The minority formed a new group, dedicated to serving German-Israeli understanding and cooperation according to its own principles. Named Deutsch-Israelische Arbeitsgruppe für Frieden im Nahen Osten (German-Israeli Working Group for Peace in the Middle East), the new body was headed by Professor Rolf Rendtorff, a Social Democrat, who was one of the founders of the German-Israeli Society and who vigorously denied pro-Arab tendencies. In October and November, the German-Israel Society and its Israeli sister organization conducted a workshop conference to discuss joint tasks and objectives. On this occasion, the German body sharply protested the Bonn government's attitude vis-à-vis Israel in the UN and in the European Economic Community.

Yad Vashem in Jerusalem awarded the honorary title "Righteous Among the Peoples" to three German citizens, Gerhard Radke, the late Carl Hermann, and Eva Hermann, for helping persecuted Jews under the Nazi regime. To date, about 100 Germans have been awarded this distinction.

The president of the Federal Republic, Walter Scheel, honored another West German citizen, the publisher Axel Springer, for his consistent championing of German-Jewish and German-Israeli reconciliation and cooperation. In May, on the occasion of his 65th birthday, the publisher was awarded the Grand Cross of the Federal Order of Merit. In January 1978, Springer was the first German citizen, other than a diplomat, to be received by Prime Minister Begin.

Thousands of West German citizens visited Israel. The volume of German tourism jumped with the inauguration of charter flights. In March, a delegation of the

German Union of Teachers and Scholars met in Israel with representatives of the Israel Union of Teachers to discuss revision of school textbooks in Germany and Israel. About 100 German book publishers joined in a display at the International Book Fair in Jerusalem during April and May. In June, the president of the Bavarian Youth League, Adolf Waibel, together with a leadership delegation of the German Federal Youth League, came to Israel as guests of the Council of Youth Movements. The president of the German Athletic Federation, Willi Weyer, and the organization's secretary general, Karlheinz Gieseler, were guests at the Tenth Maccabiah Games during July. They also met with Israeli government representatives and took part in the consecration of a memorial for the Israeli athletes killed at the Munich Olympics.

Restitution

September 10, 1977 marked the 25th anniversary of the signing, in Luxemburg, of the agreements by which Bonn obligated itself to pay a total indemnity of DM 3 billion to the Jewish State, and DM 450 million to the Conference on Jewish Material Claims Against Germany. Annemarie Renger, a prominent SPD politician, wrote in the government weekly *Das Parlament:*

> The Federal Republic of Germany has sought to stress the special nature of the Restitution Agreement and to keep it apart from commercial settlements with other creditor nations. The Republic did not look upon restitution as a way of lessening Germany's guilt; rather, it was to help the Germans come to grips with their past . . . In addition to its moral significance, the Luxemburg agreement carried much political weight. From the destruction and expulsion of the Jews, the State of Israel had arisen. Therefore, restitution was a form of aid, born of a special obligation, to the building and the survival of the State of Israel . . . The Restitution Agreement and its correct implementation, especially in political situations difficult for Israel, was the premise for a new beginning between Jews and Germans. Since then, many personal encounters have awakened an awareness in Israel of a different, democratic Germany and have led to a changed attitude. With the establishment of diplomatic relations in 1965, the political relationship between the two states became normalized. Yet a moral obligation vis-à-vis the Jewish people remains. The agonizing experiences of history cannot, and shall not, be forgotten.

Of 4,318,000 applications for indemnification filed under the Federal Indemnification Law, which governs recompense for persecution suffered by individuals, 4,298,000 had been settled. Approximately DM 42 billion had been disbursed for this purpose. Future obligations under this law, especially annuities to be paid, could amount to an additional DM 30 billion. Under the Federal Restitution Law, which governs compensation for illegally confiscated property, some 732,000 applications had been filed. Of these, 730,000 had been settled, at a cost of about DM 3.9 billion. After a change in the law in 1964, an additional 291,000 applications for special benefits in hardship cases were received. About 237,000 of these had so far been settled. In the future, approximately DM 400 million more was to be disbursed under this law. Pursuant to other restitution laws and special arrangements, about DM 4.3 billion had been paid out, among other things, for restitution to former members of the public service, in benefits to war victims, in social insurance, to provide for former employees of Jewish communities, and to look after racial persecution victims not of the Jewish faith, as well as survivors of medical experiments on humans. It was expected that DM 2.4 billion more would be paid out on behalf of these victims. In addition, the Federal Republic had concluded restitution agreements with 12 European states for the benefit of persecuted nationals of these states and of their survivors. About DM 1 billion had been disbursed on this account. Total expenditures for righting Nazi wrongs had thus far come to about DM 54 billion. By the time the annuities expired, the total was expected to exceed DM 85 billion.

Nazi Trials

The Central Office for the Investigation of National Socialist Crimes in Ludwigsburg reported in July that since the end of World War II a total of 6,425 persons had been sentenced in Nazi trials held on West German soil; 151 of them had received life sentences. Since May 1945, well over 80,000 Germans had been charged with participation in Nazi crimes. Since 1958, 352 legal proceedings had ended in a verdict, involving 832 defendants; 560 of these had been sentenced (128 to life imprisonment), while 218 were acquitted, and proceedings against 54 were terminated. Early in 1977, the Central Office was still investigating 289 cases of Nazi crimes against 4,600 persons. New proceedings were added during the year, partially because new incriminating evidence continued to arrive from Poland. The work of the Central Office was to officially terminate on December 31, 1979, when the Statute of Limitations would take effect.

Kiel: In July, a former police captain, Werner Heinrich Pöhls, 61, was acquitted of having assisted in the murder of several hundred Jews in the Soviet Union in 1942. The reasons given for the verdict were that the defendant had acted "under wartime conditions" and out of a "sense of duty," and that no cruelty on his part could be proved. The prosecutor's office in Kiel filed accusations against three former SS officers, Ernst Ehlers, Konstantin Canaris, and Kurt Asche, who were charged with having assisted in the deportation of some 26,000 Jews to the Auschwitz extermination camp between 1942 and 1944.

Darmstadt: In April, a former police sergeant, Friedrich Rondholz, was acquitted of having murdered four Soviet prisoners of war.

Hanover: In September, a trial began against former SS officers Kurt Heinemeyer, 69, and Max Olde, 69, who were charged with jointly committing murder in extermination actions against Jews in southern Poland between 1942 and 1944. Proceedings against Rudolf Körner, 70, were separated from the trial and temporarily suspended, on grounds that he was ill. In October, a criminal court which since August 1976 had been trying three former police officers, Heinrich Rathje, Reinhold

Witt, and Friedrich Keller, for mass murder of Jews in Poland suspended proceedings against the chief defendant, Johannes von Dollen, 78, because he was ill. For the same reason, proceedings against two other co-defendants, Michael Gerhardt and Karl Irle, had been halted earlier.

Frankfurt: In July, former *SS* sergeant Hubert Gomerski, 65, was sentenced, in a retrial, to 15 years' incarceration for abetting the murder of more than 100,000 Jews in the Sobibor extermination camp. Gomerski had already received a life sentence for the same crimes in 1950. In September, former *SS* members Horst Czerwinski and Josef Schmidt went to trial. They were accused of murdering several inmates in the Lagischa sub-camp at Auschwitz and during an evacuation march from a camp at Golleschau to Loslau.

Hamburg: In July, former *SS* and police major Viktor Arajs, 67, went to trial for abetting the murder of more than 35,000 Latvian Jews and other civilians in the Riga district. In August, a former police and *SS* officer, Gerhard Maywald, 64, was sentenced to four years' detention for abetting the murder of 320 Jews from Riga. In November, the Federal Constitutional Court ruled that the case of former *SS* sergeant Wilhelm Eickhoff must be retried because of a grave procedural error. A Hamburg court, in 1976, had sentenced Eickhoff to 12 years' detention for murdering Jews, and the Federal Court had subsequently imposed a life sentence. Wilhelm Rosenbaum, a former *SS* member who had been sentenced to lifetime detention for the murder of more than a hundred Jews, but had been released for six months under a clemency grant in December 1976, had to go back to prison in June, when the Hamburg Senate refused further clemency.

Düsseldorf: A trial of 14 former guards at the Majdanek extermination camp, begun in November 1975, continued with no end in sight. In April, the court began to examine surviving camp inmates, mainly Poles. By the end of the year, about 150 witnesses had been examined; well over 100 remained on the waiting list. All of the defendants were free on bail. The court traveled to Poland to examine witnesses and visit the site of the former Majdanek camp.

Aschaffenburg: Proceedings commenced in September against former *SS* members Hans Olejak, 59, and Ewald Pansegrau, 56, for murdering at least 50 internees in the Jaworzno sub-camp at Auschwitz. The defendants received greetings in the form of flowers from unnamed "fellow veterans." The head of the neo-Nazi German Soldiers' Combat League, Erwin Schönborn, distributed pamphlets outside the courthouse, as he had done elsewhere during Nazi trials. The pamphlets denied that Jews were killed in gas chambers, and offered a DM 10,000 reward to anyone who could conclusively prove that one Jew had been gassed. Schönborn also accused Jewish witnesses of lying. He was, nevertheless, heard by the court as a witness concerning the gassing of Jews in Auschwitz. In his testimony, he again called the gassings the biggest lie in history.

On August 15, Herbert Kappler, former *SS* police chief of Rome, who was serving a life sentence in Italy for his responsibility in the shooting of hostages, some of them Jews, was removed by his wife from a prison hospital in Rome and taken to Germany. He subsequently lived there as a free man, and was given police protection after threats were made against his life. The Bonn Government, on constitutional grounds, refused to extradite him to Italy. Chancellor Schmidt and the SPD expressed disapproval of Kappler's abduction to freedom and condemned his crimes. Groups of foreign persecution victims and resistance fighters, as well as others, accused the Federal Republic of sympathy for Nazi criminals, especially after the freeing of Kappler was widely hailed by the West German public.

In August, a former *SS* officer, Eduard Roschmann, died in Asunción, Paraguay. He had been wanted for crimes against Jews in Riga, and had lived in South America under the name of Federico Wegener.

JEWISH COMMUNITY

Demography

On January 1, the Jewish community in the Federal Republic numbered 27,379 members, 12,976 of them women. Their average age was 45 years. During 1977, 922 immigrants and 408 emigrants were registered, as were 74 births and 491 deaths. Thirty-nine persons converted to Judaism. The largest communities were in West Berlin (5,626), Frankfurt (5,033), Munich (3,859), Düsseldorf (1,671), Hamburg (1,344), and Cologne (1,213). Jews living in the Federal Republic without being registered as members of Jewish communities were estimated to number between 10,000 and 15,000. It was estimated that the intermarriage rate in the Federal Republic was as high as 60 per cent.

Communal Activities

The effects of right- and left-wing extremist acts in the Federal Republic were repeatedly discussed and scored by the Zentralrat der Juden in Deutschland (Central Council of Jews in Germany). The Council regarded the flood of antisemitic pamphlets, attempts in sectors of the press to minimize or deny the mass murders in ghettos and concentration camps, and frequent rallies of former *SS* members as serious causes of concern. At its annual meeting, held in Hanover during June, the Council stated its "unconditional determination to strengthen the Jewish community in the Federal Republic" and resist any attack on freedom and democracy.

In February, Werner Nachmann was elected to his fifth consecutive term as chairman of the Central Council's board. In the spring, Nachmann accompanied Foreign Minister Genscher on his visit to Israel. He and the Council's general secretary, Alexander Ginsburg, represented the organization at the convention of the Conference on Jewish Material Claims Against Germany and the Memorial Foundation for Jewish Culture, held in Amsterdam during June, as well as at the meeting of the General Council of the World Jewish Congress in Washington during

October and November. In December, at the invitation of the Hungarian Government and the Central Federation of Hungarian Jewish Communities, Nachmann and Ginsburg took part in a celebration marking the 100th anniversary of the founding of the Rabbinical Seminary in Budapest.

Representatives of the Central Council entered into frequent conversations with leading politicians and attended the conventions of the CDU, SPD, and Free Democratic Party (FDP). In October, a conversation with Federal Defense Minister Georg Leber dealt with various antisemitic and anti-democratic manifestations in the West German armed forces. In June, the Council affirmed its readiness to support any measures that might ease the plight of Syrian Jewry. During the same month, the Council appealed to the West German government and to President Tito of Yugoslavia to use their influence at the Belgrade Conference on behalf of security, cooperation, and the reduction of tensions in Europe, so that Jews might be accorded their internationally recognized human rights.

Late in November, representatives of the Central Council met in Bonn with Israeli Foreign Minister Moshe Dayan. In December, the Council appealed to the German government and the European Economic Community to support the initiatives taken by prime ministers Sadat and Begin.

In January, Hans Filbinger, prime minister of the state of Baden-Württemberg, paid an official visit to the Jewish community in Stuttgart. In February, the president of the Berlin Chamber of Deputies, Peter Lorenz, visited the Berlin Jewish community; and in June the federal minister for economic cooperation, Marie Schlei, was a guest there. In December, the prime minister of Hesse, Holger Börner, visited the Jewish community in Frankfurt.

Religion

At a plenary meeting held in Munich during January, the Rabbinerkonferenz in der Bundesrepublik Deutschland (Rabbinical Conference in the Federal Republic of Germany), numbering 10 members, decided that in view of the small number of rabbis in the country and the large territory each had to serve, it would limit itself to specifically religious tasks.

In November, members of the Rabbinical Conference and the United Lutheran Church of Germany held a workshop in Hanover. The session focused on ways of representing Jews and Judaism in Protestant religious teaching, particularly in textbooks. It was felt that, in view of the growing number of antisemitic incidents, efforts had to be made to overcome the widespread ignorance of Judaism among Lutherans, and to reduce deep-seated prejudices that were often unconscious. The Lutheran representatives were asked to request of the appropriate church agencies that future ministers and teachers of religion be given basic information on Judaism and Christian-Jewish relations while in training. Furthermore, they were requested to urge that these matters receive greater attention in advanced and in-service training of church functionaries, and in the various branches of church-sponsored programs for young people and adults.

Education and Youth Work

"The Future of Our Communities" was the theme of a youth convention of the Central Council of Jews in Germany, held in Würzburg during March. Seventy young Jews from the Federal Republic and West Berlin were given an opportunity to discuss their problems with rabbis, educators, and experienced community members. The participants agreed that Jewish survival depended primarily on the quality of religious life. At the same time, it was noted that young people tended to be alienated from Judaism. To bring about any improvement in this situation, it was argued, more rabbis and teachers would have to be put to work at the congregational level, and regular study seminars would have to be conducted at the regional level. One such seminar, on the subject "The Sabbath and Its Various Aspects," took place during June in Cologne.

A conference of delegates of the Bundesverband Jüdischer Studenten in Deutschland (Federal Association of Jewish Students in Germany), meeting in Munich during May, reaffirmed the tasks of the organization: to work for effective cooperation among Jewish organizations; to promote the well-being of the Jewish people; to support the State of Israel as the cultural and national home of the Jewish people; and to combat antisemitism. The apathy of many Jewish students was deplored. In July in Aachen, the Association conducted a weekend seminar on the current political situation, focusing mainly on the Middle East. "Policies for Israel's Security" was the theme of another weekend seminar of the Association, held in West Berlin in November.

The Bundesverband Jüdischer Jugend (National Federation of Jewish Youth), centered in the Ruhr region, also conducted a variety of programs. A one-day seminar was devoted to "Pairing Problems of Jewish Youth," a theme which had great urgency in view of the high rate of intermarriage.

In March in Munich, a seminar of the European Young Leadership Cabinet was conducted on the theme "Jewish History from 1880 to 1980." Eighty delegates from 11 European countries participated.

In July, Maccabiah Germany, the Jewish sports organization, took part in the Tenth Maccabiah Games in Israel, with a delegation of 45 persons. The delegation won six gold medals, four silver, and three bronze, and took seventh place in the team standings. The most successful athletes were Hanka Rohan, Blanka Rohan, and Hanna Slama, who won four gold medals in table tennis. Dany Leder, a gymnast, took the other two gold medals, as well as two silver and one bronze.

Christian-Jewish Cooperation

In July, the Ullstein publishing house in Berlin celebrated its 100th anniversary. The occasion was marked by a gathering of persons prominent in German public life and representatives of the Jewish community. A message from President Walter Scheel noted that Jews had brought the house its prestige, influence, and prosperity, and that Jewish journalists, scholars, and artists had contributed significantly to its success. At the 17th German Protestant Church convention in West Berlin, during June, a working group on "Jews and Christians," with Jewish participants, discussed problems of German-Jewish and Christian-Jewish coexistence. A joint Jewish-Christian service was also held. The Coordinating Council of Societies for Christian-Jewish Cooperation chose "Martin Buber: Dialogue Today" as its theme for 1978. The 1978 Brotherhood Week, scheduled for early March, was also to be devoted to this theme.

The President awarded the Federal Order of Merit to several German citizens who had risked their lives to help persecuted Jews during the Nazi era: Gerda Knöfler, who had provided asylum and other aid to numerous Jews between 1937 and her arrest in 1941; Georgette Gruschke, who for two years of the war hid a Jewish writer; and Anton Skerlownik, who hid three Jews in his home during the war years.

In June, the Hebrew Union College-Jewish Institute of Religion in New York awarded an honorary doctorate to Dr. Gertrud Luckner, 76, a German Catholic who risked her life during the Nazi years to aid Jews, and who, since the war, has championed Christian-Jewish understanding.

Publications

German-language publishers issued many new books dealing with Jewish life during the Nazi era: Leo Sievers, *Juden in Deutschland: Die Geschichte einer 2000-jährigen Tragödie* ("Jews in Germany: The History of a 2,000-Year Tragedy"; Stern Buch-Verlag, Hamburg); Gerda Luft, *Heimkehr ins Unbekannte: Eine Darstellung der Einwanderung von Juden aus Deutschland nach Palästina vom Aufstieg Hitlers zur Macht bis zum Ausbruch des Zweiten Weltkrieges 1933–1939* ("Going Home Into the Unknown: An Account of Jewish Immigration from Germany to Palestine, from Hitler's Ascent to Power Until the Outbreak of the Second World War, 1933–1939"; Hammer, Wuppertal); Margarete Sallis-Freudenthal, *Ich habe mein Land gefunden: Erinnerungen* ("I Have Found My Land: Memoirs"; Knecht, Frankfurt); Rolf Vogel, *Ein Stempel hat gefehlt: Dokumente zur Emigration deutscher Juden* ("A Stamp Was Missing: Documents of the Emigration of German Jews"; Droemer Knaur, Munich); Charlotte E. Zernik, *Im Sturm der Zeit: Ein persönliches Dokument* ("In the Tempest of the Times: A Personal Document"; Econ, Düsseldorf); Jürgen Serke, *Die verbrannten Dichter* ("The Burned Poets"; Beltz, Weinheim); Hans Sahl, *Die Wenigen und die Vielen: Roman einer Zeit* ("The

Few and the Many: Novel of an Era"; Fischer, Frankfurt); Kurt Tucholsky, *Briefe aus dem Schweigen 1932–1935* ("Letters from Out of the Silence, 1932–1935"; Rowohlt, Reinbek).

On Jewish history: Carl Cohen, *The Impact of the Protestant Reformation on the Jews* (Schneider, Heidelberg); Bruno Kirschner, *Deutsche Spottmedaillen auf Juden* ("German Medals Satirizing Jews"; Battenberg, Munich); Hans Liebeschütz and Arnold Paucker, *Das Judentum in der deutschen Umwelt 1800–1850* ("Jewry in the German Environment, 1800–1850"; Mohr, Tübingen); Eugen Taeubler, *Aufsätze zur Problematik jüdischer Geschichtsschreibung 1908–1950* ("Essays on Problems of Jewish Historiography, 1908–1950"; Mohr, Tübingen); Jacob Toury, *Soziale und politische Geschichte der Juden in Deutschland 1847–1871: Zwischen Revolution, Reaktion und Emanzipation* ("Social and Political History of the Jews in Germany, 1847–1871: Amid Revolution, Reaction and Emancipation"; Droste, Düsseldorf); Ulrich Dunker, *Der Reichsbund Jüdischer Frontsoldaten 1919–1938: Geschichte eines jüdischen Abwehrvereins* ("The National League of Jewish Combat Veterans: History of a Jewish Defense Agency"; Droste, Düsseldorf); Joachim Freyburg and Hans Wallenberg, *Hundert Jahre Ullstein* ("A Hundred Years of the House of Ullstein"; Ullstein, Berlin).

On National Socialism: Adalbert Rückerl, *Nationalsozialistische Vernichtungslager im Spiegel deutscher Strafprozesse: Belzec, Sobibor, Treblinka, Chelmno* ("Nazi Extermination Camps in the Mirror of German Criminal Trials: Belzec, Sobibor, Treblinka, Chelmno"; Deutsche Verlagsanstalt, Stuttgart); Hans Robinsohn, *Justiz als politische Verfolgung: Die Rechtsprechung in "Rassenschandefällen" beim Landgericht Hamburg 1936–1943* ("Administration of Justice as Political Persecution: Court Rulings in 'Miscegenation' Cases Before the Hamburg Regional Court, 1936–1943"; Deutsche Verlagsanstalt, Stuttgart); Avraham Barkai, *Das Wirtschaftssystem des Nationalsozialismus: Der historische und ideologische Hintergrund 1933–1936* ("The Economic System of National Socialism: The Historical and Ideological Background, 1933–1936"; Wissenschaft und Politik, Cologne); Werner Maser, *Nürnberg: Tribunal der Sieger* ("Nuremberg: Tribunal of the Victors"; Econ, Düsseldorf); Viktor E. Frankl, . . . *Trotzdem ja zum Leben sagen: Ein Psychologe erlebt das Konzentrationslager* (". . . And Yet Say Yes to Life: A Psychologist Experiences the Concentration Camp"; Kösel, Munich); Karl Sauer, *Die Verbrechen der Waffen-SS* ("The Crimes of the Waffen *SS*"; Röderberg, Frankfurt); Lieselotte Maas, *Handbuch der deutschen Exilpresse 1933–1945,* Band II ("Handbook of the German Press in Exile, 1933–1945," Vol. II; Hanser, Munich).

Ancient Jewish History: Shmuel Safrai, *Das jüdische Volk im Zeitalter des Zweiten Tempels* ("The Jewish People in the Era of the Second Temple"; Neukircher, Neukirchen-Vluyn); Gerhard Prause, *Herodes der Grosse: König der Juden* ("Herod the Great: King of the Jews"; Hoffmann und Campe, Hamburg); Svend Holm-Nielsen, *Die Psalmen Salomons: Jüdische Schriften aus hellenistisch-römischer Zeit* ("The Psalms of Solomon: Jewish Writings from the Hellenist-Roman Age"; Mohn, Gütersloh); *Gott sprach zu Abraham: Die Geschichte des biblischen Volkes und seines Glaubens* ("God Spoke to Abraham: The Story of the People of the Bible and Its Faith"), with 72 pictures in full color by Erich Lessing and introductory text by Claus Westermann (Herder, Freiburg).

The Jewish religion: Pinchas Lapide, *Auferstehung: Ein jüdisches Glaubenserlebnis* ("Resurrection: An Experience in Jewish Faith"; Kösel, Munich); Simon Schoon and Heinz Kremers, *Nes Ammim: Ein christliches Experiment in Israel* ("Nes Ammim: A Christian Experiment in Israel"; Neukircher, Neukirchen-Vluyn); Hugo S. Bergmann, *Die dialogische Philosophie von Kierkegaard bis Buber* ("The Philosophy of Dialogue from Kierkegaard to Buber"; Schneider, Heidelberg); Bernhard Uhde, *Judentum im Religionsunterricht: Sekundarstufe II—Einführung, Unterrichtsmodell, Arbeitsmaterial* ("Judaism in Religious Instruction: Secondary Level II—Introduction to the Subject; Model Study Plan; Study Materials"; Don Bosco, Munich).

Biography: Rivka Horwitz, *Buber's Way to "I and Thou": An Historical Analysis and the First Publication of Martin Buber's Lectures*; Schneider, Heidelberg); Wiebrecht Ries, *Transzendenz als Terror: Eine religionsphilosophische Studie über Franz Kafka* ("Transcendence as Terror: A Study of Franz Kafka in Terms of the Philosophy of Religion"; Schneider, Heidelberg); Heinrich Graetz, *Tagebuch und Briefe* ("Diary and Letters"; Mohr, Tübingen); Ernst Pinchas Blumenthal, *Diener am Licht: Eine Biographie Theodor Herzls* ("Servant of the Light: A Biography of Theodor Herzl"; Europäische Verlagsanstalt, Cologne); W.P. Eckert, H.L. Goldschmidt, and L. Wachinger, *Martin Bubers Ringen um Wirklichkeit* ("Martin Buber's Struggle for Reality"; Bund, Cologne); Gerhard Wehr, *Der deutsche Jude: Martin Buber* ("A German Jew: Martin Buber"; Kindler, Munich); Margarete Buber-Neumann, *Milena, Kafkas Freundin* ("Milena, Kafka's Woman Friend"; Langen-Müller, Munich).

Prose and Poetry: I.Z. Kanner, *Jüdische Märchen* ("Jewish Fairy Tales"; Fischer, Frankfurt); Edgar Hilsenrath, *Der Nazi und der Friseur* ("The Nazi and the Hairdresser," a novel; Literarischer Verlag Braun, Cologne); Heinrich Heine, *Die Wahl-Esel: Ein satirisches Lesebuch* ("The Donkey Electors: A Satirical Reader"; Satire Verlag, Cologne); Heinrich Heine, *Gedichte* ("Poems"; Diogenes, Zurich); Ephraim Kishon, *Mein Freund Jossele: Auch Schwindeln will gelernt sein* ("My Friend Yossele: Also Fakery Needs to Be Learned," satires; Langen-Müller, Munich); Salcia Landmann, *Marienbad: Ein Roman in Briefen nach Scholem Alejchem* ("Marienbad: A Novel in Letters, after Sholom Aleichem"; Herbig, Munich); Mascha Kaleko, *Der Gott der kleinen Webefehler: Spaziergänge durch New Yorks Lower East Side und Greenwich Village* ("The God of Small Flaws: Walks Through New York's Lower East Side and Greenwich Village"; Eremiten-Presse, Düsseldorf); Jurek Becker, *Schlaflose Tage* ("Sleepless Days," a novel; Suhrkamp, Frankfurt).

Personalia

Rose Ausländer, 70, a poet, originally from Czernowitz and now residing in Düsseldorf, was awarded the DM 10,000 Andreas Gryphius Prize for East German Literature by the Artists' Guild in Esslingen. She also received the Ida Dehmel Prize for Literature of the Federation of Societies of Women Artists and Friends of the Arts in Hamburg.

The DM 20,000 Lessing Prize of the city of Hamburg was awarded to writer Jean Amery, born in Vienna in 1912, a resident of Brussels since 1945. The writer Hermann Kesten, born in 1900, now living in the United States, received the DM 20,000 Nelly Sachs Prize of the city of Dortmund for his services in promoting understanding and reconciliation among nations. Lorin Maazel, now leader of the Cleveland Orchestra, was awarded the Federal Cross of Merit, First Class, by President Scheel, in recognition of his services to the cultural life of Berlin, where he was chief music director of the German Opera and conducted the Berlin Radio Symphony Orchestra from 1965–1971.

The Central Council of Jews in Germany awarded its DM 3,000 Leo Baeck Prize for 1977 to a former member of its board of directors, the late Josef Neuberger, an SPD politician and former minister of justice in the state of North Rhine-Westphalia. Hermann Lewy, 72, of Düsseldorf, the long-time editor-in-chief of the *Allgemeine jüdische Wochenzeitung,* the only national Jewish weekly in West Germany, was awarded the Great Cross and Star of the Federal Order of Merit by the President for his services to German-Jewish reconciliation. The Federal Cross of Merit, First Class, was awarded to Heinz Bär of Düsseldorf, for his services in reviving Jewish sports in postwar Germany and in consolidating Jewish communal life. Max Willner, director of the Central Welfare Agency of Jews in Germany, was named an honorary fellow of Tel Aviv University in appreciation of his services on behalf of the university, and his activities in support of culture and research for the benefit of Israel and the Jewish people.

Hans Wallenberg, a journalist who had played a significant role in the revival of a free press in postwar Germany, had been editor-in-chief of the *Neue Zeitung,* and for years had occupied leading positions at the daily *Die Welt* and other major publications, died in Berlin on April 13, at the age of 69.

FRIEDO SACHSER

German Democratic Republic

THE EAST BERLIN Jewish community had 369 members at the end of June, 248 of them 60 years or older. The other seven communities in the country had about 350 additional members.

In November, a Jewish communal library was opened in East Berlin in the presence of numerous public officials. The library comprised about 1,000 volumes and was to be expanded. At the opening, Peter Kirchner, chairman of the East Berlin Jewish community, expressed the hope that the new library would help promote Jewish cultural life in the country.

Representatives of the Federation of Jewish Communities in the German Democratic Republic took part in the World Conference of Religious Representatives for a Durable Peace, Disarmament, and Just Relationships Among Nations, held in Moscow during June; in the regional convention of the European Section of the World Jewish Congress in Milan in September; and in the Third European Conference of the International Council of Jewish Women in London during October. Also in October, the president of the Federation, Helmut Aris, stated in a message to the 14th party congress of the Christian Democratic Union of Germany: "Antisemitism and racism have been overcome and no longer have a place in our republic, in contrast to events of fascist and racist cast in the Federal Republic of Germany and other capitalist countries." In May, the new Jewish cemetery in Dresden had been desecrated.

During a visit to the Netherlands in February, Foreign Minister Oskar Fischer stated that the problem of restitution to victims of Nazi persecution had been concluded, as far as his government was concerned. The German Democratic Republic, he said, had met all its obligations.

On December 19, Jurek Becker, 40, a well-known Jewish writer who had grown up in the Lodz ghetto and been interned in a German concentration camp with his parents, left East Germany for political reasons. Becker, a winner of the East German National Prize, is best known for *Jacob the Liar,* which was made into a film.

In the area of foreign policy, the German Democratic Republic continued to support the radical forces in the Arab campaign against Israel. East Germany accused Israel of numerous crimes against the Palestinians. The press compared Israelis to Nazis; cartoons repeatedly pictured Moshe Dayan as a disciple of Hitler. The PLO was enthusiastically supported. In a congratulatory telegram to Yasir Arafat on his reelection as chairman of the PLO Executive Committee, Party Secretary Erich Honecker praised the "long-standing fraternal cooperation and anti-imperialist solidarity" between East Germany and the PLO.

In connection with the Israeli-Egyptian peace negotiations, the German Democratic Republic openly backed the opponents of President Sadat, especially Syria and Libya. The Foreign Ministry voiced "surprise and regret" over the "unexplained and unjustified" closing of the East German consulate in Alexandria, Egypt. In the opinion of Werner Lamberz, a member of East Germany's Politburo, the solution of the Middle East conflict was not to be found in an "imperialist-Zionist sham peace," which "in reality would contain the germ of new wars, but only in a comprehensive peace settlement." For this reason, Lamberz said, the German Democratic Republic would continue to favor reconvening the Geneva Conference.

FRIEDO SACHSER

Eastern Europe

Poland

Among the Jewish communities of Eastern Europe, Poland, as the ancient center of Jewish religious and secular life, occupies a special place. Today it contains a small Jewish remnant valiantly trying to preserve some semblance of Jewish life. It is difficult to predict if such efforts will prove successful; much depends on general political conditions and the attitude of the authorities.

In 1977, there were no changes in the top leadership of the country. Edward Gierek was secretary of the PPZR (Polish Communist Party), and Piotr Jaroszewicz was prime minister. The head of state, whose power was limited, was Henryk Jablonski. The crisis of June 1976, when workers rioted in protest against increases in food prices, subsided, but the essential problems of the Polish economy remained unsolved. The continuing contradictions within industrial enterprises, some 75 per cent of which were integrated into large corporations, resulted in a growing bureaucracy without affecting productivity or helping to stop the upward spiral of prices. In fact, the authorities quietly introduced price increases, which in some sectors reached 20 to 45 per cent.

At the end of 1977, 14 top members of the Party, including former head of state Edward Ochab, demanded radical revision of domestic policy with a view to resolving the problem of a continuing lack of essential food products. At the same time, Polish dissidents gained increased support among both intellectuals and workers. The Congress of Polish Writers, which met in April 1978 in Katowice, provided an interesting illustration of the oppositionist spirit prevailing among Polish intellectuals. Speakers openly demanded changes in the political line—more freedom and the abolition of censorship. A list of some 80 writers in official disgrace was made public.

Professor Edward Lipinski, an economist, was active in the Workers Defense Committee, created to defend workers who were fined, jailed, or dismissed from their jobs following the 1976 riots. Professor Lipinski, a Marxist, protested against what he called the "Russian type" of socialism.

There were some moves toward reconciliation between the authorities and the Catholic Church. In the fall of 1977, there was a meeting between Gierek and Stefan Cardinal Wyszynski. In December 1977, Gierek visited Pope Paul VI at the Vatican. In January 1978, during the visit of United States President Jimmy Carter, his wife

Rosalyn, and Zbigniew Brzezinski, Carter's adviser on national security had an unusual meeting with the Catholic Primate. In October 1978, the Communist leadership of Poland hailed the election of Polish Cardinal Karol Wojtyla as Pope. The Polish head of state went to Rome for the Pope's investiture.

JEWISH COMMUNITY

The Jewish population of Poland was estimated to be 6,000. This number included some Jews who did not identify with the Jewish community. There were varied estimates of the number of Jews who had changed their names and integrated into Polish society. Some local observers believed that their number was considerable.

Officially, some 1,500 Jews were affiliated with the Cultural and Social Union of Polish Jews, which held its seventh annual congress in October 1977 in Szrudborow. Delegates representing 17 local affiliates participated in the congress; they were greeted by a representative of the PPZR. Ruta Gutkowska, executive head of the Union, continued in the post of secretary. The Union, which was based in Warsaw, undertook efforts in, among other places, Wroclaw, Katowice, Zary, Walbrzych, Dzierzoniow, Krakow, Szczecin, and Lodz. These activities were limited mainly to lectures, amateur theatricals, and the like. There are no Jewish schools in Poland. The younger generations of Polish Jews do not understand Yiddish.

Folksztyme, the official Yiddish weekly, also published a Polish edition. The Jewish Historical Institute in Warsaw maintained its activities and was in contact with the Memorial Foundation for Jewish Culture in New York. *The Bulletin,* a periodical issued by the Institute, included articles on the Holocaust and the Jewish situation in Poland before World War II; studies dealing with the former subject strictly followed the Communist Party line.

The Jewish State Theater, under the direction of Szimon Szurmily, presented its repertoire in Yiddish, but audiences were provided with Polish translations. The theater added to its repertoire a new play, *Widerstand* ("Resistance"), by the late Soviet Yiddish writer Noah Luria. The play, directed by Jacob Rotboim, deals with Jewish life in the ghetto under German occupation.

In addition to the secular Cultural and Social Union, there was a Union of Religious Congregations which was based in Warsaw and claimed several local affiliates. There were no rabbis, no *mohalim,* and very few open synagogues. Religious life is deteriorating to a critical stage. During the Passover holiday, *matzot* were made available, but it was difficult under the existing conditions to observe *kashrut.* There was in Warsaw, however, a Jewish communal kitchen, sponsored by the Union of Religious Congregations, which distributed kosher meals. Little, if anything, was done to maintain old Jewish cemeteries in places where Jews no longer lived.

In April 1978, there was a commemoration of the 35th anniversary of the Warsaw Ghetto uprising. Some 15 countries, including the United States, Israel, West Germany, France, and the Soviet Union, were represented at the ceremonies. The Israeli delegation was headed by Gideon Hausner, the prosecutor of Adolf Eichmann, and included the Polish-Jewish resistance fighter Stefan Grayek. General Yitzhak Arad represented Yad Vashem. On April 17 Janusz Wieczorek, the minister in charge of war veterans, reopened the Jewish pavilion at Auschwitz, which had been closed since 1967, when the antisemitic policy of the government resulted in an exodus of many Jewish activists and intellectuals from the country. Dr. Nahum Goldmann, representing the World Jewish Congress, delivered an address in Yiddish.

On April 18, Yad Vashem awarded Righteous Gentile medals to 19 Poles who, during the occupation, at great personal risk, saved the lives of many of their Jewish compatriots. On the same day, a memorial meeting took place in Philharmonic Hall in Warsaw, with Ruta Gutkowska as the principal speaker representing the Polish Jewish community. On April 19, foreign delegations to the commemoration laid wreaths at the Warsaw Ghetto monument, which was surrounded by a military guard. This was the first time in many years that the annual commemoration of the Warsaw Ghetto revolt assumed a distinctly Jewish character.

In the city of Rypin, in the region of Wroclaw, the authorities opened a home for orphans in the name of Janusz Korczak. Representatives of the Cultural and Social Union participated in the dedication ceremony, which included a presentation of *Korczak and His Children,* a play about the great Jewish educator and his martyrdom under the Nazis, presented by the local drama circle of the Teachers Union.

LEON SHAPIRO

Yugoslavia

Having adopted a new constitution in 1974, the Yugoslav Assembly in 1976 promulgated a new labor law which, according to its sponsors, codified the Yugoslav concept of "self-managing socialism." Marshal Tito, president-for-life of Yugoslavia, and his collaborators viewed this "self-managing" approach as totally different from the "centralist" type of Communist management found in the USSR and China. The Belgrade model is based on the assumption that workers should directly control the government and economy.

The authorities were faced with dissent on many fronts: intellectuals calling for greater freedom; separatists, particularly among the Croatians, putting forth nationalist claims; and "hardliners" advocating the return of Yugoslavia to the Soviet bloc and, concomitantly, to Soviet methods of administration. Yugoslav leaders also had to deal with various religious groups, including the Serbian Orthodox Church, the Roman Catholic Church, and Moslems, who were promoting educational activities and distributing religious literature. The official press repeatedly called the attention of the authorities to the fact that children of members of the Communist League were being baptized, sometimes without the knowledge of their parents.

While the authorities were combating pro-Soviet tendencies and protesting "Soviet meddling" in the affairs of Yugoslavia, Soviet boss Leonid Brezhnev visited Belgrade (November 1976). Brezhnev decried the "fairy tales" about Soviet designs on Yugoslavia, and repeatedly pledged to honor Yugoslav sovereignty. In any event, Yugoslav leaders made it clear that they would fight for their freedom and their "own way to socialism." The political situation was further complicated by the advancing age of Tito, who is in his mid-80's.

Yugoslavia continued its support of Yasir Arafat and the PLO. Arafat, during a visit to Belgrade in December 1976, was received with the honor accorded a chief of state. Although Yugoslav-Israeli relations had been terminated following the Six-Day War in 1967, the authorities did not interfere with the Jewish community's support of the State of Israel. The aging president was frequently reported as seeking to promote a peaceful solution to the Israel-Arab conflict.

In January 1977, the Yugoslav prime minister, Dzemal Bijedic, was killed in an airplane crash. He was replaced by Veslin Djuranowic, a Montenegran by birth.

JEWISH COMMUNITY

The Jewish population of Yugoslavia was estimated to be 6,000, with 1,500 in the capital city of Belgrade, 1,200 in Zagreb, and 1,100 in Sarajevo. Jewish communal activities were conducted by the Federation of Jewish Communities, an officially recognized body. Lavoslav Kadelburg, an eminent Jewish leader, continued to serve as president of the Federation; its executive head was the secretary, Lucy Petrovic. The Federation promoted Jewish activities in, among other places, Belgrade, Dubrovnik, Zagreb, Skopje, Split, Sarajevo, Subotica, Novi Sad, Ljubliana, and Zemun. According to official data, many cities with a Jewish population did not have a synagogue. In fact, the Federation was essentially a secular body dealing only peripherally with religious matters. In some places, Sabbath and holiday services were conducted by qualified laymen, mostly older people. There was no formal system of religious education, and the absence of trained religious personnel made it difficult to maintain religious life. Intermarriage was widespread in most of the communities.

The Federation was affiliated with the World Jewish Congress and was in close contact with the American Jewish Joint Distribution Committee and the Memorial Foundation for Jewish Culture in New York, both of which supported its social and cultural activities.

The Federation of Jewish Communities maintained a wide variety of cultural activities. In the ten largest communities, it sponsored Jewish youth clubs and children's groups that met regularly. From time to time, these groups attended lectures given by persons from abroad. The Federation operated summer camps at which children from Yugoslavia joined with others from Hungary, Rumania, Czechoslovakia, and Israel. Included in the camp experience were visits to Jewish historical sites. The Federation organized seminars for young lay leaders. It maintained a central Judaica library which supplied Jewish literature to at least nine community libraries.

Jewish publications appeared regularly. Five issues of *Zbornik,* an anthology devoted to Jewish concerns, were published. Other publications included *Jevrejski Pregled* ("Jewish Review"); *Kadima,* a youth magazine; *Jevrejski Almanah* ("Jewish Almanac"); and a *luah* (calendar), edited by Rabbi Cadik Danon, containing some prayers printed in Hebrew and transliterated into Latin letters. The Federation was preparing a short history of the Jewish people in the Serbo-Croatian language, a volume on the Sephardic tradition in Yugoslavia, and, in collaboration with Hitahdut Olei Yugoslavia in Tel Aviv, a Jewish guide to Yugoslavia. In Belgrade and Zagreb, two Jewish choirs continued their activities, presenting programs of Jewish music to Yugoslav audiences, as well as audiences abroad. Courses in Hebrew for teenagers and young adults were provided through the Federation.

The Jewish Historical Museum and the Historical Archives, both in Belgrade, had accumulated a large number of artifacts and documents relating to the Jewish past in Yugoslavia. Much of this material, however, still remained to be classified and catalogued. Concern was expressed as to whether the oldest Yugoslav synagogue, in Dubrovnik, was being properly maintained. As in other East European countries, many old Jewish cemeteries were in urgent need of repair.

LEON SHAPIRO

Israel

NINETEEN SEVENTY-SEVEN was a year of great political upset in Israel, and of a new era in the quest for peace. The elections on May 17 put an end to a generation of Labor dominance in the Knesset and government, bringing the veteran Herut leader Menachem Begin to power at the head of an anti-socialist coalition. A month later, however, Labor retained its position in the elections to the quadrennial convention of the Histadrut, the General Federation of Labor.

At the end of October, the new Begin government announced a drastic reversal in economic policy, based on the abolition of foreign currency controls and the free floating of the Israeli pound. At the beginning of 1978, there were signs of a developing clash with various groups of workers demanding higher wages to compensate for price increases.

Meanwhile, in November 1977, President Anwar Sadat of Egypt dropped a bombshell by offering to conclude a permanent peace with Israel—the first time such an offer had been made by an Arab leader. His conditions were that Israel withdraw from all territories taken in the Six-Day War of 1967 and agree to self-determination for the Palestinians. It was later disclosed that the visit had been prepared by a secret Israeli offer to restore the whole of Sinai to Egyptian sovereignty.

At the end of December, Prime Minister Begin presented his peace proposals, based on withdrawal of Israeli forces from Sinai and self-rule for Palestinian Arabs, to United States President Jimmy Carter in Washington, and to President Sadat in Ismailiyah. Egypt and Israel agreed to continue negotiations in a military committee in Cairo, and in a political committee in Jerusalem.

The Elections

(For the early stages of the events leading up to the elections, see AJYB 1978 [Vol. 78], pp. 475–7.)

Shortly before nominations day, there were signs of unrest among hawkish members of the Labor Party. Mordecai Ben-Porat resigned and formed an independent list. Former Defense Minister Moshe Dayan met with Menachem Begin, leader of the Likud, to discuss the possibility of running on his list, but nothing came of it, reportedly because Begin would not agree that there be no annexation of Judea and Samaria as long as peace discussions were proceeding. To appease Dayan, a score of Labor Party leaders stated that, when the next government was formed, they would insist that the nation be consulted before any territory in Judea and Samaria be ceded. Dayan agreed to run on the Labor ticket.

Seven Labor leaders, including Knesset Speaker Israel Yeshayahu and Israel Galili, minister without portfolio, failed to secure places on the Labor-Mapam Alignment's list. Twenty of the first 50 names, regarded as having a fair prospect of being elected, were nominated by the party's regional groupings, and the other 30 by an appointments committee, which also decided on the order of listing. Heading the list were Defense Minister and acting Prime Minister Shimon Peres, Foreign Minister Yigal Allon, and former Foreign Minister Abba Eban.

On March 1, the council of the Likud approved its election platform on foreign affairs, which declared that a Likud government would participate in the Geneva Peace Conference and invite the neighboring Arab states "to conduct direct negotiations for the signature of peace treaties between them without prior conditions." It would "strive for an agreement" with Syria and Egypt, "taking into consideration the interests and needs of the parties" (a formula which left the way open for territorial concessions). In regard to the "West Bank," the platform declared: "Judea and Samaria will not be handed over to any foreign rule; between the sea and the Jordan there shall be only Israeli sovereignty." Each of the Likud's components chose its leading candidates separately by secret ballots in several stages.

The governing bodies and list of parliamentary candidates of the Democratic Movement for Change (DMC) were elected directly by the entire membership on February 18. The 33,000 registered members were asked to pick 30 candidates out of 151 names, in order of preference. The results aroused some surprise and controversy. DMC's opponents insinuated that organized groups had succeeded in manipulating the voting, pointing out that the first ten names on the list included three former leaders of the Free Center, that two Druzes (representing little more than one per cent of the population) were in 12th and 13th places, and that women, former members of the Shinui movement, and the poorer neighborhoods were under-represented. DMC leaders retorted that their example had induced other parties to adopt more democratic methods of choosing their nominees.

The main plank in DMC's elections platform was the reform of the electoral system. On peace policy, DMC declared that Israel's defense border should be "the River Jordan, including areas west of it essential for Israel's defense. In order to retain its Jewish and democratic nature," the plank continued, "Israel must be ready for territorial compromise while safeguarding its security needs." Security considerations would be "the guiding principle in determining settlement priorities." The economic planks, which were somewhat similar to those of the Likud, called for more opportunity for individual initiative, and a reduction in government interference. DMC representatives would be given freedom of action on questions concerned with the relations between religion and state.

In the nominations of the National Religious Party (NRP), Yitzhak Raphael, former minister of religious affairs, was ousted in favor of two of his younger lieutenants. Rabbi Hayim Druckman, closely associated with the Gush Emunim religious activists, was added to the list in second place by common consent, reinforcing the influence of the younger, more hawkish, circles in the party.

Tourism Minister Moshe Kol, the veteran leader of the Independent Liberal Party (ILP), gave way to Gideon Hausner. Shortly before the election, Hillel Seidel, one of ILP's Knesset members, joined the Likud.

Public meetings played a small part in the election campaign. Appeals by the parties were made primarily through the press, radio, and television. The party campaigns were financed, in large part, by statutory allocations from the Treasury, in proportion to the Knesset strength of the parties, and under the supervision of the state comptroller.

The Likud mounted a vigorous and effective election campaign, carried out by a prominent advertising agency under the direction of General (Reserves) Ezer Weizman. Its two main watchwords were "Force No. 1" and "Change the Government"—claiming that, after 29 years of Labor domination, it was time to try an alternative government, and that the Likud was the only political force capable of playing that role. It concentrated on domestic affairs, especially scandals (see AJYB, 1978 [Vol. 78], pp. 476–7), and portrayed Labor as riddled with corruption. It claimed to be a party of peace, playing down its opposition to withdrawal from Judea and Samaria. A special effort was made to build up the image of its leader, Menachem Begin, as a sympathetic personality and a statesman of world stature.

The Labor-Mapam Alignment, whose campaign was conducted by Yosef Sarid, a young Knesset member, pointed to the inclusion of 14 candidates from the Oriental communities and eight women in the first 50 names on its list, as showing Labor's broad-based representative character. The Alignment's main slogan was "We are the Address"—admitting responsibility for past shortcomings, but claiming credit for achievements, and asking for renewed confidence in its capacity to provide a re-invigorated leadership. It portrayed the Likud as a "one-man-show," and Menachem Begin as a man who had failed in eight election attempts. In the event of large Likud gains, Labor forecast political deadlock and national chaos.

NRP appealed to broader circles on the lines of "You don't have to be religious to vote NRP," and presented itself as a positive alternative to the Labor-dominated regime, rather than—as in past years—a potential partner.

DMC presented Professor Yigal Yadin as the most suitable candidate for prime minister, backed by a capable and experienced team, with a comprehensive program of social and political reform. Its main barbs were aimed at Labor, although it also attacked the Likud as an old-style party.

General (Reserves) Ariel Sharon led a list called Shlomzion (Peace of Zion) with a strongly nationalist platform.

Two left-wing parties, Hadash (Front for Democracy, Peace, and Equality), which appealed mainly to Arab voters, and Shelli (Peace and Equality for Israel) called for the establishment of a Palestinian state, and readiness to withdraw to the June 1967 lines as part of a peace settlement. The former came out for recognition of the Palestine Liberation Organization (PLO) as the representative of the Palestinian people, while the latter stressed the compatibility of its policy with essential Zionist aims.

An unusual candidate was Samuel Flatto-Sharon (see AJYB 1978 [Vol. 78], p. 472), who employed paid vote-getters and conducted a lavish campaign of press advertising based on the watchword "The Solitary Man in the Knesset."

Public opinion polls taken in the first four months of 1977 indicated that the Alignment retained a slight lead over the Likud, with 10–20 seats going to DMC. A very high proportion—around 40 per cent—of those polled, however, either refused to answer or expressed no opinion. The polls also showed a striking contrast between general approval of the government's record on foreign affairs and defense, and even more pronounced disapproval of its economic and social policies.

After Prime Minister Yitzhak Rabin's retirement from the contest (AJYB, 1978 [Vol. 78], p. 477), Shimon Peres was left with little more than a month to impress himself on the electorate as a potential prime minister. His image as a successful minister of defense was damaged by the publication, on April 26, of the state comptroller's annual report, which pointed out, *inter alia,* a number of instances of inefficiency and waste in the administration of the Israel Defense Forces (IDF). On May 11, less than a week before the elections, 54 paratroopers and airmen were killed in a helicopter crash during a training exercise, and the Likud hinted that Peres had been too busy with party politics to look after the armed forces. In a television confrontation between the Likud and Labor leaders, Begin was confident and incisive, while Peres was subdued and unimpressive.

The results of the election, as compared with those of 1973, are given below. Likud's first-place finish, with a percentage of the popular vote approaching that gained by Labor in the past, and Labor's relegation to second place, with little more than a quarter of the seats, astonished both parties. The results were a disappointment to DMC, because they dashed its hopes of holding the balance between the two major parties. Hadash's gain of one seat was less than had been expected, but it polled a majority of the Arab votes. Shelli won a smaller percentage of the votes than its constituent parts had in 1973. The most crushing defeat was suffered by the Independent Liberals, who had played a modest but influential role in Israel's political history, and had participated in almost all cabinets.

An analysis of the voting showed that the Likud and the religious parties gained especially among the communities of Oriental origin, while the Alignment's losses went mainly to DMC in the areas with a larger population of European origin, and to the Likud among the Oriental communities. Most commentators believed that the results were due not merely to the events and actions of the immediate past, but to deep-seated social developments, particularly the tendency among the Oriental communities, native-born Israelis, and young people to vote against the ruling party, whose hold had been weakened by the gradual depoliticization of the government and other public bureaucracies.

ELECTIONS TO 8TH KNESSET (December 31, 1973) AND 9TH KNESSET (May 17, 1977)

	1973	1977
Eligible voters	2,037,478	2,236,293
Votes cast (%)	1,601,098 (78.6)	1,771,726 (79.2)
Invalid votes (%)	34,243 (2.1)	23,906 (1.3)
Valid votes[a]	1,566,855	1,747,820
Valid votes cast for parties not qualifying[a]	75,887	46,969
Valid votes counting in allocation of seats[a]	1,490,968	1,700,851
Quota per Knesset seat[b]	12,424	14,173

Party	Popular Vote (%) 1973	Popular Vote (%) 1977	Net gain or loss	Knesset Seats 1973	Knesset Seats 1977	Net gain or loss
Likud	473,309 (30.2)	583,075 (33.4)	+(3.2)	39	43	+4
Alignment	621,183 (39.6)	430,023 (24.6)	−(15)	51[c]	32[d]	−19
Democratic Movement for Change .	— —	202,265 (11.6)	—	—	15	+15
National Religious Party	130,349 (8.3)	160,787 (9.2)	+(0.9)	10	12	+2
Agudat Israel	60,012 (3.8)[e]	58,652 (3.4)	+(1.0)		4	
Poalei Agudat Israel		23,956 (1.4)		5	1	
Democratic Front for Peace & Equality	53,353 (3.4)[f]	79,733 (4.6)	+(1.2)	4	5	+1
Flatto-Sharon	— —	35,049 (2.0)	—	—	1	+1
Shlomzion	— —	33,947 (1.9)	—	—	2	+2
Shelli	32,616 (2.1)[g]	27,281 (1.6)	+(0.2)	1	2	+1
United Arab List ..	39,012 (2.5)[h]	24,185 (1.4)	−(1.1)	3	1	−2
Independent Liberals	56,560 (3.6)	21,277 (1.2)	−(1.0)	4[i]	1	−3
Citizens' Rights Movement	35,023 (2.2)	20,621 (1.2)	−(1.0)	3	1	−2
Zionist & Social Renewal	— —	14,516 (0.8)				
Bet Israel (Yemenites)	3,195 (0.2)	9,505 (0.5)	+(0.3)			
Arab Reform Movement	— —	5,695 (0.3)				
Women's Party	— —	5,674 (0.3)				
Kach (Meir Kahane)	12,811 (0.8)	4,396 (0.2)	−(0.55)			
Workers' Front	13,332 (0.9)	2,498 (0.14)	−(0.8)			
New Generation ...	— —	1,802 (0.1)				
Zionist Panthers ...	5,945 (0.4)	1,798 (0.1)	−(0.3)			
Coexistence with Justice (Arab) ...	— —	1,085 (0.06)				
Other Lists (1973) ..	30,155 (1.9)					

[a] Only lists receiving at least one per cent of the valid votes cast—i.e. 17,478 in 1977—are entitled to share in the allocation of seats.

[b] The quota for one Knesset seat is the number of valid votes cast for the lists qualifying—i.e. 1,700,851 in 1977—divided by 120.

[c] Arie Eliav and Mordecai Ben-Porat withdrew from the party before the elections.

[d] Moshe Dayan withdrew from the party after the elections.

[e] In 1973, Agudat Israel and Poalei Agudat Israel formed one list: the Torah Religious Front.

[f] In 1973, Rakah—New Communist List

[g] In 1973, Moked (Focus) and Meri (Radicals)

[h] In 1973, Progress & Development (Arab) and Bedouins' List

[i] Hillel Seidel withdrew and joined the Likud.

The Histadrut Elections

The Labor-Mapam Alignment's supporters, particularly in the kibbutzim, reacted to the party's parliamentary debacle by redoubling their campaign efforts for the election of delegates to the 13th convention of the Histadrut, which would determine the composition of its governing bodies for the next four years.

Yeruham Meshel, the incumbent secretary-general, was renominated to head the Labor list, which included leaders of some of the larger workers' committees, but not prominent political figures. The Likud list was headed by David Levi, a young father of ten from the new immigrants' town of Beit Shean, who had come from Morocco during the period of mass immigration. Eleven lists were submitted, representing the major political parties except the religious ones, which had their own labor federations.

As in the Knesset elections, lavish press advertising was a prominent feature of the campaign, but unlike 1973, there was no television propaganda. The Likud called upon voters to complete its parliamentary victory by giving it control of the Histadrut, while the Alignment stressed the need for a strong Histadrut under its leadership, as a counterweight to a Likud dominated government.

Sixty-nine per cent of the 1,354,794 members voted, and the valid votes totaled 917,126. The results (see p. 266) were a surprise to both sides. Not only did Labor's share of the total drop much less than had been expected, leaving it in firm control, but it gained almost 60,000 more votes than it had on May 17. (In 1973, it had received about 150,000 more votes for the Knesset than for the Histadrut.) The Likud, though failing to achieve its declared objective, considerably improved its strength. The big losers, as in the Knesset elections, were the smaller parties. The Alignment also maintained its majority in Na'amat (Women Workers and Volunteers)—formerly Mo'etzet Hapo'alot (Working Women's Council)—and almost all the local labor councils, the elections to which were held simultaneously.

ELECTIONS TO THE 13TH CONVENTION OF THE HISTADRUT, THE
GENERAL FEDERATION OF LABOR, 1973 AND 1977.
(with Knesset votes, 1977, for main parties)

	1973		1977			
	Votes	%	Votes	Dele-gates	%	Knesset 1977
Alignment	447,541	58.35	507,236	841	55.31	430,023
Likud	174,038	22.69	258,466	428	28.18	583,075
DMC	—	—	73,594	122	8.02	202,265
Hadash	18,240[a]	2.38	27,781	46	3.03	79,733
Religious Workers	32,782	4.27	16,491	27	1.80	—
ILP and CRM ...	45,811	5.97	11,685	19	1.27	41,898
Shelli	21,118[b]	2.75	10,162	16	1.11	27,281
Others	27,470	3.61	11,711	—	1.28	—

[a] In 1973, Rakah (New Communist List)
[b] In 1973, Moked (Focus), Meri (Radicals) and Left Union

The New Government

The results of the elections dictated the composition of the new government within fairly narrow limits. The Likud, together with Shlomzion (whose two members joined Herut on May 29), NRP, and Flatto-Sharon, could command 58 votes, but needed the support of either Agudat Israel or DMC to have a majority. Labor firmly declined to join a government of national unity. While Begin was in the hospital, to which he had been admitted for a rest after the strains of the election, he startled the country by offering Moshe Dayan the post of foreign minister in his new cabinet. The appointment aroused fierce public controversy. Both the Liberals and DMC had expected to receive the post, while Labor spokesmen denounced Dayan's readiness to serve under Begin so soon after the elections, in which he had stood on the Alignment list, and demanded his resignation from the Knesset. The ferment soon died down, however, and the Likud started negotiations with NRP and Agudat Israel, which submitted numerous conditions concerned mainly with religious affairs.

On June 7, after the publication of the official election results and the statutory consultations with representatives of the parties, President Ephraim Katzir entrusted Begin with the task of forming a government. After seeing the President, Begin recited a psalm at the Western Wall in Jerusalem and paid a visit to Rabbi Zvi Yehuda Kook, spiritual mentor of Gush Emunim. The negotiations with NRP and Agudat Israel were rapidly concluded, but the Council of Sages, composed of recognized authorities on rabbinic law, whose rulings were binding on Agudat Israel in all matters, authorized only its joining the coalition but not accepting a cabinet portfolio. The talks with DMC raised many problems concerning foreign policy, settlement in the administered areas, and cabinet posts for its nominees.

Begin, anxious to form his government as quickly as possible, so that he could go to Washington to meet President Carter, concluded the negotiations with NRP and Agudat Israel, and the coalition agreement among the three parties was signed on June 12. It envisaged a number of social reforms, but 35 out of the 43 clauses were concerned with religious matters, such as legislation to provide that no autopsy be performed without the written consent of the deceased's family, stricter implementation of Sabbath work laws, and the amendment of the recently passed Termination of Pregnancy law to prohibit abortions on the grounds of difficult family or social conditions. A particularly controversial clause promised that any woman would be exempt from army service without further investigation, as customary hitherto, upon submitting a duly attested declaration that service would be incompatible with her religious mode of life. Prime Minister Begin undertook to make every effort to secure the passage of a private members' bill providing that only conversions in accordance with Orthodox religious law would be recognized under the Law of Return. A committee was to draft a bill, subject to the consent of all three parties, to reform the electoral system.

Begin presented his cabinet, consisting of 13 members, to the Knesset on June 20. Police was incorporated into the Ministry of Interior; Tourism was combined with Commerce and Industry; a new Ministry of Energy and Infrastructure was established; Labor was merged with Social Welfare to form a Ministry of Social Betterment, Communications, and Transport. For the first time, an NRP nominee was appointed minister of education and culture. The deputy premiership and three ministries—Labor and Social Betterment, Justice, and Transport and Communications—were left open for nominees of DMC in case it later decided to join the coalition; in the interim, they were managed by Yoram Eridor, deputy minister in the prime minister's office.

An opening clause in the new government's basic policy guide lines, presented to the Knesset for approval together with the list of ministers, declared: "The Jewish people has an eternal, historic right to the Land of Israel, the inalienable heritage of its forefathers." The government would "plan, establish, and encourage urban and rural settlement on the soil of the homeland." It would be ready to take part in the Geneva Conference "on the basis of Security Council Resolutions 242 and 338" and would not invoke its authority (under a law passed in June 1967) to apply Israeli law and jurisdiction to further parts of the Land of Israel "so long as negotiations are being conducted on a peace treaty between Israel and her neighbors." The Knesset gave the government a vote of confidence, 63 to 53.

The talks with DMC, suspended during Prime Minister Begin's visit to the United States in July, broke down in August over the question of electoral reform, as NRP objected to DMC's proposals, which would have endangered its parliamentary representation. Begin announced that he would fill the vacant cabinet posts with Likud nominees; but on October 21, a few days before the new appointments were due, DMC decided to join the government on the terms already offered. If DMC ministers objected to proposals for settlement in the administered territories, the final decision would be made by the Knesset Foreign Affairs and Security Committee; DMC members would have freedom of conscience on religious matters; and an electoral reform scheme, acceptable to the coalition parties, would be enacted before the next elections. Professor Yadin explained that he had become convinced that Israel faced "the toughest test since 1948" in connection with the reconvening of the Geneva Conference and that, therefore, DMC must join the government to strengthen it. Opponents within DMC argued that this would be a betrayal of the movement's basic principles and its promises to the voters; but the DMC council approved the proposal 68 to 45, and its representatives joined the cabinet on October 24. In order to maintain a balance between the parties, two additional Likud ministers, without portfolio, were added to the cabinet on January 10, 1978.

THE BEGIN CABINET
(installed on June 20, 1977)

Prime Minister	Menachem Begin (Likud-Herut)
Deputy Prime Minister	Yigael Yadin (DMC)[a]
Agriculture	Ariel Sharon (Likud-Herut)
Construction	Gideon Pat (Likud-Liberal)
Defense	Ezer Weizman (Likud-Herut)
Education & Culture	Zevulun Hammer (NRP)
Energy & Infrastructure	Yitzhak Moday (Likud-Liberal)
Finance	Simha Ehrlich (Likud-Liberal)
Foreign Affairs	Moshe Dayan (Independent)
Health	Eliezer Shostak (Likud-La'am)
Immigrant Absorption	David Levi (Likud-Herut)
Industry, Commerce, & Tourism	Yigael Hurwitz (Likud-La'am)
Interior & Police	Yosef Burg (NRP)
Justice	Shmuel Tamir (DMC)[a]
Labor and Social Betterment	Israel Katz (DMC)[a]
Religious Affairs	Aharon Abu-Hatzeira (NRP)
Transport & Communications	Meir Amit (DMC)[a]
Without Portfolio	Haim Landau (Likud-Herut)[b]
	Moshe Nissim (Likud-Liberal)[b]

[a]   Took office on October 24 (see text).
[b]   Took office on January 10, 1978.

Deputy Ministers

In the P.M.'s Office	Yoram Eridor (Likud-Herut)
Defense	Mordecai Zippori (Likud-Herut)
Finance	Yehezkel Flomin (Likud-Liberal)
Industry, Commerce, & Tourism	Yitzhak Peretz (Likud-La'am)

The Quest for Peace

Israel's foreign relations during the year were dominated by the quest for peace with her Arab neighbors, and the reconvening of the Geneva Peace Conference.

At the end of a visit to Israel in February (the first stage in a tour of six Middle East countries), the new United States secretary of state, Cyrus Vance, pledged "full consultations" with the Israeli government, reiterated America's commitment to a strong and secure Israel, and delivered an invitation to Prime Minister Rabin to visit Washington. (For an account of the visit, see AJYB 1978 [Vol. 78], p. 466.)

Foreign Minister Allon told the cabinet on May 8 that Israel had expressed concern to Washington about the Jewish state's exclusion from the list of favored nations for the purpose of arms supplies and joint weapons production (AJYB 1978 [Vol. 78], pp. 103–4). After President Carter reassured a Senate delegation that Israel would still be included in the list, and Allon and Secretary of State Vance met in London, Allon told the cabinet on May 15 that Israel was "thoroughly satisfied" with Carter's statement of firm commitment to Israel's deterrent strength.

Further statements by President Carter and United States spokesmen after the Knesset elections aroused renewed concern. At a cabinet meeting on June 5 to sum up the outgoing government's work, Rabin said that Carter's statements about the need for a "homeland" for the Palestinians were "a serious retreat" from past American policy.

Statements by Likud leader Menachem Begin, in the first flush of enthusiasm after his election victory, indicated a hard line over the future of Judea and Samaria. Begin sent Shmuel Katz, a close friend later appointed his advisor on overseas information, to the United States to explain his outlook. He established cordial relations with the new United States ambassador, Samuel Lewis and with Senator Richard Stone, chairman of the Senate subcommittee on the Middle East and South Asia.

When presenting his cabinet to the Knesset on June 20, Begin declared that a national consensus rejected withdrawal to the 1967 borders and the establishment of a Palestinian state. Moshe Dayan, who was to become foreign minister, appealed to all Zionist parties not to squabble with each other until the Arabs, the United States, or someone else presented concrete proposals. Government circles were very pleased with President Carter's cordial message to Begin on his accession as prime minister.

While reiterating his opposition to the establishment of a Palestinian state and a return to 1967 borders, Begin told the Zionist General Council on June 23: "The words 'not negotiable' are not in our dictionary. Everything is negotiable. The negotiations, however, must be free . . . without any externally devised formula for a settlement."

Begin was given a ceremonial send-off when he left for his visit to the United States on July 15. According to unofficial reports, he was prepared to tell President Carter that Israel would not agree to withdraw its forces from any part of the West

Bank and Gaza Strip, but would be ready to make a substantial withdrawal in Sinai, and adjust the lines on the Golan Heights. Israel was prepared to attend a renewed Geneva Conference, which could meet on October 10 or later.

The first three days of Begin's visit were spent in meetings with Jewish leaders in New York. The talks with President Carter in Washington on July 19 and 20 were marked by the obviously cordial relations established between the two leaders, who were reported to have agreed that there was no need to resolve their outstanding differences in advance of the Geneva Conference. Despite previous apprehensions, Begin declared that there had been no confrontation.

In a briefing of Israeli correspondents in Washington, a "senior Israeli official" contrasted Begin's policy with that of the previous government. He stated that Rabin, in trying to secure American agreement to Israel's positions, had only invited pressure for concessions. In a parliamentary debate on July 27, Labor Party leader Shimon Peres warned against "groundless optimism" and said that, by avoiding substantive political issues in favor of short-term agreements with the United States on procedure, Begin had waived American support and might well have set a snare for future Israel-U.S. relations.

Secretary of State Vance visited Israel again on August 9 and 10, after talks in Egypt, Syria, Jordan, and Saudi Arabia, to discuss arrangements for the reconvening of the Geneva Conference. It was agreed that the discussions with the U.S. would continue during the UN General Assembly in September. Begin declared that there had been a "breakthrough in the peacemaking process," but Vance stated that there had been "no narrowing of gaps."

Begin announced in a September 6 radio interview that Foreign Minister Dayan would be taking with him to the United States the draft of a peace treaty with Egypt, which would also apply to Syria, Jordan, and Lebanon. In Dayan's talks, which started on the 19th in Washington, a central issue was the American proposal for a united Arab delegation including Palestinians. The aim of this proposal was to avoid the difficulty of Palestinian representation at the Geneva Conference. This idea was first opposed by the Israelis, but was later accepted with certain conditions.

On October 1, America dropped a bombshell by issuing, together with the Soviet Union, a joint statement of principles favorable to the Arab cause. The Israeli government declared that the joint statement could only "further harden the positions of the Arab states and make the Middle East peace process still more difficult." On the 5th, however, while American Jewry was girding itself for a massive protest against the U.S.-USSR statement, Carter, Vance, and Dayan agreed, during a marathon session at the White House, on a working paper for the resumption of the Geneva Conference. The Arabs would be represented at the opening session by a unified Arab delegation, including "Palestinian Arabs." The negotiations would then be conducted by working groups. The West Bank and Gaza issues would be discussed in a working group consisting of Israel, Jordan, Egypt, and Palestinian Arabs. There would be separate discussions of the problem of "the Arab refugees and the Jewish refugees." The working paper was unanimously approved by the cabinet on October 11, and by a 41–28 vote in the Knesset on the 13th.

Four weeks later, while the discussions were continuing, President Sadat startled the world. At the opening session of the Egyptian Peoples' Assembly, on November 9, he declared his unprecedented intention to go to the Knesset in Jerusalem. The next day, Prime Minister Begin said that if Sadat came to Jerusalem, he would be received with all honor. On the 15th, an official written invitation to Sadat was delivered to U.S. Ambassador Lewis for transmission to Cairo. On the 17th, Sadat accepted Begin's invitation, and the next morning 60 Egyptian officials, most of them security men, arrived at Ben-Gurion airport to prepare for the visit. Within 48 hours, communications facilities, with direct telephone links to Cairo and world centers, were installed at the airport, the King David Hotel (where the main Egyptian delegation was to be housed), and the Jerusalem Theater, for hundreds of media correspondents.

Sadat arrived at Ben-Gurion airport after the end of the Sabbath on November 19, and was welcomed by President Katzir, the prime minister, and the entire cabinet. Together with the president and the prime minister, he stood at attention as the Egyptian and Israeli national anthems were played. Sadat reviewed a guard of honor and received a 21-gun salute. Crowds, waving Egyptian and Israeli flags, lined the road and cheered as Sadat's motorcade approached Jerusalem. The two leaders held their first talk the same evening in Sadat's hotel suite.

Next day, Sadat attended prayers at the al-Aqsa mosque, visited the Church of the Holy Sepulchre, and toured Yad Vashem, the Holocaust memorial to European Jewry, where he wrote in the visitor's book: "May God guide our steps for peace. Let us end all suffering for mankind." In the afternoon, after a working lunch with Begin, he went to the Knesset, where he laid a wreath at the foot of the monument to the fallen soldiers of IDF.

Addressing the Knesset in Arabic, Sadat opened with a passionate call for peace, but warned that he had not come to Jerusalem to conclude a separate peace between Egypt and Israel. He admitted that the Arabs had previously rejected Israel, but urged a new beginning: "We refused to meet with you anywhere; yes . . . We used to brand you as 'so-called Israel'; yes . . . Yet today I tell you, and I declare it to the whole world, that we accept living with you in permanent peace based on justice . . . We accept all the international guarantees . . . you want . . ."

"Peace for Israel," he stated, would mean that "Israel could live within her borders with her Arab neighbors in safety and security . . ." However, Sadat added, "There are Arab territories which Israel has occupied, and still occupies by armed force. We insist on complete withdrawal from these territories, including Arab Jerusalem." The "Palestine cause," he stressed, was "the crux of the entire problem." A peace agreement in Geneva would have to be based on, among other things, the "achievement of the fundamental rights of the Palestinian people and their right to self-determination, including the right to establish their own state." (It was noted, however, that Sadat made no mention of the PLO in his speech.)

In his reply, which was delivered without notes, Begin paid tribute to Sadat's courage, recalled that Israel's leaders had always wanted peace, and offered friendship and cooperation to the Arabs. He declared: "We seek a real, full peace, with complete reconciliation between the Jewish people and the Arab people . . . Let us negotiate . . . as free men for a peace treaty."

Begin invited the President of Syria and King Hussein of Jordan to follow in Sadat's footsteps; he also invited "genuine spokesmen of the Arabs of the Land of Israel to come and hold talks with us about our common future . . ." Sadat had been aware, Begin said, even before he came to Jerusalem, that "we have a different position from his on the permanent borders between ourselves and our neighbors." But he continued, "I call upon the President of Egypt and all our neighbors. Do not say that on any subject whatsoever there will be no negotiations . . . Everything can be negotiated . . . No side shall present prior conditions . . . Let us start the negotiations; let us continue with them, resolutely, until we succeed . . . in signing a treaty for peace."

Shimon Peres, chairman of the Labor Party, and the only other speaker, said, "Peace must be based on a reciprocal compromise, in contrast to war, which is built on a unilateral victory. We are prepared for [territorial] compromise with each of the Arab states . . . so long as they do not affect security . . . We are aware of the existence of the Palestinian identity."

In the evening, after the historic Knesset session and a working dinner, the two leaders met for a private talk. On Monday the 21st, Sadat had private meetings with Begin and Defense Minister Ezer Weizman, and went on to the Knesset to meet separately with party representatives. A basic concern, he told the coalition factions, must be "security for Israel." At the same time, however, Israel would have to make "very hard decisions."

At the beginning of a press conference given jointly by Sadat and Begin to sum up the visit, Begin read a mutually acceptable statement: "In response to the sincere and courageous move by President Sadat, the government of Israel proposes that this hopeful step be further pursued through dialogue between the two countries concerned, thereby paving the way towards successful negotiations leading to the signing of peace treaties in Geneva with all the neighboring Arab states." During Sadat's visit, Begin said, "a momentous agreement was already achieved, namely, no more war, no more bloodshed, no more threats." Both leaders replied "Yes" to the question: "Are you now both convinced of the sincerity of the desire for peace of each of you?" One of the main motives behind his visit to Israel, Sadat indicated, was "to give the peace process new momentum and to get rid of the psychological barrier that, in my idea, was more than seventy per cent of the whole conflict . . ." Sadat expressed his deep gratitude to the Israeli people, "whose welcome I can never forget."

On November 27, a few days after Sadat's return home, Egypt invited Israel, Syria, Jordan, Lebanon, the United States, and the USSR to attend an "informal" conference in Cairo to prepare the way for the Geneva Conference. Despite the efforts of Secretary of State Vance, who went to Amman and Damascus, Jordan and Syria refused to attend. The Cairo conference opened on December 14 under the chairmanship of General Ensio Siilasvuo, the UN chief of staff in the Middle East, with only Egypt, Israel, and the United States represented.

Israelis were profoundly impressed by the atmosphere surrounding the conference. The Israeli delegation, accompanied by approximately 50 journalists, was warmly greeted by the Egyptians. In a telephone survey in Israel, 41.2 per cent of those polled indicated that they were willing to give up the whole West Bank "in return for true peace and appropriate security guarantees"; 16.4 per cent were prepared to give up part of the area. In another poll, 46 per cent stated that they did not expect another war, and an unprecedented 90 per cent thought that Egypt was sincerely interested in peace with Israel. Over 100,000 people participated in a peace "happening" in Tel Aviv.

Working parties were set up in Cairo to discuss the agenda in detail, while Begin and his advisors prepared detailed peace proposals, which Begin presented to President Carter on the 16th. On the following day, Sadat invited Begin to visit Egypt for further talks, and there was a second Begin-Carter meeting on the 18th. Begin was clearly delighted at the reception of his proposals, which, he said, Carter considered "a fair basis" for negotiations. "I am leaving here a happy man," he declared.

On December 25–26, after a brief visit to Cairo by Defense Minister Ezer Weizman, Begin discussed the proposals with Sadat at Ismailia. At the end of the talks, Sadat announced that the negotiations would be continued through two ministerial-level committees: one on political affairs, headed by Foreign Minister Dayan, in Jerusalem, and one on military matters, chaired by Defense Minister Gamasy, in Cairo. There were differences regarding Judea and Samaria (the West Bank) and the Gaza Strip. While Israel offered self-rule for the Arabs of these areas, Egypt demanded the establishment of a Palestinian state.

Begin's peace plan was disclosed in detail, for the first time, in the Knesset on December 28. With reference to Judea, Samaria, and Gaza, the plan called for "self rule." Military government would be abolished, and an eleven-man administrative council, elected by the residents, would direct all affairs "relating to the Arab residents of the areas." Security and public order in the areas would be the responsibility of the Israeli authorities. Residents would be free to choose either Israeli or Jordanian citizenship, and would be entitled to vote in the elections to the respective legislatures. Residents of Israel would be entitled to acquire land and settle in the areas, and residents of the areas who opted for Israeli citizenship would be assured "freedom of movement and freedom of economic activity" in Israel.

Two committees representing Israel, Jordan, and the administrative committee would be established—one to decide questions involving legislation in the areas, the other to determine norms of immigration to the areas by Arab refugees "in reasonable number." Both committees would adopt rulings by unanimous decision only. Israel stood by "its right and its claim to sovereignty of Judea, Samaria, and the

Gaza district," but proposed, "for the sake of agreement and peace, that the question of sovereignty in these areas be left open." The final clause read: "These principles will be subject to review after a five-year period."

The central feature of the plan in terms of the future of Sinai was the withdrawal of Israeli forces to the international boundary.

The Sinai II agreement of September 1975 for the thinning out of forces between the Suez Canal and the Gidi-Mitla line was to remain valid, and the Egyptian army was not to cross the line. Jewish settlements in the Rafa area, south of the Gaza district were to "remain in place." They were to be linked with Israel's administration and courts and protected by "an Israeli force." For a transition period of several years, IDF forces would be stationed on a defensive line in central Sinai, and airfields and early warning systems would be maintained, until the withdrawal of the forces to the international boundary. Freedom of navigation in the Straits of Tiran was to be guaranteed.

In the Knesset debate, Labor leader Shimon Peres stressed the advantages of seeking a solution in cooperation with Jordan, including territorial compromise. The proposals were hotly denounced by Geula Cohen (Likud-Herut) and Moshe Shamir (Likud-Land of Israel Movement), while doubts were expressed by some NRP members. They were, however, approved by a vote of 64 to 8 (Communists, Cohen, Shamir, and one NRP), with 40 abstentions (Labor, three NRP, two Likud, and Shelli).

Lebanese Border

The "Good Fence" policy of humanitarian aid to the inhabitants of southern Lebanon (see AJYB 1978 [Vol. 78], pp. 467–8) continued, and was deeply appreciated by the Maronite Christians in the area. Francis Rizzak, political advisor to Major Sa'ad Hadad (commander of the mainly Christian forces in south Lebanon), told the press on April 18, during one of his frequent visits to Israel: "The people of Lebanon have entered into a fraternal alliance with Israel, from which they will not deviate and for which they are ready to pay with their blood." Hadad himself wrote: "Our former enemy, Israel, is today the only and the last support we have."

A close watch was kept on the situation in the area to prevent the approach of Palestinian guerrillas and Syrian forces. Toward the end of January, Israel complained about the deployment of a Syrian battalion around Nabatiya, and in mid-February, the Syrians started withdrawing their forces northward from the town.

In April, tension rose again. Shells fell in Misgav Am, just south of the border, and Israeli artillery fired several rounds at Palestinian forces. The situation quieted down, and Syria agreed to the extension of the mandate of the UN Disengagement Observation Force (established in 1974), which was approved by the Security Council on May 24.

Prime Minister Begin was outspoken about Israel's support for the Lebanese Christians. On August 9, he told an American Jewish delegation: "It shouldn't be a secret. When a barrage is opened on Christian villages, we aim our fire at the source of the hostile fire." On September 16, when the struggle between the Christians and Palestinians intensified, Israeli troops were sent to protect women and children in Christian villages, while the men were fighting. Katyusha rocket shells were fired from Lebanese territory during the next few days on Naharyia, Safad, and Kiryat Shmona, injuring several persons. A ceasefire went into effect on the 26th, and Defense Minister Weizman warned that Israel would not allow the situation to deteriorate again.

On the whole, the situation was quiet until early November, when three persons were killed and five injured by Katyusha rockets fired at Naharyia. In retaliation, Israeli planes and artillery strafed PLO bases near Tyre.

Other Foreign Relations

Resentment was felt at the statement of the European Economic Community (EEC), issued in London on June 29, supporting the Palestinian people's "legitimate right to a homeland" and rejecting "territorial conquests by force." Foreign Minister Moshe Dayan said on July 3 that the statement represented a further erosion of the EEC attitude toward Israel and would hamper the peace-making process.

Friendly contact was maintained with European organizations, and there were a number of official visits by European statesmen and delegations. Dayan visited the German Federal Republic in November, and Begin visited Britain in December.

On February 8, Israel signed an additional protocol to the 1975 agreement with EEC, providing for cooperation in the fields of industry, science and technology, as well as a financial protocol for investment aid from the European Bank.

Israel's relations with France improved somewhat after Foreign Minister Louis De Guiringaud's visit at the end of April, but there was still dissatisfaction with France's role in shaping EEC's unfavorable policies toward Israel. At the beginning of August, Israel protested against the French government's decision that an anti-boycott law would not apply to Arab-imposed restrictions on trade with Israel.

After the agreement between Portugal and Israel to establish diplomatic relations (see AJYB 1978 [Vol. 78], p. 472), the Israeli consulate in Lisbon became an embassy. The opening of a Portuguese embassy in Israel, however, was delayed.

There was no change during the year in the unfriendly attitude of the Soviet Union and the Soviet bloc countries, with the exception of Rumania. Prime Minister Begin paid a five-day visit (August 25–30) to the latter country. He described his meetings with the Rumanian Jewish community as "the most moving day in my life since the day Israel declared its independence."

There were numerous visits to Israel by Latin-American groups and public figures. President Katzir's cordial reception on a state visit to Mexico in November and December eliminated the last vestiges of tension arising out of Mexico's support of anti-Zionist resolutions at the United Nations in 1975.

Israel maintained varied economic ties with Black African countries, and, in some of them, had representatives serving as interest officers in the embassies of third countries. On February 4, Prime Minister Rabin had a secret three-hour conference in Geneva with President Felix Houphouet-Boigny of the Ivory Coast, and a joint communiqué issued after the talks declared that "dialogue is the best method for achieving peace in the region." Relations with South Africa were kept low-key during the year, and government spokesmen repeatedly denied reports of military links between the two countries.

Administered Territories

Between June 1967 and September 1977, 77 new settlements had been established in the administered territories; 26 on the Golan Heights; 21 in the lower Jordan valley and on the eastern slopes of Samaria; seven in the Etzion bloc, north of Hebron; three in western Samaria; 17 in the Rafah area (north-eastern Sinai) and the southern tip of the Gaza Strip; and three on the east Sinai coast. Prime Minister Rabin said on January 6 that these settlements enhanced the country's security, and provided a firm basis for Israel's demand for peace with defensible borders. The government's aim was to strengthen the confrontation lines along the Golan Heights, on the Jordan River, and at Ophira (Sharm al Sheikh), to protect Jerusalem and the Hebron hills, and to ensure a blocking zone south of the Gaza Strip. In May, a settlement was established on the West Bank, but it was only a short distance east of the former armistice lines.

Two days after the elections, Begin made some far-reaching statements at Elon Moreh, a settlement established by the Gush Emunim religious activist movement on the grounds of the army camp at Kadum (see AJYB 1977 [Vol. 77], p. 495 and AJYB 1978 [Vol. 78], p. 482). "In a few weeks or months," he averred, "there will be many Elon Morehs; there will be no need for a Kadum." In reply to a question whether the government would "annex" the administered territories, he retorted, "We don't use the word 'annexation'; you 'annex' foreign land, not your own country." In an ABC interview broadcast on May 22, he declared that Judea and Samaria were "an integral part of our sovereignty." On July 26, the cabinet Committee on Settlement officially recognized the Gush Emunim settlements at Kadum, Ophra, and Ma'alei Adumim. On August 17, the Joint (government and Zionist Organization) Settlement Committee approved the establishment of three new settlements in the territories close to the former armistice lines. In reply to American criticism, government sources pointed out that the settlements were all within the limits of the "minor adjustments" in the borders which even the United States was prepared to endorse; and on August 21 the Cabinet stated, "Israel does not and cannot accept the assertion that settlement by Jews in the Land of Israel is illegal." Speaking in a television interview on September 2, Agriculture Minister Ariel Sharon, chairman of the government Settlement Committee, outlined a 20-year plan to settle two million people in the administered areas, mainly in a new belt of settlements running from the Golan Heights along the River Jordan to the southern tip of Sinai.

Early in September, it was reported that Gush Emunim, tired of waiting for the new government to act, was preparing to establish 12 new settlements in the heart of the West Bank. The government asked it to exercise restraint, in view of the negotiations with the United States; but on September 28, after a long discussion with Prime Minister Begin, it was agreed that its groups be allowed to settle on the grounds of army and police camps. Six settlements were established in this way; but one group, which set out without permission to settle near Jericho, was stopped by the army with Begin's approval. The Treasury allocated funds to reimburse Gush Emunim for past outlays and new expenditures.

On September 30, during a visit by Prime Minister Begin, plans were announced to expand the population of Yamit (a coast town in the Rafah area) from about one to thirty thousand within the next two years. At his request, Begin was allocated a home in the settlement of Ne'ot Sinai, 2 kms. east of El-Arish. On August 14, the cabinet announced a policy of "equalization of services" for the inhabitants of the administered territories. Several local Arab leaders denounced the decision, and Yossi Sarid, a Labor member of the Knesset, declared that it "smells of annexation." Cabinet Secretary Arie Na'or, on the other hand, termed the move "humanitarian, not political," its object being to provide the population with the same standard of governmental services as that afforded citizens of Israel. He added, however, that the coalition parties were committed to the total integration of the areas into Israel "when the time is ripe."

Speaking at the UN Assembly debate on October 10, Foreign Minister Dayan said that Israel aimed at equal rights and full coexistence for Israelis and Palestinians in the Gaza Strip, Judea, and Samaria. "The settlements will not decide the final borders between Israel and its neighbors," he emphasized. "The border will be decided upon in the negotiations."

Economic Affairs

Nobel prize-winner Milton Friedman, of the University of Chicago, was invited to advise the new government on economic policy, as his advocacy of the elimination of government intervention conformed to one of the Likud's central planks. At the beginning of July he came to Israel to receive an honorary degree from the Hebrew University in Jerusalem, but met only once with Finance Minister Simha Ehrlich.

On June 29, Prime Minister Begin called for a program of "Social Justice without Socialism," and invited the Histadrut and the employers to join the government in negotiating a "social contract" to bring about economic stability and combat inflation. The proposal, however, was opposed by some ministers, and by the Manufacturers Association. As the previous Knesset had passed only an interim budget for April-July, a further two-month interim budget was introduced to enable the new government to consider its fiscal policy. On July 17, Finance Minister Erhlich announced a series of drastic measures, including cuts in subsidies and state expenditures, to reduce inflationary pressure and prevent depletion of foreign-currency reserves. The Histadrut called for a one-hour work stoppage in protest against the price increases, but the response was limited. In August, the Knesset approved a budget of IL 124 billion (about $12 billion) for the entire financial year 1977–78, comprising the two interim budgets. It became clear, however, that further measures would have to be taken to cope with inflation. By the end of September, currency in circulation had grown by over IL 10 billion, nearly twice as much as envisaged for the entire fiscal year, and an 8.8 per cent cost-of-living allowance was paid from October. On October 23, the cabinet decided on further subsidy cuts, which would immediately increase the prices of staple commodities and public transport by up to 10 per cent.

On October 28, Finance Minister Ehrlich announced a radically new economic policy, based on the free convertibility of the Israeli pound, and the abolition of control on foreign-currency accounts in local banks, cash holdings of up to $3,000 per person, and accounts of up to $3,000 in foreign banks. The 15 per cent defense duty on imports and the premium on exports were abolished, and the value added tax was raised from 8 to 12 per cent, with corresponding reductions in purchase taxes. Subsidies were further reduced, involving price increases of 15 per cent, but the foreign-travel tax was abolished. Welfare payments, pensions, and children's allowances were raised by 12 per cent, to compensate lower-income groups. Ehrlich said the plan would usher in a new era of economic growth, stabilize the economy, stimulate exports, attract foreign investments, and eliminate bureaucratic impediments to economic activity. Israel would now "join the club" of western nations and could become an important financial center.

The new policy was announced on the Sabbath eve. When the banks reopened on Monday, October 31, they sold dollars freely to the public for 15.5 pounds per dollar, rather than the previous rate of 10.35 pounds per dollar; but there was no rush on foreign currency. Many work committees and labor councils protested the new policy. Histadrut Secretary-General Yeruham Meshel described it as "a declaration of class war by a government that concerns itself only with the problems of the moneyed classes." The Histadrut estimated that about half a million people took part in demonstrations and strikes throughout the country; but some groups refused to stop work, and Likud spokesmen charged that some workers had been coerced into striking. Prime Minister Begin declared on November 2: "This government, which was formed on the basis of the people's will, will not be frightened by threats from without or within. The bolshevik-like tones heard these days will quickly disappear."

The new economic policy dominated the Histadrut's quadrennial convention on November 7–9, which was the stormiest in its history. However, Absorption Minister David Levi, who had headed the Likud list at the Histadrut elections and had voted against the new policy in the cabinet, made a conciliatory speech; and Meshel was given a standing ovation when he was re-elected secretary-general and promised to be the servant of all members regardless of party.

The main features of the economy during the year were: growth of only 1–3 per cent in the GNP, continuing the slow-down which had started in 1973 after increases of 11–12 per cent in 1971 and 1972; a drop of one per cent in the resources at the disposal of the economy, owing to a fall in imports; a rise of 13 per cent in exports; a rise of 3–4 per cent (1 per cent per capita) in personal consumption; a drop of 14 per cent in public consumption (expenditure by government and local authorities), due to a 20 per cent fall in defense expenditure as against a 2–5 per cent increase in civilian spending; a drop of 10–11 per cent in gross local investment; and increases of 9 per cent in agricultural output and 4–5 per cent in industrial production, counteracted by a drop of 15.5 per cent in construction.

Prices of goods and services at the disposal of the economy rose by an average of 43 per cent, after a rise of 31 per cent in 1976; while those of goods and services for private consumption rose by only 35–36 per cent (29 per cent in 1976). Over a million tourists arrived, a 25 per cent increase over 1976.

Other Domestic Affairs

At the end of the year, the population totalled 3,650,000—3,076,000 Jews and 574,000 non-Jews. This meant a 2.1 per cent increase during the year (1.8 per cent for Jews and 3.5 per cent for others). The estimated balance of immigration over emigration was only 4,000, and the growth in the rest of the Jewish population— 56,000—was due to natural increase.

The Termination of Pregnancy law, legalizing abortions on the grounds of, *inter alia,* serious social or family hardship, was passed on January 31, although bitterly opposed, before and after, by the religious parties.

In March, the Likud and Labor Party agreed on the terms of the latter's electoral reform bill, which had been given a preliminary reading in 1974 but had been held up in committee. Filibustering by representatives of Mapam, NRP, and Agudat Israel, however, prevented further progress.

Two proposals by Prime Minister Begin met with considerable public criticism and were ultimately dropped. One was to combine Holocaust Memorial Day and the memorial day for the war dead with the fast of Tish'a Be'av. The other, at first adopted by the cabinet, was to hold a military parade on Israel's 30th Independence Day.

There was heated controversy over President Katzir's remission, on Begin's recommendation, of part of the prison sentence of Joshua Bension on grounds of ill-health. Bension was released on September 8 after serving two years of a 12-year prison sentence for embezzling $39 million from the funds of the Israel British Bank, of which he was manager. The prime minister's office stated that Bension had been released on purely medical grounds, but opposition spokesmen insinuated that the motivation was political, as Bension was a supporter of Gush Emunim. Justice Joel Sussman, president of the Supreme Court, took the unprecedented step of labeling the decision a use of presidential prerogative to short-cut normal legal processes.

A police committee, headed by Assistant Commander Michael Bochner, was appointed in August to examine allegations that organized crime existed in Israel.

In its report, published on September 4, the committee said that there was no "super-organization" like the "syndicate" in the United States; nor was there any organized penetration of the police, courts, or government by criminals. There were, however, groups specializing in particular crimes on a basis of mutual aid and internal discipline. The committee also reported that police morale was low, owing to poor pay, and that there was a shortage of investigators. Interior and Police Minister Joseph Burg announced immediate measures to improve the situation at a cost of IL 140 million, and a public committee was appointed to make long-term recommendations.

Catholic Archbishop Hilarion Capucci, who was sentenced on December 9, 1974 to 12 years' imprisonment for supplying arms and explosives to Palestinian terrorists, was liberated on November 7 in response to a request for clemency from Pope Paul VI.

The terms of the Sephardi and Ashkenazi chief rabbis, which expired on October 15, were extended for up to nine months. On November 13, Rabbi Shalom Mashash, chief rabbi of Morocco, and Rabbi Bezalel Zolti were elected Sephardi and Ashkenazi chief rabbis of Jerusalem, respectively. The posts had been vacant for many years.

Israeli Arabs

In the Knesset elections, the Democratic Front for Peace and Equality (DFPE), led by the Communists, won 49 per cent of the Arab and Druze votes, in comparison to 37 per cent for the New Communist List (Rakah) in 1973. The Labor-Mapam Alignment's percentage fell from 13 to 11 per cent, its losses presumably going to DMC, which had four per cent. The United Arab List, associated with the Alignment, received 16 per cent, compared to 26 per cent for the corresponding Arab lists in 1973. In the Histadrut elections, the Alignment, with 60 per cent of the Arab votes, kept its strength; while the DFPE, with 32 per cent, made only slight gains.

There was some unrest among Israeli Arabs over government land policy and efforts to combat illegal building, especially in the Galilee and Negev. Ariel Sharon, minister of agriculture in the new government, alleged on August 23 that Negev Bedouin, moving northward with their flocks in search of pasture, had set up some 800 encampments in the coastal area. He warned Bedouin sheikhs on September 28 that the government would not tolerate illegal construction. On October 16, the government agreed to halt the demolition of nine illegally-built Bedouin houses in the Negev, and the Bedouin promised to stop unlicensed building.

On November 8, a riot in the Galilee Arab village of Majd al-Kurum over the demolition of an illegally-built house led to the death of one Arab; the arrest of 30 people, four of whom were hospitalized for injuries; and the injuring of two Jewish workers and 22 policemen. In reply to a Knesset demand for an inquiry, Interior Minister Burg stated that all Arab localities had received more building land, and that Majd al-Kurum's land reserves had been increased by 30 per cent. Over 3,000 structures had been erected in the north without permits, and legal action had been taken against only 167 of them, he added.

In response to the efforts of an Israeli Arab delegation which went to Amman in February to offer condolences to King Hussein on the death of his wife Alya, the Jordanian government persuaded Saudi Arabian authorities to allow Israeli Muslims—defined as "Moslems of Arab land occupied since 1948"—to go to Mecca for the *haj* (pilgrimage) with Jordanian travel documents.

Israel and World Jewry

Of the 21,500 *olim* in 1977—nine per cent more than in 1976—12,500 registered as immigrants and 9,000 (mainly from the western countries) as potential immigrants. Two-fifths—8,400—came from the Soviet Union, compared to 7,000 in 1976. There was also an increase of some 30 per cent in the number of *olim* from North America, to over 4,000. Some 3,000 *olim* came from Latin America.

The most serious problem in regard to immigration from the USSR was that of the "drop-outs"—those opting, on arrival at the transit station in Vienna, to go to some country other than Israel. About half of the Jews who left the USSR "dropped-out" in this way—most of them going to the United States—and the Hebrew Immigrants Aid Society (HIAS) was blamed, in Israel, for helping them to do so. Discussions of the problem between the Jewish Agency and American Jewish organizations were inconclusive. In Israel, there were frequent demands by representatives of the government, the Jewish Agency, and other public bodies for the removal of all restrictions on the departure of Jews from the Soviet Union.

The Zionist General Council, meeting on June 22, pledged support for the new government's efforts to achieve peace, and called for world support for the rights of Jews in the Soviet Union and Syria. The Jewish Agency assembly, meeting on June 26–30, devoted considerable attention to the solution of Israel's domestic social problems.

Over a million Jews outside Israel—10 per cent more than in 1971—registered in the World Zionist Organization's membership drive in preparation for the 29th Zionist Congress, to be held in Jerusalem on February 20, 1978. Among Jewish bodies holding conferences in Israel during the year were the Women's International Zionist Organization, the World Union of Jewish Journalists, and the World Congress of Jewish Community Centers. Two thousand sportsmen from abroad, as well as 450 from Israel, took part in the 10th Maccabiah Games, which opened on July 12. There was an increase of 50 per cent in the participation of young people from Europe and North America in the Zionist Organization's annual summer projects.

Prime Minister Begin established close and cordial relations with American Jewry. Rabbi Alexander Schindler, chairman of the Conference of Presidents of Major Jewish Organizations, paid frequent visits to Israel for consultations on foreign policy. During Begin's visit to the United States in July, he paid his respects to religious leaders, including the Lubavitcher Rebbe and Rabbi Joseph Solo-veitchik.

A delegation of rabbis representing the Conservative and Reform movements in the United States came to Israel in mid-August to express concern about concessions by the new government to the Orthodox religious parties. The delegation was particularly agitated over a proposed change in the Law of Return that would recognize only Orthodox conversions to Judaism. They met with the chief rabbis and Prime Minister Begin, who told them that he was bound by the coalition agreement to support the change in the law. He suggested, however, that they try to reach a compromise over the question with the Orthodox rabbinate in the United States.

Personalia

Moshe Rivlin was elected chairman of the Jewish National Fund Directorate; Rabbi Simha Bunim Alter was acclaimed Rebbe of Gur; Brigadier General Moshe Levi was appointed head of the Central Command; and Avraham Kidron presented his credentials as Israeli ambassador in London.

Avraham Ofer, minister of housing, died in Tel Aviv, January 3, at the age of 55; Abraham Dickenstein, founder of Ampal, died in Tel Aviv, February 16, at the age of 76; Rabbi Israel Alter, Rebbe of Gur, died in Jerusalem, February 20; Ezra Z. Shapiro, chairman of Keren Hayesod, died in Jerusalem, May 15, at the age of 75; Professor Haim Hillel Ben-Sasson, historian, died in Jerusalem, May 17, at the age of 63; Aviad Yaffe, director-general of the Jewish Agency, died in Kfar Sava, May 19, at the age of 54; Arye Nir, retired commissioner of prisons, died in Jerusalem, June 6, at the age of 65; Avraham Cygiel, former member of Jewish Agency Executive, died in Herzlia, June 24, at the age of 67; Oedoen Partos, composer and violist, died in Tel Aviv, July 7, at the age of 70; Julian Meltzer, veteran journalist and executive vice-chairman of the Weizmann Institute of Science, died in Jerusalem, August 6, at the age of 73; Nahum Nardi, composer of popular songs, died in Tel Aviv, September 9, at the age of 76; Meyer W. Weisgal, chancellor of the Weizmann Institute of Science, died in Rehovot, September 28; Professor Raphael Mahler, historian, died in Tel Aviv, October 4, at the age of 78; Zvi Yaron, writer and editor, died in Jerusalem, October 8, at the age of 56.

MISHA LOUVISH

South Africa

Domestic Affairs

Moves were made in 1977 to lessen discriminatory practices, especially in such areas as sports and public entertainment, where integrated audiences and mixed participation were permitted by the authorities. The moves were welcomed, but the feeling was expressed, particularly in the South African press, that much more basic changes were needed. In general, the problems of the colored (mulatto), Asiatic (mainly Indian), and urban Black populations remained unresolved.

Suggestions were made by the ruling National Party that the country's constitution be revised and that the Westminster system of government be replaced by a form of government more in keeping with the contemporary exigencies of South African life. The proposals that were put forward, however, did not gain wide popularity.

The mounting international pressure directed against South Africa, the government's race policy, and the proposal for a new constitution, were the central issues in the general election (in which only whites participated) held at the end of November. The National Party, under the leadership of Balthazar John Vorster, was returned to Parliament with 134 seats, the largest majority in the country's history. The Progressive Federal Party, which gained 17 of the 30 seats of the combined opposition, became the official opposition party.

Other significant domestic events during the year were the formation of Inkatha, a Black political alliance under the leadership of Chief Gathsa Buthelezi, chief executive minister of the KwaZulu government; the emotional response to the trial of Afrikaans poet Breyten Breytenbach, who was acquitted of charges of planning to overthrow the government while serving a prison sentence imposed upon him a year earlier for other security offenses; the banning of some highly acclaimed Afrikaans literary works, most notably *Magersfontein, O Magersfontein,* a satire by Ettienne Le Roux; and the detention without trial of a number of persons including student leaders, Black spokesmen, and journalists.

During the cold and wet winter, a group of Blacks were evicted from a squatter camp at Modderdam in the Cape. The Cape Committee of the South African Jewish

283

Board of Deputies (SAJBD) and the Cape rabbinate joined the widespread protest against this action.

The economic situation remained troubled, and many large companies showed smaller profits. Bankruptcies caused widespread losses by the public, especially in the real estate area. It was noted, however, that despite South Africa's difficulties (for political and other reasons) in competing in overseas markets, the long range economic outlook was positive, because measures had been introduced to fight inflation and restore a more favorable balance of payments.

Foreign Relations

International criticism of South Africa mounted. At the same time, attention was increasingly drawn to the whole of southern Africa because of developments in Angola, Namibia, Rhodesia, and Mozambique, most especially the presence of Cuban troops in some of these countries. Some observers, including former United States Secretary of State Henry Kissinger, viewed developments in the African subcontinent as an extension of the East-West conflict.

There was widespread reaction abroad to the riots in the Black township of Soweto, and the subsequent rioting elsewhere. Outrage was expressed at the judicial finding that no one could be held responsible for the death of the young Black leader Steve Biko, while in detention. There was strong criticism of the detention without trial of a number of people, including Percy Qoboza, editor of the banned Black newspaper *The World,* and members of the so-called "Committee of Ten," a Soweto leadership group. Finally, protests were made against the banning of the editor of the *Eastern Province Herald,* Donald Woods, who subsequently fled the country.

International opprobrium isolated South Africa politically, economically, and culturally. Toward the end of 1977, the United Nations agreed to the imposition of a ban on the sale of arms to South Africa. Andrew Young, United States ambassador to the UN, and David Owen, British foreign secretary, emphasized demands by the international community for basic changes in the Republic, including a call for majority rule. The South African government, however, rejected these demands, and continued to put forward its own solution to the volatile race problem: the separate development in independent states of all Black ethnic groups in South Africa.

Namibia (South West Africa), previously administered by South Africa, was placed under the direct control of an administrator general, Justice Marthinus T. Steyn. Formulas were advanced for its independence by the end of 1978, including free elections in the territory. Disputes concerning the continued presence of South African troops in the area, and other matters, continued to prevent wide acceptance of plans advanced by the international community, the South West Africa People's Organization (SWAPO), and the Democratic Turnhalle Alliance (DTA). Both SWAPO and DTA claimed to represent the views of the Namibian majority.

Relations with Israel

The election of Menachem Begin as prime minister had no significant effect on relations between South Africa and Israel. Begin was reported to have said: "While we reject racism, we see no reason to shun a hand of friendship that has been reaching to us from a forest of hatred and violence."

The long-awaited visit of a minister of Israel to South Africa took place when Finance Minister Simha Ehrlich came to the Republic in February 1978. During the visit, details concerning trade, the opening of mutually beneficial investment opportunities, and other financial agreements were ratified by Ehrlich and South African Finance Minister Owen Horwood. It also became possible, for the first time, for South Africans to purchase Israel bonds. A double taxation agreement was entered into by the two countries.

Frequent cultural and scientific exchanges continued. Among these were the highly acclaimed visit to South Africa of the Bat Dor Ballet Company, and similar visits to Israel by South African performers; exchanges of art exhibitions; and the exchange of scientists involved in such areas as water conservation, industrial technology, and medicine.

Israel agreed to obey the UN arms embargo against South Africa. Commenting on this, *Die Vaderland,* a leading Afrikaans daily, stated: "Although Israel has to obey the UN sanctions embargo—something for which we cannot blame her—she will not allow herself to be prescribed to with regard to what her relationship to a friend should be."

In November, on the eve of the general elections, *The Star,* a Johannesburg newspaper, published the transcript of a conversation in which Minister of Justice J.T. Kruger was alleged to have said: "You cannot deny your own homeland. You cannot deny the fact that there are Jews outside Israel and Israel is still a homeland. They are sending money to Israel and then they run away from other places . . ." The Minister later claimed that his remarks were quoted out of context. Reaction in Israel was sharp, since the remark was taken to imply that South African Jews send money to Israel and then leave at the first signs of difficulty in their own country. *Davar,* the Israeli daily, commented: "The statement of Minister Kruger cannot go unanswered. He has offended South African Jewry as well as the State of Israel . . . It is necessary to demand a full retraction from the government in Pretoria." South African Foreign Minister Roelof F. Botha sent a note of explanation to the Israeli Foreign Ministry, in which he completely disassociated the government from the "reported negative remarks" about the South African Jewish community.

Most South African newspapers, and particularly the Afrikaans press, showed understanding of Israel's problems, and devoted extensive space to reports of affairs in the Middle East. This was particularly so during the visit of President Sadat to Jerusalem.

The ambassador of Israel, Itzhak Unna, enjoyed great popularity in South Africa, most especially because he learned to speak fluent Afrikaans. He put Israel's position on a number of issues before the public, and appeared on the national television service.

Antisemitism

Antisemitism was not prevalent in South Africa, and was particularly eschewed by the government and all official public bodies. However, small neo-Nazi and other extreme right-wing groups continued to propagate antisemitic views in cheap monthly broadsheets distributed at random or to subscribers. These groups were rabidly anti-Black and anti-Jewish. They earned the contempt of most people, and were roundly condemned as sowers of hatred by the general press, both English and Afrikaans. Newly established among these groups was a South African branch of the British National Front. There were reports as well of the existence of a branch of the Ku Klux Klan. Antisemitic material from abroad, including Arthur Butz's notorious *The Hoax of the 20th Century,* continued to be distributed on a small scale.

Other manifestations of anti-Zionism and antisemitism continued in three journals: *Die Afrikaner,* official organ of the ultra-right Herstigte Nasionale Party; *The SA Observer,* edited by S.E.D. Brown; and *Muslim News,* a paper which enjoyed a fair circulation among Moslems, mainly in the Cape Town area, and espoused the views of Arab propagandists.

During the election there were some attempts to drum up anti-Jewish sentiment in certain quarters. By and large, they were of little moment, except in the Cape, where two Jewish candidates were assaulted by unknown extremists.

For the first time, a Jew, Abe Hoppenstein, stood for election to Parliament as a National Party candidate. Attempts were made to introduce a Jewish element into the election. SAJBD issued a statement deploring these attempts, stressing that Jews participated in politics as individual citizens.

The credibility of pro-Nazi propaganda which sought to deny the Holocaust was greatly undermined by events surrounding the banning of Richard Harwood's *Did Six Million Really Die?* When attempts were made to appeal the banning, Arthur Suzman presented an affidavit to the Appeal Board completely refuting Harwood's calumnies. Suzman's evidence was widely reported, and served to discredit those who supported Harwood and other writers espousing similar views.

A book based on the whole matter and containing the substance of Suzman's affidavit was subsequently published by SAJBD. The first edition of this book, *Six Million Did Die—The Truth Shall Prevail,* by Arthur Suzman and Denis Diamond, was completely sold out. A second edition containing important additional material was prepared. The book enjoyed an especially favorable reception in West Germany, where a partial translation was being prepared for wide distribution by an agency of the German government. A number of public lectures on the book drew large audiences in South Africa.

JEWISH COMMUNITY

Communal Activities

The tensions in South Africa had their effects on the Jewish community, which numbered 118,000.

There was considerable speculation about increased emigration from South Africa. While no statistics singling out Jewish emigration were available, it could be assumed that Jewish emigration was at least proportional to the general trend, which showed a decided increase in the number of people leaving the country. Most such people were professionals. There has been a noticeable increase in South Africans taking up residence in Israel since 1976.

The emigration of members of the community, and a fairly difficult financial climate, had deleterious effects on communal funding. The United Communal Fund (UCF), which provided for the financial needs of local institutions, experienced increased difficulties in meeting its growing commitments, even though it showed every sign of increasing its overall income.

The two major fund-raising organizations were UCF and the Israel United Appeal (IUA). During 1977, IUA's men's campaign was launched by Haim Zadok, former Israel minister of justice, and Akiva Hoffman. UCF's women's campaign was launched by Chaim Potok, the American writer. The chairman of IUA was I.A. Maisels; Mendal Kaplan was chairman of UCF.

At its various public meetings, and in its two publications, *Jewish Affairs* (English) and *Buurman* (Afrikaans), the South African Jewish Board of Deputies (SAJBD) continued to stress the need for harmonious intergroup relations, help for the underprivileged, and the removal of all discrimination based on race, color, or creed. Contact with Black leaders in the political and cultural spheres was encouraged by SAJBD. The Board itself met with Chief Lennox Sebe of the Ciskei, Chief Cedric Pathudi of Baphuta Tswana, and Chief Gatsha Buthelezi of KwaZulu. Chief Sebe visited Israel and spoke very positively of his experiences there.

Representatives of SAJBD attended a number of conferences of Jewish organizations abroad, most notably meetings of the Material Claims Conference and the Memorial Foundation for Jewish Culture. A large delegation under the leadership of the Board's president, D.K. Mann, attended the meeting of the General Assembly of the World Jewish Congress in Washington in October. Mann delivered a paper on South African Jewry that was widely acclaimed.

With the extension of the period of compulsory military service from one to two years, SAJBD saw the need for a well-coordinated chaplaincy service. It broadened the work it had undertaken for many years in this area by establishing a Joint National Jewish Chaplaincy Council under the chairmanship of Cecil Meltz. The chief chaplain was Rabbi L.D. Sandler; Hilton Kaplan was appointed administrative director. A regular magazine for servicemen, *Daf LaChayal* was produced by SAJBD. To meet the religious requirements of many Jewish servicemen, the army provided full kashrut facilities at a number of bases throughout the country. The Union of Jewish Women sent festival packages to men who were unable to spend holidays at home.

Zionism

The South African Zionist Federation (SAZF) was particularly active in the area of *aliyah* because of the growing interest in settlement in Israel. Through its well-organized network of Zionist associations and parties, especially the Women's Zionist Council, SAZF engaged in widespread educational programs, and conducted numerous tours to Israel. The work of various Zionist youth movements was supported. Close organizational contact was maintained with Israel through an active and well-organized committee and office of SAZF in Tel Aviv. The president of SAZF was Edel Horwitz; Julius Weinstein served as chairman.

Religion

As it became increasingly difficult to fill rabbinical posts in South Africa, particularly in small towns, a number of congregations began to employ Hebrew teachers in a rabbinical capacity. Four new Orthodox synagogues were established in the Linksfield, Victory Park, Randburg, and Edenvale areas around Johannesburg. These areas had gained in Jewish population as a result of shifts away from older areas such as Berea and Yeoville.

The Lubavitch movement showed signs of growth, and exerted influence among certain groups of university students and young people. No appointment was made to replace Rabbi Arthur S. Super as chief minister of the United Progressive Jewish Congregation, after his departure for Israel. The Progressive movement was represented on the South African Jewish Board of Deputies by Rabbi Walter Blumenthal and on the South African Zionist Federation by Rabbi Ben Isaacson. Rabbi Bernard M. Casper was chief rabbi of the Federation of Synagogues of South Africa (Orthodox); Rabbi Eugene J. Duschinsky was the Av Beth Din (Cape Town).

Jewish Education

The community was well served by ten day schools located in all the major cities. These schools were financed totally by the community, and were the major beneficiaries of the United Communal Fund. Their teaching syllabi were designed by the

South African Board of Jewish Education (SABJE), whose educational outlook was Zionist and Orthodox. Rabbi Isaac Goss served as director. The day schools served some 45 per cent of all Jewish children in Johannesburg, and about 65 per cent in the Cape area. In Durban and Port Elizabeth the proportion was estimated to be even higher. In addition to the day schools there were a number of afternoon schools. The Avida/Zlotnick Seminary, under the direction of Rabbi Moshe Kurtstag, trained Hebrew teachers and rabbis.

Jewish Culture

Two significant books that appeared were *The Celibacy of Felix Greenspan* by Lionel Abrahams and *B'ikvei HaParshayot* by Rabbi Eugene J. Duschinsky.

A major amount of SAJBD's work was in the cultural sphere, with the result that SAJBD was recognized as one of the most important sponsors of cultural events in Johannesburg. In October, it organized the first Johannesburg Film Festival, at which many internationally acclaimed films made their South African debuts. Notable among these was *Hester Street,* which went on to enjoy considerable popular success on the commercial circuit. Proceeds from the festival were donated to the Urban Foundation, an organization dedicated to the improvement of the quality of life within urban Black areas.

At its museum, SAJBD held a number of exhibitions, most notably one entitled "Shtetl Life," centering around a collection of eight oil paintings by Raphael Mandelzweig. They were donated to the museum by the well-known local Judaica collectors Abel and Sarah Shaban. Other valuable acquisitions were two important bronzes by the South African sculptors Moses Kottler and Herman Wald. SAJBD was establishing a collection of contemporary works of art by South African Jewish artists.

Personalia

The University of the Witwatersrand awarded honorary doctorates to Emmanuel P. Bradlow, Israel A. Maisels, and Ellen Hellman. Leslie Frankel was appointed a director of the United Mizrachi Bank, Ltd. (Israel); Ted Mauerberger was elected mayor of Cape Town; Professor M.F. Kaplan was appointed to the advisory committee of the Council for Scientific and Industrial Research; Harry Hurwitz was appointed adviser to the Israel prime minister. A number of Jews were appointed judges: Henry J. Preiss, David Friedman, Namie Philips, and Richard Goldstone.

People appointed to important communal offices included: Rachiel Rapaport, president, Women's Zionist Council; Aubrey Zabow, chairman, Cape Committee of SAJBD; David Drutman, administrative director, Federation of Synagogues of South Africa; Selwyn Franklin, rabbi, Durban United Hebrew Congregation; Steven Rein, national chairman, South African Jewish Ex-Service League; Franz

Auerbach, chairman, South African National Yad Vashem; Rose Norwich, president, and Anna Morris, executive director, Union of Jewish Women; Mike Belling, organizing secretary, Western Province Zionist Council; and Bernard Lazarus, president, Council of Natal Jewry.

Among prominent Jews who died during the year were: Dr. Harry Abt, distinguished figure in religious, cultural, and educational life, in April; Geoff Josman, general secretary, Eastern Cape Zionist Council, in April; Mrs. Len Davis, broadcaster and journalist, in May; Arnold Golembo, chairman, South African Revisionist Organization, and honorary officer of SAZF, in August; and Sam Cohen, philanthropist and pioneer of South West Africa, in October.

DENIS DIAMOND

World Jewish Population

THERE ARE NO PRECISE DATA on Jewish population in the various countries. The figures presented below represent the best possible estimates for 1977. They are based on local censuses, communal registration figures, and data obtained from a special inquiry conducted in Spring, 1977 (AJYB, 1978 [Vol. 78], p. 517). Some figures were obtained from local informants, mostly people involved in Jewish communal affairs. These figures are of varying degrees of accuracy, and are subject to a substantial margin of error. They will be revised when more precise data become available.

DISTRIBUTION BY CONTINENTS

The estimated world Jewish population at the end of 1977 was 14,286,000. Of the total number, about 6,698,000 (47 per cent) lived in the Americas, some 4,163,000 (29 per cent) in Europe, including the Asian parts of Turkey and the USSR, and over 3,172,000 (22 per cent) in Asia. Only some 177,000 (1.5 per cent) remained in Africa, and 75,000 (0.5 per cent) in Australia and New Zealand.

TABLE 1. DISTRIBUTION OF JEWISH POPULATION BY CONTINENTS, 1977

Continent	Number	Per Cent
Europe (including Asiatic USSR and Turkey)	4,163,370	29.0
America, (North, Central, and South)	6,698,070	47.0
Asia	3,172,410	22.0
Africa	177,770	1.5
Australia and New Zealand	75,000	0.5
TOTAL	14,286,620*	100.0

*Because sources and dates were not always identical, there may be discrepancies between figures given in the tables below and those in other sections of this volume.

Europe

Of the approximately 4,163,000 Jews in Europe, some 2,840,000 were in the Communist area, including 2,678,000 in the Soviet Union, 80,000 in Hungary, some 60,000 in Rumania, and about 6,000 in Poland. There was a continuing debate about the number of Jews in the USSR (see the article "Soviet Jewry Since the Death of

Stalin" in this volume). Some 1,320,000 Jews lived in non-Communist countries. France had about 650,000, making it not only the largest Jewish community in Western Europe, but also the fourth largest in the world. Great Britain had 410,000; Belgium, 41,000; Italy, 39,000, and Germany (including both West and East Germany) 34,000, about 5,500 of whom lived in West Berlin.

TABLE 2. ESTIMATED JEWISH POPULATION IN EUROPE, BY COUNTRIES, 1977

Country	Total Population[a]	Jewish Population
Albania	2,550,000	300
Austria	7,510,000	13,000[x]
Belgium	9,890,000	41,000
Bulgaria	8,760,000	7,000
Czechoslovakia	14,920,000	13,000
Denmark	5,070,000	7,500[x]
Finland	4,730,000	1,320
France	52,920,000	650,000
Germany	79,210,000[b]	34,000[b]
Gibraltar	30,000	650[x]
Great Britain	55,930,000	410,000[x]
Greece	9,170,000	6,000
Hungary	10,600,000	80,000
Ireland	3,160,000	4,000
Italy	56,170,000	39,000[x]
Luxembourg	360,000	1,000
Malta	300,000	50
Netherlands	13,770,000	30,000[x]
Norway	4,030,000	950
Poland	34,360,000	6,000
Portugal	9,450,000	600
Rumania	21,450,000	60,000
Spain	35,970,000	10,000
Sweden	8,220,000	16,000[x]
Switzerland	6,350,000	21,000
Turkey	40,160,000	27,000[xc]
USSR	256,670,000	2,678,000[c]
Yugoslavia	21,560,000	6,000
TOTAL		4,163,370

[a]United Nations Statistical Office, *Monthly Bulletin of Statistics,* and other sources, including local publications.

[b]Includes West Germany, East Germany, and both sectors of Berlin.

[c]Includes Asian regions of the USSR and Turkey.

[x]Reply to 1977 inquiry.

North, Central, and South America

The number of Jews in the United States, including all persons living in Jewish households, was estimated at about 5,781,000 (see the article "Jewish Population in the United States, 1978" in this volume). Canada had an estimated 305,000 Jews, and Central America about 574,000. The Jewish population figure for Argentina was 300,000. While this estimate was accepted by some local informants, it was contested by others.

TABLE 3. ESTIMATED JEWISH POPULATION IN NORTH, CENTRAL, AND SOUTH AMERICA AND THE WEST INDIES, BY COUNTRIES, 1977

Country	Total Population[a]	Jewish Population
Canada	23,140,000	305,000[x]
Mexico	62,330,000	37,500
United States	215,120,000	5,781,000
Total North America		6,123,500
Barbados	250,000	70[x]
Costa Rica	2,020,000	2,500[x]
Cuba	9,460,000	1,500
Curacao	150,000	700
Dominican Republic	4,840,000	200
El Salvador	4,120,000	350[x]
Guatemala	6,260,000	2,000
Haiti	4,670,000	150
Honduras	2,830,000	200
Jamaica	2,060,000	500
Nicaragua	2,230,000	200
Panama	1,720,000	2,000
Trinidad	1,080,000	300
Total Central America and West Indies		10,670
Argentina	25,720,000	300,000
Bolivia	5,790,000	2,000
Brazil	109,180,000	150,000[x]
Chile	10,450,000	27,000
Colombia	24,330,000	12,000
Ecuador	7,310,000	1,000
Paraguay	2,720,000	1,200
Peru	16,090,000	5,200[x]
Surinam	440,000	500
Uruguay	2,800,000	50,000
Venezuela	12,360,000	15,000
Total South America		563,900
TOTAL		6,698,070

[a]See Table 2, note[a].
[x]See Table 2, note[x].

Asia, Australia, and New Zealand

The Jewish population of Asia was over 3,171,000. Of these, 3,076,000, or approximately 97 per cent, were in Israel, the second largest Jewish population center in the world. There were 80,000 Jews in Iran and 8,000 in India. It was difficult to ascertain if events in Lebanon had any impact on the number of Jews in Lebanon and Syria.

The Jewish population of Australia was estimated at about 70,000, and that of New Zealand at 5,000.

TABLE 4. ESTIMATED JEWISH POPULATION IN ASIA, BY COUNTRIES, 1977

Country	Total Population[a]	Jewish Population
Afghanistan	19,800,000	200
Burma	30,830,000	200
China	852,130,000	30
Cyprus	640,000	30
Hong Kong	4,380,000	250
India	610,080,000	8,000[x]
Indonesia	139,620,000	100
Iran	33,400,000	80,000
Iraq	11,510,000	350
Israel	3,650,000	3,076,000
Japan	112,420,000	400[x]
Lebanon	2,960,000	400
Pakistan	72,370,000	250
Philippines	43,750,000	200
Singapore	2,280,000	500
Syria	7,600,000	4,500
Yemen	6,870,000	1,000
TOTAL		3,172,410

[a]See Table 2, note[a].
[x]See Table 2, note[x].

TABLE 5. ESTIMATED JEWISH POPULATION IN AUSTRALIA AND NEW ZEALAND, 1977

Country	Total Population[a]	Jewish Population
Australia	13,640,000	70,000[x]
New Zealand	3,140,000	5,000
TOTAL		75,000

[a]See Table 2, note [a].
[x]See Table 2, note[x].

Africa

The Jewish population of Africa stood at about 177,000, including some 118,000 in South Africa. It was not clear whether events in Rhodesia had a substantial impact on the number of Jews there. An estimated 28,000 were in Ethiopia. The Jewish communities of the Maghreb were very small—some 18,000 in Morocco, 7,000 in Tunisia, and about 1,000 in Algeria. Egypt had 400 Jews and Libya 20.

TABLE 6. ESTIMATED JEWISH POPULATION IN AFRICA, BY COUNTRIES, 1977

Country	Total Population[a]	Jewish Population
Algeria	17,300,000	1,000
Egypt	38,070,000	400
Ethiopia	28,680,000	28,000
Kenya	13,850,000	400
Libya	2,440,000	20
Morocco	17,830,000	18,000
Republic of South Africa	26,130,000	118,000[x]
Rhodesia	6,530,000	3,800[x]
Tunisia	5,740,000	7,000
Zaire	25,630,000	750
Zambia	5,140,000	400
TOTAL		177,770

[a]See Table 2, note[a].
[x]See Table 2, note[x].

COMMUNITIES WITH LARGEST JEWISH POPULATION

The largest Jewish community was in the United States, followed by Israel and the Soviet Union. Together they accounted for some 81 per cent of the world Jewish population. France, Great Britain, Canada, and Argentina had Jewish communities of 300,000 or over. Brazil had a Jewish population of 150,000, while that of South Africa stood at 118,000. The balance of the countries had Jewish communities of less than 100,000 each.

TABLE 7. COUNTRIES WITH LARGEST JEWISH POPULATION

Country	Jewish Population
United States	5,781,000
Israel	3,076,000
Soviet Union	2,678,000
France	650,000
Great Britain	410,000
Canada	305,000
Argentina	300,000

TABLE 8. ESTIMATED JEWISH POPULATION, SELECTED CITIES*

City	Jewish Population
Adelaide	1,600[x]
Amsterdam	20,000[x]
Ankara	550[x]
Antwerp	13,000
Athens	2,800
Auckland	1,500
Basel	2,300
Belgrade	1,500
Berlin (both sectors)	6,000
Bern	800
Bogota	5,500
Bombay (and district)	6,970[x]
Bordeaux	6,400[x]
Brisbane	1,500[x]
Brussels	24,500
Bucharest	40,000
Budapest	65,000
Calcutta	300[x]
Cape Town	25,650[x]
Cochin	500
Copenhagen	7,000[x]
Durban	5,990[x]
Florence	1,400
Geneva	3,250
Glasgow	13,000[x]
Goteborg	4,000[x]
Guatemala City	1,500
Haifa	210,000
Helsinki	1,000
Istanbul	23,000[x]

Izmir	2,500[x]
Jerusalem	266,000
Johannesburg	57,500[x]
Kiev	170,000
Kobe	80[x]
Leeds	18,000[x]
Leningrad	165,000
Lima	5,000[x]
Lisbon	550
Liverpool	6,500[x]
London (greater)	280,000[x]
Luxembourg	850
Lyons	20,000
Madrid	3,000
Malmo	4,000[x]
Manchester (greater)	35,000[x]
Manila	300
Marseille	65,000
Melbourne	34,000
Mexico, D. F.	32,500
Milan	9,000[x]
Montevideo	48,000
Montreal	115,000[x]
Moscow	285,000
Nice	20,000
Oslo	750
Ottawa	7,500[x]
Paris	300,000
Perth	3,200[x]
Plovdiv	1,000
Porto Alegre	12,000[x]
Prague	3,000
Rabat	2,500
Recife	3,000[x]
Rio de Janeiro	55,000[x]
Rome	10,000[x]
Salisbury	2,000[x]
Salonika	1,300
San Jose	2,500[x]
Sao Paulo	75,000[x]
Sarajevo	1,100
Sofia	4,000

Stockholm	8,000[x]
Strasbourg	12,000
Subotica	250
Sydney	28,500[x]
Teheran	50,000
Tel Aviv-Jaffa	394,000
Tokyo	320[x]
Toronto	115,000[x]
Toulouse	18,000
Trieste	1,200
Vancouver	12,000[x]
Valparaiso	4,000
Vienna	9,000
Wellington	1,500
Warsaw	4,500
Winnipeg	20,000[x]
Zagreb	1,200
Zurich	6,150

*For cities in the United States, see Table 3 of section, "Jewish Population in the United States" in this volume.

[x]See Table 2, note[x].

LEON SHAPIRO

Directories
Lists
Necrology

National Jewish Organizations[1]

UNITED STATES

Organizations are listed according to functions as follows:

COMMUNITY RELATIONS

AMERICAN COUNCIL FOR JUDAISM (1943). 309 Fifth Ave., Suite 303–6, N.Y.C., 10016. Pres. Clarence L. Coleman, Jr.; Sec. Alan V. Stone. Seeks to advance the universal principles of a Judaism free of nationalism, and the national, civic, cultural, and social integration into American institutions of Americans of Jewish faith. *Brief: Special Interest Report.*

AMERICAN JEWISH ALTERNATIVES TO ZIONISM, INC. (1968). 133 E. 73 St., N.Y.C., 10021. Pres. Elmer Berger; V. Pres. Mrs. Arthur Gutman. Applies Jewish values of justice and humanity to the Arab-Israel conflict in the Middle East; rejects nationality attachment of Jews, particularly American Jews, to the State of Israel as self-segregating, inconsistent with American constitutional concepts of individual citizenship and separation of church and state, and as being a principal obstacle to Middle East peace. *Report.*

AMERICAN JEWISH COMMITTEE (1906). Institute of Human Relations, 165 E. 56 St., N.Y.C., 10022. Pres. Richard Maass; Exec. V. Pres. Bertram H. Gold. Seeks to prevent infraction of civil and religious rights of Jews in any part of the world; to

[1]Information in this directory is based upon replies to questionnaires circulated by the editors. Inclusion in this list does not necessarily imply approval of the organizations by the publishers, nor can they assume responsibility for the accuracy of the data. An asterisk (*) indicates that no reply was received and that the information, which includes title of organization, year of founding, and address, is reprinted from AJYB, 1978 (Vol. 78).

advance the cause of human rights for people of all races, creeds, and nationalities; to interpret the position of Israel to the American public; and to help American Jews maintain and enrich their Jewish identity and, at the same time, achieve full integration in American life; includes Jacob and Hilda Blaustein Center for Human Relations, William E. Wiener Oral History Library, Leonard and Rose Sperry International Center for the Resolution of Group Conflict. AMERICAN JEWISH YEAR BOOK (with Jewish Publication Society of America); *Commentary; Present Tense; What's Doing at the Committee.*

AMERICAN JEWISH CONGRESS (1918). Stephen Wise Congress House, 15 E. 84 St., N.Y.C., 10028. Pres. Arthur Hertzberg; Exec. Dir. Naomi Levine. Works to foster the creative religious and cultural survival of the Jewish people; to help Israel develop in peace, freedom, and security; to eliminate all forms of racial and religious bigotry; to advance civil rights, protect civil liberties, defend religious freedom, and safeguard the separation of church and state. *Congress Monthly; Judaism.*

————, WOMEN'S DIVISION OF (1933). Stephen Wise Congress House, 15 E. 84 St., N.Y.C., 10028. Pres. Leona Chanin; Exec. Dir. Esther H. Kolatch. Committed to the achievement of social justice through its international and domestic programs; works for a free and secure Israel, world peace, human dignity, and the creative continuity of the Jewish people; supports Louise Waterman Wise Youth Hostel in Jerusalem.

ANTI-DEFAMATION LEAGUE OF B'NAI B'RITH (1913). 315 Lexington Ave., N.Y.C., 10016. Nat. Chmn. Burton M. Joseph; Nat. Dir. Benjamin R. Epstein. Seeks to combat antisemitism and to secure justice and fair treatment for all citizens through law, education and community relations. *ADL Bulletin: Face to Face; Fact Finding Report; Israel Backgrounder; Law Notes; Rights.*

ASSOCIATION OF JEWISH CENTER WORKERS (1918). 15 E. 26 St., N.Y.C., 10010. Pres. Hans Mayer; Exec. Dir. Debbie Schwartz. Seeks to enhance and improve the standards, techniques, practices, scope, and public understanding of Jewish community center and kindred work. *The Kesher; Viewpoints.*

ASSOCIATION OF JEWISH COMMUNITY RELATIONS WORKERS (1950). 55 W. 42 St., Suite 1530, N.Y.C., 10036. Pres. Joel Ollander; Sec. Harold Adler. Aims to stimulate higher standards of professional practice in Jewish community relations; encourages research and training toward that end; conducts educational programs and seminars; aims to encourage cooperation between community relations workers and those working in other areas of Jewish communal service.

COMMISSION ON SOCIAL ACTION OF REFORM JUDAISM (1953) (under the auspices of the Union of American Hebrew Congregations). 838 Fifth Ave., N.Y.C., 10021. Chmn. Alex Ross; Co-Dirs. Albert Vorspan, Balfour Brickner. Develops materials to assist Reform synagogues in setting up social-action programs relating the principles of Judaism to contemporary social problems; assists congregations in studying the moral and religious implications in social issues such as civil rights, civil liberties, church-state relations; guides congregational social-action committees. *Issues of Conscience; Newsletter.*

CONFERENCE OF PRESIDENTS OF MAJOR AMERICAN JEWISH ORGANIZATIONS (1955). 515 Park Ave., N.Y.C., 10022. Chmn. Alexander M. Schindler; Exec. Dir. Yehuda Hellman. Coordinates the activities of 32 major American Jewish organizations on the American scene as they relate to American-Israeli affairs, and problems affecting Jews in other lands. *Annual Report; Middle East Memo.*

CONSULTATIVE COUNCIL OF JEWISH ORGANIZATIONS-CCJO (1946). 61 Broadway, N.Y.C., 10006. Hon. Chmn. René Cassin (Alliance Israélite Universelle); Co-Chmn: Jules Braunschvig (Alliance Israélite Universelle), Harry Batshaw (Canadian Friends of Alliance Israélite Universelle), Victor Lucas (Anglo-Jewish Association); V. Chmn. Marcel Franco (American Friends of Alliance Israélite Universelle); Sec.-Gen. Moses Moskowitz. A nongovernmental organization in consultative status with the UN, UNESCO, International Labor Organization, UNICEF, and the Council of Europe; cooperates and consults with, advises and renders assistance to the Economic and Social Council of the United Nations on all problems relating to human rights and economic, social, cultural, educational, and related matters pertaining to Jews.

*COORDINATING BOARD OF JEWISH ORGANIZATIONS (1947). 1640 Rhode Island Ave., N.W., Washington, D.C., 20036. Pres. David M. Blumberg (B'nai B'rith), Lord Fisher of Camden (Board of Deputies of British Jews), Maurice Porter (South African Jewish Board of Deputies); Exec. V. Pres. Daniel Thursz (U.S.). As an organization in consultative status with the Economic and Social Council of the United Nations, represents the three constituents (B'nai B'rith, the Board of Deputies of British Jews, and the South African Jewish Board of Deputies) in the appropriate United Nations bodies for the purpose of promoting human rights, with special attention to combatting persecution or discrimination on grounds of race, religion, or origin.

COUNCIL OF JEWISH ORGANIZATIONS IN CIVIL SERVICE, INC. (1948). 45 E. 33 St., N.Y.C., 10016. Pres. Louis Weiser; Sec. Robert H. Gottlieb. Supports merit system; combats discrimination; promotes all Jewish interest projects; sponsors scholarships; is member of Greater N.Y. Conference on Soviet Jewry, Jewish Labor Committee, America-Israel Friendship League. *CJO Digest.*

INSTITUTE FOR JEWISH POLICY PLANNING AND RESEARCH (see Synagogue Council of America, p. 319).

INTERNATIONAL CONFERENCE OF JEWISH COMMUNAL SERVICE (1966). 15 E. 26 St., N.Y.C., 10010. Pres. Charles Zibbell; Sec.-Gen. Miriam R. Ephraim. Established by Jewish communal workers to strengthen their understanding of each other's programs and to communicate with colleagues in order to enrich quality of their work. Conducts quadrennial international conferences in Jerusalem and periodic regional meetings. *Proceedings of International Conferences; Newsletter.*

JEWISH LABOR COMMITTEE (1934). Atran Center for Jewish Culture, 25 E. 78 St., N.Y.C., 10021. Pres. Jacob Sheinkman; Exec. Dir. Emanuel Muravchik. Serves as a link between the Jewish community and the trade union movement; works with the AFL-CIO and other unions to combat all forms of racial and religious discrimination in the United States and abroad; furthers

labor support for Israel's security and Soviet Jewry, and Jewish communal support for labor, social, and economic change; supports Yiddish cultural institutions. *JLC News.*

————, NATIONAL TRADE UNION COUNCIL FOR HUMAN RIGHTS (1956). Atran Center for Jewish Culture, 25 E. 78 St., N.Y.C., 10021. Chmn. Edward Schneider; Exec. Dir. Betty Kaye Taylor. Works with trade unions on programs and issues affecting labor and the Jewish community.

————, WOMEN'S DIVISION OF (1947). Atran Center for Jewish Culture, 25 E. 78 St., N.Y.C., 10021. Nat. Chmn. Eleanor Schachner. Supports the general activities of the Jewish Labor Committee; provides secondary school and college scholarships for needy Israeli students; participates in educational and cultural activities.

————, WORKMEN'S CIRCLE DIVISION OF (1939). Atran Center for Jewish Culture, 25 E. 78 St., N.Y.C., 10021. Chmn. Saul Charow; Co-Chmn. Samuel Perel. Promotes aims of, and raises funds for, the Jewish Labor Committee among the Workmen's Circle branches; conducts Yiddish educational and cultural activities.

JEWISH WAR VETERANS OF THE UNITED STATES OF AMERICA (1896). 1712 New Hampshire Ave., N. W., Washington, D.C., 20009. Nat. Comdr. Herman H. Moses; Nat. Exec. Dir. Irwin R. Ziff. Seeks to foster true allegiance to the United States; to combat bigotry and prevent defamation of Jews; to encourage the doctrine of universal liberty, equal rights, and full justice to all men; to cooperate with and support existing educational institutions and establish new ones; to foster the education of ex-servicemen, ex-servicewomen, and members in the ideals and principles of Americanism. *Jewish Veteran.*

————: NATIONAL MEMORIAL, INC; NATIONAL SHRINE TO THE JEWISH WAR DEAD (1958). 1712 New Hampshire Ave., N.W., Washington, D.C., 20009. Pres. Meyer J. Abgott; Treas. Cherie Siegel. Administers shrine in Washington, D.C., a repository for medals and honors won by Jewish men and women for valor from Revolutionary War to present; maintains *Golden Book* of names of the war dead.

NATIONAL CONFERENCE ON SOVIET JEWRY (formerly AMERICAN JEWISH CONFERENCE ON SOVIET JEWRY) (1964; reorg. 1971). 11 W. 42 St., Rm. 1075, N.Y.C., 10036. Chmn. Eugene Gold; Exec. Dir. Jerry Goodman. Coordinating agency for major national Jewish organizations and local community groups in the U.S., acting on behalf of Soviet Jewry through public education and social action; stimulates all segments of the community to maintain an interest in the problems of Soviet Jews by publishing reports and special pamphlets, sponsoring special programs and projects, organizing public meetings and forums. *News Bulletin, Leadership Wrap-Up Series.*

_____: SOVIET JEWRY RESEARCH BUREAU. Organized by NCSJ to monitor emigration trends. Primary task is the accumulation, evaluation, and processing of information regarding Soviet Jews, especially those who apply for emigration.

NATIONAL JEWISH COMMISSION ON LAW AND PUBLIC AFFAIRS (COLPA) (1965). 66 Court St., Bklyn., 11201. Pres. Sidney Kwestel; Sec. Martin B. Cowan. Voluntary association of attorneys whose purpose is to represent the Orthodox Jewish community on legal matters and matters of public affairs.

NATIONAL JEWISH COMMUNITY RELATIONS ADVISORY COUNCIL (1944). 55 West 42 St., N.Y.C., 10036. Chmn. Theodore R. Mann; Exec. V. Chmn. Albert D. Chernin; Sec. Raymond Epstein. Consultative, advisory, and coordinating council of national Jewish organizations and local Jewish councils that seeks cooperatively the promotion of understanding of Israel and the Middle East; freedom for Jews in the Soviet Union; equal status and opportunity for all groups, including Jews, with full expression of distinctive group values and full participation in the general society. Through the processes of the Council, its constituent organizations seek agreement on policies, strategies, and programs for most effective utilization of their collective resources for common ends. *Guide to Program Planning for Jewish Community Relations.*

NORTH AMERICAN JEWISH YOUTH COUNCIL (1965). 515 Park Ave., N.Y.C., 10022. Chmn. David Stiefel; V. Chmn. Lynn Goldstein. Provides a framework for coordination and exchange of programs and information among national and local Jewish youth organizations to help them deepen the concern of American Jewish youth for world Jewry with special emphasis on Soviet and Israeli Jews; represents Jewish youth in the Conference on Presidents, National Conference on Soviet Jewry, United States Youth Council, etc.

STUDENT STRUGGLE FOR SOVIET JEWRY, INC. (1964). 200 W. 72 St., N.Y.C., 10023. Nat. Dir. Jacob Birnbaum; Nat. Coord. Glenn Richter. Provides information and action guidance to adult and student organizations, communities and schools throughout U.S. and Canada; assists individual Soviet Jews financially and by publicity campaigns; helps Russian Jews in the U.S.; aids Rumanian Jews seeking emigration; maintains speakers bureau. *Soviet Jewry Action Newsletter.*

WORLD JEWISH CONGRESS (1936; org. in U.S. 1939). Stephen Wise Congress House, 15 E. 84 St., N.Y.C., 10028. Pres. Philip M. Klutznick; Chmn. Gov. Bd. Lord Fisher of Camden; Chmn. Amer. Sect. Jacob Katzman; Chmn. No. Amer. Sect. Edgar N. Bronfman; Sec. Gen. Gerhart M. Reigner (Geneva); Dir. No. Amer. Branch, Exec. Dir. Amer. Sect. Max Melamet. Seeks to intensify bonds of world Jewry with Israel as central force in Jewish life; to strengthen solidarity among Jews everywhere and secure their rights, status, and interests as individuals and communities; to encourage development of Jewish social, religious, and cultural life throughout the world and coordinate efforts by Jewish communities and organizations to cope with any Jewish problem; to work for human rights generally. Represents its affiliated organizations—most representative bodies of Jewish communities in more than 60 countries and 18 national organizations in Amer. section—at UN, OAS, UNESCO, Council of Europe, ILO, UNICEF and other governmental, intergovernmental, and international authorities. Publications (including those by Institute of Jewish Affairs, London): *Christian Attitudes on Jews and Judaism; Compendium of Current Jewish Research; Folk, Velt un Medinah; Gesher; Jewish Journal of Sociology; Patterns of Prejudice; Soviet Jewish Affairs.*

CULTURAL

AMERICAN ACADEMY FOR JEWISH RE-SEARCH (1920). 3080 Broadway, N.Y.C., 10027. Pres. Salo W. Baron; Sec. Isaac E. Barzilay. Encourages research by aiding scholars in need and by giving grants for the publication of scholarly works. *Proceedings, American Academy for Jewish Research.*

AMERICAN BIBLICAL ENCYCLOPEDIA SOCI-ETY (1930). 24 West Maple Ave., Monsey, N.Y., 10952. Pres. Leo Jung; Exec. V. Pres. Bernard Greenbaum; Author-Ed. Menachem M. Kasher. Fosters biblical-talmudical research; sponsors and publishes *Torah Shelemah* (the Encyclopedia of Biblical Interpretation) and related publications; disseminates the teachings and values of the Bible. *Hatkufah Hagdola; Noam.*

AMERICAN HISTADRUT CULTURAL EX-CHANGE INSTITUTE (1962) 33 E. 67 St., N.Y.C., 10021. Nat. Chmn. Herbert Levine; Exec. Dir. Nahum Guttman. Serves as a vehicle for promoting better understanding of the efforts to create in Israel a society based on social justice. Provides a forum for the joint exploration of the urgent social problems of our times by American and Israeli labor, academic and community leaders. Publishes pamphlets and books on various Israeli and Middle East topics.

AMERICAN JEWISH HISTORICAL SOCIETY (1892). 2 Thornton Rd., Waltham, Mass., 02154. Pres. David R. Pokross; Dir. Bernard Wax. Collects, catalogues, publishes and displays material on the history of the Jews in America; serves as an information center for inquiries on American Jewish history; maintains archives of original source material on American Jewish history; sponsors lectures and exhibitions. *American Jewish Historical Quarterly; Newsletter.*

AMERICAN JEWISH PRESS ASSOCIATION (formerly AMERICAN ASSOCIATION OF ENGLISH JEWISH NEWSPAPERS) (1943) c/o American Jewish World, 9 North 4 St., Minneapolis, Minn. 55401. Pres. Norman Gold; Sec. Doris Sky. Seeks the advancement of Jewish journalism, the attainment of the highest editorial and business standards for members, and the maintenance of strong Jewish press in the U.S. and Canada. *AJPA Bulletin.*

AMERICAN SOCIETY FOR JEWISH MUSIC (1974). 155 Fifth Ave., N.Y.C. 10010. Pres. Albert Weisser; Sec. Hadássah B. Markson. Seeks to raise standards of composition and performance in Jewish liturgical and secular music; encourages research in all areas of Jewish music; publishes scholarly journal; presents programs and sponsors performances of new and rarely heard works and encourages their recording; commissions new works of Jewish interest. *Musica Judaica Journal.*

ASSOCIATED AMERICAN JEWISH MUSEUMS, INC. (1971). 303 LeRoi Road, Pittsburgh, Pa., 15208. Pres. Walter Jacob; V. Pres. William Rosenthall; Sec. Robert H. Lehman; Treas. Jason Z. Edelstein. Maintains regional collections of Jewish art, historical and ritual objects, as well as a central catalogue of such objects in the collections of Jewish museums throughout the U.S.; helps Jewish museums acquire, identify and classify objects; arranges exchanges of collections, exhibits, and individual objects among Jewish museums; encourages the creation of Jewish art, ceremonial and ritual objects.

ASSOCIATION FOR THE SOCIOLOGICAL STUDY OF JEWRY (1971). Dept. of Sociology, University College, Rutgers University, New Brunswick, N.J. 08903. Pres. Celia S. Heller; Sec.-Treas. Chaim I. Waxman. Arranges academic sessions among social scientists studying Jewry; facilitates communication among social scientists studying Jewry through meetings, newsletter, and related materials. *Contemporary Jewry: A Journal of Sociological Inquiry.*

ASSOCIATION OF JEWISH LIBRARIES (1966). c/o National Foundation for Jewish Culture, 408 Chanin Bldg., 122 E. 42 St., N.Y.C., 10017. Pres. Margot S. Berman; Sec. Edith Degani. Seeks to promote and improve services and professional standards in Jewish libraries; serves as a center for the dissemination of Jewish library information and guidance; promotes publication of literature in the field; encourages the establishment of Jewish libraries and collections of Judaica and the choice of Jewish librarianship as a vocation. *AJL Bulletin; Proceedings.*

ASSOCIATION OF JEWISH PUBLISHERS (1962). 838 Fifth Ave., N.Y.C., 10021. Pres. Jacob Steinberg. As a nonprofit group, provides a forum for discussion of mutual problems by publishers, authors, and other individuals and institutions concerned with books of Jewish interest.

CENTER FOR HOLOCAUST STUDIES, INC. (1974). 1605 Ave. J., Bklyn, N.Y., 11230. Dir. Yaffa Eliach; Chmn. Adv. Bd. Allen J. Bodner. Collects and preserves documents and memorabilia, oral histories and literary works on the Holocaust period for purpose of documentation and research; arranges lectures and exhibits; maintains speakers bureau and audio-visual department. Newsletter.

CENTRAL YIDDISH CULTURE ORGANIZATION (CYCO), INC. (1943). 25 E. 78 St., N.Y.C., 10021. Pres. Noah Singman; Sec. Jona Gutkowicz. Promotes and publishes Yiddish books; distributes books from other Yiddish publishing houses throughout the world; publishes annual bibliographical and statistical register of Yiddish books, and catalogues of new publications. Zukunft.

CONFERENCE ON JEWISH SOCIAL STUDIES, INC. (formerly CONFERENCE ON JEWISH RELATIONS, INC.) (1939). 250 W. 57 St., N.Y.C., 10019. Pres. Jeannette M. Baron; Hon. Pres. Salo W. Baron; V. Pres. Joseph L. Blau, J. M. Kaplan. Publishes scientific studies on the Jews in the modern world, dealing with such aspects as antisemitism, demography, economic stratification, history, philosophy, and political developments. Jewish Social Studies.

CONGRESS FOR JEWISH CULTURE, INC. (1948). 25 E. 78 St., N.Y.C., 10021. Pres. Joseph Landis; Exec. Dir. Hyman B. Bass. Seeks to centralize and promote Jewish culture and cultural activities throughout the world, and to unify fund raising for these activities. Bulletin fun Kultur Kongres; Zukunft; Leksikon fun der Nayer Yiddisher Literature; Pinkos far der Forshung fun der Yiddisher Literature un Presse; World of Yiddish.

HEBREW ARTS SCHOOL FOR MUSIC AND DANCE (1952). 15 W. 65 St., N.Y.C., 10023. Bd. Chmn. and Pres. Abraham Goodman; Dir. Tzipora H. Jochsberger; Hon. Sec. Benjamin W. Mehlman. Chartered by the Board of Regents, University of the State of New York. Provides children with training in instrumental and vocal skills as well as musicianship, combining instruction in Western music with musical heritage of the Jewish people; adult division offers instrumental, vocal, and dance classes, music workshop for teachers, ensemble workshops, and classes of special interest covering many areas of music-making, dance, and theatre; has Jewish Music Teacher-Training Institute, a part-time program for professional musicians or music majors; sponsors Hebrew Arts Chamber Players, Hebrew Arts Chamber Orchestra, Jewish Young People's concerts in schools. Notes & Quotes.

HEBREW CULTURE FOUNDATION (1955). 515 Park Ave., N.Y.C., 10022. Chmn. Milton R. Konvitz; Sec. Moshe Avital. Sponsors the introduction of the study of Hebrew language and literature in institutions of higher learning in the United States.

HISTADRUTH IVRITH OF AMERICA (1916; reorg. 1922). 1841 Broadway, N.Y.C., 10023. Pres. Myron Fenster; Exec. Dir. Shlomo Shamir. Emphasizes the primacy of Hebrew in Jewish life, culture, and education; aims to disseminate knowledge of written and spoken Hebrew in the Diaspora, thus building a cultural bridge between State of Israel and Jewish communities throughout the world. Hadoar; Lamishpaha.

JEWISH ACADEMY OF ARTS AND SCIENCES, INC. (1925). c/o Sec'y, 123 Gregory Ave., West Orange, N.J., 07052. Headquarters: Dropsie University, Philadelphia, Pa. 19132. Pres. Jewish Center, N.Y.C. Leo Jung; Pres. Emeritus Dropsie Univ. Abraham I. Katsh. Scholarship, contributions, accomplishments of Jews in the arts and sciences; recognition by election to membership and/or fellowship; publishes papers delivered at annual convocations. Annals.

JEWISH BOOK COUNCIL OF JWB (1925). 15 E. 26 St., N.Y.C., 10010. Pres. Sidney B. Hoenig; Dir. Sharon Strassfeld. Promotes knowledge of Jewish books through dissemination of booklists, program materials; stimulates observance of Jewish Book Month; presents literary awards and library citations; cooperates with publishers of Jewish books, and gives advice on general Jewish literature. Jewish Book Annual; Books in Review.

JEWISH INFORMATION BUREAU, INC. (1932). 250 W. 57 St., N.Y.C., 10019. Chmn. Judah A. Richards; Sec. Bruce Graeber. Serves as clearing house of information for inquiries regarding Jews, Judaism, and Jewish affairs; refers inquiries to communal agencies. *Index.*

JEWISH MUSEUM (1904) (under auspices of Jewish Theological Seminary of America). 1109 Fifth Ave., N.Y.C., 10028. Dir. Joy Ungerleider-Meyerson; Admin. Henry Korn. Main repository in U.S. of Jewish ceremonial objects. Collection ranges from Biblical archaeology to Italian Judaica to contemporary silver. Offers changing contemporary exhibitions of paintings, sculpture and photography, in addition to films, lectures, children's programs, walking tours of Lower East Side. Dedicated to exploring richness and diversity of past and present Jewish life; publishes catalogues of contemporary exhibitions.

JEWISH MUSIC COUNCIL OF JWB (1944). 15 E. 26 St., N.Y.C., 10010. Chmn. Shalom Altman; Dir. Mrs. Irene Heskes. Promotes Jewish music activities nationally, annually sponsors and promotes the Jewish Music Festival, and encourages participation on a community basis. *Jewish Music Notes* and numerous music resource publications for national distribution.

JEWISH PUBLICATION SOCIETY OF AMERICA (1888). 117 S. 17th St., Philadelphia, Pa., 19103. Pres. Edward B. Shils; Ed. Maier Deshell; Exec. V. Pres. Bernard I. Levinson. Publishes and disseminates books of Jewish interest on history, religion, and literature for the purpose of helping to preserve the Jewish heritage and culture. AMERICAN JEWISH YEAR BOOK (with American Jewish Committee).

JUDAH L. MAGNES MEMORIAL MUSEUM— JEWISH MUSEUM OF THE WEST (1962). 2911 Russell St., Berkeley, Calif., 94705. Pres. Marvin Weinreb; V. Pres. Alfred Fromm; Dir. Seymour Fromer. Serves both as museum and library, combining historical and literary materials illustrating Jewish life in the Bay Area, the Western States, and around the world; provides archives of world Jewish history and Jewish art; repository of historical documents intended for scholarly use; changing exhibits, facilities open to the general public.

LEO BAECK INSTITUTE, INC. (1955). 129 E. 73 St., N.Y.C., 10021. Pres. Max Gruenewald; Sec. Fred Grubel. Engages in historical research, the presentation and publication of the history of German-speaking Jewry, and in the collection of books, manuscripts and documents in this field; publishes monographs. *LBI Quarterly Bulletin; LBI News; LBI Year Book; LBI Library and Archives News.*

MEMORIAL FOUNDATION FOR JEWISH CULTURE, INC. (1964). 15 E. 26 St., N.Y.C., 10010. Pres. Nahum Goldmann; Exec. Dir. A.J. Sherman. Supports Jewish cultural and educational programs all over the world, in cooperation with universities and established scholarly organizations; conducts annual scholarship and fellowship program. *Annual Report.*

NATIONAL FOUNDATION FOR JEWISH CULTURE (1960). 1512 Chanin Bldg., 122 E. 42 St., N.Y.C., 10017. Pres. Amos Comay; Exec. Dir. Harry I. Barron. Provides consultation, guidance, and support to Jewish communities, organizations, educational and other institutions, and individuals for activities in the field of Jewish culture; awards fellowships and other grants to students preparing for careers in Jewish scholarship and to established scholars; makes awards for creative efforts in Jewish cultural arts and for Jewish programming in small and intermediate communities; encourages teaching of Jewish studies in colleges and universities; serves as clearinghouse of information on American Jewish culture; administers Joint Cultural Appeal among local Jewish welfare funds in behalf of 9 national cultural organizations, and administers Council for Archives and Research Libraries in Jewish Studies. *Jewish Cultural News.*

*NATIONAL HEBREW CULTURE COUNCIL (1952). 1776 Broadway, N.Y.C., 10019. Pres. Frances K. Thau; Exec. Dir. Judah Lapson. Cultivates the study of Hebrew as a modern language in American public high schools and colleges, providing guidance to community groups and public educational authorities; annually administers National Voluntary Examination in Hebrew Culture and Knowledge of Israel in the public high schools, and conducts summer seminar and tour of Israel for teachers and other educational personnel of the public school system, in cooperation with

Hebrew University and WZO *Hebrew in Colleges and Universities.*

RESEARCH FOUNDATION FOR JEWISH IMMIGRATION, INC. (1971). 570 Seventh Ave., N.Y.C., 10018. Pres. Curt C. Silberman; Sec. Herbert A. Strauss. Studies and records the history of the migration and acculturation of Jewish Nazi persecutees in the various resettlement countries; is in process of preparing world-wide biographical handbook of outstanding emigrés, in partnership with the Institut für Zeitgeschichte, Munich, Germany.

SOCIETY FOR THE HISTORY OF CZECHOSLOVAK JEWS, INC. (1961). 87–08 Santiago St., Holliswood, N.Y., 11423. Pres. Lewis Weiner; Sec. Joseph Abeles. Studies the history of the Czechoslovak Jews, collects material and disseminates information through the publication of books and pamphlets. *The Jews of Czechoslovakia* book series, Vol. I (1968), Vol. II (1971); Vol. III in prep. *Annual Reports and Pamphlets.*

YESHIVA UNIVERSITY MUSEUM (1973). 2520 Amsterdam Ave., N.Y.C., 10033. Curator Mrs. Dalia Tawil. Dir. of Admin. Sylvia A. Hershkowitz. Collects, preserves, interprets, and displays ceremonial objects, rare books and scrolls, models, paintings, and other works of art expressing the Jewish religious experience historically, to the present.

YIDDISHER KULTUR FARBAND—YKUF (1937). 853 Broadway, Suite 2121, N.Y.C., 10003. Exec. Sec. Ruth Baharas. Publishes a monthly magazine and books by contemporary and classical Jewish writers; conducts cultural forums and exhibits works by contemporary Jewish artists and materials of Jewish historical value. *Yiddishe Kultur.*

YIVO INSTITUTE FOR JEWISH RESEARCH, INC. (1925). 1048 Fifth Ave., N.Y.C., 10028. Chmn. Morris Laub. Engages in Jewish social and humanistic research; maintains library and archives of material pertaining to Jewish life; serves as information center for organizations, local institutions, information media, and individual scholars and laymen; publishes books. *Yedies fun Yivo—News of the Yivo; Yidishe Shprakh; Yivo Annual of Jewish Social Science; Yivo Bleter.*

———: MAX WEINREICH CENTER FOR ADVANCED JEWISH STUDIES (1968). 1048 Fifth Ave., N.Y.C., 10028. Pres. Nathan Reich; Act. Dean Marvin I. Herzog. Trains scholars in the fields of Eastern European Jewish life and culture; the Holocaust; the mass settlement of Jews in the U.S. and other countries; Yiddish language, literature, and folklore through inter-university courses and seminars and its panel of consultants. *Annual Bulletin.*

OVERSEAS AID

AMERICAN COUNCIL FOR JUDAISM PHILANTHROPIC FUND (1955). 386 Park Ave. S., 10th fl., N.Y.C., 10016. Pres. Charles J. Tanenbaum; Exec. Dir. Mrs. Anna Walling Matson. Through offices in Austria, France, West Germany, Italy and the United States, maintains programs offering freedom of choice and resettlement assistance in Western Europe and the United States to Jewish refugees from the Soviet Union, Eastern Europe and Arab countries.

AMERICAN FRIENDS OF THE ALLIANCE ISRAÉLITE UNIVERSELLE, INC. (1946). 61 Broadway, N.Y.C., 10006. Pres. Marcel Franco; Exec. Dir. Saadiah Cherniak. Helps networks of Jewish schools in Europe, Asia, and Africa. *Alliance Review; Revista de la Alliance.*

AMERICAN JEWISH JOINT DISTRIBUTION COMMITTEE, INC.—JDC (1914). 60 E. 42 St., N.Y.C., 10017. Pres. Donald M. Robinson; Exec. V. Pres. Ralph I. Goldman. Organizes and finances rescue, relief, and rehabilitation programs for imperiled needy Jews overseas; conducts wide range of health, welfare, rehabilitation, education assistance and aid to cultural and religious institutions, programs for 430,000 needy Jews in 25 countries overseas. Major areas of operation are Israel, North Africa, Iran and Europe. *Guidelines for Services Needed for the Aged; Helping the Blind in Israel; JDC Annual Report; JDC in Israel; JDC Overseas Guide; JDC World.*

AMERICAN ORT FEDERATION, INC.—ORGANIZATION FOR REHABILITATION THROUGH TRAINING (1924). 817 Broadway, N.Y.C., 10003. Pres. Harold Friedman; Exec. Dir. Paul Bernick. Teaches vocational skills in 24 countries around the world, particularly in Israel, to over 83,000 persons annually, with the largest program of 50,000 trainees in Israel. The teaching staff numbers about 3,400. Annual cost of program is over $52 million. *ORT Bulletin; ORT Yearbook.*

———: AMERICAN AND EUROPEAN FRIENDS OF ORT (1941). 817 Broadway, N.Y.C., 10003. Pres. Simon Jaglom; Chmn. Exec. Com. Jacques Zwibak. Promotes the ORT idea among Americans of European extraction; supports the Litton ORT Auto-Mechanics School in Jerusalem.

———: AMERICAN LABOR ORT (1937). 817 Broadway., N.Y.C., 10003. Chmn. Shelley Appleton; Exec. Sec. Samuel Milman. Promotes ORT program of vocational training among Jews.

———: BUSINESS AND PROFESSIONAL ORT (formerly YOUNG MEN'S AND WOMEN'S ORT) (1937). 817 Broadway, N.Y.C., 10003. Pres. Rose Seidel Kalich; Exec. Sec. Helen S. Kreisler. Promotes work of American ORT Federation.

———: NATIONAL ORT LEAGUE (1914). 817 Broadway, N.Y.C., 10003. Pres. Bruce B. Teicholz; Chmn. Exec. Bd. Jack Weinstein; Exec. V. Pres. and Sec. Jacob Zonis. Promotes ORT idea among Jewish fraternal *landsmanshaften,* national and local organizations, congregations; helps to equip ORT installations and Jewish artisans abroad, especially in Israel. *ORT Bulletin.*

———: WOMEN'S AMERICAN ORT (1927). 1250 Broadway, N.Y.C., 10001. Pres. Ruth Eisenberg; Exec. V. Pres. Nathan Gould. Represents and advances the program and philosophy of ORT among the women of the American Jewish community through membership and educational activities; supports materially the vocational training operations of World ORT; contributes to the American Jewish community through participation in its authorized campaigns and through general education to help raise the level of Jewish consciousness among American Jewish women; through its American Affairs program, cooperates in efforts to improve quality of education and vocational training in U.S. *Facts and Findings; Highlights; Insights; The Merchandiser; Women's American ORT Reporter.*

A.R.I.F.—ASSOCIATION POUR LE RÉTABLISSEMENT DES INSTITUTIONS ET OEUVRES ISRAÉLITES EN FRANCE, INC. (1944). 119 E. 95 St., N.Y.C., 10028. Pres. Baroness Robert de Gunzburg; Sec.-Treas. Simon Langer. Helps Jewish religious and cultural institutions in France.

CONFERENCE ON JEWISH MATERIAL CLAIMS AGAINST GERMANY, INC. (1951). 15 E. 26 St., N.Y.C., 10010. Pres. Nahum Goldmann; Sec. A.J. Sherman. Utilizes balance of funds received from the German Federal Republic under Luxembourg agreement for relief to needy Jewish victims of Nazi persecution and needy non-Jews who risked their lives to help such victims. *Annual Report.*

FREELAND LEAGUE (1935). 200 W. 72 St., N.Y.C., 10023. Pres. Nathan Turak; Exec. Sec. Mordkhe Schaechter. Promotes development and use of Yiddish as a living language. *Afn Shvel* (in Yiddish).

HIAS, INC. (1884; reorg. 1954). 200 Park Ave. S., N.Y.C., 10003. Pres. Carl Glick; Exec. V. Pres. Gaynor I. Jacobson. Worldwide Jewish migration agency with offices, affiliates, committees in United States, Europe, North Africa, Latin America, Canada, Australia, Israel, and New Zealand. Assists migrants and refugees from Eastern Europe, the Middle East, North Africa, and Latin America to find new homes in the United States and other countries. Responsible for premigration planning, visa documentation, consular representation and intervention, transportation, reception, initial adjustment and reunion of families; carries on adjustment of status and naturalization programs; provides protective service for aliens and naturalized citizens; works in the United States through local community agencies for the integration of immigrants; conducts a planned program of resettlement for Jewish immigrants in Latin America; has worldwide location service to assist in locating missing friends and relatives; conducts educational campaigns on opportunities for migration and resettlement, with particular emphasis on family reunion. *F.Y.I.; HIAS Annual Report; HIAS Bulletin; Statistical Abstract.*

JEWISH RESTITUTION SUCCESSOR ORGANIZATION (1948). 15–19 E. 26 St., N.Y.C., 10010. Pres. Monroe Goldwater; Sec. Saul Kagan. Acts to discover, claim, receive, and assist in the recovery of Jewish heirless or unclaimed property; to utilize such assets or to provide for their utilization for the relief, rehabilitation, and resettlement of surviving victims of Nazi persecution.

UNITED JEWISH APPEAL, INC. (1939). 1290 Ave. of the Americas, N.Y.C., 10019. Gen. Chmn. Leonard R. Strelitz; Pres. Frank R. Lautenberg; Exec. V. Chmn. Irving Bernstein. Channels funds for overseas humanitarian aid, supporting immigration and settlement in Israel, rehabilitation and relief in 30 nations, and refugee assistance in U.S. through Joint Distribution Committee, United Israel Appeal, United HIAS Service and New York Association for New Americans.

————, FACULTY ADVISORY CABINET (1975). 1290 Ave. of the Americas. Chmn. Michael Walzer; Dir. Melvin L. Libman. To promote faculty leadership support for local and national UJA campaigns through educational and personal commitment; to make use of faculty resources and expertise on behalf of UJA and Israel.

————, RABBINICAL ADVISORY COUNCIL (1972). 1290 Ave. of the Americas, N.Y.C., 10019. Chmn. Joseph H. Lookstein; Dir. Melvin L. Libman. To promote rabbinic leadership support for local and national UJA campaigns through education and personal commitment; to make use of rabbinic resources on behalf of UJA and Israel.

————, UNIVERSITY PROGRAMS DEPT. (1970). 1290 Ave. of the Americas, N.Y.C., 10019. Student Advisory Board. To crystallize Jewish commitment on the campus through an educational fund-raising campaign involving various programs, leadership training, and opportunities for participation in community functions.

————, WOMEN'S DIVISION OF (1946). 1290 Ave. of the Americas, N.Y.C., 10019. Pres. Mrs. Merrill L. Hassenfeld; Nat. Chmn. Marilyn Brown, Peggy Steine; Dir. Rena Button. *Ideas That Click; Right Now; Women's Division Record.*

————, YOUNG LEADERSHIP CABINET (1977). 1290 Ave. of the Americas, N.Y.C., 10019. Exec. Dir. Laurence H. Rubinstein; Chmn. Ralph J. Stern. Committed to the creative survival of Jews, Judaism, and Israel through dialogues with leading scholars and writers, and through

peer exchanges at retreats, conferences, and special programs. *Cabinet Communiqués.*

————, YOUNG WOMEN'S LEADERSHIP CABINET (1977). 1290 Ave. of the Americas, N.Y.C., 10019. Pres. Jane Sherman. Encourages young Jewish women to become involved with their local Jewish communities.

WOMEN'S SOCIAL SERVICE FOR ISRAEL, INC. (1937). 240 W. 98 St., N.Y.C., 10025. Pres. Rosi Michael; Sec. Dory Gordon. Maintains in Israel apartments for the aged, old age homes, nursing home, hospital for incurable diseases, rehabilitation department, department for bone injuries, soup kitchens. *Annual Journal; Newsletter.*

RELIGIOUS AND EDUCATIONAL

AGUDAS ISRAEL WORLD ORGANIZATION (1912). 471 West End Ave., N.Y.C., 10024. Chmn. Central Com. Am. Sect. Isaac Lewin. Represents the interests of Orthodox Jewry on the national and international scenes.

AGUDATH ISRAEL OF AMERICA (1912). 5 Beekman St., N.Y.C., 10038. Exec. Pres. Morris Sherer; Exec. Dir. Boruch B. Borchardt. Mobilizes Orthodox Jews to cope with Jewish problems in the spirit of the Torah; sponsors a broad range of constructive projects in fields of religion, education, children's welfare, protection of Jewish religious rights and social services. *Jewish Observer; Dos Yiddishe Vort.*

————, CHILDREN'S DIVISION—PIRCHEI AGUDATH ISRAEL (1925). 5 Beekman St., N.Y.C., 10038. Pres. Avrohom Portowitz; Nat. Dir. Joshua Silbermintz. Educates Orthodox Jewish children in Torah; encourages sense of communal responsibility; communal celebrations, learning groups, and welfare projects. *Darkeinu; Leaders Guide.*

————, GIRLS' DIVISION—BNOS AGUDATH ISRAEL (1921). 5 Beekman St., N.Y.C., 10038. Natl. Coordinator Esther Weisberger. Educates Jewish girls to the historic nature of the Jewish people; encourages greater devotion to and understanding of the Torah. *Kol Bnos.*

————, WOMEN'S DIVISION—N'SHEI AGUDATH ISRAEL OF AMERICA (1940). 5

Beekman St., N.Y.C., 10038. Pres. Mrs. Esther Bohensky, and Mrs. Josephine Reichel. Organizes Jewish women for philanthropic work in the U.S. and Israel and for intense Torah education, seeking to train Torah-guided Jewish mothers.

———, YOUTH DIVISION—ZEIREI AGUDATH ISRAEL (1921). 5 Beekman St., N.Y.C., 10038. Pres. Joseph Ashkenazi; Exec. Dir. Yaakov Bender. Educates Jewish youth to realize the historic nature of the Jewish people as the people of the Torah and to seek solutions to all the problems of the Jewish people in Israel in the spirit of the Torah. *The Zeirei Forum; Am Hatorah, Daf Chizuk, Yom Tov Publications.*

AMERICAN ASSOCIATION FOR JEWISH EDUCATION (1939). 114 Fifth Ave., N.Y.C., 10011. Pres. Arthur Brody; Exec. V. Pres. Isaac Toubin. Coordinates, promotes, and services Jewish education nationally through 18 constituent national organizations and 49 affiliated Bureaus of Jewish Education; conducts and administers exchange program for Israeli teachers; offers fellowships in Jewish educational leadership; sponsors and supports the National Curriculum Research Institute, including the Dept. of Methods & Materials, the National Board of License, and the Commission on Teaching About Israel. National Council on Jewish Camping engages in statistical and other educational research, provides community consultations, and conducts community studies. *Information and Research Bulletins; Jewish Education News; Jewish Education Directory; Pedagogic Reporter; Curriculum Newsletter.*

ASSOCIATION FOR JEWISH STUDIES (1969). Widener Library M. Harvard University, Cambridge, Mass., 02138. Pres. Marvin Fox; Exec. Sec. Charles Berlin. Seeks to promote, maintain, and improve the teaching of Jewish studies in American colleges and universities by sponsoring meetings and conferences, publishing a newsletter and other scholarly materials, setting standards for programs in Jewish studies, aiding in the placement of teachers, coordinating research and cooperating with other scholarly organizations. *AJS Review; Newsletter.*

ASSOCIATION OF JEWISH CHAPLAINS OF THE ARMED FORCES (1946). 15 E. 26 St., N.Y.C., 10010. Pres. Reuven Seigel; Sec.

Joseph J. Weiss. An organization of former and current chaplains of the armed forces of the U.S. which seeks to enhance the religious program of Jewish chaplains in the armed forces of the U.S. and in Veterans' Administration hospitals.

ASSOCIATION OF ORTHODOX JEWISH SCIENTISTS (1947). 116 E. 27 St., N.Y.C., 10016. Pres. Herbert Goldstein; Bd. Chmn. Nora Smith. Seeks to contribute to the development of science within the framework of Orthodox Jewish tradition; to obtain and disseminate information relating to the interaction between the Jewish traditional way of life and scientific developments—on both an ideological and practical level; to assist in the solution of problems pertaining to Orthodox Jews engaged in scientific teaching or research. *Intercom; Proceedings.*

BETH MEDROSH ELYON (ACADEMY OF HIGHER LEARNING AND RESEARCH) (1943). 73 Main St., Monsey, N.Y., 10952. V. Pres. Ira Miller; Chmn. of Bd. Arthur Sternfield. Provides postgraduate courses and research work in higher Jewish studies; offers scholarships and fellowships. *Annual Journal.*

B'NAI B'RITH HILLEL FOUNDATIONS, INC. (1923). 1640 Rhode Island Ave., N.W., Washington, D.C., 20036. Chmn. B'nai B'rith Hillel Com. Seymour Martin Lipset; Internat. Dir. Norman E. Frimer. Provides a program of cultural, religious, educational, social, and counseling content to Jewish college and university students on 350 campuses in the United States, Australia, Canada, England, Israel, the Netherlands, South Africa, Switzerland, Italy, Colombia, Brazil, Venezuela and Sweden. *Clearing House; Campus;* Hillel "Little Book" series; *Inside Hillel.*

B'NAI B'RITH YOUTH ORGANIZATION (1924). 1640 Rhode Island Ave., N.W., Washington, D.C., 20036. Chmn. Youth Com. Horace Stern; Internat. Dir. Sidney Clearfield. To help Jewish teenagers achieve self-fulfillment and to make a maximum contribution to the Jewish community and their country's culture; to help the members acquire a greater knowledge and appreciation of Jewish religion and culture. *BBYO Advisor; Monday Morning; Shofar.*

BRANDEIS-BARDIN INSTITUTE (1941). 1101 Peppertree Lane, Simi Valley, Calif.,

93064. Chmn. of Bd. Steve Broidy; Pres. Richard Gunther; Dir. Dennis Prager. Maintains Brandeis Camp Institute (BCI) for college students as a leadership training institute; Camp Alonim for children 8–16, and House of the Book Association weekend institutes for married adults, in an effort to instill an appreciation of Jewish cultural and spiritual heritage and to create a desire for active participation in the American Jewish community. *Brandeis-Bardin News.*

CANTORS ASSEMBLY (1947). 150 Fifth Ave., N.Y.C., 10011. Pres. Kurt Silbermann; Exec. V. Pres. Samuel Rosenbaum. Seeks to unite all cantors who are adherents to traditional Judaism and who serve as full-time cantors in bona fide congregations, to conserve and promote the musical traditions of the Jews, and to elevate the status of the cantorial profession. *Annual Proceedings; Journal of Synagogue Music.*

CENTRAL CONFERENCE OF AMERICAN RABBIS (1889). 790 Madison Ave., N.Y.C., 10021. Pres. Rabbi Ely E. Pilchik; Exec. V. Pres. Rabbi Joseph B. Glaser. Seeks to conserve and promote Judaism and to disseminate its teachings in a liberal spirit. *CCAR Journal; CCAR Yearbook.*

CENTRAL YESHIVA BETH JOSEPH RABBINICAL SEMINARY (in Europe 1891; in U.S. 1941). 1427 49 St., Brooklyn, N.Y. 11219. Pres. and Dean Jacob Jofen. Maintains a school for teaching Orthodox rabbis and teachers, and promoting the cause of higher Torah learning.

CLEVELAND COLLEGE OF JEWISH STUDIES (1964). 26500 Shaker Blvd., Beachwood, Ohio, 44122. Pres. Martin Goldstein; Bd. Chmn. Maurice Terkel; Sec. Mrs. Elsa Konigsberg. Trains Hebrew- and religious-school teachers; serves as the department of Hebraic and Judaic studies for Cleveland area colleges and universities; offers intensive Ulpan and Judaic studies for community; serves as Jewish information center through its library; grants teachers diplomas and degrees of Bachelor of Hebrew Literature, Bachelor of Judaic Studies, and Master of Hebrew Literature. *Index to Jewish Periodicals.*

DROPSIE UNIVERSITY (1907). Broad and York Sts., Philadelphia, Pa., 19132. Acting Pres. Leon J. Perelman; Sec. Joseph B. Saltz. The only nonsectarian and nontheological graduate institution in America completely dedicated to Hebrew, Biblical and Middle Eastern studies; offers graduate programs in these areas. Course study includes the cultures and languages of Arabic, Aramaic, Ugaritic, Akkadian, and ancient Egyptian peoples; offers Ph.D. degree. *Jewish Quarterly Review.*

———, ALUMNI ASSOCIATION OF (1925). Broad and York Sts., Philadelphia, Pa. 19132. Pres. Sidney B. Hoenig; Sec. Hanoch Guy. Enhances the relationship of the alumni to the University. *Newsletter.*

GRATZ COLLEGE (1895). 10 St. and Tabor Rd., Philadelphia, Pa., 19141. Chmn. Bd. of Overseers Daniel C. Cohen; Pres. Daniel Isaacman; Dean Saul P. Wachs. Prepares teachers for Jewish schools and teachers of Hebrew for public high schools; grants Master of Hebrew Literature, Bachelor of Hebrew Literature and Bachelor of Arts in Jewish Studies degrees; is accredited by the Middle States Association of Colleges and Secondary Schools and the Association of Hebrew Colleges; provides studies in Judaica and Hebraica, maintains a Hebrew high school, two college preparatory departments for cadet teachers, and a school of observation and practice; provides Jewish studies for adults; community-service division (central agency for Jewish education) coordinates Jewish education in the city and provides consultation services to Jewish schools of all leanings. *Alumni Newspaper; College Bulletin; DCS Bulletin; Gratz Chats; GC Annual of Jewish Studies; 75th Anniversary Volume; Kinnereth; Telem Yearbook; What's New.*

HEBREW COLLEGE (1921). 43 Hawes St., Brookline, Mass., 02146. Pres. Eli Grad; Assoc. Dean Herbert Rosenblum. Provides intensive programs of study in all areas of Jewish culture from the high-school through college and graduate-school levels, also at branches in Hartford, New Haven, Providence, and Springfield; maintains ongoing programs with most major local universities; offers the degrees of Bachelor and Master of Hebrew Literature, and Bachelor and Master of Jewish Education, with teaching certification; trains men and women to teach, conduct and supervise Jewish schools; offers extensive Ulpan program; offers courses designed to deepen the community's awareness of the Jewish heritage. *Hebrew College Bulletin.*

HEBREW THEOLOGICAL COLLEGE (1921). 7135 N. Carpenter Rd., Skokie, Ill., 60076. Pres. Irving J. Rosenbaum; Exec. Bd. Chmn. Seymour J. Abrams; Sec. Joseph R. Friedman. An institution of higher Jewish learning which includes a division of advanced Hebrew studies, a school of liberal arts and sciences, a rabbinic ordination program, and a graduate school in Judaic studies. Trains rabbis, teachers, educational administrators, communal workers, and knowledgeable lay leaders for the Jewish community. *HaSofer; Yeshiva Women Bulletin.*

HEBREW UNION COLLEGE—JEWISH INSTITUTE OF RELIGION of Cincinnati, New York, Los Angeles, and Jerusalem (1875; 1922; merged 1950; 1954; 1963). 3101 Clifton Ave., Cincinnati, Ohio, 45220; 40 W. 68 St., N.Y.C., 10023; 3077 University Ave., Los Angeles, Calif., 90007; 13 King David St., Jerusalem, Israel. Pres. Alfred Gottschalk; Bd. of Govs. Chmn. Jules Backman; Sec. Henry H. Hersch. Prepares students for rabbinate, cantorate, religious-school teaching, community service, academic careers; promotes Jewish studies; maintains libraries and a museum; offers Ph.D. and D.H.L. degrees in graduate school; engages in archaeological excavations; publishes scholarly books through Hebrew Union College Press. *American Jewish Archives; Bibliographica Judaica; HUC—JIR Catalogue; Hebrew Union College Annual; Studies in Bibliography and Booklore.*

————, ALUMNI ASSOCIATION OF THE (1889). 3101 Clifton Ave., Cincinnati, Ohio, 45220. Pres. Norman Kahan. Promotes the welfare of the Hebrew Union College-Jewish Institute of Religion, and of its graduates.

————: AMERICAN JEWISH ARCHIVES (1947). 3101 Clifton Ave., Cincinnati, Ohio, 45220. Dir. Jacob R. Marcus; Assoc. Dir. Abraham Peck. Maintained for the preservation and study of North and South American Jewish historical records. *American Jewish Archives.*

————: AMERICAN JEWISH PERIODICAL CENTER (1957). 3101 Clifton Ave., Cincinnati, Ohio, 45220. Dir. Jacob R. Marcus; Exec. Dir. Herbert C. Zafren. Maintains microfilms of all American Jewish periodicals, 1823–1925; selected periodicals, since 1925. *Jewish Periodicals and Newspapers on Microfilm (1957); First Supplement (1960).*

————: RHEA HIRSCH SCHOOL OF EDUCATION (1967). 3077 University Mall, Los Angeles, Calif., 90007. Pres. John Adler. Dean Lewis M. Barth; Dir. William Cutter. Serves national and local needs in religious education through teacher training, consultation, laboratory research; offers M.A. program in Jewish and Hebrew education; conducts summer institutes and joint programs with University of Southern California. *Newsletter.*

————: SCHOOL OF EDUCATION (1947). 40 W. 68 St., N.Y.C., 10023. Pres. Alfred Gottschalk; Dean Paul M. Steinberg. Trains and certifies teachers and principals for Reform religious schools; offers M.A. degree with specialization in religious education.

————: SCHOOL OF JEWISH COMMUNAL SERVICE (1968). 3077 University Ave., Los Angeles, Calif., 90007. Pres. Dr. Alfred Gottschalk; Dir. Gerald B. Bubis. Offers certificate and master's graduate studies in Jewish psychological, sociological, cultural, historical, and valuation materials to those employed in Jewish communal services, or preparing for such work, regardless of setting or professional discipline; offers M.S.W. and M.A. in Jewish educational and communal service through HUC and M.A. in conjunction with University of Southern California.

————: SCHOOL OF SACRED MUSIC (1947). 40 W. 68 St., N.Y.C., 10023. Dean Paul M. Steinberg. Trains cantors and music personnel for congregations; offers B.S.M., M.A., and Ph.D. degrees. *Sacred Music Press.*

————: SKIRBALL MUSEUM (1913; 1972 in Calif.). 3077 University Mall, Los Angeles, Calif., 90007. Dir. Nancy Berman. Collects, preserves, researches and exhibits art and artifacts made by or for Jews, or otherwise associated with Jews and Judaism. Provides opportunity to faculty and students to do research in the field of Jewish art.

HERZLIAH-JEWISH TEACHERS SEMINARY (1967). 69 Bank St., N.Y.C., 10014. Pres. Eli Goldstein; Exec. Dir. Aviva Barzel; V. Pres. for Academic Affairs Meir Ben-Horin. Offers undergraduate and graduate programs in Jewish studies; continuing education courses for teachers in Hebrew and Yiddish schools; academic and professional programs in major disciplines of Judaism, historic and contemporary, with emphasis on Hebrew language and literature; Yiddish language and literature, Jewish education, history, philosophy, and sociology.

_____: GRADUATE DIVISION (1965). Dean Meir Ben-Horin. Offers programs leading to degree of Doctor of Jewish Literature in Hebrew language and literature, Yiddish language and literature, Jewish education, history, philosophy, and sociology. Admits men and women who have bachelor's degree and background in Hebrew, Yiddish, and Jewish studies. Annual Horace M. Kallen lecture by major Jewish scholars.

_____: HERZLIAH HEBREW TEACHERS INSTITUTE, INC. (1921). V. Pres. for Academic Affairs Meir Ben-Horin. Offers four-year, college-level programs in Hebrew and Jewish subjects, nationally recognized Hebrew teachers diploma, preparatory courses, and Yiddish courses.

_____: JEWISH TEACHERS SEMINARY AND PEOPLE'S UNIVERSITY, INC. (1918). V. Pres. for Academic Affairs Meir Ben-Horin. Offers four-year, college-level programs leading to Yiddish teachers diploma and Bachelor of Jewish Literature; offers preparatory courses and Hebrew courses.

_____: MUSIC DIVISION (1964). Performing Arts Div. Dir. Cantor Marvin Antosofsky. Offers studies in traditional and contemporary music, religious, Yiddish, secular and Hebraic; offers certificate and degree programs in Jewish music education and cantorial art, and artist diploma.

INDEPENDENT RABBINATE OF AMERICA (1970). 130 W. 42 St., Suite 1305, N.Y.C., 10036. Dir. Rabbi Henry Lieberman; Exec. Dir. Rabbi Chaim Lieberman. Maintains active placement service for the three branches in Judaism; seeks to improve the professional and economic standing of its members; screens the authenticity of their ordinations. *Monthly Newsletter; Rabbinical Registry and Directory.*

INTERNATIONAL ASSOCIATION OF HILLEL DIRECTORS (1949). 5715 S. Woodlawn Ave., Chicago, Ill., 60637. Pres. Daniel I. Leifer; Sec. Richard Marker. Seeks to promote professional relationships and exchanges of experience, develop personnel

standards and qualifications, safeguard integrity of Hillel profession; represents and advocates before National Hillel Staff, National Hillel Commission, B'nai B'rith Supreme Lodge, Jewish Federations and Welfare Funds.

JEWISH CHAUTAUQUA SOCIETY, INC. (sponsored by NATIONAL FEDERATION OF TEMPLE BROTHERHOODS) (1893). 838 Fifth Ave. N.Y.C., 10021. Pres. Robert E. Katz; Exec. Dir. Av Bondarin. Disseminates authoritative knowledge about Jews and Judaism; assigns rabbis to lecture at colleges; endows courses in Judaism for college credit at universities; donates Jewish reference books to college libraries; sends rabbis to serve as counselor-teachers at Christian Church summer camps and as chaplains at Boy Scout camps; sponsors institutes on Judaism for Christian clergy; produces motion pictures for public service television and group showings. *Brotherhood.*

JEWISH MINISTERS CANTORS ASSOCIATION OF AMERICA, INC. (1900). 236 Second Ave., N.Y.C., 10003. Pres. Shaye Pinsky; V. Pres. S. Mandel. To further and propagate traditional liturgy; to place cantors in synagogues throughout the U.S. and Canada; to develop the cantors of the future. *Kol Lakol.*

JEWISH RECONSTRUCTIONIST FOUNDATION (1940). 432 Park Ave. S., N.Y.C., 10016. Pres. Ira Eisenstein; Exec. V. Pres. Ludwig Nadelmann; Chmn. of Bd. Benjamin Wm. Mehlman. Dedicated to the advancement of Judaism as an evolving religious civilization, to the upbuilding of Eretz Yisrael as the spiritual center of the Jewish people, to the furtherance of universal freedom, justice, and peace and the fostering and establishment of Reconstructionist foundations and fellowship movements; sponsors Reconstructionist Rabbinical College in Philadelphia, Pa.; publishes books through the Reconstructionist Press; maintains Reconstructionist Federation (congregations and *havurot*). *Reconstructionist.*

_____: RECONSTRUCTIONIST FEDERATION OF CONGREGATIONS AND FELLOWSHIPS (1954). 432 Park Ave. S., N.Y.C., 10016. Pres. Leonard Leveton; Exec. Dir. Ira Eisenstein; Assoc. Dir. Ludwig Nadelman. Committed to the philosophy and program of the Reconstructionist movement. *Newsletter.*

———: RECONSTRUCTIONIST RABBINICAL ASSOCIATION (1975). 432 Park Ave. So., N.Y.C., 10016. Pres. Rabbi Arnold Rachlis; Secs. Rabbis Lee Friedlander, Mitchell Smith. Advances the principles of Reconstructionist Judaism; provides a forum for fellowship and exchange of ideas for Reconstructionist rabbis; cooperates with Reconstructionist Rabbinical College, and Reconstructionist Federation of Congregations and Havurot. *RRA Newsletter.*

JEWISH TEACHERS ASSOCIATION—MORIM (1926). 45 E. 33 St., N.Y.C., 10016. Pres. Michael Leinwand; Sec. Dorothy G. Posner. Promotes the religious, social, and moral welfare of children; provides a program of professional, cultural, and social activities for its members; cooperates with other organizations for the promotion of goodwill and understanding. *JTA Bulletin.*

JEWISH THEOLOGICAL SEMINARY OF AMERICA (1886; reorg. 1902). 3080 Broadway, N.Y.C., 10027. Chancellor Gerson D. Cohen; Chmn. Bd. of Dir. Sol. M. Linowitz. Organized for the perpetuation of the tenets of the Jewish religion, cultivation of Hebrew literature, pursuit of biblical and archaeological research, advancement of Jewish scholarship; maintains a library with extensive collections of Hebraica and Judaica, a department for the training of rabbis, a pastoral psychiatry center, the Jewish Museum, and such youth programs as the Ramah Camps and the Leaders Training Fellowship. *Conservative Judaism.*

———: AMERICAN STUDENT CENTER IN JERUSALEM (1962). P.O. Box 196, Jerusalem, Israel. Dean Shamma Friedman; Dir. Reuven Hammer. Offers programs for Rabbinical students, classes in Judaica for qualified Israelis and Americans, and an intensive program of Jewish studies for undergraduates.

———: CANTORS INSTITUTE AND SEMINARY COLLEGE OF JEWISH MUSIC (1952). 3080 Broadway, N.Y.C., 10027. Dir. David C. Kogen; Dean Morton J. Waldman. Trains cantors, music teachers, and choral directors for congregations. Offers programs leading to degrees of B.S.M., M.S.M., and D.S.M., and diploma of *Hazzan.*

———: DEPARTMENT OF RADIO AND TELEVISION (1944). 3080 Broadway, N.Y.C.,

10027. Exec. Prod. Milton E. Krents. Produces radio and TV programs expressing the Jewish tradition in its broadest sense, with emphasis on the universal human situation: "Eternal Light," a weekly radio program; 7 "Eternal Light" TV programs, produced in cooperation with NBC; and 12 "Directions" telecasts with ABC: distributes program scripts and related reading lists.

———: FANNIE AND MAXWELL ABBEL RESEARCH INSTITUTE IN RABBINICS (1951). 3080 Broadway, N.Y.C., 10027. Co-Dirs. Louis Finkelstein, Saul Lieberman. Fosters research in Rabbinics; prepares scientific editions of early Rabbinic works.

———: INSTITUTE FOR ADVANCED STUDY IN THE HUMANITIES (1968). 3080 Broadway, N.Y.C., 10027. Dean Ismar Schorsch; Chmn. Bd. of Trustees Stanley H. Fuld. A graduate program leading to M.A. degree in all aspects of Jewish Studies and Ph.D. in Bible, Jewish education, history, literature, philosophy, or rabbinics.

———: INSTITUTE FOR RELIGIOUS AND SOCIAL STUDIES (N.Y.C. 1938; Chicago 1944; Boston 1945). 3080 Broadway, N.Y.C., 10027. Pres. Gerson D. Cohen; Dir. Jessica Feingold. Serves as a scholarly and scientific fellowship of clergymen and other religious teachers who desire authoritative information regarding some of the basic issues now confronting spiritually-minded men.

———: MELTON RESEARCH CENTER (1960). 3080 Broadway, N.Y.C., 10027. Exec. Dir. Elaine Morris. Devises new curricula and materials for Jewish education; has intensive program for training curriculum writers; recruits, trains and retrains educators through seminars and in-service programs; maintains consultant and supervisory relationships with a limited number of pilot schools. *Melton Newsletter.*

———: SCHOCKEN INSTITUTE FOR JEWISH RESEARCH (1961). 6 Balfour St., Jerusalem, Israel. Librarian Yaakov Katzenstein. Incorporates Schocken library and its related research institutes in medieval Hebrew poetry and Jewish mysticism. *Schocken Institute Yearbook (P'raqim).*

———: SEMINARY COLLEGE OF JEWISH STUDIES-TEACHERS INSTITUTE (1909).

3080 Broadway, N.Y.C., 10027. Dean Ivan
G. Marcus. Offers complete college pro-
gram in Judaica leading to B.H.L. degree;
conducts joint program with Columbia
University, enabling students to receive
B.A. from Columbia and B.H.L. from the
Seminary, after four years.

———: UNIVERSITY OF JUDAISM (1947).
15600 Mulholland Dr., Los Angeles,
Calif., 90024. Pres. David L. Lieber; V.
Pres. Max Vorspan, David Gordis. West
Coast school of JTS. Serves as center of
undergraduate and graduate study of
Judaica; offers pre-professional and professional programs in Jewish education and
allied fields, including a pre-rabbinic program and joint program enabling students
to receive B.A. from UCLA and B.H.L.
from U. of J. after 4 years, as well as a
broad range of adult education and Jewish
activities.

MACHNE ISRAEL, INC. (1940). 770 Eastern
Parkway, Bklyn., N.Y., 11213. Pres.
Menachem M. Schneerson (Lubavitcher
Rebbe); Dir., Treas. M.A. Hodakov; Sec.
Nissan Mindel. The Lubavitcher move-
ment's organ dedicated to the social,
spiritual, and material welfare of Jews
throughout the world.

MERKOS L'INYONEI CHINUCH, INC. (THE
CENTRAL ORGANIZATION FOR JEWISH
EDUCATION) (1940). 770 Eastern Parkway, Bklyn., N.Y., 11213. Pres. Menachem M. Schneerson (the Lubavitcher
Rebbe); Dir. Treas. M.A. Hodakov; Sec.
Nissan Mindel. The educational arm of the
Lubavitcher movement. Seeks to promote
Jewish education among Jews, regardless
of their background, in the spirit of Torah-
true Judaism; to establish contact with
alienated Jewish youth, to stimulate concern and active interest in Jewish education on all levels, and to promote religious
observance as a daily experience among all
Jews; maintains worldwide network of regional offices, schools, summer camps and
Chabad-Lubavitch Houses; publishes Jewish educational literature in numerous languages and monthly journal in five languages: *Conversaciones con la juventud;
Conversations avec les jeunes; Schmuessen
mit kinder un yugent; Sihot la No-ar; Talks
and Tales.*

MESIVTA YESHIVA RABBI CHAIM BERLIN
RABBINICAL ACADEMY (1905). 1593
Coney Island Ave., Bklyn., N.Y., 11230.

Pres. Pincus Iseson; Exec. V. Pres. Rabbi
Bezalel Reifman. Maintains elementary division in the Hebrew and English departments, lower Hebrew division and Mesivta
high school, rabbinical academy, and post-
graduate school for advanced studies in
Talmud and other branches of rabbinic
scholarship; maintains Camp Morris, a
summer study camp. *Igud News Letter;
Kol Torah; Kuntrasim; Merchav; Shofar.*

MIRRER YESHIVA CENTRAL INSTITUTE (in
Poland 1817; in U.S. 1947). 1791-5 Ocean
Parkway, Brooklyn, N.Y., 11223. Pres.
and Dean Rabbi Shrage Moshe Kalmano-
witz; Exec. Dir. and Sec. Manfred Han-
delsman. Maintains rabbinical college,
postgraduate school for Talmudic research, accredited high school, and Kollel
and Sephardic divisions; dedicated to the
dissemination of Torah scholarship in the
community and abroad; engages in rescue
and rehabilitation of scholars overseas.

NATIONAL COMMITTEE FOR FURTHER-
ANCE OF JEWISH EDUCATION (1951). 824
Eastern Parkway, Brooklyn, N.Y., 11213.
Exec. V. Pres. Jacob J. Hecht; Sec. Morris
Drucker. Seeks to disseminate the ideals of
Torah-true education among the youth of
America; aids poor, sick and needy in U.S.
and Israel; maintains camp for under-
privileged children; sponsors Hadar Ha
Torah and Machon Chana, seeking to win
back college youth and others to the fold of
Judaism; maintains schools and dormitory
facilities; sponsors Heroes Fund to aid wid-
ows and orphans of heroes fallen in recent
Israeli wars. *Panorama; Passover Hand-
book; Seder Guide; Spiritual Suicide;
Focus.*

NATIONAL COUNCIL FOR JEWISH EDUCA-
TION (1926). 114 Fifth Ave., N.Y.C.,
10011. Pres. Leivy Smolar; Exec. Sec. Jack
M. Horden. Fellowship of Jewish education profession, comprising administrators
and supervisors of national and local Jewish educational institutions and agencies,
and teachers in Hebrew high schools and
Jewish teachers colleges, of all ideological
groupings; conducts annual national and
regional conferences in all areas of Jewish
education; represents the Jewish education
profession before the Jewish community;
co-sponsors, with American Association
for Jewish Education, a personnel committee and other projects; cooperates with
Jewish Agency department of education
and culture in promoting Hebrew culture

and studies; conducts lectureship at Hebrew University. *Jewish Education; Sheviley Hahinuch.*

*NATIONAL COUNCIL OF BETH JACOB SCHOOLS, INC. (1945). 1415 E. 7 St., Bklyn, N.Y., 11230. Pres. Israel M. Zaks; Chmn. of Bd. Shimon Newhouse; Sec. David Rosenberg. Operates Orthodox all-day schools from kindergarten through high school for girls, a residence high school in Ferndale, N.Y., a national institute for master instructors, and a summer camp for girls. *Baís Yaakov Digest; Pnimia Call.*

NATIONAL COUNCIL OF YOUNG ISRAEL (1912). 3 W. 16 St., N.Y.C., 10011. Nat. Pres. Herman Rosenbaum; Exec. V. Pres. Ephraim H. Sturm. Maintains a program of spiritual, cultural, social and communal activity towards the advancement and perpetuation of traditional, Torah-true Judaism; seeks to instill in American youth an understanding and appreciation of the ethical and spiritual values of Judaism. Sponsors kosher dining clubs and fraternity houses and an Israel program. *Viewpoint; Hashkofa Series; Massoeah Newspaper.*

———, AMERICAN FRIENDS OF YOUNG ISRAEL SYNAGOGUES IN ISRAEL (1926). 3 W. 16 St., N.Y.C., 10011. Chmn. Marvin Luban; Exec. V. Pres. Ephraim H. Sturm. Promotes Young Israel synagogues and youth work in synagogues in Israel.

———, ARMED FORCES BUREAU (1912). 3 W. 16 St., N.Y.C., 10011. Dir. Stanley W. Schlessel; Assoc. Dir. David Rinzler. Advises and guides the inductees into the armed forces with regard to Sabbath observance, *kashrut,* and Orthodox behavior. *Guide for the Orthodox Serviceman.*

———, EMPLOYMENT BUREAU (1912). 3 W. 16 St., N.Y.C., 10011. Exec. V. Pres. Ephraim H. Sturm; Employment Dir. Dorothy Stein. Operates an on-the-job training program under federal contract; helps secure employment, particularly for Sabbath observers and Russian immigrants; offers vocational guidance. *Viewpoint.*

———: INSTITUTE FOR JEWISH STUDIES (1947). 3 W. 16 St., N.Y.C., 10011. Pres. Herman Rosenbaum; Exec. V. Pres. Rabbi Ephraim H. Sturm. Introduces students to Jewish learning and knowledge; helps form adult branch schools; aids Young Israel synagogues in their adult education programs. *Bulletin.*

———: INTERCOLLEGIATE COUNCIL AND YOUNG SINGLE ADULTS (formerly MASSORAH INTERCOLLEGIATES OF YOUNG ISRAEL; 1951). 3 W. 16 St., N.Y.C., 10011. Pres. Leon Shepshaievitz; Dir. Stanley W. Schlessel. Organizes and operates kosher dining clubs on college and university campuses; provides information and counseling on *kashrut* observance at college; gives college-age youth understanding and appreciation of Judaism and information on issues important to Jewish community; arranges seminars and meetings; publishes pamphlets and monographs. *Hashkafa.*

———: YISRAEL HATZAIR (reorg. 1968). 3 W. 16 St., N.Y.C., 10011. Pres. Jackie Goldstein; Nat. Dir. Arnold Grant. Fosters a program of spiritual, cultural, social, and communal activities for the advancement and perpetuation of traditional Torah-true Judaism; strives to instill an understanding and appreciation of the high ethical and spiritual values and to demonstrate compatibility of ancient faith of Israel with good Americanism.

NATIONAL FEDERATION OF JEWISH MEN'S CLUBS, INC. (1929). 475 Riverside Dr., Suite 244, N.Y.C., 10027. Pres. Morton R. Lang; Exec. Dir. David L. Blumenfeld. Promotes principles and objectives of Conservative Judaism by organizing, sponsoring, and developing men's clubs or brotherhoods; supports Leaders' Training Fellowship national youth organization. *Torchlight.*

NATIONAL JEWISH CONFERENCE CENTER (1974). 250 W. 57 St., N.Y.C., 10019. Chmn. Lee Javitch; Dir. Irving Greenberg; Exec. Dir. John S. Ruskay. Devoted to leadership education for the American Jewish community. Conducts weekend retreats and community gatherings, as well as conferences on various topics. *Newsletter.*

———, HOLOCAUST RESOURCE CENTER (1978). 250 W. 57 St., N.Y.C., 10019. Assoc. Dir. Michael Berenbaum. Disseminates information on the Holocaust to the American Jewish community; develops Holocaust memorial projects. *Shoah: A Review of Holocaust Studies and Commemorations.*

NATIONAL JEWISH HOSPITALITY COMMITTEE (1973). 201 S. 18 St., Rm. 1519, Philadelphia, Pa., 19103. Pres. Allen S. Maller; Exec. Dir. Steven S. Jacobs. Assists converts and prospective converts to Judaism, persons involved in intermarriages, and the parents of Jewish youth under the influence of cults and missionaries, as well as the youths themselves. *Our Choice.*

NATIONAL JEWISH INFORMATION SERVICE FOR THE PROPAGATION OF JUDAISM, INC. (1960). 5174 W. 8th St., Los Angeles, Calif., 90036. Pres. Moshe M. Maggal; V. Pres. Lawrence J. Epstein; Corr. Sec. Rachel D. Maggal. Seeks to convert non-Jews to Judaism and revert Jews to Judaism; maintains College for Jewish Ambassadors for the training of Jewish missionaries and the Correspondence Academy of Judaism for instruction on Judaism through the mail. *Voice of Judaism.*

NER ISRAEL RABBINICAL COLLEGE (1933). 400 Mt. Wilson Lane, Baltimore, Md., 21208. Pres. Rabbi Jacob I. Ruderman; V. Pres. Rabbi Herman N. Neuberger. Trains rabbis and educators for Jewish communities in America and worldwide. Offers bachelors, masters and doctoral degrees in talmudic law as well as Teachers Diploma. College has four divisions: Mechina High School, Rabbinical College, Teachers Training Institute, Graduate School and a branch in Toronto, Canada. Maintains an active community service division. *Ner Israel Bulletin; Alumni Bulletin; Bito'one Chanecha Yeshivas Ner Yisroel; Ohr Hanair Talmudic Journal; Zacher L'Avrohom Torah Journal.*

OZAR HATORAH, INC. (1946). 411 Fifth Ave., N.Y.C., 10016. Pres. Joseph Shalom; Intl. Pres. S.D. Sassoon; V. Pres. Moshe Milstein. Establishes and maintains elementary, secondary and boarding schools, combining a program of religious and secular education for Jewish youth in Morocco, Iran, Syria and France. *Bulletin.*

P'EYLIM—AMERICAN YESHIVA STUDENT UNION (1951). 3 W. 16 St., N.Y.C., 10011. Pres. Nisson Alpert; Dir. Avraham Hirsch. Aids and sponsors pioneer work by American graduate teachers and rabbis in new villages and towns in Israel; does religious, organizational, and educational work and counseling among new immigrant youth; maintains summer camps for poor immigrant youth in Israel; belongs to worldwide P'eylim movement which has groups in Argentina, Brazil, Canada, England, Belgium, the Netherlands, Switzerland, France, and Israel; engages in relief and educational work among North African immigrants in France and Canada, assisting them to relocate and reestablish a strong Jewish community life. *P'eylim Reporter; N'she P'eylim News.*

*RABBINICAL ALLIANCE OF AMERICA (IGUD HARABONIM) (1944). 156 Fifth Ave., Suite 807, N.Y.C., 10010. Pres. Rabbi Abraham B. Hecht. Seeks to promulgate the cause of Torah-true Judaism through an organized rabbinate that is consistently Orthodox; seeks to elevate the position of Orthodox rabbis nationally, and to defend the welfare of Jews the world over. Also has Beth Din Rabbinical Court. *Perspective.*

RABBINICAL ASSEMBLY (1900). 3080 Broadway, N.Y.C., 10027. Pres. Rabbi Stanley S. Rabinowitz; Exec. V. Pres. Rabbi Wolfe Kelman. Seeks to promote Conservative Judaism, and to foster the spirit of fellowship and cooperation among rabbis and other Jewish scholars; cooperates with the Jewish Theological Seminary of America and the United Synagogue of America. *Beineinu; Conservative Judaism; Proceedings of the Rabbinical Assembly.*

RABBINICAL COLLEGE OF TELSHE, INC. (1941). 28400 Euclid Ave., Wickliffe, Ohio, 44092. Pres. Rabbi Mordecai Gifter; Sec. Moshe Helfan. College for higher Jewish learning specializing in talmudic studies and rabbinics; maintains a preparatory academy including secular high school, a postgraduate department, a teachers training school, and a teachers seminary for women. *Pri Etz Chaim; Peer Mordechai; Alumni Bulletin.*

RABBINICAL COUNCIL OF AMERICA, INC. (1923; reorg. 1936). 1250 Broadway, Suite 802, N.Y.C., 10001. Pres. Walter S. Wurzburger; Exec. V. Pres. Israel Klavan. Promotes Orthodox Judaism in the community; supports institutions for study of Torah; stimulates creation of new traditional agencies. *Hadorom; Record; Sermon Manual; Tradition.*

RECONSTRUCTIONIST RABBINICAL COLLEGE (1968). 2308 N. Broad St., Philadelphia, Pa., 19132. Pres. Ira Eisenstein.

Trains rabbis for all areas of Jewish communal life: synagogues, academic and educational positions, Hillel centers, Federation agencies; requires students to pursue outside graduate studies in religion and related subjects; confers title of rabbi and grants degree of Doctor of Hebrew Letters.

*RESEARCH INSTITUTE OF RELIGIOUS JEWRY, INC. (1941; reorg. 1954). 471 West End Ave., N.Y.C., 10024. Chmn. Isaac Strahl; Sec. Marcus Levine. Engages in research and publishes studies concerning the situation of religious Jewry and its problems all over the world.

SHOLEM ALEICHEM FOLK INSTITUTE, INC. (1918). 3301 Bainbridge Ave., Bronx, N.Y., 10467. Pres. Burt Levey; Sec. Noah Zingman. Aims to imbue children with Jewish values through teaching Yiddish language and literature, Hebrew and the Bible, Jewish history, the significance of Jewish holidays, folk and choral singing, and facts about Jewish life in America and Israel. *Kinder Journal* (Yiddish).

SOCIETY OF FRIENDS OF THE TOURO SYNAGOGUE, NATIONAL HISTORIC SHRINE, INC. (1948). 85 Touro St., Newport, R.I., 02840. Pres. Seebert J. Goldowsky; Sec. Theodore Lewis. Assists in the maintenance of the Touro Synagogue as a national historic site.

SPERTUS COLLEGE OF JUDAICA (1925). 618 N. Michigan Ave., Chicago, Ill., 60605. Pres. David Weinstein; Bd. Chmn. Philip Spertus. Educates teachers of Hebraica and Judaica for elementary and secondary Jewish schools; certifies Hebrew teachers for public and private Illinois schools; provides Chicago area colleges and universities with specialized undergraduate and graduate programs in Judaica and serves as a Department of Judaic Studies to these colleges and universities; serves as Midwest Jewish information center through its Asher Library and Maurice Spertus Museum of Judaica; grants degrees of Master of Arts in Jewish Education and in Jewish Communal Service, Bachelor of Arts, and Bachelor of Judaic Studies. *Journal of Jewish Art.*

SYNAGOGUE COUNCIL OF AMERICA (1926). 432 Park Ave. S., N.Y.C., 10016. Pres. Rabbi Saul I. Teplitz; Exec. V. Pres. Rabbi Henry Siegman. Serves as spokesman for, and coordinates policies of, national rabbinical and lay synagogal organizations of Conservative, Orthodox, and Reform branches of American Judaism. Sponsors Institute for Jewish Policy Planning and Research. *SCA Report.*

————: INSTITUTE FOR JEWISH POLICY PLANNING AND RESEARCH OF (1972). 1776 Massachusetts Ave., N.W., Washington, D.C., 20036. Chmn. Philip M. Klutznick; Dir. Max Singer. Seeks to strengthen American Jewry by conducting and promoting systematic study of major issues confronting its future vitality, for which it enlists informed academic and lay people; sponsors research and analysis on the subject and disseminates findings to synagogues and other Jewish organizations. *Analysis; Background.*

TORAH UMESORAH—NATIONAL SOCIETY FOR HEBREW DAY SCHOOLS (1944). 229 Park Ave. S., N.Y.C., 10003. Nat. Pres. Samuel C. Feuerstein; Nat. Dir. Joseph Kaminetsky. Establishes Hebrew day schools throughout U.S. and Canada and services them in all areas including placement and curriculum guidance; conducts teacher training institutes, a special fellowship program, seminars, and workshops for in-service training of teachers; publishes textbooks and supplementary reading material; conducts education research and has established Fryer Fdn. for research in ethics and character education; supervises federal aid programs for Hebrew day schools throughout the U.S. *Olomeinu— Our World; Tempo; Torah Umesorah Report; Machberet Hamenahel.*

————: INSTITUTE FOR PROFESSIONAL ENRICHMENT (1973). 229 Park Ave. S., N.Y.C., 10003. Dir. Bernard Dov Milians. Provides enriched training and upgraded credentials for administrative, guidance, and classroom personnel of Hebrew day schools and for Torah-community leaders; offers graduate and undergraduate programs, in affiliation with accredited universities which award full degrees: M.A. in geriatric counseling, early childhood and elementary education, applied human relations (adult, family, alcoholism counseling), health, nutrition; M.B.A. in management; M.S. in special education, reading; B.S. in education; B.A. in liberal arts, social sciences, business, gerontology. *Professional Enrichment News (PEN).*

_____: NATIONAL ASSOCIATION OF HE-
BREW DAY SCHOOL ADMINISTRATORS
(1960). 229 Park Ave. S., N.Y.C., 10003.
Pres. David H. Schwartz; Bd. Chmn.
Rabbi Saul Wolf; Exec. Coord. Bernard
Dov Milians. Coordinates the work of the
fiscal directors of Hebrew day schools
throughout the country. *NAHDSA Review.*

_____: NATIONAL ASSOCIATION OF HE-
BREW DAY SCHOOL PARENT-TEACHER
ASSOCIATIONS (1948). 229 Park Ave. S.,
N.Y.C., 10003. Nat. Pres. Mrs. Henry C.
Rhein; Exec. Secy. Mrs. Samuel Brand;
Chmn. of Bd. Mrs. Clarence Horwitz. Acts
as a clearinghouse and service agency to
PTAs of Hebrew day schools; organizes
parent education courses and sets up pro-
grams for individual PTAs. *National Pro-
gram Notes; PTA Bulletin; Fundraising
With a Flair; PTA With a Purpose for the
Hebrew Day School.*

_____: NATIONAL CONFERENCE OF YE-
SHIVA PRINCIPALS (1956). 229 Park Ave.
S., N.Y.C., 10003. Pres. Joel Kramer;
Exec. Sec. Rabbi Joshua Fishman; Bd.
Chmn. David Mykoff. A professional organization of primary and secondary yeshiva
day-school principals which seeks to make
yeshiva day-school education more effective. *Machberet Hamenahel.*

_____: NATIONAL YESHIVA TEACHERS
BOARD OF LICENSE (1953). 229 Park Ave.
S., N.Y.C., 10003. Bd. Chmn. Elias
Schwartz; Ex. Consult. Zvi H. Shurin. Issues licenses to qualified instructors for all
grades of the Hebrew day school and the
general field of Torah education.

_____: SAMUEL A. FRYER EDUCATIONAL
RESEARCH FOUNDATION (1966). 229 Park
Ave. S., N.Y.C., 10003. Chmn. Bd. of
Trustees Jack Sable; Dir. Louis Nulman.
Strengthens the ethics programs of Hebrew
day, afternoon, and Sunday schools, summer camps, and Jewish centers through
moral sensitivity-training program; provides extensive teacher-training program;
publishes monographs, newsletter, and
teachers' bulletin. *Fryer Foundation Newsletter.*

TOURO COLLEGE (1970). 30 W. 44 St.,
N.Y.C., 10036. Pres. Bernard Lander.
Chartered by the N.Y. State Board of Regents to operate and maintain nonprofit,
four-year college with liberal arts programs leading to B.A. and B.S. degrees,
with an emphasis on the relevance of the
Jewish heritage to the general culture of
Western civilization. *Annual Bulletin.*

UNION OF AMERICAN HEBREW CONGREGA-
TIONS (1873). 838 Fifth Ave., N.Y.C.,
10021. Pres. Rabbi Alexander M. Schindler. Serves as the central congregational
body of Reform Judaism in the Western
Hemisphere; serves its approximately 740
affiliated temples and membership with religious, educational, cultural, and administrative programs. *Keeping Posted; Reform
Judaism.*

*_____: AMERICAN CONFERENCE OF CAN-
TORS OF (1956). 838 Fifth Ave., N.Y.C.,
10021. Pres. Ramon Gilbert; Exec. Dir.
Raymond Smolover. Members receive investiture and commissioning as cantors at
ordination-investiture ceremonies at Hebrew Union College-Jewish Institute of
Religion-Sacred School of Music. Through
Joint Placement Commission, serves congregations seeking cantors and music directors. Dedicated to creative Judaism,
preserving the best of the past, and encouraging new and vital approaches to religious ritual, music and ceremonies.

_____: COMMISSION ON SOCIAL ACTION OF
REFORM JUDAISM (see p. 302).

_____: NATIONAL ASSOCIATION OF TEM-
PLE ADMINISTRATORS OF (1941). 838
Fifth Ave., N.Y.C., 10021. Pres. Walter C.
Baron; Adm. Sec. Harold Press. Fosters
Reform Judaism; prepares and disseminates administrative information and
procedures to member synagogues of
UAHC; provides and encourages proper
and adequate training of professional synagogue executives; formulates and establishes professional ideals and standards
for the synagogue executive. *NATA Journal.*

_____: NATIONAL ASSOCIATION OF TEM-
PLE EDUCATORS (1955). 838 Fifth Ave.,
N.Y.C., 10021. Pres. Raymond Israel;
Exec. Sec. Harvey Kaye. Represents the
temple educator within the general body of
Reform Judaism; fosters the full-time profession of the temple educator; encourages
the growth and development of Jewish religious education consistent with the aims of
Reform Judaism; stimulates communal interest in and responsibility for Jewish religious education. *NATE News; Compass
Magazine.*

_____: NATIONAL FEDERATION OF TEMPLE BROTHERHOODS (1923). 838 Fifth Ave., N.Y.C., 10021. Pres. Robert E. Katz; Exec. Dir. Av Bondarin. Promotes Jewish education among its members, along with participation in temple, brotherhood, and interfaith activities; sponsors the Jewish Chautauqua Society. *Brotherhood.*

_____: NATIONAL FEDERATION OF TEMPLE SISTERHOODS (1913). 838 Fifth Ave., N.Y.C., 10021. Pres. Lillian Maltzer; Exec. Dir. Eleanor R. Schwartz. Serves more than 600 sisterhoods of Reform Judaism; inter-religious understanding and social justice; scholarships and grants to rabbinic students; braille and large type Judaic materials for Jewish blind; projects for Israel, Soviet Jewry and the aging; is women's agency of UAHC and cooperates with World Union for Progressive Judaism. *Notes for Now.*

*_____: NATIONAL FEDERATION OF TEMPLE YOUTH (1939). 838 Fifth Ave., N.Y.C., 10021. Dirs. Daniel Freelander and Leonard Troupp. Seeks to train Reform Jewish youth in the values of the synagogue and their application to daily life through service to the community and congregation; runs department of summer camps and national leadership training institutes; arranges overseas academic tours and work programs, international student exchange programs, college student programs in the U.S. and Israel, including an accredited study program in Israel.

_____, AND CENTRAL CONFERENCE OF AMERICAN RABBIS: COMMISSION ON JEWISH EDUCATION OF (1923). 838 Fifth Ave., N.Y.C., 10021. Chmn. Martin S. Rozenberg; Dir. Rabbi Daniel B. Syme. Develops curricula and teachers' manuals; conducts pilot projects and offers educational guidance and consultation at all age levels to member congregations and affiliates and associate bodies. *What's Happening; Compass; E³.*

_____, AND CENTRAL CONFERENCE OF AMERICAN RABBIS: JOINT COMMISSION ON SYNAGOGUE ADMINISTRATION (1962). 838 Fifth Ave., N.Y.C., 10021. Chmn. Mrs. Lillian Maltzer; Dir. Myron E. Schoen. Assists congregations in management, finance, building maintenance, design, construction, and art aspects of synagogues; maintains the Synagogue Architectural Library consisting of photos, slides, and plans of contemporary and older synagogue buildings. *Synagogue Service.*

UNION OF ORTHODOX JEWISH CONGREGATIONS OF AMERICA (1898). 116 E. 27 St., N.Y.C., 10016. Pres. Harold M. Jacobs; Exec. V. Pres. Pinchas Stolper. Serves as the national central body of Orthodox synagogues; provides educational, religious, and organizational guidance to congregations, youth groups, and men's clubs; represents the Orthodox Jewish community in relationship to governmental and civic bodies, and the general Jewish community; conducts the national authoritative U Kashruth certification service. *Jewish Action; Jewish Life; Keeping Posted; U News Reporter.*

_____: NATIONAL CONFERENCE OF SYNAGOGUE YOUTH (1954). 116 E. 27 St., N.Y.C., 10016. Pres. Meir Weinman; Nat. Dir. Baruch Taub. Serves as central body for youth groups of traditional congregations; provides such national activities and services as educational guidance, Torah study groups, Chavrusa-community service, programs consultation, Torah library, Torah fund scholarships, Ben Zakkai Honor Society, Friends of NCSY; conducts national and regional events including week-long seminars, summer Torah tours in over 200 communities, Israel summer seminar for teens and collegiates, Camp NCSY in Israel for preteens. Divisions include Senior NCSY in 18 regions and 465 chapters; Junior NCSY for preteens, CYT-College Youth for Torah; B'nai Torah Day School and NCSY in Israel. *Keeping posted with NCSY; Advisors' Newsletter; Mitsvos Ma'asiyos; Holiday Series; Jewish Thought Series; Leadership Manual Series; Texts for Teen Study.*

_____: NATIONAL ORGANIZATION OF ORTHODOX SYNAGOGUE ADMINISTRATORS (1964). 116 E. 27 St., N.Y.C., 10016. Pres. Harold M. Jacobs. Seeks to utilize the experience and knowledge of the synagogue administrator in establishing specific professional standards and practices for Orthodox congregations.

_____: WOMEN'S BRANCH (1923). 84 Fifth Ave., N.Y.C., 10011. Pres. Mrs. Samuel A. Turk; Exec. V. Pres. Mrs. Mordecai A. Stern. Seeks to spread knowledge for the understanding and practice of Orthodox Judaism, and to unite all Orthodox women and their synagogal organizations, services affiliates with educational and programming materials, leadership and organizational guidance and has an NGO representative at UN. *Hachodesh; Newsletter.*

UNION OF ORTHODOX RABBIS OF THE UNITED STATES AND CANADA (1900). 235 E. Broadway, N.Y.C., 10002. Pres. Rabbi Moshe Feinstein; Chmn. Rabbi Symcha Elberg, Dir. Rabbi Hersh M. Ginsberg. Seeks to foster and promote Torah-true Judaism in U.S. and Canada; assists in the establishment and maintenance of *yeshivot* in the United States; maintains committee on marriage and divorce and aids individuals with marital difficulties; disseminates knowledge of traditional Jewish rites and practices and publishes regulations on synagogal structure; maintains rabbinical court for resolving individual and communal conflicts. *Hapardes.*

UNION OF SEPHARDIC CONGREGATIONS, INC. (1929). 8 W. 70 St., N.Y.C., 10023. Pres. The Haham, Solomon Gaon; Sec. Joseph Tarica; Bd. Chmn. Victor Tarry. Promotes the religious interests of Sephardic Jews; prepares and distributes Sephardic prayer books and provides religious leaders for Sephardic congregations.

UNITED LUBAVITCHER YESHIVOTH (1940). 841–853 Ocean Parkway, Brooklyn, N.Y., 11230. Pres. Eli N. Sklar; Chmn. Exec. Com. Rabbi S. Gourary. Supports and organizes Jewish day schools and rabbinical seminaries in the U.S.A. and abroad.

UNITED ORTHODOX SERVICES, INC. (1971). 1311–49 St., Brooklyn, N.Y., 11219. Coordinator Rabbi Zev Perl; Adm. Dir. Ira Axelrod; Exec. Sec. Mrs. Lillian Deutsch. Centralized religious administrative umbrella organization, with 35 affiliates worldwide; acts as liaison between various religious groups with specialized functions and the Jewish community; initiates projects of its own.

UNITED SYNAGOGUE OF AMERICA (1913). 155 Fifth Ave., N.Y.C. 10010. Pres. Simon Schwartz; Exec. V. Pres. Rabbi Benjamin Z. Kreitman. National organization of Conservative Jewish congregations. Maintains 12 departments and 20 regional offices to assist its affiliated congregations with religious, educational, youth, community, and administrative programming and

guidance; aims to enhance the cause of Conservative Judaism, further religious observance, encourage establishment of Jewish religious schools; embraces all elements essentially loyal to traditional Judaism. *Program Suggestions; United Synagogue Review; Yearbook Directory and Buyers' Guide.*

————, **ATID, COLLEGE AGE ORGANIZATION OF** (1960). 155 Fifth Ave., N.Y.C., 10010. Student Advisory Board. Seeks to develop a program for strengthening identification with Judaism, based on the personality development, needs and interests of the collegian. *ATID Curricula Judaica; ATID Bibliography. ATID Bookmobile Project.*

————: **COMMISSION ON JEWISH EDUCATION** (1930). 155 Fifth Ave., N.Y.C., 10010. Chmn. Rabbi Joel H. Zaiman; Dir. Morton Siegel. Promotes higher educational standards in Conservative congregational schools and Solomon Schechter Day Schools and publishes material for the advancement of their educational program. *Briefs; Impact; In Your Hands; Your Child.*

————, **JEWISH EDUCATORS ASSEMBLY OF** (1951). 155 Fifth Ave., N.Y.C., 10010. Pres. Jay Stern; Admin. Herbert L. Tepper. Promotes, extends, and strengthens the program of Jewish education on all levels in the community in consonance with the philosophy of the Conservative movement. *Annual Yearbook; Quarterly Bulletin; Newsletters.*

————: **JOINT COMMISSION ON SOCIAL ACTION** (1958). 155 Fifth Ave., N.Y.C. 10010. Co-chmn. Jerry Wagner, Dolly Moser; Dir. Muriel Bermar. Consists of representatives of United Synagogue of America; Women's League for Conservative Judaism; Rabbinical Assembly, and National Federation of Jewish Men's Clubs; reviews public issues and cooperates with civic and Jewish community organizations to achieve social action goals. *Judaism in Social Action.*

————, **KADIMA OF** (formerly **PRE-USY**; reorg. 1968). 155 Fifth Ave., N.Y.C., 10010. Int. Co-ordinator Carol Chapnick Silk. Dir. Robert J. Leifert. Involves Jewish pre-teens in a meaningful religious, educational, and social environment; fosters a sense of identity and commitment to the Jewish community and Conservative

Movement; conducts synagogue-based chapter programs and regional Kadima days and weekends. *KADIMA; Mitzvah of the Month; Kadima Kesher; Advisors Aid Series; Chagim series.*

———, NATIONAL ACADEMY FOR ADULT JEWISH STUDIES OF (1940). 155 Fifth Ave., N.Y.C., 10010. Chmn. Bd. of Gov. Morris Fond; Dir. Marvin S. Wiener. Provides guidance and information on resources, courses, and other projects in adult Jewish education; prepares and publishes pamphlets, study guides, tracts, and texts for use in adult-education programs; publishes the Jewish Tract series and distributes El-Am edition of *Talmud*. Distributes black-and-white and color films of "Eternal Light" TV programs on Jewish subjects, produced by Jewish Theological Seminary in cooperation with NBC. *Bulletin.*

———, NATIONAL ASSOCIATION OF SYNAGOGUE ADMINISTRATORS OF (1948). 155 Fifth Ave., N.Y.C. 10010. Pres. Burton D. Shanker. Aids congregations affiliated with the United Synagogue of America to further aims of Conservative Judaism through more effective administration; advances professional standards and promotes new methods in administration; cooperates in United Synagogue placement services and administrative surveys. *NASA Newsletter; NASA Journal.*

———, UNITED SYNAGOGUE YOUTH OF (1951). 155 Fifth Ave., N.Y.C., 10010. Pres. David Marcu; Exec. Dir. Paul Freedman. Seeks to develop a program for strengthening identification with Conservative Judaism, based on the personality development, needs, and interests of the adolescent. *Achshav; HaMadrich: A Journal of Informal Jewish Education; Tikun Olam; USY Alumni Assn. Newsletter.*

———, WOMEN'S LEAGUE FOR CONSERVATIVE JUDAISM (formerly NATIONAL WOMEN'S LEAGUE) (1918). 48 E. 74 St., N.Y.C., 10021. Pres. Ruth Perry. Constitutes parent body of Conservative women's groups in U.S., Canada, Puerto Rico, Mexico, and Israel; provides them with programs in religion, education, social action, leadership training, Israel affairs, and community affairs; publishes books of Jewish interest; contributes to support of Jewish Theological Seminary and Mathilde Schechter Residence Hall. *Women's League Outlook.*

WEST COAST TALMUDICAL SEMINARY (Yeshiva Ohr Elchonon) (1953). 851 No. Kings Rd., Los Angeles, Calif., 90069. Pres. Abraham Linderman; Dean S. Wasserman; Sec. David Bass. Provides facilities for intensive Torah education as well as Orthodox rabbinical training on the West Coast; conducts an accredited college preparatory high school combined with a full program of Torah-Talmudic training and a graduate Talmudical division on college level.

WORLD COUNCIL OF SYNAGOGUES (1957). 155 Fifth Ave., N.Y.C., 10010. Pres. David Zucker; Dir. Muriel M. Bermar; Exec. Dir. in Israel Pesach Schindler. International representative of Conservative organizations and congregations (Hatenuah Hamasoratit); promotes the growth and development of the Conservative movement in Israel and throughout the world; supports new congregations and educational institutions overseas; holds biennial international convention; represents the world Conservative Movement in the World Zionist Organization.

WORLD UNION FOR PROGRESSIVE JUDAISM, LTD. (1926). 838 Fifth Ave., N.Y.C., 10021. Pres. David H. Wice; Exec. Dir. Richard G. Hirsch; Sec. Jane Evans; N.A. Bd. Dir. Ira S. Youdovin. Promotes and coordinates efforts of Reform, Liberal, and Progressive congregations throughout the world; supports new congregations; assigns and employs rabbis overseas; sponsors seminaries and schools; organizes international conferences of Liberal Jews. *International Conference Reports; News and Views; Shalhevet* (Israel); *Teshuva* (Argentina).

YAVNE HEBREW THEOLOGICAL SEMINARY, INC. (1924). 510 Dahill Road, Brooklyn, N.Y., 11218. Pres. Nathan Shapiro; Exec. Dir. Solomon K. Shapiro. School for higher Jewish learning; trains rabbis and teachers as Jewish leaders for American Jewish communities; maintains branch in Jerusalem for Higher Jewish Education-Machon Maharshal and for an exchange student program. *Yavne Newsletter.*

YAVNEH, NATIONAL RELIGIOUS STUDENTS ASSOCIATION (1960). 25 W. 26 St., N.Y.C., 10010. Pres. Eleanor Swift; V. Pres. Robert Adler. Seeks to promote religious Jewish and Zionist education on the college campus, to facilitate full observance of halakhic Judaism, to integrate the insights gained in college studies, and to become a force for the dissemination of Torah Judaism in the Jewish community; initiated *kiruv* programs aimed at drawing into the established Jewish community alienated and assimilated Jewish students; publishes occasional monographs in *Yavneh Studies Series;* conducts summer tours to Israel and Western Europe and an Eastern Europe holocaust study tour. *Kol Yavneh, Parshat Hashavua Series; Yavneh Shiron, Guide to Jewish Life on the College Campus.*

YESHIVA UNIVERSITY (1886). 500 W. 185 St., N.Y.C., 10033. Pres. Norman Lamm; Chmn. Bd. of Trustees Herbert Tenzer. The nation's oldest and largest private university founded under Jewish auspices, with a broad range of undergraduate, graduate, and professional schools, a network of affiliates, publications, a widespread program of research, community service agencies, and a museum. Curricula lead to bachelor's, master's, doctoral, and professional degrees. Undergraduate schools provide general studies curricula supplemented by courses in Jewish learning; graduate schools prepare for careers in medicine, law, mathematics, physics, social work, education, psychology, Semitic languages, literatures, and cultures, and other fields. It has five undergraduate schools, nine graduate schools, and ten affiliates, with its four main centers located in Manhattan and the Bronx. *Inside Yeshiva University; Yeshiva University Report.*

Undergraduate schools for men at Main Center: Yeshiva College (Dean Daniel C. Kurtzer) provides liberal arts and sciences curricula; grants B.A. degree. Erna Michael College of Hebraic Studies (Dean Jacob M. Rabinowitz) awards Hebraic Studies and Hebrew Teacher's diplomas, B.A., and B.S. James Striar School of General Jewish Studies (Dir. Morris J. Besdin) grants Associate in Arts degree.

Undergraduate schools for women at Midtown Center, 245 Lexington Ave., N.Y.C., 10016; Stern College for Women (Dean Karen Bacon) offers liberal arts and sciences curricula supplemented by Jewish studies courses; awards B.A., Jewish Studies certificate, Hebrew Teacher's diploma. Teachers Institute for Women (Dir. Baruch N. Faivelson) trains professionals for

education and community agency work; awards Hebrew Teacher's diploma and B.S. in Education.

Sponsors two high schools for boys and two for girls (Manhattan and Brooklyn).

Auxiliary services include: Stone-Saperstein Center for Jewish Education, Sephardic Studies Program, Brookdale Foundation Programs for the Aged, Maxwell R. Maybaum Institute of Material Sciences and Quantum Electronics.

————, ALBERT EINSTEIN COLLEGE OF MEDICINE (1955). 1300 Morris Pk. Ave., Bronx, N.Y., 10461. Dean Ephraim Friedman. Prepares physicians and conducts research in the health sciences; awards M.D. degree; includes Sue Golding Graduate Division of Medical Sciences (Dir. Jonathan R. Warner), which grants Ph.D. degree. Einstein College's clinical facilities and affiliates encompass five Bronx hospitals, including Bronx Municipal Hospital, Montefiore Hospital and Medical Center, and the Rose F. Kennedy Center for Research in Mental Retardation and Human Development. *AECOM News; AECOM Newsletter; Kennedy Newsletter.*

————. ALUMNI OFFICE, 500 West 185th Street, N.Y.C., 10033. Dir. Rabbi Abraham Avrech. Seeks to foster a close allegiance of alumni to their alma mater by maintaining ties with all alumni and servicing the following associations: Yeshiva College Alumni, Pres. Sam Bloom; Erna Michael College of Hebraic Studies Alumni; James Striar School of General Jewish Studies Alumni; Stern College Alumnae, Pres. Mrs. Doina L. Bryskin, Mrs. Marga Marx; Teachers Institute for Women Alumnae, Pres. Rivka Brass Finkelstein; Albert Einstein College of Medicine Alumni, Pres. Robert M. Chaflin; Ferkauf Graduate School of Humanities and Social Sciences Alumni, Pres. Alvin I. Schiff; Wurzweiler School of Social Work Alumni, Pres. Neva Rephun, Norman Winkler; Bernard Revel Graduate School —Harry Fischel School Alumni, Pres. Bernard Rosensweig; Rabbinic Alumni Pres. Max N. Schreier; Alumni Council, Chmn. Abraham S. Guterman, offers guidance to Pres. and Bd. of Trustees on university's academic development and service activities. *Alumni Review; AECOM Alumni News; Jewish Social Work Forum; Stern College Alumnae Newsletter; Wurzweiler*

School of Social Work Alumni Association Newsletter; Yeshiva College Alumni Bulletin.

_____, BELFER GRADUATE SCHOOL OF SCIENCE (1958). 500 W. 185 St., N.Y.C., 10033. Dir. Dr. David Finkelstein. Offers programs in mathematics and physics, including college teaching in those areas; conducts advanced research projects; confers M.A. and Ph.D. degrees.

_____, BENJAMIN N. CARDOZO SCHOOL OF LAW (1976). 55 Fifth Ave., N.Y.C., 10003. Dean Monrad G. Paulsen. Prepares students for the professional practice of law or other activities in which legal training is useful; grants L.L.D. degree.

_____, BERNARD REVEL GRADUATE SCHOOL (1937). 500 W. 185 St., N.Y.C., 10033. Dean Haym Soloveitchik. Offers graduate work in Judaic studies and Semitic languages, literatures, and cultures; confers M.S., M.A., and Ph.D. degrees.

_____, FERKAUF GRADUATE SCHOOL OF HUMANITIES AND SOCIAL SCIENCES (1957). 55 Fifth Ave., N.Y.C., 10003. Dean Morton Berger. Offers graduate programs in elementary and secondary education, administration, psychology, Jewish education, and special education; grants M.S., M.A., Specialist's Certificate, Doctor of Education, and Ph.D. degrees.

_____, HARRY FISCHEL SCHOOL FOR HIGHER JEWISH STUDIES (1945). 500 W. 185 St., N.Y.C., 10033. Dean Haym Soloveitchik. Offers summer graduate work in Judaic studies and Semitic languages, literatures, and cultures; confers M.S., M.A., and Ph.D. degrees.

_____, (affiliate) RABBI ISAAC ELCHANAN THEOLOGICAL SEMINARY (1896). 2540 Amsterdam Ave., N.Y.C., 10033. Chmn. Bd. of Trustees Charles H. Bendheim; Dir. Rabbi Zevulun Charlop. Offers comprehensive training in higher Jewish studies; grants *semikha* (ordination) and the degrees of Master of Religious Education, Master of Hebrew Literature, Doctor of Religious Education, and Doctor of Hebrew Literature; includes Kollel (Institute for Advanced Research in Rabbinics; Dir. Rabbi Hershel Schachter), and auxiliaries. Cantorial Training Institute (Dir. Macy Nulman) provides professional training of cantors and other musical personnel for the Jewish community; awards Associate Cantor's certificate and cantorial diploma. Sephardic Community Activities Program (Dir. Rabbi Solomon Gaon): serves the specific needs of 70 Sephardi synagogues in the U.S. and Canada; holds such events as annual Sephardic Cultural Festival; maintains Sephardic Home Study Group program. *American Sephardi.* Community Service Division (Dir. Victor B. Geller) makes educational, organizational, programming, consultative, and placement resources available to congregations, schools, organizations, and communities in the U.S. and Canada, through its youth bureau, department of adult education, lecture bureau, placement bureau, and rabbinic alumni. National Commission on Torah Education (Dir. Robert S. Hirt); Camp Morasha (Dir. Zvi Reich) offers Jewish study program; Educators Council of America (Dir. Robert S. Hirt) formulates uniform educational standards, provides guidance to professional staffs, rabbis, lay leaders with regard to curriculum, and promotes Jewish education.

_____, SOCIETY OF THE FOUNDERS OF THE ALBERT EINSTEIN COLLEGE OF MEDICINE (1953). 55 Fifth Ave., N.Y.C., 10003. Exec. Dir. Edwin Cohen. Seeks to further community support of Einstein College.

_____, WOMEN'S ORGANIZATION (1928). 55 Fifth Ave., N.Y.C., 10003. Pres. Mrs. Stanley Schwartz; Exec. Dir. Mrs. Malkah Isseroff. Supports Yeshiva University's national scholarship program for students training in education, community service, law, medicine, and other professions, and its development program. *YUWO News Briefs.*

_____, WURZWEILER SCHOOL OF SOCIAL WORK (1957). 55 Fifth Ave., N.Y.C., 10003. Dean Lloyd Setleis. Offers graduate programs in social casework, social group work, community social work; grants Master of Social Work and Doctor of Social Welfare degrees.

_____, (affiliate) YESHIVA UNIVERSITY OF LOS ANGELES (1977). 9760 West Pico Blvd., Los Angeles, Calif., 90035. Bd. Chmn. Samuel Belzberg; Co-chmn. Roland E. Arnall; Dean of Admin. Rabbi Marvin Hier. Offers Jewish studies program for college-age men with limited Hebrew background, Yeshiva program for day-school and yeshiva high-school graduates, and Bet Medrash program of Torah scholarship; students encouraged to pursue B.A. or B.S. degree at college of their choice; completion of YULA program leads to additional degree or diploma. *Response.*

YESHIVATH TORAH VODAATH AND MESIVTA RABBINICAL SEMINARY (1918). 425 E. 9 St., Brooklyn, N.Y., 11218. Pres. Henry Hirsch; Chmn. of Bd. Fred F. Weiss; Sec. Earl H. Spero. Offers Hebrew and secular education from elementary level through rabbinical ordination and post-graduate work; maintains a teachers institute and community-service bureau; maintains a dormitory and a nonprofit camp program for boys. *Chronicle; Mesivta Vanguard; Thought of the Week; Torah Vodaath News.*

*———, ALUMNI ASSOCIATION (1941). 425 E. 9 St., Brooklyn, N.Y., 11218. Pres. Marcus Saffer; Chmn. of Bd. Seymour Pluchenik. Promotes social and cultural ties between the alumni and the schools through fund raising; offers vocational guidance to students; operates Camp Torah Vodaath; and sponsors research fellowship program for boys. *Annual Journal; Hamesivta Torah Periodical.*

SOCIAL, MUTUAL BENEFIT

AMERICAN FEDERATION OF JEWISH FIGHTERS, CAMP INMATES AND NAZI VICTIMS, INC. (1971). 315 Lexington Ave., N.Y.C., 10016. Pres. Solomon Zynstein; Exec. Dir. Adele Grubart. Seeks to perpetuate memory of victims of the Holocaust and make Jewish and non-Jewish youth aware of the Holocaust and resistance period. *Martyrdom and Resistance.*

AMERICAN FEDERATION OF JEWS FROM CENTRAL EUROPE, INC. (1942). 570 Seventh Ave., N.Y.C., 10018. Pres. Curt C. Silberman; Exec. V. Pres. Herbert A. Strauss. Seeks to safeguard the rights and interests of American Jews of Central European descent, especially in reference to restitution and indemnification; through its Research Foundation for Jewish Immigration sponsors research and publications on the history of Central European Jewry and the history of their immigration and acculturation in the U.S.; sponsors a social program for needy Nazi victims in the U.S. in cooperation with United Help, Inc. and other specialized social agencies. Undertakes cultural activities, annual

conferences, publication, and lecture programs. Member, Council of Jews from Germany.

AMERICAN SEPHARDI FEDERATION (1972). 521 Fifth Ave., N.Y.C., 10017. Pres. Liliane L. Winn; Exec. Dir. Gary Shaer. Seeks to preserve the Sephardi heritage in the United States, Israel, and throughout the world by fostering and supporting religious and cultural activities of Sephardi congregations, organizations and communities, and uniting them in one overall organization; supports Jewish institutions of higher learning and those for the training of Sephardi lay and religious leaders to serve their communities everywhere; assists Sephardi charitable, cultural, religious and educational institutions everywhere; disseminates information by the publication, or assistance in the publication, of books and other literature dealing with Sephardi culture and tradition in the United States; supports efforts of the World Sephardi Federation to alleviate social disparities in Israel. *Sephardi News.*

AMERICAN VETERANS OF ISRAEL (1949). c/o Samuel E. Alexander, 548 E. Walnut St., Long Beach, N.Y., 11561. Pres. Nathan Nadler; Sec. Samuel E. Alexander. Maintains contact with American and Canadian volunteers who served in Aliyah Bet and/or Israel's War of Independence; promotes Israel's welfare; holds memorial services at grave of Col. David Marcus; is affiliated with World Mahal. *Newsletter.*

ASSOCIATION OF YUGOSLAV JEWS IN THE UNITED STATES, INC. (1940). 247 W. 99 St., N.Y.C., 10025. Pres. Sal Musafia; Sec. Mile Weiss. Assists members and Jews and Jewish organizations in Yugoslavia; cooperates with organization of former Yugoslav Jews in Israel and elsewhere. *Bulletin.*

BNAI ZION—THE AMERICAN FRATERNAL ZIONIST ORGANIZATION (1908). 136 E. 39 St., N.Y.C., 10016. Pres. William Berkowitz; Exec. V. Pres. Herman Z. Quittman. Fosters principles of Americanism, fraternalism, and Zionism; fosters Hebrew culture; offers life insurance, Blue Cross hospitalization, and other benefits to its members; sponsors settlements, youth centers, medical clinics, and Bnai Zion Home for Retardates in Rosh Ha'ayin, Israel. Program is dedicated to furtherance of America-Israel friendship.

Bnai Zion Foundation Newsletter; Bnai Zion Voice.

BRITH ABRAHAM (1887). 853 Broadway, N.Y.C., 10003. Grand Master Samuel F. Schwab. Protects Jewish rights and combats antisemitism; supports Israel and major Jewish organizations; maintains foundation in support of Soviet Jewry; aids Jewish education and Camp Loyaltown for Retarded. *Beacon.*

BRITH SHOLOM (1905). Adelphia House, 1235 Chestnut St., Philadelphia, Pa., 19107. Nat. Pres. David E. Molish; Nat. Exec. Dir. Albert Liss. Fraternal organization devoted to community welfare, protection of rights of Jewish people and activities which foster Jewish identity and provide support for Israel; sponsors Brith Sholom House for senior citizens in Philadelphia and Brith Sholom Beit Halochem under construction in Haifa, a rehabilitation center for war-wounded. *Community Relations Digest; Brith Sholom News.*

CENTRAL SEPHARDIC JEWISH COMMUNITY OF AMERICA (1940). 8 W. 70 St., N.Y.C., 10023. Pres. Solomon Altchek; Sec. Isaac Molho. Seeks to foster Sephardic culture, education and communal institutions. Sponsors wide range of activities; raises funds for Sephardic causes in U.S. and Israel.

FREE SONS OF ISRAEL (1849). 932 Broadway, N.Y.C., 10010. Grand Master Harry Pavony; Grand Sec. Murray Birnback. Promotes fraternalism; supports State of Israel, UJA, Soviet Jewry, Israel Bonds, and other Jewish charities; fights antisemitism; awards scholarships. Local lodges have own publications.

JEWISH LABOR BUND (Directed by WORLD COORDINATING COMMITTEE OF THE BUND) (1897; reorg. 1947). 25 E. 78 St., N.Y.C., 10021. Exec. Sec. Jacob S. Hertz. Coordinates activities of the Bund organizations throughout the world and represents them in the Socialist International; spreads the ideas of Socialism as formulated by the Jewish Labor Bund; publishes pamphlets and periodicals on world problems, Jewish life, socialist theory and policy, and on the history, activities, and ideology of the Jewish Labor Bund. *Unzer Tsait* (U.S.); *Foroys* (Mexico); *Lebns-Fragn* (Israel); *Unser Gedank* (Argentina);

Unser Gedank (Australia); *Unser Shtimme* (France); *Tsait-Fragn* (Uruguay).

JEWISH PEACE FELLOWSHIP (1941). Box 271, Nyack, N.Y., 10960. Pres. Naomi Goodman; Hon. Chmn. Isidor B. Hoffman. Unites those who believe that Jewish ideals and experience provide inspiration for a nonviolent philosophy and way of life; offers draft counseling, especially for conscientious objection based on Jewish "religious training and belief"; encourages Jewish community to become more knowledgeable, concerned, and active in regard to the war/peace problem. *JPF Newsletter.*

JEWISH SOCIALIST VERBAND OF AMERICA (1921). 45 E. 33 St., N.Y.C., 10016. Pres. Morris Bagno; Nat. Sec. Maurice Petrushka. Promotes ideals of democratic socialism and Yiddish culture; affiliated with Social Democrats, USA. *Der Wecker.*

RUMANIAN JEWISH FEDERATION OF AMERICA, INC. (1958). 210 W. 101 St., N.Y.C., 10025. Pres. Charles H. Kremer; Sec. Jacob Zonis. Serves as a representative body for Rumanian Jewry throughout the world and intervenes on their behalf; cooperates with all national Jewish and non-Jewish organizations for purpose of aiding Rumanian Jews economically, socially and politically here or abroad; disseminates information about Rumanian Jewish activities.

SEPHARDIC JEWISH BROTHERHOOD OF AMERICA, INC. (1915). 97–29 64th Rd., Rego Park, N.Y., 11374. Pres. Bernard Ouziel; Sec. Jack Ezratty. Promotes the industrial, social, educational, and religious welfare of its members, offers funeral and burial benefits, scholarships and aid to needy. *Sephardic Brother.*

UNITED ORDER TRUE SISTERS, INC. (1846). 150 W. 85 St., N.Y.C., 10024. Nat. Pres. Mrs. Bernard S. Weinberg; Nat. Sec. Mrs. Martin Sporn. Philanthropic, fraternal, community service; nat. projects; cancer service; aids handicapped children, deaf, blind, etc. *Echo.*

WORKMEN'S CIRCLE (1900). 45 E. 33 St., N.Y.C., 10016. Pres. Bernard Backer; Exec. Dir. William Stern. Provides insurance benefits and fraternal activities, Jewish educational programs, secularist Yiddish schools for children, community activities, both in Jewish life and on the

American scene, cooperation with the labor movement. *The Call; Inner Circle; Kinder Zeitung; Kultur un Lebn.*

————, DIVISION OF JEWISH LABOR COMMITTEE (see p. 303).

SOCIAL WELFARE

AMERICAN JEWISH CORRECTIONAL CHAPLAINS ASSOCIATION, INC. (formerly NATIONAL COUNCIL OF JEWISH PRISON CHAPLAINS) (1937). 10 E. 73 St., N.Y.C., 10021. (Cooperating with the New York Board of Rabbis and Jewish Family Service.) Pres. Frederic S. Nathan; Exec. Dir. Ely Saltzman. Seeks to provide a more articulate expression for Jewish chaplains serving the needs of Jewish men and women in penal and correctional institutions, and to make their ministry more effective through exchange of views and active cooperation.

AMERICAN JEWISH SOCIETY FOR SERVICE, INC., (1949). 15 E. 26 St., Rm. 1302, N.Y.C., 10010. Pres. E. Kenneth Marx; Exec. Dir. Elly Saltzman. Conducts four voluntary work service camps each summer to enable young people to live their faith by serving other people. *Newsletter.*

*AMERICAN MEDICAL CENTER AT DENVER (formerly Jewish CONSUMPTIVES' RELIEF SOCIETY, 1904; merged with EX-PATIENT'S SANITARIUM, 1966). 6401 West Colfax, Lakewood, Colo., 80215. Pres. Robert A. Silverberg; Exec. V. Pres. Manfred L. Minzer, Jr. A national hospital for cancer treatment and research, supported by private donations from all parts of the U.S.; provides free treatment to all in need; offers long-term treatment for advanced and recurrent cancer, combined with extensive basic and clinical research. *Sponsor's Report.*

————: NATIONAL COUNCIL OF AUXILIARIES (1904; reorg. 1936). 6401 W. Colfax, Lakewood, Colo., 80215. Pres. Sue Snyder. Provides support for the American Medical Center program by disseminating information, fund raising, and acting as admissions officers for patients from chapter cities throughout the country. *Bulletin.*

BARON DE HIRSCH FUND, INC. (1891). 386 Park Ave. S., N.Y.C., 10016. Pres. Robert Simons; Mng. Dir. Theodore Norman. Aids Jewish immigrants and their children in the U.S., Israel, and elsewhere by giving grants to agencies active in educational and vocational fields; has limited program for study tours in U.S. by Israeli agriculturists.

B'NAI B'RITH (1943). 1640 Rhode Island Ave., N.W., Washington, D.C., 20036. Pres. David M. Blumberg; Exec. V. Pres. Daniel Thursz. International Jewish organization, with affiliates in 40 countries. Programs involve community relations and service; international public affairs programs with emphasis on Israel and Soviet Jewry; teen and college age youth movements; adult Jewish education; civic and social welfare. *The National Jewish Monthly; Shofar.*

————, ANTI-DEFAMATION LEAGUE OF (see p. 302).

————, CAREER AND COUNSELING SERVICES (1938). 1640 Rhode Island Ave., N.W., Washington, D.C., 20036. Chmn. Stanley M. Kaufman; Nat. Dir. S. Norman Feingold. Conducts educational and occupational research and engages in a broad publications program; provides direct group and individual guidance services for youths and adults through professionally staffed regional offices in many population centers. *B'nai B'rith Career and Counseling Services Newsletter; Catalogue of Publications; Counselors Information Service.*

————. HILLEL FOUNDATIONS, INC. (see p. 311).

————: INTERNATIONAL ASSOCIATION OF HILLEL DIRECTORS (see p. 314).

————, WOMEN (1897). 1640 Rhode Island Ave., N.W., Washington, D.C., 20036. Pres. Evelyn Wasserstrom; Exec. Dir. Edna J. Wolf. Participates in contemporary Jewish life through youth and adult Jewish education programs, human rights endeavors, and community-service activities; supports a variety of services to Israel; conducts community service programs for the disadvantaged and the handicapped, and public affairs programs. *Women's World.*

————, YOUTH ORGANIZATION (see p. 311).

CITY OF HOPE—A NATIONAL MEDICAL CENTER UNDER JEWISH AUSPICES (1913). 208 W. 8 St., Los Angeles, Calif., 90014. Pres. M. E. Hersch; Exec. Dir. Ben Horowitz. Admits on completely free, nonsectarian basis patients from all parts of the nation suffering from cancer and leukemia, blood, heart, and respiratory ailments, and certain maladies of heredity and metabolism including diabetes; makes available its consultation service to doctors and hospitals throughout the nation, concerning diagnosis and treatment of their patients; as a unique pilot medical center, seeks improvements in the quality, quantity, economy, and efficiency of health care. Many hundreds of original findings have emerged from its staff who are conducting clinical and basic research in the catastrophic maladies, lupus erythematosus, Huntington's disease, genetics, and the neurosciences. *Pilot; President's Newsletter; City of Hope Quarterly.*

CONFERENCE OF JEWISH COMMUNAL SERVICE (1899). 15 E. 26 St., N.Y.C., 10010. Pres. William Kahn; Exec. Dir. Matthew Penn. Serves as forum for all professional philosophies in community service, for testing new experiences, proposing new ideas, and questioning or reaffirming old concepts. Concerned with advancement of professional personnel practices and standards. *Concurrents; Journal of Jewish Communal Service.*

COUNCIL OF JEWISH FEDERATIONS AND WELFARE FUNDS, INC. (1932). 575 Lexington Ave., N.Y.C., 10022. Pres. Jerold C. Hoffberger; Exec. V. Pres. Philip Bernstein. Provides national and regional services to more than 215 associated Federations embracing 800 communities in the United States and Canada, aiding in fund raising, community organization, health and welfare planning, personnel recruitment, and public relations. *Directory of Jewish Federations, Welfare Funds and Community Councils; Directory of Jewish Health and Welfare Agencies* (triennial); *Jewish Communal Services: Programs and Finances; Yearbook of Jewish Social Services.*

HOPE CENTER FOR THE RETARDED, INC. (1965). 3601 E. 32 Ave., Denver, Colo., 80205. Bd. Chmn. John Fischer; Exec. Dir. George E. Brantley; Sec. Lorraine Faulstich. Provides services to developmentally disabled of community: preschool training, day training and work activities center, speech and language pathology, occupational arts and crafts, and recreational therapy, social services.

INTERNATIONAL COUNCIL ON JEWISH SOCIAL AND WELFARE SERVICES (1961). 200 Park Ave. S., N.Y.C., 10003. (N.Y. liaison office with UN headquarters.) Chmn. Donald M. Robinson; V. Chmn. William Haber; The Rt. Hon. Lord Nathan; Exec. Sec. Leonard Seidenman; Dep. Exec. Sec. Theodore D. Feder. Provides for exchange of views and information among member agencies on problems of Jewish social and welfare services, including medical care, old age, welfare, child care, rehabilitation, technical assistance, vocational training, agricultural, and other resettlement, economic assistance, refugees, migration, integration and related problems, representation of views to governments and international organizations. Members: six national and international organizations.

JEWISH BRAILLE INSTITUTE OF AMERICA, INC. (1931). 110 E. 30 St., N.Y.C., 10016. Pres. Mrs. David M. Levitt; Exec. Dir. Jacob Freid. Seeks to serve the religious and cultural needs of the Jewish blind by publishing braille prayer books in Hebrew and English; provides Yiddish, Hebrew, and English records for Jewish blind throughout the world who cannot read braille; maintain worldwide free braille lending library. *Jewish Braille Review.*

JEWISH CONCILIATION BOARD OF AMERICA, INC. (1922). 33 W. 60 St., N.Y.C., 10023. Pres. Herbert A. Schneider; Dir. Sarah F. Gillman. Evaluates and attempts to resolve conflicts within families, organizations, and businesses to avoid litigation; offers, without charge, mediation, arbitration, and counseling services by rabbis, attorneys, and social workers; refers cases to other agencies, where indicated.

JWB (NATL. JEWISH WELFARE BOARD) (1917). 15 E. 26 St., N.Y.C. 10010. Pres. Robert L. Adler; Exec. V. Pres. Arthur Rotman. Major service agency for Jewish community centers and camps serving more than a million Jews in the U.S. and Canada; U.S. Government accredited agency for providing services and programs to Jewish military families and hospitalized veterans; promotes Jewish culture through its Book and Music Councils, JWB lecture bureau, and Jewish educational, cultural and Israel-related projects. *JWB Circle; Jewish Community Center Program Aids; Books in Review; Jewish Music Notes; Running the Center; Contact; JWB Facts; Public Relations Idea Exchange; JWB Personnel Reporter; Sherut;*

The Jewish Chaplain; Jewish Lay Leader; Mail Call.

_____: COMMISSION ON JEWISH CHAPLAINCY (1940). 15 E. 26 St., N.Y.C., 10010. Chmn. Rabbi Judah Nadich; Dir. Rabbi Gilbert Kollin. Recruits, endorses, and serves Jewish military and Veterans Administration chaplains on behalf of the American Jewish community and the three major rabbinic bodies; trains and assists Jewish lay leaders where there are no chaplains, for service to Jewish military personnel, their families, and hospitalized veterans. *Jewish Chaplain; Jewish Lay Leader.*

_____, JEWISH BOOK COUNCIL (see p. 306).

_____, JEWISH MUSIC COUNCIL (see p. 307).

LEO N. LEVI MEMORIAL NATIONAL ARTHRITIS HOSPITAL (sponsored by B'nai B'rith) (1914). 300 Prospect Ave., Hot Springs, Ark., 71901. Pres. Mrs. Leonard A. Bagen; Adm. D. E. Wagoner. Maintains a nonprofit nonsectarian hospital for treatment of sufferers from arthritis and related diseases.

NATIONAL ASSOCIATION OF JEWISH FAMILY, CHILDREN'S AND HEALTH PROFESSIONALS (1965). 4131 S. Braeswood Blvd., Houston, Texas 77205. Pres. Solomon Brownstein; Sec. Peter Glick. Brings together Jewish caseworkers and related professionals in Jewish family, children, and health services. Seeks to improve personnel standards, further Jewish continuity and identity, and strengthen Jewish family life; provides forums for professional discussion at national conference of Jewish communal service and regional meetings; takes action on social policy issues; provides a vehicle for representation of Jewish caseworkers and others in various national associations and activities.

NATIONAL ASSOCIATION OF JEWISH HOMES FOR THE AGED (1960). 2525 Centerville Road, Dallas, Texas, 75228. Pres. Sidney Friedman; Exec. V. Pres. Herbert Shore. Serves as a national representative of voluntary Jewish homes for the aged. Conducts annual meetings, conferences, workshops and institutes. Provides for sharing information, studies and clearinghouse functions. *Directory; Progress Report.*

NATIONAL ASSOCIATION OF JEWISH VOCATIONAL SERVICES (formerly Jewish Occupational Council) (1940). 600 Pennsylvania Ave., S.E., Washington, D.C. 20003. Pres. Bruce E. Thal; Exec. Dir. Mark J. Ugoretz. Acts as coordinating body for all Jewish agencies having programs in educational vocational guidance, job placement, vocational rehabilitation, skills-training, sheltered workshops, and occupational research. *Newsletter;* Information bulletins.

THE NATIONAL ASTHMA CENTER (1907). 1999 Julian St., Denver, Colo., 80204. Bd. Pres. Charles M. Shayer; Exec. V. Pres. Jack Gershtenson. Administers care and treatment to children from the ages of 5–16 suffering from chronic, intractable asthma; performs outpatient services for people of all ages; research and dissemination of information. *National Asthma Center News.*

NATIONAL COUNCIL OF JEWISH PRISON CHAPLAINS, INC. (see AMERICAN JEWISH CORRECTIONAL CHAPLAINS ASSOCIATION, INC.).

NATIONAL COUNCIL OF JEWISH WOMEN, INC. (1893). 15 E. 26 St., N.Y.C., 10010. Nat. Pres. Esther R. Landa; Exec. Dir. Marjorie M. Cohen. Operates programs in education, social and legislative action, and community service for children and youth, the aging, the disadvantaged in Jewish and general communities; conducts nationwide study of juvenile justice system as basis for legislative reform and community projects; promotes education in Israel through NCJW Research Institute for Innovation in Education at Hebrew University, Jerusalem; provides educational materials to kindergartens. *NCJW Journal; Washington Newsletter; Children Without Justice; Manual for Action; Symposium on Status Offenders Proceedings; Windows on Day Care.*

NATIONAL JEWISH COMMITTEE ON SCOUTING (1926). Boy Scouts of America. North Brunswick, N.J., 08902. Chmn. Melvin B. Neisner; Exec. Dir. Harry Lasker. Seeks to stimulate Boy Scout activity among Jewish boys. *Ner Tamid for Boy Scouts and Explorers; Scouting in Synagogues and Centers.*

NATIONAL JEWISH HOSPITAL AND RESEARCH CENTER (1899). 3800 E. Colfax Ave., Denver, Colo., 80206. Pres. Richard N. Bluestein; Natl. Chmn. Andrew Goodman. Offers nationwide, nonsectarian care for adults and children suffering from tuberculosis, asthma, emphysema, chronic bronchitis, cystic fibrosis, and other immunological and pulmonary disorders. *NJH Report.*

WORLD CONFEDERATION OF JEWISH COMMUNITY CENTERS (1947). 15 E. 26 St., N.Y.C., 10010. Pres. Morton L. Mandell; Exec. Dir. Herbert Millman. Serves as a council of national and continental federations of Jewish community centers; fosters development of the JCC movement worldwide; provides a forum for exchange of information among Centers. *Newsletter.*

ZIONIST AND PRO-ISRAEL

AMERICAN ASSOCIATES OF BEN-GURION UNIVERSITY OF THE NEGEV. (1973). 342 Madison Ave., Room 1923, N.Y.C., 10017. Pres. Aron Chilewich; Chmn. Exec. Com. Bobbie Abrams; Exec. Dir. Jerry Kramer. Serves as the University's publicity and fund-raising link to the United States. The Associates are committed to publicizing University activities and curriculum, securing student scholarships, transferring contributions, and encouraging American interest in the University. *The Messenger.*

AMERICAN COMMITTEE FOR SHAARE ZEDEK HOSPITAL IN JERUSALEM, INC. (1949). 49 W. 45 St., N.Y.C., 10036. Pres. Leo Jung; Bd. Chmn. Max Stern; Sec. Isaac Strahl; Treas. Norbert Strauss. Raises funds for the various needs of the Shaare Zedek Hospital, Jerusalem, such as equipment and medical supplies, a nurses training school, research, and construction of the new Shaare Zedek Medical Center. *At the Hospital.*

AMERICAN COMMITTEE FOR THE WEIZMANN INSTITUTE OF SCIENCE, INC. (1944). 515 Park Ave., N.Y.C., 10022. Pres. Stephen L. Stulman; Chmn. of Bd. Morris L. Levinson; Exec. Dir. Harold Hill. Secures support for basic and applied scientific research. *Interface; Rehovot; Research.*

AMERICAN FRIENDS OF HAIFA UNIVERSITY (1969). 60 E. 42 St., N.Y.C., 10017. Hon. Pres. Charles J. Bensley; V. Pres. Sigmund Strochlitz. Supports the development and maintenance of the various programs of the University of Haifa, among them the Arab Jewish center, Yiddish department, Bridging The Gap project, department of management, school of education, kibbutz

movement, and fine arts department; arranges overseas academic programs for American and Canadian students. *Newsletter.*

AMERICAN FRIENDS OF RELIGIOUS FREEDOM IN ISRAEL (1963). P.O. Box. 5888, Washington, D.C., 20014. Exec. Dir. Alex Hershaft. Calls for complete religious freedom and separation of church and state in Israel; publicizes violations of religious freedom to bring the influence of the benevolent opinion of the American Jewish community to bear on solution of this problem; assists other groups and individuals working toward these goals.

AMERICAN FRIENDS OF THE HEBREW UNIVERSITY (1925; Inc. 1931). 11 E. 69 St., N.Y.C., 10021. Pres. Max M. Kampelman; Exec. V. Pres. Seymour Fishman; Chmn. of Bd. Julian B. Venezky; Chmn. Exec. Comm. Henry Sonneborn III. Fosters the growth, development, and maintenance of the Hebrew University of Jerusalem; collects funds and conducts programs of information throughout the United States interpreting the work of the Hebrew University and its significance; administers American student programs and arranges exchange professorships in the United States and Israel. Created, and recruits support for, Truman Research Institute. *American Friends Bulletin; News from the Hebrew University of Jerusalem; Scopus Magazine.*

AMERICAN FRIENDS OF THE ISRAEL MUSEUM (1968). 4 E. 54 St., N.Y.C., 10022. Pres. Arnold Maremont; Exec. Dir. Michele Cohn Tocci. Raises funds for special projects of the Israel Museum in Jerusalem; solicits contributions of works of art for exhibition and educational purposes.

AMERICAN FRIENDS OF THE JERUSALEM MENTAL HEALTH CENTER—EZRATH NASHIM, INC. (1895). 10 E. 40 St., N.Y.C., 10016. Pres. Joel Finkle; Exec. Dir. S. Alvin Schwartz. Supports the growth, development, and maintenance of the Jerusalem Mental Health Center-Ezrath Nashim, a 200-bed hospital which is the only non-governmental, nonprofit, voluntary mental-health facility in Israel devoted to research in, training for, and treatment and alleviation of, problems caused by mental illness. *Progress Reports.*

AMERICAN FRIENDS OF THE TEL AVIV UNI-
VERSITY, INC. (1955). 342 Madison Ave.,
N.Y.C., 10017. Pres. Joseph H. Strelitz; V.
Pres. Yona Ettinger, Malcolm Rosenberg;
Exec. V. Pres. Zvi Almog. Supports devel-
opment and maintenance of the Tel Aviv
University. Sponsors exchange student
programs and exchange professorships in
U.S. and Israel. *Tel Aviv University Report.*

AMERICAN-ISRAEL CULTURAL FOUNDA-
TION, INC. (1939). 4 East 54 St., N.Y.C.,
10022. Bd. Chmn. Isaac Stern; Pres. William Mazer. Membership organization
supporting Israeli cultural institutions,
such as Israel Philharmonic and Israel
Chamber Orchestra, Tel Aviv Museum,
Rubin Academies, Bat Sheva Dance Co.;
sponsors cultural exchange between U.S.
and Israel; awards scholarships in all arts
to young Israelis for study in Israel and
abroad. *Hadashot; Tarbut.*

AMERICAN ISRAEL PUBLIC AFFAIRS COM-
MITTEE (1954). 444 North Capitol St.,
N.W., Suite 412, Washington, D.C.,
20001. Pres. Lawrence Weinberg; Exec.
Dir. Morris J. Amitay. Registered to lobby
on behalf of legislation affecting Israel, Soviet Jewry, and arms sales to Middle East;
represents Americans who believe support
for a secure Israel is in U.S. interest.

AMERICAN-ISRAELI LIGHTHOUSE, INC.
(1928; reorg. 1955). 30 E. 60 St., N.Y.C.,
10022. Nat. Pres. Mrs. Leonard F. Dank;
Nat. Sec. Mrs. L.T. Rosenbaum. Provides
education and rehabilitation for the blind
and physically handicapped in Israel to
effect their social and vocational integration into the seeing community; built and
maintains Rehabilitation Center for the
Blind (Migdal Or) in Haifa. *Tower.*

AMERICAN JEWISH LEAGUE FOR ISRAEL
(1957). 595 Madison Ave., N.Y.C., 10022.
Hon. Pres. Seymour R. Levine; Chmn.
Exec. Com. Eleazar Lipsky; Chmn. of Bd.
Samuel Rothberg. Seeks to unite all those
who, notwithstanding differing philosophies of Jewish life, are committed to the
historical ideals of Zionism; works, independently of class or party, for the welfare
of Israel as a whole. Not identified with any
political parties in Israel. *Bulletin of the
American Jewish League for Israel.*

AMERICAN MIZRACHI WOMEN (formerly
MIZRACHI WOMEN'S ORGANIZATION OF
AMERICA) (1925). 817 Broadway, N.Y.C.,
1003. Nat. Pres. Mrs. Sarah P. Shane;
Exec. Dir. Marvin Leff. Conducts

social-service, child care, and vocational-
educational programs in Israel in an environment of traditional Judaism; promotes
cultural activities for the purpose of disseminating Zionist ideals and strengthening traditional Judaism in America. *The
American Mizrachi Woman.*

AMERICAN PHYSICIANS FELLOWSHIP, INC.
FOR THE ISRAEL MEDICAL ASSOCIATION
(1950). 2001 Beacon St., Brookline, Mass.,
02146. Pres. Joseph Kaufman; Sec. Manuel M. Glazier. Aims to help Israel become
a major world medical center; secures fellowships for selected Israeli physicians and
arranges lectureships in Israel by prominent American physicians; supports
Jerusalem Academy of Medicine and
financially assists Israel Medical Association; supervises U.S. and Canadian medical and paramedical emergency volunteers
in Israel; maintains Israel Institute of the
History of Medicine; contributes medical
books, periodicals, instruments, and drugs.
APF News.

AMERICAN RED MAGEN DAVID FOR IS-
RAEL, INC. (1941). 888 7th Ave., N.Y.C.,
10019. Nat. Pres. Joseph Handleman; Nat.
Chmn. Emanuel Celler; Nat. Exec. V.
Pres. Benjamin Saxe. An authorized tax
exempt organization; the sole support arm
in the United States of Magen David
Adom in Israel with a national membership and chapter program. Educates and
involves its members in activities of Magen
David Adom, Israel's Red Cross Service;
raises funds for MDA's emergency medical services, including collection and distribution of blood and blood products for Israel's military and civilian population;
supplies ambulances, bloodmobiles, and
mobile cardiac rescue units serving all hospitals and communities throughout Israel;
supports MDA's 73 emergency medical
clinics and helps provide training and
equipment for volunteer emergency
paramedical corps. *Chapter Highlights;
Lifeline.*

AMERICAN TECHNION SOCIETY. (1940) 271
Madison Ave., N.Y.C., 10016. Pres. Alexander Hassan. Supports the work of the
Technion-Israel Institute of Technology,
Haifa, which trains nearly 10,000 students
in 20 departments and a medical school,
and conducts research across a broad spectrum of science and technology. *ATS
Newsletter; ATS Women's Division Newsletter; Technion Magazine.*

AMERICAN ZIONIST FEDERATION (1939; reorg. 1949 and 1970). 515 Park Ave., N.Y.C., 10022. Pres. Mrs. Faye Schenk; Exec. Dir. Carmella Carr. Consolidates the efforts of the existing Zionist constituency in such areas as public and communal affairs, education, youth and aliyah, and invites the affiliation and participation of like-minded individuals and organizations in the community-at-large. Seeks to conduct a Zionist program designed to create a greater appreciation of Jewish culture within the American Jewish community in furtherance of the continuity of Jewish life and the spiritual centrality of Israel as the Jewish homeland. Composed of 14 National Zionist organizations; 10 Zionist youth movements; individual members-at-large; corporate affiliates. Maintains regional offices in Philadelphia, Los Angeles, Chicago, Boston, Cleveland, Detroit, and New York. *News & Views.*

AMERICAN ZIONIST YOUTH FOUNDATION, INC. (1973). 515 Park Ave., N.Y.C., 10022. Bd. Chmn. David Sidorsky; Exec. Dir. Donald Adelman. Sponsors educational programs and services for American Jewish youth including tours to Israel, programs of volunteer service or study in leading institutions of science, scholarship and arts; sponsors field workers who promote Jewish and Zionist programming on campus; prepares and provides specialists who present and interpret the Israeli experience for community centers and federations throughout the country. *Activist Newsletter; Masada.*

_____: AMERICAN ZIONIST YOUTH COUNCIL (1951). 515 Park Ave., N.Y.C., 10022. Chmn. Yudie Fishman. Acts as spokesman and representative of Zionist youth in interpreting Israel to the youth of America; represents, coordinates, and implements activities of the Zionist youth movements in the U.S.

AMPAL—AMERICAN ISRAEL CORPORATION (1942). 10 Rockefeller Plaza, N.Y.C., 10020. Pres. Ralph Cohen; V. Pres. Shimon Topor. Finances and invests in Israel economic enterprises; mobilizes finance and investment capital in the U.S. through sale of own debenture issues and utilization of bank credit lines. *Annual Report; Prospectuses.*

BAR-ILAN UNIVERSITY IN ISRAEL (1955). 641 Lexington Ave., N.Y.C., 10022. Chancellor Joseph H. Lookstein; Pres.

Emanuel Rackman; Chmn. Bd. of Trustees Phillip Stollman. A liberal arts and sciences institution, located in Ramat-Gan, Israel, and chartered by Board of Regents of State of New York. *Bar-Ilan News; Academic Research; Philosophia.*

BRIT TRUMPELDOR BETAR OF AMERICA, INC. (1935). 85-40 149 St., Briarwood, N.Y., 11435. Pres. Gary Segal; V. Pres. Shari Olenberg. Teaches Jewish youth love of the Jewish people and prepares them for aliyah; emphasizes learning Hebrew; keeps its members ready for mobilization in times of crisis; stresses Jewish pride and self-respect; seeks to aid and protect Jewish communities everywhere. *Herut.*

DROR—YOUNG ZIONIST ORGANIZATION, INC. (1948). 215 Park Ave. S., N.Y.C., 10003. Pres. Robby Regev; V. Pres. Hagai Aizenberg; Sec. Mark Cohen. Fosters Zionist program for youth with emphasis on aliyah to the Kibbutz Ha'meuchad; stresses Jewish and labor education; maintains leadership seminar and work-study programs in Israel, summer camps in U.S. and Canada. Sponsors two garinim in Israel. *Alon Dror; Igeret Dror.*

_____: GARIN YARDEN, THE YOUNG KIBBUTZ MOVEMENT. (1976). Pres. Eva Rubenstein; Sec. Rachel Weisman; Exec. Off. Danny Siegal. Aids those interested in making aliyah to an Israeli kibbutz; affiliated with Kibbutz Hameuchad. *Newsletter.*

EMUNAH (formerly HAPOEL HAMIZRACHI WOMEN'S ORGANIZATION) (1948). 370 Seventh Ave., N.Y.C., 10001. Nat. Pres. Mrs. Toby Willig; Exec. Dir. Mrs. Shirley Singer. Maintains and supports religious nurseries, day care centers, and teacher training schools for the underprivileged in Israel. *The Emunah Woman.*

FEDERATED COUNCIL OF ISRAEL INSTITUTIONS—FCII (1940). 38 Park Row, N.Y.C., 10038. Chmn. Bd. Z. Shapiro; Exec. V. Pres. Julius Novack. Central fund-raising organization for 104 affiliated institutions; clearing house for information on budget, size, functions, etc. of traditional educational, welfare, and philanthropic institutions in Israel, working cooperatively with the Israel government and the overseas department of the Council of Jewish Federations and Welfare Funds, New York; handles and executes estates, wills and bequests for the traditional institutions in Israel. *Annual*

Financial Reports and Statistics on Affiliates.

FUND FOR HIGHER EDUCATION (IN ISRAEL) (1970). 1500 Broadway, Suite 1900, N.Y.C., 10036. Chmn. Louis Warschaw; Pres. Amnon Barness; Sec. Richard Segal. Supports, on a project-by-project basis, institutions of higher learning in Israel and the U.S.

HADASSAH, THE WOMEN'S ZIONIST ORGANIZATION OF AMERICA, INC. (1912). 50 W. 58 St., N.Y.C., 10019. Pres. Bernice S. Tannenbaum; Exec. Dir. Aline Kaplan. In America helps interpret Israel to the American people; provides basic Jewish education as a background for intelligent and creative Jewish living in America; sponsors Hashachar, largest Zionist youth movement in U.S., which has four divisions: Young Judaea, Intermediate Judaea, Senior Judaea, and Hamagshimim; operates eight Zionist youth camps in this country; supports summer and all-year courses in Israel. Maintains in Israel Hadassah-Hebrew University Medical Center for healing, teaching, and research; Hadassah Community College; Seligsberg/Brandeis Comprehensive High School; and Hadassah Vocational Guidance Institute. Is largest organizational contributor to Youth Aliyah and to Jewish National Fund for land purchase and reclamation. *Hadassah Headlines; Hadassah Magazine.*

_____. HASHACHAR (formerly YOUNG JUDEA and JUNIOR HADASSAH; org. 1909, reorg. 1967). 817 Broadway, N.Y.C., 10003. Nat. Pres. of Senior Judaea (high school level) Danny Spinack; Nat. Coordinator of Hamagshimim (college level) David Lehrer; Nat. Dir. Irv Widaen. Seeks to educate Jewish youth from the ages of 10–25 toward Jewish and Zionist values, active commitment to and participation in the American and Israeli Jewish communities, with *aliyah* as a prime goal; maintains summer camps and summer and year programs in Israel. *Hamagshimim Journal; Kol Hat'una; The Young Judaean; Daf L'Madrichim.*

HASHOMER HATZAIR, INC. 150 Fifth Ave., Suite 700, N.Y.C., 10011.

_____: AMERICANS FOR PROGRESSIVE ISRAEL (1951). Nat. Chmn. Bernard Harkavy; Exec. Dir. Linda Rubin. Affiliated with Kibbutz Artzi. Believes Zionism is the National Liberation Movement of the Jewish people; educates members towards an understanding of their Jewishness and progressive values; dignity of labor, social justice, and the brotherhood of nations. *Background Bulletin; For Your Information; Israel Horizons.*

_____: SOCIALIST ZIONIST YOUTH MOVEMENT (1923). Nat. Sec. Ayala Ginsburg; Dir. Itai Padan. Seeks to imbue Jewish youth with a Jewish national awareness and socialist-Zionist values in centers and camps run by, and for, youth; organizes oldest leadership in settlement groups for *aliyah* and settlement in kibbutzim of Kibbutz Federation Artzi. *Youth and Nation; Young Guard; Niv Haboger; Hayasad; Layidiatcha.*

HEBREW UNIVERSITY-TECHNION JOINT MAINTENANCE APPEAL (1954). 11 E. 69 St., N.Y.C., 10021. Chmn. Daniel G. Ross; Dir. Clifford B. Surloff. Conducts maintenance campaigns formerly conducted by the American Friends of the Hebrew University and the American Technion Society; participates in community campaigns throughout the U.S., excluding New York City.

HERUT-U.S.A. (formerly UNITED ZIONIST-REVISIONISTS OF AMERICA) (1925). 41 E. 42 St., N.Y.C., 10017. Chmn. Harry S. Taubenfeld; Exec. Dir. Steven Leibowitz. Supports Herut policy in Israel and seeks Jabotinskean solutions of problems facing American, Russian, and world Jewry; assists in the fostering of private enterprises and developments in Israel; fosters maximalist Zionism among Jews in America. Subsidiaries: Betar Zionist Youth, Young Herut Concerned Jewish Youth, Tel-Hai Fund, and For the Children of Israel. *Igeret Betar; Herut Magazine.*

THEODOR HERZL FOUNDATION (1954). 515 Park Ave., N.Y.C., 10022. Chmn. Kalman Sultanik; Sec. Isadore Hamlin. Cultural activities, lectures, conferences, courses in modern Hebrew and Jewish subjects, Israel, Zionism and Jewish history. *Midstream.*

_____: THEODOR HERZL INSTITUTE. Chmn. Jacques Torczyner. Program geared to review of contemporary problems on Jewish scene here and abroad; presentation of Jewish heritage values in light of Zionist experience of the ages; study of modern Israel; and Jewish social research with particular consideration of history and impact of Zionism. *Herzl Institute Bulletin.*

_____: HERZL PRESS. Chmn. Kalman Sultanik. Publishes books and pamphlets on Israel, Zionism, and general Jewish subjects.

ICHUD HABONIM LABOR ZIONIST YOUTH (1935). 575 Sixth Ave., N.Y.C., 10011. Sec. Gen. Yehuda Fishman; Dir. Tom Gutherz. Fosters identification with pioneering in Israel; stimulates study of Jewish life, history, and culture; sponsors community action projects, seven summer camps in North America, programs in Israel, and Garinei Aliyah to Kibbutz Grofit and Kibbutz Gezer. *Bagolah; Haboneh; Hamaapil; Iggeret L'Chaverim.*

ISRAEL MUSIC FOUNDATION (1948). 109 Cedarhurst Ave., Cedarhurst, N.Y., 11516. Pres. Oscar Regen; Sec. Oliver Sabin. Supports and stimulates the growth of music in Israel, and disseminates recorded Israeli music in the U.S. and throughout the world.

JEWISH NATIONAL FUND OF AMERICA (1901). 42 E. 69 St., N.Y.C., 10021. Pres. William Berkowitz; Exec. V. Pres. Samuel I. Cohen. Exclusive fund-raising agency of the world Zionist movement for the afforestation, reclamation, and development of the land of Israel, including the construction of roads and preparation of sites for new settlements; helps emphasize the importance of Israel in schools and synagogues throughout the world. *JNF Almanac; Land and Life.*

KEREN OR, INC. (1956). 1133 Broadway, N.Y.C., 10010. Pres. Ira Guilden; V. Pres. and Sec. Samuel I. Hendler; Exec. Dir. Jacob Igra. Funds special program at Jewish Institute for the Blind in Jerusalem that houses, clothes, feeds, educates and trains blind from childhood into adulthood; funds, in conjunction with Institute, the Keren Or Center for the Multiple Handicapped Blind Child in Jerusalem.

LABOR ZIONIST ALLIANCE reorg. (formerly FARBAND LABOR ZIONIST ORDER, now uniting membership and branches of POALE ZION—UNITED LABOR ZIONIST ORGANIZATION OF AMERICA AND AMERICAN HABONIM ASSOCIATION)

(1913). 575 Sixth Ave., N.Y.C., 10011. Pres. Judah J. Shapiro; Exec. Dir. Bernard M. Weisberg. Seeks to enhance Jewish life, culture, and education in U.S. and Canada; aids in building State of Israel as a cooperative commonwealth, and its Labor movement organized in the Histadrut; supports efforts toward a more democratic society throughout the world; furthers the democratization of the Jewish community in America and the welfare of Jews everywhere; works with labor and liberal forces in America. *Alliance Newsletter.*

LEAGUE FOR LABOR ISRAEL (1938; reorg. 1961). 575 Sixth Ave., N.Y.C., 10011. Pres. Allen Pollack; Sec. Frank Phillips. Conducts labor Zionist educational, youth, and cultural activities in the American Jewish community and promotes educational travel to Israel.

NATIONAL COMMITTEE FOR LABOR ISRAEL —ISRAEL HISTADRUT CAMPAIGN (1923). 33 E. 67 St., N.Y.C., 10021. Pres. Judah J. Shapiro; Exec. V. Pres. Bernard B. Jacobson. Provides funds for the social welfare, vocational, health, and cultural institutions and other services of Histadrut to benefit workers and immigrants and to assist in the integration of newcomers as productive citizens in Israel; promotes an understanding of the aims and achievements of Israel labor among Jews and non-Jews in America. Fund-raising arms are: Israel Histadrut Campaign and Israel Histadrut Foundation. *Histadrut Foto-News.*

_____: AMERICAN TRADE UNION COUNCIL FOR HISTADRUT (1947). 33 E. 67 St., N.Y.C., 10021. Chmn. Matthew Schoenwald; Exec. Dir. Steven M. Mrvichin. Carries on educational activities among American and Canadian trade unions for health, educational, and welfare activities of the Histadrut in Israel. *Shalom.*

PEC ISRAEL ECONOMIC CORPORATION (formerly PALESTINE ECONOMIC CORPORATION) (1926). 511 Fifth Ave., N.Y.C., 10017. Pres. Stephen Shalom; Sec.-Asst. Treas. William Gold. Investments and loans in Israel. *Annual Report.*

P.E.F. ISRAEL ENDOWMENT FUNDS, INC. (1922). 511 Fifth Ave., N.Y.C., 10017. Pres. Sidney Musher; Sec. Ruth Ginzberg. Uses funds for Israeli educational and philanthropic institutions and for constructive relief, modern education, and scientific research in Israel. *Annual Report.*

PIONEER WOMEN, THE WOMEN'S LABOR ZIONIST ORGANIZATION OF AMERICA, INC. (1925). 315 Fifth Ave., N.Y.C., 10016. Pres. Frieda Leemon; Exec. Dir. Lucette Halle. Supports in cooperation with Na'amat a widespread network of educational, vocational, and social services for women, children, and youth in Israel. Provides counseling and legal aid services for women, particularly war widows. Authorized agency of Youth Aliyah. In America, supports Jewish educational, youth, cultural programs; participates in civic affairs. *Pioneer Woman.*

POALE AGUDATH ISRAEL OF AMERICA, INC. (1948). 156 Fifth Ave., N.Y.C., 10010. Pres. David B. Hollander; Exec. Dir. Moshe Tambor; Presidium: Alexander Herman, Anshel Wainhaus. Aims to educate American Jews to the values of Orthodoxy, *aliyah,* and *halutziut;* supports kibbutzim, trade schools, *yeshivot,* teachers' college, civic and health centers, children's homes in Israel. *Achdut; PAI Views; PAI Bulletin.*

———: WOMEN'S DIVISION OF (1948). Presidium: Ethel Blasbalg, Sarah Iwanisky, Bertha Rittenberg. Assists Poale Agudath Israel to build and support children's homes, kindergartens, and trade schools in Israel. *Yediot PAI.*

RASSCO ISRAEL CORPORATION AND RASSCO FINANCIAL CORPORATION (1950). 535 Madison Ave., N.Y.C., 10022. Pres. Shmuel Lavi; Bd. Chmn. Igal Weinstein. Maintains ties with Western Hemisphere investments.

RELIGIOUS ZIONISTS OF AMERICA. 25 W. 26 St., N.Y.C., 10010.

———: BNEI AKIVA OF NORTH AMERICA (1934). 25 W. 26 St., N.Y.C., 10010. Pres. Dov A. Bloom; Sec. Rafi Neeman. Seeks to interest youth in aliyah to Israel and social justice through pioneering (*halutziut*) as an integral part of their religious observance; sponsors five summer camps, a leadership training camp for eleventh graders, a work-study program on a religious kibbutz for high school graduates, summer tours to Israel; establishes nuclei of college students for kibbutz or other settlement. *Arivon; Hamvoser; Pinkas Lamadrich; Z'raim.*

———: MIZRACHI-HAPOEL HAMIZRACHI (1909; merged 1957). 25 W. 26 St., N.Y.C., 10010. Pres. Louis Bernstein; Exec. V. Pres. Israel Friedman. Dedicated to building the Jewish state based on principles of Torah; conducts cultural work, educational program, public relations; sponsors NOAM and Bnei Akiva; raises funds for religious educational institutions in Israel. *Horizon; Kolenu; Mizrachi News Bulletin.*

———: MIZRACHI PALESTINE FUND (1928). 25 W. 26 St., N.Y.C., 10010. Chmn. Joseph Wilon; Sec. Israel Friedman. Fund-raising arm of Mizrachi movement.

———: NATIONAL COUNCIL FOR TORAH EDUCATION OF MIZRACHI-HAPOEL HAMIZRACHI (1939). 25 W. 26 St., N.Y.C., 10010. Pres. Israel Shaw; Dir. Meyer Golombek. Organizes and supervises *yeshivot* and Talmud Torahs; prepares and trains teachers; publishes textbooks and educational materials; conducts a placement agency for Hebrew schools; organizes summer seminars for Hebrew educators in cooperation with Torah department of Jewish Agency; conducts *Ulpan.*

———: NOAM-HAMISHMERET HATZEIRA (1970). 25 W. 26 St., N.Y.C., 10010. Chmn. Sarah J. Sanders; Exec. Dir. David Stahl. Sponsors three core groups to settle in Israel; conducts summer and year volunteer and study programs to Israel; organizes educational programs for young adults in the U.S., through weekly meetings, Shabbatonim, leadership seminars, etc. *Bechol Zot.*

SOCIETY OF ISRAEL PHILATELISTS (1948). c/o A. Engers, 40–67 61 St., Woodside, N.Y., 11377. Pres. Michael M. Madesker; Sec. Arthur Engers. Promotes interest in, and knowledge of, all phases of Israel philately through sponsorship of chapters and research groups, maintenance of a philatelic library, and support of public and private exhibitions. *Israel Philatelist.*

STATE OF ISRAEL BOND ORGANIZATION (1951). 215 Park Ave. S., N.Y.C., 10003. Pres. Michael Arnon; Gen. Chmn. Sam Rothberg; Exec. V. Pres. Morris Sipser. Seeks to provide large-scale investment funds for the economic development of the State of Israel through the sale of State of

Israel bonds in the U.S., Canada, Western Europe and other parts of the free world.

UNITED CHARITY INSTITUTIONS OF JERUSALEM, INC. (1903). 1141 Broadway, N.Y.C., 10001. Pres. Zevulun Charlop; Exec. Dir. S. Gabel. Raises funds for the maintenance of schools, kitchens, clinics, and dispensaries in Israel; Free Loan Foundations in Israel.

UNITED ISRAEL APPEAL, INC. (1925). 515 Park Ave., N.Y.C., 10022. Chmn. Melvin Dubinsky; Exec. V. Chmn. Irving Kessler. As principal beneficiary of the United Jewish Appeal, serves as link between American Jewish community and Jewish Agency in Israel, its operating agent; assists in resettlement and absorption of refugees in Israel, and supervises flow and expenditures for this purpose. *Briefings.*

UNITED STATES COMMITTEE—SPORTS FOR ISRAEL, INC. (1948). 130 E. 59 St., N.Y.C., 10022. Pres. Nat Holman; Exec. Dir. Leonard K. Straus. Sponsors U.S. participation in, and fields and selects U.S. team for, World Maccabiah Games in Israel every four years; promotes physical education and sports program in Israel and total fitness of Israeli and American Jewish youths; provides funds, technical and material assistance to Wingate Institute for Physical Education and Sport in Israel; sponsors U.S. coaches for training programs in Israel and provides advanced training and competition in U.S. for Israel's national sports teams, athletes and coaches; offers scholarships at U.S. colleges to Israeli physical education students. *Newsletter.*

WOMEN'S LEAGUE FOR ISRAEL, INC. (1928). 1860 Broadway, N.Y.C., 10023. Pres. Mrs. Harry M. Wiles; Exec. Dir. Mrs. Regina Wermiel. Promotes the welfare of young people in Israel, especially young women immigrants; built and maintains Y-style homes in Jerusalem, Haifa, Tel Aviv and Natanya for young women; in cooperation with Ministry of Labor, operates live-in vocational training center for girls, including handicapped, in Natanya, and weaving workshop for blind. *Bulletin; Israel News Digest.*

WORLD CONFEDERATION OF UNITED ZIONISTS (1946; reorg. 1958). 595 Madison Ave., N.Y.C., 10022. Co-Presidents Charlotte Jacobson, Kalman Sultanik, Melech Topiol. General Zionist world organization, not identified with any political party in Israel, but with Israel as a whole; supports projects identified with Israel; sponsors non-party halutzic youth movements in diaspora, Shnat Sherut and Noar Zioni Azmai in Israel; promotes Zionist education and strives for an Israel-oriented creative Jewish survival in the diaspora. *Zionist Information Views.*

WORLD ZIONIST ORGANIZATION-AMERICAN SECTION (1971). 515 Park Ave., N.Y.C., 10022. Chmn. Mrs. Charlotte Jacobson; Exec. V. Chmn. Isadore Hamlin. As the American section of the overall Zionist body throughout the world, it operates primarily in the field of aliyah from the free countries, education in the diaspora, youth and hechalutz, organization and information, cultural institutions, publications, and handling activities of Jewish National Fund; conducts a worldwide Hebrew cultural program including special seminars and pedagogic manuals; disperses information and assists in research projects concerning Israel; promotes, publishes, and distributes books, periodicals, and pamphlets concerning developments in Israel, Zionism, and Jewish history; sponsors "Panoramas de Israel" radio program in the Latin American countries. *Israel Digest; Israel y America Latina.*

———, NORTH AMERICAN ALIYAH MOVEMENT (1968). 515 Park Ave., N.Y.C., 10022. Pres. Linda Brown; Exec. Dir. Harvey G. Harth. Promotes and facilitates aliyah and klitah from the U.S. and Canada to Israel; serves as a social framework for North American immigrants to Israel. *Aliyon; NAAM Letter; Coming Home.*

———, ZIONIST ARCHIVES AND LIBRARY OF THE (1939). 515 Park Ave., N.Y.C., 10022. Dir. and Librarian Sylvia Landress. Serves as an archives and information service for material on Israel, Palestine, the Middle East, Zionism, and all aspects of Jewish life.

ZIONIST ORGANIZATION OF AMERICA (1897). ZOA House, 4 E. 34 St., N.Y.C., 10016. Pres. Joseph P. Sternstein; Nat. Exec. Dir. Leon Ilutovich. Seeks to safeguard the integrity and independence of Israel by means consistent with the laws of the U.S., to assist in the economic development of Israel, and to foster the unity of the Jewish people and the centrality of Israel in

Jewish life in the spirit of General Zionism. *American Zionist; Public Affairs Memorandum; ZINS Weekly News Bulletin; ZOA in Review.*

PROFESSIONAL ASSOCIATIONS*

AMERICAN CONFERENCE OF CANTORS (Religious, Educational)

AMERICAN JEWISH CORRECTIONAL CHAPLAINS ASSOCIATION, INC. (Social Welfare)

AMERICAN JEWISH PRESS ASSOCIATION (Cultural)

AMERICAN JEWISH PUBLIC RELATIONS SOCIETY (1957). 60 Glenwood Ave., East Orange, N.J. 07017. Pres. William Pages; Treas. Philip Gutride. Advances professional status of workers in the public-relations field in Jewish communal service; upholds a professional code of ethics and standards; serves as a clearinghouse for employment opportunities; exchanges professional information and ideas; presents awards for excellence in professional attainments. *The Handout.*

ASSOCIATION OF JEWISH CENTER WORKERS (Community Relations)

ASSOCIATION OF JEWISH CHAPLAINS OF THE ARMED FORCES (Religious, Educational)

ASSOCIATION OF JEWISH COMMUNITY RELATIONS WORKERS (Community Relations)

CANTORS ASSEMBLY OF AMERICA (Religious, Educational)

COUNCIL OF JEWISH ORGANIZATIONS IN CIVIL SERVICE (Community Relations)

EDUCATORS ASSEMBLY OF THE UNITED SYNAGOGUE OF AMERICA (Religious, Educational)

INTERNATIONAL ASSOCIATION OF HILLEL DIRECTORS (Religious, Educational)

INTERNATIONAL CONFERENCE OF JEWISH COMMUNAL SERVICE (Community Relations)

JEWISH MINISTERS CANTORS ASSOCIATION OF AMERICA, INC. (Religious, Educational)

JEWISH TEACHERS ASSOCIATION—MORIM (Religious, Educational)

NATIONAL ASSOCIATION OF JEWISH CENTER WORKERS (Community Relations)

NATIONAL ASSOCIATION OF SYNAGOGUE ADMINISTRATORS, UNITED SYNAGOGUE OF AMERICA (Religious, Educational)

NATIONAL ASSOCIATION OF TEMPLE ADMINISTRATORS, UNION OF AMERICAN HEBREW CONGREGATIONS (Religious, Educational)

NATIONAL ASSOCIATION OF TEMPLE EDUCATORS, UNION OF AMERICAN HEBREW CONGREGATIONS (Religious, Educational)

NATIONAL CONFERENCE OF JEWISH COMMUNAL SERVICE (Social Welfare)

NATIONAL CONFERENCE OF YESHIVA PRINCIPALS (Religious, Educational)

NATIONAL JEWISH WELFARE BOARD COMMISSION ON JEWISH CHAPLAINCY (Social Welfare)

WOMEN'S ORGANIZATIONS*

AMERICAN MIZRACHI WOMEN (Zionist and Pro-Israel)

B'NAI B'RITH WOMEN (Social Welfare)

BRANDEIS UNIVERSITY NATIONAL WOMEN'S COMMITTEE (1948). Brandeis University, Waltham, Mass., 02154. Exec. Dir. Esther Schwartz. Responsible for support and maintenance of Brandeis University libraries; sponsors University on Wheels and, through its chapters, study-group programs based on faculty-prepared syllabi, volunteer work in educational services, and a program of New Books for Old Sales; constitutes largest "Friends of a Library" group in U.S.

HADASSAH, THE WOMEN'S ZIONIST ORGANIZATION OF AMERICA, INC. (Zionist and Pro-Israel)

NATIONAL COUNCIL OF JEWISH WOMEN (Social Welfare)

NATIONAL FEDERATION OF TEMPLE SISTERHOODS, UNION OF AMERICAN HE-

*For fuller listing see under categories in parentheses.

BREW CONGREGATIONS (Religious, Educational)

PIONEER WOMEN, THE WOMEN'S LABOR ZIONIST ORGANIZATION OF AMERICA (Zionist and Pro-Israel)

UNITED ORDER OF TRUE SISTERS (Social, Mutual Benefit)

WOMEN'S AMERICAN ORT, FEDERATION (Overseas Aid)

WOMEN'S BRANCH OF THE UNION OF ORTHODOX JEWISH CONGREGATIONS OF AMERICA (Religious, Educational)

WOMEN'S DIVISION OF POALE AGUDATH OF AMERICA (Zionist and Pro-Israel)

WOMEN'S DIVISION OF THE AMERICAN JEWISH CONGRESS (Community Relations)

WOMEN'S DIVISION OF THE JEWISH LABOR COMMITTEE (Community Relations)

WOMEN'S DIVISION OF THE UNITED JEWISH APPEAL (Overseas Aid)

WOMEN'S LEAGUE FOR ISRAEL, INC. (Zionist and Pro-Israel)

WOMEN'S ORGANIZATION OF HAPOEL HAMIZRACHI (Zionist and Pro-Israel)

YESHIVA UNIVERSITY WOMEN'S ORGANIZATION (Religious, Educational)

YOUTH AND STUDENT ORGANIZATIONS*

AMERICAN ZIONIST YOUTH FOUNDATION, INC. (Zionist and Pro-Israel)

————: AMERICAN ZIONIST YOUTH COUNCIL

ATID, COLLEGE AGE ORGANIZATION, UNITED SYNAGOGUE OF AMERICA (Religious, Educational)

B'NAI B'RITH HILLEL FOUNDATIONS, INC. (Religious, Educational)

B'NAI B'RITH YOUTH ORGANIZATION (Religious, Educational)

B'NEI AKIVA OF NORTH AMERICA, RELIGIOUS ZIONISTS OF AMERICA (Zionist and Pro-Israel)

BNOS AGUDATH ISRAEL, AGUDATH ISRAEL OF AMERICA (Religious, Educational)

DROR YOUNG ZIONIST ORGANIZATION (Zionist and Pro-Israel)

HASHACHAR—WOMEN'S ZIONIST ORGANIZATION OF AMERICA (Zionist and Pro-Israel)

HASHOMER HATZAIR, ZIONIST YOUTH MOVEMENT (Zionist and Pro-Israel)

ICHUD HABONIM LABOR ZIONIST YOUTH (Zionist and Pro-Israel)

JEWISH STUDENT PRESS-SERVICE (1970)— JEWISH STUDENT EDITORIAL PROJECTS, INC. 15 East 26th St., Suite 1350, N.Y.C., 10010. Ed.-in-Chief Sue Berrin; Admin. Dir. Leslie Schnur. Serves all Jewish student and young adult publications, as well as many Anglo-Jewish newspapers, in North America, through monthly feature packets of articles and graphics. Holds annual national and local editors' conference for member publications. Provides technical and editorial assistance; keeps complete file of member publications since 1970; maintains Israel Bureau. *Jewish Press Features.*

KADIMA (Religious, Educational)

MASSORAH INTERCOLLEGIATES OF YOUNG ISRAEL, NATIONAL COUNCIL OF YOUNG ISRAEL (Religious, Educational)

NATIONAL CONFERENCE OF SYNAGOGUE YOUTH, UNION OF ORTHODOX JEWISH CONGREGATIONS OF AMERICA (Religious, Educational)

NATIONAL FEDERATION OF TEMPLE YOUTH, UNION OF AMERICAN HEBREW CONGREGATIONS (Religious, Educational)

NOAR MIZRACHI-HAMISHMERET (NOAM) —RELIGIOUS ZIONISTS OF AMERICA (Zionist and Pro-Israel)

NORTH AMERICAN JEWISH STUDENTS APPEAL (1971). 15 E. 26 St., N.Y.C. 10010. Pres. Steven M. Cohen; Exec. Dir. Susan C. Dessel. Serves as central fund-raising mechanism for national, independent, Jewish student organizations; insures accountability of public Jewish communal funds

*For fuller listing see under categories in parentheses.

used by these agencies; assists Jewish students undertaking projects of concern to Jewish communities; advises and assists Jewish organizations in determining student project feasibility and impact; fosters development of Jewish student leadership in the Jewish community. Beneficiaries include local and regional Jewish student projects on campuses throughout North America; founding constituents include Jewish Student Press Service, North American Jewish Students Network, Student Struggle for Soviet Jewry, *Response,* and Yugntruf; beneficiaries include Harvard Law School Jewish Students Assn., Bay Area Jewish Women's Conference, and State Univ. of N.Y. Jewish Student Union.

NORTH AMERICAN JEWISH STUDENTS' NETWORK (1969). 15 E. 26 St., N.Y.C., 10010. Chmn. Carole Stern. Coordinates information and programs among all Jewish student organizations in North America; promotes development of student-controlled Jewish student organizations; maintains contacts and coordinates programs with Jewish students throughout the world through the World Union of Jewish Students; runs the Jewish Student Speakers Bureau; sponsors regional conferences, National Jewish Women's Conference, first Pan American Jewish Students Conference, North American Jewish Students' Congress on Israel, and Conference on Alternatives in Jewish Education. *Guide to Jewish Student Groups in North America; Network.*

NORTH AMERICAN JEWISH YOUTH COUNCIL (Community Relations)

STUDENT STRUGGLE FOR SOVIET JEWRY, INC. (Community Relations)

UNITED SYNAGOGUE YOUTH, UNITED SYNAGOGUE OF AMERICA (Religious, Educational)

WOMEN'S LEAGUE FOR CONSERVATIVE JUDAISM (Religious, Educational)

YAVNEH, NATIONAL RELIGIOUS JEWISH STUDENTS ASSOCIATION (Religious, Educational)

YUGNTRUF YOUTH FOR YIDDISH (1966). 3328 Bainbridge Ave., Bronx, N.Y., 10467. Pres. Paula Teitelbaum; Exec. Dir. David Neal Miller. A worldwide, non-political organization for Yiddish-speaking high school and college students. Organizes drama and choral groups, literature clubs, picnics, dances and other social activities. Offers services of full-time field worker to assist in forming Yiddish courses and clubs. *Fum Khaver Tsu Khaver; Yugntruf.*

ZEIREI AGUDATH ISRAEL, AGUDATH ISRAEL OF AMERICA (Religious, Educational)

CANADA

CANADA-ISRAEL SECURITIES, LTD., STATE OF ISRAEL BONDS (1953). 1255 University St., Montreal, PQ, H3B 3W7. Pres. Allan Bronfman; Sec. Max Wolofsky. Sale of State of Israel Bonds in Canada. *Israel Bond News.*

CANADIAN ASSOCIATION FOR LABOR ISRAEL (HISTADRUT) (1944). 4770 Kent Ave., Rm. 301, Montreal, PQ, H3W 1H2. Nat. Pres. Bernard M. Bloomfield; Nat. Exec. Dir. Bernard Morris. Raises funds for Histadrut institutions in Israel, supporting their rehabilitation tasks. *Histadrut Foto News; Histadrut Review.*

*CANADIAN FOUNDATION FOR JEWISH CULTURE (1965). 150 Beverley St., Toronto, M5T 1Y6. Pres. Joseph L. Kronick; Exec. Sec. Edmond Y. Lipsitz. Promotes Jewish studies at university level and encourages original research and scholarship in Jewish subjects; awards annual scholarships and grants-in-aid to scholars in Canada.

CANADIAN FRIENDS OF THE ALLIANCE ISRAÉLITE UNIVERSELLE (1958). 5711 Edgemore Ave., Montreal, PQ, H4W 1V7. Pres. Harry Batshaw; Exec. Sec. Mrs. Marlene Salomon. Supports the educational work of the Alliance.

*CANADIAN FRIENDS OF THE HEBREW UNIVERSITY (1944). 1506 McGregor Ave., Montreal, PQ, H3G 1B9. Nat. Hon. Pres. Allan Bronfman; Nat. Hon. Sec. Samuel R. Risk; Exec. Dir. Daniel Ben-Natan. Represents and publicizes the Hebrew University in Canada; serves as fund-raising arm for the University in Canada; processes Canadians for study at the university. *Scopus.*

CANADIAN JEWISH CONGRESS (1919; reorg. 1934). 1590 McGregor Ave., Montreal, PQ, H3G 1C5. Pres. W. Gunther Plaut; Exec. V. Pres. Alan Rose. The official voice of Canadian Jewry at home and abroad. Acts on all matters affecting the status, rights and welfare of Canadian Jews. *Congress Bulletin; I.O.I.; Cercle Juif.*

CANADIAN ORT ORGANIZATION (Organization of Rehabilitation Through Training) (1940). 5165 Sherbrooke St. W., Suite 208, Montreal, PQ, H4A 1T6. Pres. J.A. Lyone Heppner; Exec. Dir. Max E. Levy. Carries on fund-raising projects in support of the worldwide vocational-training school network of ORT. *Canadian ORT Reporter.*

_____: WOMEN'S CANADIAN ORT (1940). 380 Wilson Ave., Downsview, Ont., M3H 1S9. Pres. Dorothy Shoichet; Exec. Dir. Diane Uslaner.

CANADIAN SEPHARDIC FEDERATION (1973). 1310 Greene Ave., Montreal PQ, H3Z 2B7. Pres. Charles Chocron; Exec. Dir. Avi Shlush. Preserves and promotes Sephardic identity, particularly among youth; works for the unity of the Jewish people; emphasizes relations between Sephardi communities all over the world; seeks better situation for Sephardim in Israel; supports Israel by all means. *Horison, Sepharadi.*

CANADIAN YOUNG JUDEA (1917). 788 Marlee Ave., Toronto, Ont., M6B 3K1. Nat. Pres. Mark Joffe; Exec. Dir. Ian Borer. Strives to attract Jewish youth to Zionism, with goal of *aliyah;* operates nine summer camps in Canada and Israel; is sponsored by Canadian Hadassah-WIZO and Zionist Organization of Canada, and affiliated with Hanoar Hatzioni in Israel. *Yedion; Judaean; Ekronot.*

CANADIAN ZIONIST FEDERATION (1967). 1310 Greene Ave., Westmount, Montreal PQ, H3Z 2B2. Pres. Philip Givens; Exec. V. Pres. Leon Kronitz. Umbrella organization of all Zionist- and Israel-oriented groups in Canada; carries on major activities in all areas of Jewish life through its departments of education and culture, aliyah, youth and students, public affairs, and fund-raising for the purpose of strengthening the State of Israel and the Canadian Jewish Community. *Canadian Zionist; The Reporter.*

_____: BUREAU OF EDUCATION AND CULTURE (1972). Pres. Philip Givens; Exec. V. Pres. and Dir. of Educ. Leon Kronitz. Provides counselling by pedagogic experts, in-service teacher training courses and seminars in Canada and Israel; operates teacher placement bureau, national pedagogic council and research centre; publishes and distributes educational material and teaching aids; conducts annual Bible contests and Hebrew language courses for adults. *Al Mitzpe Haninuch.*

HADASSAH—WIZO ORGANIZATION OF CANADA (1916). 1310 Greene Ave., 9th fl., Montreal, PQ, H3Z 2B2. Nat. Pres. Mrs. Charles Balinsky; Nat. Exec. Dir. Lily Frank. Assists needy Israeli Jews by sponsoring health, education, and social welfare services; seeks to strengthen and perpetuate Jewish identity; encourages Jewish and Hebrew culture in promoting Canadian ideals of democracy and pursuit of peace. *Orah.*

JEWISH COLONIZATION ASSOCIATION OF CANADA (1907). 5151 Cote St. Catherine Rd., Montreal, PQ, H3W 1M6. Pres. Lazarus Phillips; Sec. Morley M. Cohen; Mgr. M.J. Lister. Promotes Jewish land settlement in Canada through loans to established farmers; helps new immigrant farmers to purchase farms; or settles them on farms owned by the Association; provides agricultural advice and supervision; contributes funds to Canadian Jewish Loan Cassa for loans to small businessmen and artisans.

JEWISH IMMIGRANT AID SERVICES OF CANADA (JIAS) (1919). 5151 Cote St. Catherine Rd., Montreal, PQ, H3W 1M6. Nat. Pres. Charles Kent; Nat. Exec. V. Pres. Joseph Kage. Serves as a national agency for immigration and immigrant welfare. *JIAS Bulletin; JIAS News; Studies and Documents on Immigration and Integration in Canada.*

JEWISH LABOR COMMITTEE OF CANADA (1934). 5165 Isabella Ave., Montreal, PQ, H3W 1S9. Nat. Pres. Harry Simon; Nat. Dir. Elie Chalouh. Fights for human rights and against racism, antisemitism and other forms of discrimination; works for strengthening and continuation of Jewish life in Canada. *Bulletins.*

JEWISH NATIONAL FUND OF CANADA (KEREN KAYEMETH LE ISRAEL, INC.) (1902). 1980 Sherbrooke St. W., Suite 250, Montreal, PQ, H3H, 2M7. Nat. Pres. Nathan Scott; Exec. V. Pres. Harris D. Gulko.

Seeks to create, provide, enlarge, and administer a fund to be made up of voluntary contributions from the Jewish community and others, to be used for charitable purposes. *JNF Bulletin.*

LABOR ZIONIST MOVEMENT OF CANADA (1939). 4770 Kent Ave., Montreal, PQ, H3W 1H2. Nat. Pres. Sydney L. Wax; Nat. Exec. Dir. Leo J. Moss. Disseminates information and publications on Israel and Jewish life; arranges special events, lectures, and seminars; coordinates communal and political activities of its constituent bodies (Pioneer Women, Na'amat, Labor Zionist Alliance, Poale Zion party, Habonim-Dror Youth, Israel Histadrut, affiliated Hebrew elementary and high schools in Montreal and Toronto). *Canadian Jewish Quarterly; Viewpoints; Briefacts; Insight.*

*MIZRACHI-HAPOEL HAMIZRACHI ORGANIZATION OF CANADA (1941). 5497A Victoria Ave., Suite 101, Montreal, PQ, H3W 2R1. Nat. Pres. Kurt Rothschild; Nat. Exec. Dir. Rabbi Sender Shizgal; Sec. Zalman Stern. Promotes religious Zionism, aimed at making Israel a state based on Torah; maintains Bnei Akiva, a summer camp, adult education program, and touring department; supports Mizrachi-Hapoel Hamizrachi and other religious Zionist institutions in Israel which strengthen traditional Judaism. *Mizrachi Newsletter.*

NATIONAL COUNCIL OF JEWISH WOMEN OF CANADA (1947). 300A Wilson Ave., Suite 2, Downsview, Ont., M3H 1S8. Nat. Pres. Marjorie Blankstein; Exec. Sec. Florence Greenberg. Dedicated to furthering human welfare in Jewish and non-Jewish communities, locally, nationally, and internationally; provides essential services and stimulates and educates the individual and the community through an integrated program of education, service, and social action. *Keeping You Posted.*

NATIONAL JOINT COMMUNITY RELATIONS COMMITTEE OF CANADIAN JEWISH CONGRESS AND B'NAI B'RITH IN CANADA (1936). 150 Beverley St., Toronto, Ont., M5T 1Y6. Chmn. Rabbi Jordan Pearlson; Nat. Exec. Dir. Ben G. Kayfetz. Seeks to safeguard the status, rights, and welfare of Jews in Canada; to combat antisemitism and promote understanding and goodwill among all ethnic and religious groups. *Congress Bulletin.*

UNITED JEWISH TEACHERS' SEMINARY (1946). 5237 Clanranald Ave., Montreal, PQ, H3X, 2S5. Dir. A. Aisenbach; Sec. Mrs. M. Aspler. Trains teachers for Yiddish and Hebrew schools under auspices of Canadian Jewish Congress. YITONENU.

ZIONIST ORGANIZATION OF CANADA (1892; reorg. 1919). 788 Marlee Ave., Toronto, Ont., M6B 3K1. Nat. Pres. David Monson; Exec. V. Pres. George Liban. Furthers general Zionist aims by operating nine youth camps in Canada and one in Israel; produces two weekly TV shows, "Shalom" and "Jewish Dimensions"; maintains Zionist book club; arranges programs, lectures; sponsors Young Judea, Youth Centre Project in Jerusalem Forest, Israel.

Jewish Federations, Welfare Funds, Community Councils

THIS directory is one of a series compiled annually by the Council of Jewish Federations and Welfare Funds. Virtually all of these community organizations are affiliated with the Council as their national association for sharing of common services, interchange of experience, and joint consultation and action.

These communities comprise at least 95 per cent of the Jewish population of the United States and about 90 per cent of the Jewish population of Canada. Listed for each community is the local central agency—federation, welfare fund, or community council—with its address and the names of the president and executive officer.

The names "federation," "welfare fund," and "Jewish community council" are not definitive, and their structures and functions vary from city to city. What is called a federa-tion in one city, for example, may be called a community council in another. In the main, these central agencies have responsibility for some or all of the following functions: (a) raising of funds for local, national, and over-seas services; (b) allocation and distribution of funds for these purposes; (c) coordination and central planning of local services, such as family welfare, child care, health, recreation, community relations within the Jewish com-munity and with the general community, Jewish education, care of the aged, and voca-tional guidance; to strengthen these services, eliminate duplication, and fill gaps; (d) in small and some intermediate cities, direct ad-ministration of local social services.

In the directory, (*) preceding a listing identifies those who are *not* member agencies of the Council of Jewish Federations and Welfare Funds.

UNITED STATES

ALABAMA

BIRMINGHAM

BIRMINGHAM JEWISH FEDERATION (1935; reorg. 1971); P.O. Box 9157 (35213); Pres. Mrs. Solomon P. Kimerling; Exec. Dir. Sey-mour Marcus.

JEWISH COMMUNITY COUNCIL (1962); P.O. Box 7377, 3960 Montclair Rd. (35223); Pres. Mayer U. Newfield; Exec. Dir. Harold E. Katz.

MOBILE

MOBILE JEWISH WELFARE FUND, INC. (Inc. 1966); 1509 Government St. (36604); Pres. Melvin Stein; Exec. Dir. Richard Grant.

MONTGOMERY

JEWISH FEDERATION OF MONTGOMERY, INC. (1930); P.O. Box 1150 (36102); Pres. Perry Mendel; Sec. Mrs. Jeanette C. Waldo.

TRI-CITIES

TRI-CITIES JEWISH FEDERATION CHARI-
TIES, INC. (1933; Inc. 1956); Route 7, Florence (35632); Pres. Mrs. M. F. Shipper.

ARIZONA

PHOENIX

GREATER PHOENIX JEWISH FEDERATION
(incl. surrounding communities) (1940); 1718
W. Maryland Ave. (85015); Pres. Neal Kurn;
Exec. Dir. Herman Markowitz.

TUCSON

JEWISH COMMUNITY COUNCIL (1942); 102
N. Plumer (85719); Pres. Alvin D. Stern;
Exec. V. Pres. Benjamin N. Brook.

ARKANSAS

LITTLE ROCK

JEWISH WELFARE AGENCY, INC. (1911);
221 Donaghey Bldg; Main at 7th (72201);
Pres. Allan B. Mendel; Exec. Sec. Nancy
Goldman.

CALIFORNIA

LONG BEACH

JEWISH COMMUNITY FEDERATION (1937);
(sponsors UNITED JEWISH WELFARE
FUND); 2601 Grand Ave. (90815); Pres. Arthur Miller; Exec. Dir. Harold Benowitz.

LOS ANGELES

JEWISH FEDERATION - COUNCIL OF
GREATER LOS ANGELES (1912; reorg. 1959)
(sponsors UNITED JEWISH WELFARE
FUND); 6505 Wilshire Blvd. (90048); Pres.
Irwin H. Goldenberg; Exec. V. Pres. Alvin
Bronstein.

OAKLAND

JEWISH WELFARE FEDERATION OF
ALAMEDA AND CONTRA COSTA COUNTIES
(1918); 3245 Sheffield Ave. (94602); Pres.
Marshall Cornblum; Exec. Dir. Earnest Siegel.

ORANGE COUNTY

JEWISH FEDERATION-COUNCIL OF ORANGE
COUNTY (1964; Inc. 1965); (sponsors
UNITED JEWISH WELFARE FUND); 3303
Harbor Blvd., Costa Mesa (92626); Pres. Mel
Jaffee; Exec. Dir. Mortimer Greenberg.

PALM SPRINGS

JEWISH WELFARE FEDERATION OF PALM
SPRINGS-DESERT AREA (1971); 611 S. Palm

Canyon Dr. #210 (92262); Pres. A. S. Weiss;
Exec. Dir. Samuel J. Rosenthal.

SACRAMENTO

JEWISH FEDERATION OF SACRAMENTO
(1948). 2418 K St., Suite A (95816); Pres.
Alan Brodovsky; Exec. Dir. Ephraim Spivek.

SAN BERNARDINO

SAN BERNARDINO UNITED JEWISH WEL-
FARE FUND, INC. (1936; Inc. 1957); 3512 No.
"E" St. (92405). Pres. William Russler.

SAN DIEGO

UNITED JEWISH FEDERATION OF GREATER
SAN DIEGO (1935); 5511 El Cajon Blvd.
(92115); Pres. Bernard L. Lewis; Exec. Dir.
Donald L. Gartner.

SAN FRANCISCO

JEWISH WELFARE FEDERATION OF SAN
FRANCISCO, MARIN COUNTY AND THE
PENINSULA (1910; reorg. 1955); 220 Bush
St., Room 645 (94104); Pres. Peter E. Haas;
Exec. Dir. Brian Lurie.

SAN JOSE

JEWISH FEDERATION OF GREATER SAN
JOSE (incl. Santa Clara County except Palo
Alto and Los Altos) (1930; reorg. 1950); 1777
Hamilton Ave., Suite 201 (95125); Pres. Har-
old Witkin; Exec. Dir. Donald A. Glazer.

SANTA BARBARA

*SANTA BARBARA JEWISH FEDERATION,
P.O. Box 3314 (93105); Pres. M. Howard
Goldman.

STOCKTON

*STOCKTON JEWISH WELFARE FUND
(1972); 5105 N. El Dorado St. (95207); Pres.
Joel M. Senderov; Treas. Harry Green.

VENTURA

*VENTURA COUNTY JEWISH COUNCIL—
TEMPLE BETH TORAH (1938); 7620 Foothill
Rd. (93003); Pres. Paul Karlsberg.

COLORADO

DENVER

ALLIED JEWISH FEDERATION OF DENVER
(1936); (sponsors ALLIED JEWISH CAM-
PAIGN); 300 S. Dahlia St. (80222); Pres. Jack
Grazi; Exec. Dir. Harold Cohen.

CONNECTICUT

BRIDGEPORT

UNITED JEWISH COUNCIL OF GREATER BRIDGEPORT, INC. (1936); (sponsors UNITED JEWISH CAMPAIGN); 4200 Park Ave. (06604); Pres. Helen B. Wasserman; Exec. Dir. Sanford Lupovitz.

DANBURY

JEWISH FEDERATION OF GREATER DANBURY (1945); 8 West St. (06810); Pres. Albert Kohn; Exec. Dir. Jonathan H. Spinner.

HARTFORD

GREATER HARTFORD JEWISH FEDERATION (Incl. New Britain) (1945); 333 Bloomfield Ave., W. Hartford (06117); Pres. Arthur W. Feinstein; Exec. Dir. Don Cooper.

MERIDEN

*MERIDEN JEWISH WELFARE FUND, INC. (1944); 127 E. Main St. (06450); Pres. Joseph Barker; Sec. Harold Rosen.

NEW HAVEN

NEW HAVEN JEWISH FEDERATION (1928); (sponsors COMBINED JEWISH APPEAL) (1969); 1184 Chapel St. (06511); Pres. Josef Adler; Exec. Dir. Arthur Spiegel.

NEW LONDON

JEWISH COMMUNITY COUNCIL OF GREATER NEW LONDON, INC. (1950; Inc. 1970); 302 State St. (06320); Pres. Jerry Winter; Exec. Dir. Eugene F. Elander.

NORWALK

JEWISH COMMUNITY COUNCIL OF NORWALK (1946; reorg. 1964); Shorehaven Rd., East Norwalk (06855); Pres. Mrs. Betty Herman; Exec. Dir. Roy Stuppler.

STAMFORD

UNITED JEWISH FEDERATION (Reincorp. 1973); 1035 Newfield Ave. (06905); Pres. Bernard Samers; Exec. Dir. Sandor Sherman.

WATERBURY

JEWISH FEDERATION OF WATERBURY, INC. (1938); 1020 Country Club Rd. (06720); Pres. Donald Liebeskind; Exec. Dir. Robert Kessler.

DELAWARE

WILMINGTON

JEWISH FEDERATION OF DELAWARE, INC. (1935); 701 Shipley St. (19801); Pres. Nisson A. Finkelstein; Exec. Dir. Mike Ruvel.

DISTRICT OF COLUMBIA

WASHINGTON

UNITED JEWISH APPEAL—FEDERATION OF GREATER WASHINGTON, INC. (1935); 4701 Willard Ave., Chevy Chase, Md. (20015); Pres. Herschel W. Blumberg; Exec. V. Pres. Elton J. Kerness.

FLORIDA

FT. LAUDERDALE

JEWISH FEDERATION OF GREATER FT. LAUDERDALE (1967); 2999 N.W. 33rd Ave. (33311); Pres. Allan E. Baer; Exec. Dir. Irving L. Geisser.

HOLLYWOOD

JEWISH FEDERATION OF SOUTH BROWARD, INC. (1943); 2838 Hollywood Blvd. (33020); Pres. Lewis E. Cohn; Exec. Dir. Sumner Kaye.

JACKSONVILLE

JACKSONVILLE JEWISH COMMUNITY COUNCIL (1935); 5846 Mt. Carmel Terr. (32216); Pres. E. Theodore Cohn; Exec. Dir. Gerald L. Goldsmith.

MIAMI

GREATER MIAMI JEWISH FEDERATION, INC. (1938); 4200 Biscayne Blvd. (33137); Pres. Morton Silberman; Exec. V. Pres. Myron J. Brodie.

ORLANDO

JEWISH FEDERATION OF GREATER ORLANDO (1949); 851 No. Maitland Ave., Maitland (32751); Pres. Sy Israel; Exec. Dir. Paul Jeser.

PALM BEACH COUNTY

JEWISH FEDERATION OF PALM BEACH COUNTY, INC. (1938); 2415 Okeechobee Blvd., West Palm Beach (33409); Pres. Stanley Brenner; Exec. Dir. Norman J. Schimelman.

PENSACOLA

*PENSACOLA FEDERATED JEWISH CHARITIES (1942); 1320 E. Lee St. (32503); Pres. Gene Rosenbaum; Sec. Mrs. Harry Saffer.

PINELLAS COUNTY (incl. Clearwater and St. Petersburg)

JEWISH FEDERATION OF PINELLAS COUNTY, INC. (1950; reincorp. 1974); 8167 Elbow Lane, North, St. Petersburg (33710); Pres. Stanley Freifeld; Exec. Dir. Ron Weisinger.

SARASOTA

SARASOTA JEWISH COMMUNITY COUNCIL, INC. (1959); 1900 Main Bldg., Suite 300 (33577); Pres. Sol Levites; Exec. Dir. Florence S. Sinclair.

TAMPA

TAMPA JEWISH FEDERATION (1941); 2808 Horatio (33609); Pres. David Polur.

GEORGIA

ATLANTA

ATLANTA JEWISH WELFARE FEDERATION, INC. (1905; reorg. 1967); 1753 Peachtree Rd., N.E. (30309); Pres. David Goldwasser; Exec. Dir. Max C. Gettinger.

AUGUSTA

FEDERATION OF JEWISH CHARITIES (1937); P.O. Box 3251, Hill Station (30909) c/o Hillel Silver, Treas; Pres. Morton Wittenberg.

COLUMBUS

JEWISH WELFARE FEDERATION OF COLUMBUS, INC. (1941); P.O. Box 1303 (31902); Pres. Bernard Witt; Sec. David Helman.

SAVANNAH

SAVANNAH JEWISH COUNCIL (1943); (sponsors UJA-FEDERATION CAMPAIGN); P. O. Box 6546, 5111 Abercorn St. (31405); Pres. Aaron Levy; Exec. Dir. Stan Ramati.

IDAHO

BOISE

*SOUTHERN IDAHO JEWISH WELFARE FUND (1947); 1776 Commerce Ave. (83705); Pres. Kal Sarlat; Treas. Martin Heuman.

ILLINOIS

CHAMPAIGN-URBANA

FEDERATED JEWISH CHARITIES (1929); (member Central Illinois Jewish Federation); 1707 Parkhaven Dr., Champaign (61820); Co-Chmn. Stanley Levy, Zelda Derber; Exec. Sec. Mrs. Donald Ginsberg.

CHICAGO

JEWISH FEDERATION OF METROPOLITAN CHICAGO (1900); 1 S. Franklin St. (60606); Pres. David Smerling; Exec. V. Pres. James P. Rice.

JEWISH UNITED FUND OF METROPOLITAN CHICAGO (1968), 1 S. Franklin St. (60606); Pres. David Smerling; Exec. V. Pres. James P. Rice.

DECATUR

JEWISH FEDERATION (member Central Illinois Jewish Federation) (1942); 78 Montgomery Pl. (62522); Pres. Don Champion.

ELGIN

ELGIN AREA JEWISH WELFARE CHEST (1938); 330 Division St. (60120); Pres. Gerald Levine; Treas. Harry Seigle.

JOLIET

JOLIET JEWISH WELFARE CHEST (1938); 250 N. Midland Ave. (60435); Pres. Robert S. Krockey; Sec. Rabbi Morris M. Hershman.

PEORIA

CENTRAL ILLINOIS JEWISH FEDERATION (1969); 718 Central Bldg. (61602); Pres. Ted Century; Exec. Dir. Peretz Katz.

JEWISH COMMUNITY COUNCIL & WELFARE FUND OF PEORIA (member CENTRAL ILLINOIS JEWISH FEDERATION) (1933; Inc. 1947); 718 Central Bldg. (61602); Pres. Joseph Settler; Exec. Dir. Peretz A. Katz.

ROCK ISLAND — MOLINE — DAVENPORT — BETTENDORF

UNITED JEWISH CHARITIES OF QUAD CITIES (1938; comb. 1973); 1804 7th Ave., Rock Island (61201); Pres. Morton Kaplan; Sec. Jay Gellerman.

ROCKFORD

ROCKFORD JEWISH COMMUNITY COUNCIL (1937); 1500 Parkview Ave. (61107); Pres. Toby Toback; Exec. Dir. Daniel Tannenbaum.

SOUTHERN ILLINOIS

JEWISH FEDERATION OF SOUTHERN ILLINOIS (incl. all of Illinois south of Carlinville and Paducah, Ky.) (1941); 6464 W. Main, Suite 7A, Belleville (62223); Pres. Mrs. Frank Altman; Exec. Dir. Hyman H. Ruffman.

SPRINGFIELD

SPRINGFIELD JEWISH FEDERATION (member CENTRAL ILLINOIS JEWISH FEDERATION) (1941); 730 E. Vine St. (62703); Pres. Leonard M. Lieberman; Exec. Sec. Mrs. Lenore Loeb.

INDIANA

EVANSVILLE

EVANSVILLE JEWISH COMMUNITY COUNCIL, INC. (1936; Inc. 1964); P.O. Box 5026 (47715); Pres. Mrs. Sadelle Berger.

FORT WAYNE

FORT WAYNE JEWISH FEDERATION (1921); 227 E. Washington Blvd. (46802); Pres. Robert S. Walters; Exec. Dir. Benjamin Eisbart.

INDIANAPOLIS

JEWISH WELFARE FEDERATION, INC. (1905); 615 N. Alabama St. (46204); Pres. Walter E. Wolf, Jr.; Exec. V. Pres. Frank H. Newman.

LAFAYETTE

FEDERATED JEWISH CHARITIES (1924); P.O. Box 676 (47902); Pres. Leslie Feld; Fin. Sec. Louis Pearlman, Jr.

MICHIGAN CITY

MICHIGAN CITY UNITED JEWISH WELFARE FUND; 2800 Franklin St. (46360); Pres. Irving Loeber; Treas. Harold Leinwand.

MUNCIE

*MUNCIE JEWISH WELFARE FUND (1945); c/o Beth El Temple; P.O. Box 2792 (47302); Chmn. Edward J. Dobrow; Treas. Robert Koor.

NORTHWEST INDIANA

NORTHWEST INDIANA JEWISH WELFARE FEDERATION (1941; reorg. 1959); 4844 Broadway, Gary (46408); Pres. Alan Hurst; Exec. Dir. Barnett Labowitz.

SOUTH BEND

JEWISH COMMUNITY COUNCIL OF ST. JOSEPH AND ELKHART COUNTIES (1946); 804 Sherland Bldg. (46601); Pres. Ronald Cohen; Exec. Dir. Bernard Natkow.

JEWISH WELFARE FUND (1937); 804 Sherland Bldg. (46601); Exec. Dir. Bernard Natkow.

IOWA

CEDAR RAPIDS

*JEWISH WELFARE FUND OF LINN COUNTY (1941); 115 7 St. S.E. (52401); Chmn. Norman Lipsky; Treas. Jay Beecher.

DES MOINES

JEWISH WELFARE FEDERATION OF DES MOINES (1914); 910 Polk Blvd. (50312); Pres. Fred Lorber; Exec. Dir. Jay Yoskowitz.

SIOUX CITY

JEWISH FEDERATION (1921); 525 14 St. (51105); Pres. A. Frank Baron; Exec. Dir. Joseph Bluestein.

WATERLOO

WATERLOO JEWISH FEDERATION (1941); c/o Congregation Sons of Jacob, 411 Mitchell Ave. (50702); Pres. Irving Uze.

KANSAS

TOPEKA

TOPEKA-LAWRENCE JEWISH FEDERATION (1939); 101 Redbud Lane (66607); Pres. William Rudnick.

WICHITA

MID-KANSAS JEWISH WELFARE FEDERATION, INC. (1935); 400 N. Woodlawn, Suite 28 (67206); Pres. Joan Beren.

KENTUCKY

LOUISVILLE

JEWISH COMMUNITY FEDERATION OF LOUISVILLE, INC. (1934); (sponsors UNITED JEWISH CAMPAIGN); 702 Marion E. Taylor Bldg. (40202); Pres. Stuart Handmaker; Exec. Dir. Norbert Fruehauf.

LOUISIANA

ALEXANDRIA

THE JEWISH WELFARE FEDERATION AND COMMUNITY COUNCIL OF CENTRAL LOUISIANA (1938); 1261 Heyman Lane (71301); Pres. Harold Katz; Sec.-Treas. Mrs. George Kuplesky.

BATON ROUGE

GREATER BATON ROUGE JEWISH WELFARE FEDERATION (1971); P. O. Box 15123 (70895); Pres. Harvey Hoffman; Adm. Asst. Betty Shapiro.

MONROE

UNITED JEWISH CHARITIES OF NORTHEAST LOUISIANA (1938); 2400 Orrel Pl. (71201); Pres. Henry Gerson; Sec.-Treas. Herman E. Hirsch.

NEW ORLEANS

JEWISH FEDERATION OF GREATER NEW ORLEANS (1913; reorg. 1977); 211 Camp St. (70130); Pres. Marvin L. Jacobs; Exec. Dir. Gerald C. Lasensky.

SHREVEPORT

SHREVEPORT JEWISH FEDERATION (1941; Inc. 1967); 1021 Lane Bldg. (71101); Pres. David Greenberg; Exec. Dir. K. Bernard Klein.

MAINE

BANGOR

*JEWISH COMMUNITY COUNCIL (1949); 28 Somerset St. (04401); Pres. Sam Nyer; Exec. Dir. Alan Coren.

LEWISTON-AUBURN

JEWISH FEDERATION (1947); (sponsors UNITED JEWISH APPEAL); 134 College St., Lewiston (04240); Pres. Mrs. Bertha Allen; Exec. Dir. Robert Schwartz.

PORTLAND

JEWISH FEDERATION COMMUNITY COUNCIL OF SOUTHERN MAINE (1942); (sponsors UNITED JEWISH APPEAL); 341 Cumberland Ave. (04101); Pres. David N. Lewis; Exec. Dir. Sanford Cutler.

MARYLAND

ANNAPOLIS

*ANNAPOLIS JEWISH WELFARE FUND (1946); 601 Ridgley Ave. (21401); Pres. Anton Grobani.

BALTIMORE

ASSOCIATED JEWISH CHARITIES & WELFARE FUND, INC. (a merger of the Associated Jewish Charities & Jewish Welfare Fund) (1920; reorg. 1969); 319 W. Monument St. (21201); Pres. Bernard Manekin; Exec. V. Pres. Robert I. Hiller.

MASSACHUSETTS

BOSTON

COMBINED JEWISH PHILANTHROPIES OF GREATER BOSTON, INC. (incl. Brockton) (1895; reorg. 1961); 72 Franklin St. (02110);

Pres. Leonard Kaplan; Exec. Dir. Bernard Olshansky.

FITCHBURG

*JEWISH FEDERATION OF FITCHBURG (1939); 40 Boutelle St. (01420); Pres. Elliot L. Zide; Treas. Allen I. Rome.

FRAMINGHAM

GREATER FRAMINGHAM JEWISH FEDERATION (1968; Inc. 1969); 1000 Worchester Road, Framingham Centre (01701); Pres. Mrs. Harvey Stone; Exec. Dir. Howard G. Joress.

HAVERHILL

*HAVERHILL UNITED JEWISH APPEAL, INC., 514 Main St. (01830); Pres. Norman Birenbaum; Exec. Dir. Joseph H. Elgart.

HOLYOKE

COMBINED JEWISH APPEAL OF HOLYOKE (1939); 378 Maple St. (01040); Pres. Herbert Goldberg; Exec. Dir. Dov Sussman.

LAWRENCE

*JEWISH COMMUNITY COUNCIL OF GREATER LAWRENCE (1906); 580 Haverhill St. (01841); Pres. Michael Baker; Exec. Dir. Irving Linn.

LEOMINSTER

LEOMINSTER JEWISH COMMUNITY COUNCIL, INC. (1939); 30 Grove Ave. (01453); Pres. Marc Levine; Sec.-Treas. Edith Chatkis.

NEW BEDFORD

JEWISH FEDERATION OF GREATER NEW BEDFORD, INC. (1938; Inc. 1954); 467 Hawthorn St., North Dartmouth (02747); Pres. Alan Ades; Exec. Dir. Gerald A. Kleinman.

NORTH SHORE

JEWISH FEDERATION OF THE NORTH SHORE, INC. (1938); 4 Community Rd., Marblehead (01945); Pres. Norman S. Rosenfield; Exec. Dir. Gerald S. Ferman.

PITTSFIELD

*JEWISH COMMUNITY COUNCIL (1940); 235 E. St. (01201); Pres. Howard Kaufman; Exec. Dir. Sanford Lubin.

SPRINGFIELD

SPRINGFIELD JEWISH FEDERATION, INC. (1938); (sponsors UNITED JEWISH WELFARE FUND); 1160 Dickinson (01108); Pres. Richard Gaberman; Exec. Dir. Eli Asher.

WORCESTER

WORCESTER JEWISH FEDERATION, INC. (1947; Inc. 1957); (sponsors JEWISH WELFARE FUND, 1939); 633 Salisbury St. (01609); Pres. David F. Gould; Exec. Dir. Melvin S. Cohen.

MICHIGAN

BAY CITY

*NORTHEASTERN MICHIGAN JEWISH WELFARE FEDERATION (1940); 1100 Center Ave., Apt. 305 (48706); Sec. Hanna Hertzenberg.

DETROIT

JEWISH WELFARE FEDERATION OF DETROIT (1899); (sponsors ALLIED JEWISH CAMPAIGN); Fred M. Butzel Memorial Bldg., 163 Madison (48226); Pres. Martin E. Citrin; Exec. Dir. Sol Drachler.

FLINT

JEWISH COMMUNITY COUNCIL (1936); 120 W. Kearsley St. (48502); Pres. Murray E. Moss; Exec. Dir. Arnold S. Feder.

GRAND RAPIDS

JEWISH COMMUNITY FUND OF GRAND RAPIDS (1930); 1121 Keneberry Way S.E. (49506); Pres. Joseph N. Schwartz; Sec. Mrs. William Deutsch.

KALAMAZOO

KALAMAZOO JEWISH FEDERATION (1949); 2902 Bronson Blvd. (49001); Pres. Martin H. Kalb.

LANSING

GREATER LANSING JEWISH WELFARE FEDERATION (1939); 319 Hillcrest (48823); Pres. Marvin Hecht; Exec. Dir. Henry Jurkewicz.

SAGINAW

SAGINAW JEWISH WELFARE FEDERATION (1939); 1424 S. Washington Ave. (48607); Pres. Norman Rotenberg; Fin. Sec. Mrs. Henry Feldman.

MINNESOTA

DULUTH

JEWISH FEDERATION & COMMUNITY COUNCIL (1937); 1602 E. 2nd St. (55812); Pres. R. L. Solon; Exec. Dir. Mrs. Arnold Nides.

MINNEAPOLIS

MINNEAPOLIS FEDERATION FOR JEWISH SERVICES (1929; Inc. 1930); 811 La Salle Ave. (55402); Pres. Thomas D. Feinberg; Exec. Dir. Franklin Fogelson.

ST. PAUL

UNITED JEWISH FUND AND COUNCIL (1935); 790 S. Cleveland (55116); Pres. Annette Newman; Exec. Dir. Morris Lapidos.

MISSISSIPPI

JACKSON

*JEWISH WELFARE FUND (1945); 4135 N. Honeysuckle Lane (39211); Drive Chmn. Emanuel Crystal.

VICKSBURG

*JEWISH WELFARE FEDERATION (1936); 1210 Washington St. (39180); Pres. Richard Marcus.

MISSOURI

KANSAS CITY

JEWISH FEDERATION OF GREATER KANSAS CITY (1933); 25 E. 12 St. (64106); Pres. Donald H. Tranin; Exec. Dir. Sol Koenigsberg.

ST. JOSEPH

UNITED JEWISH FUND OF ST. JOSEPH (1915); 2903 Sherman Ave. (64506); Pres. Grace Day; Exec. Sec. Ann Saferstein.

ST. LOUIS

JEWISH FEDERATION OF ST. LOUIS (incl. St. Louis County) (1901); 611 Olive St., Suite 1520 (63101); Pres. Siegmund Halpern; V.P. David Rabinovitz.

NEBRASKA

LINCOLN

LINCOLN JEWISH WELFARE FEDERATION, INC. (1931; Inc. 1961); 809 Lincoln Benefit Life Bldg. (68508); Pres. Herbert F. Gaba; Sec. Louis B. Finkelstein.

OMAHA

JEWISH FEDERATION OF OMAHA (1903); 333 S. 132 St. (68154); Pres. Mrs. Morris Fellman; Exec. Dir. Louis B. Solomon.

NEVADA

LAS VEGAS

LAS VEGAS COMBINED JEWISH APPEAL (1973); 846 E. Sahara Ave. #4 (89104); Pres. Lloyd Katz; Exec. Dir. Jerry Countess.

NEW HAMPSHIRE

MANCHESTER

JEWISH COMMUNITY COUNCIL OF GREATER MANCHESTER (1913); 698 Beech St. (03104); Pres. Harold Cooper; Exec. Dir. Kenneth Gabel.

NEW JERSEY

ATLANTIC CITY

FEDERATION OF JEWISH AGENCIES OF ATLANTIC COUNTY (1924); 5321 Atlantic Ave., Ventnor County (08406); Pres. Esther G. Mitnick; Exec. Dir. Murray Schneier.

BERGEN COUNTY

JEWISH FEDERATION OF COMMUNITY SERVICES, BERGEN COUNTY, N.J. (incl. most of Bergen County) (1953); 20 Banta Pl., Hackensack (07601); Pres. Moshe Dworkin; Exec. Dir. Max M. Kleinbaum.

CENTRAL NEW JERSEY

JEWISH FEDERATION OF CENTRAL NEW JERSEY (sponsors UNITED JEWISH CAMPAIGN); (1940; expanded 1973 to include Westfield and Plainfield); Green Lane, Union (07083); Pres. Alan Goldstein; Exec. V. Pres. Burton Lazarow.

ENGLEWOOD

UNITED JEWISH FUND OF ENGLEWOOD AND SURROUNDING COMMUNITIES (1952); 153 Tenafly Rd. (07631); Pres. Mrs. Stanford E. Eisenberg; Exec. Dir. George Hantgan.

JERSEY CITY

UNITED JEWISH APPEAL (1939); 604 Bergen Ave. (07304); Chmn. Melvin Blum; Exec. Dir. Arthur Eisenstein.

METROPOLITAN NEW JERSEY

JEWISH COMMUNITY FEDERATION (sponsors UNITED JEWISH APPEAL) (1923); 60 Glenwood Rd., East Orange (07017); Exec. V. Pres. Carmi Schwartz.

MONMOUTH COUNTY

JEWISH FEDERATION OF GREATER MONMOUTH COUNTY (Formerly Shore Area) (1971); 100 Grant Ave. (07723); Pres. Samuel Jaffe; Exec. Dir. Clifford R. Josephson.

MORRIS COUNTY

UNITED JEWISH FEDERATION OF MORRIS-SUSSEX; 500 Route 10, Ledgewood (07852); Pres. Ralph Stern; Exec. Dir. Elliot Cohan.

NORTH JERSEY

JEWISH FEDERATION OF NORTH JERSEY (formerly Jewish Community Council) (1933); (sponsors UNITED JEWISH APPEAL DRIVE); 1 Pike Dr., Wayne (07470); Pres. Norman Zelnick; Exec. Dir. Richard Krieger.

NORTHERN MIDDLESEX COUNTY

JEWISH FEDERATION OF NORTHERN MIDDLESEX COUNTY (sponsors UNITED JEWISH APPEAL) (1975); Lord St., Avenel (07001); Pres. Ted Simkin; Exec. Dir. Charles Plotkin.

OCEAN COUNTY

OCEAN COUNTY JEWISH FEDERATION; 120 Madison Ave., Lakewood (08701); Pres. Herbert Wishnick; Exec. Dir. Marvin Relkin.

PASSAIC-CLIFTON

JEWISH COMMUNITY COUNCIL OF PASSAIC-CLIFTON AND VICINITY (1933); (sponsors UNITED JEWISH CAMPAIGN); 199 Scoles Ave. (07012). Pres. Herbert C. Klein; Exec. Dir. Max Grossman.

RARITAN VALLEY

JEWISH FEDERATION OF RARITAN VALLEY (1948); 2 South Adelaide Ave., Highland Park (08904); Pres. Jane Freedman; Exec. Dir. Howard Kieval.

SOMERSET COUNTY

JEWISH FEDERATION OF SOMERSET COUNTY (1960); 11 Park Ave., P. O. Box 874, Somerville (08876); Pres. Margit Feldman; Exec. Dir. Burt Shimanovsky.

SOUTHERN NEW JERSEY

JEWISH FEDERATION OF SOUTHERN NEW JERSEY (incl. Camden and Burlington Counties) (1922); (sponsors ALLIED JEWISH APPEAL); 2393 W. Marlton Pike, Cherry Hill (08002); Pres. Meyer L. Abrams; Exec. V. Pres. Bernard Dubin.

TRENTON

JEWISH FEDERATION OF GREATER TRENTON (1929); 999 Lower Ferry Rd., P. O. Box 7249 (08628); Pres. David Kravitz; Exec. Dir. Mark M. Edell.

VINELAND

JEWISH COMMUNITY COUNCIL OF GREATER VINELAND, INC. (1971); (sponsors ALLIED JEWISH APPEAL); 629 Wood St. (08360);

Pres. Sheldon Goldberg; Exec. Dir. Nan Goldberg.

NEW MEXICO

ALBUQUERQUE

JEWISH COMMUNITY COUNCIL OF AL-BUQUERQUE, INC. (1938); 600 Louisiana Blvd., S.E. (87108); Pres. Michael Sutin; Exec. Dir. Charles Vogel.

NEW YORK

ALBANY

ALBANY JEWISH COMMUNITY COUNCIL, INC. (1938); (sponsors JEWISH WELFARE FUND); 19 Colvin Ave. (12206); Pres. Jason Baker; Exec. Dir. Steven F. Windmueller.

BROOME COUNTY

THE JEWISH FEDERATION OF BROOME COUNTY (1937; Inc. 1958); 500 Clubhouse Rd., Binghamton (13903); Pres. Mrs. Edwin Pierson; Exec. Dir. Stanley Bard.

BUFFALO

UNITED JEWISH FEDERATION OF BUFFALO, INC. (1903); sponsors UNITED JEWISH FUND CAMPAIGN); 787 Delaware Ave. (14209); Pres. Morris Himmel; Exec. Dir. Lester I. Levin.

ELMIRA

ELMIRA JEWISH WELFARE FUND, INC. (1942); P. O. Box 3087, Grandview Rd. (14905); Pres. Irving Etkind; Exec. Dir. Louis Goldman.

GLENS FALLS

*GLENS FALLS JEWISH WELFARE FUND (1939); 6 Arbor Dr. (12801); Chmn. Orel Friedman.

HUDSON

*JEWISH WELFARE FUND OF HUDSON, N.Y., INC. (1947); Joslen Blvd. (12534); Pres. Philip Pomerantz.

KINGSTON

JEWISH COMMUNITY COUNCIL, INC. (1951); 77 East Chester St. (12401); Pres. Joseph Cohen; Exec. Dir. Marden Paru.

NEW YORK CITY

FEDERATION OF JEWISH PHILANTHROPIES OF NEW YORK (incl. Greater New York, Nassau, Suffolk, and Westchester Counties) (1917); 130 E. 59th St. (10022); Pres. Harry R. Mancher; Exec. V. Pres. Sanford Solender.

UNITED JEWISH APPEAL OF GREATER NEW YORK, INC. (incl. Greater New York, Nassau, Suffolk and Westchester Counties) (1939); 220 W. 58th St. (10019); Pres. James L. Weinberg; Exec. V. Pres. Ernest W. Michel.

UNITED JEWISH APPEAL—FEDERATION OF JEWISH PHILANTHROPIES—JOINT CAMPAIGN (1974); 220 W. 58 St. (10019); Pres. Laurence A. Tisch; Exec. V.P.s Ernest W. Michel, Sanford Solender; Bd. Chmn. Lawrence B. Buttenwieser.

NEWBURGH-MIDDLETOWN

JEWISH FEDERATION OF NEWBURGH AND MIDDLETOWN, INC. (1925); 360 Powell Ave. (12550); Pres. Florence Levine; Exec. Dir. Carol Rosengart.

NIAGARA FALLS

JEWISH FEDERATION OF NIAGARA FALLS, N.Y., INC. (1935); 209 United Office Bldg. (14303); Pres. Robert D. Wisbaum; Exec. Dir. May Chinkers.

POUGHKEEPSIE

*JEWISH WELFARE FUND-DUTCHESS CTY. (1941); 110 Grand Ave. (12603); Pres. Arthur Levinsohn; Exec. Dir. Marden Paru.

ROCHESTER

JEWISH COMMUNITY FEDERATION OF ROCHESTER, N.Y., INC. (1937); 440 Main St. E. (14604); Pres. Irving Ruderman; Exec. Dir. Darrell D. Friedman.

SCHENECTADY

JEWISH COMMUNITY COUNCIL (incl. surrounding communities) (1938); (sponsors SCHENECTADY UJA AND FEDERATED WELFARE FUND); 2565 Balltown Rd., P. O. Box 2649 (12309); Pres. Philip Ziffer; Exec. Dir. Haim Morag.

SYRACUSE

JEWISH FEDERATION, INC. (1918); (sponsors JEWISH WELFARE FUND [1933]); 321 Seitz Bldg., 201 E. Jefferson St. (13202); Pres. Norman Poltenson; Exec. Dir. Gilbert D. Orlik.

TROY

TROY JEWISH COMMUNITY COUNCIL, INC. (1936); 2500–21 St. (12180); Pres. Daniel Gotkis.

UTICA

JEWISH COMMUNITY COUNCIL OF UTICA, N.Y., INC. (1933, Inc. 1950); (sponsors UNITED JEWISH APPEAL OF UTICA); 2310 Oneida St. (13501); Pres. Mrs. Helen Sperling; Exec. Dir. Irving Epstein.

NORTH CAROLINA

ASHEVILLE

FEDERATED JEWISH CHARITIES OF ASHEVILLE, INC., 236 Charlotte St. (28801); Pres. Jerome Dave; Exec. Dir. Burt Shimanovsky.

CHARLOTTE

CHARLOTTE FEDERATION OF JEWISH CHARITIES (1940); P.O. Box 17188 (28211); Pres. Morris Speizman; Exec. Dir. Marvin Bienstock.

NORTH CAROLINA TRIAD

NORTH CAROLINA TRIAD JEWISH FEDERATION (1940); 414 Church St., Suite 11, Greensboro (27401); Pres. Robert Lavites; Exec. Dir. Sherman Harris.

OHIO

AKRON

AKRON JEWISH COMMUNITY FEDERATION (1935); 750 White Pond Dr. (44320); Pres. David Locksin; Exec. Dir. Morris Rombro.

CANTON

JEWISH COMMUNITY FEDERATION OF CANTON (1935; reorg. 1955); 2631 Harvard Ave., N. W. (44709); Pres. Stanford L. Sirak; Exec. Dir. Revella R. Kopstein.

CINCINNATI

JEWISH FEDERATION OF CINCINNATI AND VICINITY (merger of the Associated Jewish Agencies and Jewish Welfare Fund) (1896; reorg. 1967); 200 West 4th St. (45202); Pres. Morris G. Levin; Exec. V.Pres. Harold Goldberg.

CLEVELAND

JEWISH COMMUNITY FEDERATION OF CLEVELAND (1903); 1750 Euclid Ave. (44115); Pres. Albert B. Ratner; Exec. Dir. Stanley B. Horowitz.

COLUMBUS

COLUMBUS JEWISH FEDERATION (1926); 1175 College Ave. (43209); Pres. Ernest Stern; Exec. V. Pres. Ben M. Mandelkorn.

DAYTON

JEWISH COMMUNITY COUNCIL OF DAYTON (1943); 4501 Denlinger Rd. (45426); Pres.

Irvin Zipperstein; Exec. Dir. Robert Fitterman.

LIMA

FEDERATED JEWISH CHARITIES OF LIMA DISTRICT (1935); 2417 West Market St. (45805); Pres. Morris Goldberg.

STEUBENVILLE

JEWISH COMMUNITY COUNCIL (1938); P. O. Box 472 (43952); Pres. Curtis Greenberg; Exec. Sec. Mrs. Joseph Freedman.

TOLEDO

JEWISH WELFARE FEDERATION OF TOLEDO, INC. (1907; reorg. 1960); 5151 Monroe St., Suite 226 West (43623); Pres. David Katz; Exec. Dir. Alvin S. Levinson.

WARREN

JEWISH FEDERATION (1938); 3893 E. Market St. (44483); Pres. William Lippy.

YOUNGSTOWN

JEWISH FEDERATION OF YOUNGSTOWN, OHIO, INC. (1935); P. O. Box 449 (44501); Pres. Bert Tamarkin; Exec. Dir. Stanley Engel.

OKLAHOMA

ARDMORE

JEWISH FEDERATION (1934); 23 "B" St., S.W. (73401); Chmn. Ike Fishman.

OKLAHOMA CITY

JEWISH COMMUNITY COUNCIL (1941); 1100 N. Dewey, Suite 103 (73103); Pres. Sig Harpman, Jr.; Exec. Dir. Jay B. Bachrach.

TULSA

TULSA JEWISH COMMUNITY COUNCIL (1938); (sponsors TULSA UNITED JEWISH CAMPAIGN); 3314 E. 51 St., Suite T (74135); Pres. Donald Newman; Exec. Dir. Nathan Loshak.

OREGON

PORTLAND

JEWISH WELFARE FEDERATION OF PORTLAND (incl. State of Oregon and adjacent Washington communities) (1920; reorg. 1956); 6651 S. W. Capitol Highway (97219); Pres. Arden E. Shenker; Exec. Dir. David Roberts.

PENNSYLVANIA

ALLENTOWN

JEWISH FEDERATION OF ALLENTOWN, INC. (1938; Inc. 1948); 22nd and Tilghman Sts.

(18105); Pres. Robert Margolis; Exec. Dir. Leslie Gottlieb.

ALTOONA

FEDERATION OF JEWISH PHILANTHROPIES (1920; reorg. 1940); 1308 17th St. (16601); Pres. Neil Port.

BUTLER

BUTLER JEWISH WELFARE FUND (incl. Butler County) (1938); P. O. Box 992 (16001); Pres. Julius Bernstein; Sec. Maurice Horwitz.

EASTON

JEWISH COMMUNITY COUNCIL OF EASTON, PA. AND VICINITY (1939); (sponsors ALLIED WELFARE APPEAL); 660 Ferry St. (18042); Pres. Jerald Bobrow; Exec. Dir. Eugene Hurwitz.

ERIE

JEWISH COMMUNITY COUNCIL OF ERIE (1946); 32 W. 8th St., Suite 512 (16501); Pres. Sidney Wexler; Exec. Dir. Ivan C. Schonfeld.

HARRISBURG

UNITED JEWISH COMMUNITY OF GREATER HARRISBURG (1933); 100 Vaughn St. (17110); Pres. Herbert S. Abrams; Exec. Dir. Albert Hursh.

HAZELTON

JEWISH COMMUNITY COUNCIL (1960); Laurel & Hemlock Sts. (18201); Pres. Richard Chait; Exec. Dir. Steven Wendell.

JOHNSTOWN

UNITED JEWISH FEDERATION OF JOHNSTOWN (1938); 1334 Luzerne St. (15905); Pres. Isadore Glasser.

LANCASTER

UNITED JEWISH COMMUNITY COUNCIL OF LANCASTER, PA., INC. (1928); 2120 Oregon Pike (17601); Pres. Jay S. Poser; Exec. Dir. Lawrence Pallas.

LEVITTOWN

JEWISH FEDERATION OF LOWER BUCKS COUNTY (1956; Inc. 1957); 15 Stonybrook Dr. E. (19055); Pres. Arthur M. Abramsohn; Exec. Dir. Sidney Stein.

NEW CASTLE

UNITED JEWISH APPEAL OF NEW CASTLE, PA. (1967); 3218 Plank Rd. (16105); Chmn. Bruce Pickel.

NORRISTOWN

JEWISH COMMUNITY CENTER (serving Central Montgomery County) (1936); Brown and Powell Sts. (19401); Pres. Norman Kutner; Exec. Dir. Harold M. Kamsler.

PHILADELPHIA

FEDERATION OF JEWISH AGENCIES OF GREATER PHILADELPHIA (1901; reorg. 1956); 226 South 16 St. (19102); Pres. I. Jerome Stern; Exec. Dir. Robert Forman.

PITTSBURGH

UNITED JEWISH FEDERATION OF GREATER PITTSBURGH (1912; reorg. 1955); 234 McKee Pl. (15213); Pres. Sidney N. Busis; Exec. Dir. Gerald S. Soroker.

POTTSVILLE

UNITED JEWISH CHARITIES (1935); 2300 Mahantongo St. (17901); Chmn. Henry Gilbert; Exec. Sec. Gertrude Perkins.

READING

JEWISH FEDERATION OF READING, PA., INC. (1935); (sponsors UNITED JEWISH CAMPAIGN); 1700 City Line St. (19604); Pres. Benjamin J. Cutler; Exec. Dir. David Morris.

SCRANTON

SCRANTON-LACKAWANNA JEWISH COUNCIL (incl. Lackawanna County) (1945); 601 Jefferson Ave. (18510); Pres. Alvin Nathan; Exec. Dir. George Joel.

SHARON

SHENANGO VALLEY JEWISH FEDERATION (1940); 840 Highland Rd. (16146); Pres. Leon Bolotin; Treas. Irwin Yanowitz.

UNIONTOWN

UNITED JEWISH FEDERATION (1939); 406 W. Main St. (15401), c/o Jewish Community Center; Pres. Harold Cohen; Sec. Morris H. Samuels.

WILKES-BARRE

THE WYOMING VALLEY JEWISH COMMITTEE (1935); (sponsors UNITED JEWISH APPEAL); 60 S. River St. (18701); Pres. Charles M. Nelson; Exec. Dir. Monty Pomm.

YORK

YORK COUNCIL OF JEWISH CHARITIES, INC.; 120 E. Market St. (17401); Pres. Robert Erdos; Exec. Dir. Alan Dameshek.

RHODE ISLAND

PROVIDENCE

JEWISH FEDERATION OF RHODE ISLAND
(1945); 130 Sessions St. (02906); Pres. Marvin S. Holland; Exec. Dir. Dan Asher.

SOUTH CAROLINA

CHARLESTON

JEWISH WELFARE FUND (1949); 1645 Millbrook Dr. (29407); P. O. Box 31298; Pres. Melvin Solomon; Exec. Dir. Nathan Shulman.

COLUMBIA

JEWISH WELFARE FEDERATION OF COLUMBIA (1960); 4540 Trenholm Rd. (29206); Pres. Melton Kligman; Exec. Dir. Jack Weintraub.

SOUTH DAKOTA

SIOUX FALLS

JEWISH WELFARE FUND (1938); National Reserve Bldg. (57102); Pres. Richard M. Light; Exec. Sec. Louis R. Hurwitz.

TENNESSEE

CHATTANOOGA

CHATTANOOGA JEWISH WELFARE FEDERATION (1931); 5326 Lynnland Terrace (37411); Pres. Mark A. Spector; Exec. Dir. Steven Drysdale.

KNOXVILLE

JEWISH WELFARE FUND, INC. (1939); 6800 Deane Hill Dr. (37919); P. O. Box 10882; Pres. Gordon Brown; Exec. Dir. Mike Pousman.

MEMPHIS

JEWISH SERVICE AGENCY (incl. Shelby County) (1864; Inc. 1906); 6560 Poplar Ave., P. O. Box 38268 (38138); Pres. Jerrold Graber; Exec. Dir. Jack Lieberman.

MEMPHIS JEWISH FEDERATION (incl. Shelby County) (1934); 6560 Poplar Ave., P. O. Box 38268 (38138); Pres. Samuel Weintraub; Exec. Dir. Howard Weisband.

NASHVILLE

JEWISH FEDERATION OF NASHVILLE & MIDDLE TENNESSEE (1936); 3500 West End Ave. (37205); Pres. Mrs. Louis K. Fox; Exec. Dir. Martin Kraar.

TEXAS

AUSTIN

JEWISH COMMUNITY COUNCIL OF AUSTIN (1939; reorg. 1956); 8301 Balcones Dr., Suite 308-1 (78759); Pres. Marion Stahl; Exec. Dir. Charles P. Epstein.

BEAUMONT

BEAUMONT JEWISH FEDERATION OF TEXAS, INC. (Org. and Inc. 1967); P. O. Box 1981 (77704); Pres. Edwin Gale; Dir. Isadore Harris.

CORPUS CHRISTI

CORPUS CHRISTI JEWISH COMMUNITY COUNCIL (1953); 750 Everhart Rd. (78411); Pres. Madelyn Loeb; Exec. Dir. Lillian Racusin.

COMBINED JEWISH APPEAL OF CORPUS CHRISTI (1962); 750 Everhart Rd. (78411); Pres. Jule Pels; Exec. Dir. Mrs. Lillian Racusin.

DALLAS

JEWISH FEDERATION OF GREATER DALLAS (1911); 8616 Northwest Plaza-Suite 319 (75225); Pres. Morris P. Newberger; Exec. Dir. Morris A. Stein.

EL PASO

JEWISH FEDERATION OF EL PASO, INC. (incl. surrounding communities) (1939); 405 Mardi Gras, P. O. Box 12097 (79912); Pres. Mrs. Robert E. Goodman; Exec. Dir. Howard Burnham.

FORT WORTH

JEWISH FEDERATION OF FORT WORTH (1936); 6801 Grandbury Rd. (76133); Pres. Sheldon Anisman; Exec. Dir. Norman A. Mogul.

GALVESTON

GALVESTON COUNTY JEWISH COMMUNITY COUNCIL & WELFARE ASSOCIATION (1936); P. O. Box 146 (77553); Pres. Mrs. I. A. Lerner; Sec. Mrs. Charles Rosenbloom.

HOUSTON

JEWISH FEDERATION OF GREATER HOUSTON, INC. (incl. neighboring communities) (1937); (sponsors UNITED JEWISH CAMPAIGN); 5601 S. Braeswood Blvd. (77096); Pres. R. Alan Rudy; Exec. Dir. Hans Mayer.

SAN ANTONIO

JEWISH FEDERATION OF SAN ANTONIO (incl. Bexar County) (1922); 8434 Ahern Dr. (78216); Pres. Richard Goldsmith; Exec. Dir. Saul Silverman.

TYLER

*FEDERATION OF JEWISH WELFARE FUNDS (1938); P. O. Box 934 (75710); Pres. Ralph Davis.

WACO

JEWISH WELFARE COUNCIL OF WACO (1949); P. O. Box 8031 (76710); Pres. Eli Berkman.

UTAH

SALT LAKE CITY

UNITED JEWISH COUNCIL AND SALT LAKE JEWISH WELFARE FUND (1936); 2416 E. 1700 South (84108); Pres. Ralph Tannenbaum; Exec. Dir. Ernest Budwig.

VIRGINIA

NEWPORT NEWS

JEWISH FEDERATION OF NEWPORT NEWS —HAMPTON, INC. (1942); 2700 Spring Rd. (23606); P. O. Box 6680; Pres. Joe Frank; Exec. Dir. Jay Rostov.

NORFOLK

UNITED JEWISH FEDERATION, INC. OF NORFOLK AND VIRGINIA BEACH, VA. (1937); 7300 Newport Ave., P. O. Box 9776 (23505); Pres. Marvin Simon; Exec. Dir. Michael D. Fischer.

PORTSMOUTH

PORTSMOUTH JEWISH COMMUNITY COUNCIL (1919); Rm. 430, Dominion Nat'l Bank Bldg. (23704); Pres. Mrs. Joseph Ginsburg; Exec. Dir. Jeremy S. Neimand.

RICHMOND

JEWISH COMMUNITY COUNCIL (1935); 5403 Monument Ave., P. O. Box 8237 (23226); Pres. Hortense B. Wolf; Exec. Dir. Julius Mintzer.

ROANOKE

JEWISH COMMUNITY COUNCIL; 2728 Colonial Ave., S.W. (24015); Chmn. Arnold P. Masinter.

WASHINGTON

SEATTLE

JEWISH FEDERATION OF GREATER SEATTLE (incl. King County, Everett and Bremerton) (1926); Suite 525, Securities Bldg. (98101); Pres. Martin Rind; Exec. Dir. Murray Shiff.

SPOKANE

*JEWISH COMMUNITY COUNCIL OF SPOKANE (incl. Spokane County) (1927); (sponsors UNITED JEWISH FUND) (1936); 401 Paulsen Bldg. (99021); Pres. Samuel Huppin; Sec. Robert N. Arick.

WEST VIRGINIA

CHARLESTON

FEDERATED JEWISH CHARITIES OF CHARLESTON, INC. (1937); P. O. Box 1613 (25326); Pres. Robert Levine; Exec. Sec. Charles Cohen.

HUNTINGTON

FEDERATED JEWISH CHARITIES (1939); P. O. Box 947 (25713); Pres. William H. Glick; Sec. Andrew Katz.

WHEELING

UNITED JEWISH FEDERATION OF OHIO VALLEY, INC. (1933); 20 Hawthorne Court (26003); Pres. Dr. Harold Saferstein.

WISCONSIN

APPLETON

UNITED JEWISH CHARITIES OF APPLETON (1963); 3131 N. Meade St. (54911); Co-Chmn. Arnold Cohodas and Dov Edelstein; Treas. Mrs. Harold Rusky.

GREEN BAY

GREEN BAY JEWISH WELFARE FUND; P. O. Box 335 (54305); Pres. Stuart Milson; Treas. Herman J. Robitshek.

KENOSHA

KENOSHA JEWISH WELFARE FUND (1938); 6537–7th Ave. (53140); Pres. Charles Selsberg; Sec.-Treas. Mrs. S. M. Lapp.

MADISON

MADISON JEWISH COMMUNITY COUNCIL, INC. (1940); 303 Price Pl. (53705); Pres. Isadore V. Fine; Exec. Dir. Robert Gast.

MILWAUKEE

MILWAUKEE JEWISH FEDERATION, INC. (1938); 1360 N. Prospect Ave. (53202); Pres. Gerald J. Kahn; Exec. V. Pres. Melvin S. Zaret.

RACINE

RACINE JEWISH WELFARE BOARD (1946); 944 Main St. (53403); Pres. Jess Levin; Exec. Sec. Betty Goldberg.

SHEBOYGAN

JEWISH WELFARE COUNCIL OF SHEBOYGAN (1927); 1404 North Ave. (53081); Sec. Mrs. Abe Alpert.

CANADA

ALBERTA

CALGARY

CALGARY JEWISH COMMUNITY COUNCIL (1962); 102-18th Ave., S.E. (T2G 1K8); Pres. S. Bruce Green; Exec. Dir. Harry S. Shatz.

EDMONTON

EDMONTON JEWISH COMMUNITY COUNCIL, INC. (1954; Inc. 1965); 7200-156 St. (T5R 1X3); Pres. Mrs. Leon Singer; Exec. Dir. Gerald Rubin.

BRITISH COLUMBIA

VANCOUVER

*JEWISH COMMUNITY FUND & COUNCIL OF VANCOUVER (1932); 950 W. 41 Ave. (V5Z 2N7); Pres. Irvine E. Epstein; Exec. Dir. Morris Saltzman.

MANITOBA

WINNIPEG

WINNIPEG JEWISH COMMUNITY COUNCIL (incl. Combined Jewish Appeal of Winnipeg) (org. 1938, reorg. 1973); 370 Hargrave St., (R3B 2K1); Pres. Al Omson; Exec. Dir. Izzy Peltz.

ONTARIO

HAMILTON

HAMILTON JEWISH FEDERATION (incl. United Jewish Welfare Fund) (org. 1934, merged 1971); 57 Delaware Ave. (L8M 1T6); Pres. Bernard Greenbaum; Exec. Dir. Samuel Soifer.

LONDON

*LONDON JEWISH COMMUNITY COUNCIL (1932); 532 Huron St. (24), (N5Y 4J5); Pres. Gerald Klein; Exec. Dir. Lily Feldman.

OTTAWA

JEWISH COMMUNITY COUNCIL OF OTTAWA (1934); 151 Chapel St. (K1N 7Y2); Pres. Gilbert Greenberg; Exec. V.Pres. Hy Hochberg.

ST. CATHARINES

*UNITED JEWISH WELFARE FUND OF ST. CATHARINES; c/o Jewish Community Centre, Church St.; Pres. Jack Silverstein; Sec. Syd Goldford.

TORONTO

UNITED JEWISH CONGRESS (1937); 150 Beverley St. (M5T 1Y6); Pres. Rose Wolfe; Exec. Dir. Irwin Gold.

WINDSOR

JEWISH COMMUNITY COUNCIL (1938); 1641 Ouellette Ave. (N8X 1K9); Pres. Herbert Brudner; Exec. Dir. Joseph Eisenberg.

QUEBEC

MONTREAL

ALLIED JEWISH COMMUNITY SERVICES (merger of FEDERATION OF JEWISH COMMUNITY SERVICES AND COMBINED JEWISH APPEAL) (1965); 5151 Cote St. Catherine Rd. (H3W 1M6); Pres. Hillel B. Becker; Exec. V.Pres. Manuel G. Batshaw.

Jewish Periodicals[1]

UNITED STATES

ALABAMA

CONTEMPORARY JEWRY (1974 under the name Jewish Sociology and Social Research). Dept. of Sociology, Univ. of Alabama, Birmingham, 35294. Murray B. Binderman. Semi-annually. Assn. for the Sociological Study of Jewry.

JEWISH MONITOR (1948). P. O. Box 491, Tuscaloosa, 35401. Lynn G. Rosemore. Monthly.

ALASKA

*THE ALASKAN JEWISH BULLETIN (1973). 7-730 H, "J" St., Anchorage, 99506. Rabbi Israel Haber. Monthly.

ARIZONA

ARIZONA POST (1946). 102 N. Plumer Ave., Tucson, 85719. Martha K. Rothman. Bimonthly. Tucson Jewish Community Council.

PHOENIX JEWISH NEWS (1947). 1530 West Thomas Rd., Phoenix, 85015. Pearl R. Newmark. Biweekly.

CALIFORNIA

B'NAI B'RITH MESSENGER (1897). 2510 W. 7 St., Los Angeles, 90057. Joseph J. Cummins. Weekly.

HERITAGE-SOUTHWEST JEWISH PRESS (1954). 2130 S. Vermont Ave., Los Angeles, 90007. Weekly. Herb Brin. (Also SAN DIEGO JEWISH PRESS-HERITAGE, San Diego [weekly]; CENTRAL CALIFORNIA JEWISH HERITAGE, Sacramento and Fresno area [monthly]; ORANGE COUNTY JEWISH HERITAGE, Orange County area [weekly].)

ISRAEL TODAY (1973). 10340½ Reseda Blvd., Northridge, 91326. Phil Blazer. Biweekly.

JEWISH OBSERVER OF THE EAST BAY (1967). 3245 Sheffield Ave., Oakland, 94602. Bernice Scharlach. Monthly. Jewish Welfare Federation of Alameda & Contra Costa Counties.

JEWISH SPECTATOR (1935). P.O. Box 2016, Santa Monica, 90406. Trude Weiss-Rosmarin. Quarterly.

JEWISH STAR (1956). 693 Mission St. #305, San Francisco, 94105. Alfred Berger. Monthly.

SAN FRANCISCO JEWISH BULLETIN (1943). 870 Market St., San Francisco, 94102. Geoffrey Fisher. Weekly. San Francisco Jewish Community Publications.

WESTERN STATES JEWISH HISTORICAL QUARTERLY (1968). 2429 23rd St., Santa

---

[1]Information in this directory is based upon answers furnished by the publications themselves, and the publishers of the YEAR BOOK assume no responsibility for the accuracy of the data presented; nor does inclusion in this list necessarily imply approval or endorsement of the periodicals. The information provided here includes the year of organization and the name of the editor, managing editor, or publisher; unless otherwise stated, the language used by the periodical is English. An asterisk (*) indicates that no reply was received and that the information, including name of publication, date of founding, and address, is reprinted from AJYB, 1978 (Vol. 78). For organizational bulletins, consult organizational listings.

Monica, 90405. Dr. Norton B. Stern. Quarterly. Southern California Jewish Historical Society.

COLORADO

INTERMOUNTAIN JEWISH NEWS (1913). 1275 Sherman St., Denver, 80203. Mrs. Max Goldberg. Weekly.

CONNECTICUT

CONNECTICUT JEWISH LEDGER (1929). P.O. Box 1923, Hartford, 06101. Berthold Gaster. Weekly.

JEWISH DIGEST (1955). 1363 Fairfield Ave., Bridgeport, 06605. Bernard Postal. Monthly.

DELAWARE

JEWISH VOICE (1967). 701 Shipley St., Wilmington, 19801. Ruth J. Kaplan. Bimonthly. Jewish Federation of Delaware.

DISTRICT OF COLUMBIA

AMERICAN JEWISH JOURNAL (1944). 890 National Press Bldg., Washington, 20045. David Mondzac. Quarterly.

JEWISH VETERAN (1896). 1712 New Hampshire Ave., N.W., Washington, 20009. Judy Sternberg. Bimonthly. Jewish War Veterans of the U.S.A.

NATIONAL JEWISH MONTHLY (1886 under the name Menorah). 1640 Rhode Island Ave., N.W., Washington, 20036. Charles Fenyvesi. Monthly. B'nai B'rith.

NEAR EAST REPORT (1957). 444 North Capitol St., N.W., Washington, 20001. Alan M. Tigay. Weekly. Near East Research, Inc.

FLORIDA

JEWISH FLORIDIAN (1927). P.O. Box 012973, Miami, 33101. Fred K. Shochet. Weekly.

SOUTHERN JEWISH WEEKLY (1924). P.O. Box 3297, Jacksonville, 32206. Isadore Moscovitz. Weekly.

GEORGIA

SOUTHERN ISRAELITE (1925). P.O. Box 77388, 188–15 St. N.W., Atlanta, 30357. Jack Geldbart. Weekly.

ILLINOIS

CHICAGO JEWISH POST AND OPINION (1953). 6350 N. Albany, Chicago, 60659. Theodore Cohen. Weekly.

SENTINEL (1911). 323 S. Franklin St., Chicago, 60606. J. I. Fishbein. Weekly.

SOUTHERN ILLINOIS JEWISH COMMUNITY NEWS (1945). 6464 West Main, Suite 7A, Belleville, 62223. Hyman H. Ruffman. Monthly. Jewish Federation of Southern Illinois.

THE TORCH (1941). 1946 W. Hood, Chicago, 60660 Mannye London. Quarterly. Natl. Fed. of Jewish Men's Clubs, Inc.

INDIANA

INDIANA JEWISH POST AND OPINION (1935). 611 N. Park Ave., Indianapolis, 46204. Jo Ann Pinkowitz. Weekly.

JEWISH POST AND OPINION. 611 N. Park Ave., Indianapolis, 46204. Gabriel Cohen.

KENTUCKY

KENTUCKY JEWISH POST AND OPINION (1931). 1551 Bardstown Rd., Louisville, 40205. Gail Tolpin. Weekly.

LOUISIANA

THE JEWISH CIVIC PRESS (1965). P.O. Box 15500, New Orleans, 70175. Abner Tritt. Monthly.

JEWISH TIMES (1974). 211 Camp St., Suite 500, New Orleans, 70130. Peter M. Zollman. Biweekly.

MARYLAND

BALTIMORE JEWISH TIMES (1919). 2104 N. Charles St., Baltimore, 21218. Gary Rosenblatt. Weekly.

JEWISH WEEK (1965). 8630 Fenton St., Suite 611, Silver Spring, 20910. Joseph M. Hochstein. Weekly.

MASSACHUSETTS

AMERICAN JEWISH HISTORICAL QUARTERLY (1893). 2 Thornton Road, Waltham, 02154. Nathan M. Kaganoff. Quarterly. American Jewish Historical Society.

JEWISH ADVOCATE (1902). 251 Causeway St., Boston, 02114. Joseph G. Weisberg, Alexander Brin. Weekly.

*JEWISH CIVIC LEADER (1926). 340 Main St., Suite 374, Worcester, 01608. Harriet C. Israel. Weekly.

JEWISH REPORTER (1970). 1000 Worcester Road, Framingham, 01701. Howard G. Joress. Monthly. Greater Framingham Jewish Federation.

JEWISH TIMES (1945). 118 Cypress St., Brookline, 02146. Ann Kostant. Weekly.

JEWISH WEEKLY NEWS (1945). P.O. Box 1569, Springfield, 01101. Leslie B. Kahn. Weekly.

MOMENT (1975). 55 Chapel St., Newton, 02160. Leonard Fein. Monthly except Jan.-Feb., July-August.

MICHIGAN

DETROIT JEWISH NEWS (1942). 17515 W. 9 Mile Rd., Suite 865, Southfield, 48075. Philip Slomovitz. Weekly.

MICHIGAN JEWISH HISTORY (1960). 163 Madison, Detroit, 48237. Irving I. Edgar. Semi-annual. Jewish Historical Society of Michigan.

MINNESOTA

AMERICAN JEWISH WORLD (1912). 9 N. 4th St., Minneapolis, 55401. Norman Gold. Weekly.

MISSOURI

KANSAS CITY JEWISH CHRONICLE (1920). P.O. Box 8709, Kansas City, 64114. Milton Firestone. Weekly.

MISSOURI JEWISH POST AND OPINION (1948). 8235 Olive St., St. Louis, 63132. Kathie Sutin. Weekly.

ST. LOUIS JEWISH LIGHT (1947). 611 Olive St., Room 1541, St. Louis, 63101. Robert A. Cohn. Biweekly. Jewish Federation of St. Louis.

NEBRASKA

JEWISH PRESS (1921). 333 S. 132 St., Omaha, 68154. Morris Maline. Weekly. Jewish Federation of Omaha.

NEVADA

JEWISH REPORTER (1976). 846 E. Sahara Ave., Las Vegas, 89104. Jerry Countess. Monthly. Las Vegas Combined Jewish Appeal.

LAS VEGAS ISRAELITE (1965). P.O. Box 14096, Las Vegas, 89114. Jack Tell. Weekly.

NEW JERSEY

JEWISH COMMUNITY NEWS (1962). Green Lane, Union, 07083. Esther Blaustein. Fortnightly (monthly in July and August).

JEWISH JOURNAL (1956). 2 S. Adelaide Ave., Highland Park, 08904. Clifford B. Ross. Biweekly. Jewish Federation of Raritan Valley.

JEWISH NEWS (1947). 60 Glenwood Ave., East Orange, 07017. Harry Weingast. Weekly. Jewish Community Federation of Metropolitan New Jersey.

JEWISH RECORD (1939). 1537 Atlantic Ave., Atlantic City, 08401. Martin Korik. Weekly.

JEWISH STANDARD (1931). 40 Journal Sq., Jersey City, 07306. Morris J. Janoff. Weekly.

JEWISH VOICE (1975). Lord St., Avenel, 07001. Herb Rosen. Monthly. Northern Middlesex County Jewish Federation.

MORRIS/SUSSEX JEWISH NEWS (1972). 500 Route 10, Ledgewood, 07852. Rhoda Hasson. Monthly. United Jewish Federation Morris/Sussex.

VOICE (1941). 2393 W. Marlton Pike, Cherry Hill, 08002. Benn Friedman. Biweekly. Jewish Federation of Southern N.J.

NEW YORK

ALBANY JEWISH WORLD (1965). 416 Smith St., Schenectady, 12305. Sam S. Clevenson. Weekly.

BUFFALO JEWISH REVIEW (1918). 110 Pearl St., Buffalo, 14202. Steve Lipman. Weekly. Kahaal Nahalot Israel.

JEWISH CURRENT EVENTS (1959). 430 Keller Ave., Elmont, L.I., 11003. Samuel Deutsch. Biweekly.

*JEWISH LEDGER (1924). 721 Monroe Ave., Rochester, 14607. Donald Wolin. Weekly.

JEWISH WORLD OF LONG ISLAND (1971). 1029 Brighton Beach Ave., Brooklyn, 11230. Adina Michaeli. Biweekly.

REPORTER. 500 Clubhouse Rd., Binghamton, 13903. Hal Smith. Weekly. Jewish Federation of Broome County.

SH'MA (1970). Box 567, Port Washington, N.Y., 11050. Eugene B. Borowitz. Biweekly (except June, July, Aug.).

NEW YORK CITY

AFN SHVEL (1941). 200 W. 72 St., 10023. Editorial board. Quarterly. Yiddish. Freeland League.

ALGEMEINER JOURNAL (1972). 404 Park Ave., So., 10016. Gershon Jacobson. Weekly. Yiddish.

AMERICAN JEWISH YEAR BOOK (1899). 165 E. 56 St., 10022. Morris Fine, Milton Himmelfarb. Annual. American Jewish Committee and Jewish Publication Society.

AMERICAN MIZRACHI WOMAN (1925). 817 Broadway, 10003. Agatha Leifer. Irregular. English Mizrachi Women's Organization of America.

AMERICAN ZIONIST (1910). 4 E. 34 St., 10016. Elias Cooper. Monthly (except July and August). Zionist Organization of America.

AUFBAU (1934). 2121 Broadway, 10023. Hans Steinitz. Weekly. English-German. New World Club, Inc.

BITZARON (1939). 1141 Broadway, 10001. Hayim Leaf. Monthly. Hebrew. Hebrew Literary Foundation.

B'NAI YIDDISH (1968). 41 Union Sq., 10003. Itzik Kozlovsky. Bimonthly. English-Yiddish.

BOOKS IN REVIEW (1945). 15 E. 26 St., 10010. Sharon M. Strassfeld. Bimonthly. Jewish Book Council.

COMMENTARY (1945). 165 E. 56 St., 10022. Norman Podhoretz. Monthly. American Jewish Committee.

CONGRESS MONTHLY (1934). 15 E. 84 St., 10028. Herbert Poster. Monthly (except July and August). American Jewish Congress.

CONSERVATIVE JUDAISM (1945). 3080 Broadway, 10027. Myron M. Fenster. Quarterly. Rabbinical Assembly and Jewish Theological Seminary of America.

ECONOMIC HORIZONS (1953). 500 Fifth Ave., N.Y.C. 10036. Phil Opher. Quarterly. American-Israel Chamber of Commerce and Industry, Inc.

FREIE ARBEITER STIMME (1890). 33 Union Square W., 10003. P. Costan. Monthly. Yiddish. Free Voice of Labor.

HADASSAH MAGAZINE (formerly HADASSAH NEWSLETTER; 1921). 50 W. 58 St., 10019. Jesse Zel Lurie. Monthly (except June-July and Aug.-Sept.). Hadassah, Women's Zionist Organization of America.

HADAROM (1957). 1250 Broadway, 10001. Charles B. Chavel. Semiannual. Hebrew. Rabbinical Council of America, Inc.

HADOAR (1921). 1841 Broadway, 10023. Itzhak Ivry. Weekly. Hebrew. Histadruth Ivrith of America.

HISTADRUT FOTO-NEWS (1948). 33 E. 67 St., 10021. Nahum Guttman. Bimonthly. National Committee for Labor Israel.

IMPACT (1942 under the name of Synagogue School). 155 Fifth Ave., 10010. Morton Siegel. Quarterly. English-Hebrew. United Synagogue Commission on Jewish Education.

U INSTITUTIONAL AND INDUSTRIAL KOSHER PRODUCTS DIRECTORY (1967). 116 E. 27 St., 10016. Berel Wein, Admin. Irregular. Union of Orthodox Jewish Congregations of America.

ISRAEL HORIZONS (1952). 150 Fifth Ave., 10011. Richard Yaffe. Monthly (except July-August). Americans for Progressive Israel—Hashomer Hatzair.

JEWISH ACTION (1950). 116 East 27 St., 10016. Yaakov Kornreich. Bimonthly. Union of Orthodox Jewish Congregations of America.

JEWISH BOOK ANNUAL (1942). 15 East 26th St., 10010. Jacob Kabakoff. Annual. English-Hebrew-Yiddish. Jewish Book Council of the National Jewish Welfare Board.

JEWISH BRAILLE REVIEW (1931). 110 E. 30 St., 10016. Jacob Freid. Monthly. English-Braille. Jewish Braille Institute of America, Inc.

JEWISH CURRENTS (1946). 22 E. 17 St., 10003. Morris U. Schappes. Monthly.

JEWISH DAILY FORWARD (1897). 45 E. 33 St., 10016. Simon Weber. Daily. Yiddish. Forward Association, Inc.

JEWISH EDUCATION (1928). 114 Fifth Ave., 10011. Alvin I. Schiff. Quarterly. National Council for Jewish Education.

JEWISH EDUCATION DIRECTORY (1951). 114 Fifth Ave., 10011. Murray Rockowitz. Triannual. American Association for Jewish Education.

JEWISH EDUCATION NEWS (1939), 114 Fifth Ave., 10011. Gary Gobetz. Irregular. American Assn. for Jewish Education.

JEWISH FRONTIER (1934). 575 6th Ave., 10011. Judah J. Shapiro. Monthly. Labor Zionist Letters, Inc.

JEWISH GUARDIAN (1974). G.P.O. Box 2143, Brooklyn, 11202. Pinchus David. Quarterly. Neturei Karta of U.S.A.

JEWISH JOURNAL (1970). 16 Court St., Brooklyn, 11241. Earl Foreman. Weekly.

JEWISH LIFE (1946). 116 E. 27 St., 10016. Yaakov Jacobs. Quarterly. Union of Orthodox Jewish Congregations of America.

JEWISH MUSIC NOTES (1945). 15 E. 26 St., 10010. Irene Heskes. Semiannual. JWB Jewish Music Council.

JEWISH OBSERVER (1963). 5 Beekman St., 10038. Nisson Wolpin. Monthly (except July and August). Agudath Israel of America.

JEWISH POST OF NEW YORK. (1974). 101 Fifth Ave., 10003. Charles Roth. Weekly.

JEWISH PRESS (1950). 338 3rd Ave., Brooklyn, 11215. Sholom Klass. Weekly.

JEWISH SOCIAL STUDIES (1939). 250 W. 57 St., 10019. Tobey B. Gitelle. Quarterly. Conference on Jewish Social Studies, Inc.

JEWISH TELEGRAPHIC AGENCY COMMUNITY NEWS REPORTER (1962). 165 W. 46 St., Rm. 511, 10036. Murray Zuckoff. Weekly.

JEWISH TELEGRAPHIC AGENCY DAILY NEWS BULLETIN (1917). 165 W. 46 St., Rm. 511, 10036. Murray Zuckoff. Daily.

JEWISH TELEGRAPHIC AGENCY WEEKLY NEWS DIGEST (1933). 165 W. 46 St., Rm. 511, 10036. Murray Zuckoff. Weekly.

JEWISH WEEK (1876, reorg. 1970). 1 Park Ave., 10016. Philip Hochstein. Weekly.

JWB CIRCLE (1946). 15 E. 26 St., 10010. Lionel Koppman. Bimonthly. JWB.

JOURNAL OF JEWISH COMMUNAL SERVICE (1899). 15 E. 26 St., 10010. Sanford N. Sherman. Quarterly. The Conference of Jewish Communal Service.

JOURNAL OF REFORM JUDAISM. 790 Madison Ave., 10021. Bernard Martin. Quarterly. Central Conference of American Rabbis.

JUDAISM (1952). 15 E. 84 St., 10028. Robert Gordis. Quarterly. American Jewish Congress.

KINDER JOURNAL (1920). 3301 Bainbridge Ave., Bronx, N.Y., 10467. Bella Gottesman. Quarterly. Yiddish. Sholem Aleichem Folk Institute, Inc.

KINDER ZEITUNG (1930). 45 E. 33 St., 10016 Joseph Mlotek, Saul Maltz, Mates Olitzky. Bimonthly. English-Yiddish. Workmen's Circle.

KOL YAVNEH (1960). 156 Fifth Ave., 10010. Roslyn M. Sherman. Bimonthly. Yavneh, National Religious Jewish Students Association.

U KOSHER PRODUCTS DIRECTORY (1925). 116 E. 27 St., 10016. Berel Wein, Admin. Irregular. Union of Orthodox Jewish Congregations of America—Kashruth Div.

KULTUR UN LEBN—CULTURE AND LIFE (1967). 45 E. 33 St., 10016. Joseph Mlotek. Quarterly. Yiddish. Workmen's Circle.

LILITH (1976). 250 W. 57 St., 10019. Susan Weidman Schneider. Quarterly.

LONG ISLAND JEWISH PRESS (1942). 95-20 63 Rd., Rego Park, 11374. Abraham B. Shoulson. Monthly.

MIDSTREAM (1955). 515 Park Ave., 10022. Joel Carmichael. Monthly. Theodor Herzl Foundation.

MORNING FREIHEIT (1922). 22 W. 21 St., 10010. Paul Novick. Daily. Yiddish-English.

U NEWS REPORTER (1956). 116 E. 27 St., 10016. Berel Wein, Admin. Irregular. Union of Orthodox Jewish Congregations of America—Kashruth Div.

OLOMEINU—OUR WORLD (1945). 229 Park Ave. S., 10003. Nosson Scherman, Yaakov Fruchter. Monthly. English-Hebrew. Torah Umesorah National Society for Hebrew Day Schools.

U PASSOVER PRODUCTS DIRECTORY (1923). 116 E. 27 St., 10016. Berel Wein, Admin. Annual. Union of Orthodox Jewish Congregations of America—Kashruth Div.

PEDAGOGIC REPORTER (1949). 114 Fifth Ave., 10011. Mordecai H. Lewittes. Three times yearly. American Association for Jewish Education.

PIONEER WOMAN (1926). 315 Fifth Ave., 10016. David C. Gross, Judith A. Sokoloff. Bimonthly. English-Yiddish-Hebrew. Pioneer Women, Women's Labor Zionist Organization of America.

PRESENT TENSE (1973). 165 E. 56 St., 10022. Murray Polner. Quarterly. American Jewish Committee.

PROCEEDINGS OF THE AMERICAN ACADEMY FOR JEWISH RESEARCH (1920). 3080 Broadway, 10027. Isaac E. Barzilay. Annual. Hebrew, Arabic and English. American Academy for Jewish Research.

RABBINICAL COUNCIL RECORD (1953). 1250 Broadway, 10001. Louis Bernstein. Quarterly. Rabbinical Council of America.

RECONSTRUCTIONIST (1935). 432 Park Ave. South, 10016. Ira Eisenstein. Monthly (Sept.-June). Jewish Reconstructionist Foundation, Inc.

REFORM JUDAISM (1972; formerly Dimensions in American Judaism). 838 Fifth Ave., 10021. Aron Hirt-Manheimer. Monthly (Sept.-May, except Dec.). Union of American Hebrew Congregations.

RESPONSE (1967). 523 W. 113 St., 10025. Editorial board. Irregular. Jewish Educational Ventures, Inc.

SEVEN ARTS FEATURE SYNDICATE. See *News Syndicates.* p. (364).

SHEVILEY HAHINUCH (1939). 114 Fifth Ave., 10011. Matthew Mosenkis. Quarterly. Hebrew. National Council for Jewish Education.

SHMUESSEN MIT KINDER UN YUGENT (1942). 770 Eastern Parkway, Brooklyn, 11213. Nissan Mindel. Monthly. Yiddish. Merkos L'Inyonei Chinuch, Inc.

SHOAH (1978, 250 W. 57 St., 10019. Jane Gerber. Quarterly. National Jewish Conference Center and University of Bridgeport.

SYNAGOGUE LIGHT (1933). 47 Beekman St., 10038. Meyer Hager. Bimonthly. Union of Chassidic Rabbis.

TALKS AND TALES (1942). 770 Eastern Parkway, Brooklyn, 11213. Nissan Mindel. Monthly (also Hebrew, French and Spanish editions). Merkos L'Inyonei Chinuch, Inc.

TRADITION (1958). 1250 Broadway, Suite 802, 10001. Walter S. Wurzburger. Quarterly. Rabbinical Council of America.

*UJ HORIZONT (1969). P.O. Box 625, Far Rockaway, 11691. M.D. Weinstock. Monthly. Hungarian.

UNITED SYNAGOGUE REVIEW (1943). 155 Fifth Ave., 10010. Alvin Kass. Quarterly. United Synagogue of America.

UNSER TSAIT (1941). 25 E. 78 St., 10021. Jacob S. Hertz. Monthly. Yiddish. International Jewish Labor Bund.

DER WECKER (1921). 45 E. 33 St., 10016. Elias Schulman. Nine times a year. Yiddish. Jewish Socialist Verband of America.

WESTCHESTER JEWISH TRIBUNE (1942). 95-20 63 Rd., Rego Park, 11374. Abraham B. Shoulson. Monthly.

WOMEN'S AMERICAN ORT REPORTER (1966). 1250 Broadway, 10001. Elie Faust-Lévy. Bimonthly. Women's American ORT.

WOMEN'S LEAGUE OUTLOOK (1930). 48 E. 74 St., 10021. Mrs. Harry I. Kiesler. Quarterly. Women's League for Conservative Judaism.

WORKMEN'S CIRCLE CALL (1932). 45 E. 33 St., 10016. William Stern. Quarterly. Workmen's Circle.

WORLD OVER (1940). 426 W. 58 St., 10019. Stephen Schaffzin. Biweekly (October-May). Board of Jewish Education, Inc.

YAVNEH REVIEW (1963). 156 Fifth Ave., 10010. Shalom Carmy. Annual. Yavneh, National Religious Jewish Students Association.

YEARBOOK OF THE CENTRAL CONFERENCE OF AMERICAN RABBIS (1890). 790 Madison Ave., 10021. Elliot L. Stevens. Annual. Central Conference of American Rabbis.

YIDDISH (1973). Queens College, Acad. 1309, Flushing, N.Y., 11367. Joseph C. Landis. Quarterly. Queens College Press.

DI YIDDISHE HEIM (1958). 770 Eastern Parkway, Bklyn., 11213. Mrs. Rachel Altein. Quarterly. English-Yiddish. Agudas Nshei Ub'nos Chabad.

YIDDISHE KULTUR (1938). 853 Broadway. 10003. I. Goldberg. Monthly (except June-July, Aug.-Sept.). Yiddish. Yiddisher Kultur Farband, Inc.—YKUF.

DOS YIDDISHE VORT (1953). 5 Beekman St., 10038. Joseph Friedenson. Monthly. Yiddish. Agudath Israel of America.

YIDDISHER KEMFER (1906). 575 Sixth Ave., 10011. Mordechai Strigler. Weekly. Yiddish. Labor Zionist Letters, Inc.

YIDISHE SHPRAKH (1941). 1048 Fifth Ave., 10028. Mordkhe Schaechter. Three times a year. Yiddish. Yivo Institute for Jewish Research, Inc.

YIVO ANNUAL OF JEWISH SOCIAL SCIENCE (1946). 1048 Fifth Ave., 10028. David Roskies. Biannually. Yivo Institute for Jewish Research, Inc.

YIVO BLETER (1931). 1048 Fifth Ave., 10028. Joshua Fishman. Biannually. Yiddish. Yivo Institute for Jewish Research, Inc.

YOUNG ISRAEL VIEWPOINT (1952). 3 W. 16 St., 10011. C.H. Rosen. Monthly (except July, August). National Council of Young Israel.

YOUNG JUDAEAN (1912). 817 Broadway, 10003. Barbara Gingold. Monthly (Nov.-June). Hadassah Zionist Youth Commission.

YOUTH AND NATION (1934). 150 Fifth Ave., 10011. Danny Shapiro. Quarterly. Hashomer Hatzair Zionist Youth Movement.

YUGNTRUF (1964). 3328 Bainbridge Ave., Bx., 10467. Gitl Schaechter. Quarterly. Yiddish. Yugntruf Youth for Yiddish.

ZUKUNFT (1892). 25 E. 78 St., 10021. Hyman Bass, Moshe Crystal, I. Hirshaut. Monthly (bimonthly May-Aug.). Yiddish. Congress for Jewish Culture and CYCO.

NORTH CAROLINA

AMERICAN JEWISH TIMES—OUTLOOK (1934; reorg. 1950). P.O. Box 10674, Charlotte, 28234. Ronald Unger. Monthly.

OHIO

THE AMERICAN ISRAELITE (1954). 906 Main St., Cincinnati, 54202. Henry C. Segal. Weekly.

AMERICAN JEWISH ARCHIVES (1947). 3101 Clifton Ave., Cincinnati, 45220. Jacob R. Marcus, Abraham J. Peck. Semiannually. American Jewish Archives of Hebrew Union College-Jewish Institute of Religion.

CLEVELAND JEWISH NEWS (1964). 3637 Bendemeer Road., Cleveland, 44118. Jerry D. Barach. Weekly.

DAYTON JEWISH CHRONICLE (1961). 118 Salem Ave., Dayton, 45406. Anne M. Hammerman. Weekly.

HEBREW UNION COLLEGE ANNUAL (1924). 3101 Clifton Ave., Cincinnati, 45220. Sheldon H. Blank. Annual. English, Hebrew, French and German. Hebrew Union College-Jewish Institute of Religion.

INDEX TO JEWISH PERIODICALS (1963). P.O. Box 18570, Cleveland Hts., 44118. Jean H. Foxman, Miriam Leikind, Bess Rosenfeld. Semiannually.

OHIO JEWISH CHRONICLE (1921). 2831 E. Main St., Columbus, 43209. Milton J. Pinsky. Weekly.

STARK JEWISH NEWS (1920). P.O. Box 9120, Canton, 44711. David F. Leopold. Monthly.

STUDIES IN BIBLIOGRAPHY AND BOOKLORE (1953). 3101 Clifton Ave., Cincinnati,

45220. Herbert C. Zafren. Irregular. English-Hebrew-German. Library of Hebrew Union College—Jewish Institute of Religion.

TOLEDO JEWISH NEWS (1951). 2506 Evergreen St., Toledo, 43606. Burt Silverman. Monthly. Jewish Welfare Federation.

YOUNGSTOWN JEWISH TIMES (1935). P.O. Box 777, Youngstown, 44501. Harry Alter. Fortnightly.

OKLAHOMA

SOUTHWEST JEWISH CHRONICLE (1929). 324 N. Robinson St., Rm. 313, Oklahoma City, 73102. E. F. Friedman. Quarterly.

*TULSA JEWISH REVIEW (1930). 2205 E. 51 St., Tulsa, 74105. Ann R. Fellows. Monthly. Tulsa Section, National Council of Jewish Women.

PENNSYLVANIA

JEWISH CHRONICLE OF PITTSBURGH (1962). 315 S. Bellefield Ave., Pittsburgh, 15213. Albert W. Bloom. Weekly. Pittsburgh Jewish Publication and Education Foundation.

JEWISH EXPONENT (1887). 226 S. 16 St., Philadelphia, 19102. Frank F. Wundohl. Weekly. Federation of Jewish Agencies of Greater Philadelphia.

JEWISH QUARTERLY REVIEW (1910). Broad and York Sts., Philadelphia, 19132. Abraham I. Katsh. Quarterly. Dropsie University.

*JEWISH TIMES OF THE GREATER NORTHEAST. (1925). 2417 Welsh Road, Philadelphia, 19116. Leon E. Brown. Weekly.

RHODE ISLAND

RHODE ISLAND JEWISH HISTORICAL NOTES (1954). 130 Sessions St., Providence, 02906. Seebert J. Goldowsky. Annual. Rhode Island Jewish Historical Assn.

TENNESSEE

HEBREW WATCHMAN (1925). 227 Jefferson, Memphis, 38103. Herman I. Goldberger. Weekly.

OBSERVER (1934). Wilson Pike Circle, Brentwood, 37027. G. Hillel Barker. Biweekly.

TEXAS

JEWISH CIVIC PRESS (1971). P.O. Box 35656, Houston, 77035. Abner Tritt. Monthly.

JEWISH HERALD-VOICE (1908). P.O. Box 153, Houston, 77001. Joseph W. Samuels. Weekly.

TEXAS JEWISH POST (1947). P.O. Box 742, Fort Worth, 76101. 11333 N. Central Expressway, Dallas, 75243. Jimmy Wisch. Weekly.

VIRGINIA

UJF NEWS (1946). P.O. Box 9776, Norfolk, 23505. Paula S. Eisen. Weekly. United Jewish Federation of Norfolk and Virginia Beach.

WASHINGTON

JEWISH TRANSCRIPT (1924). Securities Building, Rm. 929, Seattle, 98101. Philip R. Scheier. Bimonthly. Jewish Federation & Council of Greater Seattle.

WISCONSIN

WISCONSIN JEWISH CHRONICLE (1921). 1360 N. Prospect Ave., Milwaukee, 53202. Richard B. Pearl. Weekly. Wisc. Jewish Publications Foundations, Inc.

NEWS SYNDICATES

JEWISH PRESS FEATURES (1970). 15 E. 26 St., Suite 1350, N.Y.C. 10010. Sue Berrin. Monthly. Jewish Student Press Service.

JEWISH TELEGRAPHIC AGENCY, INC. (1917). 165 W. 46 St., Rm. 511, N.Y.C., 10036. Murray Zuckoff. Daily.

SEVEN ARTS FEATURE SYNDICATE AND WORLD WIDE NEWS SERVICE (1923). 165 W. 46 St., Rm. 511, N.Y.C., 10036. John Kayston. Semi-weekly.

CANADA

BULLETIN DU CERCLE JUIF DE LANGUE FRANCAISE DU CONGRES JUIF CANADIEN (1952). 1590 McGregor Ave., Montreal, P.Q., H3G 1C5. M. Charles Dadouin. Bimonthly. French. Canadian Jewish Congress.

CANADIAN JEWISH NEWS (1960). 562 Eglinton Ave. E., Ste. 401, Toronto, Ont., M4P 1P1. Ralph Hyman. Weekly.

CANADIAN JEWISH OUTLOOK (1963). P.O. Box 65, Station B, Toronto, Ont., M5T 2T2. Editorial Board. Monthly.

CANADIAN JEWISH WEEKLY (VOCHENBLATT; formerly DER KAMPF, reorg. 1941). 430 King St. W., #209, Toronto, Ont., MV5 IL5. Joshua Gershman. Biweekly. Yiddish.

CANADIAN ZIONIST (1934). 1310 Greene Ave., Montreal, P.Q., H3Z 2B2. Dr. Leon Kronitz. Monthly (Sept.-June). Canadian Zionist Federation.

CHRONICLE REVIEW (1914). 4781 Van Horne, Montreal, P.Q., H3W 1J1. Arnold Ages. Monthly.

JEWISH DIALOG (1970). 501 Yonge St., Suite 13A, Toronto, Ont. M4Y 1Y4. Joe Rosenblatt. Quarterly.

JEWISH POST (1925). P.O. Box 3777, St. B, Winnipeg, Man., R2W 3R6. Martin Levin. Weekly.

JEWISH STANDARD (1929). Suite 507, 8 Colborne St., Toronto, Ont. M5E 1E1. Julius Hayman. Semi-monthly.

JEWISH WESTERN BULLETIN (1930). 3268 Heather St., Vancouver, V5Z 3K5, B.C. Samuel Kaplan. Weekly.

KANADER ADLER-JEWISH EAGLE (1907); 4180 De Courtrai, Suite 218, Montreal, PQ, H3S 1C3. M. Husid. Weekly. Yiddish. Combined Jewish Organizations of Montreal.

OTTAWA JEWISH BULLETIN & REVIEW (1946). 151 Chapel St., Ottawa, Ont., K1N 7Y2. Nancy Zalman. Biweekly. Jewish Community Council of Ottawa.

UNDZER VEG (1925). 272 Codsell Ave., Downsview, Ont., M3H 3R2. Joseph Kligman. Quarterly. Yiddish-English. Achdut HaAvoda-Poale Zion of Canada.

VIEWPOINTS (1966). 1590 McGregor St., Montreal, P.Q., H3W 1H2. Stanley M. Cohen. Quarterly. Canadian Jewish Congress.

WESTERN JEWISH NEWS (1925). P.O. Box 87, Winnipeg, Man., R3C 2G6. Pauline Essers. Weekly.

WINDSOR JEWISH COMMUNITY COUNCIL BULLETIN (1938). 1641 Ouellette Ave., Windsor, Ont., N8X 1K9. Joseph Eisenberg. Monthly. Windsor Jewish Community Council.

Necrology: United States[1]

ADELMAN, WILLIAM, administrator, communal worker; b. N.Y.C., Apr. 22, 1908; d. N.Y.C., July 12, 1977; exec. dir. Beth Abraham Hosp. since 1950; dir. extended care services, Montefiore Hosp.; mem. gov. bd., chmn. Long Term Care Com., Greater N.Y. Hosp. Assn.; mem. gov. bd. N.Y. Public Health Assn., Com. on Public Policy and Legislation; chmn. Citizens' Com. on Aging, Community Service Soc. of N.Y.; consultant, White House Conf. on Aging; mem. Health Com. on Chronic Diseases of N.Y.C. Health Dept.; mem. N.Y. State Senate Advisory Com. on Health; mem. Com. on Financing Continuing Health Care, Hosp. Assn. of N.Y. State; mem. Task Force on Nursing Home Code, N.Y. State Dept. of Social Welfare and N.Y.C. Dept. of Hospitals; past pres. Administrators Conf. of the Central Bureau for the Jewish Aged; v. chmn. Homes and Hospitals, Social Services, and Community and Health Services Divisions of UJA-Fed. of Jewish Philanthropies Joint Campaign; recipient: two awards from Fed. of Jewish Philanthropies for work among sick and needy; Israel and Leah Cummings Award from Fed. of Jewish Philanthropies Commission on Synagogue Relations, for service to the Jewish community; fellow: Amer. Public Health Assn., Gerontological Soc., and Royal Soc. of Health.

ARVEY, JACOB M., attorney, politician, philanthropist; b. Chicago, Ill., Nov. 3, 1895; d. Chicago, Ill., Aug. 25, 1977; Chicago Democratic Party leader; Asst. State Attorney of Cook County; Master of Chancery in Circuit Court of Cook County; Democratic natl. committeeman from Illinois; lt. col. U.S. Army, 1941–45; bd. mem.: Brandeis Univ., Mt. Sinai Hosp. of Miami, Louis A. Weiss Memorial Hosp.; contributor: Univ. of Chicago Research Fdn. for Emotionally Disturbed Children, Adlai E. Stevenson Memorial Fdn.; bd. mem. Natl. Fed. of Jewish Men's Clubs, Jewish Fed. of Metropolitan Chicago, Chicago and Miami Jewish Homes for the Aged; mem.: Amer. Friends of Hebrew Univ., Amer. Friends of Tel Aviv Univ., B'nai B'rith, UJA, Amer. ORT Fed., Jewish Welfare Bd., Jewish United Fund, Joint Distribution Com., Jewish Natl. Fund, Natl. Jewish Hosp. of Denver, Amer. Com. for the Weizmann Institute of Science, Amer. Israel Public Affairs Com., Jewish War Veterans, Assn. Talmud Torahs, Israel Publishing Institute, Encyclopedia Judaica Press, Aid Assn. for Incurable Orthodox Jews; special gifts chmn. Combined Jewish Appeal; hon. chmn. Chicago State of Israel Bonds Org.; hon. HDL, Hebrew Theological Coll.; recipient: award of merit, Decalogue Soc. of Lawyers, 1950; man-of-the-year award, Jewish Natl. Fund, 1957; bronze star, U.S. Legion of Merit, 1957; man-of-the-century award, Israel Bond Org., 1964.

---

[1]Including Jewish residents of the United States who died between January 1 and December 31, 1977.

ATLAS, SAMUEL, rabbi, educator, author, editor; b. Kamai, Lithuania, Dec. 5, 1899; d. Liberty, N.Y., July 27, 1977; in U.S. since 1942; lecturer in philosophy and Talmud, Institute of Jewish Studies, Warsaw, 1929–34, and Cambridge Univ., 1935–39; prof. Hebrew Union Coll. Jewish Institute of Religion, 1942–75; editor: *Novellae of Abraham ben David,* in Hebrew (1940); author: *Epistemological Foundations of History,* in German (1928); *To the Theory of Knowledge of Maimonides,* in Hebrew (1931); *The Philosophy of Maimonides and its Systematic Place in the History of Philosophy* (1936); *Rights of Private Property* (1944); *Legal Fictions in Talmudic Law,* in Hebrew (1945); *S. Maimon's Treatment of the Problem of Antimonies* (1948); *Maimon and Maimonides* (1952); *Maimon's Doctrine of Infinite Reason* (1952); *Solomon Maimon and Spinoza* (1952); *From Critical to Speculative Idealism, The Philosophy of Solomon Maimon* (1964); *Notes of Moses Ha-Kohen of Luxel on Maimonides' Code* (1969); articles on post-Kantian philosophical period for *Encyclopedia of Philosophy* (1967); article on the legal status of kings in Hebrew law (1968); designated prof. emeritus of philosophy and Talmud, Hebrew Union Coll., 1975.

BAUM, SHEPHARD Z., rabbi, attorney, communal leader; b. Memphis, Tenn., Sept. 20, 1903; d. N.Y.C., July 21, 1977; rabbi: Temple Ashkenazi, Cambridge, Mass., 1924–27; New Beth Israel Synagogue, Syracuse, N.Y., 1926–27; Sons of Abraham Temple, Albany, N.Y. 1927–34; chief supervisor, kosher law enforcement, N.Y. State, since 1934; capt., U.S. Chaplain Corps, 1943–45; pres. Bridge, Inc., since 1960; mem. N.Y. Jewish Conf.; pres. Albany Jewish Community Center, 1932–35; dir. Albany Community Chest, 1932–35; organizer and natl. dir. Amer. Jewish Congress, 1946–47; chmn. B'nai Zion-UJA; founder and bd. mem. Amer. Red Mogen David; mem. Rabbinical Alumni, Yeshiva Univ.; natl. v. pres. B'nai Zion; pres. Hebrew Welfare Agency; pres. upstate region, Union of Orthodox Jewish Congregations; served in high capacities in UJA and Israel Bonds.

BEN-AMI, JACOB, actor, director; b. Minsk, Russia, Dec. 23, 1890; d. N.Y.C., July 22, 1977; in U.S. since 1912; founded Jewish Art Theater, N.Y.C.; appeared in plays by Yiddish, American, British, and Russian playwrights on tours in Europe, South Africa, South America, and the U.S.; mem. Actors Equity; hon. mem. Hebrew Actors' Union.

BERMAN, MYRON, business exec., philanthropist, communal worker; b. (?), 1917; d. N.Y.C., Aug. 11, 1977; bd. chmn. Saxon Industries; mem. gov. bd. Hebrew Union Coll.; past pres. Riverdale Temple; active in Bonds for Israel, UJA, Fed. of Jewish Philanthropies, Natl. Conf. of Christians and Jews.

BLITMAN, CHARLES H., business exec., philanthropist; b. Nassau, N.Y., (?), 1894; d. N.Y.C., July 18, 1977; founded Blitman Construction Corp., 1922; responsible for construction of Custom House at World Trade Center and Journal Square Transportation Center in Jersey City, among other buildings; one of the founders, architects, and builders of a Masonic camp for underprivileged children; active in fund-raising for Fed. of Jewish Philanthropies; past v. pres. Maimonides Hosp. Center; benefactor, Kingsbrook Jewish Medical Center; recipient: Leadership Award from Jewish Guild for the Blind; awards from Anti-Defamation League and American Jewish Congress.

BLITZ, SAMUEL, communal leader; b. Lemberg, Galicia, Austro-Hungary, June 15, 1888; d. N.Y.C., May 6, 1977; in U.S. since 1890; exec. v. pres. UJA, 1939–64; organized benefit for Jewish victims of Nazi persecution, 1934; exec. dir. United Palestine Appeal of Greater N.Y.; mem. Zionist Org. of America; past sec. and fund-raising dir. Zionist Council of Greater N.Y.

BLOCH, BENJAMIN C., architect; b. Chicago, Ill., July 29, 1890; d. N.Y.C., Nov. 27, 1977; senior partner, architectural firm of Bloch & Hesse; designed more than 60 synagogues; trustee, Educational Alliance/Architectural League; honorary trustee, Stephen Wise Free Synagogue; honored by Podell House-Educational Alliance.

CHERNOWITZ, MAURICE E., educator, author, editor; b. Odessa, Russia, Dec. 24, 1908; d. N.Y.C., July 4, 1977; in U.S. since 1925; prof. of Fine Arts, Yeshiva Univ., for 27 years; editor, *Bitzaron,* a monthly Hebrew magazine, for 39 years; past district v. pres. Zionist Org. of America; author, *Proust and Painting* (1945); honored by UJA, B'nai B'rith, and State of Israel Bonds.

CHOMSKY, WILLIAM, educator, author; b. (?), Russia, Jan. 15, 1896; d. Philadelphia, Pa., July 19, 1977; in U.S. since 1913; one of the world's foremost Hebrew grammarians; Gratz Coll.: faculty mem. since 1924; prof. since 1954; faculty chmn. 1949–69; prof. emeritus since 1969; prof. of Hebrew and Jewish Ed., Dropsie Coll., 1955–77; mem.: Amer. Academy for Jewish Research; Natl. Council for Jewish Ed.; Labor Zionist Org. of America; Histadrut Ivrith; Mikveh Israel Congregation; World Union of Jewish Studies; Conf. on Jewish Studies; author: *How to Teach Hebrew* (1947); *David Kimhi's Hebrew Grammar* (1952); *Hebrew: The Eternal Language* (1957); *Teaching and Learning* (1959); *Ha-Lashon Ha-Ivrit b'Darkhei Hitpathuthah* (1967); *Darkhei Hora'ah u'Lemidah* (1968); various contributions to professional journals.

DICKENSTEIN, ABRAHAM, banker, industrialist, communal leader; b. Wishniewa, Poland, June 15, 1902; d. Tel Aviv, Israel, Feb. 16, 1977; in U.S. since 1936; pioneer laborer in Palestine, 1921–24; asst. dir. Worker's Bank, Ltd., 1924–38; founder, manager: Audit Union of Credit Coops, 1925–29; Audit Union of Consumer's Coops, 1925–29; Transportation Coops, 1927–39; delegate, World Zionist Congress, 1939, 1951; pres. Israel Development Corp.; founder, pres. AMPAL (Amer. Israel Corp.), 1941; managing dir. Bank Hapoalim; bd. chmn. Israel Amer. Industrial Development Bank; contributor to periodicals.

DLUZNOWSKY, MOSHE, author; b. Tomashov, Poland, (?), 1906; d. N.Y.C., July 30, 1977; wrote plays, novels, and essays dealing with Jewish life; author: *The Lonesome Ship, The Eleventh Inheritor, The Will of Fortune, The Well on the Road, Autumn in the Vineyard, The Blessed and the Doomed;* recipient, Jacob L. Gladstein Award of the Jewish Culture Congress, 1975.

FELDMAN, ABRAHAM J., rabbi, author, editor, communal leader; b. Kiev, the Ukraine, (?), 1893; d. West Hartford, Conn., July 21, 1977; in U.S. since 1906; natl. co-chmn. Consultative Council on Desegregation; chmn. Conn. advisory com. to U.S. Commission on Civil Rights; founder, regent, Univ. of Hartford; founder, editor, *The Connecticut Jewish Ledger* (1929); rabbi, Temple Beth Israel, West Hartford, Conn., 1925–68; past pres.: Central Conf. Amer. Rabbis, Synagogue Council of Amer.; author: *Sources of Jewish Inspiration, A Companion to the Bible, The American Jew: A Study of Backgrounds, The American Reform Rabbi: A Profile of a Profession;* honored with title of Rabbi Emeritus, Temple Beth Israel, 1968; hon. doctorates from Hebrew Union Coll. (Cinn.), Trinity Coll., Hillyer Coll., and Hartt Coll. of Music.

FISCHBACH, HENRY F., business exec., philanthropist; b. (?), Rumania, (?), 1891; d. N.Y.C., Sept. 10, 1977; in U.S. since 1903; founder, bd. chmn. Fischbach & Moore; past pres. N.Y. Electrical Contractors Assn.; benefactor: Dartmouth Coll.; Pratt Institute; Rensselaer Polytechnic Institute; Brandeis Univ. (Henry Fischbach Chair in Chemistry, Henry Fischbach Fellowship Fund supporting an interchange of Technion and Brandeis graduate students, and Henry Fischbach Scholarship and Endowment Fund for gifted and needy students seeking a career in engineering); Haifa Technion-Israel Institute of Technology; a founder: Albert Einstein Coll. of Medicine; Israel Museum; Electrical Contractor Div., UJA-Fed. of Jewish Philanthropies Joint Campaign; a fellow, Brandeis Univ.

GOLDBERG, DAVID, rabbi; b. (?), Russia, (?), 1886; d. Forest Hills, Queens, N.Y., Nov. 15, 1977; in U.S. since 1908; first Jewish chaplain U.S. Navy; only rabbi to serve as chaplain in W. W. I; entered U.S. Naval Reserve, 1925; retired as lt. commander, 1941; rabbi: Temple Beth El, Corsicana, Tex.; synagogue in Brockton, Mass.

GOLDBLOOM, MAURICE J., author, editor, translator, social activist; b. Brooklyn, N.Y., (?), 1912; d. N.Y.C., Dec. 30, 1977; before W.W.II, courier from exiled German Socialists in U.S. to the party's underground in Nazi Germany; bd. mem. Amnesty Internatl. U.S.A.; founder, exec. sec. Amer. Com. for Democracy and Freedom in Greece; mem. editorial com., *The Socialist Call,* 1942–55; associate editor, *Current* magazine; wrote for *Commentary* magazine; author, *American Security and Freedom.*

GORDON, HAROLD H., rabbi, communal leader; b. Minneapolis, Minn., (?), 1908; d. N.Y.C., May 21, 1977; delegate, White House Conf. on Children and Youth, 1960; mem. coordinating com., Governor's Com. on Scholastic Achievement; U.S.O. dir.,

Maryland; rabbi, Congregation Sons of Jacob, Waterloo, Iowa, 1935–42; chaplain, Jewish Welfare Bd., 1942–43; Army Air Force Chaplain, 1943–46, rose to rank of major; chaplaincy coordinator since 1946; N.Y. Bd. of Rabbis: gen. sec. (1946), exec. v. pres. (since 1960); co-founder: 5th Ave. Synagogue; Internatl. Synagogue at Kennedy Airport; B'rith Milah School for ritual circumcisers; Mt. Sinai Hosp. (dir., 1968); exec. sec. B'rith Milah Bd. of N.Y., since 1950; co-chmn. Com. of Religious Leaders of N.Y.; chmn. N.Y. State Interfaith Com. on Chaplaincy; spiritual advisor, Council of Jewish Organizations in Civil Service, since 1956; mem.: first delegation of rabbis to Soviet Union and other Iron Curtain countries, 1956; advisory council, Amer. Jewish Correctional Chaplains Assn.; bd. of dirs., Central Bureau of Jewish Aged; natl. exec. bd., Religious Zionists of America; Rabbinical Assembly of America; Jewish War Veterans; Assn. of Jewish Chaplains in the Armed Forces; delegate: World Jewish Congress, 1959, 1965; World Zionist Congress, 1937, 1960, 1965, 1968; honored by Fed. of Jewish Philanthropies, 1959, 1966; man-of-the-year award, Council of Jewish Organizations, 1960; citations for moral and religious leadership, N.Y.C., 1960, 1966; Avodah Award, Jewish Teachers Assn., 1961; Interfaith Movement award, 1963; honorary doctorates of Hebrew literature and divinity, Jewish Theological Seminary of America.

GREENBERG, ELIEZER, Yiddish poet, essayist, translator; b. Lipkani, Russia, Dec. 31, 1896; d. N.Y.C., June 2, 1977; in U.S. since 1913; dir. Yiddish press relations, Amer. Jewish Com., for several years; founder, past v. pres. Yiddish branch of P.E.N. Club; mem.: Workmen's Circle; I.L. Peretz Yiddish Writers Union; co-editor: the *Zukunft; Getseltn* (1946–48); *A Treasury of Yiddish Stories* (1954); *Ashes Out of Hope; A Treasury of Yiddish Poetry;* author: *Gassen un Avenues* (1928); *Foon Oometum* (1934); *Fisherdorf* (1938); *M.L. Halpern* (1942); *Die Lange Nacht* (1946); *Banachtiker Dialog* (1953), *Tsentrale Motivn in H. Leivik's Shafn* (1961); *Jacob Glatstein's Di Freid Fan Yiddishn Wort* (1964); *Eybiker Dorsht* (1968); recipient: Harry Kovner Award for Yiddish Poetry, Jewish Book Council, 1953; Jewish Book Council of America Award for Poetry, 1954; Jacob Fichman

Poetry Prize, Union of Bessarabian Jews in Israel, 1967.

ISH-KISHOR, SULAMITH, author, b. London, England, (?), 1897; d. N.Y.C., June 23, 1977; in U.S. since 1909; co-author, *Blessed Is the Daughter;* author: *A Boy of Old Prague* (1963); *Our Eddie* (1970); *The Master of Miracle: A New Novel of the Golem* (1971); *Magnificent Hadrian; The Carpet of Solomon; Everyman's History of the Jews;* recipient, Natl. Jewish Book Award, 1963, 1971; runner-up for John Newberry Medal, Amer. Library Assn., 1970.

JACOBS, JACOB, actor, director, producer, lyricist, Yiddish theater; b. Risk, Czechoslovakia, Jan. 1, 1891; d. Brooklyn, N.Y., Oct. 14, 1977; in U.S. since 1904; impresario of the Lenox, Grand, Natl., Parkway, Prospect, Anderson, Eden, and Yiddish Amer. Theaters, N.Y.C.; first v. pres. Yiddish Theatrical Alliance; mem. Amer. Soc. of Composers, Authors, & Publishers; wrote lyrics to such songs as "Bei Mir Bist du Schoen," "A Gute Heym," and "A Yiddishe Meydle Darf A Yiddishn Boy"; hon. mem. Hebrew Actors' Union; awarded "Achievement in Performing Arts" by City of N.Y., 1969.

KOHN, EUGENE, rabbi, editor, author, educator; b. (?), 1887; d. New Hyde Park, Queens, N.Y., Apr. 1, 1977; a founder of the Jewish Reconstructionist Movement and managing editor of its periodical *The Reconstructionist,* until 1960; co-editor of prayer books; author: *Religious Humanism, Good to Be a Jew, The Future of Judaism in America, A Manual for Teaching Biblical History.*

KOHN, HENRY, attorney, communal leader; b. Chicago, Ill., Nov. 9, 1902; d. Chicago, Ill., Dec. 30, 1976; mem. Adlai Stevenson Commission on Human Relations, State of Illinois; contributor, Negro Coll. Fund; active in Joint Action Bd. coalition of civic and communal groups; natl. v. pres. and past chmn. Chicago Chapter, Amer. Jewish Com.; pres. and bd. mem. Bureau on Jewish Employment Problems; bd. mem. KAM Temple; recipient, award from Natl. Conf. of Christians and Jews.

KOHN, PAULINE REDLICH, business exec., humanitarian; b. (?), Poland, (?), 1896; d. Far Rockaway, Queens, N.Y., March 13, 1977; in U.S. since 1903; pres. Durst Industries; past natl. pres. and mem. bd. of

370 / AMERICAN JEWISH YEAR BOOK, 1979

govs. Women's League for Israel; supporter of ADL; active on four wartime committees; signed affidavits of support for 250 Austrian and German Jewish refugees, 1938–40.

LEVINE, HARRY, business exec., philanthropist; b. N.Y.C., (?), 1896; d. Cambridge, Mass., May 1, 1977; founder, New England Novelty Co.; dir. Commonwealth Plastics Corp., Leominster, Mass.; chmn. U.S. Plastic & Chemical Co.; treas. Superior Plastic Co.; chief petty officer, U.S. Navy, W.W.I; established plastics factory in Israel, 1948; founding gov. Weizmann Institute of Science and treas. of its Amer. Com.

LEVINE, SAMUEL, physician, educator, editor, communal worker; b. N.Y.C., Aug. 8, 1895; d. N.Y.C., Aug. 14, 1977; house officer, Mt. Sinai Hosp., 1920–22; staff mem. Infants' & Children's Hosp., Boston, 1922–23; Cornell Univ. Medical Coll.: on faculty since 1924; prof. of pediatrics, 1936–61; named prof. emeritus, 1961; N.Y. Hosp.: on staff since 1932; attendant pediatrician-in-chief, 1936–61; consultant since 1961; taught at Institute for Psycho-Analysis, Chicago; consultant: World Health Org.; School of Social Service Admn., Western Reserve Univ.; Univ. of Pittsburgh School of Social Work; mem.: N.Y.C. Bd. of Health; Harvey Soc.; Amer. Bd. of Pediatrics; N.Y. Academy of Medicine; technical advisory com. on fluoridation of water supplies, N.Y. State Dept. of Health; Amer. Institute of Nutrition; Soc. for Experimental Biology; Amer. Assn. for the Advancement of Science; founder, Fdn. for Internatl. Child Health; pres. Soc. for Pediatric Research, 1932–33; pres. Amer. Pediatric Soc., 1959–60; active in work for Hebrew Orphan Asylum; Emanuel Settlement, N.Y.C.; Neighborhood Center, Philadelphia; exec. dir.: Bronx House; Council Educational Center, Detroit; Council Educational Alliance of Cleveland; Irene Kaufmann Center, Pittsburgh; Detroit Jewish Community Center; gen. dir. Jewish Community Centers of Chicago, 1947–66; pres.: Natl. Conf. of Jewish Communal Service; Assn. of Jewish Center Workers; editor-in-chief, *Advances in Pediatrics,* 1945; contributor to numerous medical journals; recipient: Borden Award, Amer. Academy of Pediatrics, 1944; Cornell Univ. Medical Coll. Alumni Assn. Award, 1954; Townsend Harris

Medal, City Coll. of N.Y., 1954; second annual Albert Einstein Commemorative Award, 1956; medal, N.Y. Academy of Medicine, 1966; John Howland Medal, Amer. Pediatric Soc., 1966.

LICHTENBERG, LEO, rabbi, communal leader; b. Rostock, Germany, Jan. 17, 1915; d. Cinn., Ohio, Aug. 1, 1977; in U.S. since 1935; U.S. Air Force chaplain, W.W. II, Korean War, retired as lt. col.; Hebrew instructor, Hofstra Univ., 1954–68; asst. prof. of religion, Adelphi Univ., 1954–74; dir. Hillel activities, Univ. of Virginia, Adelphi Univ., Ohio Univ., dir. Hillel Fdn., 1954–68; manuscript processor, Hebrew Union Coll., since 1976; past pres. Natl. Assn. Hillel Directors; past natl. chaplain, Amer. Legion; treas. Jewish Chaplains Armed Forces of the U.S.; mem. exec. com., Assn. of Reform Rabbis; mem. exec. bd., Central Conf. Amer. Rabbis.

LINN, IRVING, educator; b. Newark, N.J., Jan. 24, 1912; d. N.Y.C., Oct. 5, 1977; prof. of English, Yeshiva Univ., 1937–77; pres. Amer. Soc. of Geolinguistics, 1972–73; conducted WABC-TV series "This English Language of Ours," 1966–70; listed in directory of *Scholars and Outstanding Educators of America,* 1974.

LIPNICK, JEROME, rabbi, communal leader; b. Baltimore, Maryland, (?), 1918; d. Washington, D.C., March 14, 1977; dir. of ed. B'nai B'rith Youth Org.; headed Temple Beth El, Utica, N.Y.; representative, World Council of Synagogues, Jerusalem, 1965–66; hon. doctorate, Jewish Theological Seminary, 1970.

MANDELBAUM, JUDITH, educator, communal leader; b. N.Y.C., June 30, 1906; d. Brooklyn, N.Y., March 7, 1977; taught at Yeshiva Etz Chaim of Boro Park, East Midwood Jewish Center, and Flatbush Yeshiva; mem. Amer. Mizrachi Women since 1957: past sec., natl. cultural chmn., natl. v. pres., and hon. v. pres.; editor-in-chief and columnist, Amer. Mizrachi Women *Journal,* since 1945; pres. Sisterhood Congregation Talmud Torah of Flatbush, 1970–74; personal sec. of the late Rabbi Meir Bar-Ilan; past natl. pres. Mizrachi Hatzair; honored by Amer. Mizrachi Women (1971), Religious Zionists of Flatbush (1974), and Sisterhood Congregation Talmud Torah of Flatbush (1974).

MARK, JULIUS, rabbi, educator, communal leader; b. Cinn., Ohio, Dec. 25, 1898; d.

N.Y.C., Sept. 7, 1977; rabbi: Temple Beth-El, South Bend, Ind., 1922–26; Vine St. Temple, Nashville, Tenn., 1926–48; Temple Emanu-El, 1948–68; Jewish Chaplain, U.S. Navy, 1942–45, retired as lt. commander; prof. of Homiletics and Practical Theology, Hebrew Union Coll.–Jewish Institute of Religion, 1949–63; life trustee, Fed. of Jewish Philanthropies; mem.: exec. com. U.S. Commission for UNESCO; natl. bd. of Natl. Conf. of Christians and Jews; eastern bd. of ADL; bd. of govs. World Union for Progressive Judaism; Council on Foreign Relations; trustee, Union of Amer. Hebrew Colleges, 1958–62; exec. bd. Amer. Jewish Com.; exec. com. N.Y. Bd. of Rabbis; bd. of dirs. Assn. for New Americans; bd. chaplains, N.Y. Univ.; Assn. of Reform Rabbis of N.Y.; Army and Navy Chaplains Assn.; Conf. on Jewish Material Claims Against Germany; Theta Phi; pres.: Alumni Assn., Hebrew Union Coll.-Jewish Institute of Religion, 1948–50; Jewish Conciliation Bd. of America; chmn. bd. of govs. Hebrew Union Coll.; mem. com. on justice and peace, Central Conf. Amer. Rabbis, 1946–49; pres. Synagogue Council of America, 1961–63; dir. N.Y. World's Fair, 1964–65; one of three convenors, Natl. Conf. on Religion and Race, Chicago, 1963; contributing editor, *Observer*, 1934–38; author: *The Art of Preaching; Behaviorism and Religion*, (1930); *The Rabbi Faces Some Big Dilemmas* (1956); *Reaching for the Moon* (1959); hon. LLD, Cumberland Univ., 1936; hon. pres. Amer. Jewish Encyclopedia Soc.; hon. mem. Zeta Beta Tau; hon. doctorate Hebrew Union Coll., 1949; hon. v. chmn. Lighthouse of N.Y. Assn. of the Blind, since 1952; recipient: Zeta Beta Tau's man-of-the-year award, 1959; Human Relations Award, Methodist Church, 1963; Gold Medallion for Courageous Leadership, Natl. Conf. of Christians and Jews, 1966; hon. DHL, L. I. Univ., 1967; Israel Bond Plaque, 1967, 1968, 1970; Israel Tower of David Plaque, 1968; named Rabbi emeritus, Temple Emanu-El, 1968; Clergyman of the Year, Religious Heritage of America, 1969.

MERMEY, FAYVELLE, journalist, communal leader; b. (?), 1916; d. Larchmont, N.Y., March 12, 1977; feature writer and columnist, *Mamaroneck Daily Times*, 1964–70; founder, Larchmont Youth Bd.; founder, Women's Interfaith Seminar, Larchmont; dir. dues collecting agency, Union of Amer. Hebrew Congregations; pres. Larchmont Temple, 1960–62, 1972–74; first woman to serve as pres. of a synagogue in the N.Y.C. area.

MILLER, JULES, business exec.; b. Pittsburgh, Pa., Feb. 28, 1902; d. Houston, Texas, March 15, 1977; exec. business manager, *Jewish Exponent;* v. pres. Amer. Jewish Press Assn.; honored by Amer. Jewish Press Assn. (1968) and Fed. of Jewish Agencies (1974).

MINDA, ALBERT G., rabbi, communal leader; b. Holton, Kansas, July 30, 1895; d. Minneapolis, Minn., Jan. 15, 1977; leader, Temple Israel, 1922–63; past pres. Central Conf. Amer. Rabbis; internatl. v. pres. World Union for Progressive Judaism; cofounder: Minneapolis Urban League; Minneapolis Round Table Conf. of Christians and Jews; recipient, hon. DD, Hebrew Union Coll., 1947; named on list of 100 great living Minnesotans, 1940.

MODANSKY, JACOB R., business exec., philanthropist; b. Kiev, Russia, Oct. 1, 1896; d. N.Y.C., Sept. 19, 1977; in U.S. since 1912; founder, past pres., and chmn. of bd., Ajayem Lumber Corp.; past pres.: East Meadow Jewish Center; Eastern Region, Zionists of America; Knesserit Israel, Miami Beach; Apex Soc.; chmn. bd. Hebrew Academy; bd. mem. Fed. of Jewish Philanthropies; master builder, Yeshiva Univ.

MOSTEL, ZERO, actor, painter; b. (Samuel Joel Mostel), Brooklyn, N.Y., Feb. 28, 1915; d. Philadelphia, Pa., Sept. 8, 1977; debut as comedian, Cafe Soc. Downtown, 1942; U.S. Army W.W.II; appeared in such films as "The Producers" and "The Front"; received Tony Awards for his performances in the plays "Rhinoceros" (1961), "A Funny Thing Happened on the Way to the Forum" (1963), and "Fiddler on the Roof" (1964); sponsor: Natl. Negro Congress; Spanish Refugee Appeal of the Joint Anti-Fascist Refugee Com.; cochmn. Natl. Alumni Com. for City Coll. Scholar Awards; Works Progress Administration lecturer: Museum of Modern Art; Frick Museum; Museum of Science & Industry; one man art show, A.C.A. Galleries, 1973; bd. mem. Jewish Museum; recipient: Best Actor award, Theater of All Nations, Paris, 1959; Einstein medal of art.

REGENSBERG, CHAIM DAVID, rabbi, educator, author; b. Zembrova, Poland, Sept. 18,

1895; d. Jerusalem, Israel, March 28, 1977; in U.S. since 1922; prof. of Talmud and Dean of Faculty, Hebrew Theological Coll.; religious head, Chicago Rabbinical Council, 1972; chmn. Rabbinical Court, Rabbinical Council of America, 1972; author: articles in *Kerem, Hapardes, Bitzaron, Noam, Hadarom,* and the Hebrew Theological Coll. *Journal; Mishmeret Hayim Responsa,* 1966; *Giv'at Shaul,* 1936.

REMBA, ODED, educator, economist; b. (?), 1931; d. N.Y.C., Jan. 6, 1977; prof. of economics, Coll. of Staten Island, City Univ. of N.Y.; mem. bd. dirs. Amer. Academic Assn. for Peace in the Middle East; chmn. editorial advisory bd., *Middle East Review;* mem. bd. dirs., Amer. Histadrut Cultural Exchange Institute.

RHODES, IRVING, publisher; b. (?), Poland, (?), 1901; d. Milwaukee, Wisc., March 29, 1977; co-founder, co-publisher, *Wisconsin Jewish Chronicle;* founder, Amer. Jewish Press Assn.

ROBINSON, JACOB, attorney, historian, politician; b. (?), Lithuania, (?), 1889; d. N.Y.C., Oct. 24, 1977; in U.S. since 1940; served in Lithuanian Parliament, 1922–26; legal adviser to Lithuania's Foreign Office, 1932; chmn. unofficial com. of Jewish leaders in Lithuania; consultant to chief counsel at Nuremberg war crime trials, 1946; legal adviser to Jewish Agency for Palestine, 1947; founder, first dir. World Jewish Congress Institute of Jewish Affairs; mem. Israeli delegation to U.N.; appointed by Israeli Government to draft reparations agreement between Israel and West Germany, 1952; coordinator of research and documentation on the Holocaust, Conf. on Jewish Material Claims Against Germany, 1957; adviser to YIVO Institute; adviser to Memorial Fdn. for Jewish Culture; coordinated and organized much of the documentation for Yad Vashem.

ROSENBERG, ADOLPH, journalist, editor, publisher, b. Albany, Ga., Aug. 14, 1911; d. Atlanta, Ga., Jan. 17, 1977; reporter, the *Constitution,* the *Journal;* founding chmn. Georgia Communications Council; bd. mem. Atlanta District, Zionist Org. of America; bd. mem. Gate City B'nai B'rith Lodge; mem. Jewish War Veterans; editor, publisher, *The Southern Israelite;* pres. Amer. Jewish Press Assn., 1966–69; founder, pres. Atlanta Press Club, 1974–75;

treas. Sigma Delta Chi Soc. of Professional Journalists; recipient, Boris Smolar award for contributions to Jewish Journalism, 1976.

ROSENTHAL, HENRY M., author, educator; b. Louisville, Kentucky, Jan. 9, 1906; d. Ellsworth, Maine, July 29, 1977; 92nd St. YMHA, N.Y.C.: religious dir., 1930–42; dir. Adult School of Jewish Studies, 1939–42; dir. Hillel Fdn., Hunter Coll., 1942–45; lecturer in social philosophy, Cooper Union Coll., 1945–47; prof. of philosophy, Hunter Coll., 1948–73; prof. Columbia Univ., 1962; mem. Phi Beta Kappa; mem. Amer. Philosophical Assn.; author: "The Philosophy of George Santayana," *Library of Living Philosophers* (1940); *On the Function of Religion in Culture* (1941); recipient, Guggenheim fellowship, 1947–48.

SCHERER, EMANUEL, labor leader, editor; b. Cracow, Poland, (?), 1901; d. Dobbs Ferry, N.Y., May 3, 1977; in U.S. since 1939; youngest man elected to Warsaw Jewish Labor Bund's Central Committee, 1930; co-editor, several Polish-language publications of Warsaw Bund; elected to City Council of Warsaw, 1938; representative of Jewish Labor Movement, Polish Natl. Council, 1943; sec. gen. and sec. coordinating com. Amer. Jewish Labor Bund, 1946; editor, *Unser Zeit;* v. pres. Jewish Labor Com.

SCHIFRIN, ISIDOR, business exec., communal leader; b. Rochester, N.Y., Apr. 5, 1889; d. Cinn., Ohio, March 15, 1977; exec. partner, Julian J. Behr Advertising Agency, 1911–73; Federal Prison Chaplain, 1920–63; Army Chaplain, W.W.I; Air Force Chaplain, W.W.II; v. pres. Schindler-Howard Advertising Agency, 50 years; sec., bd. mem. Jewish Telegraphic Agency; natl. bd. mem. Amer. Assn. for Jewish Ed.; natl. bd. mem. Council of Jewish Federations & Welfare Funds; principal, I.M. Wise Temple Sabbath Schools; pres. Jewish Cultural & Arts Com.; pres. Bureau of Jewish Ed.; past pres. Brotherhood I.M. Wise Temple; founding mem., hon. v. pres., founding chmn. Boy Scout Com., Natl. Jewish Welfare Bd.; natl. bd. mem., Boy Scouts of America; chmn. Men's Div. ORT; natl. exec. bd., Bonds for Israel; chmn. public relations, Brandeis Univ.; Jewish Fed. of Cincinnati; public relations consultant for Mayor of Cincinnati; chmn. Boys' Week;

recipient, Shofar and Silver Beaver awards, Boy Scouts of America.

SCHINE, HAROLD L., business exec., civic leader; b. Bridgeport, Conn., Dec. 9, 1917; d. New Haven, Conn., Sept. 26, 1977; pres. City Lumber Co. of Bridgeport; U.S. staff sergeant in counter-intelligence, W.W.II; mem. Foreign Trade Zone Commission of Bridgeport; dir. State Natl. Bank of Bridgeport; bd. of associates, Univ. of Bridgeport; past pres. Bridgeport Jewish Service Bureau; bd. of dirs. North Atlantic Ports Assn.; Bridgeport Area Chamber of Commerce; bd. mem. United Jewish Council of Bridgeport; past pres. Jewish Family & Children's Bureau, Bridgeport.

SCHRAGE, SAMUEL A., rabbi, communal leader; b. Belo Horizonte, Brazil, Dec. 12, 1935; d. N.Y.C., Dec. 31, 1976; in U.S. since 1949; administrative asst. United Lubavitchen Yeshivot, 1962–64; formed Maccabees citizens' group, an anti-crime street patrol, 1964; asst. to mayor of N.Y.C., 1965–68; asst. exec. dir., N.Y.C. Youth Bd., 1966; principal human resources specialist, N.Y.C., since 1968; consultant, law enforcement agencies; dir. N.Y.C.'s Neighborhood Action Program, 1969–74.

SEGAL, ABRAHAM, educator, author; b. Philadelphia, Pa., Nov. 7, 1910; d. N.Y.C., May 24, 1977; trustee and natl. dir. Dept. of Ed., Union of Amer. Hebrew Congregations; English teacher, Philadelphia high schools, 30 years; instructor, Gratz Coll.; trustee, Israel Bonds; active in Bd. of Jewish Ed.; mem.: Natl. Assn. Temple Educators; Amer. Assn. Jewish Ed.; Natl. Council of Jewish Ed.; co-author: social studies volume, *Israel Today* (1964); *Joseph and His Brothers; The Eternal People* (1966); *Teaching Jewish History; Teaching of the Sidur; How to Conduct a Sabbath Service for Children; Guide for Jewish Youth; Holy Days and Holidays;* author, numerous magazine articles; recipient, man-of-the-year award, Gratz Coll. Alumni Assn.; honored by Jewish Natl. Fund of Philadelphia, Commission on Jewish Ed.

SHAPIRO, EZRA Z., attorney, communal leader; b. Volozhin, Poland, May 7, 1903; d. Jerusalem, Israel, May 14, 1977; in U.S. since 1906; private law practice, Cleveland, Ohio, since 1925; dir. of law, City of Cleveland, 1933–35; v. chmn. Cleveland Community Relations Bd.; chmn. natl. exec.

com. Zionist Org. of America, 1934; trustee, Cleveland Jewish Community Fed., since 1934; pres. Cleveland Jewish Community Center, 1935–70; participated in seven World Zionist Congresses, beginning in 1937; one of 19 American Jews summoned by Ben-Gurion to organize American support for Haganah, 1945; mem. natl. bd. govs. Amer. Com. for Weizmann Institute of Science, since 1950; mem. gen. council, World Zionist Org., since 1951; founder, mem. natl. bd. govs. State of Israel Bond Org., 1951–65; natl. v. pres. UJA, 1955–66; natl. bd. trustees, Amer. Friends of Hebrew Univ., since 1955; pres. Amer. Jewish League for Israel, 1957–60; v. pres., Amer. Assn. for Jewish Ed., 1959–66; bd. of govs. Hebrew Univ. and Negev Univ., since 1971; pres. Cleveland Bureau of Jewish Ed.; pres. World Confederation of Gen. Zionists; world chmn. Keren Hayesod, since 1971.

SIEGEL, SAMUEL H., author, artist, communal leader; b. Vilkovishki, Lithuania, Apr. 25, 1886; d. Edison, N.J., Oct. 6, 1977; in U.S. since 1904; co-org. Workmen's Circle Branch 300, Poland, 1909; org., sec. Yiddish Workmen's Circle, 1937–74; editor, *The Banner,* New Brunswick, N.J., 1922–25; wrote autobiography for YIVO, 1943; mosaicist and painter of Jewish and biblical themes, 1973–77.

SILBERT, SILVIA F., communal worker, philanthropist; b. N.Y.C., Jan. 31, 1910; d. N.Y.C., Nov. 16, 1977; mem. Metropolitan Museum of Art; Natl. Women's Com., Brandeis Univ.; chmn. Women's Advisory Com., Amer. Cancer Soc.; founder, Albert Einstein Coll. of Medicine; gen. chmn., dir. Women's Div., ADL Appeal; dir. N.Y.C. UJA; mem.: B'nai B'rith; Natl. Council of Jewish Women; Women's Div., Fed. of Jewish Philanthropies; patroness: Jewish Museum; Amer.-Israel Cultural Fdn.; honored at Israel Dinner of State sponsored by Park Ave. Synagogue and Temple Emanu-El.

SPIEGEL, IRVING, reporter; b. N.Y.C., Apr. 26, 1907; d. N.Y.C., March 31, 1977; staff mem., reporter, *N.Y. Times,* since 1925; covered stories about Jewish organizations and events; recipient: several publisher's awards from the *Times;* awards from B'nai B'rith (1967), Amer. Jewish Com., and numerous other Jewish organizations.

SPOTNITZ, MIRIAM, social worker, educator; b. (?), 1911; d. June 15, 1977; instructor, Center for Modern Psychoanalytic Studies; dir. managing office, Jewish Board of Guardians; psychiatric social worker: Jewish Board of Guardians; Jewish Family Service; bd. chmn. Louise Wise Adoption Agency.

STEINHARDT, MAXWELL, attorney, communal leader; b. N.Y.C., Nov. 6, 1889; d. N.Y.C., Oct. 4, 1977; practiced law privately in N.Y.C. for more than 30 years; pres.: Shaw Soc. of America; Harvard Club; Grolier Club; U.S. Army capt. W. W. I; bd. mem. Hebrew Technical Institute; natl. treas., sec., and founder of its Philanthropic Fund, Amer. Council for Judaism; past pres. Jewish Fdn. for Ed. of Women.

STERN, FREDERICK M., author; b. Dec. 1, 1889, Posen, Poland; d. N.Y.C., May 6, 1977; in U.S. since 1937; managing dir. Hinz Factory, Germany; dir. Self Help Org.; dir. Leo Baeck Institute; author: *The Junker Menace* (1945); *Capitalism in America: A Classless Society* (1951); *The Citizen Army: Key to Defense in the Atomic Age* (1957); *Life and Liberty: A Return to First Principles* (1975).

STONE, DEWEY D., business exec., industrialist, communal leader, philanthropist; b. Brockton, Mass., Aug. 31, 1900; d. Brockton, Mass., Nov. 19, 1977; pres. Harodite Finishing Co.; mem. bd. dirs. numerous companies; U.S. Army, W.W.I; trustee: Cardinal Cushing Gen. Hosp.; Stone Charitable Fdn.; associate founder, Boston Univ. (Dewey D. & Harry K. Stone Science Building, 1947) and Hebrew Teachers Coll.; headed U.S. operation to acquire boats to bring Holocaust survivors into Palestine; mem. small, secret group charged with acquisition of military equipment needed by the Haganah; played significant role in helping to secure key votes approving the UN Partition Resolution, 1947–48; mem.: Amer. Legion; Jewish War Veterans; B'nai B'rith; YMHA; Friends of Hebrew Univ.; Zionist House; Camp Young Judea; Israel Bond Corp.; Israel Economic Corp.; Amer.-Israel Cultural Fdn.; exec. bd. Jewish Agency; exec. bd. World Zionist Org.; bd. dirs. Council of Jewish Federations and Welfare Funds; Israel Foreign Trade Credits Corp.; contributor, Amer. Friends of Boys Town

Jerusalem; bd. mem. Jewish Telegraphic Agency; founder, v. pres., and hon. pres. Amer. Jewish League for Israel; past v. pres. Zionist Org. of America; founder, mem. bd. govs., and chmn. Amer. Com., Weizmann Institute of Science; bd. chmn. Brandeis Youth Fdn.; natl. chmn. UJA; natl. chmn. United Israel Appeal; man-of-the-year award, Zeta Beta Tau, 1947; recipient: hon. Dr. of Humane Letters, Boston Univ., 1950; Certificate of Merit, Jewish War Veterans, 1952; hon. Fellow, Weizmann Institute of Science, 1960.

STULBERG, LOUIS, labor union exec.; b. (?), Poland, Apr. 14, 1901; d. N.Y.C., Dec. 14, 1977; in U.S. since 1919; Internatl. Ladies' Garment Workers' Union: v. pres. 1947–66; pres. 1966–75; past v. pres. AFL-CIO; founding dir., v. pres. East River Housing Corp.; trustee, Mutual Redevelopment Houses, Inc.; mem. Public Development Corp. of N.Y.; v. pres. League for Industrial Democracy; treas. Negro Labor Com.; trustee, Fashion Institute of Technology; mem. bd. dirs. Internatl. Rescue Com.; mem. trade union com., Histadrut; mem. bd. dirs. Amer. ORT Fed.; founder, Amer. Labor ORT; mem. natl. exec. bd. Jewish Labor Com.; mem. bd. dirs. Hebrew Sheltering and Immigrant Aid Soc.; mem. Natl. Com. for Labor Israel; former trustee, Kingsbrook Jewish Medical Center; fellow, Brandeis Univ.; hon. chmn. Workmen's Circle, Cutters' Branch; honored at testimonial dinner sponsored by UJA-Fed. of Jewish Philanthropies; honored by Histadrut with construction of Louis Stulberg Hosp. at Kfar Saba.

SZOLD, ROBERT, attorney, communal leader; b. Streator, Ill., Sept. 29, 1889; d. N.Y.C., Nov. 9, 1977; asst. Attorney Gen. of Puerto Rico, 1915; asst. to Solicitor Gen. of the U.S., 1915–18; senior partner, Szold, Brandwen, Meyers, & Altman, since 1921; composed briefs that led to first federal child labor law; delegate, Round Table Conf., London, 1939; dir. numerous corporations; past pres.: United Housing Fdn.; Edward A. Filene Goodwill Fund; founder, Szold Institute of Applied Science, 1967; mem. Amer. Law Institute; founder, pres. Zionist Circle, 1915–17; mem. Zionist Commission to Palestine, 1919; mem. Zionist Reorganization Commission, 1920; treas., pres. Palestine Endowment Fund, since 1922; v. pres., pres. Palestine Economic Corp., 1925–57; chmn., past pres., hon. pres. Zionist Org. of America, since 1930; mem. Council Jewish Colonial Trust, since 1930; mem. Keren Kayemeth Leisrael, since 1930; v. chmn. Jewish Agency, since 1931; founder, Amer. Emergency Com. for Zionist Affairs, 1939; dir. Central Bank of Cooperative Institutions in Palestine, 1930–56; dir. Palestine Mortgage & Savings Bank, 1930–59; founder, co-chmn. Amer. Economic Com. for Palestine, 1939–54; first Jewish administrator of Jerusalem; treas. Amer. Zionist Council, 1940–44; mem.: Jewish Natl. Fund; the Judeans; Gen. Com., Amer. Jewish Conf., since 1943; founder, past pres. PEF (Israel Endowment Fund); cofounder, Free Synagogue of Westchester; dir. Union Bank of Israel, since 1951; dir. Israel Corp. of America, 1951–55; pres. Israel Enterprises, Inc., 1953–57; mem. Phi Beta Kappa; mem. Beta Theta Pi; hon. mem. bd. of govs., Univ. of Jerusalem; recipient: Hon. LLD, Knox Coll., 1953; hon. Dr. of Humane Letters, Brandeis Univ.; Solomon Bublick Prize, 1966; Doctor Juris Honoris Causa, Hebrew Univ., 1972.

SZTEJNWAKS, PINHUS, author, journalist, editor; b. Sokolow, Poland, July 17, 1905; d. N.Y.C., May 11, 1977; in U.S. since 1941; UN correspondent; mem. Labor Zionist movement, Warsaw; pres. Poalei Zion, 1935–77; editor, *Tzion Neiss,* World Zionist Org., 1942–51; special asst. for Yiddish press, the Jewish Agency, 1951–72; author: *Yiddishe Mames; Yidn zu Gedenken; Silhuetn Fun a Dor, Zionisten.*

WARSHAWSKY, IRVING, labor and communal leader, b. (?), d. (?), Aug. 1977; bd. mem. Jewish Natl. Fund of America; fought in Jewish Brigade, W.W.I; mem. Labor Zionist Movement; mem. Natl. Com. for Labor Israel.

WECHSLER, GABRIEL, administrator, communal leader; b. (?), 1909; d. N.Y.C., July 22, 1977; gen. sec. City Fusion Party, 1933–63; campaign dir. City of Hope; past deputy commissioner, sanitation and purchase; past asst. administrator, public affairs; exec. v. pres. Civic Fdn. of N.Y. State; veteran leader, Jabotinsky Movement, United Zionist Revisionists of America; founder, Amer. Com. for Natl. Sick Fund of Israel; founder, War Refugee Bd.; natl. sec. Emergency Com. to Save the Jewish People of Europe; founder, natl. sec. Com. for a Jewish Army of Stateless

and Palestinian Jews; directed part of negotiations with Vatican for rescue of Jews in Hungary; pres. Amer. League for a Free Palestine; former exec. dir. B'nai B'rith Council of Greater Philadelphia; pres. Natl. Haym Solomon Memorial Com.

WEISGAL, MEYER W., statesman, administrator, author, editor, communal leader; b. Kilol, Poland, Nov. 10, 1894; d. Jerusalem, Israel, Sept. 29, 1977; in U.S. 1905–49, Israel 1949–77; U.S. Army, W.W.I; founder: Amer. Jewish Conf.; Amer. section, Jewish Agency; World Zionist Org.; natl. sec. Zionist Org. of America, 1921–30; conceived and directed "The Romance of a People" (1933) and "The Eternal Road" (1936); dir. gen. Palestine Pavilion, N.Y. World's Fair, 1939–40; founder, past pres. Weizmann Institute of Science; Dr. Chaim Weizmann's personal sec. and U.S. representative; v. pres. State of Israel Bond Org., 1951; v. pres. Amer. Financial & Development Corp. for Israel, 1951; chmn. bd. Yad Chaim Weizmann natl. memorial, since 1952; chmn. world com. for Israel's tenth anniversary celebrations, 1958–59; chmn. bd. dirs. Tel Aviv's Cameri Theater; initiator, Itzik Manger Prize for Yiddish Literature; editor: *The Maccabean* (1918–21); *The New Palestine* (1921–30); *Bialik's Poems* (1926); *Herzl Memorial Book* (1929); *The Jewish Standard* (1930–32); *Chaim Weizmann: Statesman, Scientist, Builder of the Jewish Commonwealth* (1944); *Chaim Weizmann, A Biography by Many Hands* (1962); author, autobiography, *Meyer Weisgal . . . So Far* (1971); Weizmann Institute's first Ph. D. Honoris Causa, 1964; recipient: hon. doctorate, Brandeis Univ., 1969; hon. doctorate, Hebrew Univ. of Jerusalem, 1969; Rothschild Prize for Merit, 1969; Remembrance Award of World Fed. of Bergen Belsen Assns., 1974; King Solomon Award of America-Israel Cultural Fdn., 1976.

WOLFSON, ARTHUR, cantor, educator; b. Philadelphia, Pa., (?), 1912; d. (?), New Zealand, July 26, 1977; music dir. Temple Emanu-El, N.Y.C., since 1949; dir. Temple Emanu-El religious school; faculty mem.: School of Sacred Music; Hebrew Union Coll.-Jewish Institute of Religion, since 1950, faculty chmn. 1972–74; mem.: gov. bd. Amer. Soc. for Jewish Music; Amer. Musicological Soc.; Schola Musicae Liturgicae; exec. bd. Jewish Book Council of Jewish Welfare Bd.; chmn. Natl. Music Council, Jewish Welfare Bd.; pres.: Amer. Conf. of Cantors; Jewish Music Forum; Jewish Liturgical Music Soc.

ZAND, WALTER P., communal worker, educator; b. N.Y.C., Apr. 28, 1914; d. Miami, Fla., May 6, 1977; midwest regional dir., Fla. area dir. Amer. Jewish Com.; administrator, Welfare Council of Brooklyn, 1945–47; B'nai B'rith Council of Baltimore, 1947–49; chmn. Human Relations Com., City Club of Chicago, 1960; Mayor's Commission on Civil Rights, Chicago, 1960; chmn. Civil Rights Com., Natl. Assn. of Social Workers, 1961; associate prof. Human Relations, Univ. of Miami, 1967–77; taught human relations courses for U.S. Civil Service Commission and various bds. of ed. and police depts., 1968–76; author, "Training in Intergroup Relations," *Journal of Intergroup Relations* (1961); recipient: first place, Amer. Jewish Historical Soc. Award, 1956; Humanitarian Award, Broward County Chapter, Amer. Jewish Com.-Fla., 1977.

ZORN, LEWIS E., business exec., philanthropist; b. (?), 1900; d. Mount Vernon, N.Y., Oct. 12, 1977; pres. Brucks Div., Amer. Hosp. Supply Co.; founder: Amer. Friends of Hebrew Univ. in Jerusalem, v. pres. Greater Miami Chapter; Douglas Garden Jewish Home for the Aged, Miami; Mt. Sinai Medical Center, Miami Beach; recipient: Torch of Learning Award, Amer. Friends of Hebrew Univ.

Calendars

SUMMARY JEWISH CALENDAR, 5739–5743 (Oct. 1978–Sept. 1983)

HOLIDAY	5739 (1978)	5740 (1979)	5741 (1980)	5742 (1981)	5743 (1982)
Rosh Ha-shanah, 1st day	M Oct. 2	Sa Sept. 22	Th Sept. 11	T Sept. 29	Sa Sept. 18
Rosh Ha-shanah, 2nd day	T Oct. 3	S Sept. 23	F Sept. 12	W Sept. 30	S Sept. 19
Fast of Gedaliah	W Oct. 4	M Sept. 24	s Sept. 14	Th Oct. 1	M Sept. 20
Yom Kippur	W Oct. 11	M Oct. 1	Sa Sept. 20	Th Oct. 8	M Sept. 27
Sukkot, 1st day	M Oct. 16	Sa Oct. 6	Th Sept. 25	T Oct. 13	Sa Oct. 2
Sukkot, 2nd day	T Oct. 17	S Oct. 7	F Sept. 26	W Oct. 14	S Oct. 3
Hosha'na Rabbah	S Oct. 22	F Oct. 12	W Oct. 1	M Oct. 19	F Oct. 8
Shemini 'Azeret	M Oct. 23	Sa Oct. 13	Th Oct. 2	T Oct. 20	Sa Oct. 9
Simhat Torah	T Oct. 24	S Oct. 14	F Oct. 3	W Oct. 21	S Oct. 10
New Moon, Heshwan, 1st day	T Oct. 31	S Oct. 21	F Oct. 10	W Oct. 28	S Oct. 17
New Moon, Heshwan, 2nd day	W Nov. 1	M Oct. 22	Sa Oct. 11	Th Oct. 29	M Oct. 18
New Moon, Kislew, 1st day	Th Nov. 30	T Nov. 20	s Nov. 9	F Nov. 27	T Nov. 16
New Moon, Kislew, 2nd day	F Dec. 1	W Nov. 21			W Nov. 17
Hanukkah, 1st day	M Dec. 25	Sa Dec. 15	W Dec. 3	M Dec. 21	Sa Dec. 11
New Moon, Tevet, 1st day	Sa Dec. 30	Th Dec. 20	M Dec. 8	Sa Dec. 26	Th Dec. 16
New Moon, Tevet, 2nd day	S Dec. 31	F Dec. 21		S Dec. 27	F Dec. 17
Fast of the 10th of Tevet	T Jan. 9 (1979)	S Dec. 30	W Dec. 17	T Jan. 5 (1982)	S Dec. 26

	1979			1980			1981			1982			1983		
New Moon, Shevat	M	Jan.	29	Sa	Jan.	19	T	Jan.	6	M	Jan.	25	Sa	Jan.	15
Hamishshah-'asar bi-Shevat	M	Feb.	12	Sa	Feb.	2	T	Jan.	20	M	Feb.	8	Sa	Jan.	29
New Moon, Adar I, 1st day	T	Feb.	27	S	Feb.	17	W	Feb.	4	T	Feb.	23	S	Feb.	13
New Moon, Adar I, 2nd day	W	Feb.	28	M	Feb.	18	Th	Feb.	5	W	Feb.	24	M	Feb.	14
New Moon, Adar II, 1st day							F	Mar.	6						
New Moon, Adar II, 2nd day							Sa	Mar.	7						
Fast of Esther	M	Mar.	12	Th	Feb.	28	Th	Mar.	19	M	Mar.	8	Th	Feb.	24
Purim	T	Mar.	13	S	Mar.	2	F	Mar.	20	T	Mar.	9	S	Feb.	27
Shushan Purim	W	Mar.	14	M	Mar.	3	Sa	Mar.	21	W	Mar.	10	M	Feb.	28
New Moon, Nisan	Th	Mar.	29	T	Mar.	18	S	Apr.	5	Th	Mar.	25	T	Mar.	15
Passover, 1st day	Th	Apr.	12	T	Apr.	1	S	Apr.	19	Th	Apr.	8	T	Mar.	29
Passover, 2nd day	F	Apr.	13	W	Apr.	2	M	Apr.	20	F	Apr.	9	W	Mar.	30
Passover, 7th day	W	Apr.	18	M	Apr.	7	Sa	Apr.	25	W	Apr.	14	M	Apr.	4
Passover, 8th day	Th	Apr.	19	T	Apr.	8	S	Apr.	26	Th	Apr.	15	T	Apr.	5
Holocaust Memorial Day	T	Apr.	24	S	Apr.	13	F	May	1	T	Apr.	20	S	Apr.	10
New Moon, Iyar, 1st day	F	Apr.	27	W	Apr.	16	M	May	4	F	Apr.	23	W	Apr.	13
New Moon, Iyar, 2nd day	Sa	Apr.	28	Th	Apr.	17	T	May	5	Sa	Apr.	24	Th	Apr.	14
Yom ha-'Azma'ut	W	May	2	M	Apr.	21	Th	May	7	W	Apr.	28	M	Apr.	18
Lag ba-'Omer	T	May	15	S	May	4	F	May	22	T	May	11	S	May	1
New Moon, Siwan	S	May	27	F	May	16	W	June	3	S	May	23	F	May	13
Shavu'ot, 1st day	F	June	1	W	May	21	M	June	8	F	May	28	W	May	18
Shavu'ot, 2nd day	Sa	June	2	Th	May	22	T	June	9	Sa	May	29	Th	May	19
New Moon, Tammuz, 1st day	M	June	25	Sa	June	14	Th	July	2	M	June	21	Sa	June	11
New Moon, Tammuz, 2nd day	T	June	26	S	June	15	F	July	3	T	June	22	S	June	12
Fast of the 17th of Tammuz	Th	July	12	T	July	1	S	July	19	Th	July	8	T	June	28
New Moon, Av	W	July	25	M	July	14	Sa	Aug.	1	W	July	21	M	July	11
Fast of the 9th of Av	Th	Aug.	2	T	July	22	S	Aug.	9	Th	July	29	T	July	19
New Moon, Elul, 1st day	Th	Aug.	23	T	Aug.	12	S	Aug.	30	Th	Aug.	19	T	Aug.	9
New Moon, Elul, 2nd day	F	Aug.	24	W	Aug.	13	M	Aug.	31	F	Aug.	20	W	Aug.	10

CONDENSED MONTHLY CALENDAR
(1978–1980)

1977, Dec. 11—Jan. 8, 1978] ṬEVET (29 DAYS) [5738

Civil Date	Day of the Week	Jewish Date	SABBATHS, FESTIVALS, FASTS	PENTATEUCHAL READING	PROPHETICAL READING
Dec. 11	S	Tevet 1	Hanukkah, seventh day New Moon, second day	Num 28: 1–15 7: 48–53	
12	M	2	Hanukkah, eighth day	Num. 7: 54–8: 4	
17	Sa	7	Wa-yiggash	Gen. 44: 18–47: 27	Ezekiel 37: 15–28
20	T	10	Fast of the 10th of Ṭevet	Exod. 32: 11–14; 34: 1–10	Isaiah 55: 6–56: 8 (afternoon only)
24	Sa	14	Wa-yeḥi	Gen. 47: 28–50: 26	I Kings 2: 1–12
31	Sa	21	Shemot	Exod. 1: 1–6: 1	Isaiah 27: 6–28: 13; 29: 22–23 *Jeremiah 1: 1–2: 3*
Jan. 7	Sa	28	Wa-era'	Exod. 6: 2–9: 35	Ezekiel 28: 25–29: 21

*Italics are for
Sephardi Minhag.*

1978, Jan. 9—Feb. 7]   SHEVAṬ (30 DAYS)   [5738

Civil Date	Day of the Week	Jewish Date	SABBATHS, FESTIVALS, FASTS	PENTATEUCHAL READING	PROPHETICAL READING
Jan. 9	M	Shevaṭ 1	New Moon	Num. 28: 1–15	
14	Sa	6	Bo'	Exod. 10: 1–13: 16	Jeremiah 46: 13–28
21	Sa	13	Be-shallaḥ (Shirah)	Exod. 13: 17–17: 16	Judges 4: 4–5: 31 *Judges 5: 1–31*
23	M	15	Ḥamishshah-'asar bi-Shevaṭ		
28	Sa	20	Yitro	Exod. 18: 1–20: 23	Isaiah 6: 1–7: 6; 9: 5,6 *Isaiah 6: 1–13*
Feb. 4	Sa	27	Mishpaṭim	Exod. 21: 1–24: 18	Jeremiah 34: 8–22 33: 25,26
7	T	30	New Moon, first day	Num. 28: 1–15	

1978, Feb. 8—Mar. 9]   ADAR I (30 DAYS)   [5738

Civil Date	Day of the Week	Jewish Date	SABBATHS, FESTIVALS, FASTS	PENTATEUCHAL READING	PROPHETICAL READING
Feb. 8	W	Adar I 1	New Moon, second day	Num. 28: 1–15	
11	Sa	4	Terumah	Exod. 25: 1–27: 19	I Kings 5: 26–6: 13
18	Sa	11	Teẓawweh	Exod. 27: 20–30: 10	Ezekiel 43: 10–27
25	Sa	18	Ki tissa'	Exod. 30: 11–34: 35	I Kings 18: 1–39 *I Kings 18: 20–39*
Mar. 4	Sa	25	Wa-yakhel, Sheḳalim	Exod. 35: 1–38: 20; 30: 11–16	II Kings 12: 1–17 *II Kings 11: 17– 12: 17*
9	Th	30	New Moon, first day	Num. 28: 1–15	

Italics are for Sephardi Minhag.

1978, Mar. 10—Apr. 7] ADAR II (29 DAYS) [5738

Civil Date	Day of the Week	Jewish Date	SABBATHS, FESTIVALS, FASTS	PENTATEUCHAL READING	PROPHETICAL READING
Mar. 10	F	Adar II 1	New Moon, second day	Num. 28: 1–15	
11	Sa	2	Pekude	Exod. 38: 21–40: 38	I Kings 7: 51–8: 21 *I Kings 7: 40–50*
18	Sa	9	Wa-yikra' (Zakhor)	Levit. 1: 1–5: 26 Deut. 25: 17–19	I Samuel 15: 2–34 *I Samuel 15: 1–34*
22	W	13	Fast of Esther	Exod. 32: 11–14; 34: 1–10	Isaiah 55: 6–56: 8 (afternoon only)
23	Th	14	Purim	Exod. 17: 8–16	Book of Esther is read the night before and in the morning.
24	F	15	Shushan Purim		
25	Sa	16	Zaw	Levit. 6: 1–8: 36	Jeremiah 7: 21–8: 3 9: 22–23
Apr. 1	Sa	23	Shemini, Parah	Levit. 9: 1–11: 47 Num. 19: 1–22	Ezekiel 36: 16–38 *Ezekiel 36: 16–36*

Italics are for
Sephardi Minhag.

1978, Apr. 8—May 7]   NISAN (30 DAYS)   [5738

Civil Date	Day of the Week	Jewish Date	SABBATHS, FESTIVALS, FASTS	PENTATEUCHAL READING	PROPHETICAL READING
Apr. 1	Sa	Nisan 1	Tazria' (Ha-ḥodesh); New Moon	Levit. 12: 1–13: 59 Num. 28: 7–15 Exod. 12: 1–20	Ezekiel 45: 16–46: 18 *Ezekiel 45: 18–46: 15* *Isaiah 66: 1, 24*
15	Sa	8	Mezora', (Ha-gadol)	Levit. 14: 1–15: 33	Malachi 3: 4–24
21	F	14	Fast of Firstborn		
22	Sa	15	Passover, first day	Exod. 12: 21–51 Num. 28: 16–25	Joshua 5: 2–6: 1, 27
23	S	16	Passover, second day	Levit. 22: 26–23: 44 Num. 28: 16–25	II Kings 23: 1–9; 21–25
24–27	M–Th	17–20	Ḥol Ha-mo'ed	M [Exod. 13: 1–16 Num. 28: 19–25] T [Exod. 22: 24– 23: 19 Num. 28: 19–25] W [Exod. 34: 1–26 Num. 28: 19–25] Th [Num. 9: 1–14 Num. 28: 19–25]	
28	F	21	Passover, seventh day	Exod. 13: 17–15: 26 Num. 28: 19–25	II Samuel 22: 1–51
29	Sa	22	Passover, eighth day	Deut. 15: 19–16: 17 Num. 28: 19–25	Isaiah 10: 32–12: 16
May 4	Th	27	Yom ha-sho'ah weha-gevurah		
6	Sa	29	Aḥare Mot	Levit. 16: 1–18: 30	I Samuel 20: 18–42
7	S	30	New Moon, first day	Num. 28: 1–15	

Italics are for Sephardi Minhag.

1978, May 8—June 5]   IYAR (29 DAYS)   [5738

Civil Date	Day of the Week	Jewish Date	SABBATHS, FESTIVALS, FASTS	PENTATEUCHAL READING	PROPHETICAL READING
May 8	M	Iyar 1	New Moon, second day	Num. 28: 1–15	
11	Th	4	Yom ha-Azma'ut		
13	Sa	6	Ḳedoshim	Levit. 19: 1–20: 27	Ezekiel 22: 1–19 *Ezekiel 20: 2–20*
20	Sa	13	Emor	Levit. 21: 1–24: 23	Ezekiel 44: 15–31
25	Th	18	Lag Ba-'omer		
27	Sa	20	Be-har	Levit. 25: 1–26: 2	Jeremiah 32: 6–27
June 3	Sa	27	Be-ḥukḳotai	Levit. 26: 3–27: 34	Jeremiah 16: 19– 17: 14

1978, June 6–July 5]   SIWAN (30 DAYS)   [5738

Civil Date	Day of the Week	Jewish Date	SABBATHS, FESTIVALS, FASTS	PENTATEUCHAL READING	PROPHETICAL READING
June 6	T	Siwan 1	New Moon	Num. 28: 1–15	
10	Sa	5	Be-midbar	Num. 1: 1–4: 20	Hosea 2: 1–22
11	S	6	Shavu'ot, first day	Exod. 19: 1–20: 23 Num. 28: 26–31	Ezekiel 1: 1–28; 3: 12
12	M	7	Shavu'ot, second day	Deut. 15: 19–16: 17 Num. 28: 26–31	Habbakuk 3: 1–19 *Habbakuk 2: 20– 3: 19*
17	Sa	12	Naso'	Num. 4: 21–7: 89	Judges 13: 2–25
24	Sa	19	Be-ha'alotekha	Num. 8: 1–12: 16	Zechariah 2: 14–4: 7
July 1	Sa	26	Shelaḥ lekha	Num. 13: 1–15: 41	Joshua 2: 1–24
5	W	30	New Moon, first day	Num. 28: 1–15	

Italics are for Sephardi Minhag.

1978, July 6—Aug. 3] TAMMUZ (29 DAYS) [5738

Civil Date	Day of the Week	Jewish Date	SABBATHS, FESTIVALS, FASTS	PENTATEUCHAL READING	PROPHETICAL READING
July 6	Th	Tammuz 1	New Moon, second day	Num. 28: 1–15	
8	Sa	3	Ḳoraḥ	Num. 16: 1–18: 32	I Samuel 11: 14–12: 22
15	Sa	10	Ḥukkat	Num. 19: 1–22: 1	Judges 11: 1–33
22	Sa	17	Balaḳ	Num. 22: 2–25: 9	Micah 5: 6–6: 8
23	S	18	Fast of the 17th of Tammuz	Exod. 32: 11–14; 34: 1–10	Isaiah 55: 6–56: 8 (afternoon only)
29	Sa	24	Pineḥas	Num. 25: 10–30: 1	Jeremiah 1: 1–2: 3

1978, Aug. 4—Sept. 2] AV (30 DAYS) [5738

Civil Date	Day of the Week	Jewish Date	SABBATHS, FESTIVALS, FASTS	PENTATEUCHAL READING	PROPHETICAL READING
Aug. 4	F	Av 1	New Moon	Num. 28: 1–15	
5	Sa	2	Maṭṭot, Mas‘e	Num. 30: 2–36: 13	Jeremiah 2: 4–28; 3: 4 *Jeremiah 2: 4–28; 4: 1–2*
12	Sa	9	Devarim (Ḥazon)	Deut. 1: 1–3: 22	Isaiah 1: 1–27
13	S	10	Fast of the 9th of Av	Morning: Deut. 4: 25–40 Afternoon: Exod. 32: 11–14; 34: 1–10	(Lamentations is read the night before.) Jeremiah 8: 13–9: 23 Isaiah 55: 6–56: 8
19	Sa	16	Wa-ethannan (Naḥamu)	Deut. 3: 23–7: 11	Isaiah 40: 1–26
26	Sa	23	‘Eḳev	Deut. 7: 12–11: 25	Isaiah 49: 14–51: 3
Sept. 2	Sa	30	Re’eh; New Moon, first day	Deut. 11: 26–16: 17 Num. 29: 9–15	Isaiah 66: 1–24 *Isaiah 66: 1–24* *I Samuel 20: 18, 42*

Italics are for Sephardi Minhag.

1978, Sept. 3—Oct. 1]　　　　ELUL (29 DAYS)　　　　[5738

Civil Date	Day of the Week	Jewish Date	SABBATHS, FESTIVALS, FASTS	PENTATEUCHAL READING	PROPHETICAL READING
Sept. 3	S	Elul 1	New Moon, second day	Num. 28: 1–15	
9	Sa	7	Shofeṭim	Deut. 16: 18–21: 9	Isaiah 51: 12–52: 12
16	Sa	14	Ki teze'	Deut. 21: 10–25: 19	Isaiah 54: 1–55: 5
23	Sa	21	Ki tavo'	Deut. 26: 1–29: 8	Isaiah 60: 1–22
30	Sa	28	Niẓẓavim	Deut. 29: 9–30: 20	Isaiah 61: 10–63: 9

Civil Date	Day of the Week	Jewish Date	SABBATHS, FESTIVALS, FASTS	PENTATEUCHAL READING	PROPHETICAL READING
Oct. 2	M	Tishri 1	Rosh Ha-shanah, first day	Gen. 21: 1–34 Num. 29: 1–6	I Samuel 1: 1–2: 10
3	T	2	Rosh Ha-shanah, second day	Gen. 22: 1–24 Num. 29: 1–6	Jeremiah 31: 1–19 (2–20)
4	W	3	Fast of Gedaliah	Exod. 32: 11–14; 34: 1–10	Isaiah 55: 6–56: 8 (afternoon only)
7	Sa	6	Wa-yelekh (Shuvah)	Deut. 31: 1–30	Hosea 14: 2–10 Micah 7: 18–20 Joel 2: 15–27 *Hosea 14: 2–10* *Micah 7: 18–20*
11	W	10	Yom Kippur	Morning: Levit. 16: 1–34 Num. 29: 7–11 Afternoon: Levit. 18: 1–30	Isaiah 57: 14–58: 14 Jonah 1: 1–4: 11 Micah 7: 18–20
14	Sa	13	Ha'azinu	Deut. 32: 1–52	II Samuel 22: 1–51
16	M	15	Sukkot, first day	Levit. 22: 26–23: 44 Num. 29: 12–16	Zechariah 14: 1–21
17	T	16	Sukkot, second day	Levit. 22: 26–23: 44 Num. 29: 12–16	I Kings 8: 2–21
18–20	W-F	17–19	Hol Ha-mo'ed	W Num. 29: 17–25 Th Num. 29: 20–28 F Num. 29: 23–31	
21	Sa	20	Hol Ha-mo'ed	Exod. 33: 12–34: 26 Num. 29: 29–34	Ezekiel 38: 18–39: 16
22	S	21	Hosha'na Rabbah	Num. 29: 26–34	
23	M	22	Shemini 'Azeret	Deut. 14: 22–16: 17 Num. 29: 35–30: 1	I Kings 8: 54–66
24	T	23	Simhat Torah	Deut. 33: 1–34: 12 Gen. 1: 1–2: 3 Num. 29: 35–30: 1	Joshua 1: 1–18 *Joshua 1: 1–9*
28	Sa	27	Be-re'shit	Gen. 1: 1–6: 8	Isaiah 42: 5–43: 10 *Isaiah 42: 5–21*
31	T	30	New Moon, first day	Num. 28: 1–15	

Italics are for
Sephardi Minhag.

1978, Nov. 1—Nov. 30]   HESHWAN (30 DAYS)   [5739

Civil Date	Day of the Week	Jewish Date	SABBATHS, FESTIVALS, FASTS	PENTATEUCHAL READING	PROPHETICAL READING
Nov. 1	W	Heshwan 1	New Moon, second day	Num. 28: 1–15	
4	Sa	4	Noah	Gen. 6: 9–11: 32	Isaiah 54: 1–55: 5 *Isaiah 54: 1–10*
11	Sa	11	Lekh lekha	Gen. 12: 1–17: 27	Isaiah 40: 27–41: 16
18	Sa	18	Wa-yera'	Gen. 18: 1–22: 24	II Kings 4: 1–37 *II Kings 4: 1–23*
25	Sa	25	Hayye Sarah	Gen. 23: 1–25: 18	I Kings 1: 1–31
30	Th	30	New Moon, first day	Num. 28: 1–15	

1978, Dec. 1—Dec. 30]   KISLEW (30 DAYS)   [5739

Civil Date	Day of the Week	Jewish Date	SABBATHS, FESTIVALS, FASTS	PENTATEUCHAL READING	PROPHETICAL READING
Dec. 1	F	Kislew 1	New Moon, second day	Num. 28: 1–15	
2	Sa	2	Toledot	Gen. 25: 19–28: 9	Malachi 1: 1–2: 27
9	Sa	9	Wa-yeze'	Gen. 28: 10–32: 3	Hosea 12: 13–14: 10 *Hosea 11: 7–12: 12*
16	Sa	16	Wa-yishlah	Gen. 32: 4–36: 43	Hosea 11: 7–12: 12 *Obadiah 1: 1–21*
23	Sa	23	Wa-yeshev	Gen. 37: 1–40: 23	Amos 2: 6–3: 8
25–29	M-F	25–29	Hanukkah, first to fifth days	M Num. 7: 1–17 T Num. 7: 18–29 W Num. 7: 24–35 Th Num. 7: 30–41 F Num. 7: 36–47	
30	Sa	30	Mi-kez; Hannukkah, sixth day; New Moon, first day	Gen. 41: 1–44: 17 Num. 28: 9–15 Num. 7: 42–47	Zechariah 2: 14–4: 7 *Zechariah 2: 14–4: 7 Isaiah 66: 1, 23* I Samuel 20: 18, 42

Italics are for
Sephardi Minhag.

1978, Dec. 31—Jan. 28, 1979] ṬEVET (29 DAYS) [5739

Civil Date	Day of the Week	Jewish Date	SABBATHS, FESTIVALS, FASTS	PENTATEUCHAL READING	PROPHETICAL READING
Dec. 31	S	Ṭevet 1	Ḥanukkah, seventh day; New Moon, second day	Num. 28: 1–15 7: 48–53	
Jan. 1	M	2	Ḥanukkah, eighth day	Num. 7: 54–8: 4	
6	Sa	7	Wa-yiggash	Gen. 44: 18–47: 27	Ezekiel 37: 15–28
9	T	10	Fast of the 10th of Ṭevet	Exod. 32: 11–14; 34: 1–10	Isaiah 55: 6–56: 8 (afternoon only)
13	Sa	14	Wa-yeḥi	Gen. 47: 28–50: 26	I Kings 2: 1–12
20	Sa	21	Shemot	Exod. 1: 1–6: 1	Isaiah 27: 6–28: 13; 29: 22, 23 *Jeremiah 1: 1–2: 3*
27	Sa	28	Wa-era'	Exod. 6: 2–9: 35	Ezekiel 28: 25–29: 21

1979, Jan. 29–Feb. 27] SHEVAṬ (30 DAYS) [5739

Civil Date	Day of the Week	Jewish Date	SABBATHS, FESTIVALS, FASTS	PENTATEUCHAL READING	PROPHETICAL READING
Jan. 29	M	Shevaṭ 1	New Moon	Num. 28: 1–15	
Feb. 3	Sa	6	Bo'	Exod. 10: 1–13: 16	Jeremiah 46: 13–28
10	Sa	13	Be-shallaḥ (Shirah)	Exod. 13: 17–17: 16	Judges 4: 4–5: 31 *Judges 5: 1–31*
12	M	15	Ḥamishsha-'asar bi-Shevaṭ		
17	Sa	20	Yitro	Exod. 18: 1–20: 23	Isaiah 6: 1–7: 6; 9: 5, 6 *Isaiah 6: 1–13*
24	Sa	27	Mishpaṭim (Sheḳalim)	Exod. 21: 1–24: 18; 30: 11–16	II Kings 12: 1–17 *II Kings 11: 17–12: 17*
27	T	30	New Moon, first day	Num. 28: 1–15	

Italics are for Sephardi Minhag.

1979, Feb. 28–Mar. 28]   ADAR (29 DAYS)   [5739

Civil Date	Day of the Week	Jewish Date	SABBATHS, FESTIVALS, FASTS	PENTATEUCHAL READING	PROPHETICAL READING
Feb. 28	W	Adar 1	New Moon, second day	Num. 28: 1–15	
Mar 3	Sa	4	Terumah	Exod. 25: 1–27: 19	I Kings 5: 26–6: 13
10	Sa	11	Tezawweh (Zakhor)	Exod. 27: 20–30: 10 Deut. 25: 17–19	I Samuel 15: 2–34 *I Samuel 15: 1–34*
12	M	13	Fast of Esther	Exod. 32: 11–14; 34: 1–10	Isaiah 55: 6–56: 8 (afternoon only)
13	T	14	Purim	Exod. 17: 8–16	(Book of Esther is read the night before and in the morning.)
14	W	15	Shushan Purim		
17	Sa	18	Ki tissa' (Parah)	Exod. 30: 11–34: 35 Num. 19: 1–22	Ezekiel 36: 16–38 *Ezekiel 36: 16–36*
24	Sa	25	Wa-yakhel, Pekude; (Ha-ḥodesh)	Exod. 35: 1–40: 38; 12: 1–20	Ezekiel 45: 16–46: 18 *Ezekiel 36: 18–46: 15*

*Italics are for
Sephardi Minhag.*

1979, Mar. 29—Apr. 27]   NISAN (30 DAYS)   [5739

Civil Date	Day of the Week	Jewish Date	SABBATHS, FESTIVALS, FASTS	PENTATEUCHAL READING	PROPHETICAL READING
Mar. 29	Th	Nisan 1	New Moon	Num. 28: 1–15	
31	Sa	3	Wa-yikra'	Lev. 1: 1–5: 26	Isaiah 43: 21–44: 23
Apr. 7	Sa	10	Zaw (Ha-gadol)	Lev. 6: 1–8: 36	Malachi 3: 4–24
11	W	14	Fast of Firstborn		
12	Th	15	Passover, first day	Exod. 12: 21–51 / Num. 28: 16–25	Joshua 5: 2–6: 1, 27
13	F	16	Passover, second day	Lev. 22: 26–23: 44 / Num. 28: 16–25	II Kings 23: 1–9; 21–25
14–17	Sa-T	17–20	Ḥol Ha-mo'ed	Sa Exod. 33: 12–34: 26 / Num. 28: 19–25 S Exod. 13: 1–16 / Num. 28: 19–25 M Exod. 22: 24–23: 19 / Num. 28: 19–25 T Num. 9: 1–14 / 28: 19–25	Ezekiel 37: 1–15
18	W	21	Passover, seventh day	Exod. 13: 17–15: 26 / Num. 28: 19–25	II Samuel 22: 1–51
19	Th	22	Passover, eighth day	Deut. 15: 19–16: 17 / Num. 28: 19–25	Isaiah 10: 32–12: 6
21	Sa	24	Shemini	Levit. 9: 1–11: 47	II Samuel 6: 1–7: 17
24	T	27	Yom ha-sho'ah weha-gevurah		
27	F	30	New Moon, first day	Num. 28: 1–15	

1979, Apr. 28—May 26]   IYAR (29 DAYS)   [5739

Civil Date	Day of the Week	Jewish Date	SABBATHS, FESTIVALS, FASTS	PENTATEUCHAL READING	PROPHETICAL READING
Apr. 28	Sa	Iyar 1	Tazria'; Mezora'; New Moon, second day	Levit. 12: 11–15: 33 Num. 28: 9–15	Isaiah 66: 1–23
May 2	W	5	Yom ha-'Azma'ut		
5	Sa	8	Ahare Mot, Kedoshim	Levit. 16: 1–20: 27	Amos 9: 7–15 *Ezekiel 20: 2–20*
12	Sa	15	Emor	Levit. 21: 1–24: 23	Ezekiel 44: 15–31
15	T	18	Lag Ba-'omer		
19	Sa	22	Be-har, Be-hukkotai	Levit. 25: 1–27: 34	Jeremiah 16: 19– 17: 14
26	Sa	29	Be-midmar	Num. 1: 1–4: 20	I Samuel 20: 18–42

1979, May 27—June 25]   SIWAN (30 DAYS)   [5739

Civil Date	Day of the Week	Jewish Date	SABBATHS, FESTIVALS, FASTS	PENTATEUCHAL READING	PROPHETICAL READING
May 27	S	Siwan 1	New Moon	Num. 28: 1–15	
June 1	F	6	Shavu'ot, first day	Exod. 19: 1–20: 23 Num. 28: 26–31	Ezekiel 1: 1–28; 3: 12
2	Sa	7	Shavu'ot, second day	Deut. 15: 19–16: 17 Num. 28: 26–31	Habbakuk 3: 1–19 *Habbakuk 2: 20– 3: 19*
9	Sa	14	Naso'	Num. 4: 21–7: 89	Judges 13: 2–25
16	Sa	21	Be-ha'alotekha	Num. 8: 1–12: 16	Zechariah 2: 14–4: 7
23	Sa	28	Shelah lekha	Num. 13: 1–15: 41	Joshua 2: 1–24
25	M	30	New Moon, first day	Num. 28: 1–15	

*Italics are for
Sephardi Minhag.*

1979, June 26—July 24]   TAMMUZ (29 DAYS)   [5739

Civil Date	Day of the Week	Jewish Date	SABBATHS, FESTIVALS, FASTS	PENTATEUCHAL READING	PROPHETICAL READING
June 26	T	Tammuz 1	New Moon, second day	Num. 28: 1–5	
30	Sa	5	Ḳoraḥ	Num. 16: 1–18: 32	I Samuel 11: 14–12: 22
July 7	Sa	12	Ḥukkat, Balak	Num. 19: 1–25: 9	Micah 5: 6–6: 8
12	Th	17	Fast of the 17th of Tammuz	Exod. 32: 11–14; 34: 1–10	Isaiah 55: 6–56: 8 (afternoon only)
14	Sa	19	Pineḥas	Num. 25: 10–30: 1	Jeremiah 1: 1–2: 3
21	Sa	26	Maṭṭot, Mas'e	Num. 30: 2–36: 13	Jeremiah 2: 4–28; 3: 4 *Jeremiah 2: 4–28; 4: 1, 2*

1979, July 25—Aug. 23]   AV (30 DAYS)   [5739

Civil Date	Day of the Week	Jewish Date	SABBATHS, FESTIVALS, FASTS	PENTATEUCHAL READING	PROPHETICAL READING
July 25	W	Av 1	New Moon	Num. 28: 1–15	
28	Sa	4	Devarim (Ḥazon)	Deut. 1: 1–3: 22	Isaiah 1: 1–27
Aug. 2	Th	9	Fast of the 9th of Av	Morning: Deut. 4: 25–40 Afternoon: Exod. 32: 11–14; 34: 1–10	(Lamentations is read the night before.) Jeremiah 8: 13–9: 23 Isaiah 55: 6–56: 8
4	Sa	11	Wa-ethannan (Naḥamu)	Deut. 3: 23–7: 11	Isaiah 40: 1–26
11	Sa	18	'Ekev	Deut. 7: 12–11: 25	Isaiah 49: 14–51: 3
18	Sa	25	Re'eh	Deut. 11: 26–16: 17	Isaiah 54: 11–55: 5
23	Th	30	New Moon, first day	Num. 28: 1–15	

Italics are for Sephardi Minhag.

1979, Aug. 24–Sept. 21]   ELUL (29 DAYS)   [5739

Civil Date	Day of the Week	Jewish Date	SABBATHS, FESTIVALS, FASTS	PENTATEUCHAL READING	PROPHETICAL READING
Aug. 24	F	Elul 1	New Moon, second day	Num. 28: 1–15	
25	Sa	2	Shofeṭim	Deut. 16: 18–21: 9	Isaiah 51: 12–52: 12
Sept. 1	Sa	9	Ki teẓe'	Deut. 21: 10–25: 19	Isaiah 54: 1–10
8	Sa	16	Ki tavo'	Deut. 26: 1–29: 8	Isaiah 60: 1–22
15	Sa	23	Niẓẓavim; We-yelekh	Deut. 29: 9–31: 30	Isaiah 61: 10–63: 9

1979, Sept. 22–Oct. 21]   TISHRI (30 DAYS)   [5740

Civil Date	Day of the Week	Jewish Date	SABBATHS, FESTIVALS, FASTS	PENTATEUCHAL READING	PROPHETICAL READING
Sept. 22	Sa	Tishri 1	Rosh Ha-shanah, first day	Gen. 21: 1–34 Num. 29: 1–6	I Samuel 1: 1–2: 10
23	S	2	Rosh Ha-shanah, second day	Gen. 22: 1–24 Num. 29: 1–6	Jeremiah 31: 1–19 (2–20)
24	M	3	Fast of Gedaliah	Exod. 32: 11–14; 34: 1–10	Isaiah 55: 6–56: 8 (afternoon only)
29	Sa	8	Ha'azinu (Shuvah)	Deut. 32: 1–52	Hosea 14: 2–10 Micah 7: 18–20 Joel 2: 15–27 *Hosea 14: 2–10* *Micah 7: 18–20*
Oct. 1	M	10	Yom Kippur	Morning: Levit. 16: 1–34 Num. 29: 1–11 Afternoon: Levit. 18: 1–30	Isaiah 57: 14–58: 14 Jonah 1: 1–4: 11 Micah 7: 18–20
6	Sa	15	Sukkot, first day	Levit. 22: 26–23: 44 Num. 29: 12–16	Zechariah 14: 1–21
7	S	16	Sukkot, second day	Levit. 22: 26–23: 44 Num. 29: 12–16	I Kings 8: 2–21
8–11	M–Th	17–20	Ḥol Ha-mo'ed	M Num. 29: 17–25 T Num. 29: 20–28 W Num. 29: 23–31 Th Num. 29: 26–34	
12	F	21	Hosha'na Rabbah	Num. 29: 26–34	
13	Sa	22	Shemini 'Azeret	Deut. 14: 22–16: 17 Num. 29: 35–30: 1	I Kings 8: 54–66
14	S	23	Simḥat Torah	Deut. 33: 1–34: 12 Gen. 1: 1–2: 3 Num. 29: 35–30: 1	Joshua 1: 1–18 *Joshua 1: 1–19*
20	Sa	29	Be-re'shit	Gen. 1: 1–6: 8	I Samuel 20: 18–42
21	S	30	New Moon, first day	Num. 28: 1–15	

*Italics are for
Sephardi Minhag.*

1979, Oct. 22–Nov. 20]   ḤESHWAN (29 DAYS)   [5740

Civil Date	Day of the Week	Jewish Date	SABBATHS, FESTIVALS, FASTS	PENTATEUCHAL READING	PROPHETICAL READING
Oct. 22	M	Heshwan 1	New Moon, second day	Num. 28: 1–15	
27	Sa	6	Noaḥ	Gen. 6: 19–11: 32	Isaiah 54: 1–55: 5
Nov. 3	Sa	13	Lekh lekha	Gen. 12: 1–17: 27	Isaiah 40: 27–41: 16
10	Sa	20	Wa-yera'	Gen. 18: 1–22: 24	II Kings 4: 1–37 *II Kings 4: 1–23*
17	Sa	27	Ḥayye Sarah	Gen. 23: 1–25: 18	I Kings 1: 1–31
20	T	30	New Moon, first day	Num. 28: 1–15	

1979, Nov. 21–Dec. 20]   KISLEW (30 DAYS)   [5740

Civil Date	Day of the Week	Jewish Date	SABBATHS, FESTIVALS, FASTS	PENTATEUCHAL READING	PROPHETICAL READING
Nov. 21	W	Kislew 1	New Moon, second day	Num. 28: 1–15	
24	Sa	4	Toledot	Gen. 25: 19–28: 9	Malachi 1: 1–2: 7
Dec. 1	Sa	11	Wa-yeze'	Gen. 28: 10–32: 3	Hosea 12: 13–14: 10 *Hosea 11: 7–12: 12*
8	Sa	18	Wa-yishlaḥ	Gen. 32: 4–36: 43	Hosea 11: 7–12: 12 *Obadiah 1: 1–21*
15	Sa	25	Wa-yeshev; Ḥanukkah, first day	{ Gen. 37: 1–40: 23 { Num. 7: 1–17	Zechariah 2: 14–4: 7
16–19	S-W	26–29	Ḥanukkah, second to fifth day	S Num. 7: 18–29 M Num. 7: 24–35 T Num. 7: 30–41 W Num. 7: 36–47	
20	Th	30	Ḥanukkah, sixth day; New Moon, first day	Num. 28: 1–15 7: 42–47	

Italics are for Sephardi Minhag.

1979, Dec. 21–Jan. 18, 1980] TEVET (29 DAYS) [5740

Civil Date	Day of the Week	Jewish Date	SABBATHS, FESTIVALS, FASTS	PENTATEUCHAL READING	PROPHETICAL READING
Dec. 21	F	Tevet 1	Hanukkah, seventh day; New Moon, second day	Num. 28: 1–15 7: 48–53	
22	Sa	2	Mi-kez; Hanukkah, eighth day	Gen. 41: 1–44: 17 Num. 7: 54–8: 4	I Kings 7: 40–50
29	Sa	9	Wa-yiggash	Gen. 44: 18–47: 27	Ezekiel 37: 15–28
30	S	10	Fast of 10th of Tevet	Exod. 32: 11–14; 34: 1–10	Isaiah 55: 6–56: 8 (afternoon only)
1980 Jan. 5	Sa	16	Wa-yehi	Gen. 47: 28–50: 26	I Kings 2: 1–12
12	Sa	23	Shemot	Exod. 1: 1–6: 7	Isaiah 27: 6–28: 13; 29: 22–23 *Jeremiah 1: 1–2: 3*

1980, Jan. 19–Feb. 17] SHEVAT (30 DAYS) [5740

Civil Date	Day of the Week	Jewish Date	SABBATHS, FESTIVALS, FASTS	PENTATEUCHAL READING	PROPHETICAL READING
Jan. 19	Sa	Shevat 1	Wa-era' New Moon	Exod. 6: 2–9: 35	Isaiah 66: 1–24
26	Sa	8	Bo'	Exod. 10: 1–13: 16	Jeremiah 46: 13–28
Feb. 2	Sa	15	Be-shallah (Shirah)	Exod. 13: 17–17: 16	Judges 4: 4–5: 31 *Judges 5: 1–31*
9	Sa	22	Hamishsha-'asar bi-Shevat Yitro	Exod. 18: 1–20: 23	Isaiah 6: 1–7: 6 9: 5, 6
16	Sa	29	Mishpatim (Shekalim)	Exod. 21–24: 18 30: 11–16	II Kings 12: 1–17 *II Kings 11: 17–12: 17*
17	S	30	New Moon, first day	Num. 28: 1–15	*I Samuel 20: 18, 42*

Italics are for Sephardi Minhag.

Civil Date	Day of the Week	Jewish Date	SABBATHS, FESTIVALS, FASTS	PENTATEUCHAL READING	PROPHETICAL READING
Feb. 18	M	Adar 1	New Moon, second day	Num. 28: 1–15	
23	Sa	6	Terumah	Exod. 25: 1–27: 19	I Kings 5: 26–6: 13
28	Th	11	Fast of Esther	Exod. 32: 11–14 34: 1–10	Isaiah 55: 6–56: 8 (afternoon only)
Mar. 1	Sa	13	Teẓawweh (Zakhor)	Exod. 27: 20–30: 10 Deut. 25: 17–19	I Samuel 15: 2–34 *I Samuel 15: 1–34*
2	S	14	Purim	Exod. 17: 8–16	Book of Esther (night before and in the morning)
3	M	15	Shushan Purim		
8	Sa	20	Ki tissa' (Parah)	Exod. 30: 11–34: 35 Num. 19: 1–22	Ezekiel 36: 16–38 *Ezekiel 36: 16–36*
15	Sa	27	Wa-yakhel, Pekude (Ha-ḥodesh)	Exod. 35: 1–40: 38 12: 1–20	Ezekiel 45: 16–46: 18 *Ezekiel 45: 18–46: 15*

Italics are for Sephardi Minhag.

1980, Mar. 18-Apr. 16] NISAN (30 DAYS) [5740

Civil Date	Day of the Week	Jewish Date	SABBATHS, FESTIVALS, FASTS	PENTATEUCHAL READING	PROPHETICAL READING
Mar. 18	T	Nisan 1	New Moon	Num. 28: 1–15	
22	Sa	5	Wa–yiḳra'	Levit. 1: 1–5: 26	Isaiah 43: 21–44: 23
29	Sa	12	Ẓaw (Ha–gadol)	Levit. 6: 1–8: 36	Malachi 3: 4–24
31	M	14	Fast of the Firstborn		
Apr. 1	T	15	Passover, first day	Exod. 12: 21–51 Num. 28: 16–25	Joshua 5: 2–6: 1, 27
2	W	16	Passover, second day	Levit. 22: 26–23: 44 Num. 28: 16–25	II Kings 23: 1–9, 21–25
3	Th	17	Ḥol Ha-mo'ed	Exod. 13: 1–16 Num. 28: 19–25	
4	F	18	Ḥol Ha-mo'ed	Exod. 22: 24–23: 19 Num. 28: 19–25	
5	Sa	19	Ḥol Ha-mo'ed	Exod. 33: 12–34: 26 Num. 28: 19–25	Ezekiel 37: 1–15
6	S	20	Ḥol Ha-mo'ed	Num. 9: 1–14; 28: 19–25	
7	M	21	Passover, seventh day	Exod. 13: 17–15: 26 Num. 28: 19–25	II Samuel 22: 1–5
8	T	22	Passover, eighth day	Deut. 15: 19–16: 17 Num. 28: 19–25	Isaiah 10: 32–12: 6
12	Sa	26	Shemini	Levit. 9: 1–11: 47	II Samuel 6: 1–7: 17
13	S	27	Holocaust Memorial Day		
16	W	30	New Moon, first day	Num. 28: 1–15	

1980, Apr. 17–May 15]   IYAR (29 DAYS)   [5740

Civil Date	Day of the Week	Jewish Date	SABBATHS, FESTIVALS, FASTS	PENTATEUCHAL READING	PROPHETICAL READING
Apr. 17	Th	Iyar 1	New Moon, second day	Num. 28: 1–15	
19	Sa	3	Tazria', Mezora'	Levit. 12: 1–15: 33 Num. 28: 9–15	II Kings 7: 3–20
26	Sa	10	Ahare Mot, Kedoshim	Levit. 16: 1–20: 27	Amos 9: 7–15 *Ezekiel 20: 2–20*
May 3	Sa	17	Emor	Levit. 21: 1–24: 23	Ezekiel 44: 15–31
4	S	18	Lag Ba-'omer Israel Independence Day		
10	Sa	24	Be-har, Be-hukkotai	Levit. 25: 1–27: 34	Jeremiah 16: 19– 17: 14

1980, May 16–June 14]   SIWAN (30 DAYS)   [5740

Civil Date	Day of the Week	Jewish Date	SABBATHS, FESTIVALS, FASTS	PENTATEUCHAL READING	PROPHETICAL READING
May 16	F	Siwan 1	New Moon	Num. 28: 1–15	
17	Sa	2	Be–midbar	Num. 1: 1–4: 20	Hosea 2: 1–22
21	W	6	Shavu'ot, first day	Exod. 19: 1–20: 23 Num. 28: 26–31	Ezekiel 1: 1–28 3: 12
22	Th	7	Shavu'ot, second day	Deut. 15: 19–16: 17 Num. 28: 26–31	Habbakuk 3: 1–19 *Habbakuk 2: 20– 3:19*
24	Sa	9	Naso'	Num. 4: 21–7: 89	Judges 13: 2–25
31	Sa	16	Be-ha'alotekha	Num. 8: 1–12: 16	Zechariah 2: 14–4: 7
June 7	Sa	23	Shelah Lekha	Num. 13: 1–15: 41	Joshua 2: 1–24
14	Sa	30	Korah New Moon, first day	Num. 16: 1–18: 32 Num. 28: 9–15	Isaiah 66: 1–24 *I Samuel 20: 18, 42*

Italics are for Sephardi Minhag.

1980, June 15-July 13]   TAMMUZ (29 DAYS)   [5740

Civil Date	Day of the Week	Jewish Date	SABBATHS, FESTIVALS, FASTS	PENTATEUCHAL READING	PROPHETICAL READING
June 15	S	Tammuz 1	New Moon, second day	Num. 28: 1–15	
21	Sa	7	Ḥukkat	Num. 19: 1–22: 1	Judges 11: 1–33
28	Sa	14	Balak	Num. 22: 2–25: 9	Micah 5: 6–6: 8
July 1	T	17	Fast of the 17th of Tammuz	Exod. 32: 11–14 34: 1–10	Isaiah 55: 6–56: 8 (afternoon only)
5	Sa	21	Pineḥas	Num. 25: 10–30: 1	Jeremiah 1: 1–2: 3
12	Sa	28	Maṭṭot, Mas'e	Num. 30: 2–36: 13	Jeremiah 2: 4–28, 3: 4 *Jeremiah 2: 4–28, 4: 1, 2*

1980, July 14-Aug. 12]   AV (30 DAYS)   [5740

Civil Date	Day of the Week	Jewish Date	SABBATHS, FESTIVALS, FASTS	PENTATEUCHAL READING	PROPHETICAL READING
July 14	M	Av 1	New Moon	Num. 28: 1–15	
19	Sa	6	Devarim (Ḥazon)	Deut. 1: 1–3: 22	Isaiah 1: 1–27
22	T	9	Fast of the 9th of Av	Morning: Deut. 4: 25–40 Afternoon: Exod. 32: 11–14 34: 1–10	(Lamentations is read the night before.) Jeremiah 8: 13–9: 23 Isaiah 55: 6–56: 8
26	Sa	13	Wa-etḥannan (Naḥamu)	Deut. 3: 23–7: 11	Isaiah 40: 1–26
Aug. 2	Sa	20	'Ekev	Deut. 7: 12–11: 25	Isaiah 49: 14–51: 3
9	Sa	27	Re'eh	Deut. 11: 26–16: 17	Isaiah 54: 11–55: 5
12	T	30	New Moon, first day	Num. 28: 1–15	

Italics are for Sephardi Minhag.

1980, Aug. 13-Sept. 10]   ELUL (29 DAYS)   [5740

Civil Date	Day of the Week	Jewish Date	SABBATHS, FESTIVALS, FASTS	PENTATEUCHAL READING	PROPHETICAL READING
Aug. 13	W	Elul 1	New Moon, second day	Num. 28: 1–15	
16	Sa	4	Shofeṭim	Deut. 16: 18–21: 9	Isaiah 51: 12–52: 12
23	Sa	11	Ki teze'	Deut. 21: 10–25: 19	Isaiah 54: 1–10
30	Sa	18	Ki tavo'	Deut. 26: 1–29: 8	Isaiah 60: 1–22
Sept. 6	Sa	25	Nizzavim, Wa-yelekh	Deut. 29: 9–31: 30	Isaiah 61: 10–63: 9

1980, Sept. 11–Oct. 10]   TISHRI (30 DAYS)   [5741

Civil Date	Day of the Week	Jewish Date	SABBATHS, FESTIVALS, FASTS	PENTATEUCHAL READING	PROPHETICAL READING
Sept. 11	Th	Tishri 1	Rosh Ha-shanah, first day	Gen. 21: 1–34 Num. 29: 1–6	I Samuel 1: 1–2: 10
12	F	2	Rosh Ha-shanah, second day	Gen. 22: 1–24 Num. 29: 1–6	Jeremiah 31: 2–20
13	Sa	3	Ha'azinu (Shuvah)	Deut. 32: 1–52	Hosea 14: 2–10 Micah 7: 18–20 Joel 2: 15–27 *Hosea 14: 2–10* *Micah 7: 18–20*
14	S	4	Fast of Gedaliah	Exod. 32: 11–14; 34: 1–10	Isaiah 55: 6–56: 8
20	Sa	10	Yom Kippur	Morning: Levit. 16: 1–34 Num. 29: 7–11 Afternoon: Levit. 18: 1–30	Isaiah 57: 14–58: 14 Jonah 1: 1–14: 11 Micah 7: 18–20
25	Th	15	Sukkot, first day	Levit. 22: 26–23: 44 Num. 29: 12–16	Zechariah 14: 1–21
26	F	16	Sukkot, second day	Levit. 22: 26–23: 44 Num. 29: 12–16	I Kings 8: 2–21
27	Sa	17	Hol Ha–mo'ed	Exod. 33: 12–34: 26 Num. 29: 17–22	Ezekiel 38: 18–39: 16
28	S	18	Hol Ha–mo'ed	Num. 29: 20–28	
29	M	19	Hol Ha–mo 'ed	Num. 29: 23–31	
30	T	20	Hol Ha–mo'ed	Num. 29: 26–34	
Oct. 1	W	21	Hosha'na Rabbah	Num. 29: 26–34	
2	Th	22	Shemini 'Azeret	Deut. 14: 22–16: 17 Num. 29: 35–30: 1	I Kings 8: 54–66
3	F	23	Simhat Torah	Deut. 33: 1–34: 12 Gen. 1: 1–2: 3 Num. 29: 35–30: 1	Joshua 1: 1–18 *Joshua 1: 1–9*
4	Sa	24	Be-re'shit	Gen. 1: 1–6: 8	Isaiah 42: 5–43: 10 *Isaiah 42: 5–21*
10	F	30	New Moon, first day	Num. 28: 1–15	

Italics are for Sephardi Minhag.

1980, Oct. 11–Nov. 8]   ḤESHWAN (29 DAYS)   [5741

Civil Date	Day of the Week	Jewish Date	SABBATHS, FESTIVALS, FASTS	PENTATEUCHAL READING	PROPHETICAL READING
Oct. 11	Sa	Heshwan 1	Noah, New Moon, second day	Gen. 6: 9–11: 32 Num. 28: 9–15	Isaiah 66: 1–24
18	Sa	8	Lekh Lekha	Gen. 12: 1–17: 27	Isaiah 40: 27–41: 16
25	Sa	15	Wa-yera'	Gen. 18: 1–22: 24	II Kings 4: 1–37 *II Kings 4: 1–23*
Nov. 1	Sa	22	Ḥayye Sarah	Gen. 23: 1–25: 18	I Kings 1: 1–31
8	Sa	29	Toledot	Gen. 25: 19–28: 9	I Samuel 20: 18–42

1980, Nov. 9-Dec. 7]   KISLEW (29 DAYS)   [5741

Civil Date	Day of the Week	Jewish Date	SABBATHS, FESTIVALS, FASTS	PENTATEUCHAL READING	PROPHETICAL READING
Nov. 9	S	Kislew 1	New Moon	Num. 28: 1–15	
15	Sa	7	Wa-yeẓe'	Gen. 28: 10–32: 3	Hosea 12: 13–14: 10 *Hosea 11: 7–12: 12*
22	Sa	14	Wa-yishlaḥ	Gen. 32: 4–36: 43	Hosea 11: 7–12: 12 *Obadiah 1: 1–21*
29	Sa	21	Wa-yeshev	Gen. 37: 1–40: 23	Amos 2: 6–3: 8
Dec. 3	W	25	Ḥanukkah, first day	Num. 7: 1–17	
4	Th	26	Ḥanukkah, second day	Num. 7: 18–29	
5	F	27	Ḥanukkah, third day	Num. 7: 24–35	
6	Sa	28	Mi-ḳeẓ Ḥanukkah, fourth day	Gen. 41: 1–44: 17 Num. 7: 30–35	Zechariah 2: 14–4: 7
7	S	29	Ḥanukkah, fifth day	Num. 7: 36–47	

Italics are for Sephardi Minhag.

1980, Dec. 8-Jan. 5, 1981]   ṬEVET (29 DAYS)   [5741

Civil Date	Day of the Week	Jewish Date	SABBATHS, FESTIVALS, FASTS	PENTATEUCHAL READING	PROPHETICAL READING
Dec. 8	M	Ṭevet 1	Ḥanukkah, sixth day New Moon	Num. 28: 1–15 7: 42–47	
9	T	2	Ḥanukkah, seventh day	Num. 7: 48–59	
10	W	3	Ḥanukkah, eighth day	Num. 7: 54–8: 4	
13	Sa	6	Wa-yiggash	Gen. 44: 18–47: 27	Ezekiel 37: 15–28
17	T	10	Fast of the 10th of Ṭevet	Exod. 32: 11–14 34: 1–10	Isaiah 55: 6–56: 8 (afternoon only)
20	Sa	13	Wa-yeḥi	Gen. 47: 28–50: 26	I Kings 2: 1–12
27	Sa	20	Shemot	Exod. 1: 1–6: 1	Isaiah 27: 6–28: 13 29: 22–23 *Jeremiah 1: 1–2: 3*
Jan. 3	Sa	27	Wa-era'	Exod. 6: 2–9: 35	Ezekiel 28: 25–29: 21

*Italics are for
Sephardi Minhag.*

The Jewish Publication Society of America

REPORT OF NINETIETH YEAR

REPORT OF THE 90TH JPS ANNUAL MEETING

The 90th annual meeting of the Society was held on Sunday, May 21, 1978, at the Hilton Hotel in Philadelphia. Presiding was A. Leo Levin, president of the Society.

Jerome J. Shestack, associate chairman, presented the report of the Nominating Committee, which was chaired by Bernard G. Segal. The by-laws were amended, limiting the tenure of trustees to three consecutive three-year terms. The slate of officers and trustees was unanimously elected by the members in attendance.

Dr. Edward B. Shils was elected president of the Society. He served as chairman of the Department of Management at the Wharton School of the University of Pennsylvania and is currently director of the Wharton Entrepreneurial Center, which he founded. A past chairman of the Board of the Pathway School for brain-damaged children, he is currently a vice-president of the Federation of Jewish Agencies and a life trustee of the Philadelphia College of Textiles and Science. He has been a trustee of JPS for 11 years and has held office as secretary and vice-president.

Six new trustees were elected to the JPS Board: Stuart Eizenstat of Washington, D.C., who heads the domestic policy staff at the White House; Max Frankel of New York City, head of the editorial department of the New York *Times* and a Pulitzer Prize recipient for international reporting; Michael Greenblatt of Montreal, Canada, a prominent attorney who is chairman of the Commercial Law Division of the Canadian Bar, has served as president of the Corporation of the Jewish General Hospital of Montreal, and is honorary president of the Solomon Schechter Society; Roberta K.

Levy from Minneapolis, Minnesota, who serves as judge of the Hennepin County Municipality and is president of the Talmud Torah of Minneapolis; Stanley Sheerr of Philadelphia, president of Crown Textile, honorary president of Moss Rehabilitation Hospital, and a recipient of the Federation's Humanitarian Award; and Rabbi Gerald I. Wolpe, senior rabbi of Har Zion Temple of Philadelphia and assistant clinical professor of bio-ethics and medical ethics at Hahnemann Hospital and at the Medical College of Pennsylvania.

The following trustees were re-elected: Edward J. Bloustein of New Brunswick; and Alan H. Molod and Judge Charles R. Weiner, both of Philadelphia.

The following vice-presidents were also elected: Robert P. Abrams of Philadelphia, currently the chairman of the March of Dimes; Robert P. Frankel, a Philadelphia attorney and past president of Congregation Rodeph Shalom; Max M. Kampelman, an attorney from Washington, D.C., and chairman of the Board of Trustees of the American Friends of the Hebrew University; and Irwin T. Holtzman, a Detroit businessman and noted collector of books of Jewish interest, specializing in modern Hebrew literature.

Dr. Muriel M. Berman, vice-president of Hess's of Allentown, was re-elected treasurer of JPS; and Norma F. Furst, dean of student affairs at Temple University, was elected secretary.

Maier Deshell, editor of the Society, introduced Dr. Yosef H. Yerushalmi, who presented the report of the Publication Committee, which met earlier in the day.

Following the reports of the treasurer, president, and Nominating Committee, Mr. Shestack introduced the new president, Dr. Shils, to the members. Professor Levin introduced Rabbi Joseph B. Soloveitchik, who addressed the Society on "The Confused American Jew."

From the Annual Report of JPS President A. Leo Levin

It is a privilege to report that the Society is now distributing its books at a rate approaching 1,000 volumes every business day—a level unprecedented for us. Of far greater significance, the quality of our publications is generally recognized as truly superior. In recent years our books have had unusual success in commanding the attention of the book review editors of the New York *Times,* the Washington *Post,* and similar publications. The comments of the reviewers have been satisfying indeed, a legitimate source of pleasure and pride.

I note this development, not because we view either *Time* or the *Times* as the ultimate arbiter of what is "significant, worthwhile, and informative" in the field of Jewish books or Jewish values, but rather because this recognition is so helpful in making it possible for the Society to fulfill the mission set forth in its charter, to ensure that our books will be widely read.

The future offers no less promise. Credit in full measure must be given to our executive vice-president, Bernard I. Levinson; to our editor, Maier Deshell; to the chairman of the Publication Committee, Professor Yosef Hayim Yerushalmi; and through them to the entire staff they have assembled and whom they stimulate and inspire.

It is appropriate to mention a number of our special projects. Our campus membership program, now in its second year, is reaching thousands of students. We are planning a significant expansion of our efforts in this area, primarily by way of appointing JPS representatives on major campuses throughout the country.

In its first phase, two years ago, the Berman project reached out to 2,000 college and university libraries with marked success. Thousands of additional JPS books were made available to faculty and students alike, in a wide variety of educational institutions in every region of the country. In its second phase, this past year, the project required recipient libraries to participate financially, paying a portion of the cost of each volume. Hundreds of libraries took advantage of this opportunity to add JPS books to their collections. It bears emphasis that every single one of the many thousands of titles distributed to date under the Berman project was specifically requested by the recipient institutions. I am pleased to announce that the Berman project will continue this coming year, and we thank Muriel and Philip Berman for their generosity.

I turn now to describe a new project, one approved by the Board and scheduled for prompt implementation. From time to time the Society receives requests for books from communal organizations—worthy organizations that are, however, financially hard-pressed. Included are homes for the aged, golden-year programs, hospitals, new Jewish study programs, new Hillel houses, fledgling synagogues, and various groups in Israel. By the same token, many of our members and friends want to make it possible for the Society's books to reach such worthy recipients. Some would-be benefactors would like to identify recipients but not titles—and ensuring that the right titles are sent to the right recipients is by no means an unimportant task. Some would prefer to specify types of organizations to be helped, identifying neither titles nor recipients, and still others would specify only that the money be used to "do good."

To meet these needs and serve these ends, the Society is creating a Community Trust Fund, to accept gifts, large and small, and to distribute needed and wanted books to all such organizations, as resources are available.

Our charter provides that significant, worthwhile, and informative books of Jewish content be published so that our religion, history, literature, and culture will be known. This new Community Trust is designed to help us fulfill that mission by making Jewish books available to a wider audience than ever before.

Mr. Stanley Sheerr, one of the great communal leaders in this city, has accepted the chairmanship of this new project.

Permit me to conclude these brief remarks by looking both backward and forward and sharing some general thoughts concerning the proper role of the Society. It is fascinating to page through the *Year Books* of 50 to 60 years ago. In so doing, I came across the record of a debate at the annual meeting of the Society held in this city 58 years ago, March 21, 1920. Mr. Louis Marshall, at the opening of his address, stated the issue and his own view:

> I do not agree with the President when he suggests a kind of Missouri compromise between those who desire scholarly books and those who desire popular books. I do not believe in that kind of a compromise. The President will have to "show me" that that is the proper thing. There are those who desire scholarly books and would be interested only in scholarly books, just as there are those who desire and would be interested in the popular books. We have three million Jews here, and I hope that some time in the not too distant future they will all be members of this association, and every member will have a right to receive such intellectual provender as he desires and you can supply.

Variant readings of a familiar figure of speech help to understand the question. We have long been identified as the People of the Book. Is it that we are people of *the* Book, the Bible, or does the phrase imply more: people of the *book,* a people devoted to reading and learning, people who have respect for any worthwhile book?

I think back to the type of synagogue so typical 50 years ago, a synagogue of many books. There were those who could be found studying a page of Talmud with commentaries, no mean feat. Then there was a special kind of book, a book of allegories and fanciful tales, all taken from the Talmud. Here was a far simpler text, or at least one that would be dealt with at a simpler level. There tended to be more who preferred this work. Then there were those who "said Psalms." Each, please note, held a book in his hands.

I cannot say that those who said Psalms knew precisely, or even imprecisely, what the Psalmist was saying, but they all knew or felt what *they* wanted to say through the Psalmist's words. The spectrum of books and of readers ranged wide, from the most scholarly to the most simple; but each of these books enriched the lives of its readers.

I think we in the Society have reaffirmed, and should continue to reaffirm, our commitment to provide provender for all constructive elements in Jewish life. There are no Jewish souls who can be ignored. Each is precious, each worthy of our concern and our care.

I look forward with confidence to a very bright future for the Society. We come from a tradition that balances constancy and change. Every year, on the Holiday of Freedom, we reaffirm our conviction that we ourselves have been taken out of Egypt. Every day we reaffirm the rebirth of the world as a daily phenomenon and assert our own rejuvenation and rededication. Yet, we take pride in our legacy, a long and ancient tradition. So, too, for societies generally and for this Society in particular. We are proud of our 90 years and are mindful of the need for constancy, but also of the need for change, for new techniques, new methods, new approaches. And there are so many in the JPS family who are devoted, dedicated, insightful and creative, that I have no doubt about our bright tomorrow.

"The Past is Prologue" reads the inscription on the National Archives in the nation's capital. By now, the wise, albeit rather loose translation of a Washington cab driver is equally familiar: "You ain't seen nothing yet!" Our hope is that in the perspective of the future, when the present has become part of the past, it will be viewed as a worthy prologue.

JPS Treasurer's Report for 1977

I would like to begin this treasurer's report by espousing a quote of which I was reminded by the arrival of JPS's newest publication, Leo W. Schwarz's *Wolfson of Harvard—Portrait of a Young Scholar.* The entire mood of the eleventh chapter is evoked by Ralph Waldo Emerson's statement: "All men live by truth, and stand in need of expression . . . The man is only half himself, the other half is his expression."

This then, is where JPS dollars go. For this society's books run the gamut of expression . . . from novels to scholarly treatises . . . social, cultural and historical works . . . religious and spiritual expressions of all the ages, old as the Bible, and new as Hillel Halkin's expression of Zionism, 1977. These publications devoted to Judaism bring to fruition that other half of man, expression, to make him whole.

And now I am pleased to report that in 1977, income from the sale of books and membership for the Society amounted to $986,679. This represents an increase of 2.6 per cent over the $961,811 reported in 1976. Not only were revenues up in 1977, but our expenses for the year also increased at a slightly higher rate. They were $1,145,291 in 1977, as compared to $1,096,339 in 1976.

The increase in expenses reflects an increase in advertising and promotional programs; the cost of moving our office into new and more efficient quarters; the cost of a new bookkeeping machine; and the expenses incurred in advance of the publication of several new books which will produce income when released. An increase of revenue from these efforts should be seen in 1978 and in future years.

Finally, I can report that royalty payments to authors set a record in JPS history. It is gratifying for us to encourage authors to write books on Jewish themes and to know that these books are read and appreciated.

Our special purpose funds are invested conservatively to enable the Society to continue to flourish. We have recently received word of a substantial bequest that should be processed shortly. Our accountants and bankers confirm that the Jewish Publication Society's financial position continues to be sound.

JPS Publications

In 1977 JPS published the following new volumes:

Title and Author	Printed
CONTEMPORARY ISRAELI LITERATURE Edited by Elliott Anderson	4,000
THE WORLDS OF MAURICE SAMUEL Edited by Milton Hindus	4,000
LETTERS TO AN AMERICAN JEWISH FRIEND by Hillel Halkin	7,000
JOSEPH KARO: LAWYER AND MYSTIC (paperback) by R. J. Zwi Werblowsky	3,000
VIOLENCE AND DEFENSE IN THE JEWISH EXPERIENCE Edited by Salo W. Baron and George S. Wise	3,000
ZIONISM IN GERMANY 1897–1933: The Shaping of a Jewish Identity by Stephen M. Poppel	3,000

A WILL TO SURVIVE—Israel: The Faces of Terror 1948/The Faces
of Hope Today   1,500
   by John Phillips
   (Co-published with The Dial Press/James Wade)
VAGABOND STARS: A World History of the Yiddish Theater   1,500
   by Nahma Sandrow
   (Co-published with Harper & Row)
AMERICAN JEWISH YEAR BOOK (Vol. 77), 1977   3,250
   Edited by Morris Fine and Milton Himmelfarb
   Martha Jelenko, Executive Editor
   (Co-published with the American Jewish Committee)

1977 Reprints

During 1977, JPS reprinted the following books:

LEGENDS OF JERUSALEM by Zev Vilnay (3,000); LEGENDS OF THE
JEWS-Volumes I and II by Louis Ginzberg (1,500); SABBATH: The Day of
Delight edited by Abraham E. Millgram (1,500); HOLY SCRIPTURES
(25,000); GEOGRAPHY OF ISRAEL by Efraim Orni and Elisha Ofrat (1,000);
THE SECOND JEWISH CATALOG compiled and edited by Sharon Strassfeld
and Michael Strassfeld (45,000); THE TORAH (15,000); THE PROPHETS by
Abraham J. Heschel (2,000); THE JEWISH CATALOG compiled and edited by
Richard Siegel, Sharon Strassfeld, and Michael Strassfeld (30,000); PATHWAYS
THROUGH THE BIBLE by Mortimer J. Cohen (5,000); A HISTORY OF
THE JEWS by Solomon Grayzel (5,000); THE RISE AND FALL OF THE
JUDAEAN STATE-Volume II by Solomon Zeitlin (1,000); WHAT THE
MOON BROUGHT by Sadie R. Weilerstein (3,000); THE ALEPH-BET
STORY BOOK by Deborah Pessin (2,000); MASADA WILL NOT FALL
AGAIN by Sophie Greenspan (1,500); EMBATTLED JUSTICE by Ellen Nor-
man Stern (1,000); THE JEWISH MARRIAGE ANTHOLOGY by Philip and
Hanna Goodman (2,000); and MAIMONIDES by David Hartman (2,000). The
total number of books distributed by the Society during 1977 was 200,000.

SPECIAL ARTICLES IN VOLUMES 51–78
OF THE AMERICAN JEWISH YEAR BOOK

OBITUARIES

Index

AAJE (see American Association for Jewish Education)

ABC (see American Broadcasting Corporation)

Abrahams, Lionel, 289

Abramov, Zalman, 201

Abramovitch, Pavel, 198

Abt, Harry, 290

Academics for Israel Committee (Gt. Britain), 220

Academy for Jewish Studies Without Walls (see American Jewish Committee)

ACIS (see Asociación Comunidad Israelita de Buenos Aires)

ACLU (see American Civil Liberties Union)

ACTION-VISTA, 163

Adelman, William, 366

Adler, Manfred, 238

affirmative action, 108, 109–110, 160, 166

AFL-CIO, 155

Afn Shvel, 360

Die Afrikaner (S. Africa), 286

AFSC (see American Friends Service Committee)

Agudath Israel World Organization, 310

Agudath Israel of America, 36, 57, 113, 160, 161, 173, 266, 279, 310

  All-European Conference (Antwerp), 173

  Children's Division—Pirchei Agudath Israel, 310

  Girls' Division—Bnos Agudath Israel, 310

  Women's Division—N'Shei Agu-

dath Israel of America, 310–311

  Youth Division—Zeirei Agudath Israel, 311

Aguinis, Marcos, 214

Agurskii, Melik, 88n

Ain, Joe, 200

Ain, Steve, 194

AISA (see Asociación Israelita Sefaradí Argentina)

AJCS (see Allied Jewish Community Services, Canada)

AJDS (see Association of Jewish Day Schools, Canada)

Al-Arab (Gt. Britain), 220

al-Fatah, 128, 141

Al-Goumhouriah, 127

Alaiev, J.N., 84

The Alaskan Jewish Bulletin, 357

Albany Jewish World, 359

Albert Einstein College of Medicine (see Yeshiva University)

Albrecht, Ernst, 240

Aleichem, Sholem, 91

Aleksandrovich, Mikhail, 92n

Allgemeine Jüdische Wochenzeitung (W. Germany), 252

Algemeiner Journal, 360

Algeria, 150, 157, 168

Aliger, Margareta, 93

Alignment (see Labor-Mapam Alignment)

All-European Conference (see Agudath Israel of America)

Allied Jewish Community Services (AJCS; Canada), 194, 200

  Combined Jewish Appeal, 4, 11

Allilueva, Svetlana, 77, 78n

Allon, Yigal, 131, 139, 144, 261, 269

418

American Jewish Congress, 27, 107, 109, 110, 111, 139, 162, 163, 164, 165, 166, 168, 169, 174, 175, 302
Black-Jewish Information Center, 161
Women's Division, 167, 172, 302
American Jewish Correctional Chaplains Association, Inc., 328
American Jewish Historical Quarterly, 358
American Jewish Historical Society, 305
American Jewish Joint Distribution Committee—JDC, 78, 259, 308
American Jewish Journal, 358
American Jewish League for Israel, 332
American Jewish Periodical Center (see Hebrew Union College—Jewish Institute of Religion)
American Jewish Press Association, 305
American Jewish Public Relations Society, 338
American Jewish Society for Service, 328
American Jewish Times—Outlook, 363
American Jewish World, 359
American Jewish Year Book, 3, 4n, 26n, 80n, 86n, 97n, 103n, 177, 177n, 263, 269, 274, 275, 276, 360
American Labor ORT (see American ORT Federation)
American Medical Center at Denver, 328
National Council of Auxiliaries, 328
American Mizrachi Woman, 360
American Mizrachi Women, 332
American Nazi party (see National Socialist party)
American ORT Federation, 170, 308–309
American and European Friends of ORT, 309
American Labor ORT, 309
Business and Professional ORT, 309
National ORT League, 309
Women's American ORT, 309
American Physicians Fellowship, 332
American Red Magen David for Israel, 332

American Sephardi Federation, 326
American Society for Jewish Music, 305
American Student Center in Jerusalem (see Jewish Theological Seminary of America)
American Technion Society, 332
American Trade Union Council (see National Committee for Labor Israel—Israel Histadruth Campaign)
American Veterans of Israel, 326
American Yeshiva Student Union (see P'eylim)
American Zionist, 360
American Zionist Federation, 167, 175, 333
American Zionist Youth Foundation, 175, 333
American Zionist Youth Council, 333
Sherut La'am program, 175
Americans for Progressive Israel (see Hashomer Hatzair)
Amery, Jean, 252
AMIA (see Asociación Mutual Israelita Argentina)
Amichai, Yehuda, 233
Amin, Idi, 219
Amnesty International, 101
AMPAL-American Israel Corporation, 282, 333
Amsterdam News, 108
Andrews, David, 204
Andrews, Don, 195
Anglo-Jewish Chamber of Commerce (Gt. Britain)
Anti-Boycott Coordination Committee, 220
Anglo-Jewish Youth (Gt. Britain), 222
Angola, 129, 284
an-Nahar (Beirut), 148
Anti-Boycott Coordination Committee (see Anglo-Israel Chamber of Commerce)
Anti-Defamation League of B'nai B'rith (see B'nai B'rith)
Anti-Zionism Resolution (see United Nations, General Assembly, Resolution 3379)

Bialik, Hayyim Nahman, 90
Bierut, Boleslav, 93n
Bijedic, Dzemal, 258
Biko, Steve, 284
Bingham-Rosenthal Bill, 169
Binik, Sonia, 92n
Birkan, David, 202
Birobidzhan, 79, 91, 94
Birobidzhan Yiddish Folk Theater (Soviet Union), 91
Birobidzhaner Stern (Soviet Union), 89
Bitzaron, 360
Black, Misha, 228
Black Americans to Support Israel Committee (BASIC), 111
Black Hundreds (Soviet Union), 96, 102
Black-Jewish Information Center (see American Jewish Congress)
Blanch, Stuart Yarmouth, Archbishop of York, 223
Bleich, J. David, 44n
Bliachman, Claudia, 87
Blitman, Charles H., 367
Blitz, Samuel, 367
Bloc of the Faithful (see Gush Emunim)
Bloch, Benjamin C., 367
Block, Leonard, 24n
Blue, Lionel, 226
Blum, Howard, 201
Blumberg, H.M., 226
Blumenfeld, Erik, 242
Blumenthal, Ernst Pinchas, 251
Blumenthal, Walter, 288
B'nai B'rith, 27, 119, 328
　Anti-Defamation League of, 110, 114, 115, 118, 139, 160, 161, 164, 165, 166, 167, 168, 169, 170, 171, 174, 175, 302
　Holocaust Information Center, 174
　Hillel Foundations, 311, 328
　International Association of Hillel Directors, 328
　Women, 314, 328
　Youth Organizations, 311, 328
B'nai B'rith (Argentina), 211
B'nai B'rith (Canada), 195
B'nai B'rith Hillel Foundations (Gt. Britain), 220, 225

B'nai B'rith Messenger, 357
B'nai Yiddish, 360
Bnai Zion—The American Fraternal Zionist Organization, 137, 326–327
Bnei Akiva of North America (see Religious Zionists of America)
B'nos Agudath Israel (see Agudath Israel of America)
Board of Jewish Education, 6, 21n, 38, 39, 41, 76
Board of Jewish Education (Canada), 200
Bochner, Michael, 279
Bodnia, Mendel, 100
Bogomolsky, Wolf, 87
Boguslavskii, Viktor, 100
Bohn, Issy (see Levin, Benjamin)
Bolan, Marco, 228
Bolshakov, V., 96
Bolshevik Party (Soviet Union), 77, 86n, 93
Bolshevik Revolution, 77, 197
Books in Review, 360
Börner, Holger, 247
Bornfriend, Jacob, 228
Botha, Roelof F., 18
Bradlow, Emmanuel P., 289
Brandeis-Bardin Institute, 311–312
Brandeis University, 173, 233
　National Women's Committee, 338
Brandt, Willy, 237
Braude, Jacob, 228
Breira (Israel), 140
Breytenbach, Breyten, 283
Brezhnev, Leonid, 79, 87, 92, 96, 98, 102, 133, 197, 229, 258
Briggs, Kenneth, 116
Bright, Sidney, 227
Bright, William, 115
Brio, Malka, 87
Brit Trumpeldor Betar of America, 333
Britain Israel Public Affairs Committee, 220
Brith Abraham, 327
Brith Sholom, 327
British Board of Deputies, 217, 218, 220, 223, 224, 227